Developing Applications with Microsoft®

Visual Basic®

Advanced Topics

Michael V. Ekedahl

COURSE
TECHNOLOGY

ONE MAIN STREET, CAMBRIDGE, MA 02142

an International Thomson Publishing company I(T)P®

Cambridge • Albany • Bonn • Boston • Cincinnati • London • Madrid • Melbourne • Mexico City
New York • Paris • San Francisco • Singapore • Tokyo • Toronto • Washington

Developing Applications with Microsoft Visual Basic: Advanced Topics is published by Course Technology.

Managing Editor	Kristen Duerr
Product Manager	Cheryl Ouellette
Production Editor	Catherine G. DiMassa
Project Manager	Cindy Johnson
Developmental Editor	Kathleen Habib
Text Designer	Kim Munsell
Cover Designer	Efrat Reis
Cover Illustrator	Douglas Goodman

For more information contact:

Course Technology
One Main Street
Cambridge, MA 02142

ITP Europe
Berkshire House 168-173
High Holborn
London WCIV 7AA
England

Nelson ITP, Australia
102 Dodds Street
South Melbourne, 3205
Victoria, Australia

ITP Nelson Canada
1120 Birchmount Road
Scarborough, Ontario
Canada M1K 5G4

International Thomson Editores
Seneca, 53
Colonia Polanco
11560 Mexico D.F. Mexico

ITP GmbH
Königswinterer Strasse 418
53227 Bonn
Germany

ITP Asia
60 Albert Street, #15-01
Albert Complex
Singapore 189969

ITP Japan
Hirakawacho Kyowa Building, 3F
2-2-1 Hirakawacho
Chiyoda-ku, Tokyo 102
Japan

ISBN 0-7600-5852-0

Printed in the United States of America

1 2 3 4 5 6 7 8 9 10 BH 02 01 00 99 98

Preface

Developing Applications with Microsoft Visual Basic: Advanced Topics was written to provide the Visual Basic programmer with the tools to create Visual Basic programs that conform to well-adopted Windows standards. Where possible, existing Visual Basic tools are used. In some cases, Windows libraries are used to extend the functionality of Visual Basic. The intent is to provide the reader with a rich set of tools to create programs that satisfy the demands of today's business environment.

Organization and Approach

If you are familiar with Visual Basic, the first three chapters are review chapters that cover the basics of the Visual Basic development environment, language syntax, and programming in an event-driven environment. Depending upon the reader's level of experience, these chapters may be skipped or used for reference.

The book is relatively modular in design. Some readers may be interested in database-related topics, while others may want specific information about class modules and object-oriented programming. As such, some chapters are functionally related and others are not. Also, some chapters contain material required for certification and others do not.

Chapters 4 and 5 cover Database topics. Creators of business applications will find these chapters useful. Chapters 6 and 7 cover the Windows Common controls topics. These chapters are applicable to anyone who is creating a user interface that uses common Windows metaphors. Chapters 8 and 9 cover Class modules, and are the basis of the object-oriented topics necessary to complete Chapters 10 through 13.

Chapters 10 through 13 cover ActiveX components. This technology is new to Visual Basic 5.0. Chapters 14 and 15 describe the Visual Basic interface to and relationship with the Windows operating system. Chapter 16 covers Crystal Reports. Crystal Reports is not required for certification. Appendix A is intended to demonstrate how to use the Visual Basic Integrated Development Environment to locate program errors, and how to correct them.

Developing Applications with Microsoft Visual Basic: Advanced Topics is designed to provide the necessary skills to pass the Developing Applications with Microsoft Visual Basic 5.0 Certification Exam. The following table is organized by the certification topics listed in the Microsoft Exam Preparation Guide for Exam 70-165, Developing Applications with Microsoft Visual Basic 5.0. Because the organization of this book is different from the organization of the Exam Preparation Guide, the table will help you locate the section of the book corresponding to a particular Visual Basic skill.

Design Issues		
Design and create forms	**Chapter**	**Section**
Create an application that adds and deletes forms at run time	7	A
Use the Forms collection	4 7	C A
Implement drag-and-drop operations within the Microsoft Windows shell	Appendix B	
Determine when to use a specific event	**Chapter**	**Section**
Add code to the appropriate form event, such as Initialize, Terminate, Load, Unload, QueryUnload, Activate, or Deactivate	3 7	A A
Add a menu interface to an application	**Chapter**	**Section**
Dynamically modify the appearance of a menu	3	D
Add a pop-up menu to an application	3	D
Create an application that adds and deletes menus at run time	14	A
Implement user interface controls in an application	**Chapter**	**Section**
Display data by using the TreeView control	6	B
Display items by using the ListView control	6	B
Provide controls with images by using the ImageList control	6	B

Create toolbars by using the Toolbar control	7	B
Display status information by using the StatusBar control	6	A
Create an application that adds and deletes controls at run time	3	B
Use the Controls collection	4	C
Coding Issues		
Declare a variable	**Chapter**	**Section**
Define the scope of a variable by using the Public, Private, and Static statements	2	A, B
Use the appropriate declaration statement	2	A, B
Write and call Sub and Function procedures	**Chapter**	**Section**
Write and call Sub and Function procedures by using named arguments or optional arguments	2	A, B
Write and call Sub and Function procedures that require an array as an argument	2	A, B
Call procedures from outside a module	2	A, B
Create and use a class module	**Chapter**	**Section**
Add properties to a class	8	A
Add methods to a class	8	A
Identify whether a class should be public or private	9	B
Declare properties and methods as Friend	8	A
Set the value of the Instancing property	9	B
Access data by using the data controls and bound controls	**Chapter**	**Section**
Add data to a table by using the DBList or DBCombo control	5	B
Add data to a table by using the standard ListBox control	5	A
Display information by using the DBGrid control	5	B
Display information by using the MSFlexGrid control	6	A
Access data by using code	**Chapter**	**Section**
Navigate through and manipulate records in a Recordset	4	B
Add, modify, and delete records in a Recordset	4	B
Find a record in a Recordset	4	B
Use the Find or Seek method to search a Recordset	4	B
Incorporate dynamic-link libraries (DLLs) into an application	**Chapter**	**Section**
Declare and call a DLL routine	14	B
Identify when it is necessary to use the Alias clause	14	B
Create a DLL routine that modifies string arguments	14	B
Pass a null pointer to a DLL routine	14	B
Pass an argument by value and by reference	14	B
Pass a function pointer to a DLL by using a callback function	14	B
Pass a string to a DLL	14	B
Build a Microsoft ActiveX client	**Chapter**	**Section**
Use the Dim statement to reference an object	8 9	A, B A, B
Use the Set statement to create an instance of an object	8 9	A, B A, B
Use the CreateObject function to create an instance of an object	4	C
Create an Automation server that exposes objects, properties, methods, and events	**Chapter**	**Section**
Define properties for objects by using property procedures	8	A
Create a method that displays a form	12	A
Create a multithreaded component	9	B
Call an object server asynchronously by using a callback mechanism	14	B
Create, use, and respond to events	3	C
Create and use an ActiveX control	**Chapter**	**Section**
Declare and raise events	10	B
Create and enable a property page	11	A
Use control events to save and load persistent control properties	11	A
Add an ActiveX control to a Web page	11	B

Create and use ActiveX documents	Chapter	Section
Compare ActiveX documents to embedded objects	12	A
Create an ActiveX project with one or more UserDocument objects	12	A
Persist data for an ActiveX document	12	A
Automate an ActiveX document	12	B
Add an ActiveX document to a Web page	12	A
Create applications that can access the Internet	**Chapter**	**Section**
Gain access to the Internet or an intranet by using the Hyperlink object	13	A
Create an application that has the ability to browse HTML pages	13	A
Create an application that enables connections to the Internet	13	A
Implement error-handling features in an application	**Chapter**	**Section**
Raise errors from a server	8	A
Create a common error-handling routine	Appendix A	
Display an error message in a dialog box by using the Err object	4	C
Use the appropriate error-trapping options, such as Break on All Errors, Break in Class Module, and Break on Unhandled Errors	Appendix A	
Implement Help features in an application	**Chapter**	**Section**
Set properties to automatically display Help information when a user presses F1	15	C
Use the HelpFile property to set the default path for Help files in an application	15	C
Use the CommonDialog control to display the contents of a Help file	15	C
Debugging and Testing Issues		
Select appropriate compiler options	**Chapter**	**Section**
List and describe options for optimizing when compiling to native code	15	A
List and describe the differences between compiling to p-code and compiling to native code	15	A
Compile an application conditionally	**Chapter**	**Section**
Use the #If...#End If and #Const directives to conditionally compile statements	15	A
Set the appropriate conditional compiler flags	15	A
Set watch expressions during program execution	Appendix A	
Monitor the values of expressions and variables by using the debugging windows	**Chapter**	**Section**
Use the Immediate window to check or change values	Appendix A	
Explain the purpose and usage for the Locals window	Appendix A	
Implement project groups to support the debugging and development process	**Chapter**	**Section**
Debug DLLs in process	9	B
Test and debug a control in process	11	
Define the scope of a watch variable	Appendix A	
Distribution Issues		
Use the Setup Wizard to create an effective setup program	**Chapter**	**Section**
Edit the Setup.inf file	15	B
Edit the Vb5dep.ini file	15	B
Create a setup program that installs and registers ActiveX controls	11	A
Manage the Windows system registry	**Chapter**	**Section**
Use the GetSetting function and the SaveSetting statement to save application-specific information in the registry	14	A
Register components by using the Regsvr32.exe utility	14	A
Register components by using the Remote Automation Connection Manager	14	A
Edit the registry manually	14	A
Register a component automatically	14	A
Distribute an application over the Internet	11	B

Features

Developing Applications with Microsoft Visual Basic: Advanced Topics is an exceptional book because it also includes the following features:

Read This Before You Begin Page This page appears on the inside front cover of this book and is consistent with Course Technology's unequaled commitment to helping instructors introduce technology into the classroom. Technical considerations and assumptions about hardware, software, and default settings are listed in one place to help instructors save time and eliminate unnecessary aggravation.

Chapter Case and Previewing the Application Each chapter begins with a programming-related problem that the reader could expect to encounter in business, followed by a demonstration of an application that could be used to solve the problem.

The Chapter Case introduces a realistic case scenario and explains what you will learn in the course of working through the chapter.

Showing the completed application before learning how to create it is motivational and instructionally sound. By allowing you to see the type of application you will be able to create after completing the chapter, you will be more motivated to learn because you can see how the programming concepts can be used and, therefore, why the concepts are important.

Step-by-step methodology The unique Course Technology methodology keeps the reader on track. You develop programs within the context of solving the problem posed in the Chapter Case. The text constantly provides guidance, letting you know where you are in the process of solving the problem. The numerous illustrations include labels that direct your attention to what you should look at on the screen.

Objectives The Objectives call out the main concepts that will be presented in the Section.

Sections Because this text teaches both programming concepts and the Visual Basic language, the chapters are broken into Sections. Each section discusses a particular functional sub topic. Each chapter has at least two sections, but some may have up to four sections.

Syntax Windows Syntax for statements, functions, objects, etc. is presented as it appears in online Help so you will not have difficulty identifying them. Syntax is then "dissected," with a complete definition of each keyword and variable in the statement. Notes regarding peculiarities of the syntax, properties, methods, and events, code examples, and an explanation of the code example are also provided. These Syntax Windows gather important information about programming constructs and objects in an easy-to-reference format.

Code examples In addition to code examples included with the syntax, actual code is used within the text of the chapter to provide additional examples of a concept or illustrate further peculiarities. The completed application that accompanies each chapter is fully commented and will often contain additional code beyond the code entered in the step-by-step instructions included in the chapters. The intent is to demonstrate a reasonably robust example.

Tip Tips provide additional information about a procedure—for example, an alternative method of performing the procedure. Tips are an important element of the chapter pedagogy.

GUI Design Tip GUI Design Tips contain guidelines and recommendations for designing applications that follow Windows standards.

Programming Tip Programming Tips contain suggestions for you, the programmer, to either create better programs, or to help you create programs more efficiently.

Performance Tip Performance Tips contain suggestions to improve the running speed of a program

Summary Following each chapter is a section highlighting the programming concepts, commands, and controls covered in the chapter.

Questions Each chapter concludes with meaningful, conceptual Questions that test your understanding of the material presented in the chapter. Types of questions include fill-in-the-blank, multiple choice, and short programming exercises to help you evaluate your comprehension of the subject. The answers to selected questions appear on the CD-ROM.

Exercises The Questions are followed by hands-on Exercises that test your understanding of how to complete business-related programs pertaining to the chapter. The Exercises provide you with additional practice of the skills and concepts presented in the chapter.

Instructor's Manual The Instructor's Manual has been written by the author and has been quality assurance tested. It is available in printed form and through the Course Technology Faculty Online Companion on the World Wide Web. (Call your customer service representative for the URL and your password.) The Instructor's Manual contains the following items:

- Additional coverage of Visual Basic concepts such as Sorting and Binary Search.
- Cases which can be assigned as semester projects.
- Answers to all of the questions and solutions to all of the exercises.

- Chapter Notes, which contain background information from the author about the Chapter Case and the instructional progression of the chapter.
- Technical Notes, which include troubleshooting tips as well as information on how to customize the readers' screens to closely emulate the screen shots in the book.

Course Test Manager Version 1.2 Engine and Test Bank Course Test Manager (CTM) is a cutting-edge Windows-based testing software program, developed exclusively for Course Technology, that helps instructors design and administer examinations. This full-featured program allows readers to generate practice tests randomly that provide immediate on-screen feedback and detailed study guides for questions that were incorrectly answered. Instructors can also use CTM to create printed and online tests.

You can create, preview, and administer a test on any or all chapters of this textbook entirely over a local area network. CTM can grade the tests readers take automatically at the computer and can generate statistical information on individual as well as group performance. A CTM test bank has been written to accompany your book and is included on the Instructor's CD-ROM. The test bank includes multiple-choice, true/false, short answer, and essay questions.

Solution Files Solution Files contain every file that readers are asked to create or modify in the chapters and exercises.

Reader Files Reader Files, containing all of the data that readers will use to complete the chapters and exercises are provided through Course Technology's Online Companion, as well as on disk. A ReadMe file includes technical tips for lab management. See the Read This Before You Begin page on the inside front cover of this book for more information on Reader Files.

Visual Basic Developer's Kit Readers can discover more about Visual Basic's capabilities with the Visual Basic Developer's Kit CD-ROM. The CD-ROM contains the Visual Basic program files necessary to complete the hands-on steps and Exercises in each chapter. There are also demo controls, object naming conventions and other useful material. Refer to the Help files on the CD-ROM for more information.

Acknowledgments

I would like to thank all the people that helped make this book a reality. I would especially like to thank the following reviewers for their insightful comments: Michael Walton, Miami-Dade Community College; Mary Amundson-Miller, Greenville Technical College; and Matt McCaskill, Brevard Community College. I would also like to thank Cindy Johnson and Kate Habib at Publishing Services for their efforts. Thanks also to the Course Technology validation team, Brian McCooey and John Bosco, for their technical validation.

My special thanks go to Dr. William A. Newman. Without his role as mentor over the years, this book never would have been possible.

Thanks also to Mitchell Harhay, for his assistance throughout the project. I would also like to thank Mitch and the support of his company Access Nevada, an Internet provider, for their support and for providing e-mail forwarding services to be used in conjunction with this book.

Finally, I would like to thank my wife Katrina for her patience and support while I completed this book, and thanks to my dogs Rio and KC for their amusing distractions as I sat and wrote each day.

Contents

CHAPTER

Introduction to Visual Basic

1

Using an Event-Driven Visual Programming Language

case▶ Diverse Products sells household products throughout the United States. They need a user interface for a program to enter information for each of their salespeople. The user interface will display the current date when the program first is executed. The user will be able to enter the salesperson's name and address on the form. The user interface also will illustrate the use of scroll bars.

SECTION A

objectives

In this section you will:

- Identify the differences between a procedural language and an event-driven, object-oriented language
- Interact with the elements of the Visual Basic user interface
- Use the Help system
- Create, open and save a Visual Basic program
- Run a Visual Basic program
- Use the Properties window to define the characteristics of a form
- Set attributes, called properties, for the boxes and buttons you create

Getting Familiar with Visual Basic

An Introduction to Visual Basic

A computer program is made up of instructions commonly called **statements**. Statements are grouped together into **procedures**. In this book, a series of statements is referred to as **code**. The statements in a procedure perform a well-defined task. Visual Basic is an **event-driven** programming language. That is, statements in a program execute in response to some user action like clicking a mouse button. The code you write executes in response to these events. In an event-driven programming language, the statements that are executed depend on the action a user takes. An event-driven program cannot predict which statements will be executed next.

Programs written in Visual Basic have the same characteristics as other Windows programs. For example, most Visual Basic programs have windows with title bars. A title bar has a Control-menu box allowing the user to minimize, maximize, and close a window. A window can be resized and can have menus, toolbars, and boxes to enter text.

Unlike many other programming languages, Visual Basic supports most of the characteristics of an object-oriented programming language. An object can be thought of as a metaphorical representation of an everyday tool. For example, there are objects that work like on/off switches. When clicked, the switch is turned on. When clicked again, the switch is turned off. Other objects work like radio buttons. The term **radio button** is derived from car radios. Only one button (radio station) can be selected at a time. In Windows, radio buttons are called **option buttons**. As you have used the Windows interface, you have no doubt used many different objects. For example, you have clicked buttons, entered text into boxes, and selected items from lists. These are implemented as individual objects in Visual Basic. An object integrates data and the procedures that act on the data together. This coupling of data and procedures is called **encapsulation**.

An object's data are represented in Visual Basic as **properties**. An object's properties define the behavior of an object. The procedures that act on the data are implemented using **methods**. The methods of an object define all the tasks or actions the object can perform. Functionally, methods are similar to procedures in that they execute code to perform a task.

Some objects can respond to events. The concept of an event extends far beyond Visual Basic. As you know, Windows can run several programs at the same time. Each of these programs has buttons and other objects, and the user interacts with a program by clicking buttons, selecting items on a list, and so on. Every button, every list box, and any visible object on the screen, no matter which program the button or object belongs to, is viewed by the operating system as a window. When a button (window) is clicked, Windows recognizes that the button was clicked and sends a message to your program, and code is executed. This is what is known as an **event**. Events can occur because of a user action like typing a key on the keyboard or clicking the mouse button. Different objects respond to different events, and most objects respond to several events. For example, a button generates a Click event when clicked by the user, but there are additional events that occur when the mouse passes over the button or a mouse button is pressed down or released. The properties, methods, and events pertaining to an object make up its **interface**. Note that the term interface is different from the concept of a user interface. The user interface pertains to how the user interacts with a program. The object's interface pertains to how the programmer interacts with the object.

The user interacts with a program created in Visual Basic using a visual interface. The visual interface is made up of one or more forms. A **form** is a window having the same characteristics as other windows. That is, a form may or may not have a title bar or a border. A form can be resized, maximized, minimized, and closed.

The user interacts with a form using visible objects created on a form. These objects are created from **controls** and each different type of control is used to perform a specific task. Figure 1-1 shows the control instances drawn on the completed form for Diverse Products.

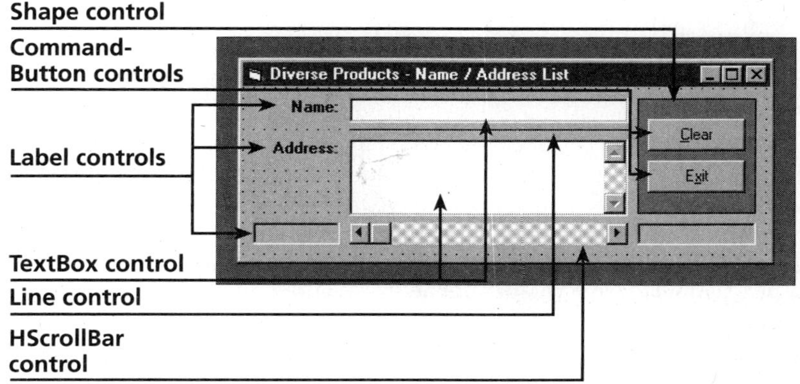

Figure 1-1: Types of controls

- The **CommandButton** object performs an action when clicked.
- The **Label** object is used to display textual information.

- The **TextBox** object displays textual information like the Label control, but also can accept input from the user.
- The **Line** and **Shape** objects are used to identify regions on the form visually. The user does not interact with these objects.
- **Scroll bars**, either vertical or horizontal, are used to represent the current position within a range. For example, they are used to indicate and change the current position in a Word document.

The only way for a program to interact with an object is through its interface; that is, setting properties, calling methods, and responding to events. There are objects that are visible in a window like buttons and boxes. There also are objects that are not visible to the user.

Using object-oriented terminology, every object is created from a **class**, which is a blueprint or template for an object. When an object is created from a class, an **instance** of the class is created. Class instances are objects that are identical copies of their class. Once an instance is created, it is possible to set the properties of the object and call its methods. Each class instance contains its own copy of data (properties). As shown in Figure 1-1, there are two text boxes in the window. In object-oriented terms, there are two instances of the TextBox class. Visual Basic supports several types of classes.

- A form is a class. One or many instances of the same form can be created from a form's class.
- A control is a type of class. Each different control performs a well-defined task. When a control instance is drawn on a form, an object is created. Most controls are visible on the form when the program runs. Others are not.
- There are classes and objects that only can be accessed programmatically. For example, there is an object called the Printer object that is used to send data to the printer.

Having defined the general characteristics of Visual Basic, and how Visual Basic differs from procedural languages, you now can see how Visual Basic stores the files that make up a program, and the structure of those files. All the information pertaining to a program is stored in a file called a project file.

Project and Module Files

At the heart of every Visual Basic program, is a project. Each program is considered a project and is identified by its project file. The **project file** contains general characteristics of a program, identifies the name of the program, its title, and how the program is compiled. The project file also contains a reference to all the different components of the program. These components are called **modules** and are stored as individual files on the disk with a reference stored in the project file. There are several types of module files, each serving a particular purpose.

- A **form module** has two parts. The first part contains the information related to the visible objects (control instances) drawn on the form and the form itself. It also can contain variable declarations and procedures. Each form module is a unique class. When a program is run, one or more instances of the form class are created. Each instance of the form's class corresponds to a visible copy of the form on the screen. Form modules have a file extension of ".frm".

- A **standard module** contains variable declarations and procedures. Standard modules commonly are used for procedures that need to be shared between modules. The procedures and variables declared in a standard module can be exposed to other modules or invisible to other modules. Standard modules commonly are referred to as **bas modules.** This name is derived from the three character extension ".bas" of the file name.
- A **class module** contains user-defined classes. Just as you can create objects from existing classes, it also is possible to create your own classes and objects from those classes. Class modules have a file extension of ".cls".
- The **user control**, **user document**, and **property page** modules are used to create your own controls.

Each of these modules is stored as a separate file on the disk. A module file is really just a text file. As such, a module could be edited using any word processing program like Notepad or WordPad. Visual Basic allows individual modules to be added and removed from a project as necessary.

The Visual Basic Environment

Visual Basic programs are created using an **Integrated Development Environment (IDE)**. That is, you add new and existing form modules and create control instances on a form to define the user interface. Standard and class modules also can be added and removed from a project as needed. All the code pertaining to the different modules can be created and edited using the IDE. Programs can be debugged, tested, and compiled into executable (.exe) files from the Visual Basic IDE. The Visual Basic IDE is made up of several windows in which you can perform these tasks as shown in Figure 1-2.

Figure 1-2 shows the Visual Basic IDE with the most common windows open and docking turned off. The windows that are open initially, their position and size, will vary based on the configuration of Visual Basic when it was last used. If more than one person uses Visual Basic on the computer you are using, you may need to open, close, and position windows each time you start Visual Basic. These windows have the following purpose:

- The **menu bar** contains the commands used to design, test, and compile Visual Basic programs.
- The **toolbar** contains buttons providing quick access to menu commands. Visual Basic can display several standard toolbars, or it is possible to create custom toolbars. The toolbars that are displayed can be changed by clicking Toolbars on the View menu, then checking the toolbars you want displayed.
- The **Form window** shows a form and the control instances created on the form, as the user will see them. One instance of the Form window can be open for each form module in the project.

- The **Code window** is used to declare variables and create procedures for a module. There can be one Code window open for each module in a project.
- The **Project Explorer** displays a hierarchical list of all the modules in a project. Each type of module is listed in a folder, which can be expanded and collapsed. The Project Explorer contains three buttons. The View Code button opens the Code window for the selected module. The View Object button opens the Form window. This button is not applicable to class modules and standard modules. The Toggle Folders button, when clicked, will display the modules in folders based on the module type. When unclicked, all the modules are displayed as a flat alphabetical list.
- The **Properties window** is used to assign and display values to the properties of a form and the control instances created on a form. Unlike the Code window, only one instance of the Properties window can be open at a time.
- The **toolbox** contains all the controls available to the currently loaded project. Creating an instance of a control is accomplished by clicking the control on the toolbox, and drawing an instance of the control on a form. The number of controls in the toolbox shown in Figure 1-2 represents only a small number of the controls available to the Visual Basic programmer.

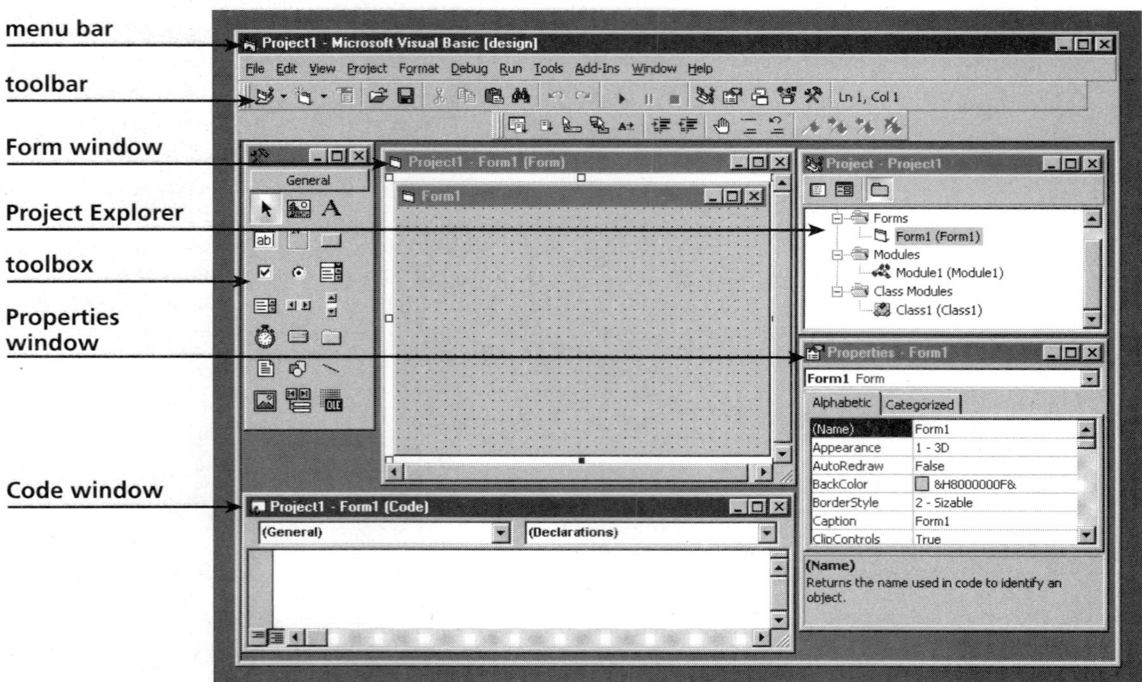

Figure 1-2: Visual Basic Integrated Development Environment (IDE)

When Visual Basic is started, a new project is created with a single form module, or the New Project dialog appears, depending on the configuration. The New

Project dialog is used to create the different types of projects supported by Visual Basic. The type of project determines how the program will be compiled. There are different types of projects to create standard .exe files and dynamic link libraries (.dll files). It also is possible to create custom controls that can be added to the toolbox. There are other types of projects that display documents on the Internet.

The programmer can customize the configuration of the Visual Basic user interface. The following list describes some of the settings that define the behavior of the user interface.

- The Visual Basic IDE can operate as a Multiple Document Interface (MDI) program or as a Single Document Interface (SDI) program. **MDI programs**, like Microsoft Word and Excel, display windows inside of a parent or container window. The windows in an **SDI program** can appear anywhere on the screen. Clicking Options on the Tools menu, clicking the Advanced tab, and then selecting or deselecting the SDI development environment check box, will change this setting. The change will take effect the next time Visual Basic is started.
- The Visual Basic IDE supports docking. This allows the border of windows to be attached or docked to the borders of other windows. Docking can be turned on or off for specific windows by right-clicking the mouse button in a window and checking or unchecking the docking option. The Docking tab in the Options dialog also can be used to change the docking settings.
- The toolbars also can be customized. Depending on whether you are debugging a program or creating a form, you can display or hide toolbars by clicking Toolbars on the View menu.

Whether to turn docking on or off, or whether to use Visual Basic in SDI or MDI mode is a matter of personal preference. Furthermore, which windows are open and closed, and the size of those windows also is a matter of personal preference. As you use Visual Basic, experiment with these settings and choose those that you find most suitable. Most of the figures in this book show a specific window rather than all the windows that make up the IDE.

Opening and Saving Projects

The modules in a project, and the project file itself, are not saved to disk automatically. Rather, these files must be saved using the File menu or the corresponding toolbar buttons. There are six commands on the File menu that open, and save, project and module files.

- The **New Project** and **Open Project** commands are used to create a new project and open an existing project, respectively. The New Project command displays the New Project dialog, which is used to specify the type of project to create. The Open Project command displays a dialog allowing you to navigate through different folders to locate an existing project file.
- The **Save Project** and **Save Project As** commands are used to save a project and its module files using the current file name and assign a new file name, respectively. If there are any unsaved module files, the Save Module As dialog

will appear for the unsaved module requesting you assign a name to the module. In this case, the word "module" is replaced with the actual module name. If the project has never been saved, the Save Project As dialog appears requesting that you specify a new file name for the project.

- The **Save *Module*** and **Save *Module* As** commands are used to save the active module. The module name appears in the command and will vary depending on which module is active. For example, when the form has not been saved, the commands read Save Form1 and Save Form1 As, respectively; if the form's name is frmDiverse, the commands read Save frmDiverse.frm and Save frmDiverse.frm As, respectively. When a form or other module is saved for the first time the Save *Module* As dialog appears, requesting you to specify a name for the module. Note that *module* is replaced with the actual module name.

Once saved, a project and all its module files can be opened by starting Visual Basic and clicking the Open Project command on the File menu. The Open Project dialog will allow you to select a folder and project file. Module files pertaining to the project file do not need to be opened one by one. Rather, they are loaded into the project because of the references in the project file.

Programming tip

It is a good idea to save both module and project files regularly as programs are developed to prevent loss of data due to system crashes and power outages. When a project is saved, any module files that have changed since the project was last saved are written on the disk in addition to the project file.

If any of the modules are missing, or moved to a different folder when you open the project file, Visual Basic will not be able to locate the module and an error message will be displayed. You can continue to load the project but the lost module will have to be located manually and then added to the project.

Each type of Visual Basic file is stored with a unique three-character file extension to identify the type of file. The default extension for a project file is ".vbp" and the default extension for a form module is ".frm". Standard modules have the extension ".bas" and class modules have the extension ".cls". Choosing meaningful, standardized names that identify the purpose of the project and module files will improve program readability.

The completed program for Diversified Products already has been created and is stored in the Complete folder in the Chapter.01 folder on your student disk. The project file contains a single module. You can open this project and see how to open and close the different windows that form the IDE.

To open an existing Visual Basic project file:

1. Click the **Start** button on the taskbar. Click **Programs, Microsoft Visual Basic 5.0,** and then **Visual Basic 5.0.** The location of Visual Basic on the Start menu may vary depending on where it was installed on your system. The Visual Basic splash screen appears, followed by the Visual Basic menu bar, toolbar, and windows.

2 If the New Project dialog appears, click the **Existing** tab. Otherwise, click **Open** on the **File** menu. Use the **Look in:** list box to locate the **Complete** folder in the **Chapter.01** folder. The project named **Diverse.vbp** appears. Click the file and click **Open** to load the project. This dialog can be disabled by checking the "Don't show this dialog in the future" check box. If the New Project dialog is disabled, Visual Basic will create a new project with a single form when started. This setting also can be changed by clicking Options on the Tools menu and clicking the Environment tab. The option buttons in the "When Visual Basic starts" section can be used to set whether or not an empty project is created when Visual Basic is started.

3 Click the form named **frmDiverse** in the Project Explorer, and then click the **View Object** button to open the Form window, if necessary.

4 Click **View** on the menu bar, **Toolbox**, **View**, then **Properties Window**, if necessary. The Toolbox and Properties window open.

Once a project is loaded, you can create objects on a form, write code, and test and run programs. Visual Basic operates in different modes depending on whether you are developing the program or running and testing the program.

Visual Basic Operating Modes

Visual Basic operates in one of three modes; design, run, or break. The current mode is displayed in brackets on the Visual Basic title bar. Control instances are drawn on a form, and the statements that make up the program are written while in **design mode**. Programs are tested and executed in **run mode**. The Visual Basic IDE allows you to suspend the execution of a program temporarily to examine the values of variables and trace the statements as they are executed by entering **break mode**. There are several ways to switch between each of these modes as shown in the following list:

- Pressing either the F5 key or clicking the Start button on the toolbar will begin executing a program. Visual Basic will enter run mode and the text "[run]" will appear on the title bar. Run mode also is referred to as **run time**.
- Pressing the Ctrl + Break keys, or clicking the Break button on the toolbar will suspend the execution of a running program temporarily. Visual Basic will enter break mode and the text "[break]" will appear on the title bar.
- Clicking the End button on the toolbar will end the running program. Visual Basic will be in design mode and the text "[design]" will appear on the title bar. Design mode also is referred to as **design time**.

The Run menu also can be used to change the Visual Basic operating mode.

To test a Visual Basic program:

1. Click the **Save Project** button on the toolbar. You have not changed anything that needs to be saved right now, but it is always a good idea to save a project before you run it.
2. Click the **Start** button on the toolbar. The words "[run]" appear on the Visual Basic title bar. Note the current date is displayed on the form.
3. Click the **text box** next to the Name label, if necessary, and enter your name.
4. Press the **Tab** key to activate the Address text box and enter your address.
5. Click the **Clear** command button. This causes an event to be generated that executes code to remove the contents from the two text boxes.
6. Click the **End** button on the toolbar. The word "[design]" title appears on the Visual Basic title bar.

Having seen how to run an existing program, you now will create a new project, and create the objects and the code for each object. The New Project and Open Project commands on the Visual Basic File menu will create new, and open existing, projects. If a project already is open, and there are unsaved changes in a module or project file, Visual Basic will prompt you to save the files before continuing. You now will create a new project file and save it. This project file and its form will contain the controls and code to implement the program you just loaded.

To create and save a project:

1. Click **New Project** on the **File** menu. If a dialog appears asking you whether or not to save changes to a list of files, click **No.**
2. When the New Project dialog appears, click the **Standard EXE** icon, then click **OK** to create a new project.
3. Use the **View** menu to open the Project Explorer and Properties window, if necessary. In the Project Explorer, click the form named **Form1**, and open the Form window, if necessary.
4. Click **File** then **Save Form1.frm As.** Click the **Startup** folder in the **Chapter.01** folder on your student disk. Change the name to **frmDiverse.frm**, then click **Save.**
5. Click **File** then **Save Project As**. Change the name to **Diverse.vbp**, then click **Save.** Make sure the project is being saved in the **Startup** folder in the **Chapter.01** folder.

   The new file names appear in the Project Explorer. Note that if you saved the project without first saving the form, Visual Basic would have displayed the dialogs for you to save both the form and the project because neither had ever been saved.

The Project menu is used to add and remove all the module types supported by Visual Basic. When adding a module to a project, a dialog is used. The dialog allows new and existing modules to be added to a project. You can create new modules from templates or from scratch. Templates contain predefined objects and code to perform common tasks. For example, there are form templates for splash screens and login dialogs.

The Add Form command on the Project menu is used to insert new empty forms, forms created from templates, and existing forms into a project. The Add Module command is used to insert a new or existing standard module. The other Add options on the Project menu pertain to modules discussed in subsequent chapters. Both the Add Form and Add Module commands display a dialog with two tabs. The New tab is used to insert a new empty form or standard module. The Existing tab allows you to browse the disk for a module file and add it to the project. Removing a module from a project is accomplished by activating the module, then clicking the Remove command on the Project menu. As modules are added and removed, the Project Explorer is updated accordingly. It is a good idea to save the project whenever you have added or removed a module.

Exploring Help

Visual Basic supports an extensive Help system that documents all the controls, their properties and methods, and all the other components that comprise the Visual Basic language. It is divided into two separate products. The Visual Basic Help system shares the same characteristics as most other Help systems. The second product, called Books Online, replaces the printed manuals historically supplied with many products.

Clicking the Microsoft Visual Basic Help Topics command on the Help menu activates the Help Topics dialog. Pressing the F1 key will activate context-sensitive help if available. Navigating through the Help system can be accomplished using the Contents, Index, and Find tabs in the dialog.

- The **Contents** tab is used like the table of contents in a book. The contents are organized as a list of books. Each book can contain other books or reference pages. Thus, the contents are hierarchical. Navigating the contents is accomplished by double-clicking a book to open it, then double-clicking another book to open it or a reference page to display the page.
- The **Index** tab is analogous to the index of a book. It contains a text box to look up a key in the index. As characters are typed, an item in a list box is highlighted that matches the text currently entered in the text box. Selecting an item then clicking Display will display a reference page for the selected topic. Navigating in the list box also can be accomplished using scroll bars and selecting a topic to display.
- The **Find** tab is used to locate a topic or topics by keyword. If Find has never been used, the Help system must build a list of words to use in the list.

Books Online is new to Visual Basic 5.0 and contains a more detailed discussion of Visual Basic than found in the Help system. In addition to providing a brief reference for a particular topic, Books Online provides informative "how to" examples to assist you. Books Online contains two main windows called the navigation area and the topic area. The navigation area works much like the Contents tab in the Help system. That is, it contains books that can be opened and closed. When a book is opened, it in turn contains other books or reference pages. The topic area contains the reference page for the currently selected topic. Books Online also supports a Find function. Entering text in the Find list box and pressing the ENTER key will search the Books Online for topics containing the search pattern. Figure 1-3 shows the Books Online product.

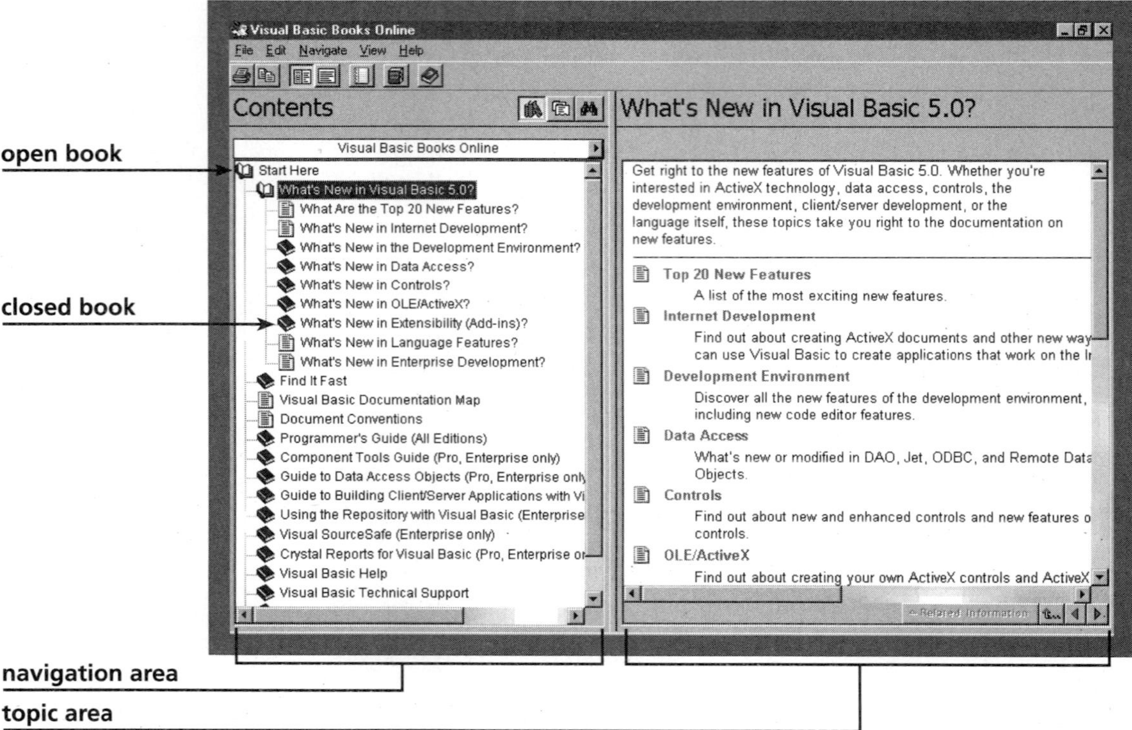

Figure 1-3: Books Online

Programming tip

The Help system is an invaluable tool to locate the syntax of statements quickly and to learn how to use different objects. It contains numerous examples showing typical uses and syntax.

Depending on the options selected when Visual Basic was installed, the Books Online option may or may not appear on the Help menu. Furthermore, it may be installed such that the actual reference pages are copied on the hard disk or remain only on the Visual Basic CD-ROM. In the second case, the CD-ROM must be present in the drive for the Books Online product to work correctly.

Understanding Properties

Each object supports a fixed set of properties. Each property contains a well-defined set of values. For example, the valid values for some properties are the Boolean values True and False. Other properties support a finite list of constant values. Still others support textual descriptions or numbers. Every form supports properties that define the general characteristics of the form including where it appears on the screen, and the characteristics of its border and title bar. Every form and visible control instance created on a form supports several properties to define the position and appearance of the form or control. These too can be set to specific values.

- The **BorderStyle** property defines how the border appears around the form, and whether or not the form can be resized. If set to 0 - None, no border is drawn around the form. If set to 1 - Fixed Single, the only way to resize the form is using the Maximize and Minimize buttons on the form's Control-menu box. If set to 2 - Sizable, the default, the form also can be resized by dragging the mouse over the border. The setting 3 - Fixed Dialog is used for dialogs. The window neither can contain Maximize and Minimize buttons nor can be resized. The settings 4 - Fixed ToolWindow and 5 - Sizable ToolWindow are used to create Tool windows. These windows do not appear on the taskbar when minimized. Also, the text on the title bar appears in a smaller font size.
- The **Caption** property defines the text that appears on the title bar.
- The **ControlBox** property can be set to True or False. If set to True, the default, a Control-menu box appears on the upper-right corner of the title bar. If set to False, no Control-menu box appears. The Control-menu box always contains a Close button, and optionally can contain Maximize and Minimize buttons.
- The **MaxButton** and **MinButton** properties each can be set to True or False to control whether the Maximize and Minimize buttons, respectively, appear on the Control-menu box.
- The **Enabled** property determines whether or not the user can interact with an object, and can be set to True or False. When the Enabled property of a form or control is set to False, the form or control will not respond to events. If set to True, the default, the form or control can respond to events.
- The **ShowInTaskbar** property can be set to True or False. If set to True, the form will appear on the taskbar when minimized. If set to False, the form will not appear on the taskbar.
- The **StartUpPosition** property can be set to one of three constant values as shown in the Properties window. If set to 0 - Manual, the default, no initial position is specified. If set to 1 - CenterOwner, the form is displayed centered in the parent form. If set to 2 - CenterScreen, the form is centered on the whole screen. If set to 3 - WindowsDefault, the form is positioned in the upper-left corner of the screen.
- The **Top** and **Left** properties define the position of the upper-left corner of a form relative to the screen, or, in the case of a control instance, the upper-left corner of the control relative to the form.

- The **Height** and **Width** properties define the size of the control instance or form.
- The **ScaleMode** property is used to determine the unit of measure applied to controls. By default, the unit of measure is a twip. A twip is a screen independent unit of measure. There are about 1,440 twips per inch.
- The **ScaleHeight** and **ScaleWidth** properties are used to create custom coordinates for an object.
- The **Visible** property determines whether an object is visible on the screen. If set to True, the form or object on the form is visible. If set to False, the form or object is invisible. The user cannot interact with objects that are not visible. It is possible, however, to reference an invisible object with code.

The Name Property

Every form and control instance has a Name property. Each time a form class is added to a project or a control instance is created on a form, Visual Basic assigns a unique name to the object. The default name for the first form created in a project is Form1. The default name for a control instance works the same way. For example, the first Label control instance has the name Label1, the second Label2, and so on. An object's name is significant for two reasons. First, the name of a form and the control instances drawn on the form provide the means for Visual Basic and Windows to locate the code associated with a specific event pertaining to the control. Second, the name of an object is the name you use to reference it with code. Thus, selecting appropriate names for the objects you create will improve the readability of the program significantly. A common strategy of assigning names to objects is to use a three-character prefix that identifies the object's type followed by a name that describes the purpose of the object. When a name contains multiple words, capitalize the first letter of each word. Also, avoid obscure abbreviations. Refer to the Student Resource CD-ROM for a complete list of these prefixes. The standard prefix for a form is "frm". The Name property of a form must:

- Begin with a letter.
- Be made up only of letters, numbers, or the underscore character (_).
- Contain no punctuation or special characters such as the dash (-) or period (.).
- Be 40 characters or less.

The naming of objects is somewhat subjective. While longer names can more fully describe the purpose of the object, long names can be tedious to type while writing code. As a general rule, keep object names to a maximum of 20 characters. Some objects like lines and labels do not generally have event procedures associated with them and are never referenced in code. When this occurs, use the default name assigned by Visual Basic as a time-saving technique.

Properties—Design Mode vs. Run Mode

You have seen that an object supports properties and those properties can be set by the programmer. Whether Visual Basic is in design mode or run mode has an effect on an object's properties. For example, there are properties that can be changed both at run time and design time. There are other properties that can be changed at design time, but not at run time. In other words, the property is read-only at run time. There are other properties that only have meaning at run time. That is, they cannot be set at design time. Other properties are entirely read-only. That is, they can never be set either at design time or at run time. They can only be read at run time. Setting properties at design time is accomplished using the Properties window.

Using the Properties Window

The Properties window works with an active module (form, standard, or class) at design time, and is unavailable at run time. If there is no module active, the Properties window is blank. When used with a form module, the Properties window displays the currently selected object (form or control instance) on its title bar as shown in Figure 1-4.

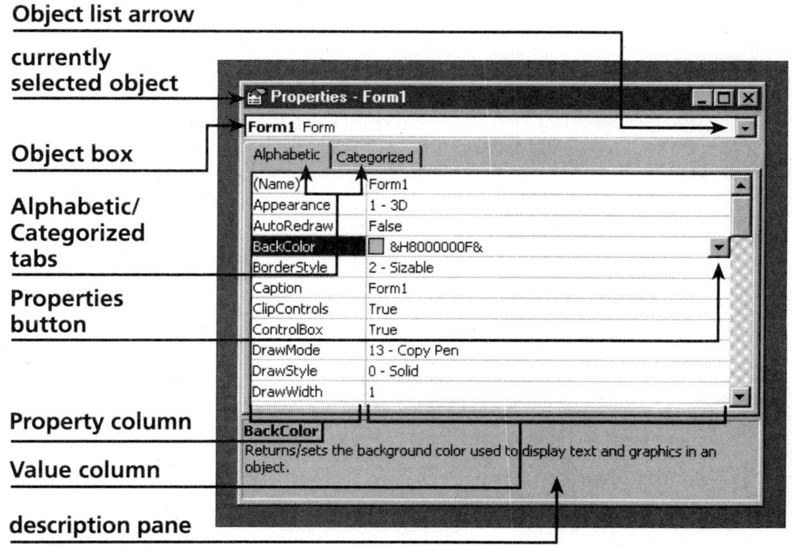

Figure 1-4: Properties window

There are several ways to select an object in the Properties window. The current object can be selected using the list arrow in the Object box. The Object box contains the name of the control instance or form followed by the name of the class from which the instance was derived. Also, you can right-click the mouse button on a form or control, then click Properties on the popup menu to activate the

Properties window for a specific object. The Properties window contains two tabs as follows:

- The Alphabetic tab displays the properties for the selected object in alphabetical order.
- The Categorized tab displays properties based on the property's purpose. The Categorized tab is implemented using a drill-down interface very similar to the Windows Explorer program. At the top level is a property category, which can be expanded or collapsed to view the properties pertaining to the selected category.

The list section of the Properties window contains two columns. The first column is known as the Property column and identifies the name of the property. The second column is called the Value column and contains the current value of the property. Properties that support a fixed set of values are assigned by clicking the Properties button at the right side of the Value column and selecting a value from the drop-down list box. If the Properties button is displayed with three dots, then clicking it will activate a dialog to set the property. The description pane is displayed at the bottom of the Properties window and contains a brief description of the selected property's purpose. Right-clicking the mouse button in the Properties window and deselecting the Description check box will hide the description and allow you to view more properties at one time in the Properties window.

As with many programs, there are multiple ways to accomplish the same task. For example, you may desire to display a form on the center of the screen when the program is started. It is possible to both explicitly set the Top and Left properties of a form, or to change the value of the StartUpPosition property. The size of a form may be changed by dragging the border of the form at design time or setting the Height and Width properties in the Properties window. The method to use largely depends on your preferences as a programmer.

To set the form's design-time properties:

1. Activate the form named **Form1** by clicking the form name in the Project Explorer, then the **View Object** button, if needed. Note that both Form1 and frmDiverse.frm are shown in Project Explorer. Form1 is the value of the form's Name property and frmDiverse.frm is the file name stored on the disk.
2. Using the Object box in the Properties window, click **Form1**, if necessary.
3. Set the Name property to **frmDiverse**.
4. Locate the **StartUpPosition** property using the scroll bars. Click the **Value column** for the property to display the Properties button. Click the **Properties** button to display the options.
5. Set the value to **2 - CenterScreen.**
6. Set the **Caption** property to **Diverse Products - Name / Address List.** Note that as you change the characters in the Properties window, the caption on the title bar is updated.

7 Set the **Height** and **Width** properties to **2385** and **6045**, respectively. The size of the form is changed accordingly.

The effect of setting the properties of a form or control is very interactive. As you change the value of a property that affects the visual part of a form or control, it is applied to the control. For example, when you set a property to change the position of a control, fonts, or colors, the change is displayed providing you with immediate feedback about the change you made.

SECTION B

objectives

In this section you will:

- Create the user interface for a Visual Basic program consisting of boxes to accept input and display output, and buttons the user can click to perform a specific task
- Create an instance of the Shape and Line controls on a form to separate sections of the form visually
- Add a Label control to display output, a TextBox control to accept input from the user, and a CommandButton control that will perform a task when clicked
- Add a scroll bar to the form
- Write code that will respond to events generated when the program is initialized and events that are created by the user
- Add comments, which are ignored by Visual Basic, to help you and other programmers understand the purpose of the program and specific statements
- Compile a Visual Basic program into an executable file
- Locate errors in a program

Building a Visual Basic Program

Creating Your First Program

To illustrate the fundamental elements of a Visual Basic program, you will create a simple program that displays the current date on the form using the form created in the previous section. The program will use an instance of the control, called the Label control, to display the date. The date will be determined by querying the system date. The value will be displayed in the label when the program is run. Note that this task is performed in response to an event. The program also will illustrate the use of the TextBox control to accept input from the user. Two instances of the CommandButton control will be used. One to clear the contents of the text boxes and the other to exit the program. Finally, you will use a scroll bar to illustrate the use of a different kind of object that can accept user input.

One step in creating a Visual Basic program is to create the user interface. You create the user interface by drawing instances of controls on a form making visible objects. Depending on the needs of the program, zero, one, or more instances of each control may be used on a form. Each control instance created on the form has a unique name. This is the value of the Name property. Each control also has a distinct set of properties. This is not to say that different controls do not share the same properties. Remember that every control has a Name property. The set of properties for each control, however, is unique.

Creating a Control Instance

Creating control instances is accomplished by clicking a control on the Toolbox, then dragging the mouse on the form to define the visible region of the control. Regardless of which control is being used, the process of creating, moving, resizing, and deleting a control is the same. The process of creating a control instance is shown in the following steps:

1. Activate the form where the control will be displayed.
2. Click the desired control on the Toolbox. The control will appear recessed on the Toolbox.
3. Drag the mouse on the desired form to define the rectangular region of the control instance. As the control is being dragged on the form, an outline of the control's visible region will appear.
4. Release the mouse button. An instance of the control is created and a unique value is assigned automatically to the Name property.

As the user interface is developed, it often is necessary to move and resize the control instances. The process of moving, resizing, and deleting a control is the same for all controls and is shown in the following list:

- Moving an object is accomplished by clicking the control instance to activate it, then dragging the mouse to the control's desired new position. As the mouse is moved, an outline of the control instance is displayed. It also is possible to set the Top and Left properties using the Properties window.
- The object can be resized by clicking the object to activate it. Then, by dragging the mouse on one of the borders, the object will be resized accordingly. As the object is moved or resized a ToolTip appears indicating the current size of the object. It also is possible to set the Height and Width properties in the Properties window.
- An object can be deleted by clicking the object to activate it, then pressing the Delete key.

As you design the user interface for a form, you will find that you frequently move and resize controls to align them, group controls into different areas on the form, and keep the spacing between controls even.

Visual Basic allows you to move and resize several controls as a group. It is possible to hold down the Shift or Ctrl key and click the mouse button on multiple control instances to select them. Each control will appear with handles at the border of the visible region. Then, you can drag the mouse while positioned inside of one of the active control instances to position several controls at once.

Visual Basic also provides considerable flexibility for setting the properties of multiple control instances at the same time. When multiple objects are selected, the Properties window can be activated. Only the properties common to all the selected objects will appear. Setting the value of these common properties will affect all the selected objects. It also is possible to create a control instance and set its properties. Then, you can activate the object by clicking it, copy it to the clipboard and paste a copy of the object back on the form. The new copy of the object will inherit the property settings of the original object. These techniques can save time creating the user interface. When you use the clipboard to copy and paste controls, a dialog box will display asking if you want to create a control array. Refer to Chapter 3 for information about control arrays.

The Line and Shape Controls

There are two controls used to identify parts of a form visually, or segment parts of a form. The user does not interact with these controls in any way. They only are used to add visual interest to the form. As such, these controls neither respond to any events nor support any methods. The **Line** control is used to draw a line on the form and has the following properties:

- The **BorderColor** property returns or sets the color of the line drawn on the form.
- The **BorderStyle** property is used to change the characteristics of the line. Valid values include a solid line, dashed line, dotted line, or a combination of the three previous options.
- The **BorderWidth** property identifies the thickness of the border.
- The starting and ending points of the line are identified by the **X1, Y1**, **X2**, and **Y2** properties. The starting point of the line is (X1,Y1), and the ending point of the line is (X2,Y2).

The **Shape** control is used to draw a rectangle, oval, square, circle, rounded rectangle, or rounded square on the form. Each shape can be filled with a color and a pattern. The Shape control supports the following properties:

- The **BackStyle** property either can be transparent or opaque. If opaque, the BackColor fills the region of the control. If transparent, the graphics and the background color of the form appear in the region of the control.
- The **BorderStyle** property is used to change the characteristics of the border surrounding the shape.
- The **Shape** property identifies the type of shape that is drawn. Valid shapes include a rectangle, square, oval, circle, rounded rectangle, and rounded square.
- The **FillColor** property is used to set the color displayed inside the region of the shape.
- The **FillStyle** property is used to draw a pattern inside the shape.

The primary purpose of the Shape and Line controls is to improve the visual appearance of the user interface. As such, its uses and the colors and patterns for lines and shapes are subjective. In general, keep the visual interface simple and uncluttered. Too many colors or objects tend to be distracting.

While the Line and Shape controls contribute to the visual appearance of the form, the Label control serves a very different purpose. It is used both to display output from the program and as a descriptive prompt for other controls on the form.

The Label Control

The primary purpose of the **Label control** is to display a prompt or message. This prompt typically is used to describe the contents of another field. The text in the prompt is stored in the Caption property of the label. The label supports the Alignment, BorderStyle, and font-related properties to control the appearance of the label.

- The **Alignment** property controls how the text is aligned inside the region of the label and accepts the values 0 - Left Justify (the default), 1 - Right Justify, and 2 - Center.

- The **Caption** property specifies the text that appears in the label.
- The **BorderStyle** property, if set to 0 - None, the default, will cause no border to be displayed. If set to 1 - Fixed Single, a single line is drawn around the control.
- The standard prefix for the Label control is "lbl".

In this example, you will create three labels. The date label will display the current date and is used for program output. The other two labels will display the descriptive prompts for the Name and Address TextBox objects you will create in a moment.

To create a control instance and set its design-time properties:

1 Click the **Label** control [A] on the Toolbox. Create an instance of the control to display the current date as shown in Figure 1-5. Position and size the label so it is the same as shown in Figure 1-5.

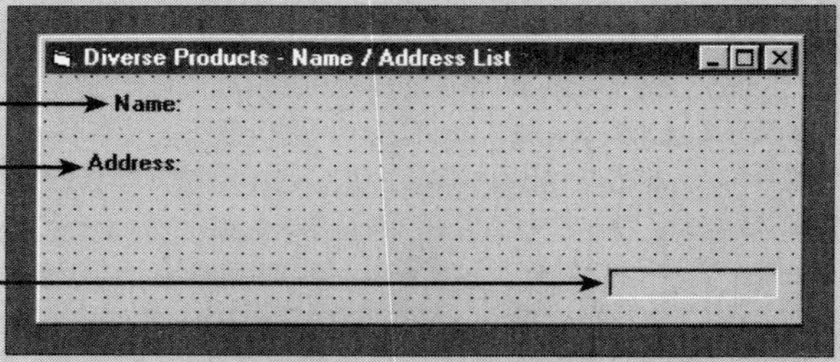

Figure 1-5: Creating the Label control instances

2 Activate the Properties window, and set the Name property to **lblDate**, the Alignment property to **2 - Center**, and the BorderStyle property to **1 - Fixed Single.** Remove the text from the Caption property.

3 Create two more labels to display the name and address prompt as shown in Figure 1-5. Set the Caption of each to **Name:** and **Address:**. Set the Alignment to **1 - Right Justify.** Note that you did not explicitly set the Name property of these labels. These labels contain descriptive prompts and will never be referenced with code. This book will follow the convention of using default names for objects when the objects will never be referenced with code.

4 Click the **Value column** of the **Font property**. Then click the **Properties** button [...] at the right side of the **Value column** to open the Font dialog. Click **Bold** in the Font Style list box and click **OK**.

At this point, your program will display the prompts in the labels and the region of the line and shapes. It will do little else, however. There is no way for the user to enter information into the program. Furthermore, none of the objects respond to any events.

Responding to an Event

If you are accustomed to writing programs in a procedural language, there is a main procedure that is executed when the program first begins. In this example, the date will not be displayed in the label because of a statement executing in the main procedure. Rather, the statement will execute in response to an event. Remember that a form is an object and that an object can respond to events. There is an event that occurs when a form is loaded into memory. It is here that you will write the statement to display the date in the label you just created. When you write code that responds to an event, you create a procedure called an **event procedure**. An event procedure has a specific syntax as shown in Figure 1-6.

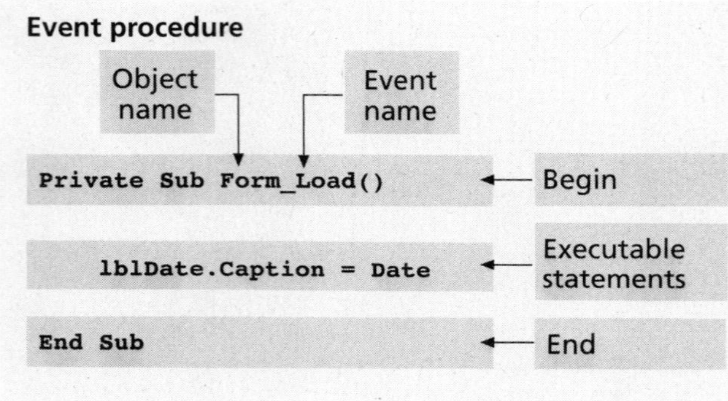

Figure 1-6: Form_Load event procedure

Figure 1-6 also illustrates that the procedure begins with the keywords Private Sub and ends with the keywords End Sub. These are keywords that mark the beginning and end of the event procedure. (They also mark the beginning and end of other procedures). Between these lines, is the code that is executed in response to the event. The event procedure has the name Form_Load( ). This name is made up of two parts. The first part indicates that the event procedure pertains to the form. The second part identifies the particular event that pertains to the form. These two parts are separated by an underscore. Typically, you would refer to this event as the Form Load event. The following list summarizes the processing that takes place in a typical event-driven Visual Basic program:

1. When a program is started, a form called the startup form is loaded and displayed on the screen. Any event procedures pertaining to initializing the startup form are executed.
2. At this time, the program waits for an event to occur and no code is executing. The code that will execute next cannot be predicted because it is impossible to predict which event will occur to which object next. That is, the program does not know whether the user will click a command button or enter characters into a text box.

3. When the user enters a keystroke, clicks a mouse button on an object, or performs some other action, an event occurs. The code in the event procedure corresponding to this event is executed. When the procedure finishes, the program waits for the next event to occur. If there is no code written for the event procedure, the event happens quietly and no code is executed.
4. There also are events that occur to a form as the program ends.

In addition to the syntax for the event procedure, consider carefully the statement inside the event procedure. This statement is called an **assignment statement**. An assignment statement contains a left-hand side followed by an equal sign (=), followed by the right-hand side. When executed, the expression on the right-hand side is evaluated and the result stored in the left-hand side. In this case, the expression on the right-hand side obtains the date from the system. The expression on the left-hand side refers to the Caption property of the Label object named lblDate. When you reference the property of an object using code, the following syntax is used:

Syntax	*objectname.propertyname*
Dissection	■ The *objectname* is the name of a form or control instance on a form. ■ The *propertyname* is the name of a property supported by the object. ■ The *objectname* and *propertyname* are separated by a dot (.).
Code Example	`lblDate.Caption = Date`
Code Dissection	The statement obtains the system date and stores it in the Caption property of the label. This causes the label to display the current date.

To create the code for an event procedure, or write any other statements, you use a window called the Code window.

The Code Window

The **Code window** is an intelligent text editor designed specifically for writing Visual Basic programs. One instance of the Code window can be open for each module in a project. Thus, if the program had two forms, two separate instances of the Code window could be open—one for each form. The Code window has features to select event procedures and other parts of a module. By default, the Code window will capitalize keywords and make consistent the case of all procedure and variable names. It also supports a technology called IntelliSense. As you write statements in the Code window, it will display ToolTips describing the syntax for procedure calls. It also displays the valid properties and methods that pertain to objects and variables. Figure 1-7 shows the Code window.

The Code window contains two list boxes, as Figure 1-7 illustrates. The Object box is used to select an object drawn on the form, the form itself, or the general procedures. The Procedures/Events box is used to select an event procedure pertaining to the selected object or a general procedure. In addition to using the Object and Procedure/Events boxes to select a procedure, it also is possible to use the **Page Up** and **Page Down** keys to scroll through the procedures in the module. The Code window will display one procedure at a time if the Procedure View button is clicked, or several procedures at a time if the Full Module View button is clicked. The mode to use is a matter of personal preference.

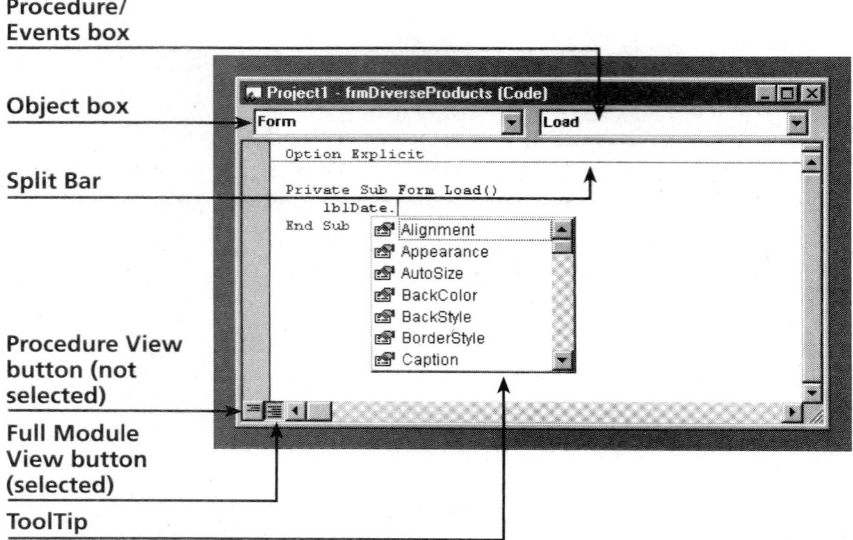

Figure 1-7: The Code window

Also, as shown in Figure 1-7, there is a ToolTip displaying a list of properties pertaining to the Label controls. Visual Basic recognizes that the lblName is an instance of the Label control. When you type the period character, Visual Basic tries to help you with the next step by displaying the list of properties. You can use the scroll bars to select a property from the list or continue to type characters.

Selecting an Event Procedure

All executable code must be in a procedure. The statement that needs to be written displays the current date on the form when the form first is loaded. Thus, the statement needs to be located in the Form_Load event procedure.

To enter code into an event procedure:

1 Make sure the Form window is active. To open the Code window for the form, click **Code** on the **View** menu or double-click the form.

2 Click the **Form** object then the **Load** procedure on the blank line below the line that begins with the word "Private," and enter the following statement into the event procedure. The statement Option Explicit appears on the first line of the Code window; it is used to require explicit declaration of variables and will be described in Chapter 2.

```
lblDate.Caption = Date
```

3 Close the Code window.

4 Save the project then run the program. The date is displayed as shown in Figure 1-8. By default, when the year is 1999 or prior, only the last two digits are displayed. Dates including and after the year 2000, however, are displayed with all four digits.

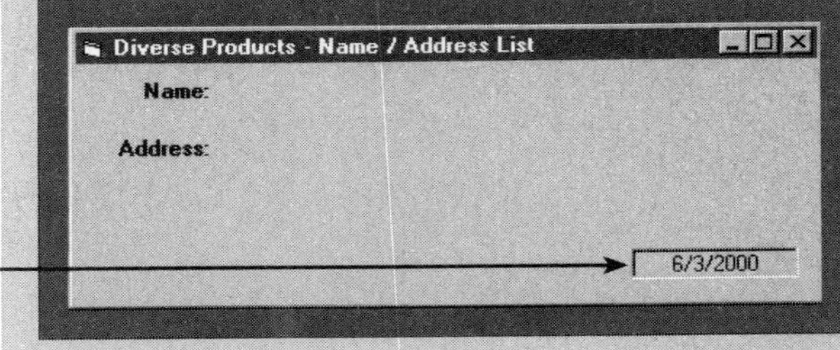

Figure 1-8: Date displayed in label

5 End the program.

The Label control is but one control that makes up a Visual Basic program. There are other controls, each suited to a particular task that make up the user interface.

The TextBox Control

The **TextBox control** is the primary way for the user to enter textual data on a form. Just as a label has properties you can set, so does the text box. The primary difference between the label and the text box is that the label cannot receive input from the user while the text box can. The TextBox control supports properties that define the text that appears inside the region of the text box. The text also can appear on multiple lines, if necessary. When text appears on multiple lines, scroll bars can be added to scroll through the contents of the text box. The value typed by the user into the text box is stored in the Text property. The text box supports the Alignment and positioning properties as supported by the Label control.

- The **Text** property contains the value displayed in the text box.
- The **Locked** property can be set to True or False. If True, the user cannot change the contents of the text box although it still can receive focus. If False, the default, the user can edit the contents of the text box. The contents of a

text box can be changed programmatically regardless of the setting of the Locked property.

- The **MultiLine** property can be True or False, the default. If set to True, the text can be displayed on multiple lines. The Alignment property has no effect unless the MultiLine property is set to True.
- The **ScrollBars** property can be set to 0 - None (the default), 1 - Horizontal, 2 - Vertical, or 3 - Both. If set to 0 - None, no scroll bars will appear. If set to 1 - Horizontal or 2 - Vertical, horizontal or vertical scroll bars will appear, respectively. If set to 3 - Both, vertical and horizontal scroll bars will appear.
- The standard prefix for a text box is "txt".

In this example, you will create two text boxes. The first will store a name and the second an address. Because the address may span multiple lines, the second text box will be a multiline text box with vertical scroll bars.

To create a TextBox control and set the design-time properties:

1 Click the **TextBox** control on the Toolbox. Create the Name text box on the form as shown in Figure 1-9.

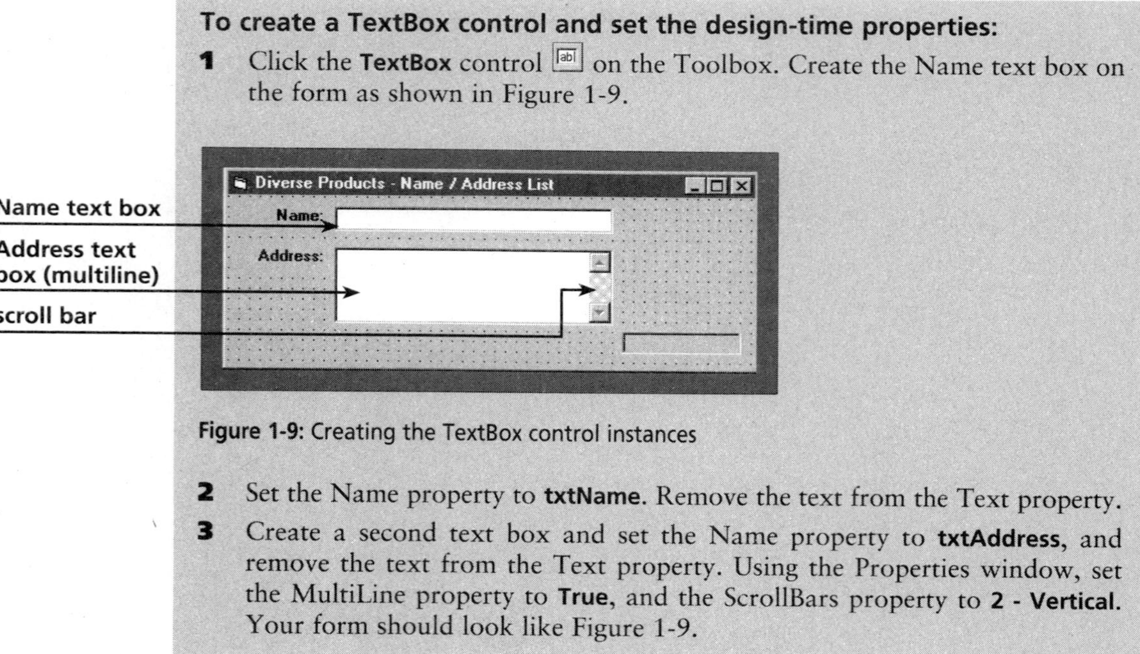

Figure 1-9: Creating the TextBox control instances

2 Set the Name property to **txtName**. Remove the text from the Text property.

3 Create a second text box and set the Name property to **txtAddress**, and remove the text from the Text property. Using the Properties window, set the MultiLine property to **True**, and the ScrollBars property to **2 - Vertical.** Your form should look like Figure 1-9.

The program now has TextBox objects where the user can enter characters. Again, if you are accustomed to programming in a procedural language, the concept of processing input characters is different in Visual Basic. Using a procedural language, your program must both know and control the destination of the input. That is, your program must determine the current input field, input the characters in that field, and control the next input field that will receive the characters.

Processing input in Visual Basic is much different. Again, some background about how Windows works with objects on a form is important. Objects can be categorized into those objects that can receive user input and those that cannot.

Put in Windows terms, there are visible objects that can get **input focus** and those that cannot. For example, a label does not process input from the user and cannot get input focus. A text box can, however. Furthermore, only one object on a form can have focus at a time. The object that currently has focus will receive the input characters. Different events occur as an object gets focus and loses focus. Two of these events are the **GotFocus** and **LostFocus** events.

There are many ways for the user to change the input focus from one object to another. The user can click the mouse on an object. This causes the input focus to be changed to the object that was just clicked. Another way to change the input focus is to use the Tab key. Objects on a form that can receive focus do so in a specific order called the **tab order**. The tab order is defined by setting the TabIndex property of an object, which contains an integer number. Values are assigned to the TabIndex property when each object is created such that the first object has a TabIndex property of zero, the second a value of one, and so on. The TabIndex property can be changed using the Properties window.

The program has two text boxes named txtName and txtAddress. To indicate visually to the user that an object has focus, you can write code for the GotFocus and LostFocus events to change the font of the text box that currently has focus.

To change the properties for an object at run-time:

1 Open the Code window.

2 Using the Object list box, click the text box named **txtName**. Using the Events/Procedures list box, click the event procedure named **GotFocus** for the text box and enter the following statement shown in bold. Note that as you enter the statement, ToolTips will appear allowing you to select a property. Also, when you enter the equal sign, a ToolTip also will appear with the options True and False. This is because Visual Basic knows that the only valid values for the FontBold property are True and False.

```
txtName.FontBold = True
```

3 Select the **LostFocus** event procedure for the same object and enter the following statement shown in bold.

```
txtName.FontBold = False
```

4 Repeat Steps 2 and 3 for the text box named **txtAddress**. Make sure to substitute the object named txtAddress for the object named txtName.

5 Test the program. Enter values in each text box. Press the **Tab** key to change focus from one text box to another. Note that as the text boxes get focus the font is set to bold, and when the text box loses focus, the font returns to normal.

The GotFocus and LostFocus events are but two events that pertain to the text box. When you selected these events using the Procedure list box in the Code window you may have noticed several other events. These events occur either as characters are typed in the text box or as the mouse is clicked in the text box.

The CommandButton Control

The primary purpose of the **CommandButton control** is to execute code in response to being clicked. In other words, the command button executes a Click event procedure when the Click event occurs. Command buttons can display either text or pictures. When pictures are used with a command button, individual pictures can be displayed depending on the button's status. Different buttons can be displayed when the button is enabled, disabled, and being clicked. The command button supports the following properties:

- The **DisabledPicture**, **DownPicture**, and **Picture** properties define the pictures displayed when the button is disabled, clicked, and enabled but not clicked, respectively. The graphical formats supported by the command button are bitmaps, icons, metafiles, GIF, and JPEG.
- The **Style** property determines whether text or a picture is displayed on the command button. If set to 0 - Standard, the button will display text. If set to 1 - Graphical, the Picture, DownPicture, and DisabledPicture properties are used to define the icons or bitmaps displayed in the button's visible region.
- The **Caption** property displays a textual caption like the Label control. Command buttons support an access key. Access keys appear underlined on the command button and allow the user to press the Alt key plus the underlined character to activate the Click event for the command button. The ampersand (&) character, when it precedes a character in the caption, causes that character to be used as an access key. Be careful not to use the same access key for more than one command button on a form.
- The **Cancel** property, when set to True, will cause the Esc key to generate a Click event for the button. Only one command button on a form can have the Cancel property set to True. The code for this button usually cancels, changes, and restores the contents of a different object to its previous value.
- The **Default** property, when set to True, will cause the Enter key to generate a Click event for the button. Only one command button on a form can have the Default property set to True. The border for the default command button appears shaded.
- The **ToolTipText** property contains text that is displayed as a ToolTip when the mouse is positioned over the button and left motionless for a few seconds.
- The **Value** property of the control is True when the button is clicked and False otherwise. Setting the Value property to True at run time causes the Click event to occur.

The **Click** event occurs when the user clicks the CommandButton object. The standard prefix for the CommandButton control is "cmd".

GUI Design ▶ tip

Command buttons can display a ToolTip to provide a more detailed description of the button's purpose. In fact, most visible controls support a property to display a ToolTip but they are used most commonly with buttons.

When using a default button, select the most commonly used command button on a form to be the default button.

To illustrate the purpose of the command button, suppose you wanted to clear the contents of the text boxes. This would be useful to clear the text boxes in preparation to add a new name to a file or database, or just after a name was deleted. To remove the contents of the text boxes you need to remove the contents of the Text property at run time. This can be achieved by setting the Text property to an empty string as shown in the following statement:

```
txtName.Text = ""
```

The left-hand side of this assignment statement has the same syntax as the one used to assign the current date to the caption of the label. That is, the object name is followed by the property name. The right hand side contains the empty string, which is specified by two double quotes.

To create a command button and set the properties:

1 Click the **CommandButton** control on the Toolbox. Create a Clear command button as shown in Figure 1-10.

new command buttons

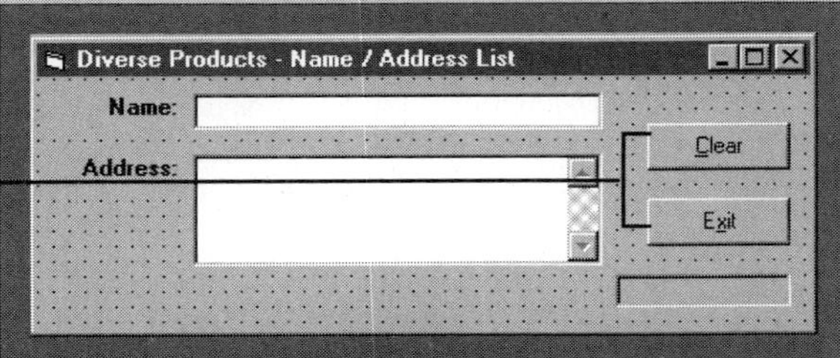

Figure 1-10: Creating the CommandButton control instances

2 Set the Name property to **cmdClear** and the Caption property to **&Clear**. Set the ToolTipText property to **Clear Text Boxes.**

3 Create a second command button as shown in Figure 1-10. Set the Name property to **cmdExit** and the Caption property to **E&xit**. Set the ToolTipText property to **Exit program.**

4 Set the Default property to **True** for the command button named **cmdClear.**

5 Open the Code window. Click the command button named **cmdClear**. Select the **Click** event procedure and enter the following statements:

```
txtName.Text = ""
txtAddress.Text = ""
```

6 Test the program. Enter information into both of the text boxes. Click the **Clear** command button. The contents of the text boxes are cleared.

You now have seen how to use five different controls each serving a very different purpose. The Line, Shape, and Label controls are used to improve the visual appearance of the form and display output but they do not respond to events. The TextBox control is used to process input and output and responds to events when the object receives or loses focus or characters are typed into the text box. The CommandButton control is used to perform a task when clicked. There are two other controls that have a very different purpose called the horizontal and vertical scroll bars.

Scroll Bars

Scroll bars are used to represent the current position within a range. This could be the current position within a document or the current record in a long list of records. This position is an integer value between –32768 and 32767. Scroll bars also are a useful way for the user to select a value from a range of values. The user can change the value of a scroll bar in one of three ways. Clicking the arrows at the endpoints of the scroll bars will increment or decrement the position by a fixed value. Clicking the region between the arrows will increment or decrement the position by a different fixed value. The user also can drag the record indicator to reposition the scroll bar. A scroll bar is divided into three regions. Figure 1-11 shows the three regions of a vertical scroll bar.

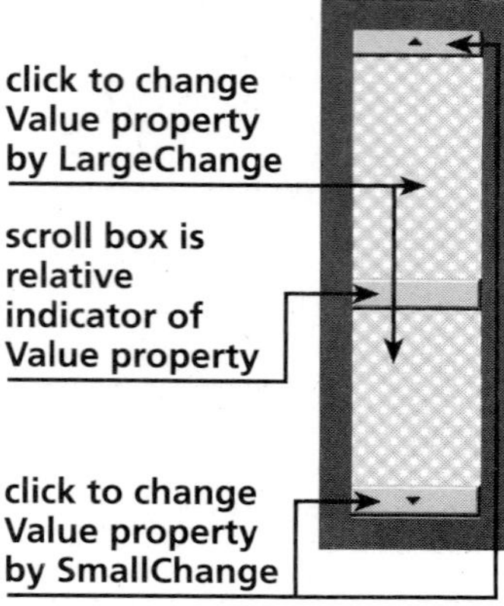

Figure 1-11: Changing the value of a vertical scroll bar

There are two types of scroll bars—vertical scroll bars and horizontal scroll bars. They both have the same properties, but one scrolls vertically and the other scrolls horizontally.

- When a user clicks the arrows, the Value property increases or decreases by the value contained in the **SmallChange** property. The default value of the SmallChange property is one (1). When a user clicks the region between the scroll box and the scroll arrow, the Value property changes by the value of the **LargeChange** property. The default value of the LargeChange property is one (1).
- The **Max** and **Min** properties control the valid range for the scroll bar, and the values can range from –32,768 to 32,767.
- The **Value** property of a scroll bar is an integer containing the current value of the scroll bar (an integer between –32,768 and 32,767).
- The **Change** event occurs whenever the Value property of the scroll bar is changed. Typically, the values of other controls are updated based on the new value of the scroll bar.
- The standard prefix for a vertical scroll bar is "vsb", and for a horizontal scroll bar it is "hsb".

By default, the value of a vertical scroll bar grows as the scroll bar moves downward. If you set the Min property to 0 and the Max property to 25, clicking the up arrow would cause the value to decrease, and clicking the down arrow would cause the value to increase. Think of using a scroll bar to scroll down through a document; the down arrow moves you from line 1 of the document to the next line. To make the value of a scroll bar grow as the scroll arrow is moved upward, reverse the values of the Max and Min properties. That is, set the Max property to 0 and the Min property to 25.

The decision of when to use a vertical scroll bar or a horizontal scroll bar is somewhat subjective. Consider the nature of the underlying data, however. If the data is a measure of distance, a horizontal scroll bar may be more appropriate. If a scroll bar were used to indicate the fullness of a tank of liquid, however, a vertical scroll bar may be more appropriate. In cases where it makes no difference, consider using the scroll bar that best visually balances the form.

The Value of a Control

Nearly every control supports a single property you can use without explicitly referencing the property. This commonly is referred to as the **value** of the control. For example, the value of a label is the Caption property. Thus, the following two statements will produce the same result:

```
lblDate.Caption = Date
lblDate = Date
```

In addition to saving typing, using the value of a control is about 20 percent faster than explicitly specifying the property name. Figure 1-12 lists the value of the controls covered in this chapter.

Control	Value/Property
CommandButton	Value
Label	Caption
Line	Visible
Shape	Shape
TextBox	Text
ScrollBar	Value

Figure 1-12: Default control values

Writing Comments

Comments can be included in any module using the apostrophe (') character. Any line beginning with a comment character is ignored. Comments also can appear at the end of a statement. When a comment appears at the end of a statement, the apostrophe must be preceded by a space. If you are accustomed to older versions of Visual Basic, you may have seen the Rem (short for remark) statement that was used to identify a comment. The Rem statement also is supported by Visual Basic. In this text, however, the apostrophe character will be used because it is more consistent with other languages like C and saves typing. The following three statements illustrate the use of comments:

```
Rem This line is ignored by Visual Basic.
' This line is ignored by Visual Basic.
txtDemo.Text = " ABC"    ' Assign the text ABC to a text box
```

Use comments liberally as you develop programs. Comments do not affect a program's performance or size, but they are an invaluable tool to help other programmers understand your code. Comments also can serve as reminders to you about tasks that still need to be completed.

Writing Continuation Lines

Statements can span multiple lines using the line continuation character, which is an underscore (_) at the end of a line. When used, the underscore must be preceded by a space. The following code is executed as one statement:

```
txtName.Text = _
    txtAddress.Text
```

Programming ▶ tip

It is a good practice to indent continuation lines as shown in the previous example. This helps visually identify that the continuation lines are part of the same statement. Continuation lines should be used when the entire line cannot be viewed in the Code window.

Unloading a Program

You have seen that the Form_Load event occurs when a form is loaded for the first time, and that different events occur as your program runs. There also are events that occur when a program ends and as a form is unloaded. A form can be unloaded using the Unload statement that has the following syntax:

Syntax	**Unload** *formname*
Dissection	■ The **Unload** keyword unloads a form. This causes the memory allocated to the form and its controls to be released to the system. ■ The *formname* must contain the name of the form instance to be unloaded.
Code Example	`Unload Form1`
Code Dissection	This statement unloads the form named Form1. If this is the only active form, the program ends.

When a form is unloaded several events occur. One of these events is the Unload event. Typically, the Unload event is used to request confirmation from the user that the form is to be unloaded, save unwritten files on the disk, or perform other housekeeping chores before exiting the program.

If you are familiar with older versions of Basic, you may have used the End statement to terminate execution of a program. While Visual Basic supports the End statement, its use is strongly discouraged. While not apparent in this introduction, when a program ends there are several "housekeeping chores" that occur. Specifically, all the memory used by the program's forms and the objects on those forms, must be deallocated and released to the system (Windows). When the End statement is used, your program may not release all the objects and their memory properly. Furthermore, the events that usually occur as forms are unloaded do not occur either. This topic is discussed more fully in Chapter 3.

To write the code to end the program:

1. Open the Code window, click the **cmdExit_Click** event procedure, then enter the following statement:

```
Unload frmDiverse
```

2 Test the program. Click the **Exit** button and notice that Visual Basic switches from run mode to design mode.

Introduction to Debugging

There are times when a program you write does not work as you intended. For example, it may end because of a run-time error. Run-time errors occur because a statement tried to perform an action that cannot be carried out. For example, your code may have tried to store a string of characters into a property that can contain only numbers. It also is possible for a program to produce incorrect results without a run-time error occurring. For example, you may have used an incorrect variable name in a statement. The statement may work, but does not produce the intended results. The process of locating and correcting these errors is called **debugging**. The Visual Basic IDE provides several tools to help you locate errors and fix them.

When you run a program, you have clicked the Run button on the toolbar or pressed the F5 key and Visual Basic enters run mode. It is possible, however, to suspend the execution of a program temporarily, enter break mode, and look at the current value of a variable or property. It also is possible to execute statements one at a time to verify the statement is performing correctly.

If a program is not producing the correct results, one technique to locate the error is to step through the program one statement at a time. This allows you to see exactly which statements in which procedures are executing. The technique is particularly useful to determine what events are occurring for an object and in what order. When you step through a program, the Code window is used to highlight the statements as they are executed. A single statement can be executed by pressing the F8 key.

Another window, called the **Immediate window**, is used to look at the current values of properties and variables. Statements you write in the Immediate window have the same effect as those written in the Code window. Thus, you assign a value to a property in the Immedate window, and the change will affect the property of the running program. You can look at the value of a property using the Print statement. The word Print is followed by an expression. The result is printed on the subsequent line in the Immediate window. Clicking Immediate on the View menu opens the Immediate window.

To execute one statement at a time and single step through the program:

1 Press **F8** to begin execution. The Code window will appear as shown in Figure 1-13. Note that the Form_Load event procedure is highlighted. This indicates that the Form_Load event is about to be executed.

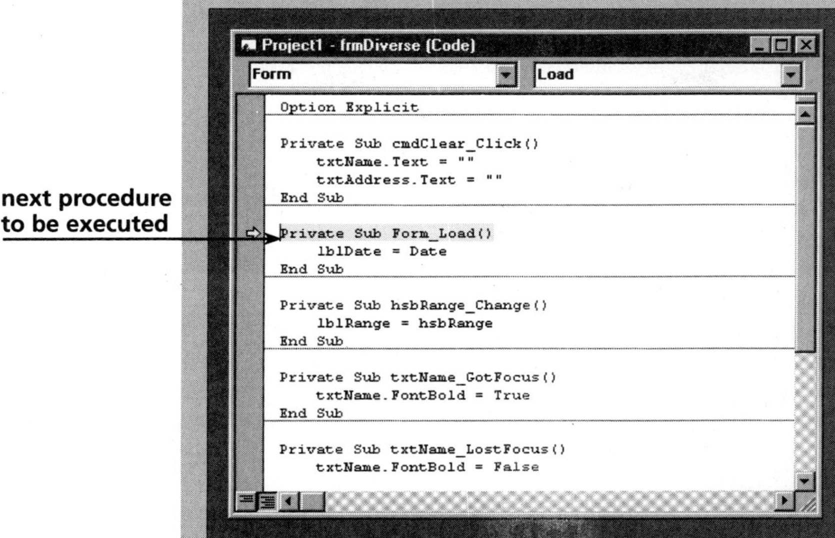
next procedure to be executed
Project1 - frmDiverse (Code)
Form
Load
Option Explicit
Private Sub cmdClear_Click()
txtName.Text = ""
txtAddress.Text = ""
End Sub
Private Sub Form_Load()
lblDate = Date
End Sub
Private Sub hsbRange_Change()
lblRange = hsbRange
End Sub
Private Sub txtName_GotFocus()
txtName.FontBold = True
End Sub
Private Sub txtName_LostFocus()
txtName.FontBold = False

Figure 1-13: Debugging using the Code window

2 Press **F8** again. The statement storing the date in the label's caption is highlighted. This is the next statement to be executed.

3 Press **F8** again to execute the statement.

4 Open the Immediate window, if necessary, and enter the print statement shown in Figure 1-14. This causes the contents of the label's Caption property to be printed in the Immediate window.

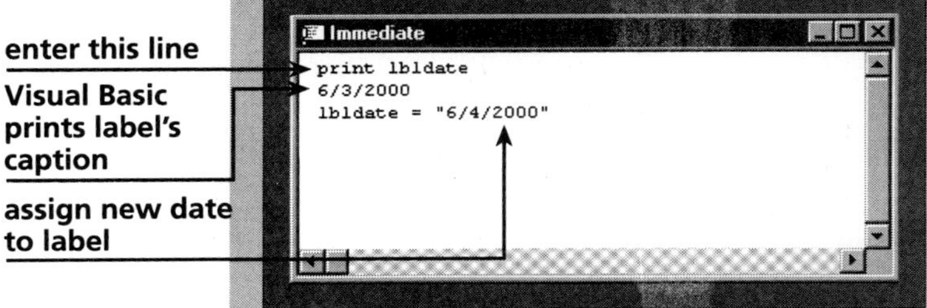
enter this line
Visual Basic prints label's caption
assign new date to label
Immediate
print lbldate
6/3/2000
lbldate = "6/4/2000"

Figure 1-14: Date displayed in label

5 Enter the assignment statement shown in Figure 1-14.

6 Continue to press the **F8** key and notice the GotFocus event procedure occurs for the first text box. As you can see, single stepping through a program is useful to see order of the events that are occurring. When the form appears, note the date in the label has changed.

Once the first text box receives focus, there are no more events to process until the text box loses focus. Thus, Visual Basic will be in run mode until the next event occurs. It also is possible to enter break mode by clicking the Break button on the toolbar.

It is also possible to display output to the Immediate window while the program is running by embedding statements into your code. The Debug.Print statement will allow you to print the values of variables and properties. For example, consider the following statements.

```
Debug.Print txtName.Text
Debug.Print lblDate.Caption
```

These are executable statements so they must appear inside of a procedure. When executed they will print the Text property of the text box named txtName and the Caption property of the label named lblDate to the Immediate window.

The topic of debugging will be revisited throughout this book to help you locate and identify the errors that occur in different programs, how to detect them, and how to correct them.

Compiling a Program

The user of a Visual Basic program seldom runs it by starting Visual Basic and then running the program. Rather, they will run the program from the command line or Start menu just like any other program. The process of converting the Visual Basic code you write into an executable file that can be run directly by Windows is called **compilation** or compiling a program. Before a program can be successfully compiled, it must be free from syntax errors. **Syntax errors** are errors that violate the rules of the Visual Basic language.

How a program is compiled depends on the type of project. In this chapter, you have used the Standard EXE project type that is used to create programs run from the command line or Start menu. Compiling a project into a standard .exe file is accomplished by setting the necessary project properties, then clicking Make EXE on the File menu.

To compile the project:

1 Click **Make Diverse** on the File menu. The Make Project dialog will appear allowing you to select the folder and file name of the executable file. Make sure the file name is **Chapter.01\Startup\Diverse.exe** on the drive where the data files are located.

2 Click **OK** to create the executable file.

3 Exit Visual Basic. Save **Diverse.vbp** if prompted.

4 Click **Run** on the **Start** menu. Enter the file name **Chapter.01\Startup\Diverse.exe** on the drive where the file is stored, then click **OK**. The project is run without Visual Basic.

SUMMARY

This chapter has presented the most fundamental concepts of Visual Basic. Visual Basic is an object-oriented, event-driven programming language. Writing a program consists of creating objects from classes. Each object has an interface made up of properties, methods, and events. Properties can be set at design time using the Properties window or at run time using code. To respond to an event, you use the Code window to create an event procedure. An event procedure contains one or more statements that execute when the event occurs.

The visual interface for a program is created by creating instances of controls on a form. Each Visual Basic control serves a particular purpose. The process of creating a control instance is the same for all controls, you click the control on the Toolbox, and draw the control on a form. The following list summarizes the controls that were discussed in the chapter:

- The Line and Shape controls are used to identify or provide emphasis to a part of a form visually.
- The Label control is used for prompts and to display output.
- The TextBox control is used for input and output. As such it can receive focus.
- The CommandButton control typically performs some action when clicked. It either can display a textual caption or pictures. ToolTips also are common for command buttons.
- Horizontal and vertical scroll bars are used to indicate the current position within a range of values.

Every control supports a default property also known as the value of a control. If you reference a control in code without identifying a specific property, the value of the control is used. Most controls also support events. You can respond to an event by entering statements into a specific event procedure.

Comments also can be included in a program by using either the apostrophe character or the Rem statement.

QUESTIONS

1. An object ___________.
   a. may have properties
   b. may have methods
   c. may support events
   d. has a well-defined interface
   e. all of the above

2. Which of the following statements is True?
   a. A form module has code and a visual interface.
   b. A standard module contains code.
   c. Form and standard modules are stored in separate files.
   d. Both a and c.
   e. All of the above.

3. Which of the following statements is False?
   a. At design time, you write code and create instances of controls on a form.
   b. At run time, you can use the Immediate window.
   c. In break mode, you can use the Immediate window.
   d. When the program is executing, Visual Basic is in run mode.
   e. Break mode is useful to debug programs.

4. The standard naming prefixes for a label, text box, and command button are: ___________.
   a. label, text, button
   b. lab, txt, cmd
   c. lbl, txt, cmd
   d. lbl, txt, com
   e. lab, txt, com

5. Which are the valid file extensions for project, form, and standard modules?
   a. .vbp, .frm, .bas
   b. .prj, .frm, .bas
   c. .prj, .frm, .std
   d. .vbp, for, .bas
   e. .vbp, .for, .std

6. The ___________ properties are used to determine the location and size of the form and objects drawn on the form.
   a. Size, Top, Left
   b. Height, Width, Top, Left
   c. Height, Width, Top, Left, Bottom, Right
   d. Width, Length, Top, Left
   e. Width, Length, Bottom, Right

7. Which of the following statements is invalid? Determine an object or variable's type by the three-character prefix.
   a. lblName = "Trevor Phipps"
   b. lblName.Caption = "Trevor Phipps"
   c. txtName.Text = "Trevor Phipps"
   d. txtName = "Trevor Phipps
   e. txtName.Caption = "Trevor Phipps

8. The ____________ window is used to set an object's properties at design time.

9. The ____________ control supports both text input and output.

10. The ____________ control typically is used to execute code when clicked.

11. To create a text box to display multiple lines of text with horizontal and vertical scroll bars, you would set the following properties: ____________.
    a. MultiLine, ScrollBars
    b. MultiLine, ScrollBar
    c. Lines, ScrollBar
    d. MultipleLine, ScrollBar
    e. MultipleLine, ScrollBars

12. Which event occurs when the user changes the value of a scroll bar?
    a. Updated
    b. Click
    c. Move
    d. Update
    e. Change

13. Write the statement to store the caption "Perfect Products" in the form named frmDemo.

14. Write the statements to set the Height and Width properties of the text box named txtDemo to 100 and 500, respectively.

15. Write the statements to clear the contents of a text box named txtDemo and a label named lblDemo. Show the correct statements by explicitly and implicitly specifying the default property.

16. Write a statement to assign the contents of the text box named txtDemo to the contents of the label named lblDemo.

17. Write the event procedure to set the value of the scroll bar named vsbDemo to zero when the command button named cmdDemo is clicked.

18. Write the event procedure to set the contents of the text box named txtDemo to the value of the scroll bar named vsbDemo whenever the value of the scroll bar changes.

19. Write the event procedure to clear the contents of the text boxes named txtOne, txtTwo, and txtThree when the form named Form1 is loaded.

20. Write the event procedure to clear the contents of a text box named txtDemo when it gets focus.

EXERCISES

1. In this exercise you will use the Line, Shape, and Label controls. For each of the controls, and the form itself, you will set the necessary properties to create the user interface shown in Figure 1-15.
   a. Create a new project.
   b. Set the Name property of the form to **frmExercise1**. Save the form using the name **frmExercise1.frm** and the project using the name **Chapter.01\Exercise\Exercise1.vbp.**
   c. Set the caption of the form to **Exercise 1 / User Interface.**
   d. Create two labels with the captions **Input Section** and **Output Section.** Select a 12-point bold font and set the foreground color to dark blue.
   e. Create a line as shown in Figure 1-15.
   f. Create two shapes as shown in Figure 1-15.
   g. Set the properties of the shapes so they are not transparent.
   h. Set the background color of the shapes to light blue.
   i. Save the project again.

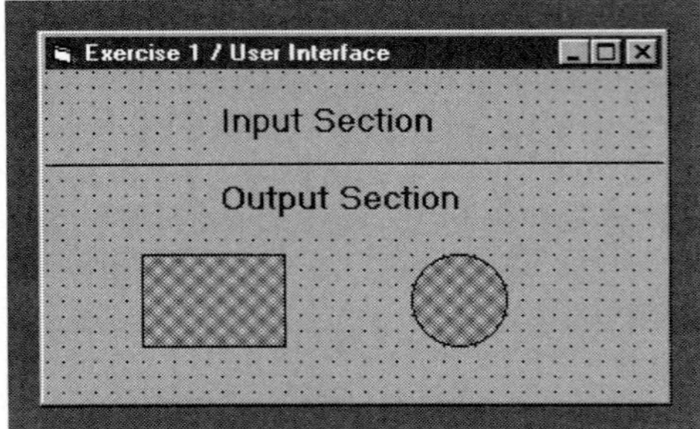

Figure 1-15

2. In this exercise you will use the Label, TextBox, and CommandButton controls to create the user interface for a program to create a mailing list.

a. Create a new project.

b. Set the Name property of the form to **frmExercise2**. Save the form using the name **Chapter.01\Exercise\frmExercise2.frm** and the project using the name **Exercise2.vbp**. Set the caption of the form to **Exercise 2 / User Interface**.

c. Create labels with the following captions: **Name**, **Address**, **City**, **State**, and **Zip Code**.

d. Create text boxes that correspond to the five labels you just created. Set the Name property as appropriate for each of the text boxes. Remove the default text.

e. When the program is loaded, write the necessary code that will store in the State text box the value "CA" for California. This process is the same as for an empty string but the text CA is enclosed in quotation marks.

f. Create a command button named **cmdClear**. When clicked, the command button should remove the contents of the text boxes. The contents of the State text box, however, should be set to CA again.

g. Create another command button to end the program.

h. Save the program again and test it.

3. In this exercise you will use the ScrollBar, Label, and CommandButton controls.

a. Create a new project.

b. Set the Name property of the form to **frmExercise3**. Save the form using the name **Chapter.01\Exercise\frmExercise3.frm** and the project using the name **Chapter.01\Exercise\Exercise3.vbp**. Set the caption of the form to **Exercise 3 / User Interface**.

c. Create a horizontal scroll bar on the form. Set the necessary properties so the minimum value for the scroll bar is 1 and the maximum value is 100.

d. Create three command buttons on the form, one having a caption of **Minimum**, the other having a caption of **Maximum**, and the last a caption of **Exit**.

e. Write the necessary statement to set the value of the scroll bar to its minimum value when the Minimum command button is clicked.

f. Write the necessary statement to set the value of the scroll bar to its maximum value when the Maximum command button is clicked.

g. Write the necessary statement to end the program when the Exit button is clicked.

h. Create a label named **lblRange**. Write the necessary code to update the contents of the label to the value of the scroll bar whenever the value of the scroll bar changes. Create a second label with a caption of **Current Value** to describe the purpose of the label you just created.

i. Save the program again and test it.

4. In this exercise you will use all the controls presented in the chapter and create an executable file.

a. Create a new project.

b. Set the Name property of the form to **frmExercise4**. Save the form using the name **Chapter.01\Exercise\frmExercise4.frm** and the project using the name **Chapter.01\Exercise\Exercise4.vbp**. Set the caption of the form to **Exercise 4 / User Interface.**

c. Create a label at the bottom of the form and store the current date in the label when the form is loaded.

d. Create a horizontal scroll bar on the form.

e. Create two text boxes on the form.

f. When the form is loaded, set the minimum value of the scroll bar and first text box to **0 (zero)**. Set the maximum value of the scroll bar and the second text box to **100**.

g. When the first text box loses focus, change the minimum value of the scroll bar to the value in the first text box.

h. When the second text box loses focus, change the maximum value of the scroll bar to the value in the second text box.

i. Create a label on the form. When the value of the scroll bar changes, store the current value in the label.

j. Create descriptive label prompts for each of the text boxes and labels.

k. Compile the program into an executable file. Save the file using the name **Exercise4.exe**.

l. Test the program. Note that if you either enter invalid data in the text boxes or enter a number that is outside the valid range of values for the scroll bar, an error will occur. You will learn how to identify and resolve these errors in Chapters 2 and 3.

CHAPTER

2

Visual Basic Language Elements

Using Visual Basic to Perform Common Tasks

case▶ Hinkley, Schmidt, and Barnes (HSB) is a public accounting firm. They are using Visual Basic to implement several software packages to be used internally. One of the requirements of all the software is to validate user input where possible. For example, some values should be dates and others should be valid numbers. Other values should be within a specific range of dates or numbers. In this chapter, you will create a standard module containing procedures that implement the various validation tasks and a sample user interface to test the validation procedures.

SECTION A

objectives

In this section you will:

- Use different modules in a project
- Create procedures that do not respond to events called general procedures
- Create general procedures that return values
- Declare variables to store information while a program is running

Declaring Variables and Procedures

Previewing the Completed Application

This chapter summarizes the fundamental elements of the Visual Basic language. If you are not familiar with another procedural or visual programming language and are unfamiliar with Visual Basic, the level of detail presented in the chapter may not be sufficient. In that case, consider reviewing a reference book on Visual Basic. If you have used Visual Basic, however, the syntactical elements presented should be a review. If you have used another procedural language, the concepts of variables, procedures, decision-making, and looping statements should be familiar and the syntax presentation adequate. Again, the Help system and Books Online can be an invaluable tool if the syntax coverage for a particular topic is not sufficient.

This chapter's completed application is intended to illustrate Visual Basic syntactical elements and the implementation of programs with multiple modules. You can load and execute this project and use it for reference as you complete this chapter.

To preview the completed application:

1. Start **Visual Basic** and load the project named **Chapter.02\Complete\HSB_C.vbp.**
2. Run the program. Enter the date and time values shown in Figure 2-1. Click the **Elapsed Date** and **Elapsed Time** command buttons. The elapsed date and time are computed.

   Minimum and maximum allowable dates are stored as constants in the form file. Refer to the form file for the current settings.

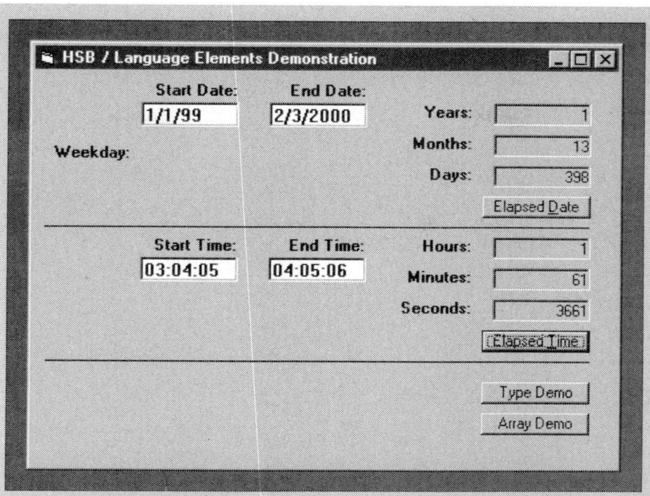

Figure 2-1: Completed application

3 End the program then exit Visual Basic.

The Structure of a Visual Basic Program

Every Visual Basic program contains one or more modules including form, standard, and class modules. Each module has a well-defined, similar structure. The start of a module is known as the **general declarations section**. The general declarations section contains variable, constant, and type declarations that can be used by the procedures in the module. Procedures typically appear after the general declarations section and can contain additional variable declarations and executable statements. There are two types of procedures: event and general. As Chapter 1 illustrated, an event procedure is executed in response to a specific event supported by an object. A general procedure is executed when explicitly called by an event procedure or another general procedure. The order of the procedures relative to each other in the Code window is not significant, although alphabetizing procedure names can improve readability.

Variables declared in a module, the arguments for procedures, and the return values for procedures all have a specific data type. This is consistent with most languages. There are specific data types to store numbers, strings of characters, True/False information, and so on. Both object properties and variables have a specific data type. Visual Basic supports several predefined data types called **intrinsic data types**.

Adopting a standard convention for naming variables and procedure arguments will make your code more readable. In this book, variables will have a three-character prefix denoting the variable's data type. This is consistent with the notion of a three-character prefix for objects. In addition to the three-character prefix to identify a variable's type, this book will precede the prefix with a single character to denote a variable's scope. For global variables, the character "g" is used. For module-level variables, the character "m" is used, and for local (procedure-level) variables, the character "p" is used. Figure 2-2 shows each intrinsic data type, the prefix, the amount of memory used to store a variable of that type, and the valid values.

Data type	Prefix	Size	Values
Byte	byt	1 byte	0 to 255
Boolean	bln	2 bytes	True or False
Integer	int	2 bytes	-32,768 to 32,767
Long	lng	4 bytes	-2,147,483,648 to 2,147,483,647
Single	sng	4 bytes	-3.402823E38 to -1.401298E-45 for negative values; 1.401298E-45 to 3.402823E38 for positive values
Double	dbl	8 types	-1.79769313486232E308 to -4.94065645841247E-324 for negative values; 4.94065645841247E-324 to 1.79769313486232E308 for positive values
Currency	cur	8 bytes	8 bytes -922,337,203,685,477.5808 to 922,337,203,685,477.5807
Date	dat	8 bytes	January 1, 100 to December 31, 9999
Object	obj	4 bytes	Any Object reference
String (variable-length)	str	10 bytes + string length	0 to approximately 2 billion
String (fixed-length)	str	Length of string	1 to approximately 65,400
Variant (with numbers)	vnt	16 bytes	Any numeric value up to the range of a Double
Variant (with characters)	vnt	22 bytes + string length	Same range as for variable-length String

Figure 2-2: Intrinsic data types

The naming conventions used in this book are guidelines. As your proficiency and experience with Visual Basic grows, you undoubtedly will develop your own style.

Procedures

Procedures can contain declarations for local variables and executable statements. All executable statements in a program must reside inside a procedure. Visual Basic does not allow procedures to be nested. That is, you cannot create a procedure inside of another procedure as you can in Pascal. Like a variable, a procedure has a defined scope. The scope of a procedure is defined using the Public and Private keywords. Public procedures are visible to other modules and Private procedures are not.

Unlike event procedures described previously, general procedures do not execute in response to an event. Rather, they must be called explicitly from an event procedure or another general procedure. There are two types of general procedures. **Function procedures** return a value of a specific data type and **Sub procedures** do not return a value. Both Function and Sub procedures have a name by which the procedure is known. Also, a procedure may accept zero or more arguments. A procedure's arguments are a list of names, separated by commas and are used to communicate information to a Function or Sub procedure.

Function Procedures

A Function procedure has the following syntax.

Syntax

[**Public|Private|Friend**] [**Static**] **Function** *name* [(*arglist*)] [**As** *type*]
    [*statements*]
    [*name* = *expression*]
    [**Exit Function**]
    [*statements*]
    [*name* = *expression*]
End Function

Dissection

- If the optional **Public** keyword is used, other modules in a project can call the Function procedure.
- If the optional **Private** keyword is used, the function is visible only to the procedure in which the function is declared.
- The optional **Friend** keyword is used with class modules to make a procedure visible to other class modules inside a project but invisible outside the project.
- The optional **Static** keyword indicates that the values of the procedure's local variables are preserved between calls.
- The required *name* argument indicates the function name and must adhere to the standard variable naming conventions. Multiple statements can assign a value to *name*. If no value is assigned to *name*, the function returns zero (0) if the return type is numeric, and an empty string ("") if the procedure returns a string. A Variant function returns the value Empty if no value is assigned to *name*.

- The *arglist* option contains a list of variables and data types representing the arguments passed to the function. A comma separates each variable.
- Functions return a value of a specific *type*. If **As** *type* is omitted, the return value is a Variant data type. If the function returns an array, the array must be of type Variant.
- The **Exit Function** keywords cause the Function procedure to exit immediately. Execution continues at the statement following the statement that called the Function procedure. A Function procedure can contain zero, one, or many Exit Function statements.
- The optional *statements* in the procedure are executed when the procedure is called.
- The optional *name* = *expression* is used to set the return value of the Function procedure. It is legal to assign a value to *name* in multiple statements. In that situation, the function returns the value of the most recent assignment to *name*.

The *arglist* contains the arguments for a function.

Syntax [**Optional**] [**ByVal|ByRef**] [**ParamArray**] *varname*[( )] [**As** *type*] [= *defaultvalue*]

Dissection

- The **Optional** keyword option indicates that an argument is not required. If used, all subsequent arguments in *arglist* also must be optional and declared using the Optional keyword. Optional arguments must have a data type of Variant.
- The optional **ByVal** keyword indicates that an argument is passed by value.
- The optional **ByRef** keyword, the default, indicates that the argument is passed by reference.
- The optional **ParamArray** keyword must be the last argument in *arglist*. It indicates that the final argument is an Optional array of Variant elements. The ParamArray keyword allows you to create Functions with an arbitrary number of arguments. It may not be used with ByVal, ByRef, or Optional keywords.
- The required *varname* contains the name of the variable representing the argument.
- The optional *type* indicates the data type of the argument passed to the procedure. If omitted, the type is a Variant.
- The optional *defaultvalue* can be any constant or constant expression and is valid for Optional parameters only. If the type is an Object, Nothing is the only valid default value.

Code Example

```
Public Function ValidDate(pvntValue As Variant, _
    Optional pvntMin As Variant, Optional pvntMax As Variant) _
    As Boolean
    Dim pblnValue As Boolean
    ' Code to validate the pvntValue and set the value of
    ' pblnValue
    ValidDate = pblnValue
End Function

' The following statement will call the function
Dim pblnResult As Boolean
pblnResult = ValidDate("12/31/2001")
```

Code Dissection

The previous code declares a function named ValidDate that accepts one required Variant argument named pvntValue. The Function procedure, although incomplete at this point, will set the value of the variable pvntValue to True or False depending on whether or not pvntValue contains correct information. By assigning the result to the function name, this result is returned by the function. The optional arguments will be used to let the user specify a minimum or maximum value. The function returns a Boolean value.

Sub Procedures

Procedures that do not return a value are called Sub procedures. Like Function procedures, Sub procedures can be Public or Private, and can accept zero or more arguments. A Sub procedure, however, cannot be used on the right-hand side of an expression.

Syntax

[**Private**|**Public**|**Friend**] [**Static**] **Sub** *name* [(*arglist*)]
  [*statements*]
  [**Exit Sub**]
  [*statements*]
End Sub

Dissection

- If the optional **Public** keyword is used, other modules in a project can call the Sub procedure.
- If the optional **Private** keyword is used, the Sub procedure is visible only to the procedure in which the Sub procedure is declared.
- The optional **Friend** keyword is used only in a class module. It is visible throughout the project, but not visible to a controller of an instance of an object.

- The optional **Static** keyword indicates that the values of the procedure's local variables are preserved between calls.
- The required *name* argument indicates that the function name must adhere to the standard variable naming conventions.
- The optional *arglist* contains a list of variables and data types representing arguments that are passed to the function. A comma separates each variable. The *arglist* has the same syntax as it does for Function procedures.
- The optional *statements* are any group of statements to be executed within the Sub procedure.
- The **Exit Sub** keywords cause the Sub procedure to exit immediately. Execution continues at the statement following the statement that called the Sub procedure. A Sub procedure can contain zero, one, or many Exit Sub statements.

Code Example

```
Private Sub FormatTextBox(txtInput As TextBox)
    txtInput.FontBold = True
    txtInput.FontSize = 10
    txtInput.FontUnderline = False
End Sub

' The following statements will call the Sub procedure
FormatTextBox Text1
' Calling procedures are discussed later in the chapter
Call FormatTextBox(Text1)
```

Code Dissection

The procedure in this example is named FormatTextBox, and takes one argument, a reference to a TextBox object. The type of the argument is the TextBox class. The procedure uses the argument to format the given text box. To call the Sub procedure, you either can use the procedure name or the Call statement. Notice that when the Call statement is used, the arguments are surrounded by parentheses.

Understanding Call by Value and Call by Reference

Procedure arguments are passed in one of two ways: by reference or by value. When an argument is passed by reference, the default, the memory address of the variable is passed as the argument. Thus, the called procedure can change the actual value of the argument. When an argument is passed by value, the current value of the variable is determined and a copy of the variable is passed to the procedure. If the procedure changes the value of the variable, only the copy is changed. The value of the actual variable is not changed. For example, consider the following Function and Sub procedures:

```
Public Sub SquareSub(ByRef pintResult As Long, _
    pintArg As Integer)
    pintResult = pintArg * pintArg
End Sub

Public Function SquareFn(pintArg As Integer) As Long
    SquareFn = pintArg * pintArg
End Function
```

These two procedures illustrate two different approaches to computing the square of a number. Using the Sub procedure, the result is passed as an argument. Using this approach, the result is declared by reference so the result can be communicated back to the calling procedure. Using the Function procedure, the result is returned by the function. When a procedure returns a single value, a Function procedure generally is preferable because the code is more intuitive. If a procedure must return multiple values, however, it must be implemented as a Sub procedure. Each value to be returned must be a ByRef argument. The following statements could be used to call the two procedures. The statements assume that txtInput and txtOutput are text boxes, and that txtInput contains a valid integer number.

```
SquareSub txtOutput, txtInput
Call SquareSub(txtOutput,txtInput)
txtOutput = SquareFn(txtInput)
```

There are two ways to create Function and Sub procedures. The first is to type the declaration into the Code window. The other is to use a tool called the Add Procedure dialog box. The Add Procedure dialog box is shown in Figure 2-3.

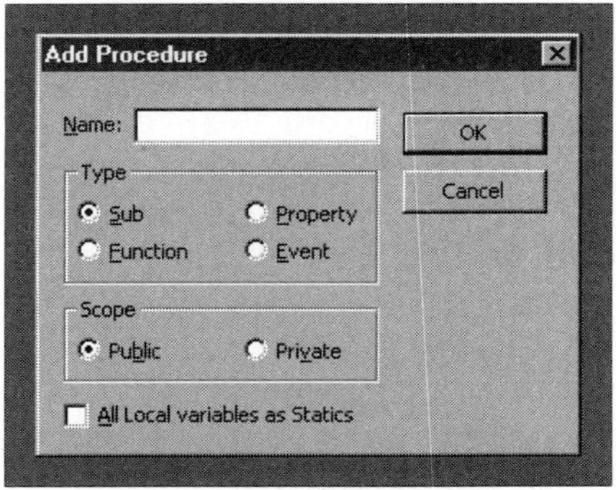

Figure 2-3: Add Procedure dialog box

The Add Procedure dialog consists of multiple sections.

- The name of the procedure should be entered into the Name text box.
- The Type section contains option buttons to indicate whether a Sub or Function procedure is created.
- The Scope section is used to specify whether the procedure is Public or Private.
- The All Local variables as Statics check box will declare the procedure with the Static keyword.

The Add Procedure dialog box has limitations. You neither can use it to declare arguments for a Function or Sub procedure, nor can you explicitly specify the return type of a Function procedure. As a result, you may find it just as easy to create a procedure by typing the declaration in the Code window. When you enter a Function or Sub procedure declaration, Visual Basic automatically inserts the appropriate End Function or End Sub statement.

Variables

Visual Basic supports variables like any other programming language. Variables allow data to be stored while a program is running. Visual Basic supports both implicit and explicit declaration of variables. If the Option Explicit statement is used, referencing a variable without previously declaring it will generate a syntax error. When omitted, referencing an undeclared variable for the first time will cause the variable to be created. The Option Explicit statement must appear in the general declarations section of a module, and it usually appears as the first statement in a module. The Option Explicit statement pertains only to the module where it is declared. Thus, if one module included the Option Explicit statement and another did not, one module would prohibit, and the other would allow, implicit variable declarations.

The Option Explicit statement can be included automatically when a new module is created by checking the Require Variable Declaration check box on the Editor tab in the Options dialog box. In this book, the Option Explicit statement will be used in all modules.

To include the Option Explicit statement in all new modules automatically:

1. Start **Visual Basic** and load the project named **Chapter.02\Startup\HSB_S.vbp**.
2. Click **Options** on the **Tools** menu to open the Options dialog box.
3. Click the **Editor** tab.
4. Click the **Require Variable Declaration** check box. This value may be checked already.
5. Click **OK** to close the dialog.

Allowing implicit variable declarations is a major cause of hard to find errors. Suppose you are using a variable named Counter to count the number of times a loop has executed. Suppose, however, that you inadvertently misspelled the word Counter as Counted. If the Option Explicit statement were not used, the misspelled word would be treated as an implicitly declared variable. Thus, if one statement referenced the variable Counter and the other the variable named Counted, the program probably would produce incorrect results. You then would need to track down the statement that was causing the error. If the Option Explicit statement was used, the compiler would detect the error for you and display a dialog box indicating that the variable was not declared.

Variables can be declared in the general declarations section of a module or inside a procedure. A variable declared in the general declarations section of a standard module exists for the life of the program. A variable declared in the general declarations section of a class or form module exists while an instance of the form or class exists. There is a unique copy of the variable for each form or class instance. A variable declared inside a procedure is allocated from the stack and exists only while the procedure is executing (unless the Static keyword is used). The **stack** is an area of memory used to store local variables and keep track of procedures called. Variables have a defined scope. The **scope** of a variable determines both the life of a variable and whether or not a variable can be referenced by other procedures in a module, or by procedures in other modules. The scope of a variable depends on where in the module a variable is declared and the statement used to declare the variable. Variables are declared explicitly with the **Public**, **Private**, **Static**, or **Dim** statements.

Syntax [**Public**|**Private**|**Static**|**Dim**] *varname* [**As** *type* [, *varname* [**As** *type*]]][, ...]

Dissection

- The optional **Public** keyword only can occur in the general declarations section of a module. Any module in a project can reference a Public variable. Public variables commonly are referred to as global variables.
- The optional **Private** keyword only can be used in the general declarations section of a module. A Private variable only can be referenced by the module in which the variable is declared. Private variables commonly are referred to as module-level variables. Private variables of the same name can be declared in multiple modules. Each is considered a separate variable whose scope is the module where it was declared.
- The optional **Dim** keyword, when used inside a procedure, creates a local variable visible only to the procedure where it is declared. Memory for the variable is allocated from the stack when the procedure starts and deallocated when the procedure exits. Thus, the value is lost between procedure calls. When used in the general declarations section of a module, the Dim keyword has the same effect as the Private keyword. It is a good coding practice to use the Private keyword rather than the Dim keyword to declare module-level variables to improve the readability of a program.
- The optional **Static** keyword is used inside a procedure to create a local variable whose value will persist between calls to the procedure. The variable is not visible to other procedures in the module or to other modules.
- The *varname* is the name by which the variable is known. Variable names must begin with a letter, be less than 255 characters in length, cannot contain an embedded period or other special characters, and must be unique within the current scope. That is, it is not legal either to have two Private variables of the same name in a module or two local variables of the same name in one procedure.

- The optional **As** *type* clause is used to specify a data type for a variable. Valid data types include Byte, Boolean, Integer, Long, Currency, Single, Double, Date, String (for variable-length strings), String * *length* (for fixed-length strings), Object, Variant, a user-defined type, an enumerated type, or an object type. If the **As** *type* clause is omitted, the data type for the variable is Variant.
- Multiple variables can be declared in the same statement by appending multiple *varname* **As** *Type* clauses to the end of the statement separated by commas.

Code Example

```
Public gsngDemo1 As Single, gvntDemo1 As Variant
Private msngDemo2 As Single, mstrDemo2 As String
Dim pintDemo1 As Integer, pintDemo2 As Integer, _
    pintDemo3 As Integer
```

Code Dissection

The first statement declares two Public (global) variables, and the second declares two module-level variables. Multiple declarations appear on the same line separated by commas, and can be of the same type or different types. The third statement is intended to be used inside a procedure and declares three variables. The final two lines are considered one statement because of the line continuation character.

Figure 2-4 illustrates the scope of variables in two modules with local, module-level, and global variables.

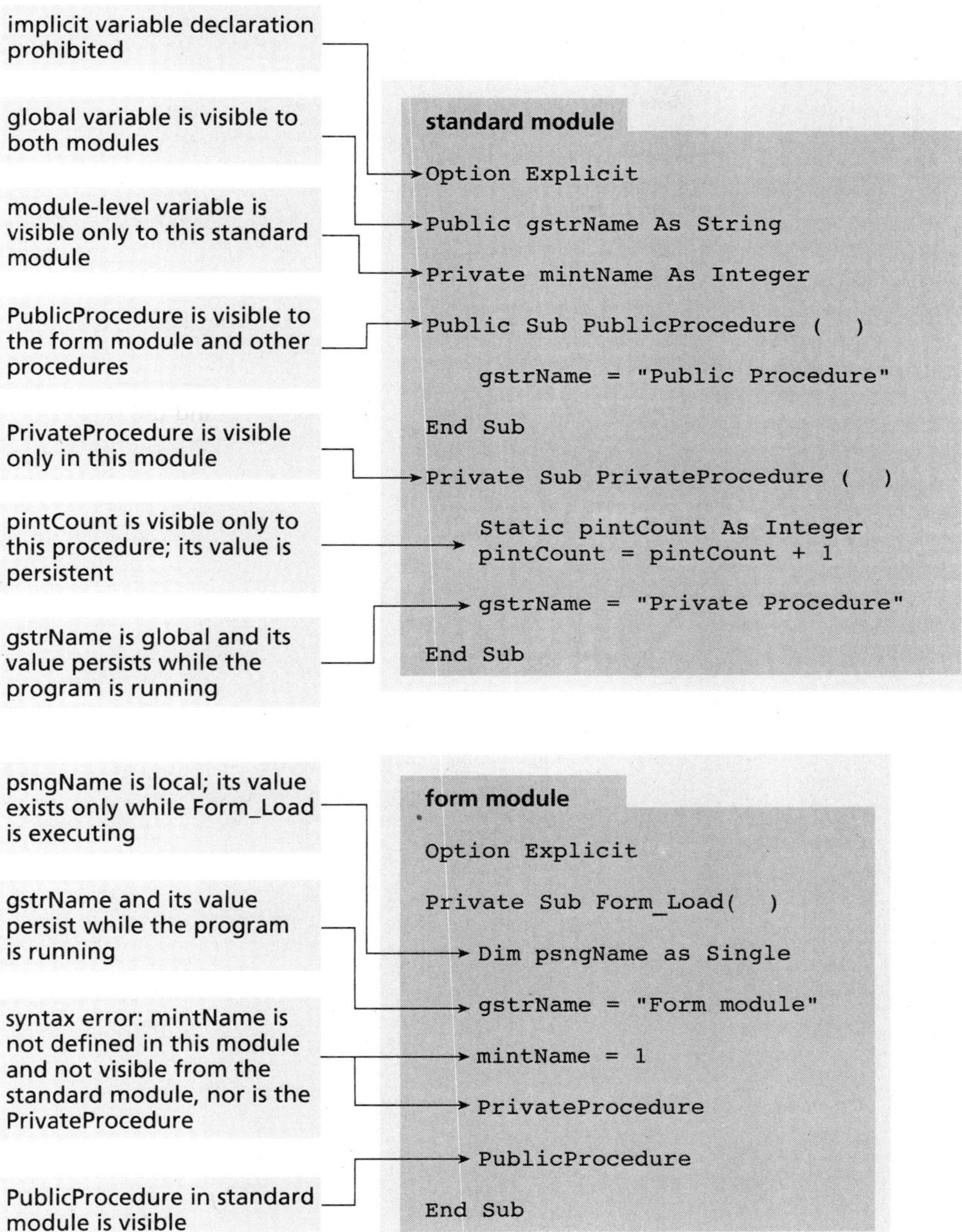
implicit variable declaration prohibited
global variable is visible to both modules
module-level variable is visible only to this standard module
PublicProcedure is visible to the form module and other procedures
PrivateProcedure is visible only in this module
pintCount is visible only to this procedure; its value is persistent
gstrName is global and its value persists while the program is running
standard module
Option Explicit
Public gstrName As String
Private mintName As Integer
Public Sub PublicProcedure ( )
gstrName = "Public Procedure"
End Sub
Private Sub PrivateProcedure ( )
Static pintCount As Integer
pintCount = pintCount + 1
gstrName = "Private Procedure"
End Sub
psngName is local; its value exists only while Form_Load is executing
gstrName and its value persist while the program is running
syntax error: mintName is not defined in this module and not visible from the standard module, nor is the PrivateProcedure
PublicProcedure in standard module is visible
form module
Option Explicit
Private Sub Form_Load( )
Dim psngName as Single
gstrName = "Form module"
mintName = 1
PrivateProcedure
PublicProcedure
End Sub

Figure 2-4: Variable and procedure scope

As shown in Figure 2-4, the variable gstrName is a global variable visible to both the standard module and form module. Changing its value in one module affects its value in all other modules. The variable mintName is a module-level variable visible only to the standard module. Attempting to use this variable in the form module will generate a syntax error. The general procedure named PrivateProcedure (because it is declared as Private), only can be used by the standard module. Trying to call the procedure from the form module will generate a syntax error. PublicProcedure is visible to the form module. The Static variable pintCount is local to PrivateProcedure. Because it is declared as Static, however, the value of the variable persists while the program is running. The next statement in the procedure adds one (1) to the variable pintCount. Thus, after the procedure is called the first time, pintCount will have a value of one (1), the second time a value of two (2), and so on.

Finally, the variable psngName is local to the event procedure named Form_Load. Memory for the variable is allocated when the procedure starts and deallocated when the procedure ends.

Assigning Values to Variables

Once a variable is declared, a value can be assigned to it using an assignment statement. An assignment statement is made up of operators and operands. Operands consist of properties, as you saw in Chapter 1, variables, and constant values. Operators like (+, -, *, /, ^) perform an action on operands. The expression on the right-hand side contains operands and operators. The right-hand side of an assignment statement also can be used to call intrinsic and user-defined functions. The left-hand side of an assignment statement can be a variable, object, or property. Assume the variables in the following statements have been declared as an Integer data type.

```
pintDemo1 = 3
pintDemo2 = pintDemo1
```

The first statement assigns the literal value 3 to the variable pintDemo1. The next statement assigns the value of pintDemo1 (3) to the variable pintDemo2. Thus, pintDemo2 will contain the value 3. When the right-hand side of an assignment contains a combination of Integer, Single, and Double data types, Visual Basic will convert the data type of any intermediate results as necessary. The implementation of the Boolean and Variant data types are unique to Visual Basic and are worthy of a more detailed explanation.

Working with Boolean Data

The Boolean data type is used to represent the values True and False. In Visual Basic, True contains the value negative one (-1) and False the value zero (0). When converting an Integer or Single data type to a Boolean value, however, the result is False, only if the numeric expression is zero (0) and True otherwise. Trying to assign a string to a Boolean variable will cause a syntax error. Consider the following statements:

```
Dim pblnDemo As Boolean
pblnDemo = -1        'True
pblnDemo = 0         'False
pblnDemo = 32.44     'False
pblnDemo = "a"       'Error
```

The first assignment statement causes pblnDemo to be True and the second False. When assigned the value of 32.44, pblnDemo is True. The final statement causes a type conversion error, because it is illegal to assign a string value to a Boolean variable. Visual Basic supports the keywords True and False that also are useful when working with Boolean data as shown in the following statements:

```
Dim pblnDemo As Boolean
pblnDemo = True
pblnDemo = False
```

In the previous example, the first assignment statement assigns the value True to the Boolean variable and the second statement assigns the value False to the variable.

Working with Variant Data

There may be times when the type of data to be stored in a variable is not known, or the data type will change at run time. In these circumstances, the Variant data type is useful. The Variant data type can store any type of data except for fixed-length strings. The Variant data type has unique characteristics that differentiate it from the other intrinsic data types.

- A Variant variable contains the value **Empty** if the variable has been declared but a value has not yet been assigned to the variable.
- It is possible to assign explicitly the value of **Null** to a Variant. A value of Null is used to indicate that the Variant contains no valid data.
- The value of **Error** also can be stored in a Variant to indicate an error has occurred.
- The special value **Nothing** is used for Variants that reference objects. When a Variant is set to Nothing, the reference to the object is destroyed.

The following statements illustrate different types of values stored in a Variant.

```
Dim pvntDemo As Variant
pvntDemo = Error
pvntDemo = Null
pvntDemo = "ABC"
pvntDemo = 123.45
```

Prior to executing the first statement, the value of the variable pvntDemo contains the special value Empty, indicating that a value has not yet been assigned to the variable. The second and third statements set the value of the Variant to Error and Null, respectively. When the Variant is assigned the value "ABC", the underlying data type is String. When the final statement is executed, the Variant contains the Single data type value of 123.45.

While variables of type Variant can store any data type, they should be used sparingly because of their impact on performance. When a Variant variable is referenced, the data type of the information stored in the variable must be determined before the variable actually is used. This causes significant overhead. Furthermore, Variant variables consume a minimum of 16 bytes. This is twice the amount of memory consumed by a Double data type.

To determine how Visual Basic treats the current value stored in a variable, you can use two different functions named TypeName and VarType.

Syntax

TypeName(*varname)*
VarType(*varname*)

Dissection

- The **TypeName** function returns a string that identifies the data type of the Variant stored in *varname*.
- The **VarType** function returns an integer number that identifies the data type of the Variant stored in *varname*.
- The required *varname* must be the name of a variable declared as Variant.

Notes

Refer to the Help topics TypeName and VarType for a list of the names and Integer data type values associated with the different data types.

Code Example

```
Dim pintType As Integer, pstrType As String
Dim pvntDemo As Variant
pstrType = TypeName(pvntDemo)
pintType = VarType(pvntDemo)
```

Code Dissection

The declaration statements create an Integer, String, and Variant variable. The TypeName function returns a string representing the type in pstrType, and the VarType function returns an integer in pintType.

Classifying and Converting Data Types

Visual Basic supports both classification and conversion functions for many data types. The classification functions all accept one argument, a Variant containing the value to be classified. They all return True, if the argument is of the selected type, and False otherwise. Figure 2-5 lists the classification functions.

Function	Description
IsArray	Determines if a variable is an array.
IsDate	Determines if a variable contains a valid date value.
IsEmpty	Determines if a Variant variable has not been initialized.
IsError	Determines if an expression represents an error value.
IsMissing	Determines if an optional Variant argument has been passed to a procedure.
IsNull	Determines if a Variant variable contains the special value Null.
IsNumeric	Determines if a variable contains a valid number.
IsObject	Determines if a variable is an object variable.

Figure 2-5: Classification functions

The IsDate and IsNumeric functions are used commonly to validate user input. The IsEmpty, IsMissing, and IsNull functions are used with Variants to determine if a Variant variable contains the values Empty, Missing, or Null, respectively. Consider the following statements:

```
Dim pvntDemo As Variant
Dim pblnResult As Boolean
pblnResult = IsEmpty(pvntDemo)        ' True
pblnResult = IsArray(pvntDemo)        ' False
pvntDemo = Null
pblnResult = IsNull(pvntDemo)         ' True
pvntDemo = 123.45
pblnResult = IsNumeric(pvntDemo)      ' True
pvntDemo = Date()
pblnResult = IsDate(pvntDemo)         ' True
```

The preceding statements illustrate the use of the classification functions. The first executable statement returns True indicating that a value has not been assigned to the variable pvntDemo, and the second returns False indicating the Variant is not an array. The next two statements assign the special value Null to the Variant then test the Variant to determine if the value contains the special value Null. The test returns True. The final four statements perform the same tests with numeric and date data. Both tests return True.

In addition to the classification functions, it also is possible to convert data types explicitly in expressions. In most cases, Visual Basic will perform type conversion automatically for you without calling these functions. The type conversion functions, however, are useful when it is desirable to coerce the evaluation of an expression to be performed on specific data types. Figure 2-6 shows the type conversion functions:

Function	Return data type	Notes
CBool*(expression)*	Boolean	The expression can be a string or numeric expression.
CByte*(expression)*	Byte	The expression must be in the range of 0 to 255.
CCur*(expression)*	Currency	
CDate*(expression)*	Date	Expression must be a valid date.
CDbl*(expression)*	Double	
CInt*(expression)*	Integer	Fractions are rounded. When the fractional part is exactly 0.5, CInt and CLng always round it to the nearest even number. For example, 0.5 rounds to 0, and 1.5 rounds to 2. CInt and CLng differ from the Fix and Int functions, which truncate rather than round the fractional part of a number. Also, Fix and Int always return a value of the same type as the one passed in.
CLng*(expression)*	Long	Fractions are rounded.
CSng*(expression)*	Single	
CVar*(expression)*	Variant	
CStr*(expression)*	String	

Figure 2-6: Data type conversion functions

The return value of the CStr conversion function depends on the data type of the expression. The following list describes the different return values:

- If expression is Boolean, the value of the string is “True” or “False”.
- If expression is Date, the value of the string is a date stored in short date format. This format depends on your system.
- If expression is Null, then a run-time error occurs.
- If expression is Empty, then a zero-length ("") string is returned.
- If expression is a number, then a string representation of the number is returned.

To illustrate the effects of data type conversion, consider the following statements:

```
Dim pdatVar As Date
Dim pstrVar As String
pstrVar = CStr(123.44)      ' pstrVar = "123.44"
pstrVar = CStr(True)        ' pstrVar = "True"
pdatVar = CDate("12/31/2002")
pdatVar = CDate("aaa")      ' Error
```

The first assignment statement converts the numeric value 123.44 to the string "123.44". The second assignment statement converts the Boolean value True to a string. Thus pstrVar contains the string "True". The next statement converts the string "12/31/2002" into a date that can be used to perform operations on the date value. The final statement generates a run-time error because the string "aaa" does not contain a valid date value.

Commonly, the classification functions and type conversion functions are used to validate user input. When the user enters text that needs to be interpreted as a numeric value, IsNumeric can be used to verify that a value contains a number. If so, the string can be converted to the appropriate data type. Otherwise, it would be appropriate to display a message to the user indicating that the data is not valid.

In this section, you have learned how to create procedures, arguments for those procedures, and the valid data types for those arguments. Next, you will see how to create procedures, variables, and statements to perform computations.

SECTION B

objectives

In this section you will:

- Create expressions made up of arithmetic, comparison, and logical operators
- Change the order in which expressions are evaluated
- Perform calculations on dates and manipulate strings
- Create constants to store literal values
- Create user-defined types
- Use the With statement to reference members of a user-defined type or the properties of an object

Creating Expressions and User-Defined Types

Writing Expressions

Visual Basic supports three types of operators—arithmetic, comparison, and logical. When several operations occur in an expression, each part is evaluated and resolved in a predetermined order called precedence. Parentheses can be used to override the order of precedence and force some parts of an expression to be evaluated before others. Operations within parentheses always are performed before those outside the parentheses. Within parentheses, however, operator precedence is maintained. Parentheses also can be nested.

Arithmetic Operators

Arithmetic operators are used to perform addition (+), subtraction (-), multiplication (*), division (/), negation (-), and exponentiation (^). There also are operators to perform integer division (\) and modulus arithmetic using the Mod operator. The Mod operator computes the integer remainder of a number. The negation operator is a unary operator; that is, it applies to one operand. All the others are binary operators; that is, the operators are applied to two operands. The integer division operator (\) causes each expression to be rounded and converted to a Byte, Integer, or Long data type before the division is performed. Consider the following statements:

```
pintResult = 8 \ 3      ' 2
pintResult = 8.1 \ 3    ' 2
pintResult = 8.8 \ 3    ' 3
```

The result of the first and second statements is 2. The fractional remainder is truncated. In the third statement, 8.8 is rounded to 9 before the division is performed, thus the result is 3. There is no remainder to truncate. The Mod operator computes the integer remainder of an expression. Like integer division, the result typically is stored in a Byte, Integer, Long, or equivalent Variant data type. Consider the following statements:

```
pintResult = 8 Mod 3      ' 2
pintResult = 8.1 Mod 3    ' 2
pintResult = 8.8 Mod 3    ' 0
```

The integer remainder of the first two statements is 2. In the third statement, 8.8 is rounded to 9 and then the operation is performed. Thus, the result is 0.

Several arithmetic operators often are combined in one statement. When using more than a single operator, the order of precedence must be considered. For each level of precedence, the operations are performed from left to right as the operators appear in the expression in the following order.

1 Exponentiation
2. Negation
3. Multiplication and division
4. Integer division
5. Modulus arithmetic
6. Addition and subtraction
7. String concatenation

The string concatenation operator is not actually an arithmetic operator but it does follow addition and subtraction in the precedence order. The following statements illustrate the effect of using parentheses to change the default precedence of an expression. For simplicity, literal values are used, but in practice these values likely would consist of variables, constants, and object properties. In the statements that follow, assume the variable pintResult has been declared as an Integer.

```
pintResult = 6/3+9*6      ' 56
```

The standard precedence in the above statement is to perform multiplication and division from left to right, in the order they appear, and then the addition and subtraction. The division (6 / 3), then the multiplication (9 * 6) is performed. The intermediate results (2 + 54) then are added together.

```
pintResult = 6/(3+9)*6    ' 3
```

This statement performs the same operations as the previous statement but the standard order of precedence is overridden. The addition (3 + 9) is performed first. Then the value 6 is divided by the intermediate result (6 / 12). Then the multiplication is performed (0.5 * 6). Consider another implication of this statement. The intermediate result (0.5) is not an integer but a floating-point number. Even though the result of the expression is an integer, the intermediate values are stored as floating-point values. Consider the following statements, which have very different results.

```
pintResult = CInt(6/(3+9))*6    '  0
pintResult = CInt(18/(3+9))*6   ' 12
```

The first statement converts the result of (6 / (3 + 9)) to an Integer data type. The result is 0.5. When the fractional part of the result is exactly 0.5, the result is rounded to the nearest even number, in this case 0. Thus, the result of (0 * 6) is zero (0). The second statement produces a different answer. (18 / (3 + 9) has a result of 1.5 so the result is rounded to 2. Thus, the result of (2 * 6) is 12.

```
pintResult = -(6/(3+9)*6)       ' -3
```

This statement uses the negation operator. Because of the parentheses, the negation is performed last. Thus, the value of the last expression (3), is negated so the result is (-3).

```
pintResult = -(6/(3+9)*6)^2     ' -9
```

In this statement, the value of the expression inside the outer parentheses evaluates to (3). This value is squared (9), then negated (-9).

The data types of the operands in an expression affect how the expression is evaluated. When the data type of the operands differ, type conversion may be performed. The following list describes some of the pertinent characteristics of type conversion.

- Adding a numeric data type like Integer or Single to a String data type will result in a type mismatch error.
- Subtracting two Date data types will result in a Double data type, but adding two Dates data types will result in a Date data type.
- Adding, subtracting, or multiplying a Single data type and a Long data type will result in a Double data type.

Expressions containing a single variable or arithmetic expressions are combined with comparison operators to create Boolean expressions. These expressions then are used typically in decision-making statements. As an example, consider the English version of a decision-making statement. "If the Last statement date plus one-month is less than the current date then print a statement." To translate this statement into expressions and operators, there is one expression to determine the last statement date plus one-month. Another expression gets the current date. The intermediate results are compared using a comparison operator (statement date + 30) is less than (today).

Comparison Operators

Comparison operators are used to compare the value of two expressions. The result of a comparison operation is True or False. Valid comparison operators include greater than (>), greater than or equal to (>=), less than (<), less than or equal to (<=), equal to (=), and not equal to (<>). Comparison operations also can return the value Null. There are two other comparison operators—Is and Like. The Is operator is used to determine the type of an object. The Is operator is an object reference comparison operator. It does not compare objects or their values;

it checks only to determine if two object references refer to the same type of object. The Like operator is equal in precedence to all comparison operators, but is actually a pattern-matching operator used with strings. Comparison operators most commonly are used in decision-making and repetition structures, although this is not a requirement. The following examples illustrate the use of the Visual Basic comparison operators. Again, literal values are used for brevity.

```
Dim pblnResult As Boolean
pblnResult = (2 < 2)              ' False
pblnResult = (2 <= 2)             ' True
pblnResult = (2 = 2)              ' True
pblnResult = (2 > 2)              ' False
```

The comments in the previous statements illustrate the result of each comparison operation. Comparison operators have a lower precedence than arithmetic operators. Thus, the following two statements are equivalent:

```
pblnResult = 1 + 7 < 1 + 8         ' True
pblnResult = (1 + 7) < (1 + 8)     ' True
```

The previous statements perform the arithmetic operations first. Thus, the intermediate result of the expression after the arithmetic is performed is (8 < 9), which is True.

Programming tip

Use parentheses liberally in expressions. They can help clarify the default precedence of the expressions and do not affect the performance of the executable program.

Expressions containing both arithmetic and comparison operators can be combined in a statement using logical operators.

Logical Operators

Logical operators are used to combine expressions. Their meaning is similar to the meaning of the same words in English. For example, the And operator is used for conjunction. The result of a logical operation is always True or False. Figure 2-7 summarizes the logical operators supported by Visual Basic.

Operator	Description
And	The And operator performs a logical conjunction. If both operands are True then the result is True, otherwise it is False. Null is the result of an explicit assignment of Null to a variable or any operation between expressions that contain Null.
Eqv	The Eqv operator determines if two statements are equivalent. If both operands are True or both operands are False, the result is True. Otherwise it is False. If either expression is Null, the result is Null.
Not	The Not operator is a unary operator that performs negation. If the operand is True the result is False. If the operand is False, the result is True. If the operand is Null, the result is Null.
Or	The Or operator performs a logical disjunction. If one or both operands is True, then the result is True. Otherwise the result is False. If both of the expressions are Null then the result is Null.
Xor	The Xor operator is used for exclusion. The result is True if and only if one operand is False and the other is True. If either expression is Null, the result is Null.

Figure 2-7: Logical operators

Refer to the Help topic for each operator to view the truth tables and see additional examples.

The following examples illustrate the use of logical operators.

```
Dim pblnResult As Boolean
pblnResult = True And True      ' True
pblnResult = False And False    ' False
pblnResult = True Or False      ' True
pblnResult = True Eqv False     ' False
pblnResult = False Eqv False    ' True
```

When expressions contain operators from more than one category, arithmetic operators are evaluated first, next comparison operators, and then logical operators last. Comparison operators all have equal precedence; that is, they are evaluated from left-to-right in the order they appear. The order of precedence for all operators is listed in Figure 2-8.

Arithmetic	Comparison	Logical
Exponentiation (^)	Equality (=)	Not
Negation (–)	Inequality (<>)	And
Multiplication and division (*, /)	Less than (<)	Or
Integer division (\)	Greater than (>)	Xor
Modulus arithmetic (Mod)	Less than or equal to (<=)	Eqv
Addition and subtraction (+, –)	Greater than or equal to (>=)	Imp
String concatenation (&)	Like	
	Is	

Figure 2-8: Operator precedence

For example, consider the following statements:

```
Dim pint1 As Integer, pint2 As Integer
Dim pblnResult As Boolean
pint1 = 2
pint2 = 4
```

The following statement performs the comparisons first. The result of (pint1 < 2) is False and the result of (pint2 < 5) is True. The result of (False Or True) is True.

```
pblnResult = pint1 < 2 Or pint2 < 5      ' True
```

The following statements apply the Not operator. Again, the comparisons are performed first resulting in the expression (Not False Or True). Because logical operators have the same precedence, the Not operator is applied first then the Or. Thus, the following statements are equivalent.

```
pbln1 = Not pint1 < 2 Or pint2 < 5          ' True
pbln1 = (Not (pint2 < 2)) Or (pint2 < 5)    ' True
```

The following statement overrides the default precedence rules, and the Or operation is performed before the Not operation. Thus, Not True is False.

```
pbln1 = Not (pint1 < 2 Or pint2 < 5)     ' False
```

The previous assignment statements operated on numbers. Visual Basic, however, allows you to perform extensive operations on both strings and dates.

Working with Dates

The Date data type can store dates from January 1, 100 to December 31, 9999. It also stores a time value. The time value is represented by a 24 hour clock having the range of 00:00:00 to 23:59:59. When you want to interpret literal values as dates, the literal is enclosed in pound signs (#). Consider the following statements to assign date and time values:

```
Dim pdatValue As Date
pdatValue = #1/10/2002 11:00:00 PM#
pdatValue = #1/10/2002#
pdatValue = #11:00:00 PM#
```

There are several intrinsic functions that return and perform calculations on date values as shown in the following list:

- The **Date**, **Now**, and **Time** functions return the current system date, current system date and time, and current system time, respectively.
- The **DateSerial** converts dates in the form of month, day, and year into a Date data type. The **TimeSerial** function has the same effect on times in the form of hours, minutes, and seconds.
- The **DateValue** and **TimeValue** functions convert String expressions to dates.
- The **Weekday** function accepts a Date or String argument and returns a constant value identifying the day of the week. See the Help topic for the Weekday function for a list of the constant values.
- The **Day**, **Month**, and **Year** functions accept one argument, a Date value or String argument that can be converted to a Date data type. The Day function returns the day of the month (a value between 1 and 31). The Month function returns the month of the year (a value between 1 and 12). The Year function returns a whole number representing the year.
- The **Hour, Minute,** and **Second** functions also accept a Date value or valid String argument. Only the time part is used. The Hour returns a value between 0 and 23. The Minute function returns a value between 0 and 59, and the Second function returns a value between 0 and 59.

The DateAdd, DateDiff, and DatePart functions perform calculations on dates.

Syntax

DateAdd(*interval, number, date*)
DateDiff(*interval, date1, date2*[, *firstdayofweek*[, *firstweekofyear*]])
DatePart(*interval, date*[,*firstdayofweek*[, *firstweekofyear*]])

Dissection

- The **DateAdd** function adds some number of seconds, or other time interval, days, or other date interval, to a Date value.
- The **DateDiff** function subtracts *date2* from *date1* and computes the number of *intervals* between the two values. The *interval* result is a Long integer.
- The **DatePart** function computes the number of the specified *intervals* in the *date.*
- The required *date, date1,* and *date2* contain a Date or String value that can be converted to a Date data type.
- The required *interval* contains a String value to identify the date or time interval to be added to a date using the DateAdd function or the interval returned by the DateDiff function.

- The optional *firstdayofweek* and *firstweekofyear* are used to change the default behavior of dates. By default, the first day of the week is Sunday. This setting can be changed using the *firstdayofweek* argument. The *firstweekofyear* setting will change what constitutes the first full week of the year. By default, the first week is assumed to be the week in which January 1 occurs. See the Help topic for the DateDiff function for a complete list of the constant settings.

Notes Refer to the Help topic for the DateDiff function for a complete list of valid interval strings. If date1 is later than date2, the interval returned is negative.

Working with Strings

In addition to supporting Date functions, there are several other functions that work with strings. When operations are performed on strings, literals are enclosed in quotes. There are two types of strings in Visual Basic; fixed-length strings and variable-length strings. Strings are concatenated together using the ampersand character (&). Consider the following statements:

```
Const cstrDemo As String = "Part"
Dim pstrDemo1 As String
pstrDemo1 = cstrDemo & " 1"     ' "Part 1"
pstrDemo1 = pstrDemo1 & " " & cstrDemo &_
    " 2"    ' "Part 1 Part 2"
```

Fixed-length strings are declared with an explicit size, which cannot be changed at run time. Consider the following statements:

```
Dim pstrDemo As String * 5
Dim pstrDemo1 As String * 5
Dim pstrResult As String * 10
pstrDemo = "One"
pstrDemo1 = "Two"
pstrResult = pstrDemo & pstrDemo1     '"One  Two  "
```

The previous code declares two, five character fixed-length strings named pstrDemo and pstrDemo1. Both variables contain two spaces after the strings "One" and "Two", respectively. When concatenated and stored into pstrResult, the embedded spaces are concatenated into the result.

There are several intrinsic functions that operate on strings. The following list describes these functions and summarizes their purpose:

- **StrConv** is used primarily to change the case of the letters in the string. The functionality of StrConv partially is supplied by the LCase and UCase functions, which convert the characters in a string to lowercase and uppercase, respectively.
- **Len** returns the length of a string.
- **LSet** and **RSet** frequently are used with fixed-length strings to left justify and right justify the characters in the string, respectively.

- **Left, Mid,** and **Right** return some number of characters from a string. Left and Right return the specified number of characters from the left-hand and right-hand side of the string, respectively. Mid returns a sub string from a search string. The arguments to the Mid function determine the first character in the string and the number of characters to be returned.
- **LTrim, RTrim,** and **Trim** all accept a string argument. They each return a copy of the string argument with leading, trailing, and both leading and trailing spaces removed, respectively.

The functions in the previous list are similar to the string manipulation statements in other languages. Refer to the Help topics for a detailed analysis of the syntax of these statements. The StrComp function compares two strings and the InStr function is used to determine whether or not a string (pattern) exists in another string.

Syntax

StrComp(*string1*, *string2*[, *compare*])
InStr([*start*,]*string1*, *string2*[, *compare*])

Dissection

- The **StrComp** function compares *string1* and *string2*. StrComp returns minus one (–1) if *string1* is less than *string2*, zero (0) if the two strings are equal, one (1) if *string1* is greater than *string2*. If either string contains Null, then the result is Null.
- The **InStr** function searches *string1* for the pattern identified by *string2*. It returns an Integer data type containing the character position of *string1* where the pattern was found. If the pattern is not found, then InStr returns zero (0).
- *string1* and *string2* must contain a valid String expression.
- The *compare* argument is used to determine how the two strings are compared. Strings can be compared using a textual or binary comparison.
- If the *start* argument is used with the InStr function, the search for *string1* in *string2* starts at the character position identified by *start*.

Code Example

```
Dim pstr1 As String
Dim pstr2 As String
pstr1 = "Smith"
pstr2 = "Smythe"
Debug.Print StrComp(pstr1, pstr2)       ' -1, Smith < Smythe
Debug.Print StrComp(pstr1, "Smith")     ' 0, Smith = Smith
Debug.Print InStr(1, pstr1, "th")       ' 4
Debug.Print InStr(1, pstr1, "then")     ' 0, No match
```

Code Dissection

These statements illustrate the StrComp and InStr functions. In the first call to StrComp, the string "Smith" < "Smythe" so the result is minus one (–1). In the second statement, the strings are equal, so the result is zero (0). The first InStr function call finds the string "th" in the string "Smythe" at the character position 4. In the final statement, the string "then" is not found in "Smythe". String comparisons are case sensitive.

A number between 0 and 255 represents each character in a string. This number is called a character code. Some of these character codes represent non-printing and special characters. For example the Tab key is represented by the character code nine (9). Visual Basic supports two functions to convert a character code to a string and a string to a character code.

Syntax

Asc(*string*)
Chr(*charcode*)

Dissection

- The **Asc** function takes one argument, a string, and returns an Integer data type containing the character code.
- The **Chr** function works in reverse. It takes one argument, a character code, and returns the corresponding string.

Code Example

```
Dim pstr1 As String * 1
pstr1 = "C"
pstr1 = Chr(Asc(pstr1) + 32)
```

Code Dissection

These statements convert an uppercase "C" to a lowercase "c". Given the order of the ASCII character set, an uppercase letter can be converted to a lowercase letter by adding the constant value 32 to the character code. Thus, the last statement in the example converts the character to its character code and adds 32 to that value. The character code then is converted back to a string.

There are many uses of the Chr and Asc functions. They can be used to embed special characters like a carriage return or a line feed into a string. They also can be used for validation. For example, you could validate that a string contained an integer by checking the character code of each character in the string. Then you could test that the character code was between 48 and 57, the character codes for the digits 0 through 9.

Visual Basic supports many intrinsic functions in addition to the Date and String functions. Mathematical functions perform trigonometric operations, generate random numbers, and other tasks. See the Help topic Math functions for a complete list. Financial functions perform common business and financial tasks like computing depreciation, payments, present and future value, and many others. See the Help topic Financial functions for a complete list.

A very common intrinsic function is the Format function. As its name implies, it is used to format output. It commonly is used to define a specific output format for numbers and dates.

Syntax 

Format(*expression*[,*format*[,*firstdayofweek*[,*firstweekofyear*]]])

Dissection

- The **Format** function reads the numeric value contained in *expression* and converts it to a string. The function allows you to control the appearance of the string by placing information in the *format* argument.

- You can specify an optional *format* argument in one of two ways. You can select from a list of named formats that already have been defined for you, or you can use special symbols to control, in more detail, the appearance of the formatted text. One of the more common named formats, the **Fixed** format, displays information with two decimal places and a leading zero (0) if the value is less than one (1). Another format, **Currency**, displays information with a leading dollar sign and two decimal places. See Help on the Format function to look at all the options for named formats.

Code Example

```
Private Sub txtType_LostFocus( )
    txtType = Format(txtType, "Currency")
End Sub
```

Code Dissection

This statement uses the LostFocus event of the text box named txtType to format the contents with the Currency format. The default Text property is used.

Constants

Visual Basic supports two kinds of constants. **Intrinsic constants** are defined by Visual Basic and are intended to make programs both more robust and readable. The intrinsic constants pertaining to a specific object can be identified using a tool called the Object Browser. The Object Browser lists all the different classes, their properties and methods, and the constants pertaining to those objects. Remember that the VarType function returns an integer indicating the data type of a Variant variable. You can use the Object Browser to find out the valid constants and their values.

To look at constants in the Object Browser:

1. Click the **Object Browser** button on the toolbar.
2. Using the scroll bars, locate and click **VbVarType** in the Classes window. The constants should be displayed in the Members of box as shown in Figure 2-9.

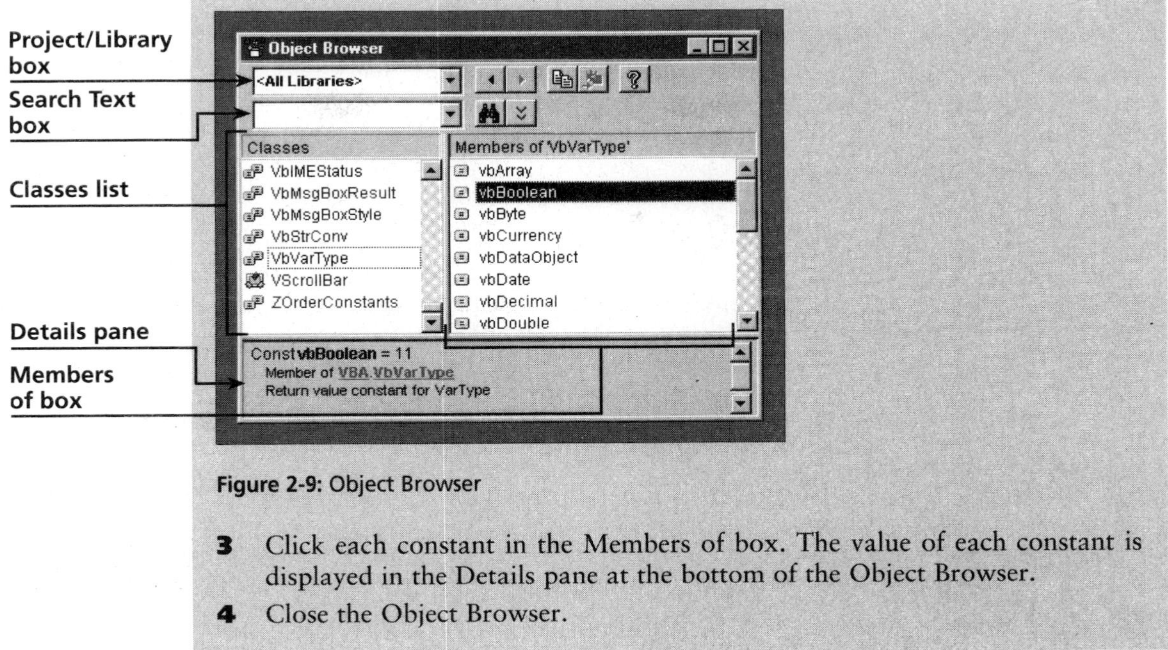

Figure 2-9: Object Browser

3 Click each constant in the Members of box. The value of each constant is displayed in the Details pane at the bottom of the Object Browser.

4 Close the Object Browser.

As shown in Figure 2-9, the constant value vbBoolean has an integer value of 11. Thus, the following two assignment statements are equivalent:

```
Dim pintBooleanType As Integer
pintBooleanType = 11
pintBooleanType = vbBoolean
```

Whenever possible, you should use intrinsic constants instead of literal values to improve the readability of a program. Both the Object Browser and the Help system can be used to determine the constants applicable to a specific function return value or argument. The practice of using constant values is followed in this book. Furthermore, when new constant values are presented, a reference to the location in the Object Browser or Help topic also will be provided.

User-defined constants are created by you, the programmer, and work the same way as intrinsic constants. User-defined constants are created with the Const statement. When a literal value is used several times in a program, using a constant in place of the literal makes the program easier to modify because the constant can be modified once, instead of searching for and changing each occurrence of the literal value. User-defined constants make a program easier to read because a constant name describes the purpose of the literal value. Its syntax is similar to the syntax used to declare variables.

Syntax	[**Public**|**Private**] **Const** *constantname* [**As** *type*] = *expression*
Dissection	■ The optional **Public** and **Private** keywords define the scope of the constant. If declared as Public, the constant is visible to all the modules in a program. If declared as Private, the constant is only visible to the module in which it is declared. Public constants cannot be declared in form or class modules. ■ The required *constantname* defines the name of the constant. It must conform to the naming conventions for variables. ■ The **As** *type* clause identifies the data type of a constant. Like variables, the *type* can be any intrinsic data type. If omitted, the constant is a Variant. ■ The *expression* can contain arithmetic operators and operands that are literal values or other constants.
Code Example	`Public Const csngPi As Single = 3.1415927` `Public Const csng2Pi As Single = csngPi * 2`
Code Dissection	The first statement creates a constant named csngPi to represent the value of Pi. The second statement creates another constant whose value is Pi, the value of the first constant, multiplied by 2. Both of these constants are visible to other modules because of the Public keyword.

You may be tempted to write the following statements to declare a constant and assign a value to it.

```
Public Const csngPi As Single
csngPi = 3.1415927
```

The previous statements will not work, however. Values assigned to constants and constant expressions are evaluated at compile time, and the value cannot be changed. Thus, attempting to declare a constant without assigning a value to it will cause an error. Furthermore, trying to assign a value to a constant at run time also will cause an error. The previous example used a prefix of "csng". This prefix conforms to the standard prefixes used for variable names. The first character "c" indicates that the value is a constant and the three-character prefix "sng" indicates the data type of the constant (Single).

Another common error is to try to use a variable name in an expression to compute a constant value. Consider the following statements:

```
Public psngRadius As Single
Public Const csngPiR As Single = 3.1415927 * psngRadius
```

These statements also will generate a syntax error. A constant's value is determined at compile time not at run time. As such, the value of the variable psngRadius cannot be determined until run time so the value of csngPiR cannot be determined at compile time. Thus, the Const statement will generate a syntax error.

User-Defined Types

In addition to creating constants to improve program readability, it also is possible to create user-defined types. User-defined types are useful when multiple variables are related together and should be treated as a unit. User-defined types can contain intrinsic data types, arrays, objects, and other user-defined types. They also can be passed as arguments to both Function and Sub procedures. Function procedures also can return user-defined types. User-defined types always are passed by reference and cannot be passed by value. User-defined types are created with the Type statement.

Syntax

[**Public**|**Private**] **Type** *varname*
  elementname [([*subscripts*])] **As** *Type*
  [*elementname* [([*subscripts*])] **As** *Type*]
  . . .
End Type

Dissection

- The **Type** and **End Type** keywords mark a block containing statements to define each element that makes up a user-defined type. User-defined types can be declared only in the general declarations section of a module.
- A user-defined type can be Public or Private. If the type is **Public**, it is visible to all the modules in a project. If it is **Private**, the type is visible only in the module in which it is declared. User-defined types declared in a standard module are considered Public if the Public or Private keyword is omitted. Public user-defined types cannot be declared in a form or class module.
- The required *varname* is the name of the new user-defined type. It must conform to the standard naming conventions for variables.
- The user-defined type can contain one or more elements identified by the required *elementname*. These elements can be any of the standard Visual Basic data types or another user-defined type. This implies that user-defined types can be nested. That is, a member of a user-defined type can itself be a user-defined type.
- You can create array elements by assigning the *elementname* an optional *subscript*. Both dynamic and fixed arrays are supported.
- The **As** *type* clause is used to specify the data type of the element. It can be any of the standard Visual Basic data types, Object (another user-defined type), or an object type.

Code Example

```
Public Type tYMDType
    Years As Long
    Months As Long
    Days As Long
End Type

Public Type tHMSType
    Hours As Integer
    Minutes As Integer
    Seconds As Integer
End Type

Public Type tYMDHMSType
    YMD As tYMDType
    HMS As tHMSType
End Type
```

Code Dissection

The first and second user-defined types are used to store the components of a date value and time value, respectively. The final type is a type made up of the other two types.

Once a user-defined type has been declared, variables of that type can be created. This is accomplished with the Dim, Private, Public, and Static statements. The data type, however, is replaced with the user-defined type. Consider the following statement:

```
Private YMDHMS As tYMDHMSType
```

The statement declares a variable named YMDHMS having the type tYMDHMSType. The syntax to reference the members of a user-defined type is similar to the syntax to reference properties.

Syntax

variablename.membername[.*membername*] ...

Dissection

- The *variablename* is a variable of some user-defined type.
- The *membername* must be a valid member of the user-defined type. If the member is itself a user defined type, the *membername* is followed by a period (.), and another *membername*.

Code Example

```
Dim YMD As tYMDType
Dim HMS As tHMSType
Dim YMDHMS As tYMDHMSType

YMD.Days = 12
HMS.Hours = 3
YMDHMS.HMS = HMS
YMDHMS.YMD = YMD
YMDHMS.YMD = HMS    ' Error — Inconsistent Type
```

Code Dissection When writing statements that involve user-defined types, variable references must resolve to the same data type. In the first and second assignment statements, YMD.Days and HMS.Hours both store an Integer value. In the third assignment statement, YMDHMS.HMS and HMS also are of type tHMSType. In the final statement, the left-hand side and right-hand side of the expression are of different types, however, so the statement will cause a run-time error.

Constants can be used in expressions. Additionally, they also can be used as both procedure arguments and as the return value for functions.

Using the With Statement

The With statement can be used as a shorthand notation to reference the members of the user-defined type or the properties of an object.

Syntax

With *object*
[*statements*]
End With

Dissection

- The **With** and **End With** statements define a block. Inside of a With block, the *object* cannot be changed.
- The required *object* argument must be the name of an object or a user-defined type.
- The *optional* statements are executed on the *object.*

Code Example

```
With YMDHMS
    .YMD.Years = 3
    .YMD.Months = 2
    .HMS.Hours = 4
End With

With YMDHMS
    With .YMD
        .Years = 3
        .Months = 2
  End With
  .HMS.Hours = 4
End With
```

Code Dissection The previous statements contain two With blocks; each perform the same task. The second With block illustrates the use of a nested With statement.

The With statement also is useful when referencing the properties and methods of the same object. For the following statements, assume lblDemo is a valid instance of the Label control.

```
With lblDemo
    .Caption = "ABC"
    .FontSize = 12
    .FontBold = True
    .FontItalic = True
End With
```

The previous statements set the Caption, FontSize, FontBold, and FontItalic properties for the object named lblDemo.

Consider the problem of a professional, like an accountant, who bills clients for time worked. This time must be accumulated each month for each client. One solution would be to account for all time using the same interval (minutes perhaps), and adding all the intervals together and billing the client by the minute. So long as the interval is the same, this solution is fine. If the accountant wanted to bill one hour, however, then the interval would have to be converted from hours to minutes. The problem can be solved using the DateDiff functions to perform the conversions automatically.

To compute the elapsed date and time intervals:

1 Activate the Code window for the module named **Valid.bas** and enter the following statements in the general declarations section of the module, following the Option Explicit statement:

```
Public Type tYMDType
    Years As Long
    Months As Long
    Days As Long
End Type

Public Type tHMSType
    Hours As Integer
    Minutes As Integer
    Seconds As Integer
End Type

Public Type tYMDHMSType
    YMD As tYMDType
    HMS As tHMSType
End Type
```

2 Create the following function procedure in the standard module:

```
Public Function YMDDiff(pdat1 As Date, pdat2 As Date) _
    As tYMDType
    Dim ymdCurrent As tYMDType
    ymdCurrent.Years = DateDiff("yyyy", pdat1, pdat2)
    ymdCurrent.Months = DateDiff("m", pdat1, pdat2)
    ymdCurrent.Days = DateDiff("d", pdat1, pdat2)
    YMDDiff = ymdCurrent
End Function
```

3 Activate the Code window for the form module named **frmHSB**. Enter the following statements in the appropriate **Click** event procedure for the command button named **cmdElapsedDate**:

```
Dim YMD As tYMDType
YMD = YMDDiff(txtStartDate, txtEndDate)
lblYears = YMD.Years
lblMonths = YMD.Months
lblDays = YMD.Days
```

4 Test the program. Enter the date as shown in Figure 2-10 and click the command button. The elapsed date output will appear as shown in Figure 2-10.

enter these dates

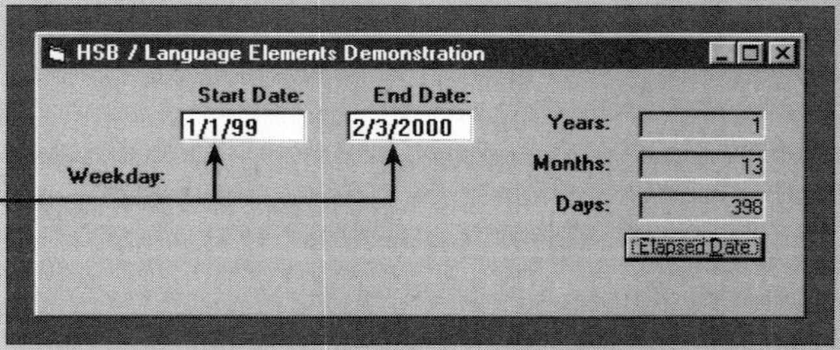

HSB / Language Elements Demonstration

Start Date:	End Date:		
1/1/99	2/3/2000	Years:	1
Weekday:		Months:	13
		Days:	398
			Elapsed Date

Figure 2-10: Testing the DateDiff functions

The first set of statements creates the necessary user-defined types. The two function procedures used the DateDiff functions to compute the elapsed date values. The code in the command button calls the function.

Enumerated Types

In addition to using intrinsic data types and constants, Visual Basic supports enumerated types also known as **enumerations**. An enumeration is useful to create a type that stores a fixed set of constant values. Each constant value has a unique name. An enumeration is created with the Enum statement.

Syntax

[**Public|Private**] **Enum** *name*
membername [= *constantexpression*]
membername [= *constantexpression*]
. . .
End Enum

Dissection

- The optional **Public** keyword, the default, specifies that the enumerated type is visible throughout the project. The optional **Private** keyword specifies that the enumerated type is visible only within the module in which it is declared. The Public and Private keywords have the same effect creating enumerated types as they do when creating variables with an intrinsic type like Integer or Single.
- The **Enum** statement declares the type for an enumeration. The Enum statement is valid only at the module level.
- The required *name* represents the name of the enumerated type. The name must adhere to the same rules as variable names.
- The required *membername* is an element of an enumerated type. The member of an enumerated type is treated like a constant.
- The optional *constantexpression* contains the value of the member and is treated as a Long integer. This value can be a number or constant value. If you do not specify a *constantexpression*, the first member is assigned the value of zero (0), the second a value of one (1), and so on.
- The **End Enum** statement exits the declaration block.

Code Example

```
Public Enum eDaysOfTheWeek
    Sunday
    Monday
    Tuesday
    Wednesday
    Thursday
    Friday
    Saturday
End Enum

Public Enum eCustomerType
    Individual = 100
    Partnership = 200
    Corporation = 300
End Enum
```

Code Dissection

The first Enum statement creates an enumerated type named eDaysOfTheWeek. It has members named Sunday, Monday, Tuesday, and so on. Each of these values has an associated constant such that Sunday = 0, Monday = 1, and so on. The second Enum statement (eCustomerType) creates an enumerated type with assigned constant values. This enumerated type represents different types of customers.

The following statements declare a variable named DayOfTheWeek of type eDaysOfTheWeek, and use the enumerated type in assignment statements:

```
Dim DayOfTheWeek As eDaysOfTheWeek
Dim Today As Single
DayOfTheWeek = Sunday
DayOfTheWeek = 0
DayOfTheWeek = Monday
DayOfTheWeek = 1
Today = 1.55
DayOfTheWeek = Today
```

The first two assignment statements have the same effect. The enumerated value Sunday is stored in DayOfTheWeek. The enumerated Value of Sunday is zero (0) so the second assignment statement has the same effect. The statements that assign Monday and the value one (1) to DayOfTheWeek are also the same. You may expect that the last assignment statement would generate an error because the Today is not a valid value in the enumeration. This is not the case. Rather, Today is converted to an integer. That is, the value 1.55 is rounded to 2. Then, the result is stored in the variable DayOfTheWeek. Thus, enumerations are strictly a programmer convenience. No validation is performed when assigning a value to the enumeration.

SECTION C

objectives

In this section you will:

- Change the order in which a procedure's statements are evaluated using an If statement
- Use a Select Case statement to execute statements conditionally
- Declare and use arrays to store variables
- Use looping structures to read and write array values

Decision-Making and Repetition Statements

Decision-Making Statements

Comparison and logical operators commonly are used in decision-making statements. Decision-making statements allow you to modify the flow of execution in a program. By default, the statements in a procedure are executed from beginning to end. Decision-making statements allow you to execute or not execute code based on some condition. Visual Basic supports two different decision-making structures—the If statement and the Select Case statement.

The If Statement

The If statement has three forms. The first form is used to execute a series of statements when a condition is True.

Syntax

If *condition* **Then**
    statements
End If

Dissection

- The *condition* is usually an expression and must evaluate to a numeric value. This numeric value is converted to a Boolean.
- If the condition is True, the statements between the If and End If statements are executed.

Code Example

```
If IsNumeric("1234.33") Then
    psngAmount = Val("1234.33")
End If

If 3 < 1 And 5 > 3 Then
    pintTest = 1
End If
```

Code Dissection

The first If statement calls the IsNumeric function, which returns True because the value is a number. Because the expression is True, the statements in the If block are executed. The second If statement first evaluates the expression (3 < 1), which is False. Then, the expression (5 > 3) is evaluated, which is True. Then, the And operator is applied (False And True) and the result is False. Thus, the statements in the If block are not executed.

The second form of the If statement is used to make a two-way decision. That is, one statement block is executed when the condition is True and another statement block is executed when the condition is False.

Syntax

If *condition* **Then**
statement-block1
Else
statement-block2
End If

Dissection

- If condition is True, then *statement-block1* is executed. If the condition is False, *statement-block2* is executed.

Code Example

```
If IsNumeric("1234.33") = True Then
    psngAmount = Val("1234.33")
Else
    psngAmount = 0
End If

If 3 < 1 And 5 < 3 Then
    pintTest = 1
Else
    pintTest = 0
End If
```

Code Dissection

These If statements are similar to the statements in the previous example. When the condition is False, however, the statements between the Else and End If statements are executed.

Programming ▶ tip

In the If blocks, the statements pertaining to a condition are indented. The If, Else, and End If statements are aligned to help visually identify the different conditions in the If statement and its bounds.

A common use of the If statement and classification functions is to validate user input. In this example, you will create a function to verify that an input value contains a valid date. This procedure will accept one required argument, the value to be verified as a date, and two optional arguments. These arguments will be used to determine if the date is between a range of dates. If the optional arguments are not specified, then the range testing is not performed.

To create an If statement to validate user input:

1. Open the Code window for the standard module named **Valid.bas**.
2. Create the following **ValidDate** function procedure:

```
Public Function ValidDate(pvntValue As Variant, _
    Optional pvntMin As Variant, _
    Optional pvntMax As Variant) As Boolean
    ValidDate = True
    If Not IsDate(pvntValue) Then
        ValidDate = False
    Else
        If Not IsMissing(pvntMin) Then
        If IsDate(pvntValue) Then
            If CDate(pvntValue) < pvntMin Then
                ValidDate = False
            End If
        Else
            ValidDate = False
        End If
    End If

    If Not IsMissing(pvntMax) Then
        If IsDate(pvntMax) Then
            If CDate(pvntValue) > pvntMax Then
                ValidDate = False
            End If
        Else
            ValidDate = False
        End If
    End If
  End If
End Function
```

3 Modify the code for the **cmdElapsedDate_Click** event procedure so it contains the following statements:

```
Dim YMD As tYMDType
If ValidDate(txtStartDate, cdatMin, cdatMax) And _
    ValidDate(txtEndDate, cdatMin, cdatMax) Then
    YMD = YMDDiff(txtStartDate, txtEndDate)
    lblYears = YMD.Years
    lblMonths = YMD.Months
    lblDays = YMD.Days
End If
```

4 Test the program. Enter an invalid date in the Start Date and End Date text boxes. Click the **Elapsed Date** command button. The output is not calculated. Enter valid dates into both text boxes and confirm that the output is calculated.

This event procedure contains a series of nested If statements. Again, the statements are indented such that each If block appears at the same level. The first If statement tests that the input value contains a valid date. If it does not, the return value of the function is set to False indicating the date is invalid. Otherwise, the Else block is executed. This block contains the statements to perform range checking if the optional minimum date or maximum date is supplied. The code to validate the minimum and maximum date is almost identical. If the optional minimum date argument is missing, the If block exits. Otherwise, the argument is tested to determine if the argument is a valid date and if so, compared against the input date. If the input date is not within the valid range, the return value is again set to False. The next If block performs the same task to determine if the input date is less than the maximum date.

The final form of the If statement is used for a multi-way decision. That is, the decision has three or more possible outcomes.

Syntax

If *condition1* **Then**
  statement-block1
ElseIf *condition2* **Then**
  statement-block2
[**ElseIf** *condition-n* **Then**
  statement-block-n]
[**Else**
  [*statements*]]
End If

Dissection

- The **If** statement tests *condition1*. If it is True, then *statement-block1* is executed. Otherwise, *condition2* is tested. If it is True, then *statement-block2* is executed. The If statement can have as many ElseIf clauses as are necessary. The *statements* in the optional Else block are executed if none of the conditions are True. Once a True condition is found, the statement block is executed and then execution continues at the statement following the If blocks.

Code Example

```
Dim pintValue As Long
Dim pintLevel As Integer
pintValue = 34435

If pintValue >= 1 And pintValue < 10000 Then
    pintLevel = 1
ElseIf pintValue < 20000 Then
    pintLevel = 2
ElseIf pintValue < 30000 Then
    pintLevel = 3
ElseIf pintValue < 40000 Then
    pintLevel = 4
Else
    pintLevel = 5
End If
```

Code Dissection

The previous If block sets the value of the variable pintLevel depending on the value of the variable pintValue. Because pintValue is greater than 30000 and less than 40000, pintLevel is assigned the value of four (4).

The Select Case Statement

The Select Case statement can be used in place of an If statement when the condition to be tested is the same for each case. The Select Case statement cannot be used when different conditions are used in the If statement. The Select Case statement is more efficient than a comparable If statement because the testexpression only needs to be evaluated once.

Syntax

Select Case *testexpression*
    Case *expressionlist1*
        statement-block1
    Case *expressionlist2*
        statement-block2
    Case *expressionlist-n*
        statement-block-n
    [**Case Else**
        [*statements*]]
End Select

Dissection

- Visual Basic executes the **Select Case** statement by evaluating the required *testexpression* once when the Select Case statement first starts. It then compares the *expressionlist1* with the *testexpression*. If they are the same, the statements in *statement-block1* are executed, then the entire Select Case statement exits. If they are not the same, the *expressionlist2* is compared with the *testexpression*. This process is repeated until there are no more expressions to be tested.
- If no expression matches the *testexpression*, the statements in the optional **Case Else** clause are executed. If no expression matched the *testexpression* and the Case Else statement is omitted, then no statement block will be executed.
- If more than one *expressionlist* is the same as the *testexpression*, only the statements in the first matching Case are executed. The *expressionlist* can be a list of values—such as 6, 7, 8—separated by commas. It also can be a range of values separated by the word To, as in 5 To 10.

Code Example

```
Select Case pintValue
    Case 1 To 9999
        pintLevel = 1
    Case 10000 To 19999
        pintLevel = 2
    Case 20000 To 29999
        pintLevel = 3
    Case 30000 To 39999
        pintLevel = 4
    Case Else
        pintLevel = 5
End Select
```

Code Dissection

This Select Case statement has the same effect as the If statement previously shown.

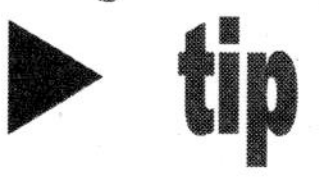

In the previous statements the Select Case and End Select statements are aligned to define the bounds of the selection structure. Each case also is aligned, and the statement(s) inside the case are indented and aligned. This helps improve the readability of the program.

Given the set of validation routines, another useful routine would be to determine the day of the week for a given date. This value will be returned as a string.

To compute the day name:

1. Enter the following function procedure in the standard module named **Valid.bas**:

```
Public Function DayName(pvntValue As Variant) As String
    Dim pdatValue As Date
    If IsDate(pvntValue) Then
        pdatValue = CDate(pvntValue)
        Select Case WeekDay(pdatValue)
            Case vbSunday
                DayName = "Sunday"
            Case vbMonday
                DayName = "Monday"
            Case vbTuesday
                DayName = "Tuesday"
            Case vbWednesday
                DayName = "Wednesday"
            Case vbThursday
                DayName = "Thursday"
            Case vbFriday
                DayName = "Friday"
            Case vbSaturday
                DayName = "Saturday"
        End Select
    End If
End Function
```

2. Inside the If statement for the **cmdElapsedDate_Click** event procedure, enter the following statements to print the day name in the labels:

```
lblStartWeekday = DayName(txtStartDate)
lblEndWeekday = DayName(txtEndDate)
```

3. Test the program. Enter two valid dates and click the **Elapsed Date** command button. The corresponding day of the week should appear in the labels.

In addition to creating variables to store a single data item, Visual Basic supports arrays to store multiple items of the same type.

Arrays

Variables of the same type can be stored as a unit in an array. An array has one or more dimensions. An array with one dimension can be thought of as a list. An array with two dimensions can be thought of as a table with rows and columns. An array is declared using the Public, Private, or Dim statements just as they are used to declare other variables. Visual Basic supports two types of arrays. Fixed-size arrays are assigned dimensions at design time. Dynamic arrays have no dimensions at design time. Rather, both the number of dimensions, and the size of each dimension, can be changed at run time as needed. To declare a fixed-size array, the array name is followed by parentheses. Inside the parentheses, the array's dimensions are specified, separated by commas. To declare a dynamic array, no values are placed inside the parentheses. By default, the lower bound of an array is zero (0). Consider the following statements:

```
Dim Array1(10) As Integer
Dim Array2(10, 10) As String
Dim Array3( ) As Single
```

The first statement declares an array with 11 elements, the second statement declares an array with 11 rows and 11 columns (121 elements). These are both fixed-size arrays. The final statement declares a dynamic array. By default, arrays have a lower bound of zero (0). That is, the 11 element array has elements numbered from 0 to 10. The upper and lower bounds of a dimension can be changed using the To keyword as follows:

```
Dim Array1(1 To 10) As Integer
Dim Array2(3 To 10, 4 To 12) As String
```

The first array declaration creates a one-dimensional array with 10 elements numbered from 1 to 10. The second statement creates a two-dimensional array with eight (8) rows and nine (9) columns. The rows are indexed from 3 to 10, and the columns are indexed from 4 to 12.

The syntax to reference an array is similar to the syntax to declare it. You specify the array name. Inside parentheses after the array name, you use a subscript for each dimension. For example, consider the following statement to reference elements in the arrays Array1 and Array2.

```
Array1(1) = 100
Array2(3, 4) = 120
```

The first statement references an element in the one-dimensional array and the second statement references an element in the two-dimensional array. Usually, the subscripts would contain a variable or constant, but numeric literal values were used for brevity.

The default lower bound for all arrays in a module can be changed from zero (0) to one (1) by including the Option Base Statement. The Option Base statement must appear in the general declarations section of a module before any procedures. It typically appears just after the Option Explicit statement. Changing the Option Base in one module does not affect the other modules in a project. This behavior is the same as the Option Explicit statement.

Syntax	**Option Base {0|1}**
Dissection	■ **Option Base 0** causes arrays to have a default lower bound of zero (0). ■ **Option Base 1** causes arrays to have a default lower bound of one (1).

To change the number of elements in an array dimension, or the number of dimensions, you use the ReDim statement. For an array to be redimensioned it must be declared as a dynamic array.

Syntax

ReDim [**Preserve**] *varname*(*subscripts*) [**As** *type*] [, *varname*(*subscripts*) [**As** *type*]] . . .

Dissection

- The **ReDim** statement changes the number of dimensions or the number of elements in an array dimension at run time. Because it is an executable statement, it must appear inside of a procedure.
- If the optional **Preserve** keyword is used, the existing contents of the array, if any, will not be destroyed. If omitted, the existing values stored in the array are destroyed. The Preserve keyword cannot be used to change the number of array dimensions but rather, only the upper bound in a dimension. When an array contains multiple dimensions, only the upper bound of the last dimension can be changed using the Preserve keyword.
- The required *varname* and optional **As** *type* clauses have the same meaning as they do when declaring variables that are not arrays. Arrays can be declared as any intrinsic or user-defined type, generic or specific object types.
- Just as you can declare multiple variables by separating each declaration by a comma, you can redimension multiple arrays by separating multiple declarations by commas.

Code Example

```
Dim Array1( ) As Integer
ReDim Array1(1 To 2)
ReDim Preserve Array1(1 To 3)
ReDim Preserve Array1(0 To 4)      ' Error

ReDim Array1(1 To 3, 1 To 3)
ReDim Preserve Array1(3, 4)
ReDim Preserve Array1(4, 4)        ' Error
```

Code Dissection

The Dim statement creates a dynamic array named Array1. The first ReDim statement increases the number of elements to two (2). The subscripts are one (1) and two (2). The second ReDim statement increases the upper bound of the array by one (1). It now has three elements. The attempt to change the lower bound of the array to zero (0) causes an error. You cannot change the lower bound of an array when the Preserve keyword is used. The statement to change the array from one to two dimensions is legal because the Preserve keyword is not used. Any existing array contents are destroyed. The first attempt to change the upper bound of the two-dimensional array is legal. The Preserve keyword is legal when only the upper bound of the last dimension is changed. The other dimensions cannot be changed. Thus, the final statement will cause a run-time error.

When using dynamic arrays, it typically is necessary to keep track of the existing size of the array. While variables can be declared and managed to keep track of the array's upper and lower bounds, Visual Basic supports two functions that allow you to determine the upper and lower bound of an array at run time. This information can be used to determine the size of the array. The UBound and LBound functions return a Long integer containing the largest and smallest available subscript in an array. If the lower bound of an array is one (1), either because it was dimensioned explicitly that way or because the Option Base 1 statement is used, the UBound function contains the number of elements in one of the array's dimensions.

Syntax

UBound(*arrayname*[, *dimension*])
LBound(*arrayname*[, *dimension*])

Dissection

- The **UBound** function returns a Long integer containing the largest available subscript for the indicated dimension of an array, and the **LBound** function returns a Long integer containing the smallest subscript in a dimension.
- The required *arrayname* argument is the name of an array that already has been declared.
- If the array has more than one *dimension*, this argument is used to identify the dimension that is returned. The first dimension has a value of one (1), the second a value of two (2), and so on. If omitted, the first dimension value of one (1) is used.

Code Example

```
Dim Array1(1 To 50, 0 To 3, -3 To 4)
UBound(Array1, 1)     ' 50
UBound(Array1, 2)     '  3
UBound(Array1, 3)     '  4
LBound(Array1, 1)     '  1
LBound(Array1, 2)     '  0
LBound(Array1, 3)     ' -3
```

Code Dissection

Given the preceding array declaration, the UBound functions will return the values 50, 3, and 4, respectively. The LBound functions will return 1, 0, and –3, respectively.

The UBound and LBound functions do not work with control arrays. Instead, a control array supports the LBound and UBound properties. Control arrays are discussed in Chapter 3.

It is possible to create arrays of user-defined types. For example, consider the following declarations.

```
Public Type tYMDType
    Years As Long
    Months As Long
    Days As Long
End Type
Private YMDArray(100) As tYMDType
Private YMD As tYMDType
```

The Private array named YMDArray contains 100 elements of type tYMDType. To reference an element, you follow the array name with a subscript. The corresponding member of the user-defined type must follow this.

```
YMDArray(0).Years = 10
YMDArray(0) = YMD
```

The first statement references the first element in the array. The value 10 is stored in the Years member of the array. The second statement stores the contents of the variable YMD in the first element of the array. Both the left-hand and right-hand sides of the expressions have the same underlying type (tYMDType).

Creating Loops to Process Arrays

Array processing tends to be performed using looping structures to examine each element of an array. Visual Basic supports two types of looping structures. The Do loop is used to execute a block of statements until the value of some condition changes from True to False or vice versa. The loop exits when a statement in the statement block changes the value of the condition from True to False or vice versa.

Syntax

Do [{**While**|**Until**} *condition*]
    statements
    [**Exit Do**]
    statements
Loop

Do
    statements
    [**Exit Do**]
    statements
Loop [{**While**|**Until**} *condition*]

Dissection

- The first form of the Do loop tests the *condition* before executing the *statements* in the loop. The second form executes the *statements* first, then tests the condition. Thus, the first form of the Do loop may not execute the *statements*, while the second form of the Do loop will execute *statements* at least once.

- The optional *condition* is an expression that must evaluate to True or False.
- The **While** keyword is used to execute *statements* whenever the *condition* is True; that is, while a condition is True.
- The **Until** keyword is used to execute *statements* whenever the *condition* is not True; that is, until a condition is True.
- The **Exit Do** keyword causes execution to continue at the statement following the Loop keyword. It typically is used to exit a Do loop prematurely as the result of an abnormal condition.

Code Example

```
Dim pintArray(10) As Integer
Dim pintCount As Integer, pintMax As Integer
pintMax = UBound(pintArray)
Do Until pintCount > pintMax
    pintArray(pintCount) = pintCount
    pintCount = pintCount + 1
Loop
```

Code Dissection

The previous statements illustrate how to reference an array and create a Do loop to iterate through all the array elements. The array is declared with 11 elements numbered 0 through 10. Option Base 0 is assumed. Before the Do loop is executed, the variable pintMax is initialized so that its value contains the subscript of the largest array element. The Do loop then processes the elements from 0 through 10. Each time through the Do loop, pintCount is stored in the current element of the array, and the current element is incremented by one (1). The loop terminates when pintCount is greater than the number of array elements.

A common error when writing Do loops is the infinite loop. An infinite loop is a loop that will never exit because the value of the condition never changes from True to False or from False to True. When an infinite loop is executed, the program may not respond to mouse or keyboard events. To stop executing the program, and return to design mode, press the Ctrl+Break keys.

Another form of looping structure is the For loop. The For loop is useful to execute statements a fixed number of times. Any For loop can be written as a Do loop. The For loop is particularly well-suited to processing arrays, because the lower and upper bounds of an array can be determined using the UBound and LBound statements.

Syntax

For *counter* = *start* **To** *end* [**Step** *increment*]
  statements
  [**Exit For**]
  statements
Next [*counter*]

Dissection	■ The **For** loop executes *statements* a fixed number of times. ■ When the loop is initialized, *counter* is set to *start*. The statements in the loop then are executed until the *counter* reaches *end*. ■ By default, *counter* is incremented by one (1) each time through the For loop. This value can be changed using the **Step** *increment* clause. ■ The For loop can be terminated prematurely using the optional **Exit For** statement. The Exit For statement typically is placed inside of a decision-making statement and executed in response to some abnormal condition.

Code Example	`For pintCount = 0 To pintMax`
	`    Debug.Print pintArray(pintCount)`
	`Next`

Code Dissection	Assuming the same declarations from the Do loop example, the For loop examines all the array elements and prints the value of the current element to the Immediate window. The For loop increments the variable pintCount automatically so there is no need to write a statement to change its value.

The techniques used to process an array with one dimension are almost the same as the techniques to process arrays with two or more dimensions. The difference is you use a subscript for each dimension. To examine all the elements in multiple dimensions, you can nest multiple For loops or Do loops. Consider the following statements:

```
Dim pint2Dim(10, 10) As Integer
Dim pintRows As Integer, pintColumns As Integer
Dim pintRCount As Integer, pintCCount As Integer
pintRows = UBound(pint2Dim, 1)
pintColumns = UBound(pint2Dim, 2)
For pintRCount = 0 To pintRows
    For pintCCount = 0 To pintColumns
        pint2Dim(pintRCount, pintCCount) = 1
    Next
Next
```

The previous statements create a two-dimensional array. The syntax of the UBound arguments have an additional argument to determine the upper bound of a specific dimension. The For Loop has the same syntax as you saw before but there is a second For loop to examine each column inside the other loop. Inside the second For loop, the array element (current row and column) is assigned a value of one (1).

SUMMARY

This chapter has presented the essential Visual Basic language elements. Although the syntax differs between Visual Basic and other languages, the concepts are the same. That is, most languages support variables, arrays, and constants. They also support decision-making and looping structures. As you proceed to the subsequent chapters, this chapter may provide a useful reference of Visual Basic syntax. Also, the IntelliSense technology used in the Code window is another helpful tool to verify the correctness of the statements you write. Finally, use the Help system and Books Online for more examples and as a syntactical reference.

QUESTIONS

1. Which of the following are valid intrinsic data types?
   a. Integer, Long, Single, Double.
   b. Number, String, Boolean.
   c. Number, String, Float.
   d. Integer, Long, String, TrueFalse.
   e. Both a and b.
2. Which of the following statements about Function procedures is True?
   a. They can return a value.
   b. They can have zero or more arguments.
   c. They do not return a value.
   d. They cannot be Public.
   e. Both a and b.
3. Which of the following statements is True pertaining to variables?
   a. Local variables exist whenever a program is running.
   b. Public variables are visible only in the module where they are declared.
   c. Private variables are visible to any module.
   d. Both b and c.
   e. None of the above.
4. Which of the following statements is True pertaining to Variant variables?
   a. Operations are slower than intrinsic data types like Integer or Boolean.
   b. They use more memory than other intrinsic data types.
   c. They can store any intrinsic data type.
   d. Both b and c.
   e. All of the above.

5. From the highest to the lowest, which is the correct order or precedence for arithmetic, comparison, and logical operators?
   a. Logical, comparison, arithmetic.
   b. Logical, arithmetic, comparison.
   c. Comparison, logical, arithmetic.
   d. Arithmetic, comparison, logical.
   e. None of the above.
6. Which of the following are valid string functions?
   a. StrConv, Left, Right, Mid.
   b. Upper, Lower.
   c. LTrim, RTrim, Trim.
   d. Both a and c.
   e. All of the above.
7. Which of the following statements is True pertaining to constants?
   a. Constants are evaluated at run time.
   b. They can have a defined data type.
   c. They are declared with the keyword Constant.
   d. Both a and b.
   e. All of the above.
8. The ______________ and ______________ statements create an enumerated and user-defined type, respectively.
   a. Enumeration, Type.
   b. Enum, Type.
   c. Enumeration, Data.
   d. Enum, Data.
   e. None of the above.
9. Which of the following is (are) considered decision-making statement(s)?
   a. If Then Else.
   b. Select Case.
   c. When.
   d. Do loop.
   e. Both a and b.
10. Which of the following is (are) considered looping or repetition statement(s)?
    a. For Next.
    b. Select Case.
    c. If Then Else.
    d. When.
    e. Both c and d.
11. Write the necessary statements to declare two variables. The scope of the first should be the module where the variable is declared. The second should be a global variable. Both should be integers. Use the correct prefix for each variable and a suffix of Count.
12. Create a user-defined type named tElapsedTime with two members named StartTime and EndTime. The StartTime and EndTime should be of the type tTime. The type tTime should have members for the elapsed hours, minutes, and seconds.

For the following three questions, assume the following type and variable declarations:

```
Private Type tFlightInfo
    AirportName As String
    AirportCode As Integer
    AirportTime As Date
End Type

Type tReservation
    FlightNumber As String
    Departure As tFlightInfo
    Arrival As tFlightInfo
End Type
Private Reservations(0 to 1000) As tReservation
Private Departure As tFlightInfo
```

13. Using the previous type and variable declarations, write the necessary statement to store the value "Los Angeles International" into the departure AirportName for the first element of the Reservations array.

14. Using the previous type and variable declarations, write the necessary statements to store the current date and time into the departure time for the first element of the Reservations array.

15. Using the previous type and variable declarations, assign the value of the departure date and time for the first element of the Reservations array to the departure time in the variable Departure.

For the next two questions, use the following code to compute the answer to the questions:

```
pintI = 3
Do Until pintI > 10
    pintI = pintI + 4
Loop
Print pintI
```

16. In the previous code, how many times does the loop execute?

17. In the previous code, what is the value of pintI when the Print statement is executed?

18. Write a function named ACount that will accept one argument, a one-dimensional array of Variants. Write the necessary statements to determine the current number of elements in the array. This value should be returned by the function. Assume that the lower and upper bounds of the array may change at run time so use the LBound and UBound functions to determine the bounds of the array.

19. Create an enumerated type named eMonths. The enumeration should have 12 members, one for each month of the year. The name of each member should be the month name. The constant value associated with the member should be the number of the month (i.e., January = 1).

20. Write a For loop to print all the array elements for the following array to the Immediate window:

```
Dim Array1(1 To 300) As String
```

EXERCISES

1. In this exercise you will create a form containing the interface for a payroll record. The form will have several text boxes whose contents need to be validated for correctness. You will use the character classification functions and string manipulation function to validate the user input.

a. Create a new project and set the Name property of the form to **frmExercise1**. Save the form using the name **frmExercise1.frm** and the project using the name **Exercise1.vbp**.

b. Set the caption of the form to **Exercise 1 / User Interface.**

c. Create two text boxes to store an employee's first name and last name. The first name can be no longer than 20 characters and the last name can be no longer than 30 characters.

d. Create a text box to store the employee's hourly wage. The hourly wage must be numeric. The minimum wage must be greater than or equal to $5.50 per hour and less than or equal to $22.50 per hour.

e. Create a text box to store the date hired. The value must be a valid date and less than or equal to the current date.

f. Create a text box to store the department identification number. Valid identification numbers are 100, 200, 300, and 400.

g. The final text box should store a Social Security number. This value has the format of XXX-XX-XXXX, where (X) is a number. The numbers should be separated by dashes as indicated. You need to use the Asc or Chr functions to examine the contents of each character in the string.

h. Create a command button with a caption of Validate. When clicked, the command button should validate the contents of the text boxes. If a text box contains invalid data, clear the contents of the text box.

i. Create a command button to exit the program.

j. Test the program and confirm that the fields are validated according to the specifications when the command button is clicked.

2. In this exercise you will use the date functions illustrated in the chapter to convert and perform calculations on date values.

a. Create a new project and set the Name property of the form to **frmExercise2**. Save the form using the name **frmExercise2.frm** and the project using the name **Exercise2.vbp**.

b. Create two text boxes. The first text box will store the starting date and the second text box will store the ending date.

c. Create a command button with the caption **Difference**. When clicked, the command button should display the number of years, months, and days between the date in the first text box and the second text box. Create three output labels to store these values.

d. Create three more command buttons with the captions **Add Years, Add Months,** and **Add Days**.

e. Create another text box to store an integer value that will contain the number of years, months, or days to add.

f. When the **Add Years** command button is clicked, add the value stored in the text box you just created to the text box containing the start date. Store the result in the text box containing the ending date.

g. Repeat the previous step for the **Add Months** and **Add Days** command button. Again, store the result in the Ending Date text box.
h. Create a command button to exit the program.
i. Test the program and confirm that the date computations are being performed correctly.

3. In this exercise you will create a standard module containing a set of utility functions that may be useful to many programs. Each of the utility functions should accept one argument, an array of single precision numbers. The functions will compute the sum, average, and count of the different array elements.

a. Create a new project and set the Name property of the form to **frmExercise3**. Save the form using the name **frmExercise3.frm** and the project using the name **Exercise3.vbp**.
b. Add a standard module to the project and save it using the name **StatArray.bas**. The standard module will support three functions. The first function will summarize the values in an array, the second will count the number of elements in the array. The final function will compute the average of the elements.
c. In the form, declare a private module-level array to store single precision numbers. The array should be a dynamic array.
d. In the form module, create a text box and command button with the caption **Add**. When clicked, the command button should increase the size of the dynamic array, and store the contents of the text box into the new array element. Make sure to validate that the text box contains a valid number.
e. In the standard module, create a public function named **SumArray**. The function should accept one argument—an array. The code in the function will need to determine the lower and upper bounds of the array. Then, using a loop, total the contents of each array element. The function should return the sum of the array contents.
f. Create a second Public function named **CountArray**. The function should accept an array as an argument and return the number of elements in the array.
g. Create a final function named **AverageArray**. The function should compute and return the average value of the array elements.
h. In the form module, create three command buttons to test the functions you just wrote. Each function should be called with the module-level array as an argument. Store the return value of the function into labels on the form. Each label should have a prompt to identify the contents of the label and a meaningful name.
i. Create a command button to exit the program.
j. Test the program. Confirm that the Add command button and the functions you wrote are working correctly.

4. In this exercise you will store data in a user-defined type and create an array of user-defined types. Assume that a company is divided into four divisions and those divisions are Marketing, Manufacturing, Accounting, and Engineering. The print shop charges each department for the time they spend on the printing projects for each department. A log is kept of the starting time, ending time, and department for each print job. At the end of each month, this log must sum the hours worked and a report must be printed containing the total number of hours for each department.

a. Create a new project and set the Name property of the form to **frmExercise4**. Save the form using the name **frmExercise4.frm** and the project using the name **Exercise4.vbp**.

b. In the form module, create three text boxes to store the starting time, ending time, and department. The user must enter the department using a code of 100, 200, 300, and 400 for the four different departments.

c. In the standard module, create a user-defined type to store the department, starting time, and ending time of a record. The starting and ending date should have a data type of Date. The department should be implemented using an enumerated type.

d. Add a standard module named **Track.bas** to the project.

e. Create a Private dynamic array of user-defined types in the standard module. Remember, dynamic arrays cannot have an initial value. Write a Sub procedure named InitializeArray that will give the array an initial dimension. This function should be called when the form is loaded (in the Form_Load) event procedure.

f. Create a Function procedure in the standard module named **RecordTime** that accepts one argument, a variable of the user-defined type you just created. The RecordTime function should verify that the ending time is greater than the starting time and should return a value indicating if the data was not valid. If the data is valid, redimension the array and add the data passed in the user-defined type argument to the new array element. If the data is not valid, do not redimension the array. The Function procedure should return True or False depending upon whether the data was added or not.

g. In the command button to add the record, store the contents of the input text boxes in a variable of the user-defined type you created. Call the Record Time function you created in the previous steps.

h. Create a Sub procedure named **SummarizeTime**. This Sub procedure should use another array to store the total amount of time for each department. This array should be passed as an argument. The array should store long integers. Because the array will store the total hours for each department the array should also have four elements. The Sub procedure should examine each element in the array of user-defined types. For each element, you need to determine the amount of time spent by subtracting the ending time from the starting time. Use the DateDiff function to compute the number of hours between the starting time and ending time. Using the department number stored in the user-defined type, locate the correct element in the second array and add the net time to the corresponding element. This function should return the array containing the total time for each department.

i. In the form module, create a command button with the caption **Add**. This command button should verify the times are valid and the department is valid. If the information is valid, store it in the variable of the user-defined type you created in the standard module. This variable should be passed as an argument to the RecordTime function.

j. Create another command button with the caption **Summarize**. The code in the command button should call the SummarizeTime Sub procedure. Pass an array as the argument.

k. Display the results into four output labels—one for each department.

l. Create a command button to exit the program.

m. Test the program by adding several records for each department, then summarize the records.

CHAPTER

3

Form Events, Keyboard Events, and Menus

Creating Programs with Multiple Forms, Dialog Boxes, and Menus

case▶ International Money Systems is developing a program to calculate information regarding loans. They want the program to support the characteristics of most Windows programs. For example, the program will display an introductory screen while the program finishes loading. The program will support dialogs to control the appearance of the objects on the form. For example, there will be a dialog to change the fonts displayed in the text boxes. This requires that the program have multiple forms instead of a single form. Furthermore, information must be communicated between different forms.

SECTION A

objectives

In this section you will:

- Set properties pertaining to the project using an object known as the App object
- Display and hide forms
- Respond to the events that occur when a form is loaded and unloaded

Working with Multiple Forms

Previewing the Completed Application

This chapter focuses on programming in an event-driven environment and is intended as a review of fundamental Windows and event-driven concepts. If you have not previously programmed in Windows or Visual Basic, a reference text will be helpful.

The applications you created in previous chapters have all used a single form. Most programs, however, contain multiple forms. The completed application for this chapter contains four forms. These forms support the characteristics of most Windows 95 programs. For example, there is an introductory splash screen. The main form has a menu under the title bar, and there are other forms that work like dialogs.

To preview the completed application:

1. Start **Visual Basic** and open the project file named **Chapter.03\Complete\ IMS_C.vbp**. Print the code for the project.
2. Run the program. An introductory form called a splash screen is displayed, then the main form is displayed as shown in Figure 3-1.

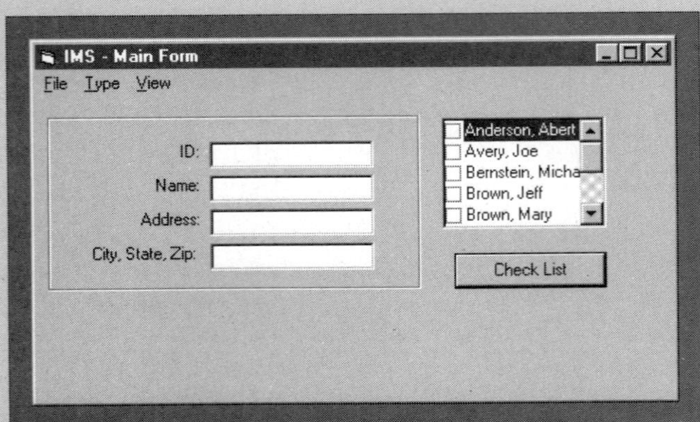

Figure 3-1: Completed main form

3 The main form has a menu. The menu works like menus in other programs. Click **Type** then **Home** on the form's menu bar. The loan form, as shown in Figure 3-2, contains three new controls—a list box, option buttons, and a frame.

The main form contains menus that are typical for most Visual Basic applications. However, some of the menus contain no code in the Click event procedure.

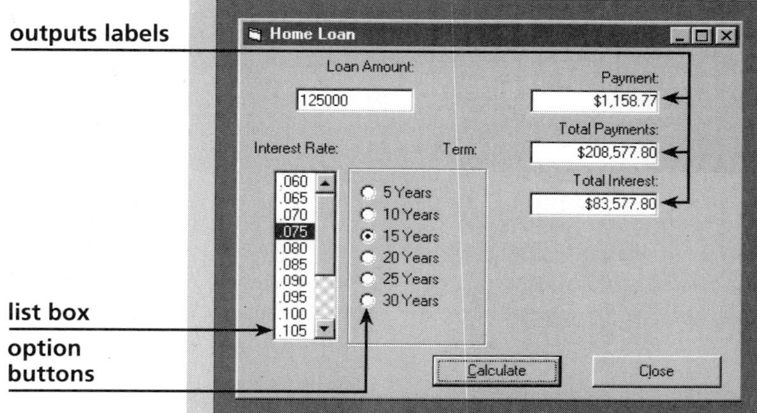

Figure 3-2: Completed loan form

4 Enter the input values shown in Figure 3-2, and click the **Calculate** command button. The loan payment amount and other output values are displayed in the output labels.

5 Click the **Close** command button to close the form.

6 Exit Visual Basic.

The App Object

Visual Basic supports a predefined global object called the **App** object. An instance of the App object exists for every project and contains information pertinent to the project. There are two ways to set the App object's properties. They can be set using the Project Properties dialog or with code.

Object	**App**
Definition	The App object specifies information about the application's title, version information, the path and name of its executable file and Help files, and whether or not a previous instance of the application is running.
Properties	■ The **CompanyName**, **LegalCopyright**, and **LegalTrademarks** properties are used to identify the company name, copyright, and trademark information pertinent to the program.

- The **Major, Minor**, and **Revision** properties are used to identify the version of the software.
- The **ProductName** and **Title** properties allow you to give the program a descriptive name and title.

Windows programs commonly display an introductory screen called a **splash screen** that displays this information. A splash screen not only identifies program information to a user but also can give the user a visual clue that the program is loading. In this example, you will use a splash screen to display the properties of the App object.

To set the properties of the App object:

1. Start **Visual Basic** and open the project file named **Chapter.03\Startup\ IMS_S.vbp.**
2. Click **Project1 Properties** on the **Project** menu to activate the dialog. Click the **Make** tab as shown in Figure 3-3.

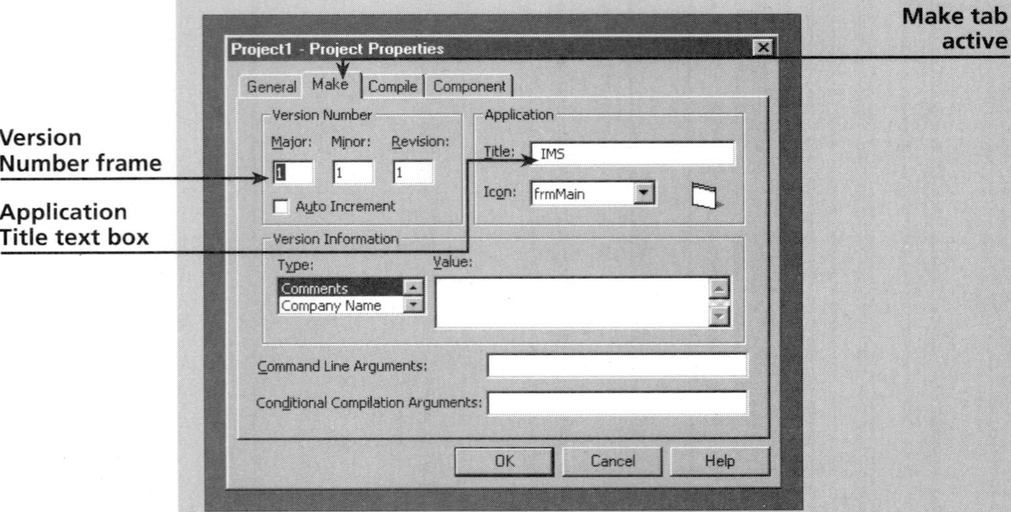

Figure 3-3: Project Properties dialog box

3. Set the **Version Number** and **Application Title** as shown in Figure 3-3.
4. Set the Company Name to **Money Systems Incorporated**, the Legal Copyright to **Unauthorized duplication prohibited**, and the Product Name to **Account List**. To accomplish this task, select the appropriate item in the **Type** list box and enter the text in the **Value** text box. Click **OK** to close the Project Properties dialog.
5. Activate the Code window for the form named **frmSplash** and enter the following statements into the **Form_Load** event procedure. The labels already have been created.

```
lblVersion = "Version " & App.Major & _
    "." & App.Minor & "." & App.Revision
lblProductName = App.Title
lblProduct = App.ProductName
lblLegalCopyright = App.LegalCopyright
```

When the form is loaded the version information and other App properties will be displayed on the splash screen.

Displaying and Hiding Forms

When a form is displayed on the screen, it is displayed in one of two ways. A form can be displayed as a **modeless** form. When a form is displayed as a modeless form, the user can interact with the other forms in the project while the modeless form is visible. A **modal** form commonly is used for forms that appear as dialogs. Dialogs can be roughly divided into four categories depending on their purpose.

- There are property dialogs to set general categories of properties. For example, you may set the fonts or colors on a form.
- Bulletin dialogs are used to get conformation from the user, or display a message alerting the user of some abnormal condition.
- Function dialogs are used to perform a specific task like finding a record or spell checking a document.
- A process dialog displays the relative completion of a task. For example, when you copy a large file with Windows Explorer, a dialog is displayed indicating how many seconds remain before the task is complete.

When a form is displayed as a modal form, the form must be unloaded or hidden before the user can interact with the other forms in the program. Displaying a form as a modal form does not prohibit the user from interacting with the windows of other programs. There are two methods used to display and hide a form. These are called the **Show** and **Hide** methods, respectively.

Syntax

object.**Show** *style*, *ownerform*
object.**Hide**

Dissection

- The optional *object* must be a valid instance of a Form object.
- The **Show** method causes the form referenced by *object* to be displayed on the screen and receive focus.
- The **Hide** method causes the form referenced by *object* to become invisible. The memory allocated to the form and its objects still exists and can be referenced with code.
- The optional *style* property determines whether the form is displayed as modal or modeless form. The constants vbModal, and vbModeless can be

used to display a form as a modal or modeless form, respectively. If this argument is omitted, the form is displayed as a modeless form.

- The optional *ownerform* identifies which form owns the new form. When using a Visual Basic form, the keyword Me should be used.

Code Example

```
Form1.Show vbModal
Me.Hide
```

Code Dissection

The first statement displays the form named Form1 as a modal form. The modal form receives focus. Until the modal form is closed, no other form in the program can get focus. The second statement hides the current form. The form still is loaded and can be referenced with code.
The Me keyword is used to provide a reference to the current form. If you are unfamiliar with the Me keyword, refer to the help topic "Me keyword."

In addition to the Show and Hide methods, there are two statements to load and unload a form.

Syntax

Load *object*
Unload *object*

Dissection

- The **Load** statement loads a form into memory. The form is not displayed until the Show method is called on the form. Even though the form is not visible, its objects can be referenced with code.
- Calling the **Unload** statement removes the form from the screen and memory. Once unloaded, the Form object no longer exists and as such cannot be referenced. Unloading all the forms from a program has the effect of ending the program.
- The *object* placeholder must be a valid instance of a Form object.

Code Example

```
Load Form1
Unload Me
```

Code Dissection

The first statement loads the form named Form1 and the second statement unloads the current form.

When a program has multiple forms, it often is necessary to reference procedures and variables in different forms. Consider this sample program with several forms. The main form can reference variables on the loan form. Assume that the loan form has the following enumeration and variable declarations.

```
Public Enum eLoanType
    Auto
    Home
End Enum
Public LoanType As eLoanType
```

Remember that a form is a class. Interestingly, when you create Public variables in a form module, they are considered properties of the form. This fact is significant because when one form references a Public variable on a second form, the syntax is the same as a property reference. Assume that the main form was responsible for setting the LoanType and displaying the loan form. This could be accomplished with the following statements:

```
frmLoan.LoanType = Auto
frmLoan.Show vbModal
```

These statements cause the form's loan type to be set to the enumeration Auto. Then, the form is displayed as a modal form. Given that Public variables are considered properties, Public procedures are considered methods. Assume that a Public general procedure named DoTask was declared in the form named frmLoan. To call this procedure from another form, the following statement would be used:

```
frmLoan.DoTask
```

The syntax is identical to the syntax used to call a method supported by an object.

The Startup Object

When a program first is run, what happens depends on the value of the Startup object. The Startup object is set using the General tab in the Project Properties dialog as shown in Figure 3-4.

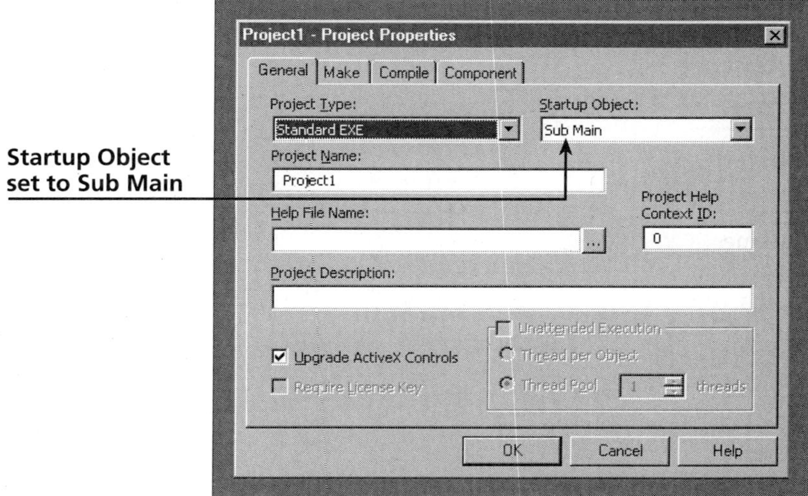

Figure 3-4: Project Properties dialog

If the Startup object is set to Sub Main, there must be a general procedure named Main in a standard module in the project. The code in the general procedure is executed when the program starts. Thus, it is possible to have a program consisting only of standard modules and no visual interface. Another common use of setting the Startup object to Sub Main, is to perform initialization functions and then load and display individual forms explicitly.

If the Startup object is set to a form, the selected form is loaded and displayed on the screen when the program loads. Then, the form waits until the user performs an action that generates an event. Code then is executed in response to the event and the program waits for another event to occur. If the Startup object is set to Sub Main, a form must be displayed on the screen explicitly.

In this example, you will load and display a form called a splash screen. This form will be displayed while the other forms in the project are loaded. After all the forms are loaded, the main form will be displayed.

To set the startup properties for your program:

1. Click **Project1 Properties** on the **Project** menu. Make sure the **General** tab is active, then click the Startup object **Sub Main.**
2. Activate the Code window for the standard module named **IMS.bas**, create a procedure named Sub Main, and enter the following statements:

```
frmSplash.Show
frmSplash.Refresh
Load frmMain
Load frmOptions
Load frmLoan
frmMain.Show
Unload frmSplash
```

3. Test the program. The splash screen is displayed and a few seconds later, the splash screen is unloaded and the main form is displayed.

The first statement calls the Show method on the form named frmSplash. This causes the splash screen to be loaded and displayed. The Refresh method is called so the form is painted on the screen completely while the other forms are being loaded. Then, the other three forms in the program are loaded into memory. Even though the forms are loaded, they are not visible on the screen. The final statements display the main form and unload the splash screen. The form is unloaded rather than hidden because it will not be used again.

Understanding Form Events

There are several events that pertain to the Form object as it is loaded and unloaded. It is possible to write code for these events to perform initialization tasks when the form is loaded, and perform housekeeping tasks when the form is unloaded. The following list summarizes the events that occur to a form as it is loaded.

1. The **Initialize** event occurs first when an instance of a form first is created. Remember that a form instance is created from a class. The visible form on the screen is considered an instance of the form class. This event commonly is used to initialize data before the form is loaded.
2. The **Load** event occurs after the Initialize event. The code in this event procedure also is used to initialize the value of controls and data.
3. The **Activate** event occurs after the Load event and happens when the form becomes the active form.

The Initialize and Load events occur when a form is loaded into memory. They do not occur repeatedly as a form gets and loses focus, however. Each time a form gets focus, the Activate event occurs. Each time a form loses focus, the **Deactivate** event occurs. When a form is unloaded, three events occur as shown in the following list:

1. The **QueryUnload** event occurs before a form is unloaded from memory.
2. After the QueryUnload event occurs, the **Unload** event occurs.
3. The **Terminate** event occurs last after the Unload event.

The QueryUnload and Unload events have the following syntax:

Syntax

Private Sub Form_QueryUnload(*cancel* As Integer, *unloadmode* As Integer)
Private Sub Form_Unload(*cancel* As Integer)

Dissection

- The *cancel* argument is an Integer value. Setting this argument to a value other than zero (0) will cause the event to be cancelled. Thus, the form will not be unloaded and execution will continue.
- The *unloadmode* argument is used to determine the cause of the QueryUnload event and is represented by five different constant values. If set to vbFormControlMenu, then the Close button on the Control-menu box was clicked. If set to vbFormCode, then the Unload statement was called from the program. If set to vbAppWindows, then Microsoft Windows is being shut down. If set to vbAppTaskManager, then the Task Manager is closing the form or application. If set to vbFormMDIForm, the MDI parent form is closing.

Code Example

```
Private Sub Form_QueryUnload(Cancel As Integer, _
    UnloadMode As Integer)
    If UnloadMode = vbFormControlMenu Then
        Cancel = True
    End If
End Sub
```

Code Dissection

These statements prevent the form from being unloaded by clicking the Close button on the form's title bar. The UnloadMode argument contains a constant value indicating the cause of the event. If the cause is the Close button on the Control-menu box, then the event is canceled. The subsequent Unload event will not occur.

SECTION B

objectives

In this section you will:

- Create control instances that share the same name and event procedures
- Use a Frame control as a container for other controls
- Create and program option buttons
- Create and program list boxes and combo boxes
- Create and program check boxes

Control Arrays and Intrinsic Controls

Creating Control Arrays

It is possible to create one or more instances of a control in such a way that each control instance has the same name and shares the same event procedures. For example, it is possible to create five instances of a TextBox control, all having the same name. In this situation, each text box would execute the same code in response to the same event. A group of controls sharing the same name and class (created from the same type of control) is called a **control array**. Conceptually, a control array is like any other array. It has multiple elements of the same type (control). Individual elements are referenced using an index (subscript).

There is a unique copy of the properties for each control in a control array. The **Index** property for each control instance in a control array has a unique value used to identify the control. When an event procedure is called, the Index property of the active object is passed as an argument to the event procedure. This value is used to determine which control in the control array is active. Figure 3-5 illustrates this process.

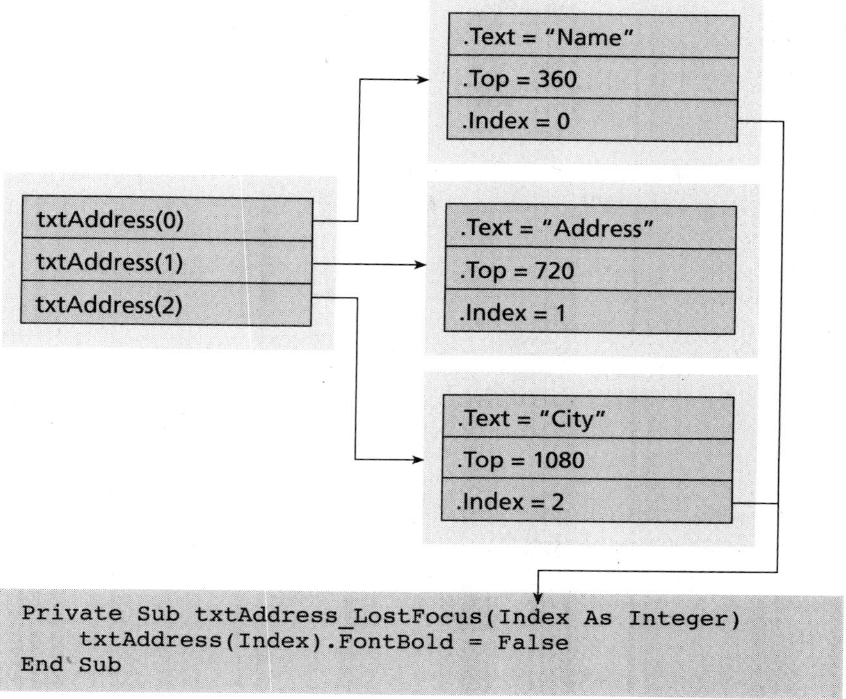

Figure 3-5: Control array

As shown in Figure 3-5, there are three text boxes in a control array named txtAddress. The elements have Index values of zero (0), one (1), and two (2). Each element has a unique copy of its properties. The Index property uniquely identifies each element in the control array. When an event procedure is executed for an element in a control array, the index of the pertinent control is passed as an argument to the event procedure. Control arrays are useful for several reasons:

- They improve program efficiency by reducing the number of event procedures and the amount of code. This causes modules to be smaller in size thereby reducing the load time.
- Performance also is improved because a control array uses fewer resources than multiple instances of the same control.
- Control arrays allow you to create and delete control instances at run time. When a new instance of a control array member is created at run time, the properties of the first element in the control array are inherited by the new control. That is, the new control has the same properties as the first element in the control array.

While adding control to a control array is possible at run time, control arrays must be created at design time. There are three ways to create a control array.

- Changing the Name property of a control to the same name as another control will cause a dialog to be displayed allowing you either to create a control array, or reset the Name property to its original value.
- Changing the Index property to a value that is not Null will create a control array.
- When copying and pasting a control using the Windows clipboard, a dialog is displayed asking whether or not to create a control array. If a control array is not created, Visual Basic assigns a default name to the object.

Programming tip

Index values typically begin at zero (0) and are incremented by one (1) for each element in the control array. It is possible, however, to assign non-sequential Index values. The maximum index for a control array is 32,767, although this limitation is seldom a problem. Control arrays most commonly are used with option buttons and menus.

When labels are used as descriptive prompts, consider using a control array for all the labels. It is slightly more efficient.

In this example, the main form has three text boxes that are members of a control array. Using a control array, it is very easy to change the typeface when each text box in the control array gets or loses focus.

To change the appearance of the controls at run time:

1. Activate the Code window for the form named **frmMain** and enter the following statement into the **txtAddress_GotFocus** event procedure:

```
txtAddress(Index).FontBold = True
```

2. Enter the following statement into the **txtAddress_LostFocus** event procedure:

```
txtAddress(Index).FontBold = False
```

3. Test the program. Enter information into the three address text boxes in the control array. As the GotFocus and LostFocus event occurs for each address text box, the typeface is changed accordingly.

   The ID text box contains an event procedure that will allow only numbers to be entered in the text box.

The event procedure has one argument named Index. This value contains the numeric index (the Index property) of the active text box in the control array. Had a control array not been used, the statements would have to be duplicated for all three controls.

Once a control array has been created at design time, additional elements can be added and removed from the control array at run time using the Load and Unload statements.

Syntax	**Load** *object*(*index-value*) **Unload** *object*(*index-value*)
Dissection	■ The **Load** statement creates a new control instance in a control array. The control array already must exist. The properties of the new control array element are inherited from the first element in the existing control array. ■ The **Unload** statement unloads a control array element. It only can be used on elements created at run time with the Load statement. ■ The *object* must be an element of an existing control array. ■ The *index-value* contains an Integer number identifying the object location in the control array. When adding an element to a control array, the *index-value* must not already be in use.

Code Example	`Load cmdDemo(1)`
	`cmdDemo(1).Caption = "Demo"`
	`Unload cmdDemo(1)`

Code Dissection	Assuming there is a control array named cmdDemo, the Load statement creates a second element in the control array with an index of one (1), and the last statement destroys the control array instance created by the Load statement. The syntax to reference an element in a control array is the same as it is for arrays. In the previous example, cmdDemo(1) provides a reference to a particular element, and Caption references the Caption property for that element.

Just as the UBound and LBound functions are used to determine the upper and lower bound of an array, a control array supports the UBound and LBound run-time properties to determine the value of the largest and smallest index value in a control array. Assuming that there is a control array named txtAddress, the following statements will reference the lower and upper bound in a control array.

```
Debug.Print txtAddress.LBound
Debug.Print txtAddress.UBound
```

There is a control called the OptionButton control that is particularly well-suited to working with control arrays. The OptionButton control commonly is used with another control called a Frame control.

The Frame Control

There exists a relationship between the form and the control instances created on it. When a control instance is created directly on a form, the form contains the controls, and is considered the container. The container for a control instance is stored in the **Container** property of the control, which is available only at run time. It contains a reference to the object, like a form, that is the container. There are two controls that can operate as containers in addition to a form. These are the

Frame and **PictureBox** controls. Each has a visible region. Controls contained by a frame or picture box appear inside the visible region of the container. Containers can be nested. That is, a frame can in turn contain frames, which in turn can contain other frames. Figure 3-6 shows this process.

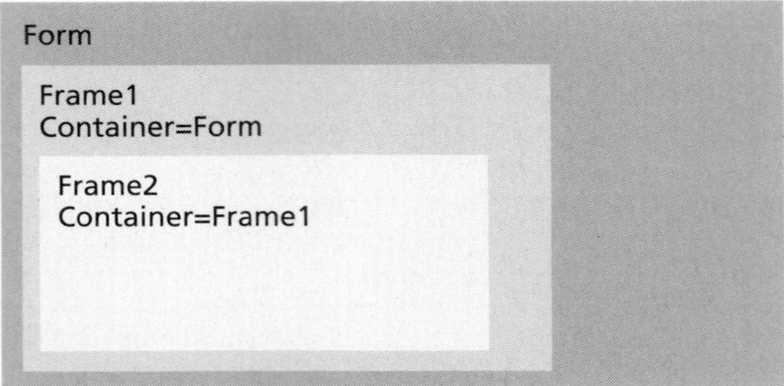

Figure 3-6: Containers

As shown in Figure 3-6, the form has two frames. The first frame is contained by the form, and the second frame is contained by the first frame. There are two reasons to use containers. By grouping controls in containers, they can be moved as a unit on the form. If the frame is moved, the control instances contained by the frame are moved accordingly. The controls also can be moved individually inside the frame but cannot be moved outside the region of the frame. The second and more important purpose of the Frame control is to make multiple instances of another control, called an OptionButton control, operate as a group.

The OptionButton Control

The **OptionButton** control allows you to create a group of buttons from which a user can click only one button at a time. Option buttons sometimes are called **radio buttons** referring to buttons in car radios that allow you to press a button to select a station. If an option button is created directly on a form, the buttons will be contained by the form and operate as an **option group**. Only one option button in an option group can be selected at a time. If a program requires multiple option groups to be maintained, a frame or picture box needs to be created for each option group, and the option buttons contained by the frame or picture box. For an option group to be contained by a frame or picture box, the frame or picture box must be created before the option buttons.

Object	**OptionButton**
Definition	An OptionButton control displays an option that can be turned on or off.
Properties	The **Caption** property defines the text displayed inside the option button.

	The **Appearance**, **Picture**, **DisabledPicture**, and **DownPicture** properties are used to create an option button with pictures instead of text. The **Value** property can be True or False indicating whether or not the option button is clicked.
Events	The **Click** event occurs when the user clicks the button.

A control array of option buttons is a common way of implementing an option group because each button performs the same action when clicked. That is, the event procedures are the same for all the option buttons in the option group. To create objects contained by a frame you can use the following steps:

1. Create a frame on the form.
2. Create an option button inside the region of the frame, and set the Index property to zero (0) to make it a member of a control array.
3. Copy the option button to the clipboard.
4. Activate the frame.
5. Paste the option button in the frame. The option button should appear at the upper-left corner of the frame rather than the form. If the option button appears at the upper-left corner of the form, delete the option button and repeat Steps 2, 3, and 4.

Option buttons consume a large amount of space on the screen. Use option buttons only when the number of choices is fewer than five. When the number of choices exceeds five, consider using a list box or combo box.

To better understand how containers work, you can look at the Container property of different objects at run time.

To examine the properties at run time:

1 Start the program, then click the **Break** button to enter break mode.

2 Activate the Immediate window and enter the statements shown in Figure 3-7.

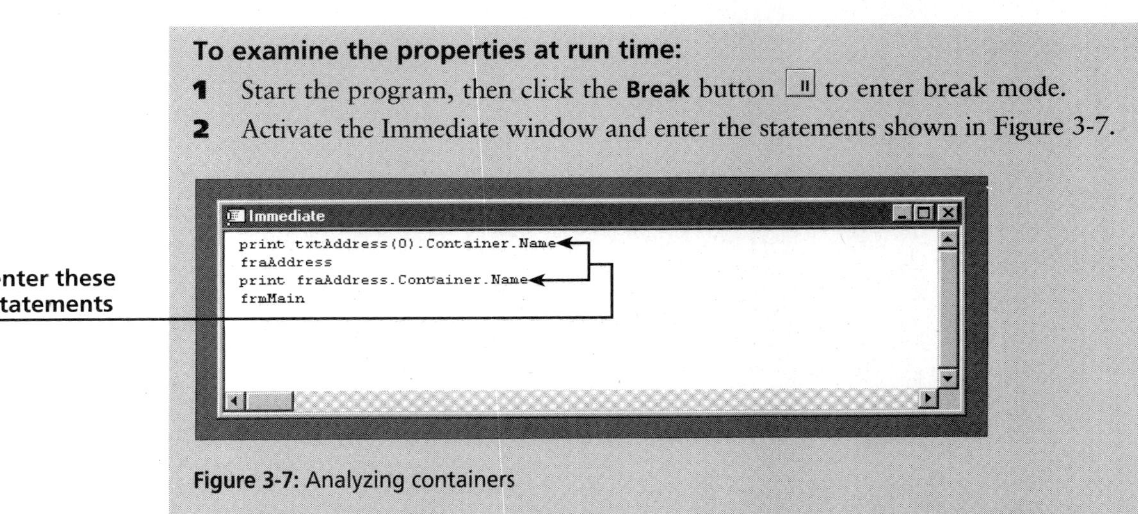
Immediate
print txtAddress(0).Container.Name
fraAddress
print fraAddress.Container.Name
frmMain
enter these statements

Figure 3-7: Analyzing containers

3 End the program.

As shown in Figure 3-7, the container for the option button is the frame named fraAddress, which is in turn contained by the form.

In this example, you will see how to create a control array of option buttons. You also will add elements to the control array at run time. The option group will be used to select the term of a loan. Assume that there are two types of loans, automobile loans having a term of between 1 and 5 years, and home loans having a term of between 5 and 30 years in increments of 5 years. The option buttons in the control array will be created dynamically at run time depending on the type of loan.

To create a dynamic control array:

1 Activate the form named **frmLoan**. Click the **Frame** control on the Toolbox and create an instance of it as shown in Figure 3-8. Make sure the Frame control is active. The handles should appear surrounding the frame.

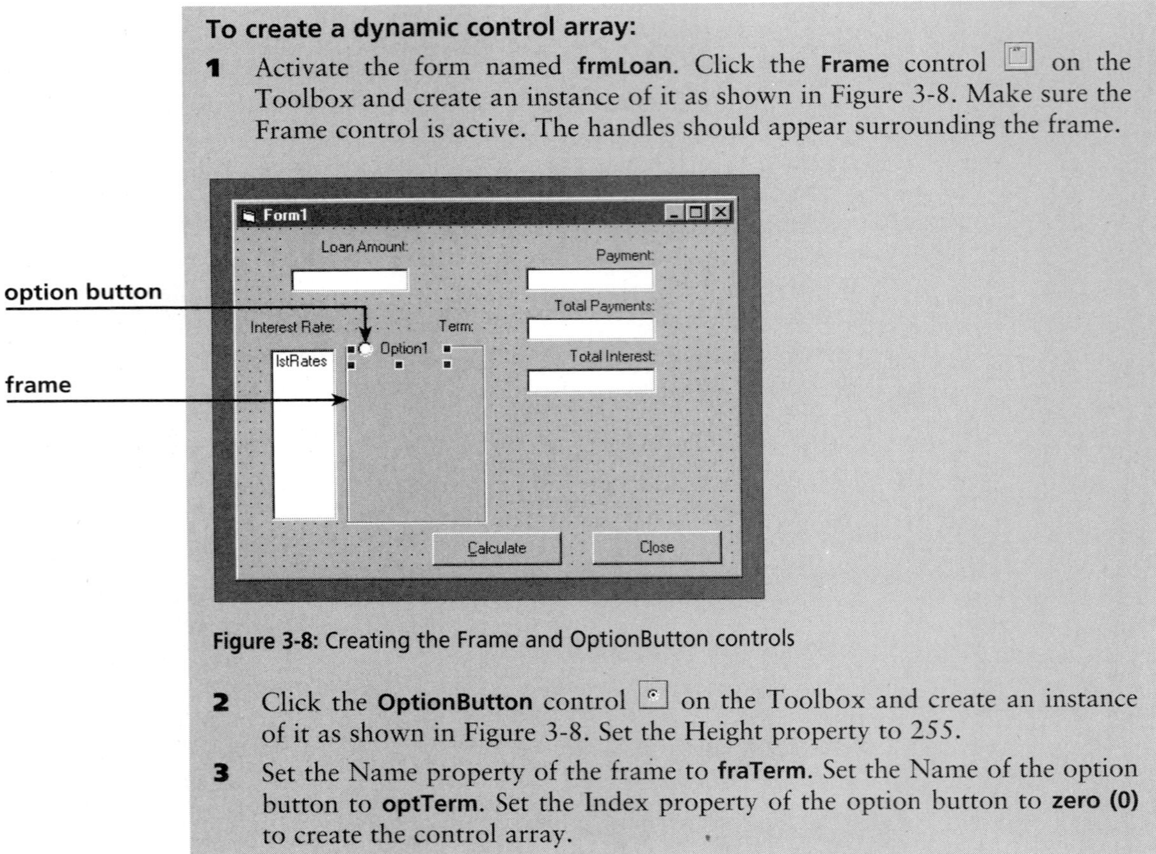

Figure 3-8: Creating the Frame and OptionButton controls

2 Click the **OptionButton** control on the Toolbox and create an instance of it as shown in Figure 3-8. Set the Height property to 255.

3 Set the Name property of the frame to **fraTerm**. Set the Name of the option button to **optTerm.** Set the Index property of the option button to **zero (0)** to create the control array.

Now that the control array is created, you must write the necessary statements to create the additional control instances in the array. This either could be done when the form is loaded or when the form is activated. Because the instances are created at run time, you must set explicitly the position and caption of each control instance at run time, and make the controls visible. Otherwise, their position would be the same and as such only one of the controls would be visible to the user. This is because each control inherits the property settings of the first element in the control array.

One of the interesting points about the implementation is the selection of the Index values. In this example, non-sequential elements will be used. The reason for this is so the index of the control array elements will have the same value as that of the loan's term. That is, the option button representing the 15-year loan will have a caption and index value of 15.

To create the instances of the control array at run time:

1 Activate the Code window for the form named **frmLoan** and enter the following statements in the **Form_Activate** event procedure:

```
Dim pintTerms As Integer, pintCount As Integer
Dim psngRate As Single

optTerm(0).Visible = False

Select Case LoanType
    Case Auto
        Me.Caption = "Auto Loan"
        For pintTerms = 1 To 5
            Load optTerm(pintTerms)
            optTerm(pintTerms).Caption = _
                CStr(pintTerms) & " Years"
            optTerm(pintTerms).Move _
                optTerm(pintTerms - 1).Left, _
                optTerm(pintTerms - 1).Top + 300
            optTerm(pintTerms).Visible = True
        Next

    Case Home
        Me.Caption = "Home Loan"
        For pintTerms = 5 To 30 Step 5
            Load optTerm(pintTerms)
            optTerm(pintTerms).Caption = _
                CStr(pintTerms) & " Years"
            optTerm(pintTerms).Move _
                optTerm(pintTerms - 5).Left, _
                optTerm(pintTerms - 5).Top + 255
            optTerm(pintTerms).Visible = True
        Next
End Select
```

2 Test the program. Click **Type** then **Home** to display the home loan form. The option buttons should have the loan terms ranging from 5 to 30 years. Click the **Close** command button. Click **Type** then **Auto** to display the form with the automobile options. The code to display the form already has been created.

This code requires careful analysis. At design time, there is one element in the control array, but it is never used. This simplifies the For loop that creates the new control array elements. The Select Case statement is used to create the control array of option buttons according to the loan type. If the loan type is an auto loan, there are five valid terms ranging from one to five years. Thus, the index values assigned are 1, 2, 3, 4, and 5. The For loop for the auto loan iterates five times. The value of the counter used is the index of the new element. Inside of the loop, the new element is created, the caption set, the control positioned, and then made visible.

The For loop for the home loan is more interesting. Home loans range from 5 to 30 years in 5-year increments. Thus, the valid terms are 5, 10, 15, 20, 25, and 30. Thus, the For loop is incremented by five (5) each time through the loop. This has the effect of creating elements with indexes that are the same as the term. The indexes are not consecutive. Again, the caption is set and the new control instance positioned as necessary.

The ComboBox Control

A **ComboBox** control displays a list of items from which the user can select one item, or enter a new item. The ComboBox is useful for tasks like selecting a font from a list of fonts or a name from a list of names. The Dropdown Combo and Dropdown List styles are particularly useful because they occupy very little space on the form. When the user activates a dropdown combo box, its visible region expands temporarily. Once an item is selected and the combo box loses focus, its visible region displays the currently selected item. There are three styles of combo boxes you can use by setting the object's Style property.

- The Style **0 - Dropdown Combo** allows a user either to select an item from a drop-down list of suggested choices or type in a new item. No options appear until the user clicks the list arrow at the right of the combo box.
- The Style **1 - Simple Combo** displays a text box and a list, which does not drop down. All the choices appear in the list at all times. Whenever the list will not fit inside the region of the object, a vertical scroll bar is displayed. The user can specify a value for the combo box that is not in the list of suggested choices.
- The Style **2 - Dropdown List** only allows a user to select an item from a preset drop-down list of choices. As in the Dropdown Combo style, no options appear until the user clicks the list arrow at the right of the combo box.

The items in the combo box can be added and removed both at design time and run time. In addition, there is a method to remove all the items in the combo box at once. The properties of the combo box are used to determine whether or not an item is selected in the list, and the text of the selected item. Every item stored in a combo box has a corresponding index ranging from 0 to the value of the property ListCount–1. The following list describes significant components of the combo box's interface. The standard prefix for a combo box is "cbo."

Object	**ComboBox**
Definition	A ComboBox control allows users to enter information into or select an item from the control.

Properties	The **List** property identifies the items stored in the combo box. It is an array of strings with a lower bound of zero (0) and an upper bound of (ListCount–1). The Properties window can be used to set the List property at design time. At run time, the List property is read-write. Attempting to use an index outside the range of values will cause a run-time error. The **ListIndex** property is an Integer value that identifies the index of the currently selected list item. The first item in the list has a ListIndex property value of zero (0), the second item has a value of one (1), and so on. If no item has been selected, the ListIndex property has a value of minus one (-1). The **ListCount** property is an Integer value that returns the number of items in the list. If the list is empty, the ListCount is zero (0). Otherwise, the value of ListCount is the number of items in the list. The **ItemData** property is an array of Long Integer values with the same number of items as the control's List property. You can use the numbers associated with each item to identify the list items. The most common use of the ItemData property is as an index into another array. The **NewIndex** property works with the ItemData property. If you are adding items to a list that is sorted, each new item is added to the list in alphabetical order. To determine where an item was inserted, you use the NewIndex property. The NewIndex property returns the ListIndex of the item most recently added to a combo box or list box. The **Sorted** property, when set to True, causes the items to be displayed in alphabetical order even if the items were not added in alphabetical order. The behavior of the **Text** property depends on the setting of the Style property. For a Dropdown List, the Text property returns the selected item. For a Dropdown Combo, or Simple Combo, the Text property is used to read or set the contents of the Edit area.
Methods	The **AddItem** method will add an item to the combo box. The **Clear** method deletes all the items from the combo box. When called, the ListIndex property is set to minus one (-1) and the ListCount property is set to zero (0). The List and ItemData arrays also are cleared. The **RemoveItem** method takes one argument—the *index* of the item you want to delete. If you want to remove the first item, the index is zero (0). If you want to remove the second item, the index is one (1), and so on.
Events	The **Click** event occurs when an item is selected by clicking the mouse button or pressing the arrow keys. The **Scroll** event occurs when the scroll bars in the control are manipulated.

One common use of the List property is to print or reference each item in a list. Assuming a combo box named cboName, the following loop will print the text of each list item in the Immediate window:

```
Dim pintCount As Integer
For pintCount = 0 To cboName.ListCount - 1
    Debug.Print cboName.List(pintCount)
Next
```

The following statements display the selected text in the combo box named cboName in the label named lblName. The If statement checks to see that an item in the list is selected. The two assignment statements have the same effect.

```
If cboName.ListIndex > -1 Then
    lblDemo = cboName.List(ListIndex)
    lblDemo = cboName.Text
End If
```

Adding and deleting items from a combo box is accomplished using the AddItem, RemoveItem, and Clear methods.

Syntax

object.**AddItem** *item*, *index*
object.**Clear**
object.**RemoveItem** *index*

Dissection

- The required *item* argument is a string expression. The value is added to the end of the list if the *index* argument is omitted.
- For the **AddItem** method, the index is optional. If specified, the value contains the row where the new item is stored. For the **RemoveItem** method, the *index* is required. The value must be between zero (0) and the value of ListCount–1 or a run-time error will occur.
- The **Clear** method removes all the items from the combo box. When this occurs, the ListIndex property is set to minus one (-1) because it is not possible to have an item selected.

Code Example

```
cboName.AddItem "Smith, John"
cboName.AddItem "Donnel, Ann", 0
cboName.RemoveItem 1
cboName.Clear
```

Code Dissection

The first call to the AddItem method adds the name to the first element (ListIndex = 0) in the combo box. The second call also adds the name to the first element in the combo box. Thus, Donnel, Ann has an index of zero (0) and Smith, John has an index of one (1). The RemoveItem method deletes the record for Smith, John, and the final statement deletes all the items from the list box.

Using the ItemData and NewIndex properties requires careful examination. The ItemData property works much like the List property. That is, it is referenced with an index from 0 to ListCount–1. Instead of storing a string, however, the ItemData property contains a Long Integer value. The ItemData property commonly is used as an index into another type of list or array. That list may be an array of user-defined types, or a reference to a specific index for another list or combo box. Figure 3-9 illustrates the use of the ItemData property.

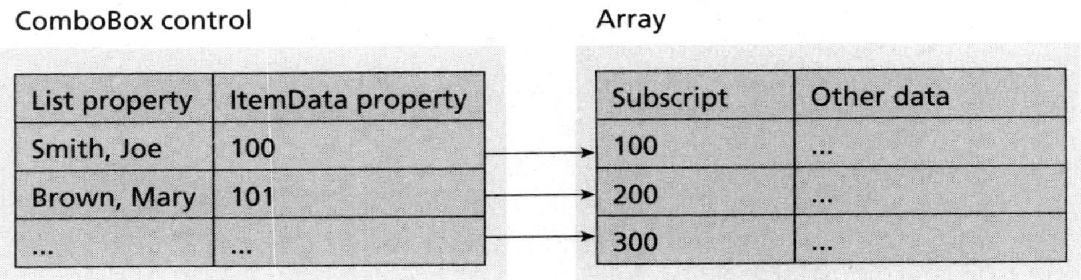

ComboBox control
Array
List property
ItemData property
Smith, Joe
100
Brown, Mary
101
...
...
Subscript
Other data
100
200
300
...
...
...

Figure 3-9: ItemData property

Imagine the following scenario: Assume that you want to display a name in a combo box. For each name, there is a corresponding Integer ID number. When adding items to the combo box, the name is stored in the List property, and the ID number is stored in the ItemData property. While the source of this information likely would be a text or database file, the following statements will use literal values for brevity:

```
cboName.AddItem "Smith, Joe"
cboName.ItemData(cboName.NewIndex) = 100
cboName.AddItem "Brown, Mary"
cboName.ItemData(cboName.NewIndex) = 101
```

The first statement adds an item to the combo box named cboName. The second statement requires careful analysis. After the AddItem method is called, the NewIndex property is set to the index of the newly added item. This is used as the index into the ItemData array. When the user clicks the combo box, the event procedure could use the ItemData property to perform a lookup operation. This would be useful if the value stored in ItemData were the same as an array index or a key of a database record.

```
Debug.Print cboName.List(cboName.ListIndex)
Debug.Print cboName.ItemData(cboName.ListIndex)
```

The previous two statements print the contents of the List and ItemData properties in the Immediate window for the currently selected list item.

The ListBox Control

The **ListBox** control is used to display a list of textual items. Each item is displayed on one line in the list. If the items will not fit in the region of the control, then scroll bars appear automatically. Items in the list only can be added at design time using the List property or at run time by calling the AddItem method. The user cannot add items to the list box. The properties and methods of the ListBox and ComboBox controls are almost identical. The following list summarizes the properties that differ between the ListBox and ComboBox controls:

Object	ListBox
Definition	A ListBox control displays a list of items from which the user can select one or more.
Properties	The **Style** property, if set to the constant 0 - Standard, displays a textual list of items. If set to 1 - CheckBox, a check box appears to the left of each item in the list box. If a ListBox control's Style property is set to 1 - CheckBox, the **Selected** property returns True only for those items whose check boxes are selected. The Selected property works like the List and ItemData properties but when used with a CheckBox style list box, the property returns a Boolean value indicating whether or not the current item is selected. The **SelCount** property is zero (0) if no items are selected. Otherwise, it contains the count of the items selected.

A checked list box can be used to select several names from a list of names. This is useful to print or perform operations on a number of items in a list at the same time.

The main form in this example contains a sample list box with check boxes named lstCheck. To illustrate the use of the Selected and SelCount properties, consider the following code segment:

```
Dim pintCount As Integer
For pintCount = 0 To lstCheck.ListCount - 1
    Debug.Print lstCheck.List(pintCount); _
        "  "; lstCheck.Selected(pintCount)
Next
```

These statements resemble the loop to look at the items in the List property for each item in the list box. The current list item is printed in the Immediate window along with the value of the Selected property, which is True if the item is checked and False otherwise.

The CheckBox Control

The **CheckBox** control has one of three states. It can be checked, not checked, or dimmed indicating the check box neither is checked nor unchecked. A dimmed check box typically is used to indicate that the user should check or uncheck the box explicitly. The standard prefix for a check box is "chk."

Object	CheckBox
Definition	A CheckBox control gives the user a True/False or Yes/No option.
Properties	■ A textual description is stored in the **Caption** property. ■ The **Value** property of a check box contains one of three constant values. If set to vbChecked, the box is checked. If set to vbUnchecked, the box is not checked. If set to vbGrayed, the check box neither is checked nor unchecked. ■ The **Style** property determines whether text or a picture is displayed in the check box. If set to 0 - Standard, the button will display text. If set to 1 - Graphical, the Picture, DownPicture, and DisabledPicture properties are used to define the icons or bitmaps displayed in the button's visible region. ■ The **DisabledPicture, DownPicture,** and **Picture** properties define the pictures displayed when the button is disabled, clicked, and enabled but not clicked, respectively. The graphical formats supported by the check box are bitmaps, icons, metafiles, GIF, and JPEG.
Events	■ The **Click** event occurs whenever the user clicks the CheckBox object. This causes the Value property to be changed accordingly. Typically, the code in the check box's Click event procedure will determine the status of the check box and perform tasks accordingly.

Typically, an If or Select Case statement is used to determine the status of a check box and perform the appropriate processing. For example, consider the following statements:

```
Private Sub chkDemo_Click( )
    Select Case chkDemo ' Value property is the default
        Case vbUnchecked
            ' Statements for unchecked
        Case vbChecked
            ' Statements for checked
        Case vbGrayed
            ' Statements for grayed
    End Select
End Sub
```

This generic Select Case statement will determine the status of a check box named chkDemo.

In this section you will:

- Write code that responds to specific mouse events
- Create keyboard handlers to respond to individual keyboard events

Keyboard and Mouse Events

Understanding Mouse Events

You have seen that many objects respond to events like Click, which is generated when the left mouse button is pressed and released. In addition to the Click event, most objects respond to several other events as the mouse is moved over an object, the mouse is pressed, and the mouse is released. These are the MouseMove, MouseDown, and MouseUp events. The MouseDown and MouseUp events have the following syntax:

Syntax

Private Sub Form_MouseDown(*button* **As Integer,** *shift* **As Integer,** *x* **As Single,** *y* **As Single)**
Private Sub *object*_**MouseDown(**[*index* **As Integer,**]*button* **As Integer,** *shift* **As Integer,** *x* **As Single,** *y* **As Single)**
Private Sub Form_MouseUp(*button* **As Integer,** *shift* **As Integer,** *x* **As Single,** *y* **As Single)**
Private Sub *object* **_MouseUp(**[*index* **As Integer,**]*button* **As Integer,** *shift* **As Integer,** *x* **As Single,** *y* **As Single)**

Dissection

- The **MouseDown** event occurs when a button on the mouse is pressed and the **MouseUp** event occurs when the button on the mouse is released.
- The *button* argument identifies which mouse button was pressed or released. The button can be represented by the following constant values: vbLeftButton, vbRightButton, or vbMiddleButton. Most PCs use a two-button mouse, which has no middle button.
- The *shift* argument commonly is used with the *button* argument to detect the state of the Shift, Ctrl, and Alt keys. These values are represented by the following masks: vbShiftMask, vbCtrlMask, and vbAltMask.
- The *x* and *y* arguments specify the current location of the mouse pointer. These values are specified using the coordinate system established by the ScaleHeight, ScaleWidth, ScaleLeft, and ScaleTop properties of the object.
- The *index* argument is used if the object is a member of a control array.

Code Example

```
Private Sub Form_MouseDown(Button As Integer, _
    Shift As Integer,  X As Single, Y As Single)
    Select Case Button
        Case vbLeftButton
            Debug.Print "Left mouse button"
        Case vbMiddleButton
            Debug.Print "Middle mouse button"
        Case vbRightButton
            Debug.Print "Right mouse button"
    End Select

    If Shift = vbShiftMask Then
        Debug.Print "Shift"
    End If

    If Shift = vbCtrlMask Then
        Debug.Print "Ctrl"
    End If

    If Shift = (vbCtrlMask + vbShiftMask) Then
        Debug.Print "Ctrl and Shift"
    End If
End Sub
```

Code Dissection The MouseDown event procedure is executed when the user presses a mouse button. It occurs for the form or a control instance on the form. The Select Case statement uses constants to determine which mouse button was pressed. The If statements determine whether the Shift, Ctrl, or Shift+Ctrl keys were pressed when the event occurred.

By using the Shift, Ctrl, and Alt masks, you can expand considerably on the available functions that can be executed when the mouse is clicked. For example, you can expand on the editing capabilities of the TextBox control. One convenience that is easy to supply to the user, is the ability to clear the contents of the text box using the Alt key with the left mouse button. To implement this functionality, you respond to the MouseDown event. Inside of the event procedure, you determine whether or not the Alt key is pressed. If so, then the contents of the text box is cleared.

To clear a control in response to an event:

1 In the form named **frmMain**, enter the following statement in the **txtAddress_MouseDown** event procedure:

```
If Button = vbLeftButton And Shift = vbAltMask Then
    txtAddress(Index) = ""
End If
```

2 Test the program. In the control array of text boxes on the main form, enter your name. Hold down the **Alt** key and click the **left mouse button.** The contents of the text box are cleared.

These statements determine if the left mouse button was clicked and the Alt key pressed. If so, the contents of the text box are cleared.

The MouseMove Event

In addition to the MouseDown and MouseUp events, you also can detect when the mouse is moved to a new point on the form. The MouseMove event occurs each time the mouse is moved to a new point on a form or control.

Syntax

Private Sub Form_MouseMove(*button* **As Integer,** *shift* **As Integer,** *x* **As Single,** *y* **As Single)**
Private Sub *object*_**MouseMove([***index* **As Integer,]** *button* **As Integer,** *shift* **As Integer,** *x* **As Single,** *y* **As Single)**

Dissection

- The **MouseMove** event occurs whenever the user moves the mouse. The event occurs for the form or control where the insertion point is positioned. If the user holds down the mouse button and moves the mouse, the MouseMove event continues to occur for the same object, even if the mouse pointer is moved off the object.
- The *button* argument is used to detect if one or more buttons on the mouse is pressed. This behavior is different from the MouseDown and MouseUp events, which only detect a single mouse button.
- The *shift*, *x*, and *y* arguments have the same purpose as they do with the MouseDown and MouseUp events.
- The *index* argument is used if the object is a member of a control array.

Code Example

```
Private Sub Form_MouseMove(Button As Integer, _
    Shift As Integer, X As Single, Y As Single)
    Debug.Print "Form insertion point at X,Y"; X, Y
End Sub
```

Code Dissection

The code for the MouseMove event prints the X and Y coordinates of the Form when the mouse is moved over the form. These events occur repeatedly as the mouse is moved.

Another important use of mouse events is to display a pop-up menu when the right mouse button is clicked. You have used pop-up menus with Visual Basic to open the Properties window and display a specific object. When clicked over a specific object, a pop-up menu can display a context-sensitive menu that lists the most common or appropriate functions for the object. The process of displaying a pop-up menu is described in the next section of this chapter.

Understanding Keyboard Events

Just as you can respond to specific mouse events, you also can respond to keyboard events. There basically are two alternatives for processing keyboard events. One alternative is to respond to the KeyPress event. The other is to respond to the KeyDown and KeyUp events.

The character set used by Windows is an 8-bit character set called ANSI, which is an acronym for the American National Standards Institute. The character set consists of 256 characters. The first 128 characters represent the letters and symbols on the keyboard. The second 128 characters represent special characters and international characters. You can get a complete list of the ANSI characters by viewing the ASCII Help topic. The digits 0 - 9 have ASCII values of 48 - 57. The lowercase letters a - z have the ASCII values 97 - 122, and the uppercase letters A - Z have the ASCII values 65 - 90.

The KeyPress event interprets the state of the keyboard and returns an ANSI character. That is, the KeyPress event determines the state of certain keys before returning a character. For example, lowercase and uppercase letters are separate characters. As such, the KeyPress event will interpret whether or not the Shift key is pressed and return an uppercase or lowercase letter accordingly.

Syntax

Private Sub Form_KeyPress(*keyascii* **As Integer)**
Private Sub *object***_KeyPress([***index* **As Integer**,] *keyascii* **As Integer)**

Dissection

- The *keyascii* argument contains an integer representing the ANSI character that was pressed. If the value of the argument is set to zero (0) in the event procedure, then the keystroke is cancelled and the object will not return the character.
- If *object* is a member of a control array, *index* contains an Integer value that uniquely identifies a control.

Code Example

```
Private Sub txtID_KeyPress(KeyAscii As Integer)
    If KeyAscii <> 8 And _
        (KeyAscii > 57 Or KeyAscii < 48) Then
        KeyAscii = 0
    End If
End Sub
```

Code Dissection

These statements determine whether the ASCII character is a digit between 0 and 9, or the backspace character (8). The character codes are used. If the input character is not in the correct range, then KeyAscii is set to zero (0) causing the keystroke to be ignored.

There are other characters used by Windows, and most computers for that matter, which are not part of the ANSI character set. For example, most keyboards have keys like Home, End, Page Up, and Page Down. To process these characters you use the KeyDown and KeyUp event procedures. As a general rule, it is more complex to process KeyDown and KeyUp events than the KeyPress event. As such, when you are programming ASCII characters, use the KeyPress event. When programming function keys, and other special keys, either the KeyDown or KeyUp events must be used.

The KeyDown and KeyUp events do not return a character. Rather, they return the state of the keyboard. For example, if the user typed an uppercase "C", the KeyDown event returns that the Shift key is pressed and the character code is for the letter "C."

Syntax

Private Sub Form_KeyDown(*keycode* **As Integer**, *shift* **As Integer)**
Private Sub *object*_**KeyDown(** [*index* **As Integer**,] *keycode* **As Integer**, *shift* **As Integer)**
Private Sub Form_KeyUp(keycode **As Integer**, *shift* **As Integer)**
Private Sub *object*_**KeyUp(** [*index* **As Integer**,] *keycode* **As Integer**, *shift* **As Integer)**

Dissection

- The **KeyDown** event occurs when a key is pressed down and the **KeyUp** event occurs when the key is released.
- The *keycode* contains a constant value for the key that was pressed. See the Help topic "Keycode constants" for a list of the constants.
- The *shift* argument contains a bit field indicating whether or not the Shift, Ctrl, or Alt keys were pressed. Bit zero represents the Shift key, bit one the Ctrl key, and bit two the Alt key. These arguments are treated as bit fields in the same way as in the MouseDown and MouseUp events.
- The *index* is used when the *object* is a member of a control array.

Code Example

```
Const cALTKEY As Integer = 4
Private Sub txtAddress_KeyDown(Index As Integer, _
    KeyCode As Integer, Shift As Integer)
    If KeyCode = vbKeyHome And (Shift And cALTKEY) Then
        txtAddress(0).SetFocus
    End If
End Sub
```

Code Dissection

This event procedure determines if the Home key was pressed while the Alt key was pressed. If so, then the first text box on the form gets focus.

Normally, keyboard events occur for the control on the form that has focus. There are times, however, when you may want the form to be able to process keyboard events. For example, consider the previous situation where the Alt+Home key combination sets the focus to the first text box. The code in the KeyDown event pertained to the control array of text boxes rather than the form. Thus, if a different object than the control array had focus, the keyboard sequence would have no effect. There are two solutions to this problem. One is to duplicate the code for the KeyDown event for all the objects on the form. The second would be to have the form intercept the keyboard events. To make a form intercept keyboard events, you set the KeyPreview property of a form to True. The keyboard events still occur for the control that has focus. They occur for the form first, however, and then to the control with focus.

When the KeyPreview property is set to True, the KeyDown and KeyUp events occur for the form before they happen to the control that has focus.

The Danger of Recursive (Cascading) Events

One of the difficulties in event-driven programming is being aware of all the different events that can occur in your program, when they occur, and why. One of the problems in event-driven programming surfaces when events occur in an order you do not expect. Consider a scenario where your program uses the SetFocus method to change the focus from one object to another. Imagine that a text box named Text1 sets the focus to another text box named Text2. Also assume that when Text2 gets focus, it performs some task, then sets the focus to Text1. When the program is run, Text1 sets the focus to Text2, which sets the focus to Text1, and so on. This is what is called a **recursive** or **cascading** event. Consider the following statements:

```
Private Sub Text1_GotFocus( )
    Text2.SetFocus
End Sub

Private Sub Text2_GotFocus( )
    Text1.SetFocus
End Sub
```

These statements illustrate cascading events. When Text1 gets focus, it sets focus to Text2, which sets the focus to Text1, and so on, and so on. Inside of the IDE, you can stop a running program by pressing Ctrl+Break. The program will enter design mode when this key sequence is pressed. This way you can stop cascading events or any other type of infinite loop.

The previous statements oversimplify the problem. It is unlikely that you would ever make a mistake like this, but it does illustrate the problem. The error of cascading events usually occurs in a complex program, which is responding to several different events.

SECTION D

objectives

In this section you will:

- Create a menu on a form using the Menu Editor
- Add shortcut and access keys to a menu
- Create dialog boxes

Menus and Dialog Boxes

Menus

Menus in Visual Basic are implemented as objects contained by a form. As such, each form can have a distinct menu. In Figure 3-10, there are different Menu objects for each of the menu titles, menus, submenus, and separator bars. Each of these objects has properties and can respond to a Click event. This behavior is analogous to a command button. Figure 3-10 identifies all the different components of a menu.

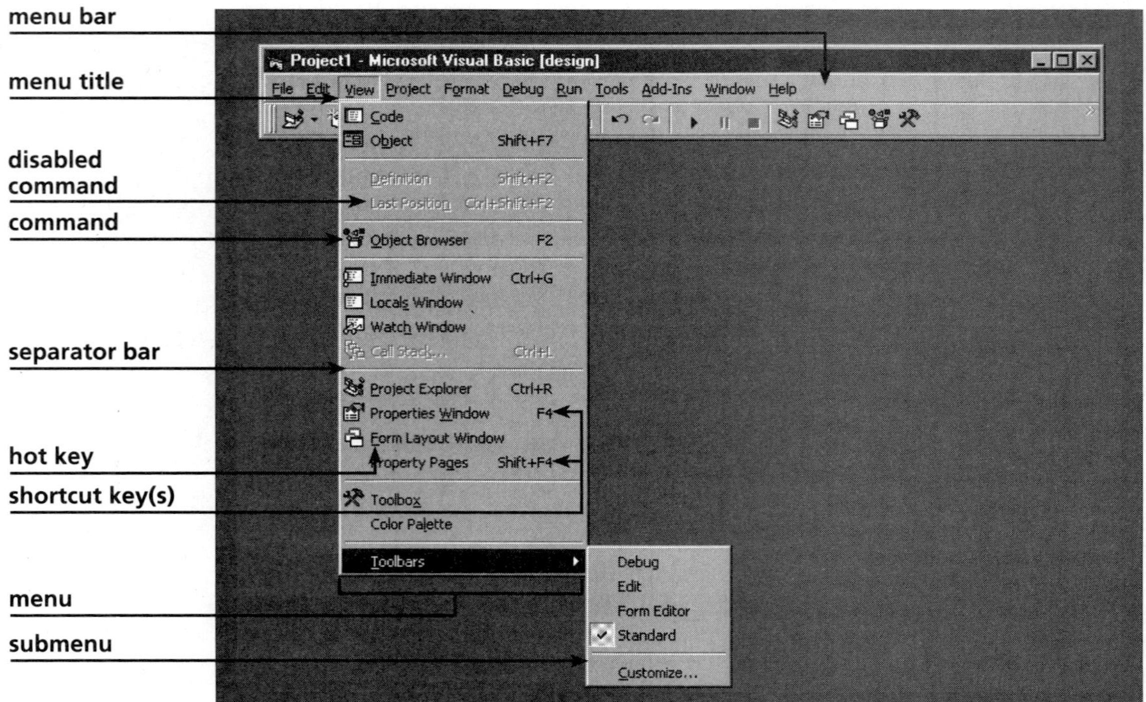

Figure 3-10: Anatomy of a menu

- The **menu bar** appears across the top of a form just below the title bar.
- **Menu titles** are displayed horizontally on the menu bar.
- A menu title contains menus. A **menu** may contain a combination of submenus, separator bars, and commands. A command is used to execute a command much like a command button.
- A menu can have a submenu. A **submenu** is a command that displays another menu, rather than executing code in an event procedure.
- A **separator bar** is a horizontal line that visually groups related commands together to make the interface easier to use. Like all components of a menu, a separator bar must have a unique name or be a member of a control array. You create a separator bar by setting a command's Caption property to a hyphen (-).
- A **shortcut key** is a function key (such as F5) or a key combination (such as Ctrl+A or Ctrl+X) that executes a command. Command buttons and menu commands support shortcut keys; you cannot create a shortcut key for a menu title.
- A **hot key**, also known as an access key, is a key you press while holding down the Alt key to open a menu or carry out a command. For example, Alt+F opens the File menu in most Windows applications.
- A **checked menu command** can work like a two-state control; that is, it can be checked or unchecked.

Several style guidelines will help you create menus that have a similar look and feel to menus in other Windows programs.

- A command's caption should be short enough to appear on one line, but it can contain multiple words to convey its purpose. In fact, a command will not appear on multiple lines.
- When commands contain multiple words, the first letter of each word should be capitalized and each word should be separated by a space.
- The first letter of a command's caption should be capitalized.
- If a command displays a dialog, or requires the user to complete other information, the command's name should be followed by an ellipsis (...).
- A separator bar should be used to group related commands on a menu.
- All menu titles, menus, and commands should have access keys, as some users prefer to use the keyboard instead of the mouse.
- Create shortcut keys for the more frequently used commands. This will minimize the number of keystrokes needed to activate a command. When selecting characters for a shortcut key, use characters that are the same as those used in other programs. For example, many programs use Ctrl+P as the shortcut key for printing. Using the first character of the menu caption also is common.

You write the code for a menu's Click event procedure the same way as you would for a command button. That is, you can locate the object and event procedure in the Code window.

You can open the Code window quickly to a command's Click event procedure while in design mode by clicking the menu title, then clicking the desired command rather than locating the event procedures in the Code window.

Menus, like other objects, have standard prefixes and naming conventions. Use the following guidelines for menu naming:

- Menu names should begin with the prefix "mnu."
- Following the prefix, a descriptive name should be used. This name should be the same as the menu title with the spaces removed.
- For menus and commands, the name should consist of the command preceded by the menu title, preceded by the menu prefix.

Using the Menu Editor

In Visual Basic, menus are created at design time using the Menu Editor. Menus can also be modified at run time. Each Menu object (menu title or command) supports a number of properties. Some of these properties only can be set using the Properties window and are not available using the Menu Editor.

Object	Menu
Properties	The **Caption** property contains the text that appears on the menu.
	The **Name** property has the same function as it does with any other control instance. It is the name you use to reference the object at run time with code.
	The **Checked** property is used to create two-state commands. Two-state commands are similar to a check box. That is, their value either can be True or False.
	The **Enabled** property can be True or False. If set to True, the menu will respond to a Click event. If False, the menu appears grayed and will not respond to the Click event.
	The **Index** property can be used to create control arrays of menus. Menu control arrays have the same characteristics as control arrays for other objects.
	The **Visible** property, when set to True, causes the menu to appear. If set to False, the Menu command is not displayed on the menu. Thus, if the menu has submenus, they will not appear on the menu either.
	The **WindowList** property is used with Multiple Document Interface (MDI) programs. When set to True, the menu will list all the open MDI child forms. Only one Menu object on a form can have the WindowList property set to True.
Events	Like a command button, Menu objects respond to the **Click** event.

The Menu Editor is an intelligent interface used to create instances of menu controls and set design-time properties. It is displayed as a modal dialog and must be closed before you can interact with other windows in the project. It consists of two main sections. The properties section is used to set the properties of a menu control. The list section displays each of the commands and their relationship to each other. Figure 3-11 shows the Menu Editor with a menu system already created.

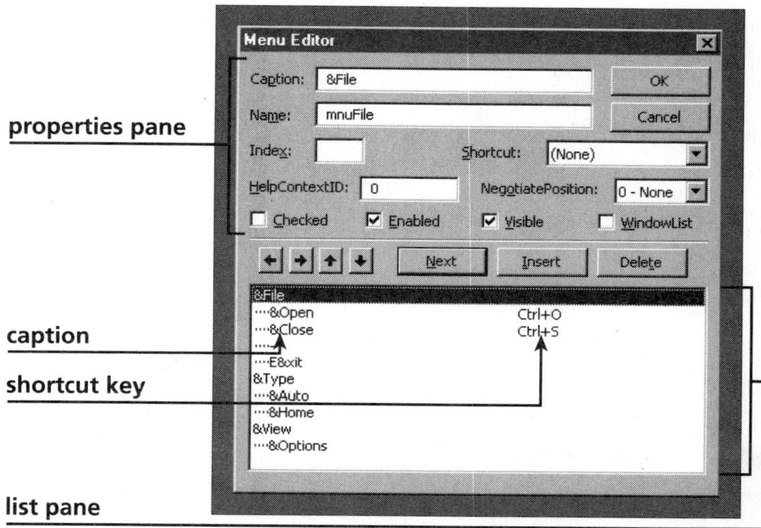

Figure 3-11: Menu Editor components

As shown in Figure 3-11, some Menu objects are indented and others are not. The order of the menus in the list section is significant.

- A menu that is not indented is considered a menu title.
- A menu that is indented once appears as a menu displayed when the menu title is selected.
- Indenting a command more than once causes the command to appear as a submenu title.
- The order of the menus in the list section is significant. Menu names indented at the same level appear on the same menu in the order they appear in the Menu Editor.

The Left and Right Arrow buttons on the Menu Editor decrease and increase the indenting of the currently selected Menu object. The Up and Down Arrow buttons are used to move the currently selected menu up or down with respect to the previous or next menu displayed in the list section. The Next button either will activate the next menu in the list section or add a new menu if the last menu currently is selected. The Insert button will insert a command just before the currently selected command, and the Delete button will remove the selected menu.

Menu Control Arrays

The only way to add and remove control instances at run time is to use control arrays. Menu control arrays share the same characteristics as other control arrays. That is, each menu in a menu control array shares the same name and event procedures. The menu is identified uniquely by its Index value. Control arrays of menus have additional rules and characteristics. The elements of a menu control array must appear sequentially in the menu control list section, and must have the same level of indentation. To create a new command at run time, you must use a control array. Menu control arrays are useful when you need to configure commands at run time. One common application is to list on the File menu recent files that have been opened.

In this example, you will modify the menu at run time to add a list of open files. Again the implementation is simplified to illustrate the concept of a menu control array. In this example, you will add a constant list of files. In practice, the list would need to be saved before the program exits. This information probably would be saved to the system registry or some initialization file. The information then would be read when the program was loaded.

To create a control array of commands:

1. Activate the **Menu Editor.**
2. Create a command named **mnuFileList** as a command on the menu named **mnuFile.** Set the Index property to **0.** This has the effect of creating a control array.
3. Close the **Menu Editor.**
4. Enter the following statements into the **Form_Load** event procedure.

```
Load mnuFileList(1)
Load mnuFileList(2)
mnuFileList(0).Caption = "File1"
mnuFileList(1).Caption = "File2"
mnuFileList(2).Caption = "File3"
```

   These statements add two items to the menu control array. Then a caption is stored in the existing control array element, and the two elements you just added. This example is simplistic. In practice, these would contain file names as loaded by the user.

5. Test the program. Click **File** on the menu bar. The file list should appear.

These statements first set the caption of the first member of the control array already created. The Load statements create two new instances of the control array, then set the caption of each new member accordingly.

Pop-Up Menus

Visual Basic supports another type of menu called a pop-up menu that does not appear at the top of the form. Rather a pop-up menu appears; usually when the mouse button is right-clicked on the form or a specific control on the form. The pop-up menu that appears when the mouse button is right-clicked depends on the position of the insertion point when it was right-clicked. Pop-up menus are useful to display different menus depending on the active object or current state of the program. Only one pop-up menu can be displayed at a time. This type of menu commonly is referred to as a shortcut menu.

Syntax *object*.**PopupMenu** *menuname*, *flags*, *x*, *y*, *boldcommand*

Dissection

- The optional *object* can be any visible object that responds to mouse events. If the argument is omitted, then the form with focus is used.
- The required *menuname* argument is used to specify the menu to be displayed. The menu must have at least one submenu to be displayed as a pop-up menu.
- The optional *flags* argument is used to control how the menu is aligned around the insertion point or x and y coordinates. It also is used to control whether or not a Click event will be generated when the left, or left and right, mouse buttons are clicked.
- The optional *x* and *y* arguments specify the x and y coordinates where the pop-up menu is displayed. If omitted, the menu is displayed at the current insertion point position.
- The optional *boldcommand* specifies the name of a menu control in the pop-up menu to display its caption in bold text. If omitted, no controls in the pop-up menu appear in bold.

Code Example

```
frmMain.PopupMenu File
```

To illustrate the creation of pop-up menus, you will display the Type menu as a pop-up menu when the right mouse button is clicked on a region of the form. This menu only should appear when the right mouse button is clicked.

To create a pop-up menu:

1. In the form named **frmMain**, activate the Code window for the **Form_MouseDown** event procedure and enter the following statements into the event procedure:

```
If Button = vbRightButton Then
    frmMain.PopupMenu mnuType, , X, Y
End If
```

2 Test the program. Right-click the form to display the **Type** menu.

These two event procedures display different pop-up menus when the right mouse button is clicked over the respective object.

Standard Dialogs

Visual Basic supports two types of dialogs also supported by the Windows operating system. These include the message box and the input box. The MsgBox function creates and displays a window, containing a title bar with a caption, a prompt, and some number of buttons. The number and caption of the buttons depends on the arguments passed to the MsgBox function. When the message box is closed, a value is returned indicating which button was clicked. An input box is much like a message box but is used to get a text string from the user. Both message boxes and input boxes are displayed as modal forms. That is, the dialogs must be closed before any other user interaction can continue with the program.

The MsgBox function

A message box is a dialog that is used to request the user for confirmation to display an informational message. A sample message box is shown in Figure 3-12.

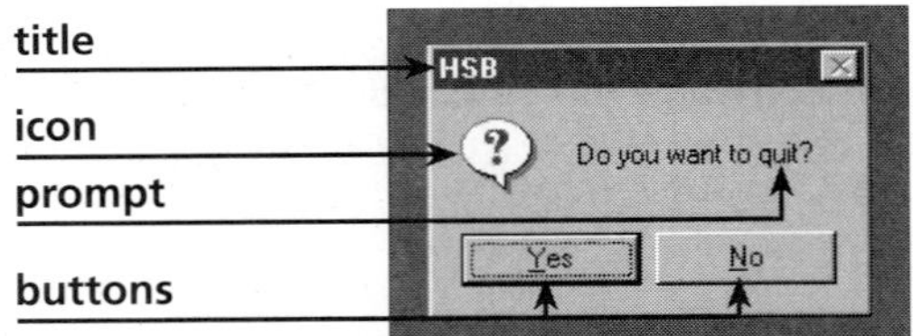

Figure 3-12: Message box

The message box shown in Figure 3-12 contains a descriptive prompt, a visual icon, a title bar, and two buttons. When the user clicks one of the buttons, the message box will be closed, and the next statement in the program can determine which button the user clicked, and then perform the appropriate action.

Syntax **MsgBox(***prompt*[, *buttons*] [, *title*] [, *helpfile*, *context*])

Dissection

- The required *prompt* argument is a string expression displayed in the message portion of the dialog. This string can span multiple lines using the carriage return and/or linefeed characters.
- The optional *title* argument is a string expression displayed in the title bar of the dialog.

- The optional *helpfile* and *context* arguments are used to display a help message.
- The optional *buttons* argument is a Long Integer value used to define all the run-time characteristics of the dialog. These characteristics are divided into six groups. Each group is represented as four bits in a Long Integer value. One value can be set from each group by adding a constant value from each group in an expression.

  The first group determines how many buttons are displayed and the caption of each button. The value is represented by the following constants: vbOKOnly, vbOKCancel, vbAbortRetryIgnore, vbYesNoCancel, vbYesNo, and vbRetryCancel.

  The second group determines the icon displayed in the message box. The valid icon constants are: vbCritical, vbQuestion, vbExclamation, and vbInformation.

  The third group is used to specify a default button. This has the same effect as setting the Default property to True for a command button. The valid button constants are: vbDefaultButton1, vbDefaultButton2, vbDefaultButton3, and vbDefaultButton4.

  The fourth group is used to make the dialog application modal or system modal. If the dialog is application modal, the user can interact with other applications when the message box is displayed. If the dialog is system modal, all applications are suspended until the message box is closed. The valid constants are: vbApplicationModal and vbSystemModal.

  The fifth group is used to add a Help button, and specify the message box as the foreground window. The valid constants are: vbMsgBoxHelpButton and vbMsgBoxSetForeground.

  The sixth group is used to right-align the text and specify that text should appear as right-to-left reading on Hebrew and Arabic systems. The valid constants are: vbMsgBoxRight and vbMsgBoxRtlReading.

Code Example

```
Dim pintReturn As Integer
pintReturn = MsgBox("Quit", vbYesNo + vbQuestion, "HSB")
pintReturn = MsgBox("Error", vbOKOnly + vbCritical, "HSB")
```

Code Dissection

The first call to the MsgBox function creates a box with Yes and No buttons, and a question mark icon. If the Yes button is clicked, the function returns the constant vbYes. The second MsgBox function displays a message box with one button with the caption OK, and a Critical icon. The MsgBox function returns an Integer value indicating which button was clicked. This value typically is used in an If or Select Case statement to determine which button was clicked, and executes code accordingly.

Figure 3-13 lists the valid return constants, their values, and the description.

Constant	Value	Description
vbOK	1	OK
vbCancel	2	Cancel
vbAbort	3	Abort
vbRetry	4	Retry
vbIgnore	5	Ignore
vbYes	6	Yes
vbNo	7	No

Figure 3-13: MsgBox return values

A common use of the MsgBox function is to request confirmation from the user before performing an action, or advising the user about some abnormal condition. It this case, a message box will be used to request confirmation before ending the program. This code is placed in the QueryUnload event for the form. This way, if the user clicks the Close button on the form, or ends the program in any way, this event will occur giving the user the opportunity to continue execution or end the program.

To display a message box before ending the program:

1 Activate the Code window for the **mnuFileExit_Click** event procedure and enter the following statement:

```
Unload Me
```

2 Enter the following statements in the **Form_QueryUnload** event procedure:

```
Dim pintReturn As Integer
pintReturn = MsgBox("Do you want to quit?", _
    vbYesNo + vbQuestion)
If pintReturn = vbYes Then
    Unload frmOptions
    Unload frmMain
    Unload frmLoan
 End If
```

These statements display a message box with the message "Do you want to quit?", Yes and No buttons, and a question mark icon. If the user clicks the Yes button all the forms are unloaded and the program ends.

3 Test the program. Click **File** then **Exit**. The message box should appear. Click **No** to continue executing the program. Click the **Close** button ☒ on the form's title bar. When the message box appears, click **Yes** to exit the program.

There is another dialog that is similar to a message box, but is used to get a text string from the user.

The InputBox Function

The InputBox function works much like the MsgBox function and is used to display a standard dialog. The dialog returns a String data type entered by the user in a text box. An input box has two buttons. If the OK button is clicked, the text string entered by the user will be returned. If the Cancel button is clicked, an empty string is returned. In addition, the programmer can control the position of the input box on the screen. Figure 3-14 shows the parts of an input box.

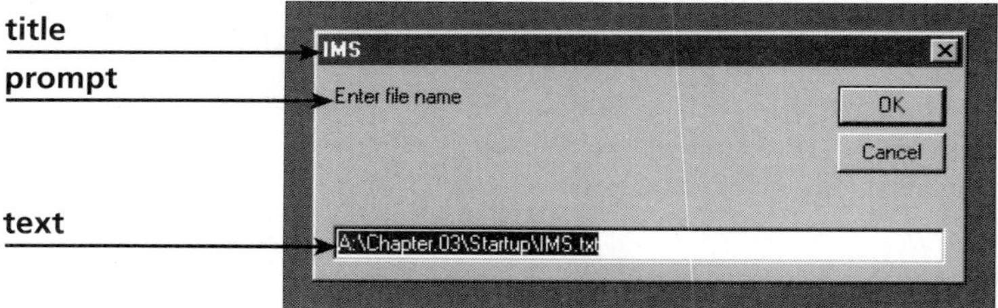

Figure 3-14: Input box

Syntax	**InputBox**(*prompt*[, *title*] [, *default*] [, *xpos*] [, *ypos*] [, *helpfile*, *context*])

Dissection

- The optional *prompt* argument is a string expression displayed in the message portion of the dialog. This string can span multiple lines using the carriage return and or linefeed characters.
- The optional *title* argument is a string expression displayed in the title bar of the dialog.
- The optional *default* argument is used to place a default string expression in the text box portion in the dialog.
- The optional *xpos* and *ypos* arguments specify the horizontal and vertical distance, in twips, from the left and top of the screen, respectively. If omitted, the dialog is centered horizontally and the top of the box appears about one-third down from the top of the screen.
- The optional *helpfile* and *context* arguments are used to display a help message.

Code Example

```
Dim pstrFileName As String
pstrFileName = InputBox("Enter file name", "IMS", _
    "A:\Chapter.03\Startup\IMS.txt")
If pstrFileName = "" Then
    Exit Sub
End If
```

Code Dissection

These statements call the InputBox function with the prompt "Enter file name," a default value of "A:\Chapter.03\Startup\IMS.txt", and the title "IMS". The If statement tests to determine whether or not the user clicked the Cancel button by testing the string returned by the InputBox function. If the string is empty, then the user clicked the Cancel button and the Sub procedure exits. Otherwise, the procedure continues to execute.

SUMMARY

In this chapter, you have seen how to create a program with multiple forms, with some of those forms being dialog boxes. You also have seen how to use control arrays, and add and remove controls from a control array at run time. You have learned how to load, display, and hide those forms. Additionally, you have learned how to process both keyboard and mouse events. You also have learned how to create programs with menus, message boxes, and dialog boxes.

QUESTIONS

1. Which of the following are valid properties of the App object?
   a. CompanyName, LegalCopyright, LegalTrademarks.
   b. Major, Minor, Revision.
   c. ProductName, Title.
   d. Both b and c.
   e. All of the above.
2. Which of the following statements are True regarding modeless and modal forms?
   a. The user cannot interact with the other forms in a program while a modal form is open.
   b. The user cannot interact with the other forms in a program while a modeless form is open.
   c. A program cannot have both modal and modeless forms.
   d. Only one modeless form can be displayed at a time.
   e. All of the above.

3. The maximum index for an element in a control array is ________.
   a. 255
   b. 32,767
   c. 32,768
   d. 64,000
   e. none of the above

4. The order of events when a form is loaded is ______________.
   a. Initialize, Load, Activate
   b. Load, Activate, Initialize
   c. Activate, Initialize, Load
   d. Initialize, Activate, Load
   e. none of the above

5. The names and order of events that occur when a form is unloaded are __________.
   a. Unload, End
   b. Unload, QueryUnload
   c. QueryUnload, Unload, Terminate
   d. QueryUnload, Cancel, Unload
   e. QueryUnload, Unload, Quit

6. The ___________ and _____________ statements are used to add and remove controls from a control array at run time.
   a. Add, Delete
   b. Load, Unload
   c. Load, Remove
   d. Add, Remove
   e. Add, Unload

7. Which property does not pertain to a Menu object?
   a. Visible.
   b. Checked.
   c. Enabled.
   d. Clicked.
   e. WindowList.

8. Which of the following is a valid menu name?
   a. mnu.File
   b. mnu.file
   c. mnu File
   d. mnuFile
   e. mnu&File

9. A ___________ is a way of accessing a command.
   a. shortcut key or hot key
   b. quick key
   c. quick key, shortcut key, or hot key
   d. quick key or hot key
   e. quick key or shortcut key

10. To create a separator bar on a menu, the caption should be set to ____________.
    a. (_)
    b. (/)
    c. (Separator)
    d. (-)
    e. (&)

11. Create a Sub Main procedure to load the forms named frmSplash, frmMain, and frmFind. Display the form named **frmSplash** but not the other two.

12. Create the QueryUnload event procedure for the form named **frmMain**. If the source of the Unload event was caused by the Task Manager, cancel the event.

13. Assuming that txtThing(0) is a control array element, create a For loop to create five more instances of the control array with Index values one (1) through five (5).

14. Assuming that lstThing is a checked list box, create a For loop to print the value of the **List**, **ItemData**, and **Selected** properties in the Immediate window for each item in the list.

15. Assuming that cboThing is a combo box, add three items to the combo box with the captions **Date**, **Text**, and **Number**.

16. Write the statements to make all the characters in the text box named txtDemo uppercase when the Alt key is pressed in the MouseUp event.

17. Write the statements to change the characters in a text box named txtDemo to uppercase whenever the user types a character.

18. Write the statement to display a message box with Yes and No buttons. The message box should display a question mark icon and the prompt "Do you want to Continue?". Store the user's response in the variable named pintReturn.

19. Write the statement to display a message box with a Critical icon, Abort, Retry, and Ignore buttons, and the prompt "Cannot open File".

20. Write the statements to display an input box with the prompt "Enter Last Name". Store the user's response in a String variable named pstrResponse. If the user presses the OK button then do nothing. Otherwise, end the program.

EXERCISES

1. In this exercise you will create code to navigate between multiple forms and create a splash screen.
    a. Create a new project and set the Name property of the form to **frmSplash**. Create a splash screen similar to the one shown in the chapter. Set the properties of the App object using the Project Properties dialog. Set the Major, Minor, and Revision numbers to **2**, **1**, and **3**, respectively. Set the Company Name to **IMS**. Save the project using the name **Chapter.03\Exercise\Exercise1.vbp**.
    b. Create a standard module named **Startup** and save the file. Set the Startup object to the Sub Main procedure in the standard module.
    c. Create a main form named **frmMain** and two other forms named **frmSub1** and **frmSub2**.

d. Create two command buttons on frmMain. One should display the form **frmSub1**, and the other should display the form **frmSub2**. Each should hide the main form. On each of the sub forms, create a command button with the caption **Close** that will hide the current form and display the main form.
e. Create the necessary code in the Sub Main procedure to load all the forms, display the splash screen, and then the main form. Unload the splash screen when the main form is displayed.
f. Create an Exit command button to unload all of the open forms and exit the program.
g. Test the program. Make sure the splash screen appears and then the main form. Test that the command buttons are displaying and hiding the other forms successfully.

2. In this exercise you will use control arrays and keyboard events to create a simple calculator program to perform addition, subtraction, multiplication, and division. The program only needs to work with integer numbers.

a. Create a new project and set the Name property of the form to **frmExercise2**. Save the form using the name **Chapter.03\Exercise\frmExercise2.frm** and the project using the name **Chapter.03\Exercise\Exercise2.vbp**.
b. Create command buttons to represent the digits zero (0) through (9) on the calculator. Use a control array.
c. Create a second control array of command buttons for the operators (+, -, *, /, =).
d. Create a label to display the number that currently is being entered or the result of the arithmetic expression.
e. When a digit is clicked, the number should be appended to the label. Thus, if the label contained the digit (1), and the digit (2) was clicked, the label would contain the value (12).
f. Remember that an arithmetic expression requires two operands. Thus, consider the following sequence of operations. The user enters the number 12, and then presses the (+) key. Because this is the first operand, the addition should not be performed yet. Rather the user should be able to enter another number. Then when an operator is entered, the two operands should be added. Suppose the current operator is multiplication. The intermediate result then would be multiplied by the next number entered by the user.
g. Create the necessary code to program the operands to perform the addition, subtraction, multiplication, and division.
h. Test the program. Test that the expressions are being evaluated correctly and at the correct time.

3. In this exercise you will use menus, message boxes, and input boxes.

a. Create a new project and set the Name property of the form to **frmExercise3**. Save the form using the name **Chapter.03\Exercise\frmExercise3.frm** and the project using the name **Chapter.03\Exercise\Exercise3.vbp**.
b. Create a menu system like the one shown in Figure 3-15. For each menu, make sure to assign a meaningful name to the Name property and use an access key.

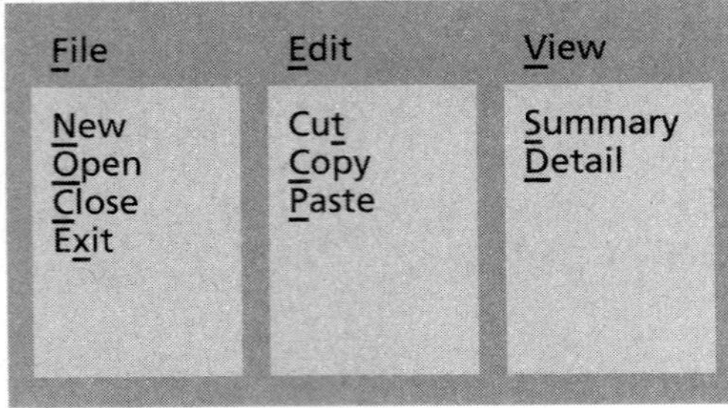

Figure 3-15: Menu

c. Create the necessary code for the Exit menu that will display a message box prompting the user to exit the program. The message box should display Yes and No buttons and a question mark icon.

d. Add a control array to the menu. The control array should appear on the File menu just before the Exit command.

e. For the File, New menu, display an input box. The input box should get a file name for the user and display the name in the control array.

f. Successive calls to the File, New menu should cause the size of the control array to be increased by one, and the text returned by the input box to be stored in the new element. Store at most five elements in the control array.

g. Test the program. Make sure that the commands appear correctly and that the File, New and File, Exit commands are working correctly.

4. In this exercise you will create a keyboard handler to change the focus between controls on the form and validate the characters displayed in a control.

a. Create a new project and set the Name property of the form to **frmExercise4**. Save the form using the name **Chapter.03\Exercise\frmExercise4.frm** and the project using the name **Chapter.03\Exercise\Exercise4.vbp**.

b. Create text boxes to store the following information: Name, Address, City, State, ZipCode, and Country.

c. When the user presses the Alt+Home key combination the focus should be set to the text box that stores the name.

d. When the user presses the Alt+End key combination the focus should be set to the text box that stores the Country.

e. When the user enters a character, it should be converted to an uppercase letter.

f. If the user enters a character other than a digit (0 - 9) or the dash key in the ZipCode text box, the character should not be returned to the text box.

g. Test the program to make sure the keyboard handler is working correctly.

CHAPTER

4

Using Visual Basic with a Database

Accessing a Database Using Controls and by Programming Objects

case▶ Magnet Distributing is a distributor of floppy disks, magnetic tapes, and other removable media. They want a program to manage orders made by their customers. The order information is stored in a database file. Magnet Distributing needs a program to add, change, and delete the orders contained in this file. In addition, the program should allow the users to locate and display specific orders. Finally, the program should allow the user to display the different objects in the database.

SECTION A

objectives

In this section you will:

- Use Visual Basic in different ways to interact with a database
- Use a Data control to establish a connection to a database
- Set properties of other controls to display read and write information in a database

Using Visual Basic Controls to Interact with a Database

Previewing the Application

You can load and execute this project and use it for reference as you complete this chapter. The data for the program is stored in a database file rather than a text file. The program for this chapter adds, changes, and deletes records stored in the database file.

To view the completed program:

1. Start **Visual Basic** and load the project named **Chapter.04\Complete\ Magnet_C.vbp**. Print the code for the project.
2. Run the program. Figure 4-1 shows the running program.
3. On the form's menu bar, click **Find** then **First** to locate the first record. On the Find menu, test the **Next**, **Previous**, and **Last** commands.
4. On the form's menu bar, click **Records** then **Add** to create a new record. The text boxes are cleared or set to zero (0). The text boxes that are initially set to zero (0) are numeric values. Enter the value **OR9999** for the order ID and the value **CU9999** for the customer ID. Use the current date for the order date. Enter valid numbers for the order cost and order sales amount.

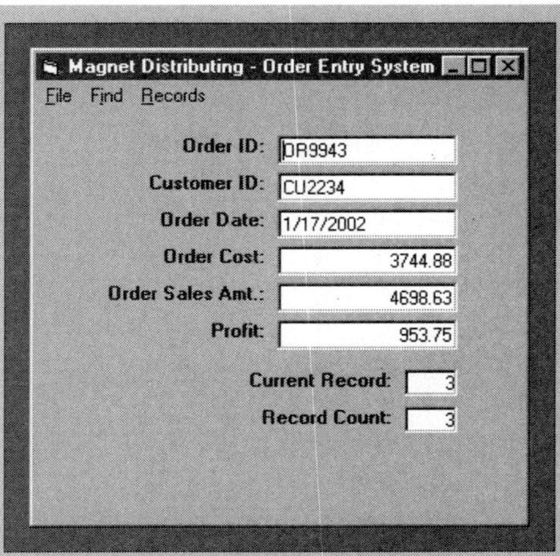

Figure 4-1: Completed application

5 Click **Records** then **Update** to record the new record to the database.

6 Click **Records** then **Delete** to remove the record you just added, then exit Visual Basic.

Fundamental Database Concepts

Current business and scientific applications often process large volumes of data. Frequently, this data must be reorganized and viewed dynamically. The complex data requirements of most programs requires more sophisticated data processing capabilities than those provided by text and random files. A **database** contains a set of information related to a particular topic or purpose. Information is stored in a database inside a table. Most databases contain several tables. A **table** consists of rows and columns. The **column** defines a name for, and characteristics of, the stored information. The columns in a table are called **fields** and the rows in a table are called **records**. Multiple tables also can be viewed as if they were a single table using a **query**. In this chapter, you will only work with tables. In the next chapter, you will work with queries.

Several companies manufacture database management programs, including Informix, Oracle, and Sybase. Visual Basic can operate with many of these programs. Visual Basic is particularly well-suited to operate with the same database management program used by Microsoft Access, the **Microsoft Jet database engine,** often referred to as just Jet or the Jet engine. Although Visual Basic also can connect to several other databases, this chapter describes only how to use Visual Basic with a Jet database. Properly designing the structure of a database requires an understanding of several key concepts.

- The tables in a database should be created such that data redundancy is eliminated. For example, a customer's address should be stored in a database once and only once. This process commonly is called **normalization**.

- Each row in a table should have a unique index so it can be located. The unique index may be made up of one or more fields.
- The data stored in a table usually is related to another table in some way. For example, consider the situation where customer information is stored in one table and that a customer can be identified by a unique customer ID. Assume that orders pertaining to customers are stored in a different table. Given this situation, the customer ID is stored in both tables and a relationship is defined between the two fields in the two different tables.

This chapter discusses how to use Visual Basic with an existing Jet database. It does not attempt to cover the topic of proper database design. If you have never used a database like Microsoft Access, consider starting Microsoft Access and reviewing the Help topic "About designing a database" using the Microsoft Office Assistant. The database for Magnet Distributing has been defined already. Figure 4-2 illustrates its structure.

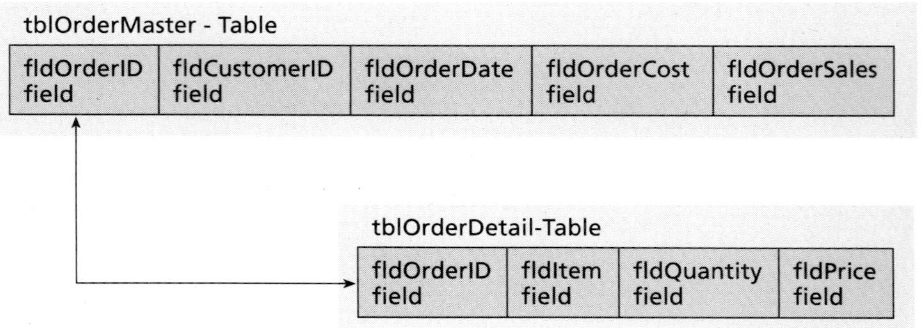

Figure 4-2: Database structure

As shown in Figure 4-2 the database has two tables named tblOrderMaster and tblOrderDetail. Just as for other objects you have created, objects in a database also should contain a three-character prefix to indicate the object's type. The three-character prefix for a table is "tbl." Each table contains several fields, which have a standard prefix of "fld." The field fldOrderID is common to both tables. In this case, information about the order is stored in the table named tblOrderMaster.

Connecting to a Database with the Data Control

There are two ways for a Visual Basic program to interact with Jet. One way is to write Visual Basic code to interact with a database. This code calls the methods and reads and writes the properties that make up the interface for the Jet. The other way is to use the **Data control.** The Data control enables you to move from record to record and to display information inside other controls on a form.

Using the properties of the Data control, you define the type of database to be used, the name and location of the database, and a table or query in the database.

At run time, the Data control will establish a connection with the database and table or query. The Data control does not itself display the records in a database table or query. Rather, it displays the individual fields of a record in other controls like text boxes and labels. The Data control can be thought of as a conduit between the controls that display a field from the current record and the database. Figure 4-3 illustrates this concept.

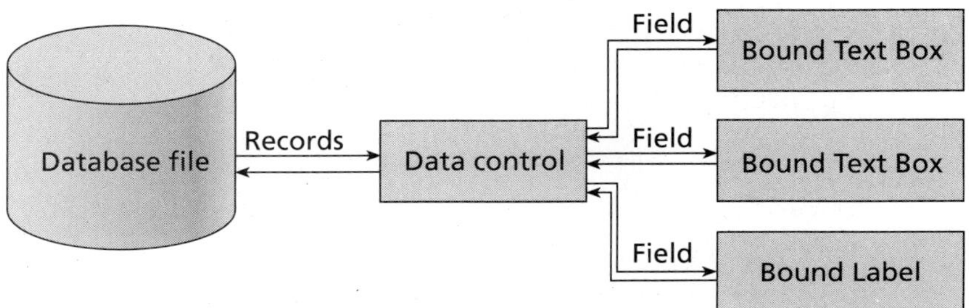

Figure 4-3: Data control

Using the Data control to navigate through records is accomplished by clicking the Data control's buttons. Using these buttons, it is possible to locate the first, last, next, and previous record in a table or query.

The Data control also supports record addition and editing. The Data control does not write records directly to the database. Rather, the data passes through a temporary storage area called the **copy buffer**. When a new record is added, a blank record is created in the copy buffer. Then, the data is stored in the blank record. The record then can be written to the database or the changes abandoned. When a record is edited, it first is read into the copy buffer, then the fields are edited, and then the record can be written back to the database or the changes abandoned.

The Data control also supports events that occur just after a record is located and just before a record is written to the database. These events allow computations to be performed on the current record and validation checks to be made before saving a record to the database.

All these tasks are performed using an object called a recordset. The Data control automatically and transparently creates an instance of the recordset for you. A **recordset** is an object representing a dynamic view of the records in an underlying database table or query. Using the methods and properties of the Recordset object, the action (addition, modification, or deletion of data) is performed. A Recordset object differs from other objects you have used in that it does not have a visual interface. A Recordset object is similar to an array of user-defined types where each element in the array represents a record. It is possible to write functions to locate the first record, next record, and identify which record is current, for example. These are the kind of tasks performed by a recordset, but instead of operating on an array the recordset operates on database tables.

Object	Data control
Properties	The **BOFAction** and **EOFAction** properties control what happens when the user tries either to locate the previous record when the first record is current or the next record when the last record is current. By default the current record is not changed. These properties can be modified, however, so a new record is added. They also can be changed to detect the beginning or end of file. The **Connect** property identifies the type of database. The Data control can operate with Access, dBASE, FoxPro, Paradox, and other types of databases. The Connect property is set to Access by default. The **DatabaseName** property identifies the name and location (folder) of a database file. Microsoft Access database files have the extension ".mdb." The **EditMode** property is read-only at run time and indicates the edit state of the current record. It can assume one of the three following constant values: dbEditNone, indicates the current record is not being edited; dbEditInProgress indicates that the current record is in the process of being edited, and the contents of the record are currently in the copy buffer; and dbEditAdd indicates that the current record in the copy buffer is a new record that has not been added to the database. The **Exclusive** property can be set to True or False, and is usually set at design time. If True, the database is opened for exclusive access meaning that no other application can open the database for processing. If False, the default, then the database is opened for shared access. The **ReadOnly** property can be set to True or False. If True, the contents of the recordset can be read but not written. If False, the default, the contents of the recordset are read-write. The **RecordSource** property identifies a database table or query. The table or query already must exist. The **RecordsetType** property determines how the recordset is created. It indirectly determines what operations can be performed on the table or query identified by the RecordSource property.
Events	The **Reposition** event occurs whenever the current record is changed. This event commonly is used to perform computations on the current record. The **Validate** event occurs before the current record changes, before a record is added, and before a record is deleted.
Methods	The **UpdateControls** method reads the current record from the underlying recordset and displays the information in the bound controls. Typically, this method is called after the user has changed the contents of one or more bound controls and then cancelled those changes.

The **UpdateRecord** method explicitly saves the changes made to the bound controls to the database. These changes are saved implicitly when the buttons on the Data control are used to reposition the current record.

To create an instance of the Data control and set its properties:

1. Open the project named **Magnet_S.vbp** located in the **Chapter.04\Startup** folder.
2. Click the **Data** control on the Toolbox and create an instance on the form.
3. Set the Caption property to **Order Master.** Set the Name and DatabaseName properties to **datOrderMaster** and **Chapter.04\Startup\Magnet.mdb**, respectively.
4. Click the **RecordSource** property then click the Properties button. Note that the list displays two tables. These are the tables in the database. The Data control connects to the database and lists the tables for you. Select the tabled named **tblOrderMaster.**
5. Note that the RecordsetType property is set to **1 - Dynaset**, the default. Note also the BOFAction and EOFAction properties are set to **0 - Move First** and **0 - Move Last**, respectively. This prevents the user from locating the beginning of file or end of file.

While the previous steps allow the Data control to establish a connection with the database named Magnet.mdb, no information will be displayed in the form's text boxes because the necessary properties of these controls have not been set.

Creating Bound Controls

A **bound control** displays a field from the current record as identified by the Data control. Many different controls that can hold text (such as the Label or ListBox control), and graphics, (such as the ImageBox or PictureBox control), can be bound to a field in a Data control. When a text box or label is bound to a Data control, changes in the current record are reflected in the bound TextBox or Label object. Each bound control corresponds to a field in a table or query. Bound controls often are referred to as **data aware** controls. The process of binding a control to a Data control requires two additional properties to be set for a control to behave as a bound control.

- The **DataSource** property of a bound control is set to an instance of a Data control typically drawn on the same form. If the properties of the Data control have been set, clicking the list arrow for this property will list the instances of Data controls created on the form. If a form will interact with multiple tables or queries, you can create multiple Data controls on a form, then select the desired Data control.

- The **DataField** property identifies the field in a table or query displayed in the bound control. When you select a field with the list arrow, Visual Basic uses the DataSource property to determine the appropriate Data control, then looks in the table or query and lists all the fields.

Programming tip

When you create instances of bound controls and set their properties at design time, it is important that you set the properties of the Data control first, then set the individual properties of the bound controls. If the Data control does not reference an existing table or query in a database, the bound control will not display the table names or field names. Set the DataSource property before setting the DataField property when creating a bound control. This way, the Properties window will list the fields in the table or query referenced by the Data control.

To create bound controls:

1. Activate the TextBox objects as shown in Figure 4-4.
2. Set the DataSource property to **datOrderMaster** for each of the text boxes except for the text box named txtOrderProfit. Selecting all the text boxes, then setting the DataSource property causes the property to be set for all the controls at once.
3. For each of the text boxes, set the DataField properties to **fldOrderID**, **fldCustomerID**, **fldOrderDate**, **fldOrderCost**, and **fldOrderSales**, as shown in Figure 4-4. Note that because you already have identified the Data control, the DataField can be set using the list arrow and selecting a field from the list.

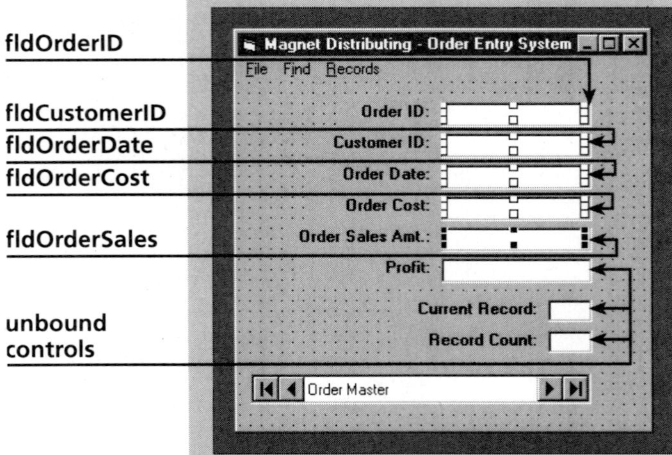

Figure 4-4: Selecting the bound controls

4. Test the program. Data from the database should be displayed as shown in Figure 4-5. Nothing appears in the unbound objects because you have not written any code yet to display the profit, current record, or record count.

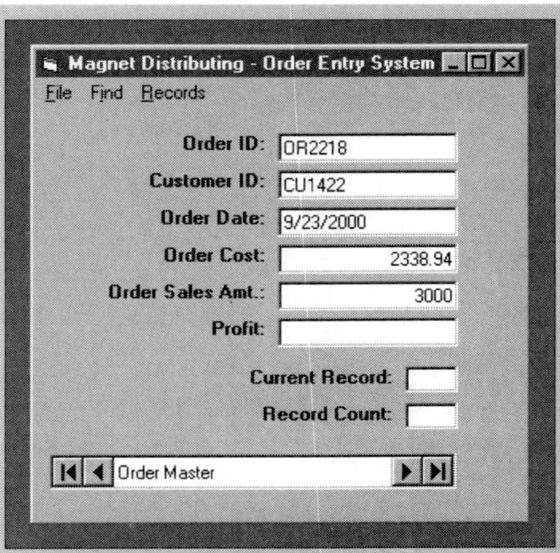

Figure 4-5: Displaying data in bound controls

The Data control works by using the design-time properties to create an object called a recordset. It then uses the underlying methods and properties of the Recordset object to locate different records, and modify data. Both the Data control and recordset support a set of properties and methods that interact with each other. For example, a recordset has specific methods to make a record available for editing and to record the changes to a record once editing is complete. The Data control calls these methods for you. When the contents of a data-aware control are changed, and then a different record is located using the buttons on the Data control, the Data control automatically enables editing on the recordset, then updates any changes made to the current record, and then locates the next record. These same actions are possible by calling the methods of the recordset individually. It is possible to use the Data control along with bound controls and never reference the underlying recordset directly even though it always exists. It is possible to use the Data control and the underlying recordset at the same time. It also is possible to create recordsets and display data in unbound controls without the aid of the Data control. Figure 4-6 illustrates these different methods of processing Jet data.

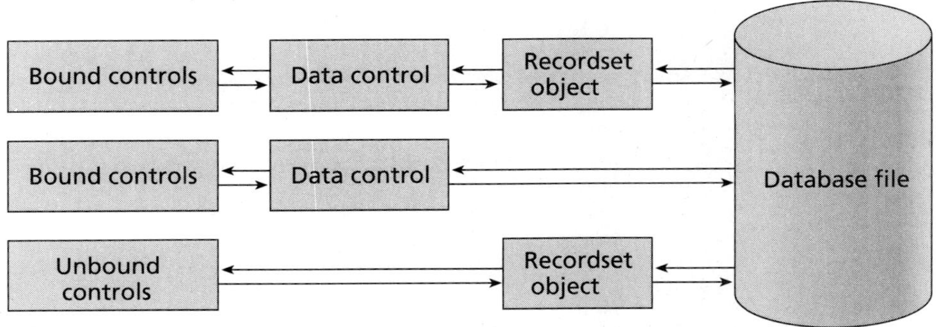

Figure 4-6: Data control and a Recordset object's relationship

A reference to the Recordset object is stored in the Recordset property of the Data control at run time. Recordsets differ from other objects you have created in that they have no visible component. Thus, the only way to interact with a recordset is programmatically. Describing the Data control and the underlying recordset presents a chicken and egg problem because the two objects are so interrelated. In this chapter, the Data control is presented first then the recordset is more fully defined. In the process of working with the Data control, however, some references are made to the underlying recordset. Thus, the properties and methods of the Recordset object are described here briefly to provide a frame of reference.

Object	Recordset
Properties	The **AbsolutePosition** property contains a value between 0 and RecordCount -1, and indicates the position of the current record pointer in the recordset. If there is no current record, the value of AbsolutePosition is minus one (-1).
	The **BOF** and **EOF** properties store Boolean values indicating whether or not the current record pointer is at the beginning or end of file, respectively. When BOF or EOF is True, there is no current record.
	The **BookMark** property allows you to create variables that are used to locate and uniquely identify an individual record in the recordset.
	The **EditMode** property can assume the constant value dbEditNone, dbEditInProgress, or dbEditAdd. These values have the same meaning as they do for the Data control's EditMode property. In fact, they represent the same values.
	The **LockEdits** property determines when and how a record is locked while it is being edited. If set to True, the record is locked as soon as the Edit method is called. If set to False, the record is not locked until the Update method is called.
	The **NoMatch** property contains the value True or False. If True, the previous Seek, FindFirst, or FindNext method did not locate a record that matched the criteria. Otherwise, it is False.
	The **PercentPosition** property contains a Single value between 0 and 100 indicating the relative percent position of the current record pointer in a recordset.
	The **RecordCount** property returns the number of records in a Recordset object.
	The **Type** property determines the type of recordset to create.
Methods	The **AddNew** method creates a new blank record in the copy buffer. The record is not written to the database until the Update method is called.
	The **CancelUpdate** method cancels the update operation initiated by the AddNew or Edit methods.
	The **Clone** method is used to duplicate a recordset from an original recordset. The new recordset has its own current record pointer. Furthermore, each recordset has its own copy buffer.

The **Delete** method deletes the current record from the recordset. After this method is called, there is no current record. Thus, it is advisable to call the MoveNext method so there is a current record.

The **Edit** method copies the contents of the current record (identified by the current record pointer) into the copy buffer, and makes the record available for editing. When the changes are complete, the Update method must be called to write the data in the copy buffer to the recordset. Attempting to edit an existing record without first calling the Edit method will cause a run-time error.

The **FindFirst**, **FindNext**, **FindPrevious**, and **FindLast** methods locate the first, next, previous, and last record matching some criteria.

The **MoveFirst**, **MoveNext**, **MovePrevious**, and **MoveLast** methods locate the first, next, previous, and last records in the recordset. The MoveNext and MovePrevious methods locate the next and previous record relative to the current record pointer.

The **Requery** method executes the query on which the recordset is based again.

The **Seek** method only applies to table-type recordsets and is used to locate a specific record.

The **Update** method writes any changes made to a record in the copy buffer to the database. This method only can be called after the AddNew or Edit methods have been called. If one of these methods have not been called, there is no data in the copy buffer and a run-time error will occur.

In this section you will use only the events and methods supported by the Data control itself. In the next section you will write code to reference the Recordset object directly.

Programming the Data Control's Events

There are two events pertaining to the Data control that commonly are used to validate data before it is saved to the database, and to detect when the current record is changed. These events are called the Validate and Reposition events. The Validate event occurs before a new record is located, and before the contents of the current record are changed in any way. At run time, when the Data control is initialized, a Reposition event occurs immediately after locating the first record. It is useful to perform computations in this event that are based on the current record, and display the result of those computations.

The statements you are about to create contain a subtle error. This was intentional so you can see the effects of events, and the importance of the order of their occurrence. The Reposition event occurs when the first record is located. When the first record is located, however, the event occurs before the data has been stored in the bound text boxes. As such, the first time the Reposition event occurs, the text boxes are empty. You will see how to fix this problem in the next section.

To program the Reposition event to compute the profit on a sale:

1. Activate the Code window for the event procedure named **datOrderMaster_Reposition** and enter the following statements:

```
Dim psngOrderCost As Single
Dim psngOrderSales As Single
txtOrderProfit = Val(txtOrderSales) - Val(txtOrderCost)
```

2. Test the program. Locate different records using the buttons on the Data control; the profit is updated whenever a new record is located. The profit on the order is computed by subtracting the value contained in the sales and cost text boxes. Note that when the program first is started, the profit text box contains no value.

The Validate Event

As the name implies, the primary purpose of the Validate event is to validate data before any changes are saved to the database, or request user confirmation before committing an action.

Syntax

Private Sub *object*_**Validate (**[*index* **As Integer**,] *action* **As Integer**, *save* **As Integer)**

Dissection

The *object* must be a valid instance of the Data control.

The *index* is used to identify uniquely the Data control if it is a member of a control array.

The *action* is an integer that describes the operation causing the Validate event to occur.

The *save* argument is used with bound controls. If the contents of a bound control have changed, the *save* argument is True. Otherwise, it is False.

Notes

Do not use any methods in this event that will change the current record. This causes the Reposition and Validate events to occur again causing the events to cascade indefinitely.

Code Example

```
Private Sub datOrder_Validate(Action As Integer, Save As
Integer)
    Dim pintReturn As Integer
    If Save = True Then
        If Action = vbDataActionDelete Then
            pintReturn = MsgBox("Delete?",vbYesNo)
            If pintReturn = vbNo Then
                Action = vbDataActionCancel
            End If
        End If
    End If
End Sub
```

Code Dissection

These statements test to see if the current record stored in the bound controls has changed. If so, then the action argument is tested to see if a delete operation caused the Validate event to occur. If so, then a message box is displayed to confirm the deletion. If the user responds no to the message box, then the delete operation is cancelled by setting the Action argument to vbDataActionCancel.

An important part of programming the Validate event is to determine the action that caused the event. It is likely that one set of statements will need to be executed if a record is being changed, and another set of statements executed if the user is trying to delete a record. These actions correspond to methods of the underlying recordset. Figure 4-7 lists the actions for the Validate event.

Constant	Value	Cause
vbDataActionCancel	0	Cancel the operation when the Sub exits
vbDataActionMoveFirst	1	MoveFirst method
vbDataActionMovePrevious	2	MovePrevious method
vbDataActionMoveNext	3	MoveNext method
vbDataActionMoveLast	4	MoveLast method
vbDataActionAddNew	5	AddNew method
vbDataActionUpdate	6	Update operation (not UpdateRecord)
vbDataActionDelete	7	Delete method
vbDataActionFind	8	Find method
vbDataActionBookmark	9	Bookmark property has been set
vbDataActionClose	10	Close method
vbDataActionUnload	11	Form is being unloaded

Figure 4-7: Data control actions

The Validate and Reposition events are closely related. Frequently, an operation like an update will cause both the Validate event and then the Reposition event to occur. For example, when the current record changes, the Validate event occurs before the new record is located, then the Reposition event occurs after the new record becomes the current record.

One common use of the Validate event is to verify that the data types of any bound controls are correct, before attempting to save the current record to the database.

This can be achieved by checking the value of the action argument. Remember that an update will occur when the user changes data and locates a different record by clicking the buttons on the Data control. You may expect that the action argument would indicate an update (vbDataActionUpdate). It does not, however. Rather, it contains a value indicating which button was clicked. You must account for this situation when you write the code for the Validate Event.

To program the Validate event:

1 Activate the Code window for the event procedure named **datOrderMaster_Validate** and enter the following statements:

```
Dim pstrMsg As String
Dim pblnError As Boolean
Select Case Action
    Case vbDataActionMoveNext, _
        vbDataActionMovePrevious, _
        vbDataActionMoveFirst, vbDataActionMoveLast, _
        vbDataActionUpdate
        If Not IsDate(txtOrderDate) Then
            pstrMsg = pstrMsg & _
                "Order date not a valid date." & Chr(13)
            pblnError = True
        End If
        If Not IsNumeric(txtOrderSales) Then
            pstrMsg = pstrMsg & _
                "Sales must be numeric." & _
                Chr(13)
            pblnError = True
        End If
        If Not IsNumeric(txtOrderCost) Then
            pstrMsg = pstrMsg & "Cost must be numeric."
            pblnError = True
        End If
        If pblnError Then
            MsgBox pstrMsg, vbOKOnly
            datOrderMaster.UpdateControls
            Action = vbDataActionCancel
        End If
    Case Else
End Select
```

2 Test the program. Enter an invalid date in the order date, then an invalid number for both the order cost and the sales amount, then click the **Move Next** button ▸ on the Data control. A message box should appear identifying the invalid fields. Test other order dates, costs, and sales, and use the other buttons on the Data control.

The Validate event occurs whenever a method pertaining to the underlying recordset causes the data in the recordset to be changed, or a different record located. The MoveNext, MoveFirst, MovePrevious, and MoveLast actions (pertaining to the Data control's Validate event) occur when a button is clicked on the Data control. In addition, explicitly calling the recordset's Update method to record changes to the current record will cause the Validate event to occur with the Update action. Thus, the changes should be validated when any of these actions occur so they are listed in the Select Case statement. The If statements are executed to determine whether or not the order date is a valid date, and if the order sales and order cost contain valid numeric values. If an error is recognized, the error variable pblnError is set to True. After all the possible error conditions have been tested, the error variable is checked. If an input error has occurred, a message box is displayed identifying all the input errors. Then the UpdateControls method is called to restore the data from the recordset. An error in one or all input fields causes a single message box to be displayed rather than one message box for each error. This is implemented by declaring a string and appending a message to the string for each error that is recognized.

SECTION B

objectives

In this section you will:

- Program a Recordset object and understand the interaction between the recordset and the Data control
- Locate records using a recordset
- Add, change, and delete records using a recordset

Using the Recordset Object to Manipulate Data

Programming the Recordset Object

As mentioned, a recordset is created automatically by the Data control when the form is loaded. In addition to using the interface of the Data control, it also is possible to use the interface provided by the underlying recordset. A reference to this object is stored in the Recordset property of the Data control. The syntax to reference the properties and methods of the recordset requires explanation. The only reference to the recordset is stored in the Recordset property of the Data control. To make the syntactical reference, the same dot notation is used as with properties and methods. There is an additional object reference, however. For example, to call the MoveFirst method of the recordset referenced by a Data control named datOrderMaster, the following syntax would be used:

```
datOrderMaster.Recordset.MoveFirst
```

This statement refers to the Recordset property of the Data control named datOrderMaster. This property contains a reference to a Recordset object which itself has methods and properties. One of the methods, MoveFirst, locates the first record in the recordset.

In the previous section, you used bound controls and the Data control to locate records and save changes to a record. As shown in the previous statement, it also is possible to reference a recordset directly. When the recordset is bound to a Data control, changes to the recordset are reflected in both the Data control and its bound controls. That is, if changes are made to the data in the recordset, the Validate event will occur for the Data control. If the methods of the recordset are called to locate a different record, the Reposition event will occur to the corresponding Data control.

The recordset itself does not respond to events. Figure 4-8 shows the relationship between the Data control and the Recordset object created by the Data control.

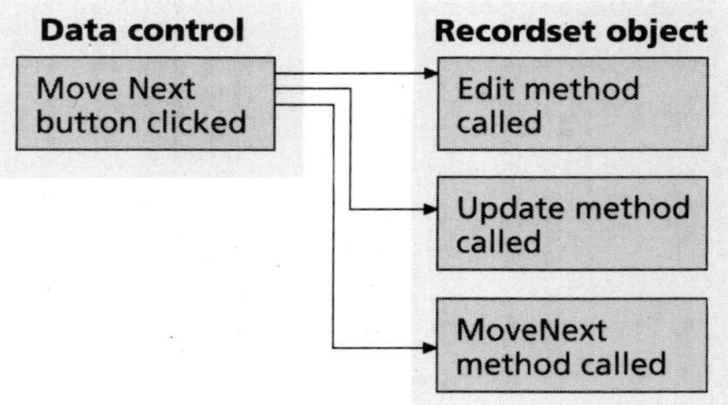

Figure 4-8: Interaction between the Data control and recordset

As you work with both the Data control and the recordset it references, you need to be aware of the effects they have on each other. When the buttons on the Data control are clicked, the Data control itself takes care of enabling a record for editing, and saving the changed record back to the database. When you program the recordset directly, however, you expressly call methods to enable editing and record or discard changes. Thus, if the user executes menu commands that expressly call the methods of a recordset and have the capability to click the buttons on the Data control, the code in your program must keep track of the edit state of a record. Otherwise, run-time errors are likely to occur.

Types of Recordsets

Different types of recordsets can be created depending on how they will be used. That is, there are types of recordsets that are read-only and others that are read-write. Using the proper type of recordset for a task has a major impact on performance. There are five types of recordsets supported by the Jet database.

- A **table-type recordset** represents a physical table stored in an Access database (Jet workspace). A table-type recordset is read-write.
- A **dynaset-type recordset** is the most common type of recordset. It can be created from a table or query. The dynaset-type recordset is updateable. That is, it is possible to add, change, and delete records.
- A **snapshot-type recordset** is a read-only recordset. It typically is used when printing reports or displaying records when data will not be changed. When printing a report or performing calculations where all the records in the recordset will be examined, a snapshot will be faster than a table or dynaset. This is because Jet does not have to maintain the necessary information to keep track of whether records need to be saved.
- A **forward-only-type recordset** is like a snapshot but the recordset, once opened, only can be processed once. That is, it is not possible to locate the

previous record in a forward-only-type recordset. This type of recordset also is very fast when all the records need to be examined.

- Another type of recordset that is only supported by ODBC is the **dynamic-type recordset.** ODBC database connectivity is not covered in this book.

If you have used earlier versions of Visual Basic and the Jet engine, you may be familiar with the Dynaset object. The Recordset object is now more generic and supports all types of recordsets including dynasets. See the Help topic "Obsolete features in DAO" for more information.

When using the Data control to create a recordset, the RecordsetType property can be used to determine the type of recordset created. The Data control, however, does not support the forward-only-type recordset. Forward-only-type recordsets must be created programmatically using the OpenRecordset method.

Programming the recordset can be divided roughly into two parts. There are properties and methods to navigate through a recordset and determine the current position of a record in the recordset. There is a second set of properties and methods used to change the data in the table or query referenced by the recordset. When you look at records stored in the Recordset object, only one record can be active at a time. The **current record pointer** indicates the active record. You do not access the current record pointer explicitly. Rather, you move the current record pointer indirectly using the Recordset object's methods. You can find out if the current record pointer is at the beginning or end of the recordset using the BOF and EOF properties of the Recordset object. The term current record pointer is slightly misleading when BOF or EOF is True, because there actually is no current record.

There are several different ways to navigate through the different records in a Recordset object. There are methods to move forward and backward through different records, and locate the first and last record. There also are methods to locate records having specific criteria.

Determining the Current Record Pointer Location

There are several properties used to indicate the current position in the recordset both in absolute and relative terms, and the number of records in a recordset. These properties are the AbsolutePosition, RecordCount, and PercentPosition. Each of these properties has unique characteristics.

- The **AbsolutePosition** property cannot be used with forward-only-type recordsets. If the current record pointer is at BOF or EOF, then the AbsolutePosition property has a value of minus one (-1). The AbsoluteProperty is zero-based so the first record has an AbsolutePosition of zero (0).
- The **RecordCount** property identifies the number of records in a recordset. This can be accomplished by calling the MoveLast method at the expense of performance. The RecordCount property also is useful to determine if the recordset contains no records, in which case the value of the RecordCount property is zero (0). Furthermore, the RecordCount may not reflect accurately the last record. Jet reads records in 2K blocks called a page, and pages

are not read until needed. The number of records on a page depends on the size of the record. The RecordCount property counts the number of records only for the pages that have been read. Thus, if three records fit on a page, the RecordCount property will have a value of three (3) when the first record is located no matter how many records are in the table. The RecordCount will not be accurate unless the recordset's MoveLast method is called.

- The **PercentPosition** property is a value between 0 and 100, but is computed based on the current value of the RecordCount property. Thus, if the last record in a recordset has not been located, then the PercentPosition property may be incorrect.

As mentioned, the Validate and Reposition events are closely related. One of the tasks to be performed is to determine the record count. This cannot be done when the form is loaded (in the Form_Load event procedure) because the Data control may not be initialized. Because the Reposition event occurs when the first record is loaded, it is possible to call the MoveLast method, which has the effect of setting the RecordCount property to its correct value. Consider the following event procedure:

```
Private Sub datOrderMaster_Reposition( )
    datOrderMaster.Recordset.MoveLast
End Sub
```

This event procedure will not work. When the Data control is initialized, the MoveLast method is called which triggers a Reposition event, which causes the MoveLast method to be called again, which triggers another Reposition event. This process continues indefinitely. The problem can be solved by using an If statement to prevent this method from being called more than once. The implementation chosen in this program is to declare a Private module-level variable to store a Boolean value that initially is False and becomes True when the last record is located. This value will be tested in an If statement so the last record will be located only once.

In this section, you will use the menus on the form rather than the buttons on the Data control so you can see the technique of manipulating the recordset with code. As such, you will make the Data control invisible at run time. To prevent the user from selecting options that would otherwise cause run time errors, certain menu commands and bound controls will be enabled or disabled depending on the edit state of the current record. This code already has been created and is stored in the general procedure named EditState. Refer to the comments in the completed program for more information. This procedure should be called when the form is loaded to set the initial edit state and whenever the edit state is changed.

To determine the number of records and current record:

1. Activate the Code window for the **Form_Load** event procedure and enter the following statement:

```
Call EditState(NotEditing)
```

2 Activate the Code window for the event procedure named **datOrderMaster_Reposition** and enter the statements shown in bold:

```
Dim psngOrderCost As Single
Dim psngOrderSales As Single
If Not mblnInitialized Then
    datOrderMaster.Recordset.MoveLast
End If
lblCurrentRecord = _
    datOrderMaster.Recordset.AbsolutePosition + 1
lblRecordCount = _
    datOrderMaster.Recordset.RecordCount
txtOrderProfit = Val(txtOrderSales) - Val(txtOrderCost)
```

3 Activate the Code window for the event procedure named **datOrderMaster_Validate** and enter the statements shown in bold:

```
Dim pstrMsg As String, pintReturn As Integer
Dim pblnError As Boolean
If mblnInitialized = False Then
    mblnInitialized = True
    Exit Sub
End If
Select Case Action
. . .
```

4 Test the program. The position and record count should be displayed on the form.

The statements to locate the last record the first time the Reposition event occurs requires code both for the Reposition and Validate events. The Reposition event calls the MoveLast method of the recordset the first time the event occurs. This causes a Validate event to occur. When the event occurs, however, the current record is not yet loaded into the text boxes. Thus, the code in the event procedure to validate the current record must not be executed. Therefore, the following If statement sets the mblnInitialized flag to True and exits the procedure immediately without executing the validation code.

```
If mblnInitialized = False Then
    mblnInitialized = True
    Exit Sub
End If
```

After locating the last record, both the AbsolutePosition and RecordCount properties can be set and the result stored in the proper labels. Because the AbsolutePosition property is zero-based, one (1) is added to the value. Because users tend to perceive the first record having a value of one (1), this is more intuitive.

If the statements that prevent the Validate and Reposition events are omitted, the Reposition event will call itself indefinitely. This will cause an error message indicating the computer is out of stack space. Again, the cause is a cascading event. One way to detect this error is to use Visual Basic's debugging tools. One of these tools lets you look at the call stack. The **call stack** contains a list of the active procedure calls; that is, procedures that have not exited. To look at the current call stack, you can enter break mode and click View, Call Stack. The Call Stack can only be viewed if there is a procedure executing. The Call Stack window appears as shown in Figure 4-9.

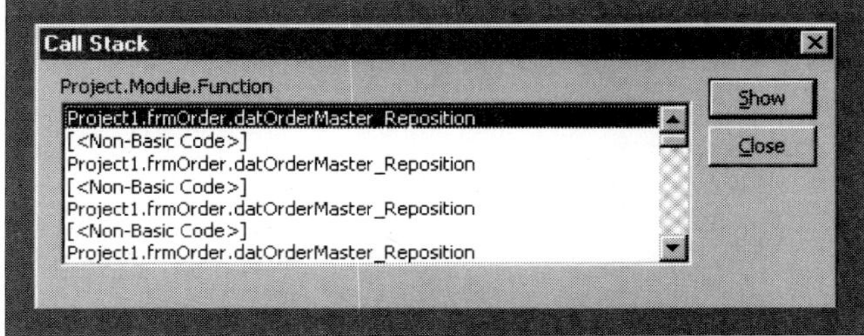

Figure 4-9: Call Stack window

As shown in Figure 4-9, the event procedure named datOrderMaster_Reposition is calling itself repeatedly. From this information, you can deduce that the out of stack space error condition was caused by the cascading Reposition event.

Programming tip

Use caution not to call a method that will cause the current record to be changed inside the Reposition event. This will cause the Reposition event to occur again which will again cause the current record to be changed and so on. This cascading event will continue to be called until the program exhausts the available stack space and then it will crash.
Avoid using the MoveLast method in large databases to determine the record count. The operation can take considerable time. Using a sample table with 500,000 records, the operation takes several seconds.

Understanding Bookmarks

Rather than using the AbsolutePosition property to identify a specific record, it often is preferable to use a bookmark to locate or identify a specific record. A bookmark works much like using bookmarks to mark the pages of a book. Like a physical bookmark, it is possible to create several bookmarks. Using bookmarks consists of setting bookmarks and locating a record by its bookmark. Every record in a recordset contains a bookmark stored in its Bookmark property. Some types of recordsets support bookmarks and others do not. The recordset's Bookmarkable property contains a Boolean value indicating whether or not the recordset supports bookmarks. The following If statement is useful to determine if a recordset can contain bookmarks.

```
If datOrderMaster.Recordset.Bookmarkable Then
    ' bookmarks are supported
Else
    ' bookmarks are not supported
End If
```

To create a bookmark, you assign the Bookmark property to a Variant data type. The following statements set a bookmark to the first record in a recordset:

```
Dim mvntBookmark As Variant
datOrderMaster.Recordset.MoveFirst
mvntBookmark = datOrderMaster.Recordset.Bookmark
```

To locate a record by its bookmark, you set the Bookmark property to the Variant variable as shown in the following statement. This statement has the effect of changing the current record to the bookmarked record.

```
datOrderMaster.Recordset.Bookmark = mvntBookmark
```

While these statements illustrate the process of creating and locating a bookmark, the statements are useful to create only a single bookmark. The following statements shown in the steps can be used with dynamic arrays to create several bookmarks as illustrated.

To create the necessary code for the bookmarks:

1. Set the Visible property of the Data control to **False**.
2. Activate the Code window for the event procedure named **mnuRecordsNewBookmark_Click** and enter the following code. (Note that the array mvntBookmarks has been declared already.)

```
ReDim Preserve mvntBookmarks(UBound(mvntBookmarks) + 1)
mvntBookmarks(UBound(mvntBookmarks)) = _
    datOrderMaster.Recordset.Bookmark
```

3. Activate the Code window for the event procedure named **mnuRecordsRestoreBookmark_Click** and enter the following code:

```
If UBound(mvntBookmarks) > 1 Then
    datOrderMaster.Recordset.Bookmark = _
        mvntBookmarks(UBound(mvntBookmarks))
    ReDim Preserve _
        mvntBookmarks(UBound(mvntBookmarks) - 1)
End If
```

4. Test the program. Click **Records** then **New Bookmark** to set a bookmark. Locate a different record. Click **Records** then **Restore Last Bookmark**. This locates the record identified by the bookmark you just created.

These event procedures operate using a Variant module-level array named mvntBookmarks. Each time a bookmark is added, the array is redimensioned and the new bookmark is stored in the newly-created array element. Thus, the array can store an indefinite number of bookmarks. When the last bookmark is restored, assigning the last element in the array (the most current bookmark) to the Bookmark property changes the current record. Then the array size is decremented by one, thus destroying the latest bookmark. An If statement is used to verify that there is a valid bookmark. This is accomplished by checking the size of the array, then locating the bookmark only if one exists.

Locating Records

There are two ways to locate records. One way is to navigate through the recordset using all the records. The other is to locate records based on specific criteria. The MoveFirst, MoveNext, MovePrevious, and MoveLast methods, navigate through a recordset and are similar to clicking the buttons on the Data control.

When you call the MovePrevious and MoveNext methods, you must be aware of the beginning of file and end of file. If the last record is the current record and you call the MoveNext method, the current record pointer is at the end of file so there is no current record. If there is no current record, editing is not possible. There are several techniques that will solve the problem. One is check that the absolute position is not the first or last record using an If statement. If it is the first or last record, the corresponding move method is not called. Another technique is to call the method and then test whether BOF or EOF is True. If it is, then call the MoveFirst or MoveLast method so there is a current record. In this example, the second approach will be used.

To program the positioning method of the recordset:

1 Activate the Code window for the event procedure named **mnuFindFirst_Click** and enter the following statement:

```
datOrderMaster.Recordset.MoveFirst
```

2 Activate the Code window for the event procedure named **mnuFindLast_Click** and enter the following statement:

```
datOrderMaster.Recordset.MoveLast
```

3 Activate the Code window for the event procedure named **mnuFindNext_Click** and enter the following statements:

```
datOrderMaster.Recordset.MoveNext
If datOrderMaster.Recordset.EOF Then
    datOrderMaster.Recordset.MoveLast
End If
```

4 Activate the Code window for the event procedure named **mnuFindPrevious_Click** and enter the following statements:

```
datOrderMaster.Recordset.MovePrevious
If datOrderMaster.Recordset.BOF Then
    datOrderMaster.Recordset.MoveFirst
End If
```

5 Activate the Code window for the event procedure named **datOrderMaster_Validate** and modify the Select Case statement so it only contains one case for updating. The others are no longer necessary because the buttons on the Data control are not visible to the user. As you will see in a moment, the menu commands will be used to enable editing and disable editing explicitly.

```
Select Case Action
    Case vbDataActionUpdate
```

6 Test the program. Select each of the menu commands and confirm that different records are being located.

In addition to navigating through the entire recordset, it is possible to locate records using specific criteria. This is accomplished using the FindFirst and FindNext methods, which pertain to the Recordset object. The FindFirst and FindNext methods have the following syntax:

Syntax

object.**FindFirst** *criteria*
object.**FindNext** *criteria*

Dissection

The *object* must be a valid instance of a Recordset object.

The *criteria* determines how the search is performed. In its simplest form, the *criteria* contains a field name, followed by an operator, followed by a value. It takes the form of an SQL WHERE clause but without the word WHERE. When specifying the criteria, strings must be enclosed in single quotes (') and Date values must be enclosed in pound signs (#). The syntax of the WHERE clause is more fully explained in the next chapter.

Code Example

```
Dim pstrName As String
pstrName = "John Smith"
prstCurrent.FindFirst "fldID = 123"
prstCurrent.FindFirst "fldName = 'John Smith'"
prstCurrent.FindFirst "fldName = " & "'" & pstrName & "'"
```

Code Dissection

The previous statements assume that prstCurrent references an existing recordset. The first statement assumes that fldID is a numeric field. After executing this statement, the first record having a fldID of 123, becomes the current record. The second statement locates the first record where fldName contains the value

"John Smith." Because this is a string, the value is enclosed in single quotation marks. The final statement performs the same task. Instead of using a literal value, however, the variable containing the string is used. The string concatenation operator is used to build the criteria, and the single quotes are inserted.

It is possible that no records will be found that match the criteria. In this case, the NoMatch property is set to True by the FindFirst or FindNext method. Otherwise, it is False. The value of the NoMatch property should be checked after the FindFirst or FindNext methods are called to verify that a record was located as shown in the following statements:

```
If datOrderMaster.Recordset.NoMatch Then
    ' error
End If
```

The difficult part of using these two methods is to create the criteria. Consider the following statements:

```
datOrderMaster.Recordset.FindFirst "fldOrderID = 'OR9441'"
datOrderMaster.Recordset.FindFirst _
    "fldOrderDate > #9/18/2000#"
datOrderMaster.Recordset.FindFirst "fldOrderCost <= 3000"
```

These statements use string, date and numeric criteria based on the underlying data type of the database field. That is, fldOrderID is a String, fldOrderDate is a date, and fldOrderCost is numeric. Note that the String is enclosed in single quotes and date is enclosed in pound signs. Conditions are applied much like the conditions are applied in an If statement and the syntax is much the same. It is possible to use both logical and relational operators in a criteria expression.

To use the FindFirst method:

1 Activate the Code window for the event procedure named **mnuFindByOrderID_Click** and enter the following statements:

```
Dim pstrOrderID As String
pstrOrderID = InputBox("Enter Order ID")
If pstrOrderID = "" Then
    Exit Sub
Else
    datOrderMaster.Recordset.FindFirst "fldOrderID = " _
        & "'" & pstrOrderID & "'"
    If datOrderMaster.Recordset.NoMatch = True Then
        MsgBox "Cannot find record.", vbOKOnly
    End If
End If
```

2 Test the program. Click **Find** then **By Order ID**. When the input box is displayed enter the Order ID **OR2318** then click the **OK** button. The corresponding record should be displayed in the text boxes.

Try to find the Order ID number **ZZZZ**. Because the record does not exist, the NoMatch property is True so the message box is displayed.

The event procedure uses an input box to get an Order ID from the user. If the Order ID is blank, then the event procedure terminates. Otherwise, the FindFirst method is called.

```
datOrderMaster.Recordset.FindFirst "fldOrderID = " _
    & "'" & pstrOrderID & "'"
```

Because the field fldOrderID is a string, the value must be enclosed in single quotation marks. This is accomplished by manually concatenating quotes around the variable pstrOrderID. For example, if the variable pstrOrderID contained the value "ABC123" then the string would be evaluated as:

```
fldOrderID = 'ABC123'
```

Looping Through the Records in a Recordset

In addition to locating a specific record, it often is necessary to create a loop to iterate through the records in a recordset to print a report or to accumulate totals. This can be accomplished with a Do loop. The condition in the Do loop typically uses the BOF and EOF properties to determine when the beginning of file or end of file is reached. These properties are False when there is a current record. Inside of the Do loop, it is possible to reference the individual fields programmatically in addition to using bound controls. The syntax to reference a field in a recordset is as follows:

Syntax *object*![*fieldname*]

Dissection The *object* must be a valid instance of a recordset object.

The *fieldname* must be a field in the recordset.

Code Example

```
Do Until datOrderMaster.Recordset.EOF
    Debug.Print datOrderMaster.Recordset![fldOrderID]
    datOrderMaster.Recordset.MoveNext
Loop
```

Code Dissection These statements use a Do loop to examine each record in a recordset. The MoveNext method is called on the recordset inside of the Do loop. Otherwise, the loop would examine the first record of the recordset indefinitely. For each record, the field named fldOrderID is printed in the Immediate window.

Recall that the code you wrote previously for the Reposition event used the contents of the text boxes to compute the gross profit. The following statements will have the same effect:

```
txtOrderProfit = Format _
    (datOrderMaster.Recordset![fldOrderSales] - _
    datOrderMaster.Recordset![fldOrderCost], "Currency")
```

These statements use the fields named fldOrderSales and fldOrderCost from the underlying recordset to compute the profit on the sales.

Programming ▶ tip

Note that one statement was used to obtain the fields from the recordset, perform the computation, then format the output. In this example, the data type of each field is guaranteed to be correct because the Jet engine will not store invalid data in a field. Thus, validating the field is redundant. Furthermore, you could have declared local variables to store the sales and cost values. Then in another statement, you could have subtracted the values storing the result in yet another variable. Finally, you still would have needed to call the Format statement with the result. This is an example where embedding expressions inside expressions cannot only save typing, but also marginally improve performance. This is because the overhead required to allocate the local variables is not necessary.

Making Changes to Data

The AddNew, Edit, Update, and Delete methods are used to add, change, and delete data in a database table referenced by a recordset. Before using these methods, there are some caveats to be aware of.

- The **AddNew method** creates a new record in the copy buffer. The data actually is not written to the underlying database table until the Update method is called. If the EOFAction property of the Data control is set to the constant vbEOFActionAddNew, then a new record will be added when the user clicks the Move Next button on the Data control when the last record is the current record.
- Before changing data in a recordset, the **Edit method** must be called to copy the current record from the database to the copy buffer. This enables the current record for editing. Once editing is complete, the Update method must be called to write the contents of the copy buffer to the underlying database table. This happens automatically when the buttons on the Data control are used to locate a different record.
- If a record has been enabled for editing, the **CancelUpdate method** will restore the contents of the current record to the values that existed before editing began.
- When the **Delete method** is called, the current record is removed. Thus, there is no current record. Typically, the MoveNext method is called so a current record exists.

Programming

tip

As you develop programs, carefully consider the interaction between the Data control and the recordset. As you have seen, clicking a button on the Data control may invoke several methods of the recordset. For example, locating the next record with the Data control will cause any changes to be recorded. This has the effect of calling the Edit and Update methods. To gain more precise control over the recordset, consider making the Data control invisible so the user cannot access its buttons. Then call the methods of the recordset for navigation and updating purposes. It also is possible to use unbound controls and still work with a database. In this situation you must write code to display the current record in text boxes, validate changes, and perform deletions. Which method to choose is subjective and depends somewhat on programmer preference.

GUI Design

tip

In this program, the menu commands are enabled and disabled as necessary. That is, when a record is being added or edited, only the Edit and Cancel Edit menu commands are enabled. When a record is not being edited, then the Add, Update, and Delete menu commands are enabled and the Edit and Cancel buttons are disabled. Disabling menu commands, when they are not applicable prevents run-time errors and clarifies the user interface.

In the Magnet Distributing example, the Data control is not visible to the user. So the user cannot select a menu command when it is not valid, the menu commands are enabled and disabled as necessary depending on the edit state of the current record. This code has been completed already and is contained in the Sub procedure EditState. The are two edit states. One edit state identifies when the current record is being edited and another when it is not. Refer to the commented code in the program for a more detailed explanation of the procedure.

Adding Data

The Recordset object allows you to add new records to a recordset, and therefore a table, in the database. The AddNew method does this by creating a new blank record in the copy buffer. Before the changes are written to the database, the Update method should be called explicitly on the recordset. Each of these methods triggers a Validate event for the Data control even though the Data control is invisible. Thus, the Validate event can be programmed to check the correctness of data before attempting to write the actual record to the database table. If records are updated manually by calling the Update method, then the code in the menu command or button that calls the method could perform the necessary validation. Again, be aware of the interaction between the Data control and the recordset. Note that some recordsets can be updated and others cannot. Furthermore some fields in a recordset may be updateable and others may not. For example, a database field can be read-only in which case it cannot be updated. Refer to the Help topic "Recordsets, updating" for more information.

To add a new record to the database using the recordset's methods:

1 Activate the Code window for the event procedure named **mnuRecordsAdd_Click** and enter the following statements:

```
EditState Editing
datOrderMaster.Recordset.AddNew
```

2 Activate the Code window for the event procedure named **mnuRecordsUpdate_Click** event and enter the following statements:

```
EditState NotEditing
datOrderMaster.Recordset.Update
```

3 Test the program. Click Records then Add to store a new record in the copy buffer. Enter an Order ID of **O2341**, then a Customer ID of **CU722**. Enter the current date for the order date and enter valid numeric values in the sales and cost fields. Finally, click **Records** then **Update** to record the new records to the database.

In addition to calling the AddNew and Update methods, these event procedures enable and disable the appropriate menu commands so the user cannot attempt to perform an impossible action. Disabling menu commands in cases like this is a good programming practice. Another option would be to set the Visible property for a menu command to False so the user will not even see the menu command.

Changing Data

There are two methods of the Recordset object used to modify the existing contents of a record. These are the Edit and Update methods. Before a record can be changed, the Edit method must be called on the recordset. This causes the contents of the record to be placed into the copy buffer for editing. After editing is complete, the Update method is called to write the contents of the copy buffer to the underlying recordset.

To enable editing for a recordset:

1 Activate the Code window for the event procedure named **mnuRecordsEdit_Click** and enter the following statements:

```
EditState Editing
datOrderMaster.Recordset.Edit
```

2 Test the program. Locate the record you just added and click **Records** then **Edit** to enable editing for the record. Change the data in the fields then click **Records** then **Update** to save the changes.

These statements enable and disable the menu commands as necessary and then call the Edit method on the recordset to enable editing on the record.

Deleting Data

Deleting data from a database is accomplished by calling the Delete method on the recordset. This causes the record identified by the current record pointer to be deleted from the database. After calling this method, there is no longer a current record. Thus, the MoveNext method commonly is called after the Delete method to locate a different record.

To program the Delete method:

1. Activate the Code window for the event procedure named **mnuRecordsDelete_Click** and enter the following statements:

```
datOrderMaster.Recordset.Delete
datOrderMaster.Recordset.MoveNext
If datOrderMaster.Recordset.EOF Then
    datOrderMaster.Recordset.MoveLast
End If
```

2. Test the program. Locate the record you just edited and delete it by clicking **Records** on the menu bar, then **Delete**. The record is deleted and a new record becomes the current record.

These statements delete the current record then locate the next record. It is possible to start editing a record and then cancel the changes.

To cancel the changes to a record being edited:

1. Activate the Code window for the event procedure named **mnuRecordsAbandon_Click** and enter the following statements:

```
EditState NotEditing
datOrderMaster.Recordset.CancelUpdate
```

2. Test the program. Click **Records** then **Edit** to enable editing. Make changes to the current record then click **Records** then **Abandon** to cancel the update process.

These statements set the edit mode, then call the CancelUpdate method of the Recordset object. This causes both the contents of the recordset and the contents of the bound text boxes to be restored.

SECTION C

objectives

In this section you will:

- Create variables that reference objects
- Program objects stored as a group in another object called a collection
- Use the collections and objects pertaining to Jet
- Handle run-time errors

Understanding Errors and Database Objects

An Introduction to Object Variables

In the previous chapters, you created variables of intrinsic and user-defined types. Variables also can be created to reference objects like command buttons and recordsets. When you declare a variable of an intrinsic data type, the data is stored in the memory address of the variable. The memory address of an object variable, however, contains a pointer to the actual object. In other words, the contents of an object variable is a Long integer number. That number represents the memory address of the actual object. You use this reference to an object variable to then call the methods and read and write the properties of the underlying object. Figure 4-10 illustrates this difference.

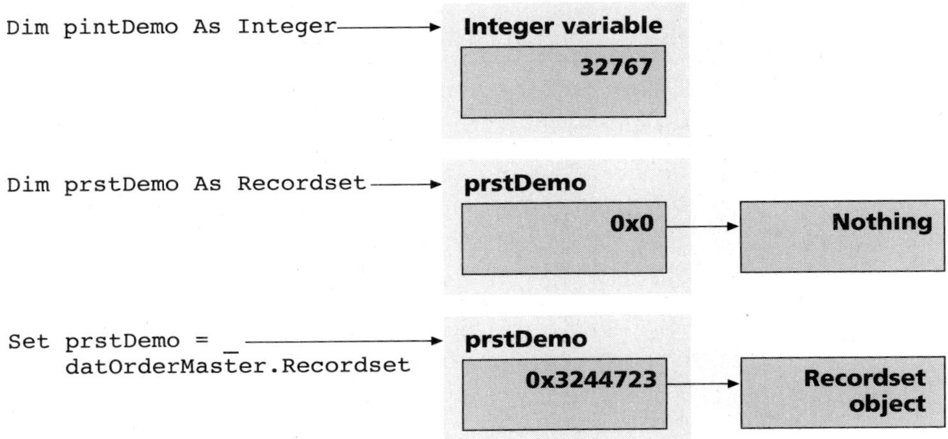

Figure 4-10: Comparing intrinsic variables to object variables

As you will see in this and subsequent chapters, the concept of a pointer is very significant in Visual Basic, because it can help you understand why object variables work. An object variable (pointer) does not contain an object but rather a reference to an object. This allows multiple object variables to reference the same object. That is, multiple object variables can point to the same object. Another distinction between an object variable and an ordinary variable is the state of the variable after it has been declared but no value has been assigned to it. In the case of an ordinary variable, numeric variables like Integers, Floats, and so on, contain the value of zero (0). Strings contain an empty string. Object variables contain nothing, however. That is, they do not reference an object and in fact point to a memory address known in Visual Basic as Nothing. Again, if you are familiar with C, you can think of this as a Null pointer. Another important consideration with object variables (pointers) is understanding when the actual objects are created and destroyed.

Object variables are created using the Dim, Private, Public, and Static statements. The As *type* clause, instead of containing an intrinsic, user-defined, or enumerated type, contains a class. Remember that all objects are created from classes. Command buttons, and all other control instances and objects like recordsets, are all created from a corresponding class.

Syntax

[Dim|ReDim|Public|Private|Static] *varname* **As** [**New**] *class*]

Dissection

The **Dim**, **ReDim**, **Public**, **Private**, and **Static** statements have the same meaning as with intrinsic variables.

The required *varname* must adhere to standard variable naming conventions.

The optional **New** keyword only can be used with externally creatable objects. When an object variable is referenced for the first time, a new instance of the object is created from the *class*. Some objects only can be created by calling the methods of other objects. Others can be created with the New keyword.

The *class* can be any class name or the types Object or Variant.

Code Example

```
Dim pcmdRef1 As CommandButton
Dim prstCurrent As Recordset
```

Code Dissection

The first statement creates an object variable named pcmdRef1 that can be used to reference a command button instance, and the second statement creates an object variable to reference a Recordset object. The declarations simply create two object variables capable of referencing two distinct types of objects. They do not create an object nor do the variables reference an existing object. Rather, the variables point to a special value Nothing. This value is used with object variables to indicate that the variable does not point to (reference) an existing object instance. To illustrate this concept, consider what happens when you draw a command button on a form. You actually are creating an instance of the command button class. The name of the instance actually is the same as the value you set for the Name property. As such, if you create a command button named cmdExit, you have created implicitly an object reference named cmdExit. The previous statements, however, do not create a class instance. Rather, they create a variable that can reference a class instance. The object variable, pcmdRef1, can be assigned to reference an existing command button like cmdExit.

Object variables are assigned, using the Set statement. The Set statement is a type of assignment statement for assigning object references and creating objects. The left-hand side of the assignment statement must contain an object variable. The right-hand side of the assignment statement must evaluate to an object.

Syntax **Set** *objectvar* = {[**New**] *objectexpression* | **Nothing**}

Dissection The required *objectvar* must be a variable declared as a specific object, generic Object type, or Variant.

The optional **New** keyword is used to create a new object instance. It only is valid with externally creatable objects.

The required *objectexpression* can be the name of an existing object like a command button. It also can be an object variable of a compatible type. Finally, the expression can be a property or method that returns an object variable of a compatible type.

The optional **Nothing** keyword is used to destroy the reference between *objectvar* and the object it referenced. If there are other references to the object, the object will continue to exist. Otherwise, the memory allocated to the object, thus the object itself, will be destroyed.

Code Example

```
Dim pcmdRef1 As CommandButton, pcmdRef2 As CommandButton
Dim mdbCurrent As Database
Set pcmdRef1 = cmdExit
pcmdRef1.Caption = "Exit"
Set pcmdRef2 = pcmdRef1
Set pcmdRef1 = Nothing
Set mdbCurrent = OpenDatabase("demodb.mdb")
```

Code Dissection The first Set statement assumes that cmdExit is an instance of a command button. It assigns pcmdRef1 to reference the existing command button. Thus, pcmdRef1 and cmdExit can be used to reference the command button interchangeably. By setting the Caption property of pcmdRef1, the Caption property of the command button named cmdExit is set. When pcmdRef1 is set to Nothing, the reference is destroyed. The command button named cmdExit continues to exist, however, and also can be referenced by the object variable named pcmdRef2. The second Set statement causes pcmdRef2 to reference the object pointed to by pcmdRef1. Thus, pcmdRef2 and pcmdRef1 both reference the same command button named cmdExit. The final statement assumes that mdbCurrent is an object variable of type Database. The OpenDatabase method creates a Database object. A reference to the Database object is stored in the object variable mdbCurrent.

Figure 4-11 illustrates object references.

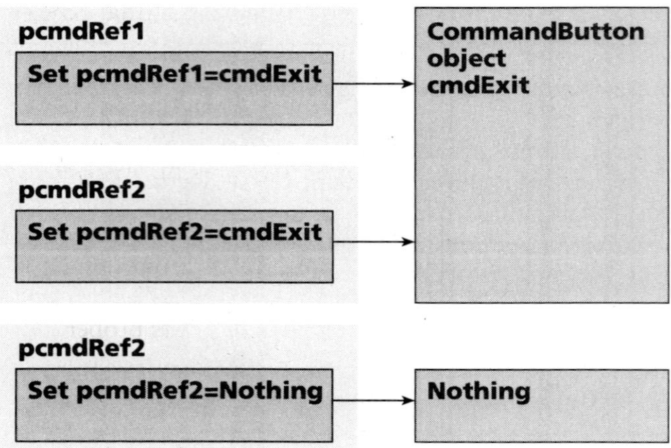

Figure 4-11: Object references

In Figure 4-11, two object variables named pcmdRef1 and pcmdRef2 reference the same CommandButton object. If an assignment statement were used to set pcmdRef2 to Nothing, then the object variable would no longer reference a command button.

Creating Instances of Objects

The New keyword can be used both when declaring object variables and with the Set statement. Whether or not the New keyword can be used depends on whether or not an object is an externally creatable object or a dependant object. Externally creatable objects can be created with the New keyword. Many applications like Microsoft Word and Excel, provide externally creatable objects. For example, the following statements are valid to create an instance of a Word and Excel application, respectively. Multiple form instances also can be created with the New keyword.

```
Dim pobjWord As Object, pobjExcel As Object
Set pobjWord = New Word.Application
Set pobjExcel = New Excel.Application
```

A dependant object only can be created using a property or method of another object. For example, a recordset only can be created by calling the OpenRecordset method of a database. Controls are considered dependant objects. It is not possible to create a new control instance with the New keyword. For example, the following Set statement will cause a syntax error:

```
Dim cmdError As CommandButton
Set cmdError = New CommandButton
```

Collections of Objects

An integral part of programming with objects in Visual Basic involves using a collection. A **collection** is similar to an array but supplies functionality beyond arrays. Arrays can store intrinsic data types like Integers and Strings. They also can store references to objects. For example, it is possible to create an array to reference command buttons, forms, or any other object. When using arrays, however, it is necessary to search an array for a particular item. Also, if the size of an array is not known at design time, it is necessary to redimension the array at run time as new elements are added. If an array element is deleted, keeping track of the deleted element also is the responsibility of the programmer.

Collections solve many of these problems. A collection can be thought of as an object-based implementation of an array. It supports properties and methods to keep track of the number of members in the collection. Collections also provide a mechanism to access a collection member using a unique string key without having to search each individual collection member. There also are methods to add and delete members from a collection. The following list describes the properties and methods of most collections. Some collections are more robust than others and supply additional properties and methods.

Object	Collection
Properties	The **Count** property contains the number of items in the collection.
Methods	The **Add** method adds a new member to a collection. The **Item** method uses either a numeric index or a string key to locate a specific item in a collection. This is typically the default method of a collection. The **Remove** method deletes an item from a collection.

There are several intrinsic collections that keep track of the control instances on a form, and the forms themselves. The printers installed on the computer also are managed using a collection.

It is possible to iterate through the items in a collection in the same way as an array. Remember that arrays are by default zero-based. That is, the first element in an array has an index of zero (0). Using the Option Base statement, the default lower bound of an array can be changed to one (1). Collections are also zero-based or one-based. The lower bound of a collection cannot be changed, however. Whether a collection is zero-based or one-based depends on the collection itself. Collections created in earlier versions of Visual Basic generally are zero-based. Collections created in newer versions of Visual Basic tend to be one-based, because it generally is agreed that one-based collections are more intuitive. Before using a collection, refer to the Help system to determine if a specific collection is one-based or zero-based.

The Controls collection, because it has been around since the beginning of Visual Basic, is zero-based. The Controls collection contains a reference to each control instance drawn on a form. It is useful for setting the properties of several controls at once. A For loop can be used to examine each element in an array or each member of a collection. Consider the following statements:

```
Dim pintCurrent As Integer
For pintCurrent = 0 to Controls.Count - 1
    Debug.Print Controls.Item(pintCurrent).Name
Next
```

These statements print the Name property of each control drawn on a form. This is accomplished with a For loop. The loop is initialized to zero (0), the first member of the Controls collection, and incremented to the value of the Count property minus one (-1). This is similar to referencing a zero-based array. The Controls collection, like other collections, supports the Item method to examine a specific element in the collection.

Because the Item method is the default method for the Controls collection, the statement inside the previous For Loop usually is abbreviated to:

```
Debug.Print Controls(pintCurrent).Name
```

Getting back to the concept of a pointer, a collection does not store the objects themselves. Rather, it stores a reference to the individual objects or in other words, pointers to the objects. The statement fragment Controls(pintCurrent) provides a reference to a specific control. Using that reference you can access any property or method, just as the control name had been used.

While the For loop is useful to iterate through the members of a collection, there is a variation of a For loop called the For Each loop that is designed specifically to examine all the members of a collection.

Syntax

For Each *element* **In** *group*
    [*statements*]
[**Exit For**]
    [*statements*]
Next [*element*]

Dissection

The required *element* must be an object variable of the same type as the objects in the collection, a general Object, or Variant. That is, if you wanted to examine each Control object in the Controls collection, *element* must be declared as a Control object type, a Variant data type, or an Object data type.

The required *group* defines the collection you want to examine.

The optional *statements* execute until there are no more *elements* in the collection.

The **Exit For** statement has the same effect as in an ordinary For loop. When executed, the For Each loop terminates and the statement following the **Next** statement is executed.

Code Example

```
Dim pctlCurrent As Control
For Each pctlCurrent In Controls
    Debug.Print pctlCurrent.Name
Next
```

Code Dissection This For Each loop performs the same task as the previous For loop. It is not necessary to create a variable to count expressly the members of the collection. The statement works by storing in the variable pctlCurrent, a reference to a control in the Controls collection. Each time through the loop, pctlCurrent references the next control in the collection.

Another keyword commonly used with a collection is the TypeOf keyword. The statement can be used to determine the underlying type of any object variable commonly used in an If statement.

Syntax **If TypeOf** *objectname* **Is** *objecttype* **Then** ...

Dissection The *objectname* can be any valid object variable reference.

The *objecttype* can be any object class.

Notes Note that the TypeOf statement is used inside an If...Then...Else statement. The full syntax of the If block has been omitted.

Code Example

```
Dim pctlCurrent As Control
For Each pctlCurrent In Controls
    If TypeOf pctlCurrent Is TextBox Then
        pctlCurrent.FontSize = 12
    End If
Next
```

Code Dissection These statements again use the Controls collection to examine each control instance on a form. If the type of the control is a TextBox (this is the class name for a text box), then the FontSize property is set to 12 points. As you can see, this is a useful way to set the same properties for several controls at once.

In addition to the Controls collection there is a Forms collection. There is one Forms collection per project and it lists each of the loaded forms. In addition to the Forms and Controls collection there are several other collections. In fact, many applications, like the Jet database engine, have an interface made up of objects and collections. These objects are organized into an inverted tree structure or hierarchy.

One way to improve the program's user interface, is to unlock the text boxes when the current record is in edit mode and lock the text boxes otherwise. This way, the user only can edit the text boxes when appropriate. In addition, it also would be reasonable to enable and disable the text boxes. The following code already exists in the EditState function:

```
If State = Editing Then
    For Each ctlCurrent In Controls
        If TypeOf ctlCurrent Is TextBox Then
            ctlCurrent.Locked = False
        End If
    Next
    . . .
Else
    For Each ctlCurrent In Controls
        If TypeOf ctlCurrent Is TextBox Then
            ctlCurrent.Locked = True
        End If
    Next
    . . .
End If
```

These statements use the Controls collection to examine each control on the form. Only the Locked property is to be changed for the text boxes so the TypeOf statement is used to determine whether or not the control is a text box.

Using a Database Programmatically

Visual Basic and nearly any other programming language can access Jet by using object variables and their properties and methods. Remember an object is defined by its interface. The interface is made up of a fixed number of properties, methods, and event responses. Accessing Jet is accomplished not by a single object like a command button, but with several objects. In this section, you will learn the fundamentals of how to open databases and recordsets without the aid of the Data control using the objects supported by Jet.

When Jet is accessed programmatically, you are referencing the objects of another program. This is accomplished using a technology known as Component Object Modules (COM). COM defines a standard for accessing the interface of another program's objects. Many different programs expose themselves using COM objects including Microsoft Office 97 programs like Excel, Word, and PowerPoint.

Before a Visual Basic program can use another program's objects, the program's objects must be made available. This is accomplished by adding to the project, a reference to the other program's object or type library. A **type library** is a file that contains the information about the exposed properties and methods that make up the interface of the class. Object libraries are added to a project using the References dialog. This dialog is shown in Figure 4-12.

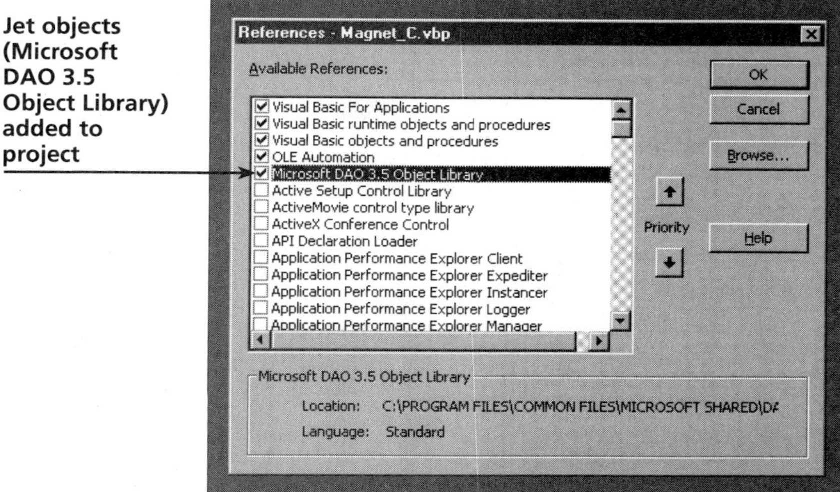

Figure 4-12: The References dialog

As shown in Figure 4-12, there are several programs on a system that expose themselves as objects programmable from Visual Basic. The list of references will differ depending on the software installed on your computer.

One such set of objects is collectively referred to as the **Data Access Object (DAO)**. DAO is a well-defined group of collections and objects that allow a Visual Basic program, and many other programs for that matter, to communicate with Jet.

To insert reference to another program's objects in a project:

1. Click **Projects** then **References** to open the References dialog.
2. Locate the item **Microsoft DAO 3.5 Object Library.**
3. Make sure the check box is checked. Click **OK** to close the dialog.

As mentioned previously, Jet's interface is made up of an exposed set of objects and collections, and these objects and collections are organized into an inverted tree structure or hierarchy. At the top of the DAO hierarchy is the DBEngine object. The DBEngine object contains all the objects in the DAO hierarchy and is the interface you use to work with the Microsoft Jet database engine. You do not create an instance of the DBEngine; rather it is predefined. This is a rare instance where you do not declare an object variable before using it.

When the Microsoft Jet database engine first is accessed, a session is created, and the session is destroyed when the Microsoft Jet database engine is closed. A **session** contains all the open databases for a user. In DAO, a session is implemented as a Workspaces collection containing one or more Workspace objects. When the DBEngine object is created for you, the Workspaces collection also is created and a single Workspace object is created in the Workspaces collection. This is known as the Default Workspace object. The **Default Workspace object** is a Workspace object, created automatically when you connect to the Microsoft Jet database engine. Usually, only one session is necessary for a user, hence one Workspace object is in the Workspaces collection. It is possible to create multiple sessions, thus creating multiple Workspace objects. Figure 4-13 shows the relationship between the DBEngine object and the Workspaces collection.

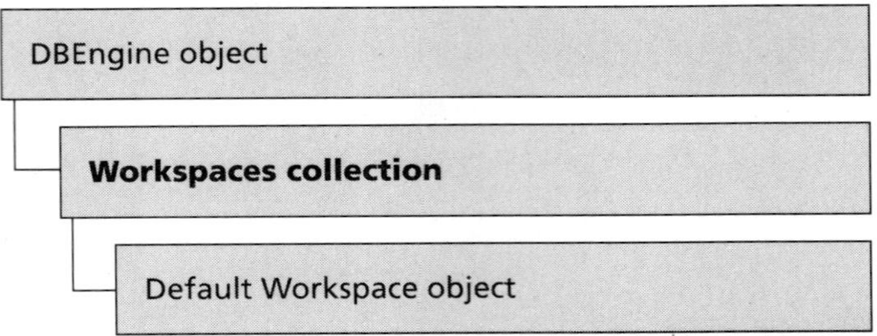

Figure 4-13: Relationship between DBEngine and Workspaces collection

To reference the Workspaces collection, you would write the following statement fragment:

```
DBEngine.Workspaces
```

Although this statement references the Workspaces collection, you need a way to reference an individual Workspace object stored in the collection. Most collections allow you to access an individual object in a collection in two ways.

- You always can use a numeric index to reference an individual object in a collection.
- Most collections allow you to reference an object using a string key. A **string key** is a string that uniquely identifies the object in a collection. A string key provides a more intuitive way to reference each object in a collection.

Because the Workspaces collection is zero-based, the Default Workspace object (the first item in the collection) has an index of zero (0). The string key for the Default Workspace object is #Default Workspace#. To reference the Default Workspace object (the Workspace object created by Jet), you could write the following equivalent statements:

```
Dim pwspCurrent As Workspace
Set pwspCurrent = DBEngine.Workspaces.Item(0)
Set pwspCurrent = DBEngine.Workspaces.Item _
    ("#Default Workspace#")
Set pwspCurrent = DBEngine.Workspaces(0)
Set pwspCurrent = DBEngine.Workspaces("#Default Workspace#")
```

Each of these statements produces the same result. The first two statements use the Item method to reference the default workspace by numeric index and by string key, respectively. The second two statements omit the Item method because it is the default method of the Workspaces collection.

The Database Object

Each Workspace object contains a reference to a collection called the Databases collection. This collection is empty until a database is opened. When a database is opened, a Database object is created and a reference to the object added to the Databases collection. If there is one open database, then the Databases collection contains a reference to one Database object. If there are two open databases, then the Databases collection contains a reference to two Database objects, and so on. Figure 4-14 shows the relationship between the Workspaces and Databases collections and the objects that they contain.

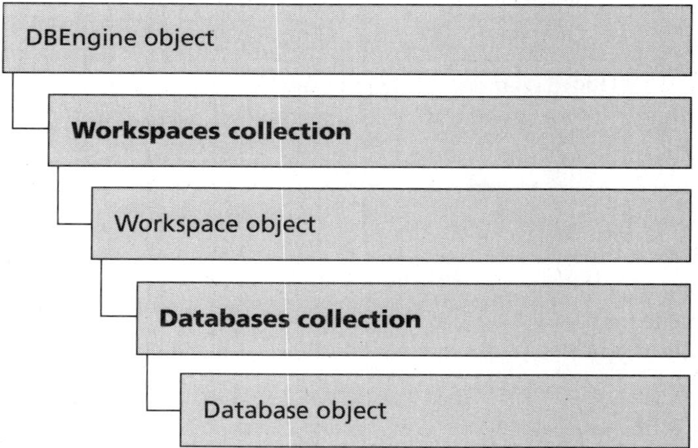

Figure 4-14: Relationship between Workspaces and Databases collection

Opening a database programmatically is accomplished by calling the OpenDatabase method, which applies to the Workspace object. This statement is executed for you automatically when the Data control is used. The OpenDatabase method has the following syntax:

Syntax — **Set** *database* = *workspace*.**OpenDatabase** (*dbname*, *options*, *read-only*, *connect*)

Dissection

The required *database* argument is an object variable. After the OpenDatabase method is called, a reference to the open database is stored in *database*.

The optional *workspace* argument, if omitted, will open the database in the *default workspace*. If specified, the database will be opened in the specified *workspace*.

The required *dbname* argument is a String data type containing the folder and file of the database to open.

	The optional *options* argument can be True or False. If True, the database is opened for exclusive access. If False, the default, the database can be opened by multiple processes. The optional *read-only* argument can be True or False. If True, data cannot be written to the database. If False, the default, the database is open for read-write access. The optional *connect* argument is a Variant data type (String subtype) that specifies various connection information, including passwords.

Code Example	`Dim pdbCurrent As Database`
	`Set pdbCurrent = _`
	`    DBEngine.Workspaces(0). _`
	`    OpenDatabase("A:\Chapter.04\Magnet.mdb")`

Code Dissection	These statements declare a variable named pdbCurrent of type Database. Because the OpenDatabase method pertains to a Workspace object, the syntax DBEngine.Workspaces(0) is used to reference the Default Workspace object. Thus, the Set statement opens a database in the Default Workspace object and assigns a reference to the newly-created Database object in the object variable pdbCurrent.

Just as an object has a default method or property, some methods are applied to a specific object unless explicitly specified. For example, the OpenDatabase method applies to the Default Workspace object unless a Workspace object is specified explicitly. Thus, the previous Set statement could be abbreviated to the following:

```
Set pdbCurrent = OpenDatabase("A:\Chapter.04\Magnet.mdb")
```

Like any other object, the Database object supports several properties and methods.

Object	**Database**
Properties	The **Name** property contains the full path and file name of the database. The **Version** property of a Database object corresponds to a version of the Microsoft Jet database engine.
Methods	The **Close** method closes an open Database object. This has the same effect as setting a Database object to Nothing. The **CreateTableDef** method creates a new table in the open database. The **Execute** method runs an SQL statement on the open database. SQL statements are discussed in the next chapter. The **OpenRecordset** method opens a recordset. This has the effect of creating a new Recordset object, which is added to the Recordsets collection.

To open a database programmatically:

1 Activate the Code window for the event procedure named **mnuFilePrint_Click** and enter the following statements:

```
Dim pdbCurrent As Database
Dim pstrFileName As String
    pstrFileName = InputBox("Enter File Name", _
    "Magnet Distributing", _
    "A:\Chapter.04\Startup\Magnet.mdb")
Set pdbCurrent = OpenDatabase(pstrFileName)
Debug.Print pdbCurrent.Name
Debug.Print pdbCurrent.Version
```

2 Test the program. On the menu bar, click **File** then **Print** to print the database name and version in the Immediate window.

These statements open the database named Magnet.mdb. The database is opened in the Default Workspace object because no Workspace object was specified explicitly. Because an object reference is being assigned, the Set statement is required. The Name and Version properties of the Database object are referenced using the object variable pdbCurrent.

The TableDef Object

Each Database object contains several other collections. For example, each Database object contains a collection named TableDefs. This collection contains zero (0) or more TableDef objects representing the different tables in your database. There is one TableDef object for each table in the database. Figure 4-15 shows the relationship between the TableDefs collection and TableDef object to the other objects in the DAO hierarchy.

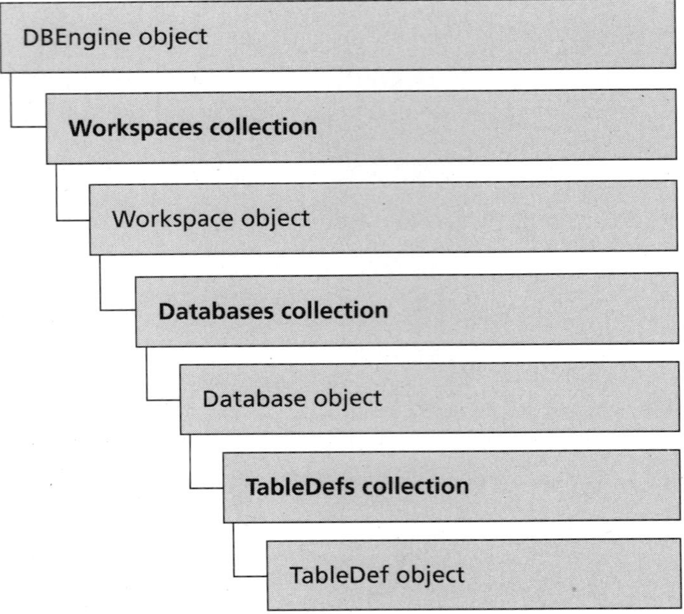

Figure 4-15: Relationship between TableDefs collection and TableDef object

The following list describes some of the common properties and methods supported by the TableDef object.

Object	TableDef
Properties	The **Name** property indicates the name of the table. This is the same name used to specify a table name to the Data control. The **RecordCount** property indicates the number of records in the table. The **DateCreated** property returns the date and time that the TableDef object was created. The **LastUpdated** property returns the date and time of the most recent change made to the TableDef object.
Methods	The **CreateField** method is used to create a new field in the table. The **CreateIndex** method is used to create a new index in the table. The **OpenRecordset** method creates a table-type recordset based on the specified table.

The syntax to reference a specific TableDef in a database requires you to reference a specific TableDef object in the TableDefs collection. Remember that objects in a collection can be referenced using a string key in addition to a numeric index. The string key of each TableDef object is the same as the value of the Name property or the name of the table. Consider the following two statements to reference the RecordCount property of the table named tblOrderMaster:

```
Debug.Print pdbCurrent.TableDefs("tblOrderMaster"). _
    RecordCount
Debug.Print DBEngine.Workspaces(0).Databases(0). _
    TableDefs("tblOrderMaster").RecordCount
```

Assuming pdbCurrent references a Database object, the first statement prints the number of records in the table named tblOrderMaster. A Database object contains a TableDefs collection, which in turn contains individual TableDef objects. In this case, the object is referenced by its string key. The second statement has the same effect as the first. Instead of using the Database object variable pdbCurrent to reference the database, the same object is referenced using the object in each collection. That is, the first database is stored in the Default Workspace object of the DBEngine object.

To examine the TableDefs collection:

1 Locate the **mnuFilePrint_Click** event procedure and append the following statements, shown in bold, to the event procedure:

```
    Dim pdbCurrent As Database
    Dim ptdfCurrent As TableDef
    . . .
    Debug.Print dbCurrent.Version
    For Each ptdfCurrent In pdbCurrent.TableDefs
        Debug.Print ptdfCurrent.Name
        Debug.Print ptdfCurrent.RecordCount
    Next
End Sub
```

2 Test the program. On the menu bar, click **File** then **Print** to print the database name and version, then the database tables in the Immediate window.

Like most collections, each object in the TableDefs collection can be examined using a For Each loop. The object variable ptdfCurrent is declared as a TableDef. This object variable references a TableDef object in the collection each time through the loop. The Debug.Print statements print the Name and RecordCount of each table in the database.

Several tables begin with the name MSys. These are called system tables and are used by Jet to manage various characteristics of the database. You neither should modify explicitly the contents or the structure of these tables, nor should these tables be removed. Doing so probably will corrupt the database making it unusable.

The Field Object

Just as each Database object has one TableDefs collection containing one TableDef object for each table, each TableDef object has a Fields collection. The Fields collection contains all the fields in a table. Each field is stored as a Field object in the Fields collection. Field objects have the "fld" prefix. Like a TableDef object, a Field object has properties. These properties define the name of the field, its data type, size, and other related attributes.

Object	Field
Properties	The **Name** property indicates the name of the field. This is the same name used to select a field name in a bound control like a text box. The **Type** property is used to set or return the data type of the field. Each data type can be represented by an intrinsic constant. For a listing of those constants, see Help on the "CreateField Method" for more information. The **Size** property sets or returns the maximum number of bytes for a Field object. For numeric fields, the size is set automatically when the Type property is set. For the Text data type, the Size property defines the maximum number of characters that can be stored in the field. The **Required** property is True if a Field object must contain a value, and False otherwise.

Figure 4-16 illustrates the relationship between the Fields collection and Field object to the other objects in the DAO hierarchy.

Each Field object in the Fields collection can be examined in the same way as each TableDef object was examined using a For Each loop.

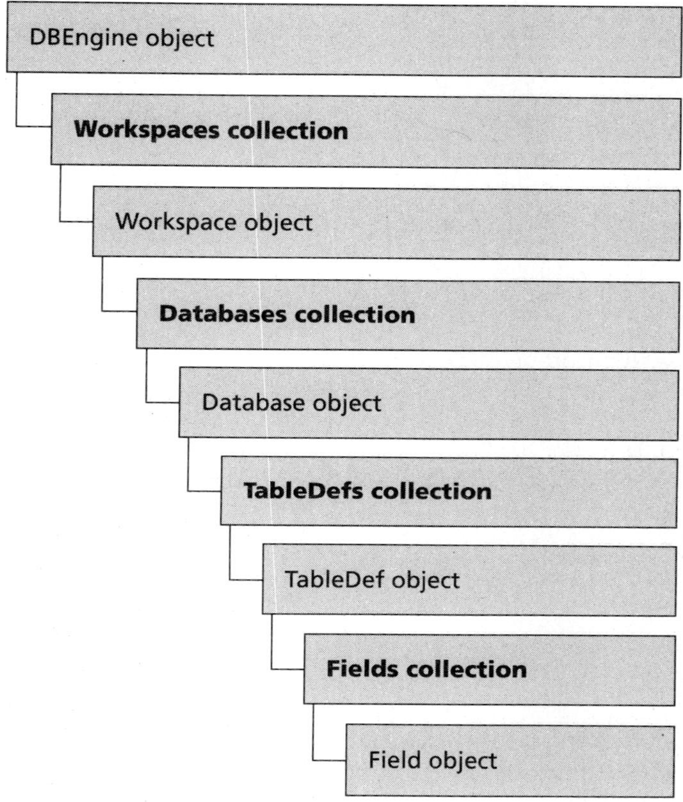

Figure 4-16: Relationship between Fields collection and Field object

To examine each field in the Fields collection:

1 Activate the Code window for the event procedure named **mnuFilePrint_Click** and enter the following statements shown in bold:

```
Dim ptdfCurrent As TableDef
Dim pfldCurrent As Field
. . .
    Debug.Print ptdfCurrent.RecordCount
    For Each pfldCurrent In ptdfCurrent.Fields
        Debug.Print pfldCurrent.Name
    Next
Next
```

2 Test the program. On the menu bar click **File** then **Print** to print the database, tables, and fields in the Immediate window.

This For Each loop examines each field in the current TableDef object. The reference to the current table is stored in the variable ptdfCurrent. The loop is nested inside the For Each loop that examines the TableDef objects. Thus, each field is examined in each table. Inside the For Each loop, the name of the field is printed.

Explicitly Opening a Recordset

The Database, TableDef, and Field objects are called persistent objects. That is, they exist while the database is open and between invocations. Recordsets, however, are not persistent objects. They only exist while the recordset is open. A recordset can be opened by the Data control or programmatically. Each Recordset object has a place in the DAO hierarchy. Each Database object contains a Recordsets collection. For each open recordset, there is an object in the Recordsets collection. Figure 4-17 shows the relationship between the Recordsets collection and the Recordset object in the DAO hierarchy.

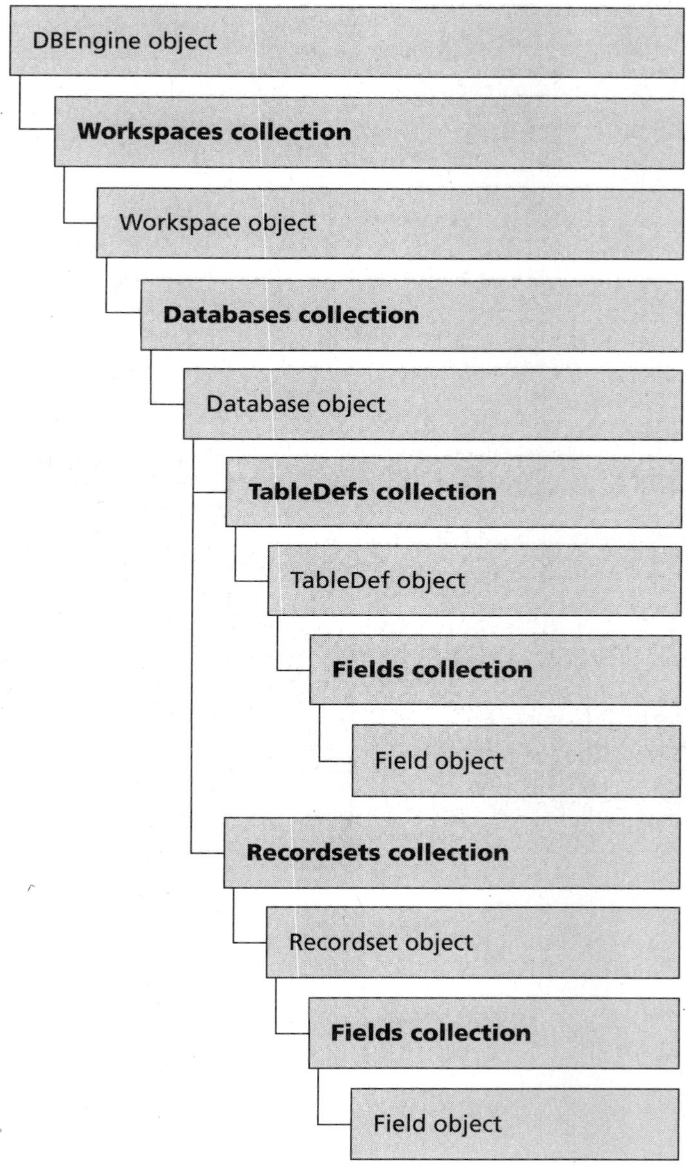

Figure 4-17: Relationship between Recordsets collection and Recordset object

Once the database has been opened, it also is possible to open a recordset. This is accomplished by calling one of the methods supported by the Database object called the OpenRecordset method.

Syntax	**Set** *recordset* = *object*.**OpenRecordset** (*source*, *type*, *options*, *lockedits*)
Dissection	The required *recordset* argument is an object variable. After the method is called, a reference to the open recordset is stored in *recordset.* The required *object* argument is typically an object of type Database. The database must have been opened previously with the OpenDatabase method. The required *source* argument is a String data type specifying the table or query from which the recordset is created. The argument can contain a table name or a query name. An SQL SELECT statement also can be used to create recordsets. This topic is described in the next chapter. The optional *type* argument indicates the type of recordset to open. Valid types of recordsets are identified by the constants dbOpenTable, dbOpenDynaset, dbOpenSnapshot, and dbOpenForwardOnly. The optional *options* argument contains the constants defining the actions allowable on a recordset. The optional *lockedits* argument contains the constants defining how records are locked. This is important when multiple users open the same database concurrently.

Code Example	`Dim pdbCurrent As Database, prstCurrent As Recordset`
	`Set pdbCurrent = _`
	`    OpenDatabase("A:\Chapter.04\Complete\Magnet.mdb")`
	`Set prstCurrent = _`
	`    OpenRecordset("tblOrderMaster",dbOpenTable)`

Code Dissection	These statements declare Database and Recordset type object variables, and then open a database. Assuming that tblOrderMaster is a table in the database, prstCurrent will contain a reference to the open recordset once the OpenRecordset method is called.

The options and lockedits arguments of the OpenRecordset method are particularly important in multi-user environments. When two or more users access a database concurrently, only one user can edit a specific record at the same time. This process is called **locking.** That is, a record is locked by a user and unavailable to other users. Jet supports a type of locking called page-level locking. Instead of working with a single record at a time, Jet views records in 2K blocks called **pages.** Thus, if a record is smaller then 2K, then multiple records are stored on a page. When a record on a page is being edited, all the records on the page are locked rather than a single record. Jet supports two types of page locking called **pessimistic** and **optimistic locking.** When pessimistic locking is used, once the edit method is called on a recordset, the page containing the record is locked and remains locked until the Update method is called. When optimistic locking is used, the record is locked only when the Update method is executing.

Error Handling

As you compile a program, the Visual Basic compiler detects syntax errors. It is possible for errors to occur at run time, however. Run-time errors can occur for several reasons as shown in the following list:

- Numeric overflow and numeric underflow errors occur when you attempt to store too large or to small a number in a variable. For example, the largest number allowable in an Integer data type is 32767. If you try to store a number larger than this in an Integer data type a run-time error will occur.
- Type conversion errors also may cause a run-time error. For example, if you try to perform arithmetic on String data types that cannot be converted to numbers, a run-time error will occur.
- Trying to perform an impossible action also will cause a run-time error. For example, if you try to open or read a file on the floppy disk and the disk is not inserted in the drive, a run-time error will occur.

In many cases, your program can prevent a run-time error from occurring by properly validating user input. For example, you could use the IsNumeric function on a string before using the value in a numeric expression. There are other cases when you cannot predict whether or not a run-time error will occur. In other words, a program cannot detect a numeric overflow condition until it happens. Nor can it detect that there is no floppy disk in the drive until the program tries to read a file on the disk.

If a run-time error occurs inside the Visual Basic IDE, a dialog will be displayed, the Code window will be activated, and the offending statement displayed. If the program has been compiled and is running outside the IDE, the user will receive a message and the program will end.

Remember that all executable statements must exist inside a procedure, whether it be a general Function, a Sub procedure, or an event procedure. While you cannot prevent run-time errors from occurring in a procedure, you can detect the error and execute code accordingly. This commonly is called **error trapping** and is implemented using an **error handler**. Error handling in Visual Basic is supported at the procedure level. That is, any procedure can implement an error handler. If a procedure implements an error handler, there is an **enabled error handler** for the procedure. When a run-time error occurs in the procedure, the code for the enabled error handler will execute. This is called an **active error handler**. An error handler is not a separate procedure. Rather, a procedure with an enabled error handler contains additional statements to process the error.

When a run-time error occurs, Visual Basic automatically sets the properties of an object called the Err object.

Object	Err
Properties	The **Number** property contains the numerical value of the error. If no error has occurred, the value of Number is zero (0). The **Source** property contains the name of the current Visual Basic project. The **Description** property contains a String data type corresponding to the error number if one exists. If not, the description contains a string like "Application-defined or object-defined error".
Methods	The **Raise** method is used to generate explicitly a run-time error inside an application. Raising an error is common in class modules and ActiveX controls.

An error hander is enabled with the On Error statement, which has the following syntax and syntax variations:

Syntax

On Error GoTo *line*
On Error Resume Next
On Error GoTo 0

Dissection

- The **On Error GoTo** *line* syntax is used to execute the statement following *line*.
- The **On Error Resume Next** syntax causes execution to resume at the statement following the statement that caused the error.
- The **On Error GoTo 0** syntax disables error handling in the current procedure.

Code Example

```
On Error Resume Next
Set pdbCurrent = OpenDatabase(pstrFileName)
If Err.Number <> 0 Then
    Call MsgBox("Cannot open database.", _
        vbOKOnly + vbExclamation, "Magnet Distributing")
    Exit Sub
End If
```

Code Dissection

These statements attempt to open a database. Assume that pdbCurrent is declared as Database and pstrFileName contains an invalid file name. If an error occurs, the value of Err is not zero (0) indicating that an error has occurred. Because the Resume Next variation of the On Error statement is used, the statement following the statement that called the error is executed next and the error is cleared.

When an error occurs in a procedure where there is an enabled error handler, the error handler is made active. The concept of an active error handler is important. Suppose a procedure generated run-time error like a numeric overflow error causing the enabled error handler to become active. If the error handler itself causes another run-time error to occur, that error cannot be trapped by the active error handler. Instead, the calling procedure is checked for an enabled error handler, and if one exists, it becomes active. It there is not an enabled error handler in the calling procedure, that procedure's calling procedure is checked for an error handler. This process continues until the entire call tree is examined.

Exiting an Error Handler

There are two statements used in an error handler that can be used to return control to a specific location in a procedure. These statements look much like the variations of the On Error statement and have the following syntax:

Syntax

Resume [0]
Resume Next
Resume *line*

Dissection

- The **Resume** statement is used in an error handler to resume execution at the statement that caused the error to occur.
- The **Resume Next** statement is used to resume execution at the statement following the statement that caused the error.
- The **Resume** *line* statement causes execution to continue at the statement following the *line* argument.

This section contains only the most fundamental concepts pertaining to error handling. The topic will be revisited throughout this book as necessary to detect the various run-time errors that can occur in your code. In addition to the Err object, there is another object named Error that is part of the DAO hierarchy. This object is discussed in Chapter 5.

SUMMARY

- A Visual Basic program can interact with a database using a Data control and Bound controls. The Data control takes care of moving data back and forth between the bound controls and the database. The Data control does this by creating a recordset at run time. The Data control supports the Validate event, which is used to verify the correctness of data before it is written to the database. The Reposition event occurs whenever a new record is located.
- The Recordset object is an integral part of reading and writing database data. It supports properties and methods to locate, add, change, and delete records. When the AddNew method is called, a new record is created in the copy buffer and written to the database when the Update method is called. Record editing is enabled when the Edit method is called. The Delete method removes records from the database.

- Like objects are grouped together in a collection. Collections are similar to arrays, but support methods to locate the objects in the collection. There are predefined collections like the Forms and Controls collections. These collections identify the loaded forms in a project and the controls on a form. The individual objects in a collection are implemented using a variation of the For loop called a For Each loop.
- The Jet database is made up of a group of objects referred to as DAO. DAO consists of collections and objects. The Databases collection contains a reference to each of the open databases. The Database object contains a TableDefs collection that lists all the tables in the database. It also contains the Recordsets collection, which contains all the open recordsets. Both the Recordset and TableDef objects contains a Fields collection that identifies the fields in the table or recordset. These are but a few of the DAO objects. There are other objects to manage the users and database security.
- Run-time errors can occur in programs that cannot be prevented. To trap a run-time error, you can create an error handler in a procedure to prevent the run-time error from terminating the program.

QUESTIONS

1. The ____________ property and the ____________ properties of the Data control identify the name of the database and table in the database that will be used to create a recordset.
   a. Database, Table
   b. DatabaseName, Recordset
   c. DatabaseName, RecordSource
   d. Database, Recordset
   e. none of the above
2. The Reposition event pertains to the Data control and occurs ____________.
   a. each time a new record is located
   b. when the buttons are clicked on the Data control
   c. when the user changes the contents of a bound text box
   d. both a and b
   e. all of the above
3. The ____________ and ____________ properties are used to bind a control, such as a text box to a Data control.
   a. Database, DataControl
   b. DataField, DataSource
   c. Table, Field
   d. DatabaseName, DataField
   e. none of the above
4. ____________ can be used as bound controls.
   a. Text boxes
   b. Labels
   c. Picture boxes
   d. Both a and b
   e. All of the above

5. The action argument of the Data control's Validate event is used to ___________.
   a. determine what caused the event to occur
   b. cancel the action that caused the Validate event to occur
   c. save the current record to the database
   d. both a and b
   e. all of the above
6. To locate a record in the recordset, you could use the following methods: ___________.
   a. FindFirst, MoveFirst, LocateFirst, MoveUp
   b. FindFirst, MoveFirst, FindNext, MoveNext
   c. FindLast, MoveLast
   d. both a and c
   e. either b or c
7. The ___________, ___________, and ___________ methods of the recordset are used to add, change, and delete records from the recordset.
   a. Add, Change, Delete
   b. Add, Update, Delete
   c. AddNew, Update, Delete
   d. Add, Update, Remove
   e. AddNew, Change, Delete
8. The ___________ keyword is used to destroy an object variable's reference to the underlying object.
   a. Nothing
   b. None
   c. Null
   d. Empty
   e. Variant
9. The ___________ property is used to determine the number of items in a collection.
   a. Index
   b. Item
   c. Count
   d. Number
   e. none of the above
10. ___________ are all valid DAO objects.
    a. Database, Table, Field
    b. Database, Table, Workspace, Field
    c. db, tbl, fld
    d. Database, TableDef, Field
    e. Both a and b
11. Write the statements to locate the first, next, previous, and last records in the recordset identified by the data control named **datCurrent**.
12. Create two If statements to determine whether the recordset named prstCurrent is at the beginning of file or end of file.
13. Write the statements to declare an object variable named **pcmdRef** of type CommandButton. Assign the object variable to an instance of a command button named **cmdExit**.

14. Write the statement to determine the number of items in the collection named **Controls** and store the result in the variable **pintControlCount**.
15. Write the necessary statements to declare a variable named **pdbCurrent** of type Database. Then open a database named **A:\Demo.mdb** and store the reference to the database in the variable pdbCurrent. Print the Name and Version properties in the Immediate window.
16. Write the Necessary statements to create a recordset named **prstCurrent** based on the table named **tblList**. Assume that an open database is stored in Database object variable pdbCurrent. For each record in the recordset, print the fields named **fldLastName** and **fldFirstName** in the Immediate window.
17. Write the necessary statements to find the text "John Smith" in the field named **fldName**. Use the Recordset named **prstCurrent**.
18. Write a For Each loop to print the Caption of all the labels on a form.
19. Assuming that pdbCurrent is an instance of a Database object, write the necessary statements to print the name of each table in the database.
20. Create a procedure named OpenDB that takes one argument, a file name to open, and then returns a Database object. The code in the procedure should open the database.

EXERCISES

1. In this exercise you will use the Controls collection to set the properties of different types of controls.
   a. Create a new project and set the Name property of the form to **frmExercise1**. Save the form using the name **Chapter.04\Exercise\frmExercise1.frm** and the project using the name **Chapter.04\Exercise\Exercise1.vbp**.
   b. Create three text boxes and three labels. There is no need to set any properties for these buttons. Their only purpose is to provide control instances so you can iterate the Controls collection.
   c. Create a command button named **cmdPrintName**. Write a For Each loop in the command button's Click event procedure to print the name of each control in the Immediate window.
   d. Create a Sub procedure named **SetVisible** that takes a Boolean argument. If the value is True, set the Visible property of all the text boxes on the form to Visible. Otherwise, set the property to False. Set the function to **False**.
   e. Create a command button named **cmdSetInvisible**. The code for this procedure should call the SetVisible function.
   f. Save the project and test that the loops are working correctly.

For each of the following exercises, use the Database named **Chapter.04\Exercise\ Lida.mdb**. The database has the following structure:

tblSales		**tblCustomers**	
fldSalesID	Integer	fldCustomerID	Integer
fldSalesAmount	Single	fldCustomerName	String
fldSalesCost	Single	fldCustomerAddress	String
fldSalesDate	Date		

2. In this exercise you will use the Data control to display each of the different fields in the table named **tblSales**.
   a. Create a new project and set the Name property of the form to **frmExercise2.** Save the form using the name **Chapter.04\Exercise\frmExercise2.frm** and the project using the name **Chapter.04\Exercise\Exercise2.vbp.**
   b. Create an instance of the Data control on the form. Set the properties so the Data control will connect to the database named **Chapter.04\Exercise\Lida.mdb** and the table named **tblSales.**
   c. Create text boxes to display the fields in the table named **tblSales.**
   d. Create prompts for each of the text boxes.
   e. Write the code for the Reposition event to compute the sales profit. The sales profit can be computed by subtracting the sales amount from the sales cost.
   f. Write the code for the Validate event to verify that the fields are valid before changes are written to the database. That is the sales date must be a valid Date value and the other fields must contain numbers.
   g. Test the program as necessary. As you make changes to the database as you test it, you may want to make a copy of the Database file Lida.mdb before proceeding.
3. In this exercise you will use the methods of the Recordset object to locate, add, change, and delete records in a database.
   a. Create a new project and set the Name property of the form to **frmExercise3.** Save the form using the name **Chapter.04\Exercise\frmExercise3.frm** and the project using the name **Chapter.04\Exercise\Exercise3.vbp.**
   b. Create an instance of the Data control on the form. Set the properties so the Data control will connect to the database named **Chapter.04\Exercise\Lida.mdb** and the table named **tblSales.** Set the Visible property to False. The user will not interact with the Data control at run time.
   c. Create the necessary bound text boxes to display the four fields in the table **tblSales.**
   d. Create a menu named **Find** with the following menu commands: **First, Next, Previous,** and **Last.**
   e. Write the code for these menu commands to locate the first, next, previous, and last record, respectively.
   f. Write the necessary code to disable the **Next** menu command when the last record is the current record and disable the **Previous** menu command when the first record is the current record.
   g. Create another menu with the following menu commands: **Add, Edit, Update, Delete,** and **Abandon.**
   h. Write the code for these menu commands to add a new record, enable editing on the current record, record the changes to the current record, delete the current record, and abandon the changes made to the current record.
   i. Create a function named **EditState** like the one used in the completed program in this chapter so the commands are enabled or disabled as necessary depending on whether or not the current record is being edited or not.
   j. Test the program as necessary.

4. In this exercise you will examine the objects in a database.

a. Create a new project and set the Name property of the form to **frmExercise4**. Save the form using the name **Chapter.04\Exercise\frmExercise4.frm** and the project using the name **Chapter.04\Exercise\Exercise4.vbp**.

b. Create a menu named **File** with two commands—**Open** and **Exit**.

c. When the Open command is executed, display an input box to get a file name from the user.

d. Write the necessary code to open the database specified by the user. If the action causes an error because the file does not exist or because the file is not a database file, trap the error and display an error message to the Immediate window.

e. If the database is opened successfully, display all the tables in a list box.

f. In the Click event procedure for the list box, write the necessary code to display all the fields pertaining to the selected table.

g. Test the program as necessary.

CHAPTER

5

Accessing a Database with SQL and ActiveX Controls

case▶ IGA Travel is a travel agency with offices in 37 states. Their existing payroll system is no longer adequate for the size of their business. In this chapter, you will help IGA create a new program to manage their payroll processing. The tasks for this project include computing payroll, updating the salaries of employees, and deleting obsolete payroll records. The system also includes functions to select employees and view their corresponding payroll records.

SECTION A

objectives

In this section you will:

- Use SQL
- Create a recordset using a SELECT statement
- Add, change, and delete data using the INSERT, UPDATE, and DELETE statements
- Use unbound controls with a database
- Group database statements into transactions

Introduction to the SQL Programming Language

Previewing the Completed Application

The completed payroll application for IGA Travel contains three new controls that you have not used before. These controls are called: the DBGrid, DBCombo, and DBList boxes. They work like other bound controls. The DBCombo and DBList boxes, however, display multiple rows from a single field in a table, and the DBGrid control displays multiple rows and columns from a specific table. In addition, the program uses a language called the Structured Query Language (SQL) to perform operations on the records in a table. **SQL** is a language specifically designed to manipulate database information. SQL statements can be used to add, update, and delete records.

To review the completed program:

1 Start **Visual Basic** and open the project named **Chapter.05\Complete\ IGA_C.vbp.**

2 Run the program. The main form in the program is shown in Figure 5-1. Click the list arrow on the Category DBCombo control to display all the different categories.

3 Click the buttons on the Payroll Master Data control. The category corresponding to the selected payroll record is changed automatically.

DBCombo control

Payroll Master Data control

Figure 5-1: IGA Startup form

4 Click **View** then **Payroll Detail** to view the Payroll Detail form. Figure 5-2 shows the Payroll Detail form with the employee named "Andy Wilson" selected. The payroll detail records for Andy Wilson are displayed in the DBGrid control.

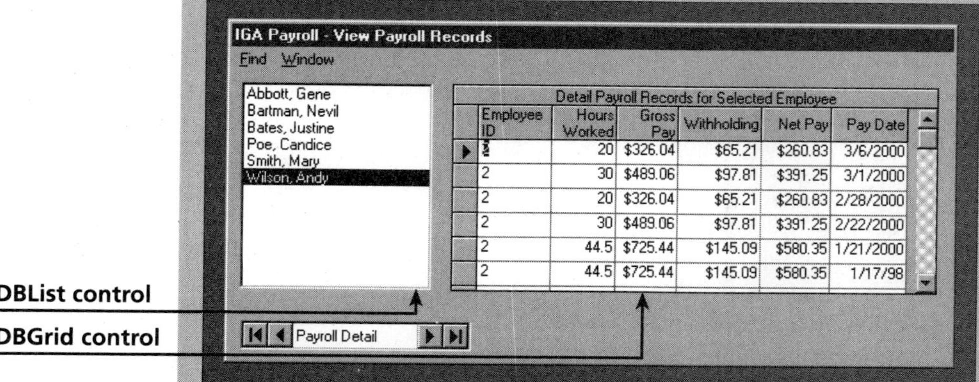

Employee ID	Hours Worked	Gross Pay	Withholding	Net Pay	Pay Date
2	20	$326.04	$65.21	$260.83	3/6/2000
2	30	$489.06	$97.81	$391.25	3/1/2000
2	20	$326.04	$65.21	$260.83	2/28/2000
2	30	$489.06	$97.81	$391.25	2/22/2000
2	44.5	$725.44	$145.09	$580.35	1/21/2000
2	44.5	$725.44	$145.09	$580.35	1/17/98

Figure 5-2: Payroll Detail form

5 As shown in Figure 5-2, the form contains two new controls. The DBList control obtains the rows in the list directly from a field in the database. The DBGrid control displays the payroll detail records corresponding to the selected name.

6 Select different names in the list box by clicking the name. The records corresponding to the selected name are displayed in the DBGrid control. DBGrid controls also can be linked together. Close the form by clicking **Window** then **Close**.

7 Then, from the menu on the main form, click **View** then **Linked DBGrids**. This form is shown in Figure 5-3.

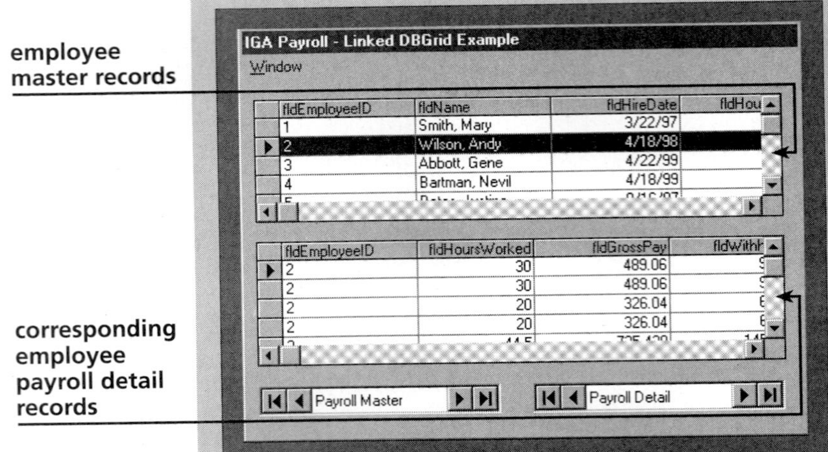

Figure 5-3: Linking DBGrid controls

As shown in Figure 5-3, there are two DBGrid controls. The first DBGrid control displays all the employee master records. When the user selects a master record, the payroll detail records corresponding to the selected employee are displayed in the second DBGrid control.

8 Click the different rows in the DBGrid control at the top of the form. As different employees are selected, the payroll records are displayed in the DBGrid control at the bottom of the form. Close the form.

9 Click **View** then **Unbound Controls**. This form contains a list box and output labels. Click items in the list box. The information pertaining to the name displayed in the list box appears in the output labels. While you have seen these controls previously, they are used in an unbound mode and the code for the program explicitly manages which is the current record and synchronizes the current record with the output labels.

The Form_Load event procedure for this form assumes that the database has a path name of A:\Chapter.05\Complete\. If you are using a different drive, change the path name as needed.

10 Exit Visual Basic.

The database for this program contains three tables named tblPayrollMaster, tblPayrollDetail, and tblCategory.

- The table named tblPayrollMaster contains the name, hourly wage, and other information pertaining to an employee. There is one record in this table for each employee.
- The table named tblCategory can be thought of as a lookup table. The field fldCategoryID in the table tblPayrollMaster contains an Integer value that corresponds to a description stored in the field fldCategoryDescription in the table named tblCategory.

- The table named tblPayrollDetail contains multiple records for one employee. That is, it contains a record for each employee each time the employee was paid.

Figure 5-4 illustrates the structure of the database.

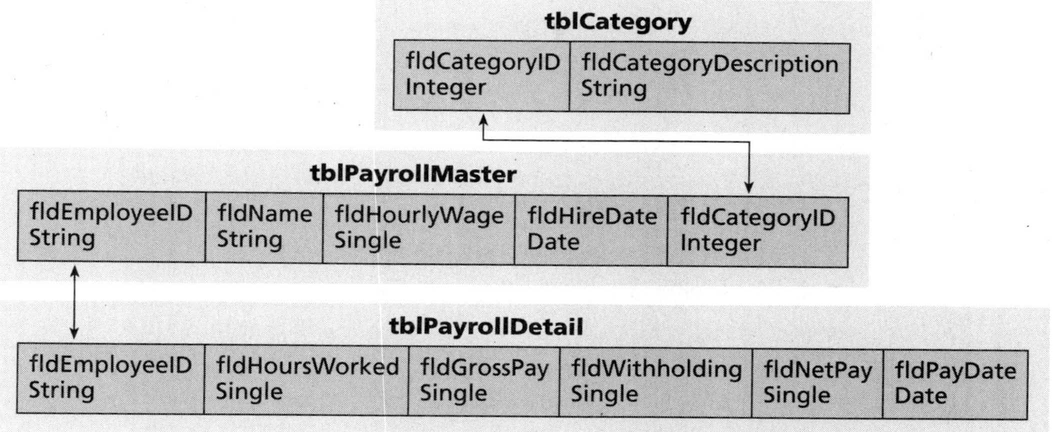

Figure 5-4: Database structure

The SQL Language

In the previous chapter, you learned how to use the Data control along with bound controls to view a record in a table, and navigate through the records in a table. You also saw how to create programmatically a recordset from an underlying table. Record insertion and modification were accomplished using bound controls and the underlying methods of the Recordset object. In each case, the program added, changed, and deleted data, one record at a time. Furthermore, locating a specific record was accomplished by moving from one record to the next. While this type of interface is fine for tasks that operate on a single record, performing the same task on several records would require a loop. While this approach works, it requires more coding. For example, imagine a payroll table where each employee needs to receive a 10% salary increase. Using a recordset, it is necessary to examine each record in a Do loop and update the appropriate field. Consider a similar situation where it is necessary to delete or archive obsolete information like old sales or accounts payable history. Again, it would be necessary to examine each record with a Do loop. Inside of the Do loop, an If statement would be necessary to determine whether or not the current record should be deleted. In each case, performing the same operations on a number of records requires a Do loop to examine all the records and statements inside the Do loop to perform a specific task on each record. This form of database access commonly is referred to as the **navigational model** or **navigational access**, because navigating from record to record performs tasks.

In addition to the navigational model, it also is possible to create a single statement that will modify the contents of several database records at the same time based on some criteria. In other words, a single statement can be written to update the salary field of the payroll table for all records or perform the same task on specific records, like those having a specific pay date. That is, you can write one statement to update only those records where the length of employment is greater than five years or specify some other criteria. Record deletion can be performed similarly. That is, you can delete all payroll records with a pay date that is seven-years-old or older. This method of data access is called **relational access** or the **relational model**.

IBM originally developed the Structured Query Language (SQL) in the early 1970s. Since that time, SQL has evolved into the de facto standard language for manipulating database information. Today, nearly every manufacturer of database management systems provides support for the SQL language. Visual Basic allows you to tap into the power of SQL using the same Jet engine objects used in the previous chapter.

When creating programs that operate with the Jet engine, you must decide when to use the Data control and bound controls, and when to write SQL statements. In situations where the user needs to navigate through different records and edit those records one at a time, using the Data control and bound controls is more suitable. In other situations, where the same task can be performed on many records at the same time, using the SQL statements may be more appropriate. Using SQL does not preclude using the Data control or vice versa. In fact, the two techniques can complement each other. In the previous chapter, you set the RecordSource property to the name of an existing table or query in a Jet database. SQL statements can be built dynamically at run time, however. Setting the RecordSource property to a valid SQL statement at run time and calling the Refresh method of the Data control, will cause the SQL statement to be executed, and the recordset recreated based on the results of the SQL statement. Any changes to the recordset are reflected in any controls bound to the Data control. The following guidelines will help you determine when to use the Data control and when to use SQL statements:

- When using bound controls including text boxes, DBList, DBCombo, or DBGrid controls, a Data control must be used. The Data control's active recordset, however, can be replaced by changing the RecordSource property at run time.
- When the rows selected in a recordset need to be changed at run time, an SQL statement should be used.
- When performing the same operations on a number of rows, an SQL statement should be used.
- It is possible to use controls like text boxes in an unbound mode. Data can be copied from a recordset into the text boxes by writing code. Using this method, however, it is necessary to write statements to retrieve the information from the recordset and display it in the contents of the text boxes when the current record changes. Furthermore, it is necessary to write code to locate, add, change, and delete records. This option is most suitable when you want to control, with finer granularity, the processing of a recordset than that provided by the Data control.

There are two ways to execute SQL statements from Visual Basic. The first is to use the Data control and set the RecordSource property to a valid SQL statement instead of a table name. After setting the RecordSource, the Data control's Refresh method should be called to execute the SQL statement and recreate the recordset. The second is to use the OpenRecordset and Execute methods supported by the Database object. The OpenRecordset method was described in the previous chapter. Whether to use the OpenRecordset or Execute method depends on whether or not the SQL statement creates a recordset; that is, returns records. There are two types of SQL queries. One, called an **action query**, performs an action like updating or deleting records but does not return any records. An action query is suitable for inserting, updating, or deleting records. The other, called a **select query** or **selection query,** executes an SQL statement and returns a Recordset object. This Recordset object can be manipulated in the same way as the recordsets created by the Data control at run time. A select query is suitable any time when you want to display records in bound controls, or use a loop to process records individually.

SQL statements are divided into two groups. The first group of statements is used to modify the structure of a database; these statements are referred to collectively as Data Definition Language (DDL) statements. The second group is used to retrieve, insert, update, and delete the data contained in a database. These statements are referred to as Data Manipulation Language (DML) statements. SQL consists of four DML statements as shown in Figure 5-5.

The four DML statements appear as all uppercase characters. This is a common convention used when writing SQL statements. The convention of capitalizing SQL statements and clauses will be followed in this book. Refer to the Help topics "CREATE TABLE statement" and "CREATE INDEX statement" for more information on DDL statements.

Statement	Description
INSERT	Inserts a row or rows in a table
UPDATE	Updates a row or rows in a table or query
DELETE	Deletes a row or rows from a table
SELECT	Selects rows from a table or query

Figure 5-5: DML statements

This chapter describes each of the DML statements and how to use them with the Jet engine. SQL, as presented here, is an overview of the SQL language. Much more complex and sophisticated queries can be created than those presented in this text. The means by which queries are executed from Visual Basic is the same. That is, all SQL statements are executed using the OpenRecordset or Execute methods, or by setting the RecordSource property of a Data control to an SQL statement that returns a recordset.

One common task is to select records from a database to display their contents in visible controls or in a report. While this can be accomplished by setting the RecordSource property to a table in the database, this method does not allow records to be selected dynamically. Consider the payroll example: A user may want to select only those records for a given pay period, which can change. This requires that instead of selecting all the rows from a table, only specific rows should be selected. Selecting only specific rows can be accomplished using an SQL SELECT statement.

Retrieving Data with the SELECT Statement

The SELECT statement is used to retrieve a set of records from a database and can be used to retrieve records from multiple tables or queries. When you use a SELECT statement with a database like Microsoft Access, you can type the statement into one window and view the results of the statement in another window. When you use the SELECT statement with Visual Basic, the statement typically is stored in a String data type and passed as an argument to the OpenRecordset method of the Database object or stored in the RecordSource property of a Data control. When the OpenRecordset method is called, the SELECT statement is executed and the resultant rows are retrieved and stored in a Recordset object. The same SELECT statement also can be stored in the Data control's RecordSource property and executed by calling the Data control's Refresh method. You can scroll through the records and make changes to a recordset by calling the recordset's methods as you have done in the past.

Syntax	**SELECT * FROM** *tablename*
Dissection	■ The *tablename* indicates the name of a table or query in the database.
Code Example	`SELECT * FROM tblPayrollMaster`
Code Dissection	This simple form of the SELECT statement is analogous to setting the RecordSource property of the Data control to a table in the database. That is, it selects all the records from the table named tblPayrollMaster.

To illustrate how a SELECT statement can be used with a Data control, you can replace a table name with a SELECT statement to achieve the same result. So you can visualize the SELECT statement in action, the form named frmSelect contains a text box in which you can enter SELECT statements. When the Select Records command button is clicked, the following code is executed to process the statement. This code has been written already.

```
Private Sub cmdSelect_Click( )
    With datPayrollMaster
        .RecordSource = txtSelect
        .Refresh
```

```
            .Recordset.MoveLast
            .Caption = .Recordset.RecordCount & _
                "Records Selected"
        End With
End Sub
```

To use the Data control with a SELECT statement:

1 Start Visual Basic and open the project named **Chapter.05\Startup\IGA_S.vbp**. Open the form named **frmSelect**. Set the DatabaseName property for the Data control named **datPayrollMaster** to **Chapter.05\Startup\IGA.mdb**. Be sure to add the drive designator to the path name as necessary. Set the RecordSource property to the following string using the Properties window:

```
SELECT * FROM tblPayrollMaster
```

Both the DataSource and DataField properties of the text boxes and labels have been set already.

2 Test the program. On the main form's menu bar, click **View** then **Select Form**.

3 When the Data control is initialized, it will pass the SELECT statement to the Jet engine for processing. This will cause a recordset to be created as identified by the SELECT statement. Locate the different records by clicking the buttons on the Data control.

4 The form and SELECT statement are shown in Figure 5-6. Enter the statement shown in Figure 5-6, then click the **Select Records** command button to execute the statement, and then end the program.

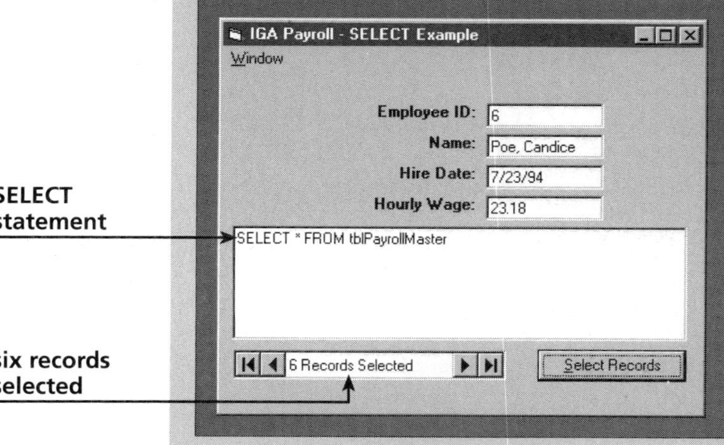

Figure 5-6: Select form

This event procedure retrieves the value stored in the multiline text box named txtSelect and assigns the value to the RecordSource property of the Data control. The Refresh method then is called, which causes the SELECT statement to be executed. Then, the last record is located so the number of records can be displayed in the visible Data control's caption. While this simple form of the SELECT statement is useful, it can be expanded to return rows in a specific order, select specific rows from a table, or select only specific fields. Expanding the SELECT statement requires that additional clauses be added. While the previous SELECT statement returned all the rows from the table, the records are returned in the same order they originally were added to the table. Typically, the records should be sorted. For example, it is common to order records by name. For a sales report, you may want to order the records by the sales amount. In other situations, records may be ordered by date. This is possible by adding the ORDER BY clause to the SELECT statement.

Syntax

SELECT * FROM *tablename*
[**ORDER BY** *field1* [**ASC | DESC**][,*field2* [**ASC | DESC**][,*fieldn* [**ASC | DESC**]]

Dissection

- The optional **ORDER BY** clause causes rows to be returned in a specific order. The order is determined by the field name specified in *field*.
- The optional **ASC** keyword will cause the records to be returned in ascending order. If omitted, this is the default.
- The optional **DESC** keyword will cause the records to be returned in descending order. Both the ASC and DESC keywords cannot be used on the same fields.
- Multiple fields may be sorted by specifying multiple fields separated by commas. Sorting a Date value in ascending order will return the records from the oldest date to the newest date. Sorting a numeric value in ascending order will return records from the smallest value to the largest value.

Code Example

```
SELECT * FROM tblPayrollMaster ORDER BY fldName
SELECT * FROM tblPayrollMaster ORDER BY fldName, fldCategoryID
SELECT * FROM tblPayrollMaster ORDER BY fldHireDate DESC
```

Code Dissection

The first SELECT statement returns the same records as shown in the previous steps but the records are returned in ascending order by name. The second SELECT statement will have the same effect as the first unless there are two records with the same name. In this case, records with the same name will be further sorted by category. The final SELECT statement will return the records according to the date hired. Records are returned from the most current date to the least current date.

You now will use the Select form again and use the ORDER BY clause to view records in a particular order.

To select records in a specific order:

1 Test the program. On the startup form's menu bar, click **View** then **Select Form** to display the Select form. Enter the first SELECT statement into the text box and then click the **Select Records** command button. Use the buttons on the Data control to navigate through the records to verify the sort order is correct. Replace the first SELECT statement with the second SELECT statement and click **Select Records.**

```
SELECT * FROM tblPayrollMaster ORDER BY fldCategoryID
     DESC, fldName
SELECT * FROM tblPayrollMaster ORDER BY fldHourlyWage
     DESC, fldName
```

Note: Both SELECT statements should be entered on one line even though the statement appears on two lines in this text.

The first statement selects all six records ordered by name, and the second statement orders the records by hourly wage. If two records have the same hourly wage, then the records are further sorted by name in descending order.

The SELECT statements in the previous steps select all the records from the table. It also is possible to restrict which rows are selected.

When you sort records with the ORDER BY clause, the performance of the statement can be improved considerably if the underlying field name is indexed. Indexes can be created on a field using Microsoft Access, or using DAO objects. For more information, refer to the Index topic in Microsoft Access Help. This requires that you have Access installed on your computer.

Restricting the Rows Returned with the WHERE Clause

One of the most powerful capabilities of the SELECT statement is the capability to select only those rows matching specific criteria. In the previous chapter, you used a limited form of this type of functionality using the FindFirst and FindNext methods of the Recordset object. In this case, the underlying recordset contained all the rows in a specific table, and the methods were used to search through the recordset to find a specific record. A SELECT statement with a WHERE clause produces a similar result but only those records matching the criteria are included in the recordset regardless of how many records are in the underlying table.

This capability allows the user to perform complex queries like selecting only those payroll records that have a specific date paid or only those employees with an hourly wage greater than some number.

The WHERE clause is used to restrict the rows returned by an SQL statement. In the case of the SELECT statement, it restricts the rows returned in the record-set. The WHERE clause consists of the keyword WHERE followed by a condition list, as shown in the following syntax diagram.

Syntax

SELECT * **FROM** *tablename*
  WHERE *conditionlist*
  [**ORDER BY** *field1* [**ASC** | **DESC**][,*field2* [**ASC** | **DESC**][,*fieldn*] [**ASC** | **DESC**]]

Dissection

- The optional **WHERE** clause typically follows the SELECT statement and precedes the ORDER BY clause. It consists of the keyword WHERE followed by the *conditionlist*.
- The *conditionlist* is a condition that evaluates to True or False and is similar syntactically to the condition in an If statement. The *conditionlist* is made up of individual conditions separated by logical operators like And, Or, Xor, among others. The *conditionlist* is applied to each row in *tablename*. If the *conditionlist* is True, then the record matches the criteria and is returned by the SELECT statement. Otherwise, the record is ignored and not returned by the SELECT statement. In other words, it will not appear in the recordset.

Notes

The syntax is identical to the syntax you used in the previous chapter with the FindFirst and FindNext methods. When the data type of a field is a String, the value must be enclosed in single quotation marks. When the data type of a field is a Date or Time, the value must be enclosed in pound signs. Numeric values are not enclosed by any characters.

Code Example

```
SELECT * FROM tblPayroll WHERE fldEmployeeID = 'A32'
SELECT * FROM tblPayroll WHERE fldHireDate > #3/22/2001#
SELECT * FROM tblPayroll WHERE fldHourlyWage < 10.22
```

Code Dissection

These three SELECT statements all use a WHERE clause to restrict the number of rows returned. The condition looks just like a condition in an If statement. The Employee ID is enclosed in single quotes, however, because it is a String data type and the hire date is enclosed in pound signs because it is a Date data type.

The first statement selects only those records having an Employee ID of "A32." The second selects only those records where the date hired is more recent then 3/22/2001, and the final statement selects only those records where the hourly wage is less than $10.22.

The WHERE clause is very powerful and flexible. In addition to using relational operators like < or >, it is possible to use logical operators to create more complex expressions. Logical operators in a WHERE clause have the same syntax as they do in an If statement. Consider the following statements:

```
SELECT * FROM tblPayrollMaster
    WHERE fldHireDate > #3/22/90# And
    fldHourlyWage > 12.00
SELECT * FROM tblPayrollMaster
    WHERE fldHireDate > #3/22/90# Or
    fldHourlyWage > 12.00
    ORDER BY fldName
```

The first SELECT statement selects only those records where both the date hired is more recent that 3/22/90 and the hourly wage is greater than $12.00. The second SELECT statement selects those records where either of the conditions is True.

To restrict the records selected using a WHERE clause:

1 Test the program. On the startup form's menu bar, click **View** then **Select Form**, if needed. Enter each of the following SELECT statements into the text box and click the **Select Records** command button to execute each statement. *Note:* The second SELECT statement appears on three lines but should be entered as a single statement.

```
SELECT * FROM tblPayrollMaster
    WHERE fldHireDate > #3/23/97#
SELECT * FROM tblPayrollMaster
    WHERE fldHireDate > #3/22/99#
    Or fldHourlyWage > 23.00
    ORDER BY fldName
```

Note: The previous SELECT statements should be entered on one line even though they appear on multiple lines in this text. The first SELECT statement should return four (4) records and the second should return three (3) records.

Selecting Records Using Ranges and Patterns

There are two special operators that can be used to create conditions in the WHERE clause. These are the Like and Between operators. These operators allow a range of values to be selected or to use pattern matching to select records.

Syntax *expression* [**NOT**] **Between** *value1* **And** *value2*

Dissection

- The *expression* typically contains the field name you want to evaluate.
- *value1* and *value2* are applied to the expression to determine whether or not *expression* is between *value1* and *value2*. If it is, then the value is True and the record is returned by the SELECT statement.
- The **Between** operator is used as a condition in the WHERE clause's *condition-list*. Thus, multiple operations can be concatenated using logical operators.

Code Example

```
SELECT * FROM tblPayrollMaster
    WHERE fldHireDate Between #3/22/90# And #3/22/91#
SELECT * FROM tblPayrollMaster
    WHERE fldHourlyWage Between 10.00 And 11.00 And
    fldHireDate Between #3/22/90# And #3/22/91#
```

Code Dissection	These SELECT statements use the Between operator to select records within a range of values. The first returns those records where the date hired is between 3/22/90 and 3/22/91. The second returns those records where the hourly wage is between $10.00 and $11.00 per hour and the date hired is between 3/22/90 and 3/22/91.

The Like operator is a pattern-matching operator used with strings. That is, it is used with string fields to determine if a string field contains a specific pattern. To perform pattern matching, a set of special characters is used as wildcard characters. Figure 5-7 illustrates the different pattern-matching characters.

Character	Operation
*	Matches multiple characters
?	Matches a single character
[*a*-*b*]	Matches a range of characters from *a* to *b*
![*a*-*b*]	Matched characters are excluded
#	Matches a single digit

Figure 5-7: Pattern-matching operators

These characters can be combined to form complex patterns as shown in Figure 5-8.

Pattern	Match	No match
smi*	smith, smitty	smythe
th	the, then, smith	tih
the*	then, them	the, than
1#3	123, 133	1a3
[A-L]	A, B, L	M, N, Z
[!A-L]	M, N, Z	A, B, L
[S-T]?i*	This, Sting, Thin	The, Then

Figure 5-8: Pattern-matching examples

To select a range of records and use the pattern-matching operators:

1 Test the program. On the startup form's menu bar, click **View** then **Select Form**. Enter the following SELECT statements into the text box. For each SELECT statement you enter, click the **Select Records** command button to execute the SELECT statement. For each statement you enter, use the buttons on the Data control to view the selected records.

```
SELECT * FROM tblPayrollMaster WHERE fldName
    Like 'B*' ORDER BY fldName
SELECT * FROM tblPayrollMaster
    WHERE fldHireDate Between #8/1/97#
    And #12/22/2001# ORDER BY fldName
```

The first SELECT statement returns two (2) records and the second returns four (4) records.

Selecting Specific Fields

The preceding SELECT statements have retrieved all the fields from a table or query. In situations where only specific fields are needed, however, the performance of the SELECT statement can be improved only by selecting those fields that will be used. This form of the SELECT statement has the following syntax:

Syntax

SELECT [*predicate*] { * | *table*.* | [*table*.]*field1* [**AS** *alias1*] [, [*table*.]*field2* [**AS** *alias2*] [, ...]]}
FROM *tablename*
WHERE *conditionlist*
ORDER BY *field1* [**ASC** | **DESC**] [,*field2* [**ASC** | **DESC**] [,*fieldn*] [**ASC** | **DESC**]]

Dissection

- The *table* contains the name of the table containing the field.
- The * specifies that all fields from the specified table or tables are selected.
- The names of each field to be retrieved are represented by the variables *field1*, *field2*, and *fieldn*. Fields are retrieved in the order they are listed in the SELECT statement.
- The **As** *alias* clause is used to assign a name to a column that is different from the field name.

Code Example

```
SELECT fldEmployeeID AS ID, fldName AS FullName FROM
    tblPayrollMaster
```

Code Dissection

The preceding SELECT statement selects two fields from the table named tblPayrollMaster. The first field named fldEmployeeID is renamed ID in the recordset. The second field is renamed to FullName in the recordset.

The examples of the SELECT statements you have used so far have all used the Data control to execute the SELECT statement. Recall that the Data control performs this task by creating a Recordset based on the contents of the RecordSource property. Just as it is possible to open explicitly a recordset based on a table, a SELECT statement can be used as an argument to the OpenRecordset method. Consider the following statements:

```
Dim pdbCurrent As Database, prstCurrent As Recordset
Dim pstrSQL As String
pstrSQL = "SELECT * FROM tblPayroll"
Set pdbCurrent =
    OpenDatabase("A:\Chapter.05\Startup\IGA.mdb")
Set prstCurrent = pdbCurrent.OpenRecordset(pstrSQL)
```

These statements have nearly the same effect as using a SELECT statement with the Data control to open a recordset. These statements explicitly open the database and then the recordset. Instead of a table name, the SQL statement is passed as the argument to the OpenRecordset method. While this statement is fairly simple, consider SELECT statements with complex WHERE clauses. Also, consider the situation where the values for the WHERE clause are specified by the user rather than being coded explicitly into the SELECT statement. Thus, if a WHERE clause needs to contain Date values or String values, you must insert the single quote (') and pound signs (#) manually into the SELECT statement. In these situations, the SELECT statement can get extremely long. Instead of using several continuation lines, the code may be more readable if you create separate variables for each clause, and concatenate the variables into one variable containing the entire SQL statement and passing that variable as the argument to the OpenRecordset method.

Consider the situation where the user wants to select payroll records for a specific date. The user needs to specify different dates each time the query is run, however. Most likely, the user will enter the value into a text box. This value then will need to be used to create and execute the proper SELECT statement. The following statements accomplish this task. Assume the database has been opened and a reference to the Database object stored in pdbCurrent.

```
Dim pstrSQL As String, pstrSELECT As String, _
    pstrWHERE As String
Dim pdbCurrent As Database, prstCurrent As Recordset
pstrSELECT = "SELECT * FROM tblPayroll"
pstrWHERE = "WHERE fldPayDate = " & "#" txtPayDate & "#"
pstrSQL = pstrSELECT & pstrWHERE
Set prstCurrent = pdbCurrent.OpenRecordset(pstrSQL)
Do Until prstCurrent.EOF
    Debug.Print prstCurrent![fldLastName]
    prstCurrent.MoveNext
Loop
```

These statements perform a query to select all records from tblPayroll where the field named fldPayDate is the same as the value stored in the text box named txtPayDate. Pound signs were concatenated into the string. Thus, if the txtPayDate contained the value 3/22/99, the variable pstrSQL would contain the following string:

```
SELECT * FROM tblPayroll WHERE fldPayDate = #3/22/99#
```

Use caution when building String variables for use with the SELECT statement. If the keywords are not separated by spaces, the SQL statement will be invalid and a run-time error will occur. In the previous statement, the first line of the assignment statement appends a space after the table named tblPayroll, and a space also follows the equal sign. It is imperative that SQL keywords be separated by spaces.

A useful technique to debug SELECT statements is to store the statement in a variable. Just before the recordset is opened, print the value of the variable in the Immediate window to verify the syntax.

Processing Database Errors

Database errors can occur because of many conditions. A user may try to add a record with invalid information like trying to store character data in a numeric field, or add or make changes to records that would violate the underlying rules of the database. In these circumstances, an error will occur that must be dealt with. Handling the error requires an understanding of the cause of the error and the proper way to deal with it. As you saw in the previous chapter, the Data control will raise an Error event when a database error occurs. When a Visual Basic statement causes an error, an error handler must be written to trap the error. As you saw in the previous chapter, when the execution of a Visual Basic statement causes a run-time error, you can create an error handler. When the run-time error occurs, the Number, Source and Description properties are set. The error handler uses the information to determine if it makes sense to continue processing, display a message to the user, or some other action.

In this program, a run-time error will occur if an invalid SELECT statement is stored in the Data control's RecordSource property when the Refresh method is called on the recordset.

When the Jet engine cannot process an SQL statement, a run-time error is generated that can be trapped. For each run-time error, there actually may be several different database errors. So the program can determine the individual database errors that have occurred, the DBEngine object stores each of the errors leading up to the run-time error in the Errors collection. The Errors collection contains one Error object for each database error that occurred. The last Error object in the Errors collection corresponds to the error value stored in the Visual Basic Err object. Note that the Error object and the Err object are separate objects. When a Database error occurs that pertains to objects in the DAO hierarchy, the Jet engine creates an Error object in the Errors collection. After this process is complete, an error is raised and detected by Visual Basic. This causes the trappable run-time error to occur and the properties of the Err object set to the last error in the DAO Errors collection.

Object	Error
Properties	■ The **Description** property contains a string describing the cause of the error. ■ The **Number** property contains a Long integer identifying the error. A complete list of the error numbers can be found by selecting the Help topic "Trappable Microsoft Jet and DAO Errors." ■ The **Source** property contains the name of the object or program that caused the error to occur.

Figure 5-9 shows the relationship of the Errors collection and Error object in the DAO hierarchy.

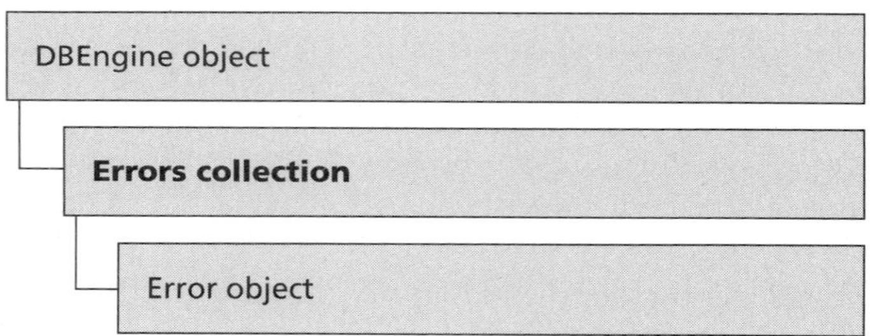

Figure 5-9: The Errors collection

So an invalid SQL statement will not cause a run-time error to occur, the code for the Select Records command button can be expanded to trap the error and display the errors in a message box.

To create an error handler that uses the DAO Errors collection:

1 Locate the **cmdSelect_Click** event procedure for the form named **frmSelect** in the Code window. Modify the event procedure by adding the following statements shown in bold:

```
Dim perrSelect As Error, pstrMessage As String
On Error GoTo cmdSelect_Error:
    With datPayrollMaster
        .RecordSource = txtSelect
        .Refresh
        .Recordset.MoveLast
        .Caption = .Recordset.RecordCount & _
            " Records Selected"
    End With
    Exit Sub
cmdSelect_Error:
    For Each perrSelect In Errors
        pstrMessage = perrSelect.Description & _
            Chr(13) & pstrMessage
    Next
    MsgBox pstrMessage, vbOKOnly + vbInformation, _
        "Database Error"
```

2 Test the program. Display the Select form then enter the following invalid SELECT statements, then click the **Select Records** command button.

```
SELECT * FROZ tblPayroll
SELECT * FROM tblInvalid
```

A message box should appear. Click **OK** to acknowledge the message, then end the program.

The statements you added create an error handler for the event procedure.

```
cmdSelect_Error:
    For Each perrSelect In Errors
        pstrMessage = errSelect.Description & _
            Chr(13) & pstrMessage
    Next
    MsgBox pstrMessage, vbOKOnly + vbInformation, _
        "Database Error"
```

Like most collections, the Errors collection can be enumerated using a For Each loop. In this case, the variable perrSelect is declared as an Error object. Thus, each time through the loop, the object variable perrSelect references the next error in the Errors collection. The error messages are concatenated into the message that will ultimately be displayed in the message box. After all the errors have been examined, the message box is displayed.

Performing Action Queries

All the queries you have performed with the SELECT statement returned records, so the OpenRecordset method was used. Remember, there is another type of query called an action query that does not return records. Action queries perform operations on data like inserting a new row, changing the records in a table, or deleting records. In each case, the action is performed without returning a recordset. Rather, the task is performed then a value is returned indicating whether or not the operation was successful.

The **Execute** method executes an SQL statement that runs an action query. If the statement returns rows from a database table or query (a select query), you instead open a recordset using the OpenRecordset method of the Database object.

Syntax *object*.**Execute** *source*, *options*

Dissection

- The *object* is usually a Database object. The Database object usually is created using the OpenDatabase method.
- The **Execute** method runs the SQL statement stored in *source*.
- The *source* is a String data type containing the SQL statement or the Name property value of a QueryDef object.
- The optional *options* argument contains one or more constants to determine characteristics of the statement. The dbFailOnError option causes a trappable run-time error to occur if the SQL statement cannot be executed. See the Help topic "Execute method" for more information about these constants. If this option is not included, the Jet engine will not generate a run-time error.

Code Example

```
Dim pdbCurrent As Database
pdbCurrent = OpenDatabase("A:\Chapter.05\Startup\IGA.mdb")
pdbCurrent.Execute actionQuery, dbFailOnError
```

Code Dissection

These statements execute an SQL action query. In this example, the *actionQuery* would be replaced with a valid INSERT, UPDATE, or DELETE statement. Unlike the previous statements, the Execute method is used instead of the OpenRecordset method. The first argument of the Execute method is the SQL statement to execute. The *options* argument contains the constant dbFailOnError. If the statement cannot be executed, the Jet engine will raise a run-time error.

Programming tip

Whenever the dbFailOnError constant is used, the procedure should contain an error handler to process any errors caused by the Jet engine. The error handler should determine if it is possible to continue.

When the DELETE statement is executed, there is no way to undo the changes. Thus, it is common to display a message box to request confirmation from the user before performing the deletion.

The INSERT Statement

There are two forms of the INSERT statement. The first is used to append a single record to a table, while the second is used to append multiple records based on the contents of some other table. The following describes the first form of the INSERT statement:

Syntax

INSERT INTO *target* [(*field1*[, *field2* [, ...]])]
VALUES (*value1*[, *value2*[, ...])

Dissection

- The *target* is the name of the table or query where the records will be appended.
- For each *field* in the target, the INSERT statement will store data in the *field*. The list of fields are enclosed in parentheses, and a comma separates each *field*.
- The values stored in the fields are specified using the VALUES clause followed by the values *value1*, *value2*, and so on. Each value is inserted such that *value1* corresponds to *field1*, *value2* corresponds to *field2*, and so on.

Notes

The number of fields and values must be the same. Commas must separate each value and the values must be enclosed in parentheses. Text data must be enclosed by quotation marks but numeric data should not. A pound sign (#) must enclose Date fields.

Code Example

```
Dim pstrSQL As String
pstrSQL = "INSERT INTO tblDemo (fldString, fldDate," & _
    "fldNumber) VALUES ('Marty Smith', #3/22/2001#," & _
    23884.33)"
pdbCurrent.Execute pstrSQL, dbFailOnError
```

Code Dissection

These statements insert a record into the table named tblDemo. Three fields are inserted named fldString, fldDate, and fldNumber having the values 'Marty Smith,' 3/22/2001, and 23884.33, respectively. The INSERT statement is built and stored in the String variable pstrSQL and then the Execute method is called with the String argument as a variable. If the statement fails because of an improper date or numeric value, an error will be raised because the dbFailOnError option is used.

In reality, records will seldom be inserted with literal values. Rather, variables will be used to store input values. It also is common to insert records into a database from a text file. In this case, a Do loop is necessary to read each of the records in the text file. Inside of the Do loop, the string containing the proper input statement must be created then executed for each record. For example, assume the values in the previous statement are stored in the variable pstrName, pstrDate, and psngValue. The following statements would be used to perform the same insert operation instead of literal values:

```
Dim pstrSQL As String
pstrSQL = "INSERT INTO tblDemo " & _
    "(fldString, fldDate, fldNumber) " & _
    "VALUES ( & "'" & pstrName & "'," & "#" & pstrDate & _
    "#," & psngValue & ")"
pdbCurrent.Execute pstrSQL, dbFailOnError
```

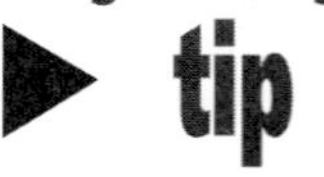

A run-time error will occur if you try to insert invalid data into a file. Consider validating all input fields before trying to insert them into the database. Also create an error handler to trap any unavoidable run-time errors.

The payroll for IGA arrives at the Payroll office in the form of a text file containing two fields: Employee ID and Hours Worked. This information needs to be inserted into the database before the payroll can be processed. To accomplish the task, a Do loop is needed to read the text file. For each record in the text file, the information needs to be inserted into the table named tblPayrollDetail. Once this is complete, the payroll can be computed.

To insert the payroll data into the database:

1 Locate the **mnuPayrollReadTextFile_Click** event procedure for the form named **frmIGA**, and enter the following statements into the event procedure.

```
Dim pstrFileName As String, pstrEmployeeID As String
Dim psngHoursWorked As Single, pstrPayDate As String
Dim pstrSQL As String
pstrPayDate = CStr(Date)
pstrFileName = InputBox("Enter Payroll File Name")
Open pstrFileName For Input As #1
Do Until EOF(1)
    Input #1, pstrEmployeeID, psngHoursWorked
    pstrSQL = "INSERT INTO tblPayrollDetail " & _
        "(fldEmployeeID,fldHoursWorked,fldPayDate) " & _
        "VALUES " & "('" & pstrEmployeeID & "'," & _
        psngHoursWorked & "," & "#" & pstrPayDate & _
        " #)"
    datPayrollMaster.Database.Execute pstrSQL, _
        dbFailOnError
Loop
```

2 Test the program. Click **Payroll** then **Read Text File**. When the input box is displayed, enter the file named **A:\Chapter.05\Startup\Payroll.txt**. Click **OK**. The file will be opened and the records inserted into the table.

These statements open the text file, read the records into variables, then insert the record into the database. The syntax for the String variable containing the INSERT statement requires careful analysis.

```
pstrSQL = "INSERT INTO tblPayrollDetail " & _
    "(fldEmployeeID,fldHoursWorked,fldPayDate) " & _
    "VALUES " & "('" & pstrEmployeeID & "'," & _
    psngHoursWorked & "," & "#" & pstrPayDate & "#)"
```

Building the String variable requires extensive string concatenation. Because the String variable must be enclosed in single quotation marks, and the Date value must be enclosed in pound signs, these characters must be embedded into the string expression by manually concatenating the characters. Thus, in the previous example, the variable pstrEmployeeID is evaluated, and surrounded by quotation characters. Because fldPayDate is a Date data type, pound signs surround the variable pstrPayDate. The parentheses also are inserted into the VALUES clause. Assuming that the EmployeeID was '1A', the hours worked has a value of 32, and the current date is 3/22/2001, then the value of pstrSQL would contain the following text:

```
INSERT INTO tblPayrollDetail
    (fldEmployeeID,fldHoursWorked,fldPayDate)
    VALUES ('1A',32,#3/22/2001#)
```

The previous statement is stored as a string on one line, although it appears formatted on multiple lines to improve readability.

The UPDATE Statement

In the previous chapter, you updated records using the Edit and Update methods of the Recordset object. Using these methods, one record was updated at a time. Thus, to update all the records in a recordset, you would need to again create a Do loop to examine each record, then manually update the record. You also can use the relational model to update several records in a table at once using the UPDATE statement. The UPDATE statement is used to change the contents of one or more fields from one or more rows in a database.

Syntax

UPDATE *tablename*
SET *fieldname* = *newvalue* [,*fieldname* = *newvalue*]
WHERE *criteria*

Dissection	■ The *tablename* is the name of an existing table or query. ■ The *fieldname* is a field from the table or query specified by *tablename*. ■ The *newvalue* can be a literal value or expression. ■ The WHERE clause has the same syntax as used with the SELECT statement. ■ The *criteria* is an expression that determines which records will be updated.

Code Example	`pstrSQL = "UPDATE tblPayrollDetail " & _`
	`    "SET fldGrossPay = fldHourlyWage * fldHoursWorked"`
	`pdbCurrent.Execute pstrSQL, dbFailOnError`

Code Dissection	These statements update the Gross Pay field in the table named tblPayrollDetail. The value of the field is set to the value of the field fldHourlyWage multiplied by fldHoursWorked. Once again, the result is stored in a String data type, then the statement is executed by passing the string as an argument to the Execute method.

It is possible to create these statements dynamically using variables and/or literal values as shown in the following statements:

```
Dim pdbCurrent As Database, pstrSQL As String
Set pdbCurrent = _
    OpenDatabase("A:\Chapter.05\Startup\IGA.mdb")
pstrSQL = "UPDATE tblPayrollMaster " & _
    "SET fldHourlyWage = fldHourlyWage * 1.10"
pdbCurrent.Execute pstrSQL, dbFailOnError
```

These statements increase the value of the column fldHourlyWage by 10 percent. This is achieved by multiplying the current value of the field by 1.10 and storing the result in the same field. The statement is executed for all the rows in the database. To restrict the rows that are updated, a WHERE clause can be supplied as shown in the following statements:

```
pstrSQL = "UPDATE tblPayrollMaster " & _
    "SET fldHourlyWage = fldHourlyWage * 1.10 " & _
    "WHERE fldHourlyWage < 10.00"
pdbCurrent.Execute pstrSQL, dbFailOnError
```

This WHERE clause restricts the rows so only those employees having an hourly wage of less then $10.00 per hour are updated. The payroll needs to be computed for the records that were just added. This can be accomplished by performing the following tasks for the records having a date paid equal to the current date:

- The gross pay is computed by multiplying the hourly wage by the hours worked.
- The withholding tax is computed by multiplying the gross pay by 20 percent.
- The net pay is computed by subtracting the withholding tax from the gross pay.

To perform an action query with the UPDATE statement:

1 Locate the **mnuComputePayroll_Click** event procedure for the form named **frmIGA**, and enter the following statements into the event procedure:

```
Dim pstrSQL As String, pstrDate As String, _
    pstrWHERE As String
pstrDate = InputBox("Enter Payroll Date")
pstrWHERE = " WHERE fldPayDate = " & "#" & _
    pstrDate & "#"
pstrSQL = "UPDATE qryPayroll " & _
    "SET fldGrossPay = fldHoursWorked * " & _
    fldHourlyWage & pstrWHERE
datPayrollMaster.Database.Execute pstrSQL, _
    dbFailOnError
pstrSQL = "UPDATE qryPayroll " & _
    "SET fldWithholding = fldGrossPay * .20 " & _
    pstrWHERE
datPayrollMaster.Database.Execute pstrSQL,
    dbFailOnError
pstrSQL = "UPDATE qryPayroll " & _
    "SET fldNetPay = fldGrossPay - fldWithholding " _
    & pstrWHERE
datPayrollMaster.Database.Execute pstrSQL, _
    dbFailOnError
```

2 Before testing the program, consider making a copy of the database file.

3 Test the program. Click **Payroll** then **Compute Payroll**.

When the input box appears, enter the current date. The payroll records for the current date are updated.

These UPDATE statements compute the gross pay, withholding, and net pay. This set of statements executed three UPDATE statements rather than creating one UPDATE statement that set all three fields. This is because of the order in which the UPDATE is performed. Rather than computing the value for the first field and then using the result in the second computation, the UPDATE statement reads the values only once. That is, fldGrossPay is used as the result in the first UPDATE statement. This result must be computed before it can be used as an operand to compute the gross pay in the second UPDATE statement. Each UPDATE statement contains a WHERE clause to change only those records having a specific date paid.

Deleting Database Records

The DELETE statement allows you to remove one or more rows from a table. Again, a recordset could be created, then the Delete method called for each record to be deleted. You can call the DELETE statement once, however, to remove several records just like you can call the UPDATE statement once to update several records. The syntax of the DELETE statement is:

Syntax

DELETE *
  FROM *table*
  WHERE *criteria*

Dissection

- The *table* is the name of the table from which records are deleted.
- The *criteria* is an expression that determines which records to delete and has the same format as the WHERE clause in the UPDATE and SELECT statements. That is, the expression contained in *criteria* must evaluate to True or False. If True, then the record is deleted. If False, the record is ignored.

Code Example

```
Dim pstrSQL As String
pstrSQL = "DELETE * FROM tblPayroll " & _
    "WHERE fldPayDate < #3/10/95#"
pdbCurrent.Execute pstrSQL, dbFailOnError
```

Code Dissection

These statements delete the payroll records from the table named tblPayroll where the date paid is less than the value 3/10/95. Again, it is common for the values of the WHERE clause to be specified by the user.

This section on the SQL language only describes the fundamental concepts of the language. Much more complicated SQL statements can be written to join multiple tables, group together and summarize the contents of specific fields in a record, and perform many other tasks. As you develop SQL queries, be careful to consider the database engine you are using as each vendor supplies slightly different versions of SQL.

Transactions

In the previous examples using the UPDATE statement, you executed multiple UPDATE statements to compute the payroll. One statement was executed to compute the gross pay, another to compute the withholding, and another to compute the net pay. In this situation, all the UPDATE statements must execute successfully for the payroll processing to be complete. That is, if one of the UPDATE statements executed, then the power failed or some other system error occurred preventing the remaining UPDATE statements from completing, the payroll would not be correct and the database would be in an inconsistent state. The problem is magnified as the number and complexity of statements grows that collectively perform a task. A series of database statements like the UPDATE statements you just wrote can be thought of as a **transaction**. The Jet engine allows you to view a group of statements as a unit using transactions. Transactions are implemented using three statements.

Syntax

workspace.**BeginTrans**
workspace.**CommitTrans [dbFlushOSCacheWrites]**
workspace.**Rollback**

Dissection

- *workspace* must be a valid Workspace object.
- The **BeginTrans** method should be called before the first action query, and identifies the start of the transaction.
- The **CommitTrans** method causes the action queries performed between the BeginTrans and CommitTrans methods to be saved to the database. Once the CommitTrans method is called, the changes cannot be undone. The dbFlushOSCacheWrites option causes the transaction to be written to disk immediately instead of being cached in memory. This ensures that a power outage or other system problem will not cause the transaction to be lost.
- The **Rollback** method is used to undo the changes made by any action query up to the last BeginTrans method.

Notes

Calling the CommitTrans or Rollback methods without first calling the BeginTrans method will generate a run-time error. Note that if a Workspace object is closed without explicitly committing pending transactions, the transactions are rolled back. Transactions can be nested up to five levels.

Code Example

```
Dim pwsCurrent As Workspace
Set pwsCurrent = Workspaces(0)
pwsCurrent.BeginTrans
' Statements
pwsCurrent.CommitTrans

pwsCurrent.BeginTrans
' Statements
pwsCurrent.Rollback
```

Code Dissection

The first statement block illustrates the use of a transaction that gets committed to the database. The second block illustrates the use of a transaction that is rolled back. As such, the statements are not written to the database.

Using Unbound Controls with a Database

It is possible to use controls in an unbound mode without the aid of a Data control. The technique you use to process an unbound control is fairly simple. First, you must open explicitly the database and create the recordset. As you have seen, the recordset can be created from a table or SELECT statement. Once the recordset is opened, you must synchronize the current record in the recordset with the records displayed in labels or text boxes. Thus, whenever the recordset is repositioned with one of the move or find methods, you must write explicitly the code to display the fields in the current record into the visible objects. Furthermore, you must call explicitly the methods of the recordset to insert, update, and delete data.

In this example, you will see how to create a recordset and display an employee name in a list box for each employee name in the recordset. The list box will be loaded with employee names when the form is loaded. The example demonstrates a pertinent use of the ItemData property. The EmployeeID is a unique field in the table. When the employee name is added to the visible part of the list box, the EmployeeID is stored in the corresponding ItemData property. When the user clicks one of the employee names, finding the corresponding EmployeeID will change the current record. The information pertaining to the current record will be displayed in corresponding labels. This simple example is not complete. It does not provide for any data to be added, updated, or deleted. It only illustrates the use of unbound controls to navigate a recordset.

This example does not present any new syntax. Rather, it just uses a different technique to manage database data.

To use unbound controls:

1 Open the form named **frmUnbound**. The form is shown in Figure 5-10.

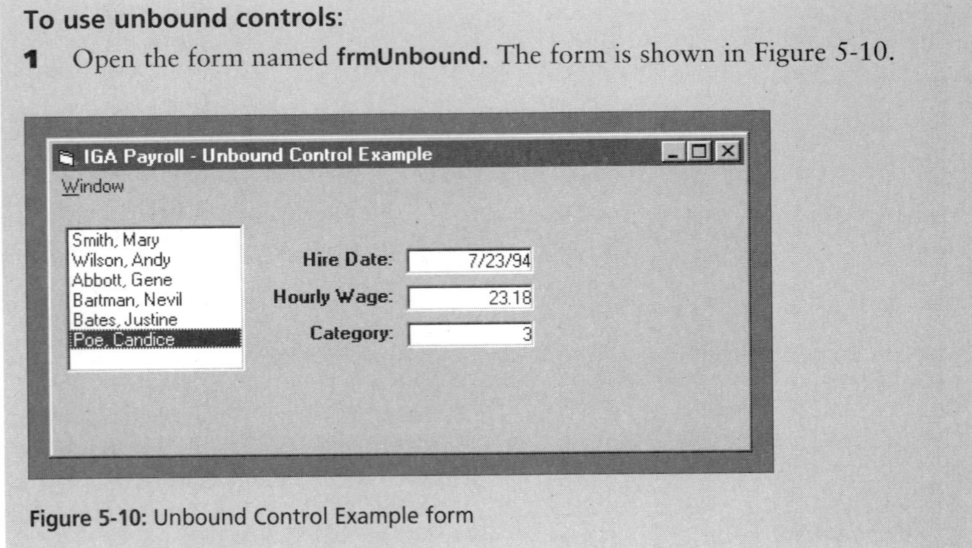

Figure 5-10: Unbound Control Example form

2 Enter the following declarations in the general declarations section to declare the variables that will store the Database and Recordset object references:

```
Private pdbCurrent As Database
Private prstCurrent As Recordset
```

3 Enter the following statements in the **Form_Load** event procedure to open the database and recordset:

```
Set pdbCurrent = _
    OpenDatabase("A:\Chapter.05\Startup\IGA.mdb")
Set prstCurrent = _
    pdbCurrent.OpenRecordset("tblPayrollMaster", _
    dbOpenDynaset)
Do Until prstCurrent.EOF
    lstName.AddItem prstCurrent![fldName]
    lstName.ItemData(lstName.NewIndex) = _
        prstCurrent![fldEmployeeID]
    prstCurrent.MoveNext
Loop
```

4 Enter the following statements in the **lstName_Click** event procedure to display the current record when one is selected:

```
Dim pintEmp As Integer
pintEmp = lstName.ItemData(lstName.ListIndex)
prstCurrent.FindFirst _
    "fldEmployeeID = '" & CStr(pintEmp) & "'"
lblHireDate = prstCurrent![fldHireDate]
lblHourlyWage = prstCurrent![fldHourlyWage]
lblCategoryID = prstCurrent![fldCategoryID]
```

5 Test the program. Click **View** then **Unbound Controls**. The employee names should be displayed in the list box when the form is loaded. Click different employee names. When a new name is selected, the information pertaining to the employee is displayed in the corresponding output labels.

The syntax for the Do loop requires some analysis.

```
Do Until prstCurrent.EOF
    lstName.AddItem prstCurrent![fldName]
    lstName.ItemData(lstName.NewIndex) = _
        prstCurrent![fldEmployeeID]
    prstCurrent.MoveNext
Loop
```

The Do loop examines each of the records in the recordset. For each record, the employee name (fldName) is added to the list. Remember that when the AddItem method is called, the NewIndex property contains the index of the list item that was just added. This is used as the argument to the ItemData property to store the EmployeeID field into the ItemData property.

```
pintEmp = lstName.ItemData(lstName.ListIndex)
prstCurrent.FindFirst _
    "fldEmployeeID = '" & cstr(pintEmp) & "'"
lblHireDate = prstCurrent![fldHireDate]
```

These statements use the ItemData property of the currently selected list item to find the first record matching the criteria. Here the criteria is the employee ID. The final statements store the hire date of the current record in the output label.

To complete this example, the labels could be converted to text boxes used for input and output. Your code would need to synchronize the text boxes with the current record as shown in this example. It also would need to add, change, and delete records.

SECTION B

objectives

In this section you will:

- Use a type of control called an ActiveX control
- Add an ActiveX control to a project
- Program a type of list box and combo box called the DBList and DBCombo controls
- Program an ActiveX control that displays multiple rows and columns called a DBGrid control
- Use SELECT statements to change the rows contained in these controls dynamically

Using Data Bound ActiveX Controls

ActiveX Controls—A Definition

Visual Basic supports two types of controls: intrinsic controls and ActiveX controls. Consider the intrinsic TextBox control you have been using. This control is not unique to Visual Basic. Rather, Visual Basic uses a control supported by the Windows operating system. When a program is compiled, the code to call the appropriate Windows functions is embedded in the executable file produced by Visual Basic. Refer to the chapter on the Windows Application Programming Interface for more information on the interaction between Visual Basic and its intrinsic controls.

An ActiveX control differs from an intrinsic control in many ways. The code that contains the methods and events for an ActiveX control is not stored in the executable file produced by Visual Basic. Rather, it is stored in a separate file with the file extension ".ocx." To execute a program that uses an ActiveX control, this .ocx file must exist on the computer running the program. Figure 5-11 illustrates this distinction.

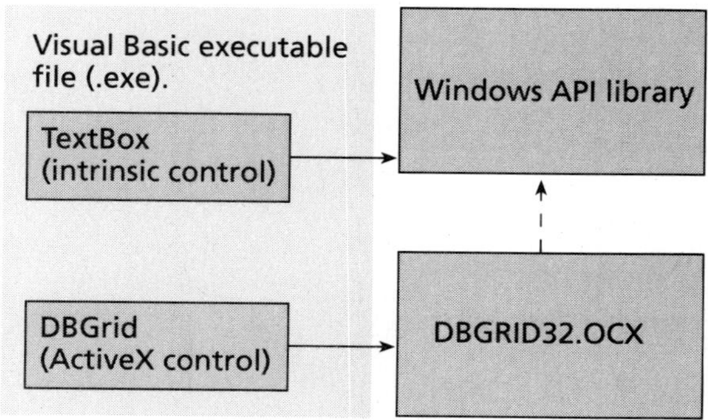

Figure 5-11: Intrinsic and ActiveX controls

Because an ActiveX control is independent of Visual Basic itself, ActiveX controls can be used with many different programming languages. They also are suitable for use over the Internet. That is, it is possible to create ActiveX controls that are downloaded over the Internet to a Web browser and executed. The reason ActiveX controls can operate with multiple languages is because the mechanism for a program to interact with an ActiveX control is defined clearly. ActiveX is part of a technology called Component Object Modules (COM). **COM** defines a standard interface by which objects interact. It is the foundation for interaction with programs like Jet using DAO objects.

The current release of Visual Basic allows you to create ActiveX controls. This capability previously has been limited to other languages like C++. The topic of ActiveX controls is discussed fully in subsequent chapters.

Adding an ActiveX Control to a Project

The Professional Edition of Visual Basic is shipped with a number of controls in addition to the intrinsic controls you have been using. All of these are ActiveX controls. In this chapter, you will learn about three of these ActiveX controls: the DBGrid, DBList, and DBCombo. Before an ActiveX control can be used in a program, it must be added explicitly to the project file. This is accomplished using the Components dialog shown in Figure 5-12.

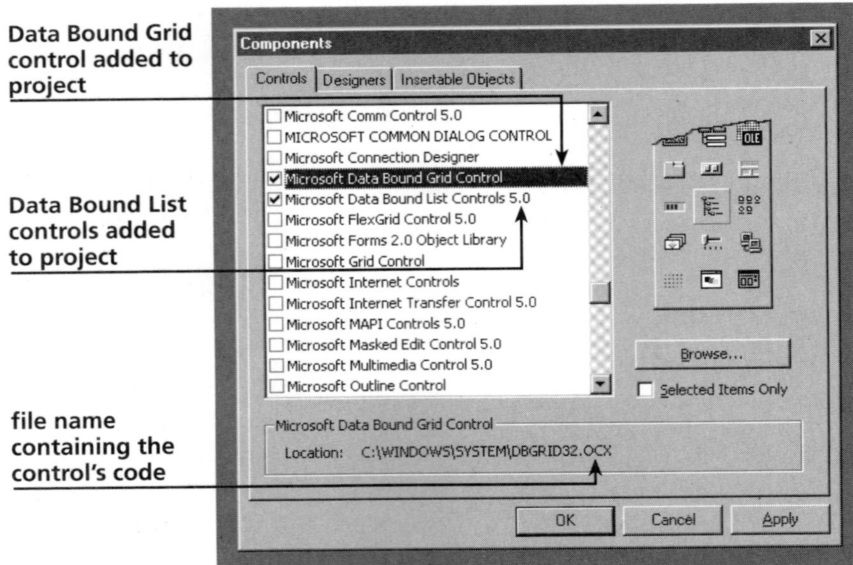

Figure 5-12: Components dialog

The list of controls shown in Figure 5-12 may differ from those displayed on your system. There are ActiveX controls that implement fax machines, electronic mail, and many others. These controls can be purchased from third party vendors and used to extend the power of Visual Basic. When an ActiveX control is added to a project, the project file is updated to indicate that the ActiveX control is used by the project.

To add an ActiveX control to the project file:

1. Click **Project** then **Components** to open the Components dialog.
2. Make sure the **Microsoft Data Bound Grid Control 5.0** and **Microsoft Data Bound List Controls 5.0** check boxes are checked, then click the **OK** button to add the controls to the project and close the dialog. This causes the control to be added on the Toolbox. Once added, the control can be used on a form just like any other control.

In Figure 5-12, the file name containing the code for the control is listed when the control is selected. This file must exist on the computer running the program that uses the control. Furthermore, it is possible to store multiple controls in the same .ocx file. For example, both the DBCombo and DBList controls are stored in the file named dblist32.ocx. Once an ActiveX control is added to the project and the project saved, it does not need to be added each time the project is loaded.

One difference between an ActiveX control and an intrinsic control is the way design-time properties are set. In addition to the Properties window, ActiveX controls support a type of dialog called Property Pages. Figure 5-13 shows the Property Pages for the DBGrid control.

each tab is referred to as a Property Page

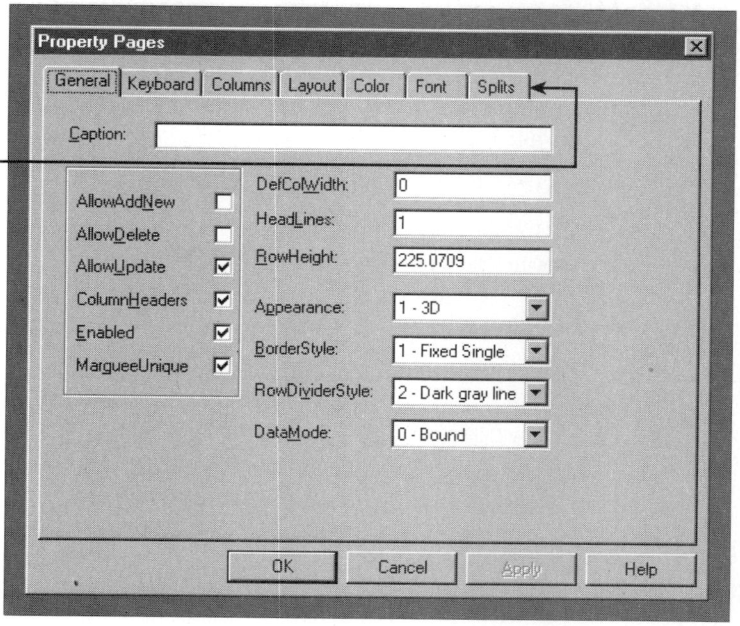

Figure 5-13: DBGrid Property Pages

As shown in Figure 5-13, the Property Pages contains several tabs. Each tab is called a Property Page. Property Pages are used to set the design-time properties for an ActiveX control that are not supported in the Properties window. Some properties can be set both by the Property Pages and the Properties window. When this occurs, it does not matter whether the Property Pages or Properties window are used.

When using ActiveX controls, the Properties pop-up menu will activate the Property Pages, rather than the Properties window. To use the Properties window with an ActiveX control, click the control to activate it, then press the F4 key. While the interface for all Property Pages are the same, the number and content of each Property Page depends on the specific control.

The DBCombo and DBList Controls

The **DBList** and **DBCombo** controls work like the intrinsic ListBox and ComboBox controls but they support several other properties allowing you to read and write data from and to a database table. Both are bound controls that, like a text box, will display information obtained from a Data control's recordset.

The DBList and DBCombo controls work like the intrinsic list and combo box boxes. The DBList control displays information like a list box does; that is, multiple lines always are visible on the screen. If the size of the object, as it is drawn on the form, cannot display all the lines, then scroll bars will appear. The DBCombo control, works like a combo box in that the DBCombo control supports a drop-down combo box from which the user can select an item.

Like other bound controls you have used, the DBCombo control obtains its information from a Recordset object created by the Data control. Thus, you set properties to identify a Data control, and a field name. Each row in the field is displayed in the list automatically when the program is run. In addition to displaying a field from a single Data control, it is possible to use two Data controls to perform lookup operations. That is, by selecting an item from the list, it is possible to lookup another record in a second Data control. The standard prefix for the DBList control is "dls" and "dbc" for the DBCombo control. The following list summarizes the properties pertaining to the DBCombo and DBList controls:

Object	**DBCombo** **DBList**
Properties	■ The **DataSource** property contains the name of a Data control. It is used to specify a recordset to be updated.

- The **DataField** property works with the DataSource property. It specifies the field in the DataSource that will be updated. Typically the DataField and BoundColumn properties refer to the same field in two different Data controls.
- The **RowSource** property identifies the Data control whose records will be displayed in the list.
- The **ListField** property identifies the field in a recordset that will be displayed. The recordset is determined using the RowSource property.
- The **BoundColumn** property identifies a second field in the Data control identified by RowSource. It typically is used to supply a value to a second Data control. The second Data control and field is specified using the DataSource and DataField properties.
- When an item in the list is selected, the **BoundText** property is updated to the value of the BoundColumn property.
- The **Text** property contains the text of the currently selected item in the control.
- The **MatchEntry** property is used to determine how the search is performed. If set to the constant dblBasicMatching, typing a character will search the list for the first item that matches the character typed by the user. If set to dblExtendedMatching, the search is refined as each character is typed.
- The **SelectedItem** property specifies the bookmark of the selected item in the Recordset object specified by the RowSource property.
- The **VisibleCount** property contains a number indicating the number of items appearing in the visible region of the control.
- The **VisibleItems** property specifies an array of bookmarks with a maximum number of items equal to the VisibleCount property.

In the simplest example, the DBList and DBCombo controls are used to display a list of rows from a field in a recordset. Each row from the underlying recordset created by the Data control is displayed on a single line in the DBList and DBCombo controls. To connect the DBList or DBCombo controls to a recordset, the RowSource and ListField properties are used. In this example, the DBCombo control will be used to display the employee category description pertaining to an employee. The first step is to display a list of valid employee categories.

To create a bound DBCombo control:

1 Create an instance of the DBCombo control on the form named **frmIGA** as shown in Figure 5-14 and set the following properties: RowSource to **datCategory**, ListField to **fldCategoryDescription**, Name to **dbcCategory**, Style to **2 – dbcDropdownList**.

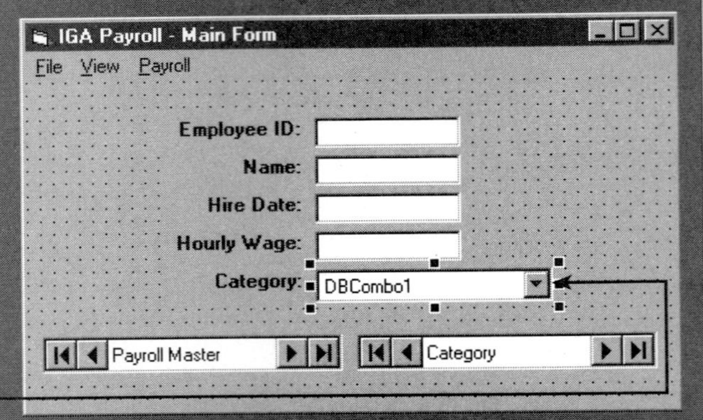

Figure 5-14: Creating a DBCombo control

2 Test the program. The rows should be displayed in the combo box when the list arrow is clicked.

While this example is useful to display a list of items, the DBCombo control most commonly is used to lookup values from one table and update a value in another table. Each employee has a Category ID assigned in the table named tblPayrollMaster. This value is an Integer data type. The number corresponds to a description stored in the table named tblCategory. While the Category ID can be displayed in a bound text box, the user interface would be more intuitive if the descriptive text is displayed. This can be accomplished using the DBCombo control. As the user selects different employee records, the category description corresponding to the numeric Category ID can be displayed in the DBCombo control. In addition, by selecting a different category description in the DBCombo control, the numeric Category ID in the payroll record will be updated. To achieve this functionality, it is necessary to set the BoundColumn, DataSource, and DataField properties. The BoundColumn property will be set to the field named fldCategoryID. When the user selects a different record in the combo box, the BoundColumn property is used to set the BoundText property. In addition, the DataSource property is set to the Data control for the Payroll Master table, and the DataField property also is set to the Category ID. Thus, when a different item is selected from the list, the BoundText property is updated to the new Category ID. Then, the DataField and DataSource properties are used to update the Category ID in the Payroll Master table. Figure 5-15 illustrates the process of selecting the category description 'Manager' in the list box. Assume the Category ID corresponding to Manager is the value three (3).

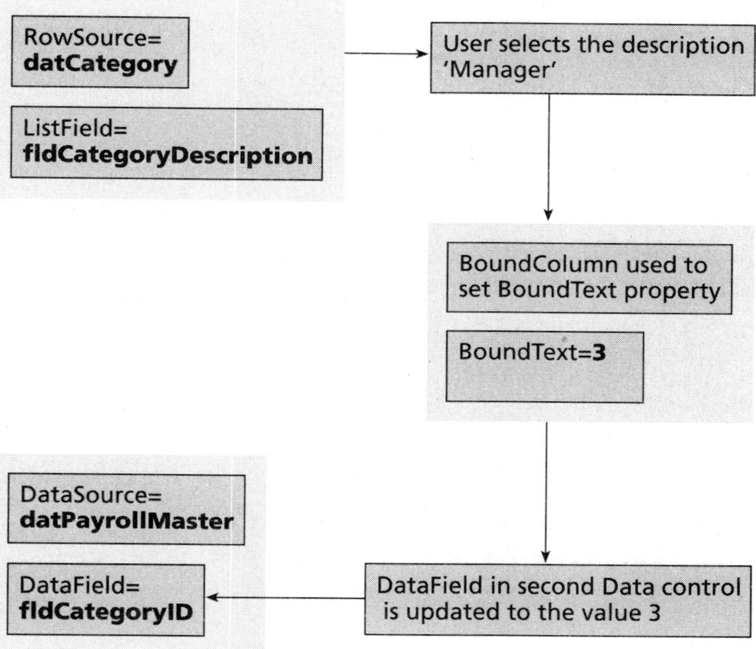

Figure 5-15: Using the DBList with two Data controls

To link two Data controls with a DBCombo control:

1. Activate the Properties window for the DBCombo control named **dbcCategory.** Set BoundColumn to **fldCategoryID**, DataSource to **datPayrollMaster**, and DataField to **fldCategoryID.**
2. Test the program. Using the buttons on the Data control for the table named tblPayrollMaster, select different records. The category description is updated for the different payroll records as they are selected.
3. Locate the first record. Change the category description to a different value. The record in the Payroll Master database is updated with the new corresponding Category ID because the DataSource and DataField properties are set.

In addition to the DBList and DBCombo controls, there is another control that, instead of displaying multiple rows from a single field, can display multiple rows from multiple fields.

The DBGrid Control

The DBGrid control displays the records in a Recordset object associated with a Data control as a grid containing multiple rows and columns. The standard prefix for the DBGrid control is "dbg." Figure 5-16 shows the anatomy of the DBGrid control.

caption

column header

current row indicator

new row indicator

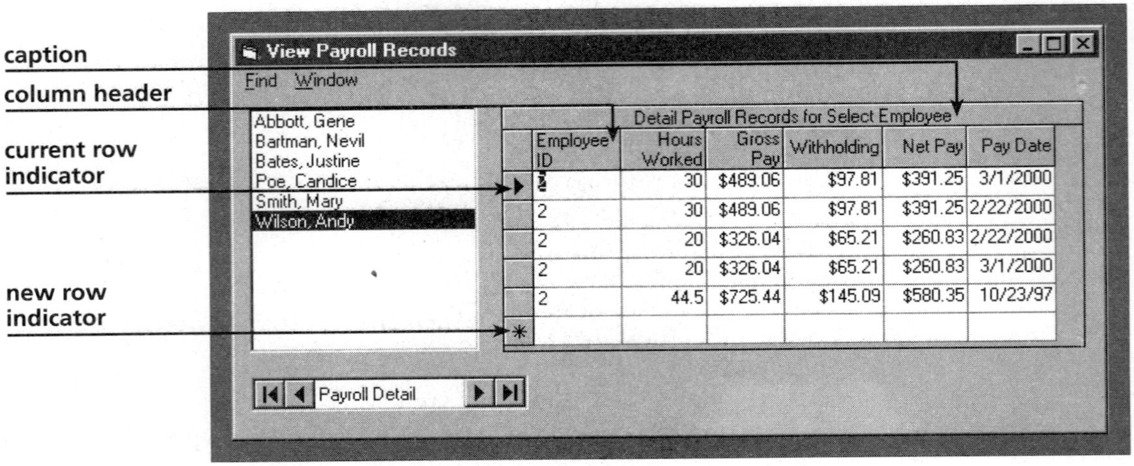

Figure 5-16: Anatomy of the DBGrid control

As shown in Figure 5-16, there is a caption typically used to describe the table or purpose of the control. Under the caption is a row of column headers. By default, these values contain the column names in the table but can be modified to include more descriptive text. An instance of the DBGrid control can have a fixed number of columns and any number of rows. The DBGrid control can store about 1,700 columns and the number of rows varies based on the configuration of your system. The intersection of a row and column in a DBGrid control is called a **cell**.

The left-hand column of the DBGrid control is used to identify the current record by displaying an arrow icon in the row. If the record is being edited, a pencil icon appears. The last row of the control contains an asterisk if record addition is enabled. Editing this row will cause a new row to be added.

Navigating through the individual cells is accomplished using the Arrow, and other keyboard, keys. The following list describes the default behavior of these keys:

- The behavior of the Right Arrow key depends on whether a cell is being edited or not. When a cell receives focus, all the characters in the cell are selected. Pressing the Right Arrow key will move the focus to the next field (column). If the current field (column) is the last visible field, the Right Arrow key has no effect. If a cell is being edited, the Right Arrow key will move forward one character position in the cell. If the insertion point is on the last character, the next field will receive focus.

- The Left Arrow key works like the Right Arrow key but the operations pertain to the previous column instead of the next column. That is, pressing the Left Arrow key while editing the first character in a cell will cause the previous field to be selected.
- The Up and Down Arrow keys locate the previous and next rows, respectively. If the first or last row is current, pressing the key has no effect.
- The Home key will locate the first field in the current row if the current cell is not being edited, and the first character in the cell if it is being edited.
- The End key will locate the last field in the current row if the current cell is not being edited, and the last character in the cell if the cell is being edited.
- The Tab key will change focus to the next object in the tab order.
- Clicking the left-hand column selects an entire row. After selecting a row, the row can be deleted, and other operations performed.

The rows and columns appearing in the DBGrid control are loaded at run time by connecting the DBGrid control to a Data control. The Data control is identifed by setting the DataSource property in the DBGrid control. This has the same effect as setting the DataSource for a text box. There is no property to specify a specific field. That is, there are no equivalent DataField or ListField properties. This is because the DBGrid control operates on all the fields in the recordset at the same time. Note that the standard prefix for the DBGrid control is "dbg."

To create an instance of the DBGrid control and navigate through the rows and columns:

1 Activate the form named **frmPayrollDetail.** Create an instance of the DBGrid control as shown in Figure 5-17 and set the properties as follows: DataSource to **datPayrollDetail** and Name to **dbgPayrollDetail.**

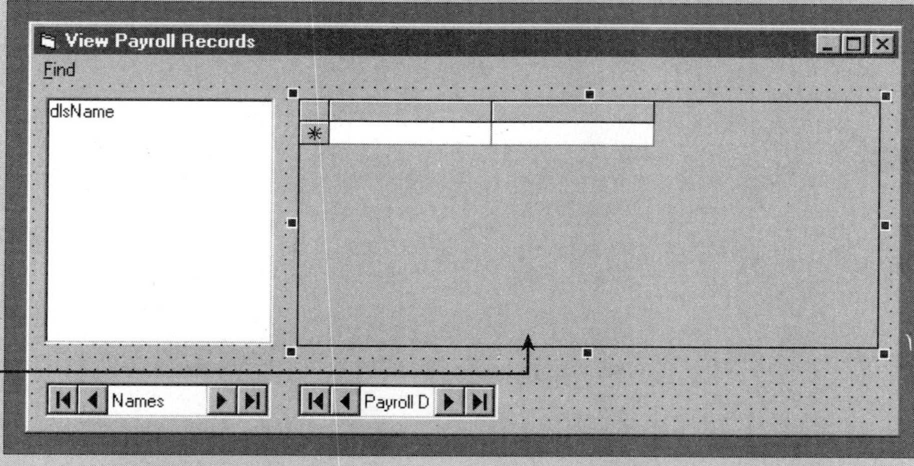

Figure 5-17: Creating the DBGrid control

2 Test the program. On the form's menu bar, click **View** then **Payroll Detail.** The DBGrid control is populated with the records retrieved by the underlying Data control.

Click the **DBGrid** control to change the focus. Press the Right and Left Arrow keys. The focus is changed to the next and previous cells.

Use the Up and Down Arrow keys to locate the next and previous rows. Press the Home and End keys to locate the first and last field in the row. As the focus moves from row to row, the current record pointer is changed. The scroll bars also can be used to change which rows and columns are visible.

Changing the Behavior of the Arrow and Tab Keys

Setting the AllowArrows and the TabAction properties modifies the behavior of the Arrow and Tab keys.

- If the **AllowArrows** property is set to False, pressing an Arrow key will change the focus to the next control on the form. If set to True, the Arrow keys will navigate through the cells in the grid. Focus will not change to another control.
- By default, pressing the Tab key will change the focus to the next control. The **TabAction** property can be set to cause the Tab key to navigate through the different cells in the control.
- If the TabAction is set to grid navigation, and the **WrapCellPointer** property is True, then pressing the Tab key will change the active cell to the first column in the next row when the last column is current. If set to False, then pressing the Tab key will have no effect.

The TabAction property has three settings. You can use the following constants at run time, or use the Property Pages to set them at design time:

- If set to the constant **dbgControlNavigation,** the default, pressing the Tab key will cause the next control on the form to receive focus.
- If set to the constant **dbgColumnNavigation**, pressing the Tab key will move the focus to the cell in the next or previous column. If the last column in the DBGrid control is active, then pressing the Tab key will cause focus to change to the next control on the form.
- If set to the constant **dbgGridNavigation**, the Tab key moves the current cell to the next or previous column. What happens when the Tab key is pressed if the last column is active, depends on the setting of the WrapCellPointer property.

To see the effects of the TabAction property:

1 Activate the Property Pages for the **DBGrid control** you just created. Activate the **Keyboard Property Page**.

2 Check the **WrapCellPointer** check box, then click **2 - Grid Navigation** from the combo box. Click **OK** to change the properties.

3 Test the program. Display the Payroll Detail form, activate the DBGrid control, and press the Tab and Shift+Tab keys. The cell focus moves from cell to cell. When the last column has focus and the Tab key is pressed, focus changes to the first column in the next row.

Formatting the DBGrid Control

When the DBGrid control is created, by default it displays two rows and two columns at design time. Each column has an empty column header, which can store a descriptive prompt. When the program was run, the field names were displayed automatically in the column headers. The Property Pages are used to define both the general appearance of the DBGrid control and the appearance of each column. The General tab on the Property Pages defines properties that apply to all the columns in the DBGrid control.

Object	DBGrid
Properties	■ The **Caption** property will cause a caption to be displayed in the DBGrid control on its own line just above the column headers. ■ The **HeadLines** property is a value between 0 and 10 and identifies the number of lines displayed in the column headers. ■ The **BorderStyle** property, if set to **1 - Fixed Single**, draws a border around the region of the DBGrid control. If set to **0 - None**, no border is drawn. ■ The **RowDividerStyle** property describes the characteristics of the line separating each row and column. For a description of the valid settings, see the Help topic "RowDividerStyle property" for more information. ■ If the **AllowAddNew** property is set to True, the DBGrid control will display an asterisk in the last row of the grid, and allow new records to be added. If the underlying recordset is not updateable, new records cannot be added even when the AllowAddNew property is True. ■ If the **AllowUpdate** property is set to True, the user can modify rows in the DBGrid control, otherwise data cannot be modified. The Recordset object may not enable updates even if AllowUpdate is True for the DBGrid control. ■ If the **AllowDelete** property is set to True, records can be deleted from the DBGrid control, otherwise records cannot be deleted. Again, if the underlying recordset is not updateable, then records cannot be deleted and a trappable error occurs when the user tries to delete the record.

	■ The **Text** property pertains to a Column object and contains a formatted version of the data. The data is formatted based on the value of the NumberFormat property. ■ The **Value** property also pertains to a Column object and contains the raw data stored as a Variant data type.
Events	■ The **BeforeDelete** event occurs just before removing a selected record from the database. If the cancel argument is set to True, the deletion will be canceled and the AfterDelete event will not occur. Displaying a message box in this event procedure to confirm deletion is common. ■ The **AfterDelete** event occurs immediately after the record is deleted.

Remember that the Recordset and TableDef objects have a Fields collection containing one Field object for each field in the Recordset or TableDef objects. When you ran the program, the number of columns, and the contents of each column is determined by using the Recordset object of the underlying Data control.

Just as the Field object and Fields collection identify the fields in a recordset, the Column object and Columns collection identifies the columns in the DBGrid control. The Columns collection is a zero-based collection containing one Column object for each column in the DBGrid control. Each Column object in the Columns collection supports the properties that pertain to an individual column like the column's caption, the field in a table or query to be displayed, a default value if any, and the format of the data displayed in the column.

Programming tip

The Columns collection contains a numeric index for each Column object in the collection. The Columns collection does not support a string key to identify a specific column unlike other collections you have used.

The Columns Property Page is used to define the title, format, and field of each column displayed in the DBGrid control. The Column list box is used to select a column. The Columns Property Page is shown in Figure 5-18.

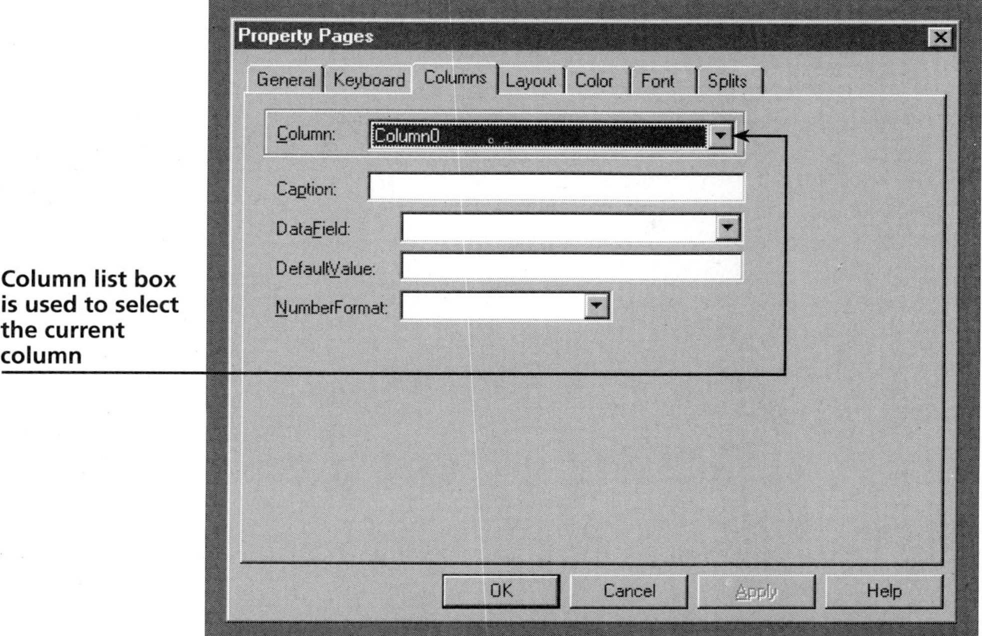

Figure 5-18: The Columns Property Page

The Layout Property Page works like the Columns Property Page. A column is selected using the Column list box to select a column, then the properties that define the layout of the column are set.

The following list summarizes the Column object of the Columns collection:

Object	Column
Properties	■ The **Caption** property contains the text displayed at the top of the column (the column header). ■ The **DataField** property works like the DataField property that applies to a text box. It identifies the field for a table or query. The DataField property is set automatically when the fields are retrieved. ■ The **DefaultValue** property is a placeholder for you to program an event that will set a default value of a column. ■ The **NumberFormat** property defines how numeric data in a column is displayed. The formats are the same as the named formats used in the Format statement. ■ The **Split** object is used to split the region of the DBGrid control into multiple panes much like you can split a spreadsheet in Microsoft Excel.

- If the **AllowSizing** property is set to True, the mouse pointer changes to a double-headed arrow when positioned over the row or column divider. The user can resize the rows and columns by dragging them at run time.
- The **Alignment**, **Locked**, and **Width** properties work like properties of the same names for the other controls you have used. The DBGrid control sets the default alignment based on the data type of the underlying field.
- The **Visible** property, if set to False, causes a column to be invisible. Even though the user cannot see the column, the data in the column can be accessed programmatically.

To change the captions for a column, it is necessary to load the field names from the Data control at design time. This can be accomplished by clicking the right mouse button while the insertion point is positioned over the DBGrid control and clicking Retrieve Fields. The fields from the table identified by the Data control are loaded into the column headings for the DBGrid control. Then, the Property Pages can be used to change the caption and size of each individual column.

In addition to setting the caption and formatting for each column, it is possible to adjust the column width at design time by making the DBGrid control user interface (UI) active. This is accomplished by activating the pop-up menu for the DBGrid control, then clicking Edit. After clicking Edit, the mouse pointer will change to a double-headed arrow when positioned over a row divider or column divider. Dragging the mouse at this time will increase or decrease the size of the row or column, respectively.

To change the column titles and sizes:

1. Click the DBGrid control on the form named **frmPayrollDetail** to activate it.
2. Click the right mouse button and click **Retrieve Fields** to load the fields into the DBGrid control. Respond **OK** to the dialog that appears.
3. Click the right mouse button and click **Properties** to activate the Property Pages for the control. Click the **General** Property Page and set the **Headlines** property to **2**. This will cause the column headers to be displayed on two lines. Click the **Columns** Property Page, then select each column using the Column list box. Change the caption so the "fld" prefix is removed and the words are separated by spaces. The NumberFormat list box contains several numeric formatting options.
4. Select the **Layout** Property Page as shown in Figure 5-19.

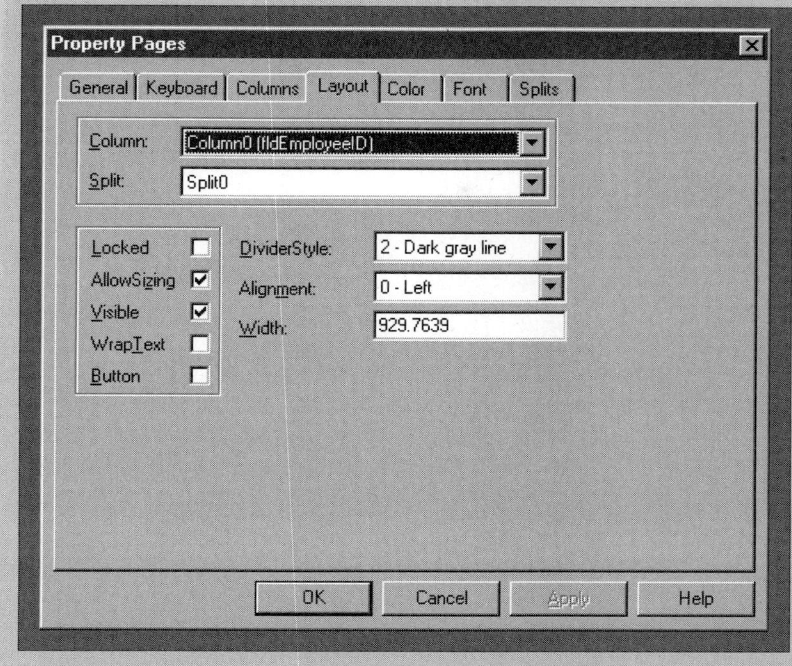

Figure 5-19: The Layout Property Page

5 Scroll through the different columns using the list box. The alignment is set based on whether the data type is a String or Numeric. Apply the changes and close the Property Pages.

Programming tip

Be careful to click the OK or Apply buttons on the Property Pages to record any changes. Clicking the Close button in the Control-menu box will cause any changes to be lost.

Selecting Records Dynamically

Another common task is to link two DBGrid controls together or to link a DBCombo or DBList control with the DBGrid control. Currently, the DBGrid control on the Payroll Detail form displays all the rows. The program can be modified easily to display in the DBGrid control only those records matching the currently selected employee. Employees are selected by name using the DBList control. When a record is selected, the Click event can be used to create a SELECT statement and recreate the recordset only for those records having the Employee ID matching the selected name. To accomplish this, the BoundText property for the DBList control can be set to the Employee ID field, and used in a SELECT statement to select the matching payroll detail records.

To display the payroll detail records for one employee in the DBGrid control:

1. Open the **Payroll Detail** form and activate the **Properties** window.
2. Set the BoundColumn property to **fldEmployeeID** for the DBList control named **dlsName**.
3. Locate the **dlsName_Click** event procedure in the Code window and enter the following statements:

```
Dim pstrSQL As String
pstrSQL = "SELECT * FROM tblPayrollDetail " & _
    "WHERE fldEmployeeID = " & "'" & _
    dlsName.BoundText & "'"
datPayrollDetail.RecordSource = pstrSQL
datPayrollDetail.Refresh
```

4. Test the program. Open the Payroll Detail form. Click each employee. The visible records are changed in the DBGrid control.

When you used bound controls like a text box and label, remember that explicitly calling the methods of the underlying recordset to navigate records updates the current record. This change was reflected in the Data control and the bound controls. The same also is True for the DBGrid control. That is, you can call the methods of the recordset to locate records. These changes are reflected in the DBGrid control. The following event procedures exist for the Find menu commands on the Payroll Detail form.

```
Private Sub mnuFindNext_Click( )
    datPayrollDetail.Recordset.MoveNext
End Sub

Private Sub mnuFindPrevious_Click( )
    datPayrollDetail.Recordset.MovePrevious
End Sub
```

When the program is run, these methods are called on the recordset affecting the current row.

To locate the records in the recordset:

1. Test the program. Open the Payroll Detail form.

   Click the **Find Next** and **Find Previous** commands to locate different records. The current record pointer in the DBGrid control is updated as the current record changes. For brevity, error handlers for these procedures have been omitted to account for BOF and EOF conditions.

Modifying Data with the DBGrid Control

The DBGrid control allows the user to add, change, and delete records. Changes made to the current record are stored in the DBGrid control's copy buffer. Remember that the DBGrid control reads and writes data to the recordset using the Data control and its recordset, and that a Data control has its own copy buffer. Data is manipulated within the DBGrid control's internal copy buffer before being passed to the copy buffer used by the Data control and the recordset. Figure 5-20 illustrates this process.

Three properties pertaining to the DBGrid control determine whether or not records can be added, changed, or deleted: the AllowAddNew, AllowUpdate, and AllowDelete properties.

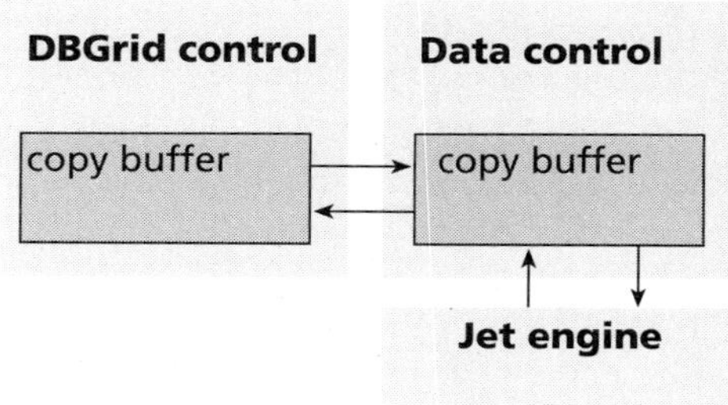

Figure 5-20: The DBGrid and Data controls interaction

Just as the Data control responds to events like Reposition and Validate allowing you to verify input before writing data to a table in the database, the DBGrid control supports several events that occur when the user moves from field to field or from one row to another. Some of these events occur for actions involving an entire record or row in the DBGrid control. Other events occur for actions involving a specific column. The DBGrid control has a copy buffer much like the Data control. When the user locates a different record, the fields in the DBGrid control's copy buffer are written to the Data control. In fact, events for the Data control occur because of actions caused by the DBGrid control. For example, when changes are made in a record, or a new record is located, a Validate event and/or Reposition event occurs on the underlying Data control. You can write code to respond to these events as necessary.

To allow record addition, changes, and deletion:

1. Activate the **General** tab of the DBGrid control's Property Pages. Use the DBGrid control on the form named **frmPayrollDetail**.
2. Click the **AllowAddNew** and **AllowDelete** check boxes, apply the changes, then close the Property Pages.

3 Test the program. Locate the first cell in the row containing the asterisk. This causes a new row to be added in the DBGrid control's internal copy buffer. Enter a payroll record in the row with an Employee ID of **1**.

Locate a different row. This causes the record to be added to the underlying recordset.

Click the border to the left of the field you just added to select the entire record and press the **Delete** key to remove the record.

Events Pertaining to the DBGrid Control

As the user enters information into cells and changes focus from row to row or column to column, several different events occur. Some of these events pertain to the entire record while other events pertain to individual cells. You can respond to these events to validate user input and possibly cancel an action like updating a record. Consider the following scenario where the user is updating two fields in the DBGrid control. The user makes changes to the first field. Then changes are made to a second field, and finally a new row is located. Several events occur as the user performs these tasks.

1. The **BeforeColEdit** event occurs when the user first makes a change to the contents of a specific cell. An integer representing the column is passed as an argument to the event procedure. This integer contains the index of the Column object in the Columns collection. If the *cancel* argument is set to True, editing the cell is cancelled and the original contents of the cell are restored.
2. Immediately after the BeforeColEdit event fires, the **ColEdit** event occurs only if the BeforeColEdit event was not cancelled.
3. When the focus either is changed to another cell in the same row or to another row, editing is complete for the column. Just before the new data in the cell is moved to the DBGrid control's internal copy buffer, the **BeforeColUpdate** event occurs. Commonly, this event is used to validate the contents of the changed cell before continuing. If the contents of the cell are invalid, the event's two arguments can be used to restore the original data to the cell and cancel the update.
4. If the BeforeColUpdate is not cancelled, the **AfterColUpdate** event occurs. This event occurs immediately after the new contents of the cell are copied to the DBGrid control's internal copy buffer.
5. The **AfterColEdit** event occurs next indicating that editing is complete in the current cell. This event occurs even if no changes were made to the current cell or if editing was cancelled. The BeforeColEdit and AfterColEdit events commonly are used to update a status message or change the insertion point while the record is being updated.
6. When the user locates a different row, the DBGrid control will try to update any changes in the record to the database. The **BeforeUpdate** event

occurs in the DBGrid control just before the row is copied to the Data control's copy buffer. The event can be used to validate the cells in the row before committing the changes. The event can be canceled by setting the *cancel* argument to True.

7. If the BeforeUpdate event is not cancelled, then the **AfterUpdate** event occurs indicating the update is complete. It is common to recompute the values of any computed columns in this event.

The events pertaining to the Data control also occur as a record is being updated. That is, when the data is copied from the DBGrid control's internal copy buffer to the Data control's copy buffer, the Validate event occurs for the Data control. Deciding whether to validate data in the Data control's Validate event or in the DBGrid control is up to the programmer as both solutions will work. Also, as different records are located in the DBGrid control, the Reposition event continues to occur to the Data control. By performing the validation in the DBGrid control, however, error checks can be performed on each column as changes are made instead of validating the entire row in the Data control's Validate event.

When inserting data into the DBGrid control, there are other events that occur in a defined sequence.

1. When the user selects a new record in the DBGrid control (identified by an asterisk (*) in the status column), and begins editing, the **BeforeInsert** event occurs.
2. As cells are edited, the events shown in the previous list occur.
3. When editing is complete, the **AfterInsert** event occurs.

The DBGrid control supports two events pertaining to record deletion: the BeforeDelete event and the AfterDelete event.

Validating Changes in the DBGrid Control

Typically, when the user changes the contents of a cell, adds or deletes a record, either the data should be validated, or the request confirmed by displaying a message box. Using the same techniques you used in the previous chapter with the Data control's Validate event, you can validate input, and request user confirmation by programming the change events pertaining to the DBGrid control. The following list summarizes the syntax of selected events:

Syntax

Private Sub *object*_**BeforeColUpdate** ([*index* **As Integer**,] *colindex* **As Integer**, *oldvalue* **As Variant**, *cancel* **As Integer**)

Private Sub *object*_**RowColChange** ([*index* **As Integer**, *lastrow* **As String**, *lastcol* **As Integer**])

Dissection

- The *index* identifies the control if it is a member of a control array. The *colindex* contains an Integer value indicating the column that is being updated. Like the Columns collection, the first column has an index of zero (0), the second a value of one (1), and so on.

- The *oldvalue* contains the value of the column before it was edited. This value commonly is used to restore the contents of the column when editing is abandoned.
- If the *cancel* argument is set to True, editing is canceled on the field.
- The *object* must be a valid instance of the DBGrid control, and the *index* is used to identify the DBGrid control uniquely if it is a member of a control array.
- The *lastrow* argument is a String data type representing a bookmark. The concept of a bookmark is the same as in the previous chapter. It is used to locate a record.
- The *lastcol* argument contains an Integer value that identifies the previously selected column. Using these two arguments, it is possible to restore the contents of a cell that previously had focus, or locate the previously selected row.
- The *index* argument is used to identify a specific control that is a member of a control array as you have seen in the past.

Code Example

```
Private Sub dbgPayrollDetail_BeforeColUpdate(ByVal ColIndex
As Integer, OldValue As Variant, Cancel As Integer)
    If ColIndex = 0 Then
        If Not _
            IsNumeric(dbgPayrollDetail.Columns(ColIndex) Then
            Cancel = True
            dbgPayrollDetail.Columns(ColIndex).Value = _
                OldValue
        End If
    End If
End Sub
```

Code Dissection

These statements examine the first column to make sure it is numeric. If it is not, the update is canceled, and the value of the column is restored to the value before editing began.

This program will use the BeforeColUpdate event to validate changes to the fields in the DBGrid control. Thus, after focus is changed from a cell whose value changed, this event will occur. Then, the current column will be validated to make sure that the column contains a numeric or Date value as needed. To accomplish this task, you need a way to reference the contents of the current cell.

Because the index of the current column is passed as an argument to the BeforeColUpdate event, the following statement fragments can be used to reference the contents of the current cell. The following two statements are equivalent because the Value property is the default property for a Column object:

```
dbgPayrollDetail.Columns(ColIndex).Value
dbgPayrollDetail.Columns(ColIndex)
```

This syntax resembles the syntax you have used to reference an item in a specific collection. Columns(ColIndex) references the contents of the current column (the Value property). Both of these properties select the value of the column for the currently selected row.

To validate changes to the DBGrid control:

1 Active the **dbgPayrollDetail_BeforeColUpdate** event procedure for the form named **frmPayrollDetail** and enter the following statements:

```
Select Case ColIndex
    Case 1, 2, 3, 4
        If Not _
            IsNumeric(dbgPayrollDetail.Columns _
                (ColIndex).Value) Then
            MsgBox "Value must be numeric"
            dbgPayrollDetail.Columns(ColIndex) = _
                OldValue
            Cancel = True
        End If
    Case 5
        If Not _
            IsDate(dbgPayrollDetail.Columns(ColIndex)) _
            Then
            MsgBox "Value must be date"
            dbgPayrollDetail.Columns(ColIndex) = _
                OldValue
            Cancel = True
        End If
End Select
```

2 Test the program. Open the Payroll Detail form.

Select the different cells and enter invalid data in a field. When locating another field, the message box should appear, and the original contents of the control should be restored.

Enter an invalid date in the Pay Date field. Again, a message box should be displayed and the original contents restored.

These statements validate the numeric columns (1, 2, 3 and 4) and the Pay Date columns. If the tests fail, the original contents of the field are restored by setting the value of the column to the old value. Remember that the old value is passed to the event procedure in the *OldValue* argument. The *cancel* argument is set to True causing the update to be aborted.

This validation task also could be performed in the BeforeUpdate event. If this event is used, all the fields must be validated at once because the event occurs only once before the entire column is updated. Furthermore, the fields also could be validated in the Data control's Validate event.

Deletion of records also can be confirmed using the BeforeDelete event. Remember, this event is generated just before the record is deleted. Setting the *cancel* argument to True causes the deletion to be aborted.

To confirm record deletion:

1 Locate the **dbgPayrollDetail_BeforeDelete** event procedure for the form named **frmPayrollDetail** and enter the following statements:

```
Dim pintReturn As Integer
pintReturn = MsgBox("Delete current record?", _
    vbQuestion + vbYesNo)
If pintReturn = vbNo Then
    Cancel = True
End If
```

2 Test the program. Locate the Payroll Detail form. Select the first record by clicking the row containing the current record indicator. Press the Delete key to attempt to delete the record. This causes the BeforeDelete event to occur and the code you just wrote to be executed. The message box should appear. Click **No** in the message box to cancel the deletion.

Creating Columns at Run Time

Another feature of the DBGrid control is the capability to add and delete columns at run time. It also is possible to modify the appearance of individual columns at run time dynamically. In this program, the Net Pay is stored in a database column. It also is reasonable, however, to compute this value in the DBGrid control and store the result in a column not bound to the database. Both implementations have advantages and disadvantages. Storing the Net Pay in a column in the database will increase the physical size of the database, but the field need not be computed from the Gross Pay and Withholding each time the record is displayed. Computing the Net Pay has the reverse effect.

The mechanics of adding a column at run time is the same as adding an item to any collection. That is, the Add method is called on the Columns collection, with one argument, an Index value indicating where the column should be inserted. The following statement will insert a new column as the first column in the DBGrid control. The index of the other columns is adjusted accordingly.

```
dbgPayrollDetail.Columns.Add 0
```

When a column is added, it initially is invisible, has no caption, and is not bound to a field in the recordset. To make the column visible, set its caption, and bind the field to the recordset, the Visible property must be set to True, the Caption property of the column set, and the DataField column set to a field in the underlying recordset as shown in the following statements:

```
With dbgPayrollDetail
    .Columns.Add 0
    .Columns(0).Caption = "New Column"
    .Columns(0).Visible = True
    .Columns(0).DataField = "fldEmployeeID"
End With
```

These statements insert a new column as the first column in the DBGrid control, set the caption in the row header to the value "New Column," make the column visible, then bind the column to the field "fldEmployeeID."

Linking Multiple DBGrid Controls

Given the master-detail relationship that exists between the two payroll tables, it would be suitable to create a user interface such that selecting a row in one DBGrid control that displays the records for the master payroll table would cause the detail records corresponding to the selected Employee ID to be displayed in a second DBGrid control. To accomplish this task, two Data controls are used on a form—one for each table. The DBGrid controls are in turn bound to the Data controls. When the user selects a record, the RowColChange event occurs. In this event procedure, it is possible to create a SELECT statement and recreate the recordset for the second Data control so only the records corresponding to the selected Employee ID field will be displayed in the second Data control.

To link two DBGrid controls:

1 Locate the **dbgPayrollMaster_RowColChange** event procedure in the Code window for the form named **frmLinked**, and enter the following statements into the event procedure:

```
Dim pstrSQL As String
pstrSQL = "SELECT * FROM tblPayrollDetail " & _
    "WHERE fldEmployeeID = '" & _
    datPayrollMaster.Recordset![fldEmployeeID] & "'"
datPayrollDetail.RecordSource = pstrSQL
datPayrollDetail.Refresh
```

2 Test the program. Open the form by clicking **View** on the menu bar, then **Linked DBGrids.** Select different master records in the first table. The detail records for the corresponding Employee ID field are displayed in the second DBGrid control.

SUMMARY

In this chapter, you have learned how to use the SQL programming language to modify data in a database table. The SQL statements introduced are intended to provide an introduction to the SQL language. Much more complex queries certainly are possible.

You also have learned how to add ActiveX controls to a project, and use three ActiveX controls that interact with a database. These three ActiveX controls are just a few of the hundreds of ActiveX controls available to the Visual Basic programmer. In the next chapter, you will learn about several other ActiveX controls that can improve considerably a program's user interface.

- SQL is made up of two types of statements. Data manipulation statements are used to add, change, and delete records in a table. Data definition statements are used to change the structure of the database itself.
- The SELECT statement is the primary means to retrieve data from a table or query. It can contain a WHERE clause to restrict the rows that are selected. It also can contain an ORDER BY clause to specify in what order the selected records are returned. The SELECT statement also allows specific records to be selected. In Visual Basic, a SELECT statement typically returns records and is used as an argument to the OpenRecordset method.
- DAO supports the Errors collection and Error object to store information about any database errors that have occurred. In some situations, a database operation may generate several errors in which case the Errors collection contains several Error objects.
- Another type of query is an action query. Action queries do not return records. Rather, they perform an action like record addition or deletion. In Visual Basic, action queries are run using the Execute method which pertains to the Database object.
- There are three statements used to perform action queries. The INSERT statement adds a row to a table. The UPDATE statement will update one or more rows as defined by the WHERE clause. In a single UPDATE statement, multiple columns can be updated at the same time. The DELETE statement removes rows from a table. Again, it can contain a WHERE clause to select which rows are deleted.

- The DBList and DBCombo controls are data-aware ActiveX controls, and can be thought of as a superset of the intrinsic ListBox and ComboBox controls. Both can be bound to two Data controls. This technique is useful to perform lookup operations.
- The DBGrid control also is a data-aware control. It displays multiple rows and columns at the same time. The DBGrid control supports several properties to control the behavior of the keyboard keys used to navigate through the DBGrid control. It also supports extensive properties to control how the rows and columns are formatted.

QUESTIONS

1. The ___________ statements are all valid SQL DML statements.

a. SELECT, UPDATE, INSERT, DELETE
b. SELECT, CHANGE, INSERT, REMOVE
c. SELECT, CHANGE, INSERT, DELETE
d. RECORDSET, UPDATE, INSERT, DELETE
e. none of the above

2. When using a WHERE clause, values must be enclosed in special characters depending on the data type. ___________ variables are enclosed in single quotes, ___________ variables are enclosed in pound signs, and ___________ variables are not enclosed by any special characters.

a. Date, String, Numeric
b. Numeric, Date, String
c. String, Date, Numeric
d. Numeric, String, Date
e. None of the above.

3. The ___________ characters are all pattern-matching characters used with the Like keyword.

a. *, [,], #, !
b. *, {, }, #, !
c. *, [,], ^, !
d. &, [,], ^, !
e. all of the above

4. When using an ActiveX control, design time properties can be set using: ____________.
   a. the Properties window
   b. Property Pages
   c. a pop-up menu
   d. both a and b
   e. all of the above
5. The ____________ dialog is used to add an ActiveX control to a project.
   a. Project
   b. References
   c. Components
   d. ActiveX
   e. Insert ActiveX
6. In which order do the following events occur when updating the contents of the DBGrid control ____________.
   a. BeforeColUpdate, BeforeColEdit, AfterColEdit, AfterColUpdate
   b. BeforeUpdate, BeforeColUpdate, AfterColUpdate, AfterUpdate
   c. BeforeColEdit, BeforeColUpdate, AfterColUpdate, AfterColEdit
   d. both a and c
   e. none of the above
7. The ____________ property contains the field displayed in the DBList and DBCombo controls. The table (Data control) used is specified by the ____________ property.
   a. DataSource, DataField
   b. ListField, BoundColumn
   c. ListField, RowSource
   d. DataField, BoundText
   e. DataSource, ListField
8. The ____________ property and the ____________ property are used to change the behavior of the Tab and Arrow keys in the DBGrid control.
   a. TabKey, ArrowKey
   b. Tab, Arrow
   c. TabAction, ArrowKey
   d. TabAction, AllowArrows
   e. Tab, AllowArrows
9. What are the properties that control whether or not records can be added, changed, and deleted from the DBGrid control?
   a. AddNew, Update, Delete
   b. Add, Update, Delete
   c. AllowAdd, AllowUpdate, AllowDelete
   d. AllowAddNew, AllowUpdate, AllowDelete
   e. AllowNew, AllowUpdate, AllowDelete

10. Write a SELECT statement to retrieve all the rows from the table named tblPayrollMaster where the hourly wage (fldWage) is greater than or equal to $5.50 and less then $10.00. Return the rows sorted in descending order by hourly wage.

11. Write a SELECT statement to retrieve all the rows from the table named tblPayrollMaster where the field named fldDatePaid is equal to 10/22/2001.

12. Write a SELECT statement to retrieve all the rows from the table named tblPayrollMaster where fldHireDate, a Date data type, is between 3/1/90 and 3/1/97.

13. Write a SELECT statement to retrieve all the rows from the table named tblPayrollMaster where the field named fldLastName begins with the character "C."

14. Write an INSERT statement to insert the value **A10** into the field named fldEmployeeID, the value **7/17/2000** into the field named fldDate, and **2874.22** into the field named fldValue. The data should be inserted into the table named tblPayrollMaster.

15. Write an UPDATE statement to increase the value of fldHourlyWage by 5 percent where fldName is **John Smith**.

16. Write a DELETE statement to delete the row from tblCategory where the value of the field fldCategoryID is **3**.

17. Write the necessary Visual Basic statements to open the database named **A:\Chapter.05\Startup\IGA.mdb** and create a recordset based on the following SELECT statement.

    ```
    SELECT * FROM tblCategory
    ```

18. Write the event procedure that will execute just before the selected record in the DBGrid control named **dbgPayroll** is deleted. The code in the event procedure should display a message box requesting confirmation and cancel the deletion depending on the user's response.

19. Write a For Each loop that will examine the Error objects in the Errors Collection. For Each Error object, add the error description to the contents of the list box named lstErrors.

20. Write a For Each loop that will examine all the Column objects in the Columns collection for the DBGrid control's object named dbgTest. For each column, set the Alignment property so the text is centered in the column.

EXERCISES

All of the following exercises use the database named **Chapter.05\Exercise\Inventory.mdb.** Figure 5-21 illustrates the structure of the database.

1. In this exercise you will use SQL statements to add, change, and delete different rows in the database.

a. Create a new project and set the Name property of the form to **frmExercise1**. Save the form using the name **Chapter.05\Exercise\frmExercise1.frm** and the project using the name **Chapter.05\Exercise\Exercise1.vbp**.

b. Use the Components dialog to add the DBGrid control to the project.

c. For all the objects you create, set the Name property such that it uses the standard prefix followed by a descriptive name.

d. Write the necessary statements to open the database and store a reference to the object in a Private form-level variable.

e. Assume that there are three valid Category ID's numbered 1, 2 and 3. Create an option group to represent the different categories.

f. Create a text box to store the percent amount of a price increase. This value will be used to update the field **fldCost** in the table **tblInventory**.

g. Create a command button that, when clicked, will increase the cost of the specified category by the amount indicated in the text box.

h. Create another command button that uses an input box to obtain a part number. If a part number is entered, write statements to delete all the records in the tables named **tblSales** and **tblInventory** having the selected part number.

i. Create two DBGrid controls to display the changes and deletions that occur for the two tables. Remember that the DBGrid controls must be bound to a Data control.

j. Save the form using the name **frmSQL** and the project using the name **SQL.vbp**.

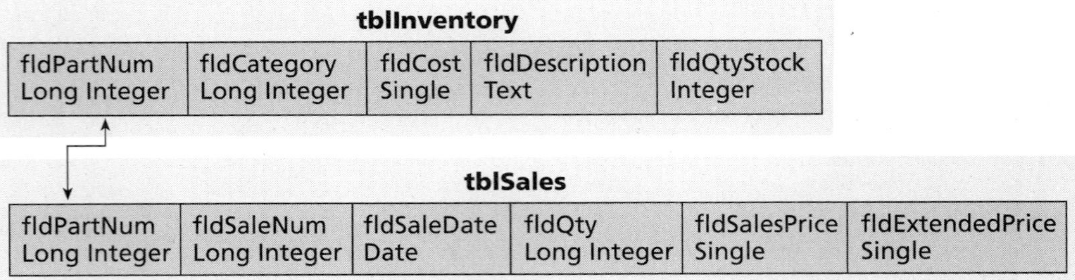

Figure 5-21: Database structure

2. In this exercise you will use unbound controls to locate, add, change, and delete records from the table named tblInventory.

a. Create a new project and set the Name property of the form to **frmExercise2**. Save the form using the name **Chapter.05\Exercise\frmExercise2.frm** and the project using the name **Chapter.05\Exercise\Exercise2.vbp**.

b. Add the necessary text boxes and label controls to display the field in the table named tblInventory.

c. Write the statements to open the database named **Chapter.05\Exercise\Inventory.mdb**. Create an updateable recordset based on the table named tblInventory.

d. Create a menu that has commands to locate records in the recordset. For each menu command, write the necessary code to locate the record and display the current record in the text boxes.

e. Create menu commands to add and change records. It should be possible to cancel changes.

f. When a new record is added, update the text boxes as needed. If the user wants to commit the addition, add the record to the database and make the newly-added record the current record.

g. To process the record changes, verify that the data types are correct before trying to record the changes to the recordset. If the data is valid, record the changes to the recordset. Otherwise, restore the text boxes to their previous state before editing began. The user also should be able to cancel the changes.

h. Test the program. Make sure the text boxes are synchronized properly with the current record and the record addition and updating is working properly.

3. This exercise requires that you use the DBList and DBGrid controls.

a. Create a new project and set the Name property of the form to **frmExercise3**. Save the form using the name **Chapter.05\Exercise\frmExercise3.frm** and the project using the name **Chapter.05\Exercise\Exercise3.vbp**.

b. Add the DBList and DBGrid controls to the project.

c. Create two Data controls on the form. The first Data control should reference the table named **tblSales** and the second should reference the table named **tblInventory**.

d. Create a DBList control that displays the field named **fldPartNumber** from the table named **tblInventory**.

e. Create a DBGrid control that displays the rows from the table **tblSales**.

f. Use the Property Pages for the DBGrid control to update the column captions and set the numeric format to Currency for the Single data types.

g. Resize the columns as needed.

h. Code the appropriate event procedure so when the user clicks a part number in the DBList control, the sales records corresponding to the part numbers are displayed in the DBGrid control.

i. Set the necessary properties to prohibit the user from editing the contents of the DBGrid control at run time.

j. Make the column containing the part number invisible at run time in the DBGrid control.

4. The following exercise requires that you link two DBGrid controls together.

a. Create a new project and set the Name property of the form to **frmExercise4**. Save the form using the name **Chapter.05\Exercise\frmExercise4.frm** and the project using the name **Chapter.05\Exercise\Exercise4.vbp.**

b. Add the DBGrid control to the project.

c. Create two Data controls on the form. The first Data control should reference the table named **tblInventory** and the second should reference the table named **tblSales.**

d. Create two DBGrid controls to display the data from the two Data controls.

e. Load the fields for each DBGrid control and format the columns.

f. Create a caption for both DBGrid controls.

g. Write the necessary statements that will execute when the user selects a row in the first DBGrid control. When a row is selected, only those sales records corresponding to the selected part number should be displayed in the second DBGrid control.

h. Write the code for the appropriate event procedure in the second DBGrid control that will verify that the fields **fldQtySold**, **fldSalesPrice**, and **fldExtendedPrice** all contain valid numbers as the fields are being edited. If a field contains invalid data, cancel the update and restore the contents of the fields to their previous values.

i. Test the program. Make sure the DBGrid controls are synchronized.

CHAPTER

6

Using the Windows Common Controls

Creating a Spreadsheet and Drill-Down Interface for ETC Incorporated

case▶ ETC Incorporated is a multinational corporation with 10 worldwide offices. In this chapter, you will create two separate programs. The first will use a control that resembles the DBGrid control in that it contains rows and columns. This grid will not be bound to a database, however. Rather, it will work something like a spreadsheet in that the user will display and edit data in rows and columns. The second program will display the names, phone numbers, and extensions of all employees in the organization, hierarchically.

SECTION A

objectives

In this section you will:

- Use the MSFlexGrid control that operates much like a spreadsheet
- Apply formatting to the MSFlexGrid control
- Add and delete rows and columns to the MSFlexGrid control at run time
- Write code to iterate through the rows and columns of the MSFlexGrid control to summarize values
- Integrate a text box with the MSFlexGrid control to edit the contents of the grid
- Use a StatusBar control to display information about the state of keyboard keys and other information related to the current status of the program

Programming the MSFlexGrid Control

Previewing the Completed Application

The completed application allows the user to order the various ETC Incorporated internal forms. The user will select a form from a description contained in a list box, specify the quantity ordered in a text box, and then click a command button to add the form to a grid containing all the forms ordered. If an error is made, the user has the capability to remove a form that was ordered, or to change the quantity ordered for a specific form. So a new order can be created, there is a button to remove all the forms from the existing order. Notably, part of the implementation is absent. There neither is a facility to print the order, nor is there any information about who is receiving the order. As such, the focus of the chapter remains on using the MSFlexGrid control. These features could be implemented easily using the database techniques presented in the previous chapters.

To preview the completed application:

1. Start **Visual Basic** and open the project named **Chapter.06\Complete\ETCGridC.vbp**.
2. Run the program. The main form, as shown in Figure 6-1, contains a list box to select items, a text box to select the quantity ordered for a particular item, and command buttons to add and remove items. At the bottom of the form, there is a status bar to display the status of the editing keys. When the MSFlexGrid control has focus, the status bar is updated to display the current row and column selected in the grid.

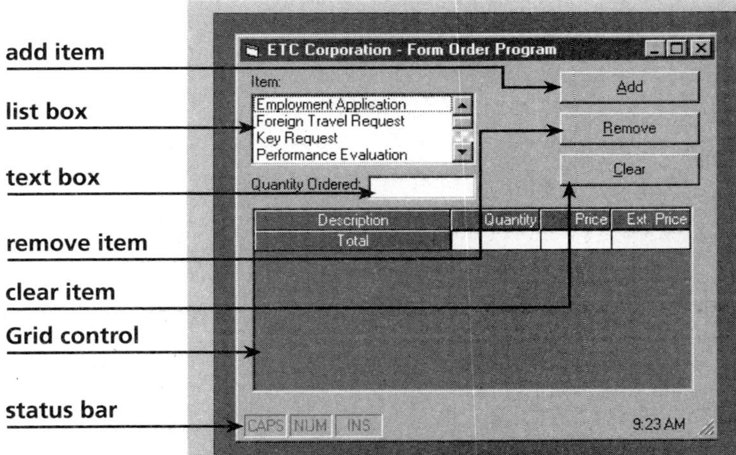

Figure 6-1: Completed program

3 Click an item in the list box, then enter a numeric value for the quantity ordered. Click the **Add** command button to add the item to the grid. Repeat this process for several different items. As new items are added, the dollar amount of the order total is updated. If enough items are added to the order, and they cannot all be displayed in the grid, scroll bars will appear automatically.

4 Click a row in the grid, then click the **Remove** command button. The row is removed and the total again is updated.

5 Double-click the quantity ordered for a specific row, then modify the quantity ordered value. Press the **Enter** key to record the change. After pressing the Enter key, the new value is displayed, the extended price of the item is updated, and the order total is updated. When the grid has focus, the status bar displays the current row and column on the left-hand side.

6 Click the **Clear** command button to remove the items from the grid in preparation for another order.

7 Note that the status bar has inset regions to identify the status of the Caps, Num, and Ins keys. These regions indicate the status of these keys. When disabled, the values appear shaded. When the keys are enabled, they appear in a normal typeface. Click the **Caps Lock**, **Num Lock**, and **Ins** keys to see the effect on the status bar.

8 End the program then exit Visual Basic.

The MSFlexGrid control was used in the previous example to display information in rows and columns. It is supplied with the Professional Edition of Visual Basic and can be added to a project just like any other ActiveX control.

The MSFlexGrid Control

The MSFlexGrid control works with tabular data; that is, it has rows and columns much like a two-dimensional array. In this chapter, the term **grid** refers to the MSFlexGrid control, to reduce wordiness. The maximum number of rows and columns that can be stored in a grid varies depending on the amount of memory and swap space available on the computer. The grid can be bound to a Data control, but the data in the grid is read-only at run time. Typically, the DBGrid control is better suited to working with data in a database. In this chapter, you will create a grid that will list the items for an invoice. While this information is not recorded to a database or text file, the program could be extended easily to perform this task.

The grid supports properties to define the number of rows and columns, and the appearance of the data in the rows and columns. The grid is like a two-dimensional array of rows and columns. The intersection of a row and column is called a **cell** just as with the DBGrid control. Rows and columns are zero-based. That is, the first row and column each have an index of zero (0). A cell can contain either text or a picture. Formatting also can be applied to individual cells. Data always is stored in the grid as a String data type. Even if the data is numeric, it still is represented in the grid as a String data type. Thus, before storing a numeric value in a cell, it is a good idea to convert the data to a String data type, and to convert the data back to its Numeric data type when retrieving the value. The MSFlexGrid control is an ActiveX control, so a reference to the control must be added to the project file using the Components dialog. The component name for the control is Microsoft FlexGrid Control 5.0. As with other ActiveX controls, the .ocx file for the control must be distributed with the program. The .ocx file for the MSFlexGrid control is "msflxgrd.ocx." Figure 6-2 shows a grid on a form.

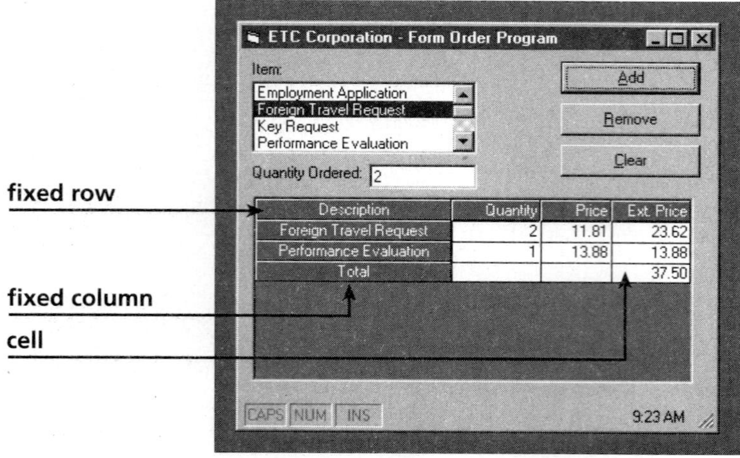

Figure 6-2: MSFlexGrid components

As shown in Figure 6-2, the grid contains four (4) rows and four (4) columns. The top row and the left-hand column are treated differently than the other rows and columns. These are called a **fixed row** and a **fixed column**. A fixed row and column usually contain the titles or headings for the row or column and do not move as the row or column is scrolled. Other rows and columns contain data. When setting the number of rows and columns, the number of rows must be at least one greater than the number of fixed rows, and the number of columns must be at least one greater than the number of fixed columns.

By default, a grid is created with two rows and two columns, the first of which are fixed. The number of fixed and normal rows and columns can be set at design time using the Property Pages or at run time using code.

The program in the ETC example requires one fixed row and column as shown in Figure 6-2. You now can create the grid, use the design-time properties to create the initial number of rows and columns, and then assign the fixed rows and columns.

To create the grid:

1. Start **Visual Basic** and open the project named **Chapter.06\Startup\ETCGridS.vbp.**
2. Click **Project** then **Components** to open the Components dialog. Check the box to the left of **Microsoft FlexGrid Control 5.0**, then click the **OK** button. The control will be added to the project and on the Toolbox.
3. Create an instance of the **MSFlexGrid** control as shown in Figure 6-3, then set the Name property to **msgOrder**.

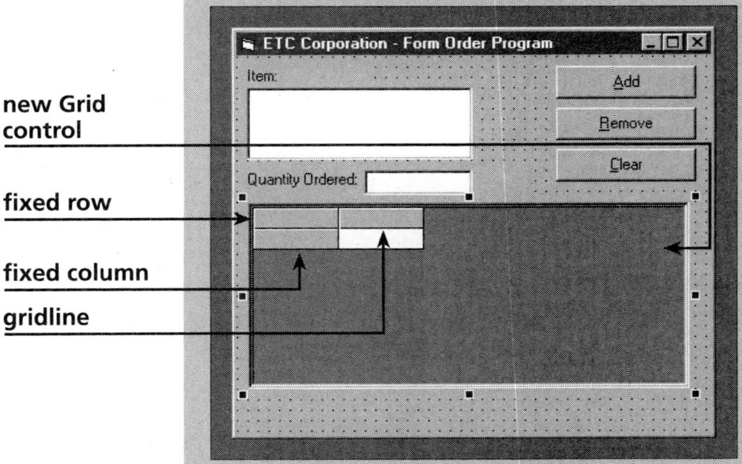

Figure 6-3: Creating the grid

Like the DBGrid control, the MSFlexGrid control supports a long list of properties and methods.

Object	MSFlexGrid

Properties

- The **AllowUserResizing** property determines whether or not the user can resize the rows and columns at run time using the mouse. If set to flexResizeNone, the default, resizing is prohibited. If set to flexResizeColumns or flexResizeRows, the columns or rows can be resized, respectively. If set to flexResizeBoth, both columns and rows can be resized.
- Just as most controls support the **Top**, **Left**, **Height**, and **Width** properties to define the upper-left corner of the control, and the height and width of the control, the grid supports the same properties. Additionally, there are properties to define the same attributes for the current cell. The **CellLeft**, **CellTop**, **CellWidth**, and **CellHeight** properties identify the upper-left corner of the current cell, in relation to the grid, and the width and height of the current cell. These properties are useful to overlay another control in the grid for cell editing purposes.
- The **TextStyle** and **TextStyleFixed** properties determine the three-dimensional appearance of the text in the rows and fixed rows. If set to flexTextFlat, the default, text appears flat in a cell. If set to flexTextRaised or flexTextInset, the text appears raised off the cell or recessed in the cell. flexTextRaisedLight and flexTextInsetLight apply a softer shadowing to the raised or inset text.
- By default, lines, called gridlines, divide the rows and columns. The **GridLines** and **GridLinesFixed** properties determine the format of the lines for normal cells and fixed cells, respectively. The default format of Gridlines is flexGridFlat; the default format of GridLinesFixed is flexGridInset. If set to flexGridNone, no lines appear between the cells. Setting the properties to flexGridInset or flexGridRaised causes the gridlines to appear inset or raised off the surface of the grid.
- The **Rows** and **Cols** properties set or return the total number of rows and columns in the grid.
- The **Row** and **Col** properties specify the currently selected row and column, respectively. Setting these properties changes the current row or column. Row and column numbers are zero-based. That is, the first row and column each has a value of zero.
- The **RowSel** and **ColSel** properties are run-time properties that set or return the starting or ending row or column for a range of cells.
- The **FormatString** is used to define the contents of the fixed rows and columns, and the justification of the text in the fixed rows and columns.
- The **ColWidth** property defines the width of the specified column. The ColWidth property is used with an index, an integer representing the column to resize. Thus, to resize the first column, the syntax ColWidth(0) would be used.

- The **Sort** property is a run-time property that is used to sort selected rows according to specific criteria. Entire rows are sorted. By default, all non-fixed rows are sorted. Specific rows can be sorted, however, by setting the Row and RowSel properties.
- The format of the current cell can be set using the **CellFontBold**, **CellFontSize**, and **CellFontUnderline** properties. Each of these properties can be set to True or False to apply the specific format of the current cell. Setting the **CellFontName** property will also change the font. These properties only can be set at run time. These properties commonly are set in response to an EnterCell or LeaveCell event.
- The **TextArray** and **TextMatrix** properties serve the same purpose. They are used to reference a particular cell in the grid. Which to use is a matter of programmer preference, although the **TextMatrix** property is more intuitive because the syntax is much easier to use.
- The **Color** Property Page can be used to change the foreground and background colors of the fixed rows, normal rows, and selected cell. The properties also can be set at run time. Refer to the Property Page for a list of the property names or to the Help topic "MSFlexGrid control" for more information.

Events

- The **EnterCell** and **LeaveCell** events occur when a cell becomes the current cell and when a cell is no longer the current cell.
- The **Scroll** event occurs when the visible rows or columns change, either because the user clicked the scroll bars, or because code is executed to change the visible region of the grid.
- The **SelChange** event occurs when the user selects a range of cells.
- The **RowColChange** event occurs whenever the selected cell changes. When the user selects a different cell, the order of the events is LeaveCell, EnterCell, RowColChange.

Methods

- The methods of the grid are similar to those supported by the ListBox. The **AddItem** method adds a new row to the grid.
- The **Clear** method deletes the contents from all the rows and columns in the grid. Neither the height of the rows nor the width of the columns is affected, nor are the number of rows and columns. The contents are cleared for all rows and columns including the fixed rows and columns.
- The **RemoveItem** method deletes a row from the grid. Its syntax is the same as that of a list box. The method takes one argument—the row to remove.

The grid you have created contains one fixed column and one fixed row. At this time, you can use the Property Pages to set the number of columns, and color of the rows and columns. In the ETC example, the text in the fixed columns will be defined at run time although the property could be set at design time using the Style Property Page.

To set the design-time properties for the grid:

1. Open the **Property Pages** for the grid, set the number of rows and columns to **1**, then click **Apply**. A message box is displayed because the number of rows must be greater than the number of fixed rows. The same error also will occur if you try to click the OK button to exit the Property Pages. The error message will be displayed, and the Property Page will not close.
2. Close the message box, set the Cols property to **4** and the Rows property to **2**, then click **Apply**. The grid now has four columns instead of two.
3. Activate the **Color** Property Page. Select the **BackColorFixed** property and, using the **Standard Colors** choice in the Color Set list box, set the color to **Dark Cyan** and the ForeColorFixed property to **White.** Remember to click the **Apply** button before changing the active Property Page.
4. Activate the **Style** Property Page, then set the GridLines property to **3 - Raised** and the GridLinesFixed property to **2 - Inset**. Click **OK** to close the Property Pages.

While the grid supports extensive formatting, use care with inset and raised characters. Also, if changing colors, make sure there is enough contrast between the foreground and background colors. In general, keep it simple.

Formatting the Fixed Rows and Fixed Columns

The FormatString property contains a string value that is displayed in a fixed column, fixed row, or both. A vertical bar (|) separates the text for each column. The following statement defines a format string with three fixed columns. The first fixed column is blank, the second contains the string "Description," and the third column contains the string "Value." This format string also could be applied by setting the Format property on the Style Property Page. If the Style Property Page is used, the quotes surrounding the string are omitted.

```
msgDemo.FormatString = "|Description|Value"
```

The text in a column can be aligned using special characters to the right of the vertical bar. The less than (<), caret (^), and greater than (>) symbols are used to left-justify, center, or right-justify the text in the fixed column. The following format string is the same as the previous with the exception that the second column is left-justified and the third column is right-justified.

```
msgDemo.FormatString = "|<Description|>Value"
```

A format string also can be expanded to store values in fixed rows by appending a semicolon to the string followed by strings of text separated by vertical bars. Each string following the semicolon then is displayed in a fixed row. Consider the following format string:

```
pstrFormatString = "|<Description|>Value;|Row1|Row2|Row3"
msgDemo.FormatString = pstrFormatString
```

The preceding format string defines the text for a grid with one fixed column and one fixed row. The semicolon separates the column from the row format. Also, the first character for the column and the first character for the row are a vertical bar (|). This causes the first cell in the grid to be blank. Figure 6-4 shows the fixed rows and columns displayed with the above format string.

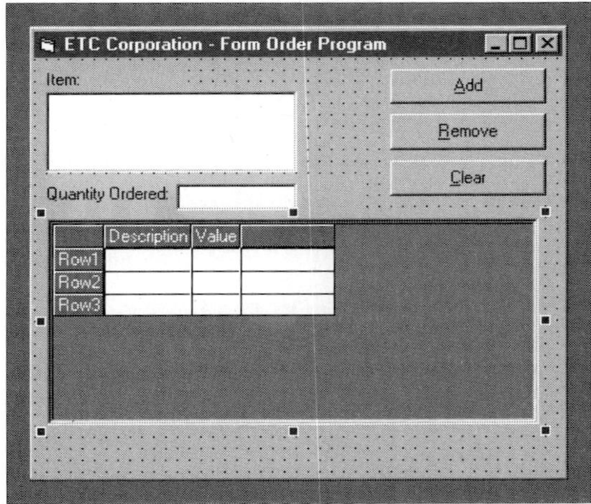

Figure 6-4: Formatting fixed columns

Using a format string to assign values to the fixed rows is much less common than using a format string to assign values to a fixed column. The number of rows and the contents of the rows, usually are added and deleted at run time. In situations where the rows and columns are fixed at run time, the format string is useful to set contents of both the fixed rows and columns. When a format string is applied, the width of the column is changed automatically so the contents of the format string will fit in the column. It also is possible to set the ColWidth property to define exactly the width of a column.

Programming ▶ tip

If a format string is created that has more rows or columns than already exist in the grid, the number of rows or columns will be increased as needed to store the values. This will not generate an error.

When you apply a format string as shown in the previous examples, the widths of the columns are adjusted automatically so the text will fit in the column. This may not be the desired effect, however. In the ETC example, the columns will have the following values: Description, Quantity, Price, Ext. Price. The automatic column widths set by the format string will not be wide enough to hold the actual data. This is true especially for the Description column. Thus, after setting the format string for the four columns, the width of each column will be adjusted manually by setting the ColumnWidth property.

To create the FormatString property for the grid:

1 Locate the **Form_Load** event procedure and enter the following statements shown in bold:

```
Private Sub Form_Load( )
    InitializeList    ' Load the list box
    txtEdit.Visible = False
    msgOrder.FormatString = _
        "^Description|>Quantity|>Price|>Ext. Price"
    msgOrder.ColWidth(0) = 2200
    msgOrder.ColWidth(1) = 1000
    msgOrder.ColWidth(2) = 800
    msgOrder.ColWidth(3) = 900
End Sub
```

2 Test the program. The format string that appears should look like that shown in Figure 6-5.

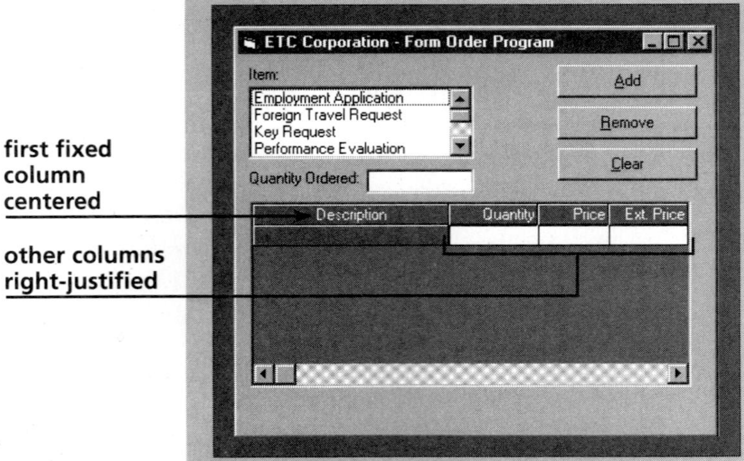

Figure 6-5: Setting the FormatString at run time

The preceding statements define a format string. The first column has the caption "Description" centered in the column. The next three columns are right-justified. The column width is adjusted explicitly by setting the ColWidth property. In this example, the setting for the column widths is somewhat arbitrary. The widths were defined such that the data and description would fit into the column.

Adding and Removing Rows at Run Time

Rows containing data are added and deleted at run time using the AddItem and RemoveItem methods. These methods are similar to the methods of the same name pertaining to the ListBox control.

Syntax

object.**AddItem** (*item* **As String**, *index*)
object.**RemoveItem** *index*

Dissection

- The **AddItem** method adds a new row to the grid. If the *index* argument is omitted, the new row is inserted immediately after the fixed rows. If the *index* argument is used, the row must not be a fixed row or a run-time error will occur.
- The **RemoveItem** method removes a row from the grid. The *index* must contain an existing row in the grid. This method cannot be used to remove a fixed row. To remove a fixed row, the value of the FixedRows property must be changed to make the row a normal row, and then the RemoveItem method called.
- The *object* must be an instance of the MSFlexGrid control.
- The optional *index* contains a Long integer indicating where the new row is added or the row to be removed. The first row has an index value of zero (0). When adding a new row, the largest valid value for *index* is the same as the value of the Rows property. In this case, the new row is added just after the last current row. If the value of *index* is greater than Rows, then an error will occur.
- The required *item* is a string expression containing the text for the new row. The text is made up of character strings separated by Tab characters. Tab characters can be represented by the constant vbTab.

Code Example

```
pstrRow = "Employment Application" & vbTab & "9.84"
msgOrder.AddItem pstrRow
```

Code Dissection

When the AddItem method is called, by default it will add a new row to the first non-fixed row. The row contains two columns. One has the contents of "Employment Application" and the other the value "9.84".

The program you are writing has four columns. Thus, to create a string representing four columns, the following statements could be used:

```
pstrRow = "Employment Application" & vbTab & "1" & _
    vbTab & "9.84" & vbTab & "9.84"
msgOrder.AddItem pstrRow 1
```

The previous statement assigns to the string variable, the values for the four columns. The numeric values are treated as strings by the grid so they are enclosed in quotes. The Tab character (vbTab) separates each string. Row number one was specified so the row will be inserted as the second row. Remember that row numbers are zero-based, but the AddItem method inserts rows at the first non-fixed row.

In the ETC example, a new order item will be added to the first non-fixed row by selecting an item from the list box, then entering the quantity ordered. When the Add command button is clicked, the new row needs to be added to the grid. This is accomplished by calling the AddItem method. The list box containing the descriptions has been initialized already by reading a text file. For each item in the list box, there is a corresponding price stored in the array named msngPrices. The information is initialized such that the ListIndex property of an item in the list box corresponds to the element in the price array. The code to load the list box and initialize the array is in the general procedure named InitializeList. Refer to the general procedure in the program for a more detailed analysis of the code. When the Add command button is clicked, the code for the Click event procedure needs to add a row to the grid. The first column should contain the description from the selected item in the list box. The second column contains the quantity ordered specified in the text box. The third column contains the price, which is found by looking up the value in an array. Finally, the extended price is computed by multiplying the price by the quantity ordered. For the Add command to work correctly, an item in the list box must be selected and the quantity order must contain a valid number. Both of these conditions are validated before attempting to add an item to the grid.

To add an item to the grid:

1 Locate the **cmdAdd_Click** event procedure in the Code window and enter the following statements:

```
Dim pstrItem As String, pstrPrice As String, _
    pstrExtPrice As String
If IsNumeric(txtQuantity) _
    And lstForms.ListIndex > -1 Then
    pstrPrice = _
        Format(msngPrices(lstForms.ListIndex), "Fixed")
    pstrExtPrice = Format(txtQuantity * _
        msngPrices(lstForms.ListIndex), "Fixed")
```

```
        pstrItem = lstForms & vbTab & txtQuantity & vbTab & _
            pstrPrice & vbTab & pstrExtPrice
        msgOrder.AddItem pstrItem, 1
    Else
        Call MsgBox("Cannot Add", vbInformation)
    End If
    lstForms.ListIndex = -1
    txtQuantity = ""
```

2 Test the program. Select items from the list and different values for the quantity ordered, then click the **Add** button to add items to the grid. Each item is added to the first row of the grid and the other rows are adjusted downward.

All values in the grid are stored as strings. The local variables are used to store the string representation of the price and extended price. The variable pstrItem is used to store the string representation for the row to be added.

The first assignment statement retrieves the price of the currently selected item, formats the value, and stores the result in the price string. The second computes the extended price and formats the value.

```
pstrItem = lstForms & vbTab & txtQuantity & vbTab & _
    pstrPrice & vbTab & pstrExtPrice
```

The previous statement creates the string that is passed to the AddItem method. The Tab character (vbTab) is used to separate each column in the string. Thus, the first column contains the description, the second contains the quantity ordered, the third column contains the price, and the fourth contains the extended price.

Programming tip

Instead of using the AddItem method to add a new row, the Rows property can be changed at run time. In this situation, you must reference explicitly the individual cells to store values. It also is possible to add additional columns by increasing the value of the Cols property.

Removing an Existing Row

In addition to adding a row to the grid, it is possible to select a row and delete the selected row by calling the RemoveItem method with one argument—the index of the row to be deleted. When the user clicks a cell or row, the Row and Col properties are set automatically. The Row property can be used to determine the current row, which in the ETC example is the row to be deleted.

Remember, the number of rows must be one greater than the number of fixed rows. As such, if the user attempts to remove the only normal row, the number of rows would be the same as the number of fixed rows. This cannot happen and will cause a run-time error. Thus, when removing rows, your code must verify that there is a row to delete.

To remove a row:

1. Locate the **cmdRemove_Click** event procedure in the Code window and enter the following statements:

```
If msgOrder.FixedRows < msgOrder.Rows - 1 Then
    msgOrder.RemoveItem msgOrder.Row
Else
    Call MsgBox("Cannot remove row", vbInformation)
End If
```

2. Test the program. Add items to the grid, then click a row and click the **Remove** command button to remove the row.
3. Try to continue to remove all the rows. The message box will appear indicating that the last row cannot be deleted.

The If statement verifies that there is a row to be deleted. If so, the RemoveItem method is called to remove a row. Remember, this method accepts one argument (the row to be removed), which should be the current row. Reading the value of the Row property identifies the current row.

In addition to removing a row, the rows in the grid need to be cleared in preparation for another order. The Clear method can be used to remove the contents of the cells and the Rows property can be used to reset the number of rows.

To clear the contents of the grid:

1. Locate the **cmdClear_Click** event procedure in the Code window and enter the following statements:

```
msgOrder.Clear
msgOrder.FormatString = _
    "^Description|>Quantity|>Price|>Ext. Price"
msgOrder.ColWidth(0) = 2200
msgOrder.ColWidth(1) = 1000
msgOrder.ColWidth(2) = 800
msgOrder.ColWidth(3) = 900
msgOrder.Rows = 2
```

2. Test the program. Add items to the grid, then click the **Clear** command button to remove the rows.

These statements clear the contents of the grid and redefine the number of rows to 2. The Clear method deletes the contents of the rows but it does not remove the rows themselves. Because the contents of all the cells were cleared, the FormatString must be reinitialized. This is one solution to clearing the contents. You also can implement the task by setting the contents of specific cells to a null string.

In addition to adding and deleting rows, it is possible to reference specific cells in the grid and perform editing tasks.

Referencing a Specific Cell in the Grid

One common task is to read and write text to and from an arbitrary cell. This can be accomplished using the TextArray and TextMatrix properties. These two properties serve the same purpose, so which to use is a matter of programmer preference. The TextArray property requires that you execute a function to compute the index of a particular cell. The TextMatrix property allows you to specify a row and column. Thus, the TextMatrix property generally is more intuitive.

Syntax

object.**TextArray**(*cellindex*) [= *string*]
object.**TextMatrix**(*rowindex*, *colindex*) [= *string*]

Dissection

- The **TextArray** and **TextMatrix** properties read or write a string from or to a specific cell. Both properties can read or write the contents of both fixed and normal cells. Attempting to reference a cell that does not exist will cause a subscript out of range error to occur. Remember, the grid works like a two-dimensional array. Thus, the error is like referencing an invalid array element.
- The *object* must be a valid instance of the MSFlexGrid control.
- The *rowindex* and *colindex* arguments identify the row and column whose value is read or written. Remember, rows and columns have a lower bound of zero.
- The *cellindex* contains a numeric expression that determines the cell whose value is read or written. Use of this property will be explained in a moment.
- The optional *string* argument contains the value that is stored in the cell. Remember, all values are stored in the grid as string expressions.

Code Example

```
msgOrder.TextMatrix(0, 0) = "Description"
```

Code Dissection

This statement stores the string "Description" in the first row and column of the grid. Note that the TextMatrix property does not care whether or not the row or column is fixed. In this case, the text "Description" is stored in a fixed row and column.

Using the TextArray property is a little more difficult because the value of the *cellindex* must be computed. Remember, the grid is like a zero-based, two-dimensional array. As such, the cell index can be calculated by multiplying the desired row by the

Cols property and adding the desired column. The clearest and most convenient way to calculate *cellindex* is to define a function as follows:

```
Function MsgIndex(row As Integer, col As Integer) _
    As Long
    msgIndex = row * msgOrder.Cols + col
End Function
```

As you can see, this function accepts two arguments—*row* and *col*. The current row is multiplied by the number of columns and the current column is added to the intermediate result. This value is returned by the function and used as the argument in the TextArray property. Thus, to use this function and set the TextArray property for the grid named msgOrder, the following statement could be used:

```
msgOrder.TextArray(MsgIndex(row,col)) = "Description"
```

Programming tip

If multiple grids are being used, or to further generalize the function, it is reasonable to pass a reference to the grid as an argument to the function. That way, the same function can be used by multiple grids.

One of the tasks that must be performed is to update the order total each time an item is added or removed. The total should be displayed on the last row of the grid. Computing the total can be accomplished by adding the values in the extended price column together, and then displaying the result in the grid.

To compute the total:

1. Enter the following statement to display the Total caption in the first column. Enter this statement as the last statement in the **Form_Load** event procedure. This causes the caption "Total" to appear in the first column, which is a fixed column.

```
msgOrder.TextMatrix(1, 0) = "Total"
```

2. Create a general procedure named **ComputeTotal** that accepts no arguments, and enter the following statements:

```
Dim pintRows As Integer
Dim pstrTotal As String, psngTotal As Single

For pintRows = msgOrder.FixedRows To msgOrder.Rows - 2
    psngTotal = psngTotal + _
        msgOrder.TextArray(MsgIndex(pintRows, 3))
Next

pintRows = msgOrder.Rows - 1
pstrTotal = Format(psngTotal, "Fixed")
msgOrder.TextArray(MsgIndex(pintRows, 3)) = pstrTotal
```

3 Create a function procedure named **MsgIndex** as follows:

```
Private Function MsgIndex(row As Integer, _
    col As Integer) As Integer
    msgIndex = row * msgOrder.Cols + col
End Function
```

4 Add the following statement just before the Else clause for both the **cmdAdd_Click** and **cmdRemove_Click** event procedures:

```
ComputeTotal
```

5 Test the program. Add and remove items. The total should be recomputed.

The statements to compute the total require careful analysis. Remember, rows are numbered from zero. Notice the conditions in the For loop. The initial condition is msgOrder.FixedRows. There is one fixed row, so the first row to be examined is the first non-fixed row (row 1). While a constant value one (1) could be used, this loop allows for the number of fixed rows to be changed without modifying the For loop. The terminal condition is msgOrder.Rows - 2. msgOrder.Rows returns the number of rows, so msgOrder.Rows - 1 can be used to reference the last row. But the last row contains the total which should not be added to the total, so minus two (- 2) is used. Inside the For loop, the total is computed using the current row and the last column. Although the TextArray property is used in this example, the TextMatrix property also would be suitable. The final statements format the total and display the result.

Editing Cells in the Grid

The grid does not itself support editing of individual cells. Editing a cell can be accomplished, however, by using a text box in conjunction with the grid. This example illustrates the usefulness of combining one control with another. In Chapter 3, keyboard events were introduced. To perform editing on a cell, you again need to use the keyboard events to determine when to initiate editing on a cell and when editing is complete.

The process of cell editing can be divided into two steps. The first step is to position the text box so it appears on top of the current cell, copy the contents of the current cell to the text box, and then give focus to the text box. Therefore, editing is performed in the text box not the grid. The second step is to store the contents of the text box back in the current cell and make the text box invisible when editing is complete.

Enabling Editing

Expanding on the first step, a mechanism is needed to determine when editing should be performed. Editing will commence when the user double-clicks a cell or presses a character while a cell is selected. Thus, the grid needs to respond to a KeyPress event and a DblClick event. When either of these events occur, a text box needs to be displayed over the region of the current cell. This text box should be the same size as the current cell to provide the illusion to the user that they are editing a cell in the grid.

This poses an interesting problem. When two visible controls occupy the same visible region, one control may obscure another. That is, if you created two text boxes with overlapping regions, then part or all of one text box would obscure the other. In this example, the text box must obscure the grid, not the other way around. When this situation arises, you must define explicitly which object appears in front and which object appears in back. This is called the **ZOrder**. The simplest way to set the ZOrder of objects is at design time. You can click an object and right-click the mouse button to activate the pop-up menu. There are two commands on this menu pertaining to the ZOrder. The Bring to Front and Send to Back commands will cause the object to appear in front of, or in back of, other objects.

As you use the menu commands to set the ZOrder of objects, you will see that certain actions are impossible. For example, it is impossible for the region of a label to appear in front of the region of a text box. Every visible object has a place in the ZOrder. The ZOrder is divided into three different layers. Think of these as the back, middle, and front layer. Each visible control belongs to one, and only one, layer. A control that belongs to the back layer cannot visibly obscure a control belonging to the middle or front layer. A control that belongs to the middle layer cannot obscure the front layer.

- The back layer is used by drawing methods, like the Line method pertaining to the form, which are used to draw lines and rectangles on a form.
- The middle layer contains graphical objects, like the Line and Shape controls and the label. The Line method used by the back layer is different than the Line control.
- The front layer contains all the non-graphical controls. These include text boxes, command buttons, and ActiveX controls, like the grid.

The ZOrder also can be set at run time by calling the ZOrder method. This method applies to all visible objects. The method takes one argument having a value of zero (0) or one (1). If zero (0), the object is placed at the front of the ZOrder. If one (1), the object is placed at the back of the ZOrder.

A general procedure will be used to make the text box visible, position the text box at the correct location in the grid, and set focus to the text box. The location is determined using the CellLeft and CellTop properties of the grid. Both the DblClick and KeyPress event procedures will call the general procedure. A text box named txtEdit has been created already on the form. You must set its ZOrder, however.

To enable editing for a cell:

1. Create a Sub procedure named **msgEdit** and enter the following statements:

```
Private Sub msgEdit(msg As MSFlexGrid, _
    txt As TextBox, KeyAscii As Integer)
    Select Case KeyAscii
        Case 0 To vbKeySpace
            txt = msg
            txt.SelStart = len(txt)
        Case Else
            txt = Chr(KeyAscii)
            txt.SelStart = 1
    End Select
    txt.Move msg.CellLeft + msg.Left, _
        msg.CellTop + msg.Top, msg.CellWidth, _
        msg.CellHeight
    txt.Visible = True
    msgOrder.Enabled = False
    txt.SetFocus
End Sub
```

2. Enter the following statement in the **msgOrder_DblClick** event procedure:

```
If msgOrder.col = 1 And Not _
    (msgOrder.row = (msgOrder.Rows - 1)) Then
    msgEdit msgOrder, txtEdit, vbKeySpace
End If
```

3. Enter the following statement into the **msgOrder_KeyPress** event procedure:

```
If msgOrder.col = 1 And Not _
    (msgOrder.row = (msgOrder.Rows - 1)) Then
    msgEdit msgOrder, txtEdit, KeyAscii
End If
```

4. In Form window, right-click the text box named **txtEdit**, then click **Bring To Front**. Otherwise, the grid will obscure the text box when the program is run.
5. Test the program. Add an item. Then, in the quantity ordered column, double-click a value. The current value is copied to the text box, and the text is available for editing. At this point, the code has not been written to copy the contents of the text box back to the cell in the grid. Nor has the code been written to update the extended price or the total. End the program.

The general procedure takes three arguments—a grid, a text box, and the key that was pressed. By passing the grid and text box as arguments, the procedure can be used by any grid. The condition in the Select Case statement is the key that was pressed.

```
Case 0 To vbKeySpace
    txt = msg
    txt.SelStart = len(txt)
```

If the Spacebar is pressed, the contents of the current cell stored in the msg argument are copied to the text box. The insertion point position is determined by finding the last character of the text box. Note the syntax of the assignment statement. The default property of the text box is the Text property and the default property of the grid is the value of the currently selected row and column (cell). Thus, the following two statements produce the same result:

```
    txt = msg
    txt = msg.TextMatrix(msg.row, msg.col)
```

If the character pressed was not a space, the character that was pressed is stored in the text box, and the current position is just after the one and only character. This code is executed in response to the Case Else statement.

Calling the Move method causes the text box to be resized and positioned over the current cell. The CellLeft property of the grid contains the position of the left border of the cell relative to the grid rather than the form. This value is added to the Left property of the grid to obtain the correct horizontal position. The same technique is used to compute the vertical position.

Finally, the text box is made visible and gets the focus. The two event procedures call the general procedure. The DblClick event procedure simulates a Spacebar. Also, the only field that is allowed to be edited is the quantity field. This is the purpose of the If statement in both of the event procedures—to test that the current column is column one.

The msgEdit function may be called when the user double-clicks a cell or a key is pressed in a cell. These event procedures are nearly identical. Consider the DblClick event procedure.

The If statement is used for validation. Both the price and extended price are computed values. As such, they should not be able to be edited by the user. Thus, the first part of the If statement checks that the first column is being editing by checking the Col property. The second part of the If statement is more interesting. The Last row contains the total for the invoice. The cell in the first column is not used, however. As such, the user should not be able to enter a value in this cell either. The second part of the If statement used the Row and Rows properties to determine if the selected cell is in the last row.

Saving the Edits

Now that you have created the necessary code to perform editing on the grid, a mechanism is needed to copy the contents of the text box back to the current cell and return focus to the grid when editing is complete. The Enter key will be used to signify that editing is complete. Keyboard events again are used to determine when the Enter key is pressed. When this occurs, the contents of the text box need to be copied back to the current cell in the grid, and focus returned to the grid.

In addition to pressing the Enter key, the user also has the capability to click another object like one of the command buttons before pressing the Enter key. In this situation, there are two possible implementation options. One is to commit the changes made. The other is to abandon the change and restore the contents of the cell. In this example, the second choice will be used. This is a good idea because the interface should support a way for the user to abandon changes. Adding this feature is relatively simple. You can create a module-level Boolean variable to determine whether or not the text box is being edited. When the text box gets focus, the edit state should be set to True. When the user is editing the contents and presses the Enter key, the contents are written back to the grid, and the edit state is False. Inside the LostFocus event procedure, an If statement is written to determine the edit state. If True, the text box is losing focus without pressing the Enter key so the changes should be abandoned.

To complete the editing functions:

1 Enter the following statement in the form's general declarations section:

```
Private mblnEditing As Boolean
```

2 Enter the following statement in the **txtEdit_GotFocus** event procedure:

```
mblnEditing = True
```

3 Enter the following statements in the **txtEdit_LostFocus** event procedure:

```
If mblnEditing Then
    msgOrder.Enabled = True
    msgOrder.SetFocus
    txtEdit.Visible = False
    mblnEditing = False
End If
```

4 Enter the following statements into the **txtEdit_KeyPress** event procedure:

```
If KeyAscii = Asc(vbCr) Then
    KeyAscii = 0
End If
```

5 Enter the following statements in the **txtEdit_KeyDown** event procedure:

```
Dim psngExtPrice As Single
If KeyCode = 13 Then
    msgOrder = txtEdit
    txtEdit.Visible = False
    psngExtPrice = msgOrder.TextMatrix(msgOrder.row, _
        msgOrder.col) _
        * msgOrder.TextMatrix(msgOrder.row, _
        msgOrder.col + 1)
    msgOrder.TextMatrix(msgOrder.row, _
        msgOrder.col + 2) = _
        Format(psngExtPrice, "Fixed")
    ComputeTotal
    msgOrder.Enabled = True
    mblnEditing = False
    msgOrder.SetFocus
    DoEvents
End If
```

6 Test the program. Add items to the grid and enable a cell for editing by double-clicking the cell. Change the value in the text box, then press the **Enter** key. The changed value is copied back to the grid, the extended price is updated, and the order total is updated. Edit the cell again, then click the list box. The changes to the grid are discarded and the cell is restored to its original contents.

The KeyDown event occurs before the KeyPress event. If the Enter key is pressed, the contents of the text box are copied to the grid. The text box is hidden, and focus is returned to the grid. The code for the KeyPress event has the effect of removing the carriage return.

The code for the KeyDown event determines if the Enter key was pressed. If so, editing is complete, the extended price is recomputed, and then stored back in the current cell. The text box is made invisible and the focus is returned to the grid.

Programming tip

The code for these events has been simplified for brevity. It is reasonable to add code to validate that only a numeric value can be entered in the text box. Furthermore, completion of editing could be signified with different keystrokes. For example, it would be reasonable for the Esc key to abandon editing and restore the contents of the cell to its original condition. Also, the Arrow keys could be programmed to terminate editing, but instead of returning to the current cell in the grid, focus could be changed to a different cell depending on which Arrow key was clicked.

Introducing the Microsoft Windows Common Controls

The Windows 95 operating system provides much more than just an interface for users. It also provides a rich set of libraries available to the programmer. There are several ActiveX controls that give the Visual Basic programmer access to the objects defined in these libraries. One such set of controls commonly is referred to as the Windows Common Controls. These controls are stored in two different ActiveX libraries. Figure 6-6 lists these controls and a brief description of their purpose.

Control	Description
Animation	The Animation control is used to create buttons that display animations, such as .avi files, when clicked.
ImageList	The ImageList control manages a collection of bitmap and icon images. It typically is used with another control like a Toolbar, ListView, or TreeView
ListView	The ListView control is used to display items in a list.
ProgressBar	The ProgressBar control is used to display the progress of a time-consuming operation.
Slider	The Slider control is similar to a scroll bar, except it displays a slider in a range of tick marks.
StatusBar	The StatusBar control displays a status bar, typically across the bottom of the form. The StatusBar control is used to describe the current state of the program or selected keyboard keys like the Caps Lock key.
TabStrip	The TabStrip control contains tabs that work like the dividers in a notebook. Most Property Pages are implemented using an interface that looks like a TabStrip control.
Toolbar	The Toolbar control displays a toolbar containing buttons the user can click.
TreeView	The TreeView control displays information hierarchically. Each item in the hierarchy consists of a text string and an optional icon.
UpDown	The UpDown control is similar to a scrollbar. It typically is used to increment or decrement the value of another control like a TextBox control.

Figure 6-6: The Windows Common Controls

In this chapter and the next, you will use many of these controls to create programs with user interfaces that closely model the interfaces supplied by many common programs.

Improving the User Interface with a Status Bar

Visual Basic allows you to create forms with a status bar by using the StatusBar control. A status bar typically appears at the bottom of a form and commonly is used to display information like the state of specific keys; that is, whether the Caps Lock key is enabled, or Insert mode is on or off. Used in the database programs of the preceding chapters, a status bar would have been useful to display the number of the current record, whether or not the current record was being edited, or the progress of an update operation. Figure 6-7 shows a status bar and its components.

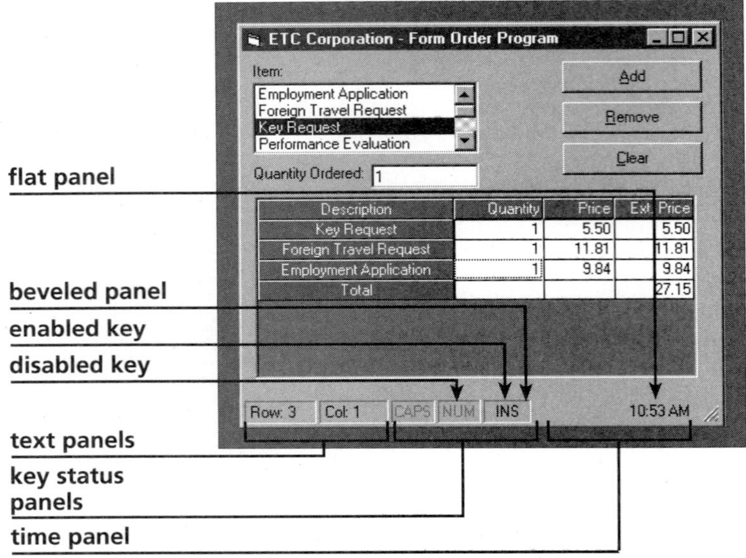

Figure 6-7: Anatomy of a status bar

The status bar is divided into regions called **panels**. Each panel is implemented as a Panel object in the Panels collection. At design time, panels are added and removed using the Property Pages. The Property Pages contain tabs to define the general characteristics of the status bar, and the characteristics of each panel on the status bar. Like any other collection, Panel objects can be added and removed at run time using the Add and Remove methods of the Panels collection. The standard prefix for the StatusBar is "sbr."

Object	**StatusBar**
Properties	■ The **Style** property can be set to one of two modes. If set to the constant value sbrSimple, the status bar is displayed with one large panel encompassing the entire region of the status bar. If set to sbrNormal, the default, then the status bar displays all the Panel objects.

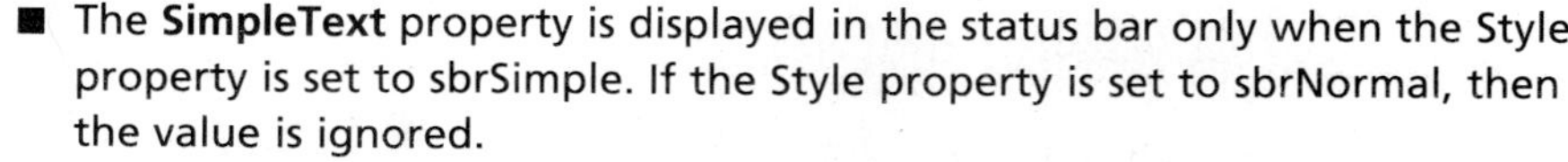

- The **SimpleText** property is displayed in the status bar only when the Style property is set to sbrSimple. If the Style property is set to sbrNormal, then the value is ignored.

Events

- The StatusBar control responds to the **Click** event like other controls although it seldom is used. The contents of the entire status bar usually are managed by the program's code.
- The **PanelClick** event occurs when the user clicks a specific panel. If a panel indicates the status of something, like whether or not a field is being edited, responding to this event allows your program to change the status. In this situation, the panel is working much like a command button.

After creating the status bar and setting the general properties, the panels are created and the Panel object's properties are set. The Panels collection is a one-based collection. Like most collections, a panel can be referenced by either a numeric index or a string key.

Object — **Panel**

Properties

- The **Index** and **Key** properties define the numeric index and string key to identify the Panel object in the Panels collection uniquely.
- The **Alignment** property determines how the text is aligned inside a specific panel. Text can be left-justified, centered, or right-justified.
- The **Style** property defines the behavior of an individual panel. This property is different from the property of the same name pertaining to the status bar itself. This property pertains to a Panel object. The Style property defines whether a Panel object contains text or an icon. It also is used to display the status of keyboard keys like the Num Lock key, the Ins key, or the Shift key.
- The **Bevel** property determines how the panel appears on the status bar. If set to sbrNoBevel, the panel appears flat on the status bar. If set to sbrInset or sbrRaised, the panel appears recessed or raised off the status bar, respectively.
- The **Text** property contains the text inside the panel.
- The **Width** and **MinWidth** properties identify the size of a panel on the status bar.
- The **AutoSize** property pertains to the Panel object and can be set to one of three constant values. If set to sbrNoAutosize, the size of the Panel object is fixed. If set to sbrSpring, the size of all panels having an AutoSize property of sbrSpring are adjusted so their width is equal. If set to sbrContents, the size of the panel is adjusted so the contents fit inside the panel. The size will not decrease below the MinWidth property when the AutoSize property is set to sbrContents.

A panel on a status bar commonly is used to indicate the current state of a program. This information may include the position within a file, or the editing status of a record. For example, Microsoft Word uses the status bar to indicate the current position within a document, while Microsoft Excel uses the status bar to inform the user when it is recalculating the spreadsheet and to provide instructional tips about what to do next. Both programs also display, in individual Panel objects, the status of specific keys. These include whether or not the Caps Lock or Num Lock keys are pressed, and whether or not the document is in Insert or Overwrite mode. By setting the Style property for a panel, it is possible to display automatically the status of these individual keyboard buttons. Figure 6-8 describes the different settings for the Style property.

sbrText	0	(Default). Text and/or a bitmap. Set text with the Text property.
sbrCaps	1	Caps Lock key. Displays the letters CAPS in bold when the Caps Lock key is enabled, and dimmed when disabled.
sbrNum	2	Num Lock. Displays the letters NUM in bold when the Num Lock key is enabled, and dimmed when disabled.
sbrIns	3	Ins key. Displays the letters INS in bold when the Ins key is enabled, and dimmed when disabled.
sbrScrl	4	Scroll Lock key. Displays the letters SCRL in bold when the Scroll Lock key is enabled, and dimmed when disabled.
sbrTime	5	Time. Displays the current time in the System format.
sbrDate	6	Date. Displays the current date in the System format.
sbrKana	7	Kana. Displays the letters KANA in bold when the Scroll Lock key is enabled, and dimmed when disabled.

Figure 6-8: Panel constants pertaining to a Panel object

The StatusBar control allows the size of a panel to be changed at run time when the form is resized. What happens to a panel when the form is resized depends on the value of the panel's AutoSize property.

In the ETC example, the status bar will contain the current row and column of the grid, along with the status of the Caps Lock, Ins, and Num Lock keys. The width of these panels will be determined automatically based on the size of the contents. The MinWidth property of these panels also must be set, because the default MinWidth is greater than the size of the actual contents. The time also will be displayed. The panel that displays the time will spring to fill the width of the status bar, hence the form.

The contents of the row and column panels will need to be updated at run time as the user selects different rows and columns. As such, you will need to reference the panel in the Panels collection, so a string key will be used to make the code more intuitive. While string keys could be assigned to the other panels, the panels are never referenced in code.

To set the properties of the different panels on the status bar:

1. Click **Project** then **Components** to open the Components dialog. Select **Microsoft Windows Common Controls 5.0**, if necessary, to add the controls to the project.
2. Create a status bar on the bottom of the form so the status bar encompasses the entire width of the form and set the Name property to **sbrForm.**
3. Activate the **Panels Property Page** for the status bar. The Panels Property Page is shown in Figure 6-9.

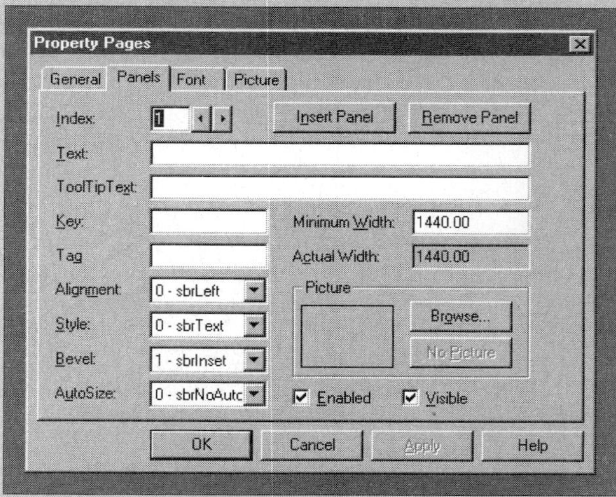

Figure 6-9: Panels Property Page

Panels are added and removed using the Insert Panel and Remove Panel command buttons. The Property Page automatically assigns an index to the Panel objects. The scroll bars next to the Index property can be used to select a specific panel.

4. As you set the properties of each panel, set the MinWidth property to **1.** The contents of most of the panels will be less than the minimum width.
5. To create the first Panel object, set Key to **Row**, alignment to **sbrLeft**, Style to **sbrText**, and AutoSize to **sbrContents**. The text will be added at run time. Click **Insert Panel** to create a second Panel object, then set the Key to **Col**. Duplicate the other property settings for the first panel. For both of these panels, set the Visible property to **False** by removing the value from the check box. You will make these panels visible when the grid gets focus.

6 The third, fourth, and fifth panels will display the status of the editing keys. Use the styles **sbrCaps**, **sbrNum**, and **sbrIns** as the Style for the respective panels. Center the text, then set the AutoSize property to **sbrContents**.

7 The last panel will display the time. Set Style to **sbrTime**, AutoSize to **sbrSpring**, and Alignment to **sbrRight**.

8 Test the program. Press the **Caps Lock**, **Num Lock**, and **Ins** keys. As the keys are enabled and disabled, the text on the status bar appears in a normal, then grayed, font. Also, the time is displayed at the right-hand side of the status bar.

In this example, you need to display the current row and column in the first two panels of the status bar. Having set the Key property of the panel to Row and Col, respectively, it is simple to reference the panels and change the text string. Whenever the user selects a row in the grid, the Row and Column panels should be made visible and the current row and column displayed in the respective panels. When the grid loses focus, the two panels should be made invisible.

To update the Row and Column panels on the status bar:

1 Locate the **msgOrder_RowColChange** event procedure and enter the following statements:

```
sbrForm.Panels("Row") = "Row: " & msgOrder.row
sbrForm.Panels("Col") = "Col: " & msgOrder.col
```

2 Locate the **msgOrder_GotFocus** event procedure and enter the following statements to make the Row and Column panels visible when the grid gets focus:

```
sbrForm.Panels("Row").Visible = True
sbrForm.Panels("Col").Visible = True
sbrForm.Panels("Row") = "Row: " & msgOrder.row
sbrForm.Panels("Col") = "Col: " & msgOrder.col
```

3 Locate the **msgOrder_LostFocus** event procedure and enter the following statements to make the Row and Column panels invisible when the grid loses focus:

```
sbrForm.Panels("Row").Visible = False
sbrForm.Panels("Col").Visible = False
```

4 Test the program. Locate different cells and notice that the status bar is updated accordingly.

These statements update the contents of the panels containing the row and column information. The other panels are updated automatically by the StatusBar control itself. When the grid has focus, the current row and column are displayed in the Row and Column panels. When the focus is changed to another control, these panels are invisible.

GUI Design tip

By default, the style of the panels is beveled. Avoid using raised panels. They look like buttons and users identify buttons as objects they can click to perform an action.

You have completed this section of the chapter, you have seen that the grid is useful for editing data not bound to a database, and how to perform in-place editing on specific cells and restrict the cells that are not able to be edited.

SECTION B

objectives

In this section you will:

- Use an ImageList control to store icons and bitmaps that can be used by other controls on the form or project
- Program a drill-down interface
- Create a TreeView control to display data that is organized hierarchically
- Create a ListView control to display data in different ways

Programming the TreeView and ListView Controls

Previewing the Completed Application

The program example in this section uses two new ActiveX controls that are part of the Windows Common Controls. These are the TreeView and ListView controls. Together, these programs have a user interface much like the Windows Explorer program.

To review the completed application:

1. Start **Visual Basic** and open the project named **Chapter.06\Complete\ETCViewC.vbp.**
2. Run the program. The main form in the program is shown in Figure 6-10.

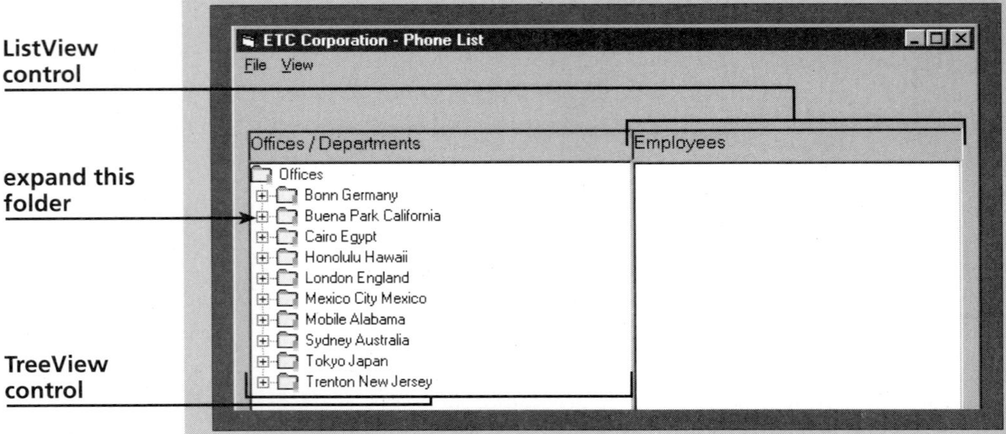

ListView control

expand this folder

TreeView control

ETC Corporation - Phone List

File View

Offices / Departments

Employees

Offices

Bonn Germany

Buena Park California

Cairo Egypt

Honolulu Hawaii

London England

Mexico City Mexico

Mobile Alabama

Sydney Australia

Tokyo Japan

Trenton New Jersey

Figure 6-10: Completed program

3 Click the plus sign to the left of the item **Buena Park California** as shown in Figure 6-10 to open the folder and display the departments pertaining to the selected regional office.

4 Double-click the folder named **Finance** to open the folder and display the employees that work in the Finance department in the ListView control. The employees are shown in Figure 6-11.

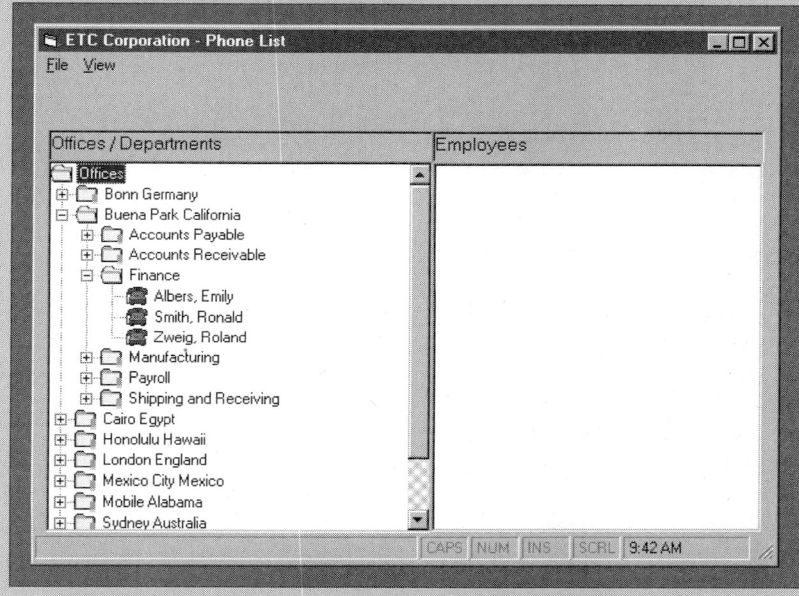

Figure 6-11: Displaying data in the ListView control

5 End the program then exit Visual Basic.

As you can see, this example is based on a database that is hierarchical in nature. There are 10 offices. Each office has one or more departments. Each employee works for one department in one office. For each employee, there are fields listing their phone number, extension, and whether or not they are in or out of the office.

Figure 6-12 shows the structure of the database.

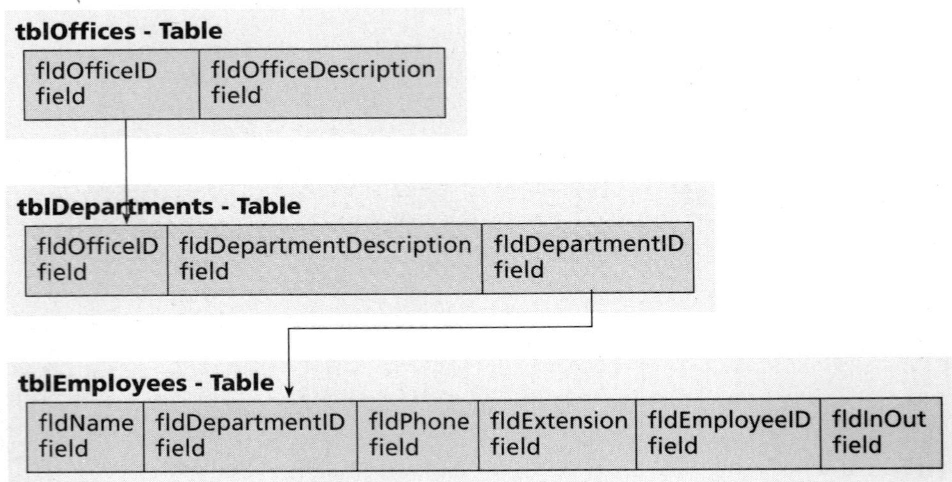

Figure 6-12: Database structure

In addition to the visible controls on the form, there is a control that is not visible at run time called the ImageList control. This control contains the bitmaps and icons used by the ListView and TreeView controls.

Storing Images in the ImageList Control

The ImageList control is not a visible control. Rather, it serves as a repository for images (bitmaps and icons). The ImageList control rarely is used by itself. Rather, it is used with other controls that display icons. Consider the Visual Basic IDE. It contains a toolbar that displays several different images. Furthermore, the Project Explorer also displays images indicating whether or not a folder is open or closed. There also are images displayed in the Project Explorer to identify the type of modules. These images could be stored in an ImageList control. When a TreeView or ListView control displays images, those images are not stored in the control itself. Rather, the images are stored in the ImageList control.

There is a good reason for separating the images from the controls that use them. Consider a program that contains both ListView and TreeView controls. Assume also that both the controls use many of the same images. Rather than storing multiple copies of the same image in the ListView and TreeView controls, one ImageList control can be used to store the actual images, and they can be shared by the multiple controls that use them.

An ImageList control tends to contain static information, so it is very uncommon for the images to change at run time. As a general rule, determine all the images your program will use, and load the images into the control at design time using the Property Pages. While it is possible to modify the images in an ImageList control at run time, there are several restrictions on changes to the images once they are used by other controls. Because the bitmaps stored in the ImageList control are usually very small, the performance impact of inserting images that are never used is minimal. Thus, if you think you may need an image, insert it at design time.

Each image in the ImageList control is stored in a ListImage object, contained in a ListImages collection. A numeric index or a string key can be used to reference ListImage objects. This is consistent with most collections. Inserting the images in the ImageList control is accomplished using the Property Pages for the ImageList control, which contains three tabs.

- The **General** Property Page is used to set the size of the images. All images in an ImageList control must be of the same size. If your program needs to use images of different sizes, create different ImageList controls, and change the image size for each control. Once an image has been added to a control, the size of the images cannot be changed. The only way to change the image size is to remove all the images, change the size, and then recreate the images.
- The **Images** Property Page is used to add and delete images to and from the list. This causes the ListImage objects to be added or removed from the ListImages collection.
- The **Color** Property Page is used to set the background color of the images.

In the ETC example, you will create the images that will be used by both the ListView and TreeView controls. The standard prefix for the ImageList control is "ils." While the images you will use are stored in the Chapter.06 folder, they also can be found in the Graphics folder of the Visual Basic folder. Many more bitmaps and icons are supplied than those used in this chapter.

To create the ImageList control and set the size of the images:

1. Start **Visual Basic** and open the project named **Chapter.06\Startup\ETCViewS.vbp.**
2. Activate the **Components** dialog. Make sure the **Microsoft Windows Common Controls 5.0** item is checked.
3. Create an ImageList control on the form and set the Name property to **ilsSmallIcons.**

   Because the ImageList control is not visible on the form at run time, it does not matter where it is placed on the form. Note that the size cannot be changed. No matter what region you select on the form when you create the ImageList control, it will be adjusted to the same size—about a ½-inch square.

4 Activate the Property Pages for **ilsSmallIcons**, and make sure the General Property Page is active.

5 Set the size of the buttons to **16 × 16**. Remember, once images are added, the size cannot be changed.

After defining the size of the images, the images themselves can be added to the image list. This is accomplished using the Images Property Page as shown in Figure 6-13.

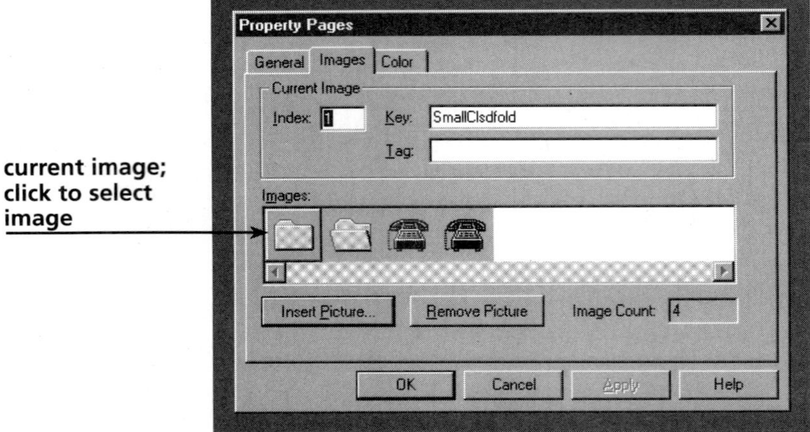

Figure 6-13: Images Property Page

The images used in this example are shown in Figure 6-13; there are two command buttons to Insert and Remove pictures from the image list. When the Insert Picture command button is clicked, the Select Picture dialog appears allowing you to select an image to insert. From this dialog, you can locate different folders in addition to the current folder. Removing a picture is accomplished by clicking an image in the Images window to activate it, and then clicking the Remove Picture command button. As you add and remove images using the Property Page, the ImageList control actually is adding and removing ListImage objects from the ListImages collection.

Like most collections, the ListImages collection supports a numeric index and string key used to reference a specific image in the collection. Using the Images Property Page, the numeric index is assigned automatically. You manually set the string key, however. The string key should be set to a meaningful name that will help describe the button. The string key is case sensitive.

To add the images to the ImageList control:

1 Activate the **Images** Property Page for **ilsSmallIcons**.

2 Click the **Insert Picture** command button. Locate the **Chapter.06\Startup** folder in the dialog box and select the icon named **Clsdfold.ico**. Click the **Open** button in the dialog to insert the picture in the ImageList control. Set the Key property to **SmallClsdfold.** Repeat the process to insert the following images: **Openfold.ico**, **Phone07.ico**, and **Phone08.ico**. As you add each image, make sure to set the Key property and that the case of the key is correct. Set the keys to **SmallOpenfold**, **SmallPhone07**, and **SmallPhone08**.

3 Close the Property Pages.

Make sure to create the ImageList control and define its images before creating the ListView, the TreeView controls, or other controls that use the images. Once another control references an ImageList control, new images can be added to the ImageList control but existing images cannot be modified or removed. Several icons are supplied with Visual Basic and are located in the Graphics folder in the Visual Basic folder (usually ProgramFiles\DevStudio\VB\Graphics). The graphics folder may or may not exist depending on the Visual Basic installation options chosen.

There is another ImageList control on the form named **ilsLargeIcons**. This image list contains the same icons that are 32 × 32 pixels instead of 16 × 16 pixels. The key names have been replaced such that the word Small has been replaced with the word Large, that is, LargePhone07. The key names could be the same for the two controls because each ImageList control contains its own ListImages collection.

Drill-Down Interfaces

Many Windows programs use a type of user interface, called a drill-down interface, to navigate through data that is organized hierarchically. One example of this drill-down type of interface is the Windows Explorer program shown in Figure 6-14.

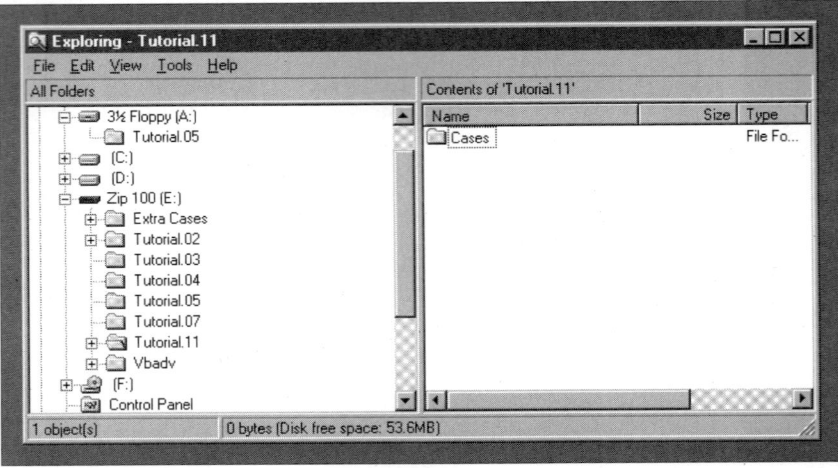

Figure 6-14: Windows Explorer

As shown in Figure 6-14, Windows Explorer consists of two separate windows. The left window is used to display folders and files in a hierarchy of folders. The interface allows individual folders to be expanded and collapsed. When a folder is expanded, the contents of the folder, including files and other folders, is displayed. The right window is used to display the specific information pertaining to the files in the selected folder. As shown in Figure 6-14, the right window consists of several columns. Each column typically displays information of the same type. In the case of Windows Explorer, the first column contains the file name, the second column contains the size, and so on. Both windows can display an icon with each item.

In Visual Basic, this type of user interface is created using two different controls. The hierarchical part (displayed in the left window in Windows Explorer) is implemented using the TreeView control, and the items in the list displayed in the right window in Windows Explorer are implemented using the ListView control.

The TreeView and ListView controls frequently are used together. In Windows Explorer, the data displayed in the ListView control is synchronized with the selected folder in the TreeView control. This process is not automatic. You must write code to update the ListView control when a different element of the TreeView control is selected.

In this program, you will use the TreeView and ListView controls to display and locate the phone numbers for employees in the organization based on the physical office location, and the department within an office.

The TreeView Control

The TreeView control displays information in a hierarchical way much like Windows Explorer. Thus, it is useful to display a hierarchy of files stored on the disk. The standard prefix for the TreeView control is "tvw." In this chapter, the TreeView control will be used to locate the phone numbers of different employees.

The TreeView control supports the Nodes property. This property is a collection that stores references to Node objects. Each element in the hierarchy is represented in the TreeView control as a Node object in the Nodes collection. That is, if a hierarchy of directories and files is created, each directory or file is represented as a Node object in the hierarchy. The visual part of a Node object consists of a textual label and an optional bitmap. The TreeView control and the Node objects it manages are very intertwined and seldom are used independently. In this section, however, the interface of the TreeView control will be presented first and then the interface of the individual Node objects will be discussed.

In the context of Visual Basic, the term Node refers to a particular Node object in a Nodes collection. However, the term node has a much more generic meaning that is used to define an element of a hierarchical data structure. In this chapter however, the term node, and Node object, are used interchangeably to refer to a Node object. The intent is to reduce wordiness.

There is a set of standard terms used to describe the relationship between individual nodes in a hierarchy. These names are based on the names used to describe genealogical relationships. This hierarchy is expressed as an inverted tree structure similar in form to the DAO hierarchy you saw in previous chapters.

At the top of the family tree is the Root node. The Root node can have zero or more children. From the child's perspective, the Root node is considered the parent of the child. All children having the same parent are considered siblings. A child node can have only one parent but a parent can have multiple children. It is possible for children to in turn have children, which in turn also can have children. The terms grandchildren and great grandchildren often are used. Figure 6-15 illustrates this process.

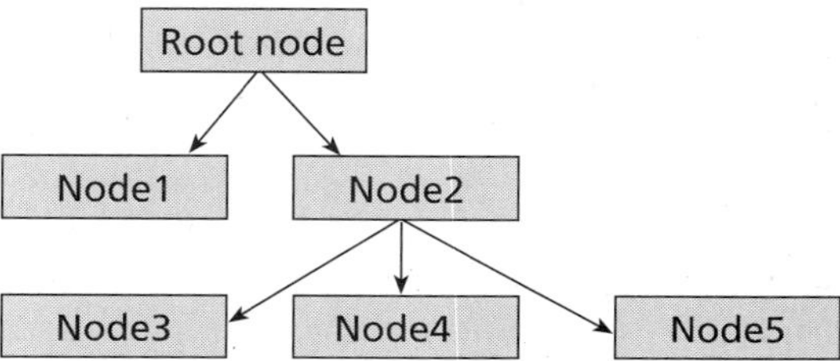

Figure 6-15: Node hierarchy

As shown in Figure 6-15, the Root node has two children (Node1 and Node2). These two nodes are siblings. Node2 has three children (Node3, Node4, and Node5). The parent of these nodes is Node2, and the parent of the Node2 is the Root node.

As you review the properties and methods pertaining to the TreeView control and Node object, you will see that both the TreeView control and Node object share some of the same properties. For example, each supports the Sorted property. One property is used to sort the immediate children of the TreeView control. The other is to sort the children of a particular node. While they have nearly identical purpose and effect, they are separate properties.

Object	TreeView
Properties	■ The **FullPath** and **PathSeparator** properties typically are used when the TreeView contains nodes that pertain to files. The PathSeparator property is a string value typically set to the backslash (\ ) character. When the FullPath property is read, it returns the fully-qualified path. Consider Windows Explorer. If a file were selected in Windows Explorer, the FullPath property would contain the full path of the file. ■ The **LabelEdit** property has the same purpose as it does with the ListView control. If set to the constant tvwAutomatic, the user can click in the text portion of the node to edit the text. If set to tvwManual, the StartLabelEdit method must be called programmatically to initiate editing. ■ The **ImageList** property contains the images that are displayed in the control. ■ The **Indentation** property defines the width of the indentation of the child nodes under the parent node. ■ The **Nodes** property contains a reference to the Nodes collection. ■ The **Sorted** property can be set to True or False and pertains to both the TreeView control and a Node object. As it pertains to the TreeView control, the child nodes of the TreeView control are sorted. If child nodes are added after setting the Sorted property, the new child nodes will not be sorted until the Sorted property is set again. Thus, the Sorted property must be set after all the child nodes are added. ■ The **Style** property is used to set the attributes that control the graphics, if any, that appear next to each node. It also controls whether plus and minus signs appear. These are used to indicate to the user whether the node is expanded or collapsed. Lines may or may not appear to visually connect the different nodes together visually.
Methods	■ The **GetVisibleCount** method returns the number of Node objects that can appear in the visible region of the TreeView control. It commonly is used to change the size of the TreeView control when a certain number of nodes need to be visible.
Events	■ There are two different events that can occur when the user clicks the mouse inside the region of the TreeView control. If the mouse is positioned over a node when clicked, a **NodeClick** event occurs. If the mouse is clicked outside the region of a node, a **Click** event is generated. The **NodeClick** event pertains to the TreeView control rather than a specific node. To determine the node that actually was clicked, the node is passed as an argument to the event procedure.

- The **BeforeLabelEdit** and **AfterLabelEdit** events occur when the user starts to edit a label and completes editing. Again, these events accept one argument—a reference to the node that is being edited. These events commonly are used to save changes to data in a database or other file.
- The **Collapse** and **Expand** events occur when a node is expanded (its children become visible), or collapsed (its children become invisible). Like the NodeClick event, the node that is being collapsed or expanded is passed as an argument to the event procedures.

While processing these events may seem complicated, it is not. Fortunately, the TreeView control itself expands and collapses nodes automatically. The most common use of these events is to synchronize the selected node in the TreeView control with a ListView control.

Each Node object supports several properties that determine the behavior of the node and its relationship to other nodes.

Object	**Node**
Properties	■ The **Expanded** property contains a Boolean value. If True, the children of the current node are displayed. Otherwise, they are not. Double-clicking a node has the effect of toggling this property. That is, double-clicking a node will cause its children to be displayed. Double-clicking the node again will cause the node to be collapsed and its children hidden. ■ Each node can display one of two icons depending upon whether or not the node is expanded. If the node is expanded, the image identified by the **ExpandedImage** property is displayed. If the node is collapsed, the image identified by the **Image** property is displayed. ■ Each node can display a different image when clicked. This image is identified by the **SelectedImage** property. ■ The **Index** and **Key** properties contain the numeric index and string key to identify uniquely a Node object within the Nodes collection. These properties have the same purpose as with other collections. The Nodes collection is a one-based collection. Also, the string keys are case-sensitive like other collections. ■ The **Sorted** property can be set to True or False. If True, the child nodes at the same level in the hierarchy will be sorted alphabetically. If False, the child nodes are not sorted. If child nodes are added after setting the Sorted property, the new child nodes will not be sorted until the Sorted property is set again. Thus, the Sorted property for a node should be set after all of the child nodes are added.

- The **Text** property contains the text displayed in the node. This text appears to the right of the image if an image is defined.
- The **Children** property returns a number indicating the number of children contained by the specified node. When examining a node's child nodes, the Children property commonly is used in an If statement to determine that child nodes exist.
- The **Child** property contains a reference to the first child of a node if a child node exists.
- Nodes at the same level are called siblings. The **FirstSibling** property contains a reference to the first node at the same level of the hierarchy, and the **LastSibling** property contains a reference to the last node at the same level of the hierarchy.
- The **Next** and **Previous** properties contain a reference to the next and the previous node at the same hierarchical level.
- The **Parent** property contains a reference to a parent node; that is, the node one level up on the hierarchy.
- The **Root** property contains a reference to the Root node.

Methods

- The **Add** method is used to add a node to the Nodes collection.
- The **Remove** method is used to remove a node from the Nodes collection.

Note that the Node objects do not respond to events. All the event processing is handled by the TreeView control itself. The event procedures all contain a reference to the specific node that is active.

In the ETC example, there will be a Root node having child nodes for the 10 different regional offices. This information is contained in the database table named tblOffices having fields named fldOfficeID and fldOfficeDescription. To display the information in the TreeView control, the database containing the information must be opened and the information in the table read. The code to open the database has been written already. For each regional office, a node then is added to the TreeView control.

To create an instance of the TreeView control:

1 Create an instance of the TreeView control as shown in Figure 6-16 and set its properties as follows: Name to **tvwETC**, Indentation to **200**, LabelEdit to **tvwManual**.

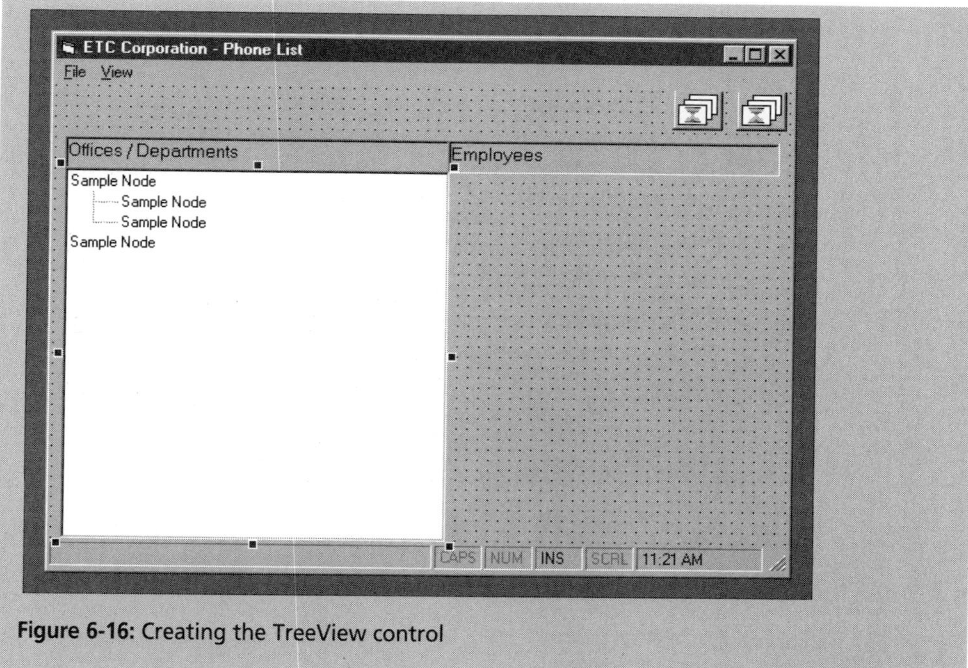

Figure 6-16: Creating the TreeView control

Once an instance of the TreeView control is created, it is possible to add nodes to the TreeView control at run time. Common sources for data include database and text files.

While both TreeView and ListView controls support editing of the textual contents, it is the programmer's responsibility to do something with the edited data. For example, if editing were enabled in this program, it would be necessary to record the changes back to the database by writing SQL statements or writing a recordset. As such, your code must respond to the BeforeLabelEdit and AfterLabelEdit events.

Adding a Node to the TreeView Control

A node is added to the collection of nodes by calling the Add method of the Nodes collection. This is consistent with other collections you have used. The Add method supports additional arguments that define the relationship of the node to another node in the hierarchy, and the images displayed in the node.

Syntax *object*.**Add**(*relative, relationship, key, text, image, selectedimage*)

Dissection

- The required *object* must be the Nodes collection in a TreeView control.
- The optional *relative* argument contains the index or string key of an existing Node object. It is used with the *relationship* argument to determine the placement of the new node in the hierarchy.
- The *relationship* argument contains a constant to define the relationship of the new node to the *relative* argument.
- The optional *key* contains a unique string key used to identify the node within the collection.
- The required *text* argument describes the text that appears to the right of the icon.
- The optional *image* argument identifies the image that is displayed to the left of the *text* argument.
- The *selectedimage* argument contains the image that is displayed when the node is selected.

Code Example

```
Dim pNode As Node
Set tvwETC.ImageList = ilsView    ' ilsView is an ImageList
Set pNode = tvwETC.Nodes.Add( )   ' Add the Root node
pNode.Key = "Unique Value"
pNode.Text = "Buena Park"
pNode.Image = "Clsdfold"
pNode.SelectedImage = "Openfold"
Set pNode = tvwETC.Nodes.Add(, , "UniqueValue", _
    "Buena Park", "Clsdfold", "Openfold")
```

Code Dissection

The preceding statements illustrate two different ways to add a Node to the Nodes collection. One uses the Add method with no arguments and sets the properties individually. The second supplies the same values using the arguments supported by the Add method.

The first statement declares an object variable named pNode to supply a reference to the Node. The second statement identifies the ImageList control that contains the images used by the node. Next, a new node is added. Because the Add method is called with no arguments, the node is added to the top level of the hierarchy. If there were other nodes at the top level, then the node would appear as the last node in the top-level of the hierarchy. Finally, the text and images for the node are specified.

The previous statements in the syntax dissection illustrate a very important concept pertaining to the nodes used by the TreeView control. While you continually have used object variables, you seldom have used multiple object variables to reference the same object. As you will see in this chapter, object variables of type Node will be created frequently to reference the nodes in the hierarchy.

Another distinction needs to be made regarding the Nodes collection and other collections you have used. While all collections are nothing more than a list of values from Visual Basic's perspective, the TreeView control views the Nodes collection much differently than a simple list. From the TreeView control's perspective, the Nodes collection is a hierarchically-organized group of elements.

In the ETC example, you will create a Root-level node. Each of the 10 offices will appear as children of the Root-level node. Each of the 10 offices in turn will have departments, which will vary depending on the office. Thus, the departments are children of the offices. Each department in turn will have some number of employees. In other words, the employees are children of the department and grandchildren of the office. The implementation to create the nodes uses four different general procedures. The first general procedure creates the Root-level node, then calls a procedure to create a node for each of the 10 offices. For each office, this procedure in turn calls another procedure to create the nodes for the departments pertaining to that office. The procedure to create the departments calls another procedure to create the nodes representing the employees working in a particular department. In summary, the processing for each level of the hierarchy is performed by a specific procedure. Figure 6-17 illustrates this process.

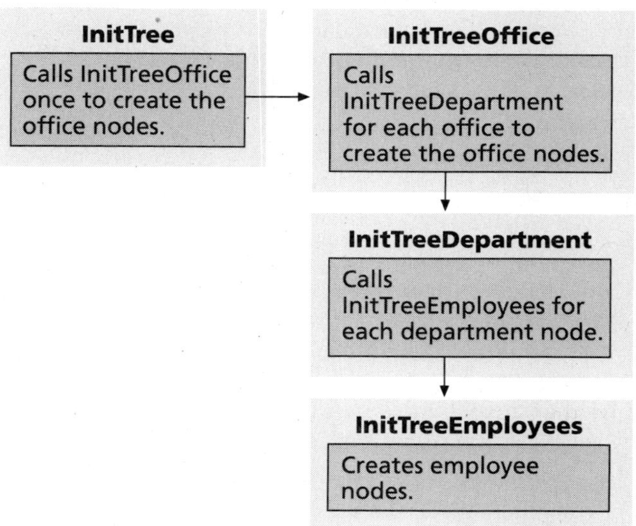
InitTree
Calls InitTreeOffice once to create the office nodes.
InitTreeOffice
Calls InitTreeDepartment for each office to create the office nodes.
InitTreeDepartment
Calls InitTreeEmployees for each department node.
InitTreeEmployees
Creates employee nodes.

Figure 6-17: Processing the node hierarchy

Creating the Root-Level Node

The first procedure is relatively simple, it creates the Root-level node and defines the text and icons for the node. Then it calls the procedure to add the child nodes representing the offices. After the offices have been added, the child nodes are sorted, and the node is expanded. This causes the children to be displayed.

To create the Root-level node:

1. Activate the **general declarations section** of the Code window and declare the following variable to store a reference to the Root-level node:

```
Dim mRootNode As Node
```

2. Locate the **InitTree** general procedure and enter the following statements:

```
tvwETC.ImageList = ilsSmallIcons
Set mRootNode = tvwETC.Nodes.Add _
    (, , "Root", "Offices", "SmallClsdfold", _
    "SmallOpenfold")
InitTreeOffice mRootNode
mRootNode.Expanded = True
mRootNode.Sorted = True
```

3. Test the program: the Root-level node with the caption "Offices" and an open folder will appear when the program is run. The procedure InitTreeOffice is declared already but contains no code. Thus, the offices will not appear as child nodes until you complete the next steps.

The code you just wrote associates the ImageList control with the TreeView control. When the Add method is called, a Node object is created in the Nodes collection. While the properties were set as arguments to the Add method, they could have just as well been set by writing the individual properties of the Node.

Creating Child Nodes

Before you can add nodes that exist at different levels of the hierarchy, you need to know how to create nodes relative to other nodes. This is accomplished using the *relative* and *relationship* arguments supported by the Add method of the Nodes collection. When a node is added, it is by default added to the top of the node hierarchy. If a Node is specified in the *relative* argument, however, the position of the new node in the hierarchy is relative to the specified node. The *relationship* argument determines the *relative* placement of the new node. Valid arguments for the *relationship* argument are listed in Figure 6-18.

Constant	Value	Description
tvwFirst	0	The node is added at the same level in the hierarchy as the node named in the *relative* argument. It is added such that the node is positioned before all other nodes at the same level.
tvwLast	1	The node is added at the same level in the hierarchy as the node named in the *relative* argument. Any node added subsequently may be positioned after all other nodes at the same level.
tvwNext	2	The node is placed at the same hierarchical level positioned immediately after the node named in the *relative* argument.
tvwPrevious	3	The node is placed at the same hierarchical level positioned immediately before the node named in the *relative* argument.
tvwChild	4	The node is placed below the node named in the *relative* argument, thus becoming a child of the node.

Figure 6-18: Valid relationship arguments

Now that the Root-level node is created, the child nodes representing the offices can be created. This task is performed in the InitTreeOffice procedure, which is called by the InitTree procedure. This general procedure creates a recordset to examine each of the different offices. For each office, a node is added as a child node of the Root node.

To add the Root node's children to the TreeView control:

1 Locate the **InitTreeOffice** general procedure in the Code window and enter the following statements. Note that the Root node is passed as an argument named pRoot:

```
Dim pCurrentNode As Node, prstOffices As Recordset
Set prstOffices = mdbCurrent.OpenRecordset("tblOffices")
Do Until prstOffices.EOF
    Set pCurrentNode = tvwETC.Nodes.Add(pRoot, tvwChild)
    With pCurrentNode
        .Text = prstOffices![fldOfficeDescription]
        .Image = "SmallClsdfold"
        .ExpandedImage = "SmallOpenfold"
    End With
    InitTreeDepartment pCurrentNode, _
        prstOffices![fldOfficeID]
    pCurrentNode.Sorted = True
    prstOffices.MoveNext
Loop
```

2 Test the program. The offices should be displayed as shown in Figure 6-19.

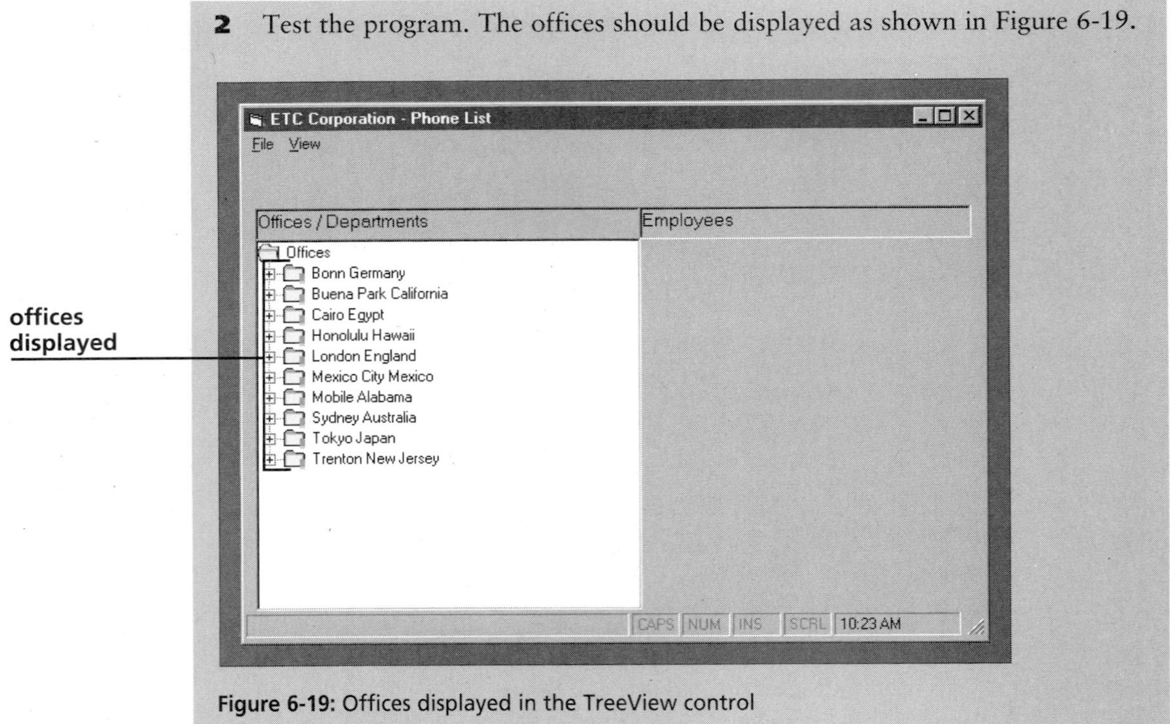

Figure 6-19: Offices displayed in the TreeView control

These statements add all the regional offices as children of the Root node. The database has been opened already and a reference stored in the object variable named mdbCurrent. This is performed in the Form_Load event procedure. The variable pCurrentNode stores a reference to the office that is being added. The first step is to call the OpenRecordset control to open the table named tblOffices. Then, a Do loop is used to step through each record in the table.

```
Set pCurrentNode = tvwETC.Nodes.Add(pRoot, tvwChild)
```

For each record in the table, a new node is added and a reference to the node stored in pCurrentNode. These nodes are added as children of the Root-level node. The relative argument, pRoot, references the Root node. Remember, the Root node is passed as an argument to this procedure. The *relative* argument, tvwChild, indicates that the new node is a child of the Root-level node.

```
With pCurrentNode
    .Text = prstOffices![fldOfficeDescription]
    .Image = "SmallClsdfold"
    .ExpandedImage = "SmallOpenfold"
End With
```

The previous statements store the remaining values in the newly-added office node. Then, the office description is stored in the Text property of the node. This value is obtained from the recordset. After setting the Text property, the images associated with the node are identified by setting the Image and ExpandedImage properties. Remember, the image will be displayed when the node is collapsed, and the expanded image is displayed when the Node is expanded.

Within each office, there are different departments. Each time an office node is added, the departments for that office need to be added so they will appear as child nodes of the current office. This can be accomplished by creating a recordset consisting of the departments corresponding to an office. Then using a Do loop, create a child node, set the text to the department description, and then set the pertinent image properties.

As you may expect, the structure of this procedure is similar to the InitTreeOffice procedure you just wrote. This procedure, however, will accept two arguments—a reference to a node and an OfficeID. Each of the departments is associated with one office. Thus, each department node will have as its parent an office node.

To add the departments as children of the respective office:

1 Locate the **InitTreeDepartment** general procedure and insert the following statements shown in bold. Note that the general procedure accepts two arguments—pParentNode is of type Node and provides a reference to the parent node and pintOfficeID is a Long integer and contains the OfficeID property of the parent node. This value is used to lookup the values pertaining to the office.

```
Dim prstDepartments As Recordset
Dim pstrSQL As String, pChildNode As Node
pstrSQL = "SELECT * FROM tblDepartments WHERE " & _
    "fldOfficeID = " & pintOfficeID
Set prstDepartments = mdbCurrent.OpenRecordset(pstrSQL)
Do Until prstDepartments.EOF
    Set pChildNode = tvwETC.Nodes.Add(pParentNode, _
        tvwChild)
    With pChildNode
        .Text = prstDepartments![fldDepartmentDescription]
        .Image = "SmallClsdfold"
        .ExpandedImage = "SmallOpenfold"
        .Tag = prstDepartments![fldDepartmentID]
    End With
    InitTreeEmployees pChildNode, _
        prstDepartments![fldDepartmentID]
    pChildNode.Sorted = True
    prstDepartments.MoveNext
Loop
prstDepartments.Close
```

2 Test the program. Double-click the offices to expand and collapse the node. The divisions should be displayed under the office as shown in Figure 6-20.

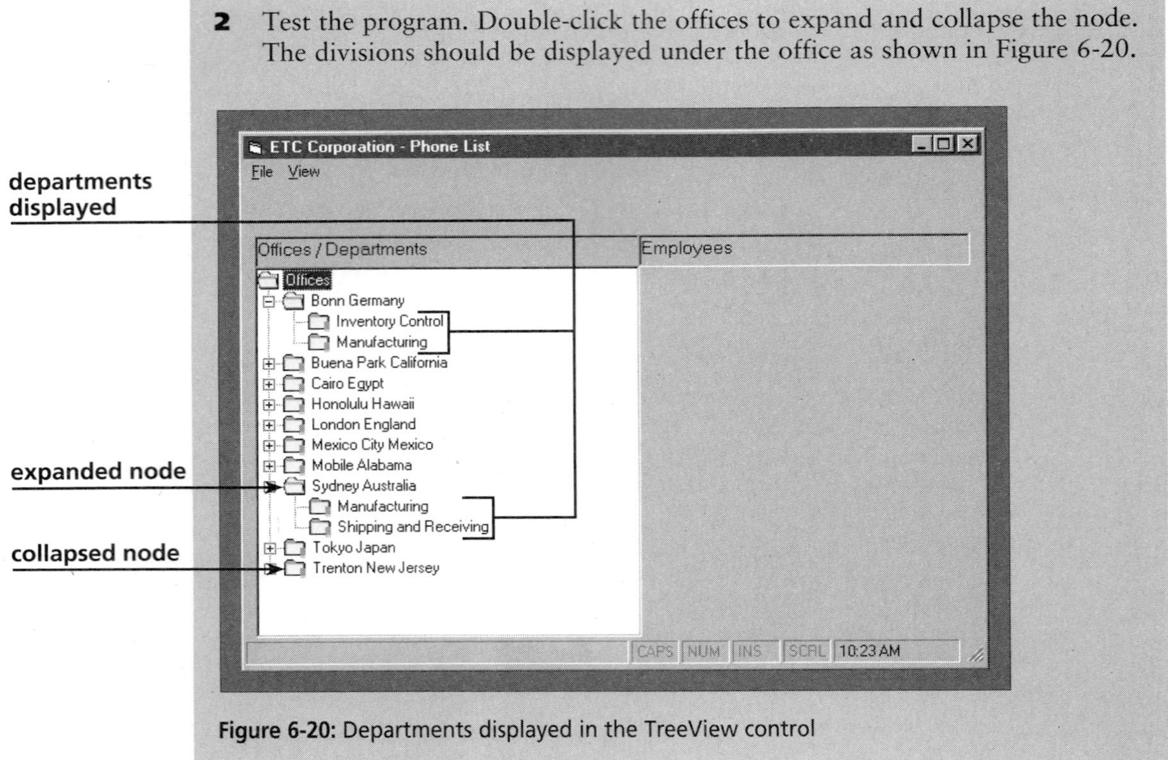

Figure 6-20: Departments displayed in the TreeView control

The statements you just wrote create a recordset containing the departments belonging to a specific office. Then a Do loop is used again to create nodes as children of the parent office node. Consider the following statements:

```
Set pChildNode = tvwETC.Nodes.Add(pParentNode,tvwChild)
```

The *relative* argument is set to pParentNode, which contains a reference to the corresponding office. The following statements also will have the same effect:

```
Set pChildNode = tvwETC.Nodes.Add(pParentNode.Key, _
    tvwChild)
Set pChildNode = tvwETC.Nodes.Add(pParentNode.Index, _
    tvwChild)
```

Note the following statement that stores the current DepartmentID in the Tag property:

```
.Tag = prstDepartments![fldDepartmentID]
```

In this example, only departments have employees. Furthermore, when a department is selected, the employees pertaining to the department ultimately will be displayed in the ListView control. Given this, when the user clicks a node, the

Tag property can be checked to see if it contains a value. If it does, then the corresponding employees should be displayed in the ListView control. If it does not, the contents of the ListView control should be cleared.

The final step in the process is to add the employees to the departments where they work. The process of adding the employees is nearly identical to the process of adding the departments. Every employee works for one, and only one, department.

To add the employees to their department:

1 Locate the **InitTreeEmployees** general procedure and insert the following statements shown in bold. The parent node (department) is passed in the argument pParentNode.

```
On Error GoTo No_Record
    Dim prstCurrent As Recordset, pCurrentNode As Node
    Dim pstrSQL As String
    pstrSQL = "SELECT * FROM tblEmployees " & _
        "WHERE fldDepartmentID = " & pintDepartmentID
    Set prstCurrent = mdbCurrent.OpenRecordset(pstrSQL)
    Do Until prstCurrent.EOF
        Set pCurrentNode = tvwETC.Nodes.Add _
            (pParentNode, tvwChild)
        pCurrentNode.Text = prstCurrent![fldName]
        pCurrentNode.Image = "SmallPhone07"
        prstCurrent.MoveNext
    Loop
    prstCurrent.Close
No_Record:
```

2 Test the program. Expand the offices and departments. Double-click various departments and the employees should be listed with an icon.

These statements are almost identical to the statements to add the departmental nodes. A SELECT statement is used to create a recordset containing the employees that work for a specific department. A node then is added for each employee as a child of the department. Again, all the variables are local to the procedure.

Navigating the Node Hierarchy

A Node object supports the following properties used for navigation: Children, Child, FirstSibling, LastSibling, Next, and Previous. These properties are useful to traverse the nodes in the tree and print the contents.

Using these properties, there are several techniques that are useful to examine the entire hierarchy of nodes, or all of a particular node's children. Assume that you wanted to list all the children (offices of the Root node) in this example. You can generalize this and create a procedure to list all the immediate children of a node.

```
Private Sub ListChildren(pNode As Node)
    Dim pintCount As Integer, pintCurrent As Integer
    Dim pCurrentNode As Node
    Set pCurrentNode = pNode.Child
    pintCount = pNode.Children
    For pintCurrent = 1 To pintCount
        Debug.Print pCurrentNode.Text
        Set pCurrentNode = pCurrentNode.Next
    Next
End Sub
```

This code illustrates the importance of using the Set statement with object references. The general procedure accepts one argument—a node. In this example, assume that the Root node for ETC is passed as the argument. pNode.Children contains the number of children in the node (in this case the 10 offices or 10 nodes). As such, the For loop will iterate 10 times. Inside the For loop, the text property of the Node is printed. The final statement is significant.

```
Set pCurrentNode = pCurrentNode.Next
```

Each node supports the Next property, which contains a reference to the next sibling. This assignment statement sets the object variable pCurrentNode so it will reference the next sibling. This process continues until all the nodes have been examined.

This example can be extended to examine multiple hierarchies. To accomplish this, you can use nested For loops. In the ETC example, the navigational properties are used to print the Text property for each object in the tree. The printout is organized such that the children are printed indented on the report much like they appear on the form.

To use the navigational properties to print the tree:

1 Locate the **mnuFilePrint_Click** event procedure and enter the following statements:

```
Dim pOfficeNode As Node, pDeptNode As Node, _
    pEmpNode As Node
Dim pintRC As Integer, pintOC As Integer, _
    pintDC As Integer
Dim pintRCount As Integer, pintOCount As Integer, _
    pintDCount As Integer
Debug.Print mRootNode.Text
Set pOfficeNode = mRootNode.Child
pintRC = mRootNode.Children
For pintRCount = 1 To pintRC
    Debug.Print "     "; pOfficeNode.Text
```

```
        Set pDeptNode = pOfficeNode.Child
        pintOC = pOfficeNode.Children
        For pintOCount = 1 To pintOC
            Debug.Print "         "; pDeptNode.Text
            Set pEmpNode = pDeptNode.Child
            pintDC = pDeptNode.Children
            For pintDCount = 1 To pintDC
                Debug.Print "            "; pEmpNode.Text
                Set pEmpNode = pEmpNode.Next
            Next
            Set pDeptNode = pDeptNode.Next
        Next
        Set pOfficeNode = pOfficeNode.Next
    Next
```

2 Test the program. On the menu bar, click **File** then **Print.** The report printed in the Immediate window should look similar to the tree with all the nodes expanded.

These statements work in much the same way as the general procedures used to create the nodes hierarchy. That is, there are three nested For loops to process each level of nodes. The first examines the offices, the second the departments, and the inner loop examines the employees for a specific department. Each loop works the same way. The Children property is used to determine if a node has any children. If so, the statements in the loop are executed. Otherwise, they are not. Inside the loop, the text of the current node is printed and then the next node is selected.

Events Pertaining to the TreeView Control

Just as with other controls you have used, the TreeView control responds to several events as the user clicks on different nodes in the tree. The Expand, Collapse, and NodeClick events are most useful when the TreeView control is synchronized with the ListView. This process will be illustrated in a moment.

You have completed the programming for the TreeView control. The next step to complete the program is to display the employee information in the ListView control when the user double-clicks a specific department.

The ListView Control

The ListView control displays its data in one of four different views as defined by the setting of the View property. It is possible to change the view at run time or design time. Each item of data contains two parts: a textual part and an associated icon. This is similar to the nodes in a TreeView control.

- In **Icon** view, each item is displayed with an icon and a text description. In Icon view, the user can arrange the icons within the visible region of the ListView control. It also is common to perform drag-and-drop operations on the icons.
- **Small Icon** view works like Icon view but allows more ListItem objects to be viewed in the visible region of the ListView control.
- In **List** view, items are presented in sorted order with one item on a line and an optional icon appearing to the left of the icon. Do not confuse List view with the ListView control.
- **Report** view is similar to List view but each item can be displayed with subitems. This allows a columnar list of items to be displayed. Subitems are discussed later in the chapter.

You have seen that collections commonly are used to keep track of the run-time objects displayed in a control. For example, the DBGrid control uses the Columns collection and individual Column objects to keep track of the columns displayed in the grid. You also saw that the ListImages collection contains ListImage objects for the ImageList control. The ListView control works similarly. Each item displayed in the ListView control is a ListItem object. The ListItems collection contains a reference to all the ListItem objects in the collection. As shown in the previous list, these ListItem objects can be displayed in one of four different views determined by the setting of the View property. The ListView control only is supported by Windows 95 and Windows NT 3.51 or higher. The standard prefix for the ListView control is "lvw."

Like the grid, the ListView control supports a long list of properties and methods. Some of these properties only are meaningful for a specific view. Thus, the presentation of the properties and methods will be discussed and ordered in the context of each individual view. The ListView control can be associated with two different ImageList controls, whereas the TreeView control can be associated with only one. This is because, depending on the view, different sized icons are displayed. Remember, one ImageList control only can display icons of the same size. The Icons and SmallIcons properties define the two image lists that appear. Each ListItem object supports several properties to identify the icon and text associated with the ListItem object as shown in the following list.

Object	ListItem
Properties	■ The **Icon** and **SmallIcon** properties contain the numeric index or string key of an image stored in a ListImage object. These properties cannot be set until the ListView control is associated with an ImageList control that is using the Icons and SmallIcons property. ■ The **Index** and **Key** properties uniquely identify the ListItem object in the ListItems collection and have the same purpose as the Index and Key properties of other collections. ■ The **Text** property identifies the text pertaining to the ListItem object.

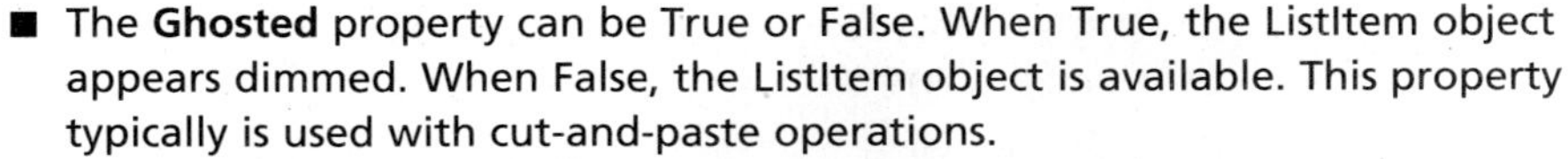

- The **Ghosted** property can be True or False. When True, the ListItem object appears dimmed. When False, the ListItem object is available. This property typically is used with cut-and-paste operations.

Methods

- The **Add** and **Remove** methods are used to add or remove ListItem objects to and from the collection. They have the same purpose as the methods of the same name for other collections.
- The **Clear** method takes no arguments. It removes all the ListItem objects from the collection thereby having the effect of removing all the items from the list.

The first step in using the ListView control is to load the ListItem objects into the ListItems collection. ListItem objects are added to the collection using the Add method, as you would expect. There are many viable sources for the data. An ASCII delimited file could be read and its contents displayed. For each record in the ASCII delimited file, the Add method would be called to insert the record in the ListItems collection. Records in a database also could be displayed. In the ETC example, you will display a list of names and phone numbers from a database. The usefulness of this list will become apparent when Report view is discussed.

Syntax *object*.**Add**(*index*, *key*, *text*, *icon*, *smallIcon*)

Dissection

- The required *object* argument must be a valid instance of the ListView control.
- The optional *index* and *key* arguments uniquely identify a ListItem object. Like other controls, the *index* argument is a numeric value and the *key* argument is a unique string key. String keys are case-sensitive.
- The optional *text* argument identifies the text associated with the ListItem object. The visual appearance of the ListItem object varies based on the current view.
- The optional *icon* and *smallIcon* arguments contain a string key or numeric index of an image in a corresponding ImageList control.

Code Example

```
lvwEmployees.Icons = ilsLargeIcons
lvwEmployees.SmallIcons = ilsSmallIcons
lvwEmployees.Add(1,"Item","String","SmallIcon", _
    "LargeIcon")
```

Code Dissection

This example assumes that an instance of the ListView control named lvwEmployees has been declared. The first two assignment statements define the two image lists that will be used to display the normal and small icons, respectively. The Add method is called to add an item to the list. Both the numeric index and string key are defined. The text that will appear in the ListItem object is "String". The last two arguments specify the string keys of the icons in the two different ImageList controls.

In the ETC example, you will create ListItem objects when the user double-clicks a department in the TreeView control. This interface is very similar to the way folders and files are displayed in the right-hand pane in Windows Explorer. Each ListItem object ultimately will contain the name, phone number, and extension of the employee. For each employee in the list, one of two icons will be displayed to indicate whether or not the employee is in the office. So you can see the appearance of the different views, commands have been created and located on the View menu. They set the View property to one of the four different views.

Integrating the ListView and TreeView Controls

As indicated earlier, the ListView control commonly is used in conjunction with the TreeView control. This requires that when different nodes are expanded or collapsed, the contents of the TreeView control must be updated to display the contents pertaining to the selected node. In the ETC example, the names, phone number, and extension for the employees in a department should be displayed when the user double-clicks a department. Remember, when you created the nodes in the TreeView control, you set the Tag property only for departments. In the NodeClick event procedure, you can determine whether or not the node has a Tag property. If it does, then the employees should be displayed in the ListView control.

To create a ListView control and synchronize it with the TreeView control:

1. Create a ListView control to the right of the TreeView control. Using the Properties window set the Name property to **lvwEmployees**.
2. Locate the **tvwETC_NodeClick** event procedure in the Code window and enter the following statements:

```
If Node.Tag <> "" Then
    InitializeList Node.Tag
Else
    ClearList
End If
```

3. Create the **ClearList** Sub procedure and enter the following statement:

```
lvwEmployees.ListItems.Clear
```

4 Insert the following statements into the **InitializeList** general procedure. Note that pintID is passed as an argument to the procedure. This argument contains the current DepartmentID.

```
Dim pitmCurrent As ListItem, pstrSQL As String
lvwEmployees.Icons = ilsLargeIcons
lvwEmployees.SmallIcons = ilsSmallIcons
lvwEmployees.View = lvwReport
lvwEmployees.ListItems.Clear
lvwEmployees.ColumnHeaders.Clear
lvwEmployees.ColumnHeaders.Add , , "Name", 1400
lvwEmployees.ColumnHeaders.Add , , "Phone", 1000
lvwEmployees.ColumnHeaders.Add , , "Ext.", 400
lvwEmployees.Sorted = True
pstrSQL = "SELECT * FROM tblEmployees WHERE " & _
    "fldDepartmentID = " & pintID
Set mrstCurrent = mdbCurrent.OpenRecordset(pstrSQL)
Do Until mrstCurrent.EOF
    Set pitmCurrent = lvwEmployees.ListItems.Add()
    pitmCurrent.Text = mrstCurrent![fldName]
    If mrstCurrent![fldInOut] = True Then
        pitmCurrent.SmallIcon = "SmallPhone07"
        pitmCurrent.Icon = "LargePhone07"
    Else
        pitmCurrent.SmallIcon = "SmallPhone08"
        pitmCurrent.Icon = "LargePhone08"
    End If
    pitmCurrent.SubItems(1) = mrstCurrent![fldPhone]
    pitmCurrent.SubItems(2) = mrstCurrent![fldExtension]
    mrstCurrent.MoveNext
Loop
```

5 Test the program. Expand the folders until a folder at the office level appears. Then double-click the icon for a particular office. This will generate a NodeClick event procedure, which calls the InitializeList procedure. The employees should be listed in the ListView control. Use the commands on the View menu to see the different views. In Icon view, the default, the large icons are displayed. In Small Icon view the other icons are displayed. This will allow more information to be displayed in the visible area of the ListView control. List view displays the items in a columnar list. The necessary properties have not yet been set for Report view to operate properly.

The NodeClick event procedure tests to determine that there is a value stored in the Tag property. If there is, the procedure to list the employees is called. Only department-level nodes have a value stored in the Tag property. If there is no value in the Tag property, the contents of the ListView control are cleared.

The InitializeList general procedure accepts one argument—the ID representing a department at a regional office. This value is used in the SELECT statement. The resulting recordset stored in mrstCurrent contains all the employees working in a specific department. For each record, an item is added to the list and the employee name is stored in the Text property of the ListItem control. Depending on the value of the field fldInOut, one of two different icons is displayed. Large and small versions of the icons are stored in the two ImageList controls.

```
Set pitmCurrent = _
    lvwEmployees.ListItems.Add(mrstCurrent![fldID])
pitmCurrent.Text = mrstCurrent![fldName]
```

The first statement adds the new ListItem object to the collection. The numeric index of the item is the same as the Employee ID. This requires that the Employee IDs are unique so the collection indexes are unique. A string key is not used. The second statement stores the employee name in the Text property of the ListItem object. This value appears in the first column in Report view and also will appear as the textual description in the other three views.

In Icon view and Small Icon view, there are several properties to control the appearance of the icon as shown in the following list.

Object	Icon
Properties	■ In Icon view, it is possible for text to appear on multiple lines if the **LabelWrap** property is set to True and on one line if the LabelWrap property is False. When the LabelWrap property is True, the maximum width of a line is set using the Appearance tab on the Display control panel. ■ The **Arrange** property is used only with Icon view and Small Icon view. If set to the constant lvwAutoLeft, the icons are aligned along the left-hand side of the ListView control. If set to the constant lvwAutoTop, the icons are aligned along the top of the ListView. If set to the default value of lvwNone, the icons are not aligned. ■ The **LabelEdit** property can be set to True or False, and determines whether or not the contents of the label (stored in the Text property of the ListItem control) can be edited. This is a slight inconsistency because one would tend to think of the property names as LabelEdit and Label or TextEdit and Text. ■ In drag-and-drop operations, it often is useful to be able to select multiple items (multiple ListItem objects). If the user should be able to select multiple ListItem objects, set the **MultiSelect** property to True. Otherwise, set the property to False.

Using Report View

Using the ListView control in Report view adds considerable functionality beyond the other three views. Along with the additional functionality comes increased programming complexity, however. Report view commonly is used to display records in a database or a text file. The information must be loaded at run time rather than creating the list at design time. Figure 6-21 shows the ListView control in report view.

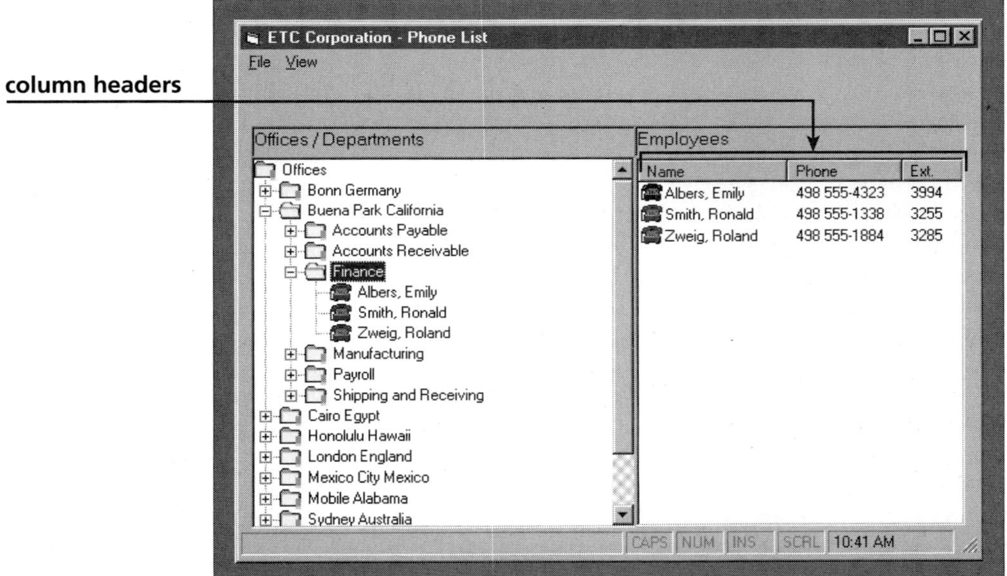

Figure 6-21: Report view

As shown in Figure 6-21, the name, phone number, and extension of an employee are displayed in columns. At the top of each column, a column header is used to identify the column. To support this functionality, a mechanism is needed to store the column headers and the information in the rows under the column headers. This is achieved using the ColumnHeaders collection, ColumnHeader object, and SubItems property. These objects are pertinent only when the View property is set to Report view.

The ColumnHeader Object

Each column is represented by a ColumnHeader object in the ColumnHeaders collection. A reference to this collection is maintained by the ColumnHeaders property in the ListView control. The following list summarizes the properties supported by the ColumnHeader object.

Object	ColumnHeader
Properties	■ The **Index** and **Key** properties contain the numeric index and string key of the ColumnHeader object in the ColumnHeaders collection. ■ The **Text** property contains the caption that is displayed in the column header. Setting the Alignment property changes the justification of the text. ■ Each column header corresponds to a subitem. The **SubItemIndex** property contains the numeric index of the subitem associated with the ColumnHeader object.

Column headers can be added at design time using the Property Pages, or at run time by calling the Add method which has the following syntax:

Syntax	*object*.**Add**(*index, key, text, width, alignment*)
Dissection	■ The required *object* must contain a reference to a ColumnHeaders collection. ■ The optional *index* and *key* arguments specify the numeric index and string key to identify the ColumnHeader object in the collection uniquely. ■ The value of the optional *text* argument is displayed in the column header. ■ The optional *width* argument defines the width of the column header. ■ The optional *alignment* argument is used to left-justify, right-justify, or center *text* in the column.
Code Example	`lvwEmployees.ColumnHeaders.Add 1 "Column1", _` `    "Description", 1500`
Code Dissection	This statement adds a column header with the string key of Column1. The text appearing in the column is "Description," and the column is 1,500 twips wide.

In the ETC example, you need to create a column header for the name, phone number, and extension. These are created using the Add method. For each column, the width of the column is set explicitly. This is accomplished using the following statements already created in the InitializeList procedure:

```
lvwEmployees.ColumnHeaders.Clear
lvwEmployees.ColumnHeaders.Add , , "Name", 1400
lvwEmployees.ColumnHeaders.Add , , "Phone", 1000
lvwEmployees.ColumnHeaders.Add , , "Ext.", 400
lvwEmployees.Sorted = True
```

These statements add three column headers that are displayed in Report view. The first column header has a caption of Name, the second Phone, and the third Ext. The final argument to the Add method sets the width of the columns. The column headers are cleared before adding the new column headers.

In Report view, the ListView control displays one ListItem object on a line. In Figure 6-21, you can see that each line consists of multiple columns. This is implemented using another property supported by the ListItem object. This property is called the SubItems property. The SubItems property is an array containing a string for each SubItem object in the list. A ListItem object can have any number of subitems. Each ListItem object in the ListItems collection must have the same number of subitems, however. The number of subitems corresponds to the number of column headers. When a ColumnHeader object is created (added to the ColumnHeaders collection), a corresponding subitem is added automatically to the ListItem control.

In the following example, the rows from the table named tblEmployees are added to the ListItems collection. When the Add method is called, a new ListItem object is added. Thus, in Report view, a new row will be displayed in the ListView control. Given the current example, the ListItem object is created with two subitems because of the creation of additional ColumnHeader objects. It is possible to create a Do loop to read all the employees into the ListView control and store the values in the subitems.

```
If mrstCurrent![fldInOut] = True Then
    pitmCurrent.SmallIcon = "SmallPhone07"
    pitmCurrent.Icon = "LargePhone07"
Else
    pitmCurrent.SmallIcon = "SmallPhone08"
    pitmCurrent.Icon = "LargePhone08"
End If
pitmCurrent.SubItems(1) = mrstCurrent![fldPhone]
pitmCurrent.SubItems(2) = mrstCurrent![fldExtension]
```

These statements load the phone number and extension into the two subitems. The array of subitems is not created explicitly. Rather, the number of subitems is determined by the number of ColumnHeader objects. Thus, by adding a column header, a subitem is added automatically.

```
    pitmCurrent.SubItems(4) = mrstCurrent![fldExtension]
```

In the ETC example, there are two subitems with index values of 1 and 2. Thus, the previous statement will generate a run-time error because the index attempts to reference a subitem that does not exist.

Column Selection

In Report view, the user can click a column header to generate a ColumnClick event. The column header that was clicked is passed as an argument to the ColumnClick event procedure. One common task performed in this event procedure is to sort the rows by the values in the selected column. Sorting the rows in the ListView control is performed using the SortKey and Sorted properties. The SortKey is set to an Integer value that determines how the rows are sorted. If set to zero (0), the rows are sorted using the Text property of the ListItem object. If the value is greater than zero (0), the rows are sorted by the subitem having the same Index value. Thus, if the value is one (1), the rows are sorted by the first subitem. Before setting the SortKey property, the Sorted property should be set to True.

In the ETC example, you will program the ColumnClick event procedure so the rows will be sorted by the column that was clicked.

To sort the columns:

1 Enter the following statements in the **lvwEmployees_ColumnClick** event procedure:

```
lvwEmployees.Sorted = True
lvwEmployees.SortKey = ColumnHeader.Index - 1
```

2 Test the program. Click each of the columns and note that the data is sorted by the selected column.

These statements provide a generic way to sort the list by the column that was clicked and can be used with any ListView control to perform the task. A ColumnHeader object is passed to the event procedure. Using the Index property of the ColumnHeader object, the column can be determined and assigned to the sort key.

You have completed this chapter. You have seen how additional ActiveX controls can be used to provide a drill-down interface. You also have seen how the grid can be implemented to work like a spreadsheet. You learned that you need to carefully consider the type of user interface that is best suited to the task, and use the appropriate controls to implement the interface. You also saw how to implement a status bar. Again, status bars are common in many applications and can improve a program's user interface by keeping the user alerted to the program's status, as well as the status of the editing keys.

SUMMARY

- In this chapter you used the MSFlexGrid control. This control has characteristics of a spreadsheet in that it is used to edit rows and columns. There are two types of rows and columns. Fixed rows and columns are used as headers. Normal rows and columns contain data. As the developer, you have considerable control over the appearance of the text in both types of columns and the gridlines that divide them. The contents of fixed rows and columns can be set using the FormatString property. Like a list box, rows are added and removed at run time using the AddItem and RemoveItem methods. To reference a cell in the grid, you used the TextArray and TextMatrix properties. The TextMatrix property works like a two-dimensional array accepting a row and column as arguments. The grid control does not directly support editing. Rather, another control, such as a TextBox, commonly is used to edit the contents of a cell.
- The StatusBar control, as its name implies, displays a status bar across the bottom of a form. The status bar is made up of panels. Each panel has a style to define its characteristics. Setting the Style property allows you to display the settings of keyboard keys and the date and time. You also can store text in a panel by writing code executed at run time.
- The ImageList control is used to store bitmaps and other graphics used as icons by other controls. It does not display these icons. Rather, they are used and displayed by other controls. Each image in the ImageList control is considered as a ListImage object in the ListImages collection. Like other collection members they can be referenced by a string key or numeric index. All the images must be of the same size. Furthermore, you cannot change images that have been bound to other controls.
- A drill-down interface is used to navigate through data like the Windows Explorer program navigates through the file system. The TreeView and ListView controls are used concurrently to implement a drill-down interface.
- The TreeView control contains a Nodes collection. Each node represents an item in the hierarchy. The TreeView control responds to events as the user clicks different visible nodes. It automatically takes care of expanding and collapsing the nodes in the hierarchy. You can write code to respond to the events to override the default actions, or to synchronize a ListView control with the currently selected node. Each node has several properties to define its relationship to other nodes in the hierarchy. These properties typically are set when the node is added to the collection.
- Commonly used with the TreeView control is the ListView control. The ListView control displays data in one of four views. The user can toggle between these four views. There are two views used to display icons, and another to display data in list form. The final view, Report view, is the most complicated. Items are displayed with the SubItems property in a columnar fashion.

QUESTIONS

1. The __________ and __________ properties set or return the number of rows and columns in the MSFlexGrid control.
   a. FixedRow, FixedColumn
   b. FixedRows, FixedColumns
   c. Row, Column
   d. Rows, Columns
   e. none of the above
2. The __________ property is used to change the width of a column in the MSFlexGrid control.
   a. ColumnWidth
   b. Size
   c. Column
   d. ColWidth
   e. Width
3. The __________ and __________ properties are used to reference an arbitrary cell in the MSFlexGrid control.
   a. Row, Column
   b. TextArray, TextMatrix
   c. Row, Col
   d. TextArray and TextMatrix, Row and Col
   e. none of the above
4. The ImageList control stores images in the __________ object.
   a. ListItem
   b. Image
   c. ListImage
   d. ImageList
   e. List
5. Which of the following statement(s) is True pertaining to the ImageList control?
   a. Images can have a numeric index or string key.
   b. Images must all be the same size.
   c. Both icons and bitmap images are supported.
   d. Images are represented by ListImage objects in the ListImages collection.
   e. All of the above.
6. What are the constants used to set the Style property in a StatusBar's Panel objects?
   a. sbrCaption, sbrNum, sbrIns
   b. sbrCaption, sbrNumLock, sbrInsert
   c. sbrText, sbrNum, sbrIns
   d. sbrDate, sbrTime
   e. both c and d

7. The ListView control supports the following views: ____________.
   a. Icon
   b. Small Icon
   c. List
   d. Report
   e. all of the above
8. What three properties are used to determine the images displayed in a TreeView control?
   a. Image, ExpandedImage, SelectedImage
   b. Image, ListImage, SelectedImage
   c. Image, ListImage, CurrentImage
   d. Images collection
   e. none of the above
9. A Node object can have ____________ parent(s), ____________ (child/children), and ____________ sibling(s).
   a. one, several, several
   b. one, one, one
   c. one, several, one
   d. zero, several, several
   e. zero, one, several
10. Displaying multiple columns in Report view relies on the ____________ and ____________ properties.
    a. SubItems, ColumnHeaders
    b. Rows, Columns
    c. List, ListItem
    d. Row, Column
    e. both a and c
11. Create a format string to define three fixed columns in an MSFlexGrid control named msgDemo. The first column should contain the caption **Title** centered in the column. The second column should contain the caption **Author** left-justified, and the third column should contain the caption **Price** right-justified.
12. Write the necessary statement(s) to add a row to a grid named mstDemo. The row should contain three columns having the following values: Joe Smith, 3/22/99, and 32.88.
13. Write a procedure that accepts one argument—the name of a grid. In the procedure, print the value in the Immediate window for all the rows in column one (1). This is the second column and column numbering begins at zero (0).
14. Write the statements to store the value 100 in the first row and third column of a grid named msgDemo using the TextMatrix property.

15. Write the statements to make visible the panel in a status bar named sbrDemo having the string key of Status and set the text to the string Editing.
16. Write the necessary statements to add a Node object to the TreeView control named tvwDemo. Set the text to NewNode.
17. Declare the necessary variables and write a For loop to print the value of the Text property for all the children of a Node object named pNodeDemo.
18. Write the statements to create a Root node with 10 children. Each child should have the caption 1, 2, 3, 4, and so on. *Hint:* use a For loop.
19. Write the statements to create three column headers for a ListView control named lvwDemo. They should have the captions First, Second, and Third. Set the width of each column to 1,000 twips.
20. Write the statements to store the value **1** in the text property, and the value **2** and **3** in the first and second subitems for a ListView control named lvwDemo.

EXERCISES

1. In this exercise you will read a text file and load the contents into the MSFlexGrid control.
   a. Look at the file named **Chapter.06\Exercise\Inventory.txt.** It contains a text file with five fields: **Part Number**, **Description**, **Quantity**, **Price**, and **Total.**
   b. Create a new project and set the Name property of the form to **frmExercise1.** Save the form using the name **Chapter.06\Exercise\frmExercise1.frm** and the project using the name **Chapter.06\Exercise\Exercise1.vbp.**
   c. Add the MSFlexGrid control to the project, then create an instance of the grid on the form. The grid should have one fixed row and five fixed columns.
   d. Create a format string so descriptive names pertaining to the five fields are displayed in the columns.
   e. Read the text file. For each record in the text file, add a row to the grid and display the proper field in the proper column.
   f. Using the techniques presented in the chapter, enable editing for the cells using a text box. Only allow editing for the Quantity field.
   g. If the quantity changes, update the extended price.
   h. Program the necessary keyboard handler so the user can use the Arrow keys to navigate from cell to cell.
   i. Create a command that will save the contents of the grid to a text file of the same format as the text file you read. Use an input box to get the file name from the user.

2. In this exercise you will create a TreeView control and a Node object's hierarchy.
   a. Create a new project and set the Name property of the form to **frmExercise2**. Save the form using the name **Chapter.06\Exercise\frmExercise2.frm** and the project using the name **Chapter.06\Exercise\Exercise2.vbp.**
   b. Add the TreeView control to the project.
   c. Create two Root-level nodes having the captions **By Letter** and **By Number.**
   d. Create a child node of the **By Letter** node for each letter of the alphabet. That is, there should be 26 Node objects, each having as its caption a letter of the alphabet. *Hint:* Use a For loop and the Chr function to do this.
   e. Create a child node of the **By Number** node for the numbers zero (0) through nine (9).
3. In this exercise you will read the contents of a text file in a ListView control. Use the same text file, **Chapter.06\Exercise\Inventory.txt**, that you used in the previous exercise.
   a. Create a new project and set the Name property of the form to **frmExercise3**. Save the form using the name **Chapter.06\Exercise\frmExercise3.frm** and the project using the name **Chapter.06\Exercise\Exercise3.vbp**.
   b. Add the ListView control to the project.
   c. Create an instance of the ListView control on the form.
   d. Create a menu title named **View** and four commands. Write the code for the commands to display the ListView control in the four different supported views.
   e. Set the necessary properties to display the ListView control in Report view and the column headers such that there are columns for each of the fields in the text file.
   f. Using the same text file as used in the previous exercise, open the text file, and read the contents in the ListView control.
   g. Write the necessary code to allow the user to click a column to sort rows by the selected column.
4. In this exercise you will use the ListView and TreeView controls in much the same way they were used in the chapter. In this example, however, you will create a drill-down interface to look up a part number in inventory. This information is stored in the database file **Chapter.06\Exercise\Inv.mdb**. The file contains a table named **tblInventory** having the following fields: **fldCategory** (text), **fldSubCategory** (text), **fldPartNumber** (Integer), **fldDescription** (text), **fldQuantity** (Integer), **fldPrice** (Single).

   While similar to the synchronized TreeView and ListView controls you created in the chapter, there are differences in the database that will force you to change how the TreeView control is loaded. All of the data is stored in a single table. Thus, there will be multiple records having the same category and subcategory. The Description field is unique. Thus, when you load the Category level of the hierarchy, you should select unique records. This can be accomplished using the SELECT DISTINCT statement. Consider organizing the procedures as shown in the chapter. One procedure should load the root node. It in turn should call a procedure to initialize each of the Category level nodes. For each category, this procedure should call another procedure that initializes all of the subcategories pertaining to the current category.

Because there are three distinct levels in the hierarchy, consider storing in the Tag property of each node a string indicating the level of the node in the hierarchy. This way you can determine at what level the node exists when it is clicked. This will allow you to select the appropriate records and display them in the ListView control.

a. Create a new project and set the Name property of the form to **frmExercise4**. Save the form using the name **Chapter.06\Exercise\frmExercise4.frm** and the project using the name **Chapter.06\Exercise\Exercise4.vbp**.
b. Add both the ListView and TreeView controls to the project.
c. Create both a ListView and TreeView control instance on the form.
d. Create a Root node with the caption **Parts**.
e. As a child of the Root node, create child nodes containing the part category.
f. As a child of the part category Node objects, create child nodes containing the part sub-category. Be sure that you only add nodes having a corresponding category.
g. As a child of the part category Node objects, create child nodes containing the part description. Be sure that you only add nodes having a corresponding category and subcategory.
h. When the user clicks on a part category, subcategory, or description, write the code to add all the corresponding part numbers to the ListView control. This ListView control should display the information in report view, with information displayed in three columns; Description, Quantity, and Price.

CHAPTER

7

Managing Multiple Forms with an MDI

Creating a Text Editor for Perfect Programming Systems

case▶ Perfect Programming Systems sells a commercial software package consisting of several utility programs. One of the utility programs they want to add to the software package is a text editor. The user interface for this program will consist of the following elements:

- Text will be displayed and edited in a RichTextBox control.
- Formatting is applied to the text using commands contained on a menu bar and toolbar. The toolbar will be used to provide quick access to the commands on the menu bar.
- Files are opened and saved using a standardized dialog that allows the user to locate different folders, create folders, and then select and change file names.
- A standard dialog also will be used to set fonts and colors and print files.
- It also will be possible to edit several files at once using multiple copies of the same form.

SECTION A

objectives

In this section you will:

- Create a type of interface called a Multiple Document Interface (MDI) program that uses multiple instances of the same form
- Add and destroy instances of a form at run time
- Keep track of the different form instances
- Understand the events that occur as the different forms in an MDI program are unloaded

Creating a Multiple Document Interface Application

Previewing the Completed Application

The completed application utilizes several new controls. The RichTextBox control is a superset of the intrinsic text box. It supports additional properties and methods to format and display text.

Another control, called the CommonDialog control, is used to provide a standard interface to open, save, and print files. The common dialog also is used to select fonts, font attributes, and font colors. The common dialog is a standard dialog supported not only by Visual Basic. Rather, it exists as a Windows library used by many applications. As you have opened files using Word or Excel, you may have noticed that the user interface for the Open dialog is identical from program to program. Visual Basic supports these same dialogs with the CommonDialog control.

To create a robust user interface a toolbar also is used. The toolbar provides quick access to common functions like opening and saving files, and setting font attributes. Like most programs that implement a toolbar, a toolbar button performs the same task as a corresponding menu command.

Unlike programs you have created in the previous chapters, this program is implemented using what is known as a Multiple Document Interface (MDI). An MDI program is not unique to Visual Basic. Programs like Word, Excel, and Visual Basic are all MDI programs. In Word, multiple files (documents) can be open at the same time, each appearing in a separate window. Each window appears inside the region of another window that is called a parent form or window. This program will have a similar user interface.

You can load and execute this project and use it for reference as you complete this chapter.

To preview the completed application:

1. Start **Visual Basic** and open the project named **Chapter.07\Complete\Text_ C.vbp**. Print the code for the project. The project consists of two form modules. One form module contains the interface for the text editor. The other form, called an MDI parent form, acts as a container for the text editor form.
2. Run the program. The MDI parent form appears on the screen. Because a new file has not yet been created or an existing file opened, however, the form used to edit data is not displayed.
3. On the form's menu bar, click **File** then **New** to create a new file. Another form called the MDI child form will appear inside the region of the parent form as shown in Figure 7-1.

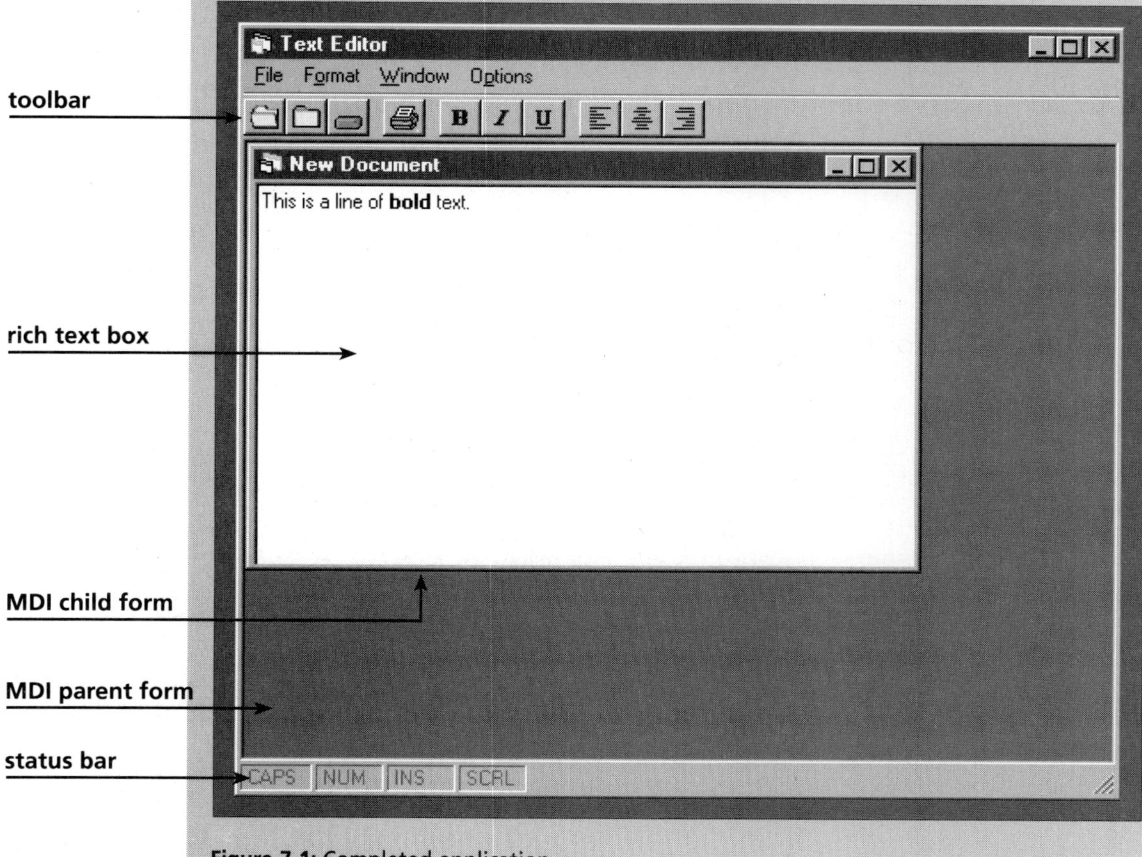

Figure 7-1: Completed application

4 Move the form inside the region of the MDI parent form. Its borders cannot extend beyond the region of the MDI parent form. This is one of the characteristics of MDI programs.

Figure 7-1 shows the toolbar and menu displayed on the MDI parent form. At this point there is one MDI child form with a rich text box and status bar on the form.

5 Enter the text shown in Figure 7-1.

6 Select text by dragging the mouse over the word bold. On the form's menu bar, click **Format** then **Bold** to apply the selected formatting. The selected text now appears in a bold typeface. Repeat the process for the **Italic** and **Underline** menu commands. As you apply these formatting characteristics, the buttons on the toolbar appear pressed or unpressed to indicate the current formatting. The menu commands also are updated such that they either contain a check mark or not to indicate the status of the formatting characteristic.

The toolbar buttons provide quick access to specific menu commands on the menu bar.

7 To test the toolbar, select text in the rich text box, then click the **Bold**, **Italic**, and **Underline** formatting buttons on the toolbar. These buttons have the same effect as the commands of the same name on the menu bar.

The CommonDialog control is used in this program to provide a standard interface for common functions like opening, saving, and printing files, and setting fonts.

8 To use the common dialog to change the font, select some text in the rich text box, then click **Format** then **Fonts** to open the Font dialog. Select a font and a size for the font. Click the **OK** button to apply the font to the selected text.

9 The common dialog also is used to save files. Click the **Save** button. The Save As dialog appears allowing you to select a folder and file name. Select the **Chapter.07\Complete** folder. Enter the name **Test** in the File name text box. Files can also be opened using the **File**, **Open** menu commands. This causes a similar dialog to appear.

10 MDI programs commonly are used when the user interface displays multiple copies of the same form at the same time. In this text editor, each file that is being edited appears in a different copy of the MDI child form. To illustrate this process, click **File** then **New**. A second form is opened. It is possible to navigate between these two forms, minimize them, and close the forms independently of each other.

11 Try to resize the MDI parent window. You can change its size, and maximize and minimize the MDI parent window as necessary.

12 MDI programs support features to arrange the open child forms automatically. The functions are implemented on the Window menu. While multiple windows are open, click **Window**, then click **Cascade**, **Tile Horizontal**, **Tile Vertical** in order. These options change the visual orientation of the different forms relative to each other.

13 Another feature of menus and MDI programs is the capability to display a list of the MDI child forms on a menu. Click **Window** then **List**. The open MDI child forms are listed on the menu.

14 End the program then exit Visual Basic.

Characteristics of MDI Programs

In all the programs you have created so far, you have created a single instance of a form that could appear anywhere on the screen. These are called Single Document Interface (SDI) programs. It also is common to create multiple instances of the same form, and create programs where forms appear inside the region of another form. These are called **Multiple Document Interface (MDI)** programs. When you create an MDI program, there are three different types of forms that you can use:

- There must be one and only one MDI parent form. An **MDI parent form** acts as a container for other forms. Other forms in the program are displayed inside the region of the MDI parent form. An MDI parent form cannot be displayed as a modal form.
- An **MDI child form** always is displayed inside the region of the MDI parent form. An MDI child form cannot be displayed as a modal form. A project may have several MDI child forms.
- You can continue to use standard forms in an MDI program. **Standard forms** can be displayed anywhere on the screen and are not contained by the MDI parent form. You can use both MDI child forms and standard forms in an MDI program. Standard forms can be displayed as modal or modeless forms.

When you create an MDI program, the MDI parent form and its MDI child forms have unique characteristics that differ from standard forms. First, an MDI child form always appears inside the region of the MDI parent form. Child forms can be moved and resized, but their visible region cannot expand beyond the region of the MDI parent form. Of course, the MDI parent form also can be resized. Depending on the desired implementation, the BorderStyle property of both the MDI parent and MDI child forms can be set to control whether or not the forms can be resized. Second, when an MDI child form is minimized, its icon appears at the bottom of the MDI parent form rather than at the bottom of the desktop. Third, when an MDI child form is maximized, the MDI child form's caption appears in brackets on the title bar of the MDI parent form. A maximized MDI child form occupies the region of the MDI parent form rather than the entire desktop. MDI programs still can contain standard forms although they typically are used as modal dialogs. When a standard form is used in an MDI program, its icon appears on the desktop when the form is minimized. A standard form also can appear anywhere on the screen. In addition, the behavior of message boxes and input boxes does not change. That is, they are displayed as modal dialogs and can appear anywhere on the screen.

Creating the MDI interface for a program is very simple. First, an MDI parent form is added to the project using the Add MDI Form command on the Project menu. Because a project can have only one MDI parent form, this option is disabled once the MDI parent form has been added to the project. After creating the MDI parent form, standard forms are converted into MDI child forms by setting the MDIChild property of the desired form to True. In this text editor, the form containing the text editor will be implemented as an MDI child form. Whether or not an instance of the MDI child form(s) is displayed when the MDI parent form is shown, depends on the value of the MDI parent form's AutoShowChildren property. This property, if True, causes one instance of each MDI child form to be displayed when the MDI parent form is shown. If False, MDI child forms must be loaded explicitly and shown.

Menus and MDI Programs

One of the most significant differences between an MDI program and a standard program is the behavior of the menu system. Remember that each form can have its own set of menus, and a form's set of menus always is displayed at the top of the form beneath the form's title bar. Menus for both MDI parent forms and MDI child forms appear just below the title bar of the MDI parent form. The menu that appears is the menu for the form that currently has focus. The menus for standard forms in an MDI program appear beneath the title bar of the standard form as usual. Thus, if a program contains one MDI parent form and two different MDI child forms, there can be three menus—one for each different form. The menu for each form appears beneath the title bar for the MDI parent form rather than beneath the title bar of the MDI child form. Which menu appears depends on which form is active. The active form's menu always appears. If there are no MDI child forms active or the MDI child form does not have a menu, then the MDI parent form's menu appears.

Remember that the menu for the MDI parent form only has options to create a new file, open an existing file, or exit the program. The menu for the MDI child form has the New, Open, and Exit commands, and additional commands pertaining to the MDI child form. This technique is important. In a typical MDI program, most of the operations pertain to a specific MDI child form, which appears whenever the child form is active. If there are no MDI child forms loaded, the MDI parent form must allow the user to create an MDI child form (load a file in this case).

GUI Design tip

Menu commands common to both the MDI parent and child form should be of the same name for both the MDI parent and child forms. That is, they should have the same caption. Because the two commands of the same name perform the same task, it is common to create a general procedure in either the MDI parent form or a standard module and call the general procedure from both menu commands. This way, the two different commands will appear to the user as one command performing one task.

The Open command in the program could be implemented two ways. The Click event procedures for the Open commands for both forms each need to call the same general procedure. The general procedure could be placed either on the MDI parent form or a standard module. Either of these techniques will work. In this text editor, the code is placed on the MDI parent form. This eliminates the need to create and load another module. You now will modify an existing program so it works as an MDI program.

To create the MDI interface:

1. Start **Visual Basic** and open the project named **Chapter.07\Startup\Text_S.vbp**.
2. Click **Project** then **Add MDI Form** to add an MDI parent form to the project. Select the existing form named **Chapter.07\Startup\MDIText.frm**. This form already has the menu interface created, and an ImageList control for the toolbar you will create later in the chapter.
3. Open the Properties window for the form named **frmText** and set the MDIChild property to **True**.
4. Open the Properties window for the form named **MDIText** and verify that the AutoShowChildren property is set to **True**.
5. Set the Startup object (the MDI parent form) to **MDIText** using the Project Properties dialog.
6. Test the program. An instance of the MDI parent form appears however the MDI child form does not.

This program will be implemented such that an MDI child form will not appear until a file has been opened or a new form created. Ultimately, this will require a new form instance to be created whenever the user opens a file, or creates a new document. Before programming these commands, however, a more thorough discussion of form modules is in order.

Forms as Classes

When you create an MDI program, it is common to show multiple instances of the same form. This process is somewhat analogous to creating multiple references to the same object or creating multiple instances of the same control. In Chapter 3, you saw how to use the Set statement to assign object references and the New keyword was mentioned briefly as the way to create new objects explicitly. Remember that every object is created from a class. That is, there is a command button class from which command buttons are created. Each instance of a command button created on a form has properties and can respond to events. A form or form module is really no different from a control. A form is a class. When a form is loaded or displayed on the screen, an instance of the form is created from the underlying class. Each form in the project is a distinct class and the name of the class is defined by the form's Name property. In this text editor, there are two form classes named MDIText and frmText. Once an instance of the form is created, you can read and write its properties and call the methods of the form. This implies that multiple instances of the same form can be created much like multiple instances of the same control. The prefix for an MDI form is "MDI" rather than frm.

Compare a form module to a standard module. A standard module is not a class, and you do not create instances of a standard module. Consequently, there is one, and only one, copy of the data (Public and Private variables) for a standard module. That is, one copy of the Public and Private variables in a standard module exist for the life of a program. There is a unique copy of the data for each form instance that is created, however. That is, if there are two instances of the MDI child form loaded, then there are two copies of the child form's data. Note the previous sentence used the term loaded rather than visible or displayed. When a form is loaded, the memory is allocated for the form, and it is possible to access the form's properties and methods even though the form is not visible. In this text editor, a copy of the MDI child form could be displayed by calling the child form's Show method using the following statements:

```
Private Sub MDIForm_Load( )
    frmText.Show
End Sub
```

When the MDI parent form is loaded, the MDI child form named frmText is displayed and receives focus. What exactly happens when the Show method is called is important. When a form is loaded, Visual Basic creates a hidden variable that has the same name as the form (class), and creates an instance of the form from the underlying class. Thus, when the program starts, the MDI parent form is loaded causing the MDIForm_Load event to occur. This event procedure explicitly loads and displays the form named frmText. Visual Basic creates an instance of both forms, and declares the equivalent of a Public variable for each form named MDIText of type MDIText and frmText of type frmText, respectively. The reason that Visual Basic declares this variable is that the name will change anytime you change the value of the form's Name property. It is as if the following variable declarations had been made.

```
Public MDIText As MDIText
Public frmText As frmText
```

Another important point needs to be made. Assume that the MDI child form (frmText) has the following general declaration:

```
Public DocumentName As String
```

If there were multiple instances of this form, there would be a separate copy of the variable DocumentName for each form instance. This concept also is significant. Public variables in a form module actually are properties and are treated just like the predefined properties like Name, Top, or Left. To demonstrate this, consider the following illegal declarations in a form module named frmText.

```
Public Name As frmText
Public Top As Integer
```

Every form has a predefined Name and Top property. These declarations will cause the following compiler error, "Member already exists in an object module from which this object module derives." When you create Public variables in a form module, they are considered properties that extend the predefined properties of the form. Syntactically, you reference these variables as properties.

Creating multiple instances of the same form differs slightly because you must create object variables to reference each form instance. To illustrate this concept, consider the following statements to create two instances of the same form. This requires that you use the New keyword with the Dim or Set statements to create an instance of the object. Without the New keyword, an object variable is created that references Nothing.

```
Private Sub MDIForm_Load( )
    Dim frmText1 As frmText, frmText2 As frmText
    Set frmText1 = New frmText
    Set frmText2 = New frmText
    frmText1.Show
    frmText2.Show
    frmText1.Caption = "One"
    frmText2.Caption = "Two"
    frmText1.DocumentName = "Document1"
    frmText2.DocumentName = "Document2"
End Sub
```

These statements declare two object variables named frmText1 and frmText2 that are used to store references to forms created from the frmText class. The two Set statements cause the two form instances to be created, and a reference to each form instance stored in the two object variables. Using the object variables, it is possible to set the form's properties, call its methods, and reference the control instances on the form. In this case, calling the Show method for each form instance causes two MDI child forms to appear in the region of the MDI parent form. The Caption property is set for each instance.

In the previous statements, the Public variable DocumentName is a property of the frmText form class. Interestingly, Public, Function, and Sub procedures in form modules are treated as methods of the form class. As such, the syntax to call the method is the same as calling the methods of any object. Assuming that the MDIText class contained a Public Sub procedure named CloseFile, to call it from the MDI child form or a standard module, you would use the following statement:

```
MDIText.CloseFile
```

To create the multiple instances of an MDI child form:

1 Locate the **MDIForm_Load** event procedure on the MDI parent form (MDIText) and enter the following statements:

```
Dim frmText1 As frmText, frmText2 As frmText
Set frmText1 = New frmText
Set frmText2 = New frmText
frmText1.Show
frmText2.Show
frmText1.Caption = "One"
frmText2.Caption = "Two"
```

2 Test the program. Two form instances, as shown in Figure 7-2, appear with different captions.

form instances with different captions

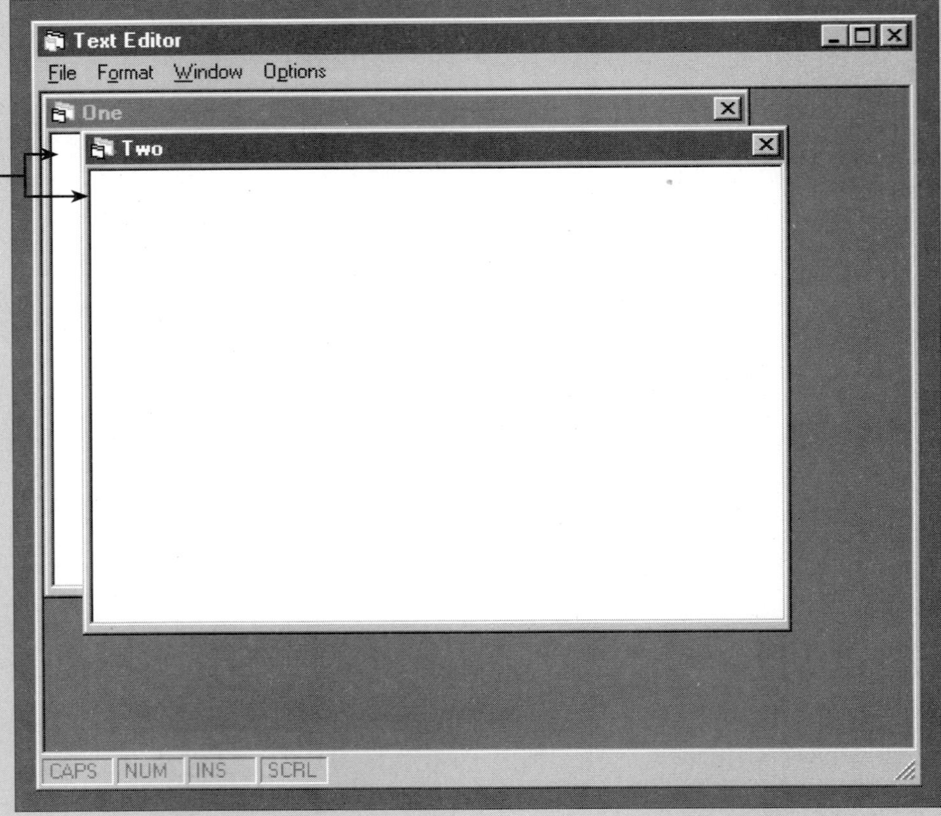

Figure 7-2: Multiple form instances

While these statements illustrate the concept of multiple form instances, they have serious limitations. There is no provision to create form instances dynamically. Furthermore, the statements can only create two instances of the same form. To create more form instances, it would be necessary to declare additional object variables and use the Set statement to create the form instances.

There is a technique to create multiple instances of the same form dynamically and keep track of those form instances by creating a dynamic array. It is the responsibility of the program to add and delete elements from the array as new form instances are created and destroyed. Adding elements to the array is fairly simple. The size of the array can be increased by one. Then, an instance of the form is created and a reference to the form is stored in the new array element. When a form is closed, the instance of the form is destroyed. Thus, the array element that referenced the form instance has no meaning. To delete the element from the array would require that you shift the array elements so the last array element referenced the deleted form and then decrease the array size by one. This process can be simplified by creating an array of user-defined types as follows:

```
Private Type tDocType
    Active As Boolean
    frmCurrent As frmText
End Type
Private Docs( ) As tDocType
```

This user-defined type contains two members. One provides a reference to the form and the other is a Boolean variable to indicate if the array element currently is being used. Thus, when a form instance is created, frmCurrent will reference the newly-created form, and the Active flag will be set to True. When the form instance is destroyed, frmCurrent can be set to Nothing, and the Active flag set to False. When a new form instance is created, the array can be searched to try to locate an inactive element. If one is found, the reference to the new form could be stored in an existing element. Otherwise, the size of the array would need to be increased by one. This array could be declared, and the procedures to add and remove elements from the array could be created either in an MDI parent form or in a standard module. The process is somewhat analogous to creating your own collection. In this text editor, an array of MDI child form references will be created and managed on the MDI parent form. Consider what would happen if you created the array in the MDI child form. There would be one copy of the array for each loaded MDI child form and no array at all if there were no loaded MDI child forms. Thus, the array must be declared either in a standard module or in the MDI parent form.

To create an array to manage child forms:

1 Locate the general declarations section of the form module named **MDIText** and enter the following statements:

```
Private Type tDocType
    Active As Boolean
    frmCurrent As frmText
End Type
Private Docs( ) As tDocType
```

2 In the MDIText form module, enter the following statements in the **GetFormIndex** Function procedure. This procedure is used to recycle an inactive array element or allocate a new element in the array. The function returns an integer indicating the element that was used.

```
Dim pintDocCount As Integer, pintCurrent As Integer
Dim pblnFound As Boolean
pintDocCount = UBound(Docs)
For pintCurrent = 1 To pintDocCount
    If Docs(pintCurrent).Active = False Then
        pblnFound = True
        Exit For
    End If
Next
If Not pblnFound Then
    pintCurrent = pintDocCount + 1
    ReDim Preserve Docs(pintCurrent)
End If
With Docs(pintCurrent)
    Set .frmCurrent = New frmText
    .frmCurrent.Tag = pintCurrent
    .frmCurrent.Show
    .Active = True
End With
GetFormIndex = pintCurrent
```

3 Locate the **NewFile** Sub procedure on the MDI parent form. This procedure calls GetFormIndex. Using the index of the newly allocated form, the Caption property is set to the text **New Document.** Enter the following statements:

```
Dim pintCurrentDoc As Integer
pintCurrentDoc = GetFormIndex( )
Docs(pintCurrentDoc).frmCurrent.Caption = "New Document"
```

4 In the **mnuFileNew_Click** event procedure for the MDI parent form, enter the following statement to call the general procedure:

```
NewFile
```

5 In the **mnuFileNew_Click** event procedure for the MDI child form, enter the following statement to call the general procedure:

```
MDIText.NewFile
```

6 In the **MDIForm_Load** event procedure, replace the statements with the following statement to initialize the array when the MDI parent form first is loaded.

```
ReDim Docs(0)
```

7 Test the program. On the menu bar click **File** then **New** several times and notice that a new instance of the MDI child form is created each time.

These procedures and statements require careful analysis. The Function procedure GetFormIndex does all the work. It returns the element in the array allocated to the new form. It makes the decision on whether to recycle an existing element or redimension the array. The For loop examines each element in the array to determine if there is an unused array element (the Active flag is False). If there is, that element is used as the index into the array. You will create the code in a moment to set this flag to False whenever a form instance is closed. The variable pblnFound is used to determine whether or not an unused array element was found. If one was not, then a new array element is created and the current element set.

```
Set Docs(pintCurrent).frmCurrent = New frmText
```

The previous statement creates the new form instance, and stores a reference to it in the current array element. Remember, this is an array of user-defined types, so the form reference is stored in the frmCurrent member of the type. Note that the New keyword causes the form instance to be created.

```
Docs(pintCurrent).frmCurrent.Tag = pintCurrent
Docs(pintCurrent).frmCurrent.Show
Docs(pintCurrent).Active = True
```

The use of the Tag property will become apparent in a moment. It will be used as a way to identify the current form. The value of the Tag property is the same as the index in the array. Finally, the form is displayed and the Active flag is set to True indicating that the array element is in use and the element references a form instance. Finally, the procedure returns the index to the array of forms so it can be used by the calling procedure, if necessary.

The NewFile Sub procedure calls the GetFormIndex function and sets the caption of the new form. This implementation could be expanded to include a number next to the text (i.e., “New Document 1”, “New Document 2”).

```
Dim pintCurrentDoc As Integer
pintCurrentDoc = GetFormIndex( )
Docs(pintCurrentDoc).frmCurrent.Caption = "New Document"
```

The GetFormIndex function is called and the caption of the current form is set. The syntax to reference the caption of the current form is Docs(pintCurrentDoc).frmCurrent; it provides the reference to the current form. This gives you the capability to set the form's properties and call its methods. The reason for separating code in the NewFile and GetFormIndex procedures is that the code you will write in a moment to open an existing file will use the GetFormIndex function, but will have additional code for the user to specify the file to open. The form's caption will be set to the file name instead of the constant text "New Document."

Finally, you called the NewFile procedure in both the menu commands for the MDI parent and child forms. The only time the menu for the MDI parent form is displayed is when there are no open MDI child forms. Otherwise, the menu for the MDI child form will appear. Thus, the two different Open menus will have the same effect and appear to the user as if the two commands were one and the same. When called from the MDI child form, the following syntax is used:

```
MDIText.NewFile
```

It is necessary to specify the MDI parent form. Otherwise, Visual Basic would not know where to look for the procedure. Remember, you are calling a method of the MDI parent form.

At this point, you have learned how to create form instances. Now you will learn how to destroy those form instances.

Destroying Form Instances

Unloading MDI parent and child forms introduces additional complexity beyond that of a single form application. In this text editor, the program keeps track of which elements in the Docs array store a reference to an active form. So, when the form is closed, the array must be updated accordingly. That is, the form element must reference Nothing and the Active flag should be set to False. Additionally, the program will determine whether or not the contents of the rich text box have changed since the file was last saved, and if so, prompt the user to confirm whether or not the changes should be discarded.

Creating a successful MDI program requires an understanding of the events that occur when forms are unloaded and the order of those events. When an MDI child form or standard form is unloaded, two events occur for each form instance. The QueryUnload event occurs just before the form is unloaded. This event takes an argument, *cancel*, which if set to True, causes the subsequent Unload event to be cancelled. If the QueryUnload event does not set the *cancel* argument to True, the Unload event will occur.

Syntax

Private Sub Form_QueryUnload(*cancel* **As Integer**, *unloadmode* **As Integer)**
Private Sub MDIForm_QueryUnload(*cancel* **As Integer**, *unloadmode* **As Integer)**
Private Sub *object*_**Unload(***cancel* **As Integer)**

Dissection

- The *cancel* argument, if set to True, causes subsequent QueryUnload or Unload events to be cancelled.

- The *unloadmode* argument contains a constant indicating what caused the event to occur. For example, the event may occur because the user clicked the Close button on the Control-menu box, Windows is shutting down, or some other cause. Refer to the "QueryUnload event" Help page for a complete list of constants.
- The Unload event must contain a reference to an MDI parent, child, or standard form.

Notes

These events occur both for the MDI parent form, when an attempt is made to unload the MDI parent form, and to each instance of the MDI child form when it is unloaded.

Code Example

```
Private Sub MDIForm_QueryUnload(Cancel As Integer, _
    UnloadMode As Integer)
    If UnloadMode = vbFormControlMenu Then
        Cancel = True
    End If
End Sub
```

Code Dissection

These statements use the UnloadMode argument to determine if the user clicked the Close button on the Control-menu box to cause the event. If so, then the event is cancelled.

The following list describes the order of the Unload events when the MDI parent form is unloaded.

1. The QueryUnload event occurs for the MDI parent form first. This event supports the cancel argument. If set to True, all other QueryUnload and Unload events for both MDI parent and child forms are cancelled.
2. If the QueryUnload event is not cancelled for the MDI parent form, the QueryUnload event occurs for each of the MDI child forms. This event also can be cancelled. If one of the form instances sets the *cancel* argument to True, no more QueryUnload events will occur for the MDI child forms. Also, all the Unload events will be cancelled for the MDI child and parent forms.
3. If none of the QueryUnload events for the MDI child forms were cancelled, then the Unload event occurs for each MDI child form. If one of the MDI child forms cancels the Unload event, the Unload events for all subsequent MDI child and parent forms will be cancelled.
4. Finally, the Unload event occurs for the MDI parent form if, and only if, none of the QueryUnload or Unload events were cancelled.

In this text editor, the QueryUnload event for the MDI child forms will be used to prompt the user whether or not to discard changes for the current form. If the user does not want to discard the changes, then the event will be cancelled. Otherwise, the Unload event(s) will occur. The Unload event procedure for the MDI child form calls a general procedure to update the array that manages the MDI child forms. This update causes the Active flag to be set indicating that the element is not currently in use, and that the reference to the form is to be destroyed for the proper element. The QueryUnload event procedure for the MDI parent form also will display a message box asking the user whether or not to exit the program.

To program the QueryUnload and Unload events for the MDI parent and child forms:

1. The statements in the MDIForm_QueryUnload event procedure will execute when an attempt is made to exit the program. The code causes a message box to appear asking for confirmation before the program exits. If the user responds No to the message box, the event is cancelled. Thus, no further attempt is made to unload any of the MDI child forms. Enter the following statements in the **MDIForm_QueryUnload** event procedure:

```
Dim pintReturn As Integer
pintReturn = MsgBox("Really Exit", vbYesNo + _
     vbQuestion)
If pintReturn = vbNo Then
    Cancel = True
End If
```

2. To cause the MDI parent form to be unloaded from either the MDI parent or child form, enter the following statement in the **mnuFileExit_Click** procedure in both forms:

```
Unload MDIText
```

3. The Form_QueryUnload event procedure occurs when an attempt is made to close an instance of the MDI child form. It also will be generated for all the MDI child forms when an attempt is made to close the MDI parent form. The code uses the variable Dirty to determine if the contents of the rich text box have been changed. You will see in a moment how the value of this variable is set. If there are unsaved changes, then a message box is displayed requesting confirmation before unloading the form. Again the *cancel* argument is used to cancel the event depending on the user's response. Enter the following statements in the **Form_QueryUnload** event procedure for the MDI child form:

```
Dim pintReturn As Integer
If Dirty Then
    pintReturn = MsgBox("Abandon Changes", _
        vbYesNo + vbQuestion)
    If pintReturn = vbNo Then
        Cancel = True
    End If
End If
```

4 The Form_Unload event procedure occurs if the QueryUnload events were not cancelled. The statement in the event procedure calls the CloseFile general procedure to make the changes to the Docs array so the array element indicates that it does not reference an active form instance. Enter the following statement in the **Form_Unload** event procedure:

```
MDIText.CloseFile Me
```

5 Enter the following statements in the **CloseFile** general procedure on the MDI parent form to update the status of the current array element: (Note the CloseFile procedure accepts one argument, a reference to an MDI child form).

```
Dim pintCurrent As Integer
pintCurrent = frm.Tag
Docs(pintCurrent).Active = False
Set Docs(pintCurrent).frmCurrent = Nothing
```

6 Test the program. Create multiple instances of the MDI child forms using the **New** command on the **File** menu. Make changes to the contents of each MDI child form. Click the **Exit** command on the **File** menu. This causes the QueryUnload event to occur first for the MDI parent form. Click the **Yes** button in the message box to continue.

7 Then the QueryUnload event occurs for each of the MDI child forms. Click **Yes** to abandon the changes for each of the forms. Because none of the QueryUnload events were cancelled, the forms are unloaded and the program exits.

The code for the QueryUnload and Unload event procedures is simple. A message box is displayed and, depending on the user's response, the event is or is not cancelled. The code for the CloseFile general procedure requires careful examination.

```
pintCurrent = frm.Tag
```

Remember, you set the Tag property when an instance of the form was created. This value contains an integer representing the index in the Docs array on the MDI parent form. The current form is passed as an argument to the general procedure and the Tag property is used to determine the desired array element.

```
Docs(pintCurrent).Active = False
```

The previous statement indicates the element is not in use. Remember, this value is used to reallocate an array element that is not currently in use when a new file is created or an existing file opened.

```
Set Docs(pintCurrent).frmCurrent = Nothing
```

This statement explicitly destroys the reference to the form.

Other Ways to Keep Track of Forms

In addition to using an array to manage a form, there are other objects to help you manage the loaded forms in a program. These include the Forms collection, the Screen object, and the Me keyword.

The **Me** keyword is a global variable that represents the current instance of a class. Because a form is considered a class, the active form always can be referenced using the Me keyword. This is very useful to pass a reference to the current form to a general procedure. You have seen the Me keyword used in previous chapters as a way to unload the current form. Consider the following event procedure, which sets the Visible property for all the controls on a form to True:

```
Dim ctl As Control
For Each ctl in Me.Controls
    ctl.Visible = True
Next
```

The **Forms collection** works like the Controls collection presented in Chapter 4. It contains a reference to each of the loaded forms. Each instance of a form class is treated as a separate form in the Forms collection. If a form has not been loaded, there is no entry for the form in the collection. Forms that are loaded and not visible can be referenced using the Forms collection. This program creates several instances of the same form. Each instance has an entry in the Forms collection. Iterating through the Forms collection is useful when the same operation needs to be performed for all the active forms, or all the active forms having the same class. In this text editor, a Save All function has been implemented that will save all unsaved files automatically. For example, the following generic loop could be used to save all the forms having the class frmText:

```
Private Sub mnuFileSaveAll_Click( )
    Dim frm As Form
    For Each frm In Forms
        If TypeOf frm Is frmText Then
            If frm.Caption = "New Document" Then
                SaveFile Me
            Else
                frm.rtfText.SaveFile frm.Caption
            End If
        End If
    Next
End Sub
```

This loop iterates through all the forms in the Forms collection. If the type of the form is frmText, then it is a candidate to be saved. The Caption property either contains the name of the file or the text "New Document" if the file has never been saved. If the file has not been saved, the SaveFile procedure is called.

This procedure is described later in the chapter. The TypeOf statement is used to test that the form is a member of the frmText class. This prevents the SaveFile procedure being called for the MDI parent form. This is necessary as it makes no sense to save the MDI parent form because it does not correspond to a file.

The Screen Object

The **Screen** object supports properties to determine the active form or the active control. The following list summarizes the properties of the Screen object.

Object	Screen
Properties	■ The **ActiveForm** and **ActiveControl** properties identify the form and control that currently have focus. ■ The **Fonts** property contains an array of the fonts for the currently selected display device. It typically is used with the **FontCount** property, which contains the number of fonts, supported by the display device. Thus, the Fonts array has index values ranging from zero (0) to FontCount minus one (-1). ■ The **MouseIcon** and **MousePointer** properties are used to change the format of the mouse pointer. In addition to the Screen object, these properties also pertain to the Form object and visible controls that can receive focus. Refer to the "MousePointer Property" Help topic for a list of the valid constants representing the different mouse pointers.

The uses of the Screen object are quite varied as the object pertains to the state of the program as managed by the operating system (Windows). Through the Screen object, you are obtaining information from Windows about which control and form have focus, and the appearance of the mouse pointer on that form. The fonts on the system also are managed by Windows and can be determined using the Screen object.

Using Word, and other Windows programs, you commonly have seen a list box containing fonts, which is used to set the font of selected text. This functionality can be duplicated in a Visual Basic program by loading the available fonts into a list or combo box. Assuming that cboFonts is a valid instance of a combo box, the following loop will load the available fonts into the combo box:

```
Dim pintCount As Integer
For pintCount = 0 To Screen.FontCount -1
     cboFonts.AddItem Screen.Fonts(pintCount)
Next
```

Another use of the Screen object is to change the mouse pointer when the insertion point is positioned over a form or particular control. Another common use is to display an hourglass while the program is performing a lengthy operation that cannot be interrupted. This provides a visual clue to the user that the program cannot accept input. In this program, reading or writing a large file may take more than a second or two so changing the mouse pointer during these operations will improve the user interface. For a list of the valid mouse pointers, refer to the "Mouse Pointer Constants" Help topic.

```
Private Sub cmdLong_Click( )
    Screen.MousePointer = vbHourglass
    For plngCurrent = 1 To 1000000
        ' Statements
    Next
    Screen.MousePointer = vbNormal
End Sub
```

The previous event procedure illustrates a long running procedure. When it begins, the mouse pointer is set to an hourglass and restored to normal when the procedure finishes.

Arranging MDI Forms

As mentioned, MDI child forms can be moved around the region of the MDI parent form. It also is possible to call the Arrange method of the MDI parent form to arrange the open MDI child forms, or manipulate the icons.

Syntax	*object*.**Arrange** *arrangement*
Dissection	■ The required *object* must be an instance of an MDI parent form. ■ The required *arrangement* argument can be one of several constants. If set to vbCascade, all the open MDI child forms are cascaded. vbTileHorizontal and vbTileVertical cause the MDI child forms to be organized horizontally or vertically. vbArrangeIcons causes the minimized child forms to be arranged across the bottom of the form.
Code Example	`MDIText.Arrange vbTileHorizontal`
Code Dissection	The previous statement arranges the open MDI child windows so each occupies the width of the MDI parent window. Each MDI child window has the same vertical size.

In the text editor form, the Window menu title contains four commands to demonstrate the four possible arrangements, which is accomplished with a control array. The index of the control array element corresponds to one of the four constant values used to define the desired arrangement.

```
Private Sub mnuArrange_Click(Index As Integer)
    MDIText.Arrange Index
End Sub
```

This code already has been written and the commands created. You can run the program to see the effect of the different arrangements.

In addition to using the above methods to arrange MDI child forms, Visual Basic supports a unique type of menu called a WindowList. One menu command on a menu can have the WindowList property set to True. At run time, selecting this menu displays another menu listing all the loaded MDI child forms. At design time, checking the WindowList check box in the menu editor identifies the menu that will act as the window list menu.

To test the Arrange method:

1. Test the program and create three different MDI child windows.
2. Click **Window** then **Tile Horizontal**, **Tile Vertical**, and **Cascade** to see the effect of the three different options.
3. Minimize the MDI child forms by clicking the **Minimize** button. Drag the icons around the MDI parent form then click **Window**, then **Arrange Icons** to arrange the icons across the bottom of the form.
4. Click **Window** then **List** and notice that all the MDI child form instances are displayed. Clicking one of the commands will activate the respective form.

You have completed this section, which introduced the techniques of working with MDI programs and multiple instances of the same form. These techniques of creating, destroying, and keeping track of form instances apply to every MDI program that you create.

SECTION B

objectives

In this section you will:

- Use a CommonDialog control to provide a standard interface for the tasks of opening and saving files, selecting fonts and colors, and printing files
- Use a RichTextBox control to format text
- Improve a program's user interface with a toolbar

Programming the RichTextBox, CommonDialog, and Toolbar Controls

In the previous section you saw how to manage the MDI parent and child forms. Now you will learn more about the specific controls drawn on the form.

Reading and Writing Files with the RichTextBox Control

At the core of the text editor in this chapter is the RichTextBox control, which can be thought of as a superset of the intrinsic TextBox control you have been using. The RichTextBox control is an ActiveX control so it must be added explicitly to the project before it can be used. The code for the control is stored in the file richtx32.ocx. The rich text box supports properties and methods to apply formatting to text including setting fonts and font attributes. The rich text box works by using a standardized file format called Rich Text Format (RTF). Embedded inside RTF files are formatting directives. These directives are not displayed in the rich text box, but are interpreted by the control to perform a desired formatting task. Figure 7-3 shows a short RTF file with formatting directives.

```
{\rtf1\ansi\deff0\deftab720{\fonttbl{\f0\fswiss MS Sans
Serif;}{\f1\froman\fcharset2 Symbol;}{\f2\fswiss MS Sans Serif;}}

{\colortbl\red0\green0\blue0;}

\deflang1033\pard\plain\f2\fs17 This is \plain\f2\fs17\b
bold\plain\f2\fs17  text.
\par }
```

Figure 7-3: RTF file

As shown in Figure 7-3, there are directives to specify the font, font size, and font attributes. Embedded in the directives, is the text that is displayed. Fortunately, you do not have to worry about these directives. Rather, the rich text box takes care of interpreting all these directives for you. In addition, when formatting is applied to specific text, the rich text box also stores the directives in the file. In addition to processing rich text files, the rich text box also can read and write ordinary text files. The text shown in Figure 7-3 will appear formatted as shown in Figure 7-4.

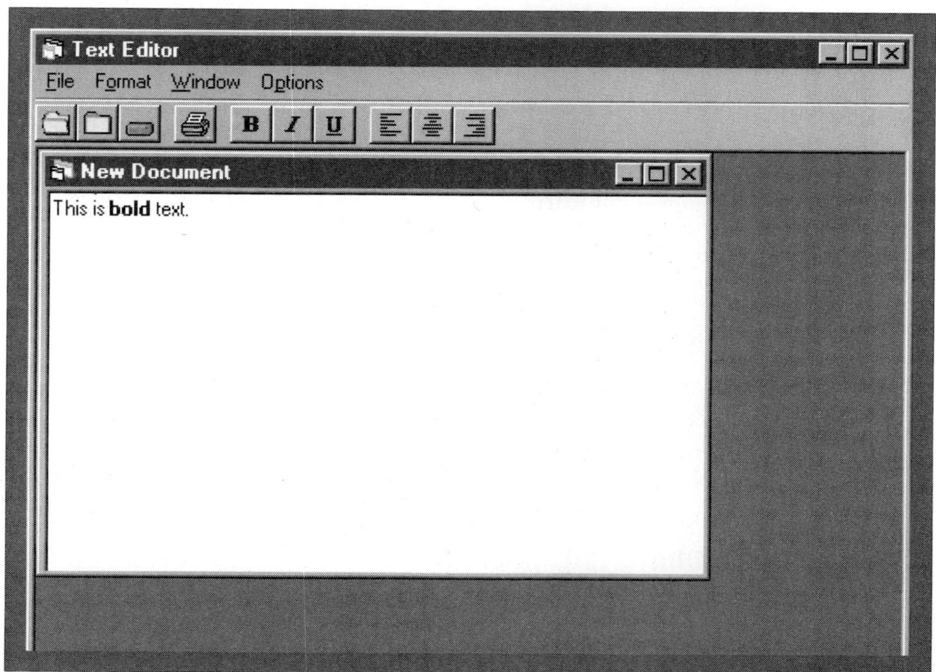

Figure 7-4: RTF file in a rich text box

One of the functions supported by the rich text box is the capability to read and write files using two methods supported by the control. Instead of writing code to open, read or write, and then close a file, all the functionality is built into the control itself.

Syntax

object.**LoadFile** *pathname*[, *filetype*]
object.**SaveFile** *pathname*[, *filetype*]

Dissection

- The required *object* must be a valid instance of a RichTextBox control.
- The **LoadFile** and **SaveFile** methods read and write text and RTF files to and from a rich text box.
- The required *pathname* argument contains the folder and file name of the file to be read or written.
- The optional *filetype* argument can contain one of two constants. If set to rtfRTF, the file is loaded as an RTF file and the formatting directives are applied. If set to rtfText, the file is interpreted as a plain text file. If the *filetype* argument is omitted, rtfRTF is assumed.

Code Example

```
rtfText.LoadFile "A:\Chapter.07\Demo.rtf"
rtfText.SaveFile "A:\Chapter.07\Demo.rtf"
```

Code Dissection

The previous statements assume that the object rtfText is a valid instance of a RichTextBox control. The standard prefix for the rich text box is "rtf." The two statements load and save the file named Demo.rtf, respectively. The file is interpreted as an RTF file because the *filetype* argument is not specified.

Until now, whenever you have read or written a file, the file name either has been coded explicitly in the statement as shown in the previous examples, or the user entered a path and file name in an input box. While both of these methods work, specifying a file name in an input box makes for a rather primitive user interface. In this chapter, you will learn how to improve a program's user interface by providing dialogs in your programs that use the same interface as programs like Word and Excel. The control that provides this interface is called the CommonDialog control.

Opening and Saving Files with the CommonDialog Control

The CommonDialog control is an ActiveX control that allows a Visual Basic program to access the Windows library that provides a standard way to open and save files, print files, change fonts, and access the Help system. The code for the CommonDialog control is contained in the file comdlg32.ocx. The code in this file in turn calls the library routines contained in the Windows system library named comdlg32.dll. This is why a standard interface to open and save files is possible.

The common dialog is not a visible control. That is, the user does not click the object drawn on the form to interact with the control instance. Rather, a dialog appears when the methods supported by the CommonDialog control are called at run time. The standard prefix for the CommonDialog control is "cdl." There are six standard dialogs you can display. These dialogs correspond to the six different methods supported by the control.

The common dialog supports several properties but most properties only pertain to a specific dialog (method). This makes sense, as the properties related to selecting a font have nothing to do with the properties to open a file. There are a few properties that pertain to all the dialogs.

Object	CommonDialog
Properties	Each dialog has at least two command buttons. One of them has the caption "Cancel," and is used to communicate back to the Visual Basic program that the user does not want to perform the desired task. The **CancelError** property is used to determine what happens when the user presses the Cancel button on the dialog. Its use will be discussed in a moment. The **DialogTitle** property contains the string that appears on the title bar of the dialog when it is displayed. If a value is not assigned explicitly to this property, the title contains a brief generic caption like Open or Print. The **Flags** property is used with all the dialogs to customize their behavior. For example, it is possible to use different flags to prohibit the user from changing directories when the Open and Save As dialogs are displayed. Flags also are used to return additional information about the state of the dialog when it was closed. The **Left** and **Top** properties determine where the dialog appears when it is displayed.
Methods	The **ShowColor** method displays the Color dialog allowing the user to select existing colors or define custom colors. The **ShowFont** method displays the Font dialog allowing the user to select fonts and font attributes like bold, italic, and underline. The **ShowHelp** method allows you to activate the Help system. The **ShowOpen** method displays a dialog allowing the user to navigate through different folders to select a file to be opened. The **ShowSave** method displays a dialog much like the Open dialog allowing the user to locate a folder and specify a file to be saved. The **ShowPrinter** method displays the Print dialog, allowing the user to select a printer, number of copies to print, and other printing characteristics.

Each dialog is displayed on the screen when one of the methods is called. That is, the Print dialog appears on the screen when the ShowPrinter method is called, the Save As dialog is called when the ShowSave method is called, and so on.

Programming

tip

These methods also can be called by setting the value of the Action property. The Action property provides backward compatibility with older versions of Visual Basic. The capability to call methods had limitations in older versions of Visual Basic so the functionality was accomplished by setting the value of a property, typically called Action.

It is important to point out that the common dialog does not actually open, save, or print files. Also it does not set the fonts or colors of text explicitly. Rather, when a specific dialog is displayed, the user selects options from the dialog, like a file name or a font and its attributes. When the dialog is closed, properties and/or flags pertaining to the dialog are set. It is up to the program to use these properties as needed. For example, if you wanted the user to be able to change the font of a text box, you could display the Font dialog by calling the ShowFont method. After the dialog is closed, you would need to set explicitly the desired font properties of the text box based on the common dialog's property settings. This is true for all the dialogs supported by the common dialog. That is, the common dialog does not actually perform the desired task. Rather, it sets specific properties that then can be used by your program to perform the task.

GUI Design

tip

Using the common dialog to open and save files, set fonts and colors, and print output helps to create a user interface that is consistent with other Windows programs. Consider using this control for all these operations.

In previous chapters, you have used the message box and input box dialogs to display messages and get text from the user. In both cases, these were modal dialogs. That is, the user cannot interact with the other forms in the program, until the dialog is closed. The common dialog also is modal.

Understanding the CancelError Property

Every dialog displayed by the CommonDialog control contains two command buttons. One is used to indicate to the program that the desired action should be performed. The other has the caption Cancel and is used to signify that the task should not be performed. For example, imagine the user wanted to open a file. In this case, the Open dialog would be displayed by calling the ShowOpen method. After displaying the dialog, however, suppose the user determined that the file did not already exist, or that the file could not be found. In this case, the user would click the Cancel button on the dialog to indicate that a file should not be opened and the operation cancelled.

The behavior of the Cancel button depends on the value of the common dialog's CancelError property. If the CancelError property is True, the CommonDialog control will generate a run-time error that your program then can trap. If False, no run-time error is generated. Examine the following event procedure:

```
Private Sub Command1_Click( )
On Error GoTo Cancel_Error
    cdl1.CancelError = True
    cdl1.ShowOpen
    ' Code to open file
    Exit Sub
Cancel_Error:
End Sub
```

This Click event procedure contains an error handler that does nothing but trap the error and exit the current procedure. The first executable statement sets the CancelError property to True, causing a run-time error to occur if the user clicks the Cancel button on the CommonDialog control. Then the ShowOpen method is called. If no error occurs, then the code to open the file will be executed, and the event procedure will exit. Otherwise, execution will continue following the Cancel_Error: label. Thus, no attempt will be made to open a file. This technique is used by all the dialogs supported by the CommonDialog control.

GUI Design ▶ tip

In all procedures that display a common dialog, an error handler should be written and the CancelError property set to True, as this is the only way the program can be notified that the user wants to abort the current action. Imagine the user's reaction if he did not actually want to print a 1000-page file.

Opening Files

The common dialog supports two nearly identical dialogs. One opens a file by name, the other saves a file by name. Programmatically, the two dialogs operate the same way. You set properties to define the initial folder, default file name, and other information, then call a method to show the dialog on the screen. After the method has been called, your code reads a property containing the file name specified by the user, and uses this name to open or save the file. Figure 7-5 shows the Open dialog.

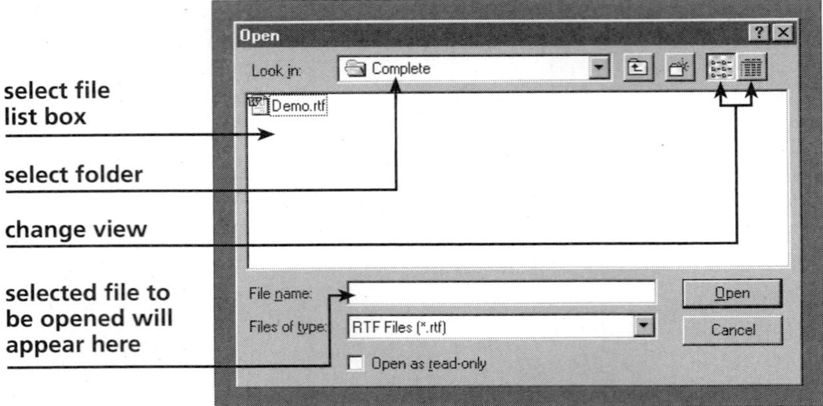

Figure 7-5: Open dialog

As shown in Figure 7-5, the Open dialog contains a list box to select a file and a button to change the current folder. There also are buttons to change the current view in the list portion of the dialog. These views are equivalent to the list and report views for the ListView control. The Files of type list box is used to restrict the files displayed to those files having a specific file extension. Ultimately, the File name text box contains the name of the file to be opened.

Setting the properties for the common dialog can be accomplished in two ways. As with other ActiveX controls, you can use the Property Pages to set the design-time properties. There is a Property Page for each different dialog with the exception of the Open and Save As dialogs. Because they are nearly identical and use the same properties, their properties are set using the same Property Page.

The properties of the common dialog also can be set at run time. In a complex program where the common dialog is used to open and save files of different types, and perform other operations like printing files and setting fonts, it is typical to set the properties pertaining to the specific dialog then call the appropriate method to display the dialog. This way, one common dialog instance can be used for all operations. This reduces the memory needed by the program because only one instance of the common dialog is used.

The following properties and methods pertain to the Open and Save As dialogs. These are the dialogs displayed when the ShowOpen and ShowSave methods are called:

- As you know, most file types have a default file extension. For example, text files have an extension of ".txt," and RTF files have an extension of ".rtf." The **DefaultExt** property will set or return the default file extension for the dialog.
- The **FileName** property contains the name of the file selected by the user. The full path name including drive, directory, and file name is stored in this property. Setting this property before displaying the dialog is useful to specify a default file name.

- The **FileTitle** property contains the name of the file with the drive and path information removed.
- The **Filter** property is used to control the file extensions that will be displayed in the dialog.
- The **FilterIndex** property is used in conjunction with the Filter property to identify the default filter. Filters are one-based. That is, the first filter has a FilterIndex property of one (1) and so on.
- The **Flags** property, as it pertains to the Open and Save As dialogs, is used to determine how directory and file selection is performed. For example, it is possible to prohibit users from creating directories, changing directories, and deleting directories. It also is possible to allow the user to select multiple files. Refer to the "Flags Property (Open, Save As Dialogs)" Help topic for a more complete list of the valid flags.
- The **InitDir** property is used to specify an initial directory to look for or save files. If the Flag cdlNoChangeDir is set, then this directory cannot be changed.

One of the most difficult parts of using the ShowOpen method is setting the Filter and FilterIndex properties. While not essential to displaying the Open dialog, they can improve significantly the user interface by only displaying files with a specific extension. This reduces clutter appearing in the list portion of the common dialog. As you well know, most files have a three-character file extension to identify the file's type. For example, Jet database files have the file extension ".mdb," and Word files have the extension ".doc." If you are creating a program that uses files of a specific type, they too should use a standardized file extension. The files displayed in the common dialog can be restricted to those having a specific extension or extensions. That is, it is possible to create multiple filters and select one of the filters at run time. In this text editor, you will create filters to display text files or RTF files. A filter consists of a description followed by a vertical bar (|) followed by the filter. Separating each filter with a vertical bar (|) creates multiple filters.

Syntax

object.**Filter** [= *description1*|*filter1*|*description2*|*filter2* ...]

Dissection

- The *object* must be a valid instance of the CommonDialog control.
- The *description* contains descriptive text that identifies the file type.
- The *filter* contains the three-character file extension of the filter preceded by the "*." characters.
- Vertical bars separate filters and descriptions. Use care not to embed spaces between the vertical bars. These characters either will be embedded into the description or the filter itself, which generally is not desirable.

Code Example

```
cdlText.Filter = "Documents (*.doc)|*.doc|" & _
    "Rich Text (*.rtf)|*.rtf|All Files (*.*)|*.*"
cdlText.FilterIndex = 2
cdlText.ShowOpen
```

Code Dissection As shown in the preceding example, there are three filters. The first displays files with the extension ".doc," the second displays files with the extension ".rtf," and the final filter displays all the files in the current folder. By setting the FilterIndex property to two (2), the default filter is ".rtf" (the second filter). After setting the Filter and FilterIndex properties, the ShowOpen method is called to display the dialog.

GUI Design tip

As shown in the previous filter, each description contains text followed by the file extension in parentheses (i.e., (*.doc)). This standard nomenclature for descriptions should be used so that the user is aware of the actual file extension, because the filter itself is not displayed in the dialog. For example, consider the following filter:

```
cdlText.Filter = "Documents|*.doc|" & _
    "Rich Text|*.rtf|All Files|*.*"
```

Also, you should usually include the *.* (All Files) filter in case the user accidentally changed the extension of a file.

The filter shown in the previous statement has the same effect as the filter shown in the syntax dissection. The user will not see the actual file extensions displayed in the Files of type list box, making the interface less intuitive.

In addition to the filter, there are several flags that pertain to the Open and Save As dialogs. These flags are used to further control the files that are displayed, and define how the user can navigate through the different folders. The following list summarizes the different flags pertaining to the Open and Save As dialogs.

- Using Word and many other programs, it is possible to select multiple files in the Open dialog. Each file selected then is opened as a separate document. If the flag **cdlOFNAllowMultiselect** is set, then the dialog will return multiple files in the FileName property. The files are listed such that the full path name is displayed in the string, followed by a space, followed by each of the file names separated by spaces. It is up to the programmer to develop the code to break the string up into the individual file names and open them.
- By default, the common dialog uses an interface that is similar to the Windows Explorer program. If the flag **cdlOFNExplorer** is set, then the Windows Explorer style interface is used. Otherwise, an interface reminiscent of the Windows 3.1 Open File dialog is used.
- If the flag **cdlOFNFileMustExist** is set, the user must specify an existing file. If not set, the user can specify files that do not exist. If an attempt is made by the user to enter a non-existent file, a dialog is displayed containing a warning message.
- If the flag **cdlOFNNoChangeDir** is set, the user only can open or save files in the initial directory, which cannot be changed. This flag is useful when you want to restrict the user to locating and saving files to a particular folder.
- The flag **cdlOFNOverwritePrompt** actually is used by the Save As dialog but the flags for both dialogs are described here because they are so similar. If this flag is set, the user will be prompted if a file is specified that already exists.

Adding the values of the different flags together and storing the result in the Flags property is the technique used to combine flags. For example, consider the following statement:

```
cdlText.Flags = cdlOFNExplorer + cdlOFNFileMustExist
```

These statements cause the dialog to be displayed using the Windows Explorer style interface. Also, the user must select a file that already exists. In this text editor, the common dialog will be used to open files with the extension ".txt" or ".rtf," so the Filter property is set accordingly. Intuitively, if a file is being opened, it should exist. Thus, the flags also are set accordingly.

To open a file with the common dialog:

1. Open the MDI parent form and click **Project** then **Components** to open the Components dialog. Make sure the **Controls** tab is active and the **Microsoft Common Dialog Control 5.0** check box is checked.
2. Create an instance of the CommonDialog control on the MDI parent form. Remember, the control is not a visible control so the placement of the control on the form is not important. Set the Name property to **cdlText**.
3. Locate the **OpenFile** general procedure on the MDI parent form. The statements for this procedure set the properties for the common dialog and then display the Open dialog. If the user did not click the Cancel button, a new form is created using the GetFormIndex function you created earlier, and the Caption is set as necessary. Enter the following statements:

```
On Error GoTo Cancel_Error
Dim pintCurrentDoc As Integer
With cdlText
    .Flags = cdlOFNExplorer + cdlOFNPathMustExist + _
        cdlOFNFileMustExist
    .Filter = "Text Files (*.txt)|*.txt|RTF Files" & _
        "(*.rtf)|*.rtf"
    .FilterIndex = 2
    .CancelError = True
    .InitDir = "A:\Chapter.07\Startup"
    .ShowOpen
End With
pintCurrentDoc = GetFormIndex( )
With Docs(pintCurrentDoc).frmCurrent
    .Caption = MDIText.cdlText.FileTitle
    .rtfText.LoadFile MDIText.cdlText.FileName
End With
Cancel_Error:
```

4 It should be possible to call the FileOpen procedure from either the MDI parent or child form. Locate **mnuFileOpen_Click** event procedure in both the MDI parent and child forms and enter the following statement:

```
MDIText.OpenFile
```

5 Test the program. To test the functionality of the Cancel button, on the form's menu bar click **File** then **Open.** Instead of opening a file, click the **Cancel** button on the dialog. The dialog will be closed causing a run-time error to be generated. This error is trapped by the handler so the statement to open the file will not be executed.

6 On the form's menu bar, click **File** then **Open**. The **Chapter.07\Startup** folder is the current folder because of the setting of the InitDir property. Click the file named **Demo.rtf**, then click the **Open** button.

These statements set the filter such that text files and rich text files having the extension ".txt" and ".rtf" can be displayed in the list portion of the dialog. By default, file names with the extension ".rtf" are displayed, which is the second filter.

```
pintCurrentDoc = GetFormIndex( )
With Docs(pintCurrentDoc).frmCurrent
    .Caption = MDIText.cdlText.FileTitle
    .rtfText.LoadFile MDIText.cdlText.FileName
End With
```

These statements are very similar to the statements in the NewFile procedure. Instead of setting the Caption property to the constant text "New Document," the name of the file appears as the form's caption. Then the LoadFile method is called for the rich text box. The file name stored in the common dialog is used to specify the file to load.

Whether or not to display the file title or file and full path name in the title bar is somewhat subjective. Because of long file names, however the length of the path may not fit on a form's title bar. Thus, consider displaying just the title.

Saving Files

The Save As dialog is very similar to the Open dialog. It contains exactly the same buttons, text, and list boxes. In this text editor, you will use the common dialog to save the contents of a rich text box to a file. This is accomplished by setting the necessary properties, then calling the ShowSave method of the common dialog. Using the file specified by the user, the SaveFile method of the rich text box is called with the file name as an argument.

To save a file using the common dialog:

1. Locate the **SaveFile** general procedure on the MDI parent form and enter the following statements:

```
On Error GoTo Cancel_Error
With cdlText
    .Filter = "Text Files (*.txt)|*.txt|" & _
        "RTF Files (*.rtf)|*.rtf"
    .FilterIndex = 2
    .InitDir = "A:\Chapter.07\Startup"
    .ShowSave
    frm.rtfText.SaveFile .filename
    frm.Caption = .filename
End With
frm.Dirty = False
Cancel_Error:
```

2. Enter the following statement into the **mnuFileSave_Click** event procedure on the MDI child form:

```
MDIText.SaveFile Me
```

   Note that this procedure does not need to be called from the MDI parent form because when the MDI parent form's menu is displayed there are no child forms (files) open.

3. Test the program. Create a new file and enter text into the file. On the menu bar click **File** then **Save**. The Save As dialog will appear. Save the file using the name **Chapter.07\Startup\NewFile.rtf**.

The code in the mnuFileSave_Click event procedure is nearly identical to the code in the mnuFileOpen_Click event procedure. It calls the ShowSave method to display the Save As dialog, however, and then calls the SaveFile method of the rich text box. It also resets the contents of the Dirty variable indicating that the file has no unsaved changes. This variable will be set to True whenever the user changes the contents of the rich text box.

Formatting the Contents of a Rich Text Box

At this point, the program is able to open and save RTF files. The next step in the process is to apply formatting to the current file. This is accomplished using several properties supported by the rich text box. The process of formatting text consists of selecting text to format, then applying a specific format to the selected text.

The rich text box supports properties to apply specific formatting to selected text.

- The **SelBold**, **SelItalic**, **SelUnderline**, and **SelStrikethru** properties are used to determine whether or not a specific font style is applied to the currently selected text. Each property can contain one of three values. If True, the font style is applied to the selected text. If False, the default, the font style is not applied to the selected text. If Null, the selected text contains characters with and without the formatting applied.
- The **SelFontName** and **SelFontSize** properties read or set the font and the size of the font for the selected text.
- The **SelFontColor** property sets or reads the color of the selected text.
- The **SelFontName** property sets or reads the font of the selected text.
- The **SelFontSize** property identifies the font size of the selected text.
- The **SelAlignment** property can contain one of four constant values: Null, rtfLeft, rtfRight, and rtfCenter. These constants left-justify, right-justify, and center text, respectively. The **RightMargin** property is used to determine the right margin when text is right-justified or centered. The RightMargin property contains the number of twips from the left border of the control.

Each of the above properties contains the value Null if the selected text contains different values for the same property. For example, if the selected text contained different font sizes, the SelFontSize property would contain the value Null. If the selected text contained a mixture of bold and regular typeface characters, the SelBold property would be Null. As you implement the program, you must decide what to do when this happens. For example, if the SelBold property was Null, you need to decide whether to apply or remove the boldface font. The choice is subjective, but whichever implementation you choose, be consistent. That is, if you decide to apply the attribute when the current value is Null, then apply the attribute for all the different properties.

In this text editor, checked menu commands are used to signify and apply the formatting to selected text. These commands appear on the Format menu and are named mnuFormatBold, mnuFormatItalic, and mnuFormatUnderline.

Before creating the procedures to accomplish the formatting, a few words about the implementation are necessary. As you will see later in the chapter, the menu commands will be but one way to apply formatting. It also will be possible to format characters using buttons on the toolbar. Also, as you will see later in the chapter, there will be multiple copies of the same form open at the same time. Thus, you will create three procedures on the MDI parent form to apply formatting—one for the bold text, another for the italicized text, and another for the underlined text. These general procedures will be called from the Click event procedure for the corresponding menu command. Furthermore, a reference to the current form will be passed as an argument to each procedure. As you have seen, the Me keyword contains a reference to the active form, and can be used to pass a form reference.

In the text editor, a formatting attribute can be thought of as being in one of two states. That is, the formatting attribute can be applied or not. Whenever the selected text is changed, the value of the toolbar buttons and commands must be updated accordingly to reflect the formatting of the currently selected text. Because the formatting can be changed in a number of ways, the formatting routines, which already have been created, are separated into their own Sub procedures.

```
Public Sub BoldStatus(frm As Form, pbln As Boolean)
    If pbln Then
        frm.mnuFormatBold.Checked = True
        MDIText.tbrText.Buttons("Bold").Value = tbrPressed
    Else
        frm.mnuFormatBold.Checked = False
        MDIText.tbrText.Buttons("Bold").Value = tbrUnpressed
    End If
End Sub
```

The previous function sets the status of the checked menu command and the state of the toolbar button. The syntax of the statements affecting the toolbar buttons will be explained in the section that describes the toolbar. The procedure takes two arguments—a reference to the MDI child form, and a Boolean variable indicating whether or not the formatting attribute should be applied. There are other nearly identical procedures named ItalicStatus and UnderlineStatus used to set the italic and underline formatting attributes.

To apply the formatting to the selected text:

1. Locate the **mnuFormatBold_Click** event procedure on the MDI child form and enter the following statement:

   ```
   MDIText.FormatBold Me
   ```

2. Enter the following statements in the **mnuFormatItalic_Click** and **mnuFormat Underline_Click** procedures, respectively:

   ```
   MDIText.FormatItalic Me
   MDIText.FormatUnderline Me
   ```

3 Create the **FormatBold**, **FormatItalic**, and **FormatUnderline** general procedures on the MDI parent form named **MDIText** and enter the following statements:

```
Public Sub FormatBold(frm As Form)
    If frm.rtfText.SelBold = True Then
        BoldStatus frm, False
        frm.rtfText.SelBold = False
    Else
        BoldStatus frm, True
        frm.rtfText.SelBold = True
    End If
End Sub

Public Sub FormatItalic(frm As Form)
    If frm.rtfText.SelItalic = True Then
        ItalicStatus frm, False
        frm.rtfText.SelItalic = False
    Else
        ItalicStatus frm, True
        frm.rtfText.SelItalic = True
    End If
End Sub

Public Sub FormatUnderline(frm As Form)
    If frm.rtfText.SelUnderline = True Then
        UnderlineStatus frm, False
        frm.rtfText.SelUnderline = False
    Else
        UnderlineStatus frm, True
        frm.rtfText.SelUnderline = True
    End If
End Sub
```

4 Test the program. Create a new document then enter a line of text. Select the text using the mouse. Then, use the **Format** menu and the **Bold**, **Italic**, and **Underline** commands to apply and remove the specified formatting.

In the previous example, you used the Me keyword as the argument to the different Format functions. It also would have been possible to pass the argument using Screen.ActiveForm. The Me keyword, however, is considerably faster (about 25 percent) than using Screen.ActiveForm.

The current form is passed to each of the procedures as an argument. As you have seen in previous chapters, it is possible to pass an object reference to a procedure. The argument name "frm" is of type Form. Form actually is a generic type that can store a reference to any form.

Each general procedure has the same structure. The If statement is used to determine if the style already is applied to the selected text. If so, the desired formatting is removed. If not, the format is applied. The command is updated to indicate the current format by setting the Checked property. If the format is applied, a check box appears next to the command because the Checked property is True.

In addition to selecting text and applying formatting to the selected text, the checked menu commands must be updated accordingly when the selected text or the insertion point is changed. The SelChange event pertaining to the rich text box occurs whenever the selected text or the insertion point is changed. In this event procedure, you need to call the BoldStatus, ItalicStatus, and UnderlineStatus procedures so the commands will be synchronized with the selected text.

To synchronize selected text with the menu commands:

1. Enter the following statements in the **rtfText_SelChange** event procedure on the MDI child form:

```
If rtfText.SelBold = True Then
    MDIText.BoldStatus Me, True
Else
    MDIText.BoldStatus Me, False
End If
If rtfText.SelItalic = True Then
    MDIText.ItalicStatus Me, True
Else
    MDIText.ItalicStatus Me, False
End If
If rtfText.SelUnderline = True Then
    MDIText.UnderlineStatus Me, True
Else
    MDIText.UnderlineStatus Me, False
End If
```

2. Test the program. Format the text with different attributes and select different text. Verify that the commands are synchronized with the selected text.

In this text editor, different fonts and font sizes also need to be applied to the selected text.

Working with Fonts

Before discussing the Font dialog, a few words about fonts are in order. Attached to your computer are several devices and some of these devices like the screen and printer are output devices. A fax modem also is considered to be an output device. Each device has unique characteristics. For example, different printers support different fonts. Programs known as device drivers perform communication with each of these different devices. The link between a program, Windows, and the actual devices is referred to as a **device context**. There is a unique device context for each printer and for the screen on the computer. In Visual Basic, a reference to a device context is performed using the hDC property supported by many objects. For example, the Printer object supports the hDC property. Remember, there can be multiple printers on a system and each printer is represented as a Printer object in the Printers collection. Thus, each printer has a device context stored in the hDC property of the Printer object. A form also supports the hDC property. The common dialog uses the device context to determine fonts supported by the device.

The Font dialog allows the user to select a font, its size, and other font attributes. Like the Open and Save As dialogs, the common dialog does not actually change the font of text. Rather, it sets properties you can read to set the font of text in a text box or other object. The Font dialog is shown in Figure 7-6.

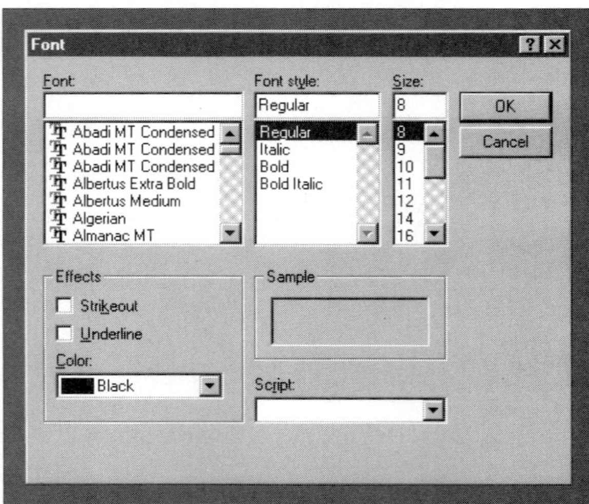

Figure 7-6: Font dialog

As shown in Figure 7-6, selecting values from the different list boxes can set the font name, style, and size. These settings are communicated to a program through the following properties pertaining to the Font dialog:

- The **FontBold**, **FontItalic**, **FontUnderline**, and **FontStrikethru** properties identify the bold, italic, underline, and strikethrough font attributes, respectively.
- The **Color** property identifies the color of the selected font.
- The **FontName** property contains the name of the selected font.
- The **FontSize** property contains the size, in points, of the selected font.
- The **ShowFont** method displays the Font dialog.
- The **Flags** property, as it pertains to fonts, is used to determine the fonts that are available, and whether or not a font must exist for the font to be selected.
- The **Min** and **Max** properties are used to specify the smallest and largest font size that can be selected in the Font dialog.

While the flags are optional for the Open and Save As dialogs, the type of fonts you want to use must be specified using the Flags property before calling the ShowFont method. Otherwise, a run-time error will occur indicating that there are no fonts selected. The following list summarizes the flags pertaining to the ShowFont dialog:

- The flag **cdlCFEffects** causes the strikethrough, underline, and color effects check boxes to be visible and enabled. If not set, these check boxes do not appear in the dialog.
- The flag **cdlCFPrinterFonts** causes the dialog to display only those fonts that apply to the currently selected printer (stored in the hDC property of the Printer object).
- The flag **cdlCFScreenFonts** causes the dialog to display those fonts that apply to the screen.
- The flag **cdlCFBoth** selects both printer and screen fonts.
- If the flag **cdlCFLimitSize** is set, the user only can select fonts within the range of the Max and Min properties.

Remember, if a font set is not selected using one of the flags cdlCFScreenFonts, cdlCFPrinterFonts, or cdlCFBoth, a run-time error will occur. You now will use the Font dialog to set fonts and font attributes. Because the Font dialog can be used to set attributes like bold, italic, and underline, you must also format the selected text in the rich text box and update the status of the checked menu commands and toolbar. This again is accomplished by calling the BoldStatus, ItalicStatus, or UnderlineStatus functions.

To set fonts and font attributes using the common dialog:

1. Locate the **mnuFormatFonts_Click** event procedure on the MDI child form and enter the following statements:

```
On Error GoTo Cancel_Error
    cdlText.Flags = cdlCFScreenFonts + cdlCFEffects
    cdlText.CancelError = True
    cdlText.ShowFont
    rtfText.SelFontName = cdlText.FontName
    rtfText.SelFontSize = cdlText.FontSize
    rtfText.SelBold = cdlText.FontBold
    If cdlText.FontBold = True Then
        MDIText.BoldStatus Me, True
    Else
        MDIText.BoldStatus Me, False
    End If
    rtfText.SelItalic = cdlText.FontItalic
    If cdlText.FontItalic = True Then
        MDIText.ItalicStatus Me, True
    Else
        MDIText.ItalicStatus Me, False
    End If
    rtfText.SelUnderline = cdlText.FontUnderline
    If cdlText.FontUnderline = True Then
        MDIText.UnderlineStatus Me, True
    Else
        MDIText.UnderlineStatus Me, False
    End If
    Exit Sub
Cancel_Error:
```

2. Test the program. On the form's menu bar, click **Format** then **Fonts.** Click different fonts and font attributes to test the procedure.

The first statement in this event procedure sets the Flags argument so the screen fonts will be displayed in the dialog. Then the Font dialog is displayed when the ShowFont method is called. If the user clicks the Cancel button, a run-time error will be generated because the Cancel property is set to True. If no error is generated, the font, size, and typeface attributes are applied to the selected text.

Justifying Text

The rich text box allows you to justify the text on a line. This is accomplished by setting the SelAlignment of the rich text box to one of several constant values. If set to rtfLeft, the text is left-justified; if set to rtfRight, the text is right-justified; and if set to rtfCenter, the text is centered. When text is right-justified or centered, the right margin must be defined so the rich text box knows where to align the text. Setting the right margin is accomplished by setting the RightMargin property pertaining to the rich text box. This property usually is measured in twips like other sizing properties. The property already has been set in the Form_Load event procedure for the MDI child form.

The function to set the justification will use the selected text like the other formatting functions you have used. It will take one argument—a string identifying how the selected text will be justified. This function will be called from the toolbar button code, which you will create in a moment.

To justify text in the rich text box:

1 Create the following general procedure on the MDI parent form:

```
Public Sub Justify(pstr As String)
    Select Case pstr
        Case "Left"
            Screen.ActiveForm.rtfText.SelAlignment = _
                rtfLeft
        Case "Right"
            Screen.ActiveForm.rtfText.SelAlignment = _
                rtfRight
        Case "Center"
            Screen.ActiveForm.rtfText.SelAlignment = _
                rtfCenter
    End Select
End Sub
```

These statements use a Select Case statement to determine the desired justification. To determine the active form, the Screen.ActiveForm object is used. The active form just as well could have been passed as an argument to the Sub procedure. You will test this procedure in the next section when the toolbar is created.

Printing Output

The Print dialog is used to select different printing characteristics. Again, the dialog does not actually print a file. Rather, it sets property and flag values, which your program can examine to determine what text to print and where to print it.

The Print dialog is shown in Figure 7-7.

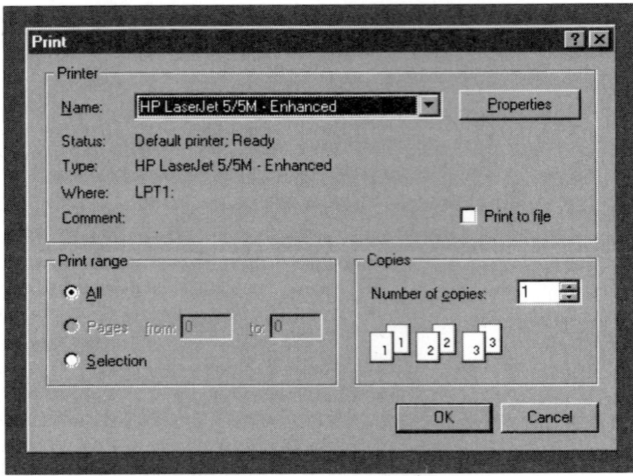

Figure 7-7: Print dialog

As shown in Figure 7-7, the Print dialog consists of three sections—the Printer section, the Print range section, and the Copies section. The various flags pertaining to the Print dialog determine which buttons are enabled in these sections, and the values selected by the user.

Like the other dialogs, the Print dialog is controlled using both the properties pertaining to the Print dialog and the flags pertaining to the dialog.

- The **Copies** property is used to determine the number of output copies to print.
- The **FromPage** and **ToPage** properties are used to determine the starting and ending pages to be printed.
- The **hDC** property specifies the device context.
- The **ShowPrint** method displays the Print dialog.

While the number of copies and starting and ending pages are determined by the above properties, much of the information about what to print, where to print, and how to print is controlled by the flags pertaining to the Print dialog. The following list summarizes the flags pertaining to the Print dialog:

- The All Pages option button is controlled by the flag **cdlPDAllPages**. If set, the button is selected. If not set, the button is not selected.
- By default, the Print to file check box is enabled. If the flag **cdlPDDisablePrintToFile** is set, then the check box is disabled. The check box can be hidden completely by setting the **cdlHidePrintToFile** flag.

- By default, the flag **cdlPDNoPageNums** is set causing the option button to select specific pages and the two text boxes containing the starting and ending page number to be disabled. Clearing this flag enables the option button and text boxes. If the user selects a starting and ending page number, the values are returned in the StartPage and EndPage properties.
- The flag **cdlPDNoSelection**, when set, disables the Selection option button. This flag typically is used to print selected text. The value of the Selection option button is returned in the flag **cdlPDSelection**.
- The flag **cldPDPrintToFile**, if set, indicates the Print to file check box is checked.

In practice, using the Print dialog requires that certain flags be set before the ShowPrinter method is called. After calling the dialog, the Flags property must be examined carefully to determine which flags are set and which are not.

To print the contents of the rich text box:

1. Create the following general procedure on the MDI parent form and enter the following statements:

```
Public Sub PrintFile (frm As frmText)
On Error GoTo Cancel_Error
    cdlText.Flags = cdlPDReturnDC + cdlPDNoPageNums
    cdlText.ShowPrinter
    frm.rtfText.SelPrint cdlText.hDC
Cancel_Error:
End Sub
```

2. Locate the **mnuFilePrint_Click** event procedure on the MDI child form and enter the following statement:

```
MDIText.PrintFile Me
```

3. Test the program. Create a new file and enter some text in the rich text box. On the form's menu bar, click **File** then **Print**. The contents of the rich text box are printed.

These statements call the ShowPrinter method to display the Print dialog. If the Cancel button is not clicked, calling the SelPrint method causes the selected text to be printed. The SelPrint method takes one argument—the device context of the printer.

Changing Colors

The CommonDialog control also allows you to select colors on a palette, which can in turn be used to change the color for an object. Like the other dialogs, the Color dialog supports properties as shown in the following list:

- The **Flags** property controls whether or not custom colors can be defined and the initial color selected.
- When closed, the selected color is returned in the **Color** property.
- The **ShowColor** method is used to display the Color dialog.

When working with color, it is important to consider the target computer where the program is run. Specifically, different computers have different color capabilities. That is, older display devices supporting the CGA standard, could display only 16 different colors. Later standards extended the number of colors to 256, and then later standards extended the number of colors into the millions. To represent a color, each pixel (dot on the screen) is represented by some number of bits. The more bits per pixel, the more colors the system can display. Common display devices in use today use 16-, 24-, and 32-bit color allowing for millions of different colors. Care must be exercised if a program will be run on a system with a limited color palette, however. That is, if the target computer cannot display a color you have selected, the color will be converted into one of the supported colors. This conversion does not always produce the desired results, causing the output to be illegible.

To change the color of the selected text:

1. Locate the **mnuOptionsColor_Click** event procedure on the MDI child form and enter the following statements:

```
On Error GoTo Cancel_Error
    MDIText.cdlText.ShowColor
    rtfText.SelColor = MDIText.cdlText.Color
    Exit Sub
Cancel_Error:
```

2. Test the program. Create a new file, enter text into the rich text box, and select it. On the form's menu bar, click **Options** then **Color** to activate the Color dialog. Click a different color then apply the color. The selected color should be applied to the selected text.

These statements cause the Color dialog to be displayed. The selected color is stored in the Color property of the common dialog. This color then is applied to the selected text in the rich text box by setting the SelColor property.

Improving the User Interface with a Toolbar

A toolbar typically contains a set of buttons the user can click. Each button can contain text or a graphical image. It is possible to create three different types of buttons. One type of button works like a command button. When clicked, the button appears recessed while an event procedure is executing and returns to normal when the procedure is finished. Buttons also can work much like a check box. That is, they can appear recessed or not recessed. In these situations, the button behaves much like a toggle switch and commonly displays status information like whether or not selected text is bolded. Buttons also can work as a group. That is, only one button can be checked from a group of buttons. For example, Word supports left, right, centered, and justified text. Only one setting is valid at a time. In this situation, a button group would be useful. It also is possible to separate buttons from each other. This has much the same effect as a separator bar on a menu but it is used visually to separate buttons rather than commands. Finally, it is possible to place an empty region on the toolbar where other controls like a drop-down combo box can be placed. Figure 7-8 shows the anatomy of a toolbar.

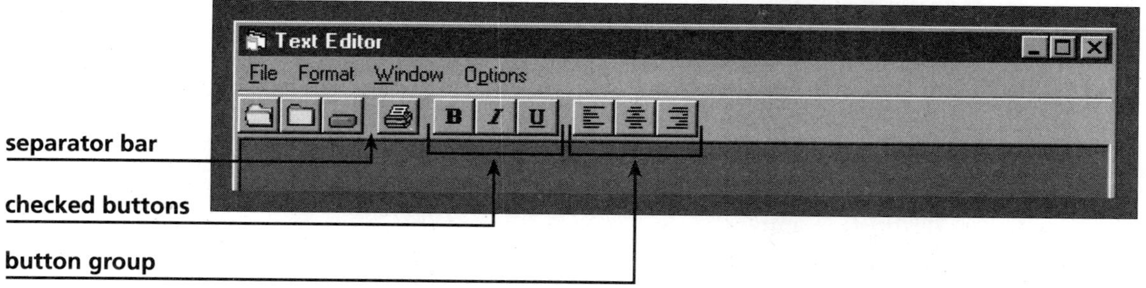

Figure 7-8: Anatomy of a toolbar

A toolbar is implemented by coupling two ActiveX controls together. These two controls are the ImageList control and the Toolbar control. The ImageList control was described in Chapter 6. To create a toolbar, the ImageList control must be created first to store the graphical images used in the toolbar. Then the toolbar is created. The toolbar is one of the Windows Common Controls and must be added to the project before it is available to the program.

Intuitively, you may think that a toolbar works like a menu when used in an MDI program. That is, different toolbars will appear for each form just under the menu bar. This is not the case, however. The toolbar for an MDI parent form appears just below the menu bar if one exists. If a toolbar is created for an MDI child form, the toolbar will appear on the MDI child form rather than under the menu on the MDI parent form. As a result, when programming toolbars with MDI programs, the toolbar is typically created as an object on the MDI parent form only. Toolbars also can be used with standard forms.

Creating the Toolbar and its Buttons

The Toolbar control is used to create a toolbar on a form. A toolbar is made up of buttons. Each button appearing on the toolbar is represented as a Button object in a Buttons collection. A button can display text or images (stored in the ImageList control).

Like other ActiveX controls, the design-time properties of the toolbar are set using the Property Pages for the control. The Property Pages for the Toolbar contains tabs to set the general properties of the toolbar and the properties pertaining to the individual buttons.

- The **General** tab is used to set the properties that define where the toolbar appears on the form, its size, and the name of the ImageList control containing the images that will be displayed in the toolbar.
- The **Buttons** tab is used to create each of the toolbar's buttons, define how the buttons behave, and which image from the ImageList control will be displayed on the button. It also is used to define the blank space that appears between the buttons.

Setting the General Characteristics of the Toolbar

Typically, the general characteristics of the toolbar are set first and then the buttons are created. The general characteristics are set using the General tab on the Toolbar control's Property Pages which is shown in Figure 7-9.

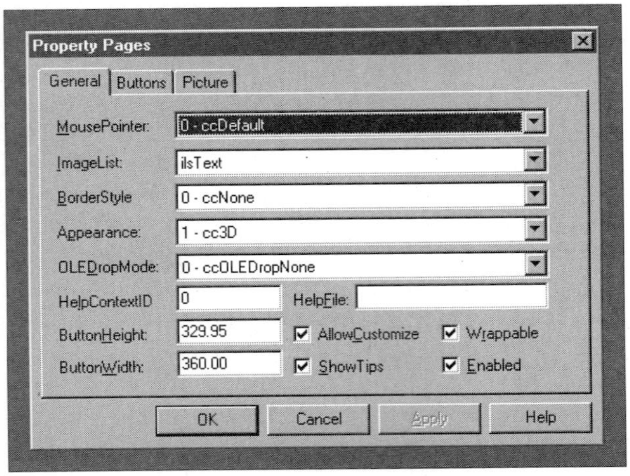

Figure 7-9: General Property Page

The Toolbar control is one of the Windows Common Controls, Thus, the Windows Common Controls must be added to the project, and the file comctl32.ocx must be distributed with the program for it to be run on a computer without the Visual Basic IDE. The three-character prefix for the toolbar is "tbr." The following properties are set using the General tab.

- The **ImageList** property is the name of an ImageList control on the form. Once this property has been set, the images in the ImageList control cannot be removed or changed. To change the images, this property must be cleared, the ImageList control changed, and this property reset. It is still possible, however, to add new images.
- The **BorderStyle** property determines whether or not a single line border appears around the region of the toolbar.
- The **Appearance** property causes the control to appear flat on the form or as a three-dimensional bar raised off the form.
- The **ShowTips** property can be True or False. If True, a ToolTip, if one is defined, will appear when the insertion point is held over a button.
- The **Enabled** property can be True or False. If False, the toolbar will not respond to events.
- The **AllowCustomize** property can be True or False. If True, double-clicking the toolbar at run time causes the Customize Toolbar dialog to appear. This dialog allows the user to change the characteristics of the toolbar.

In this text editor, the ImageList control already has been created and contains icons that will appear as buttons on the toolbar. These buttons will be used to open, save, and print files. Other buttons will be used to apply formatting and display whether the selected text is bold, underlined, or italicized.

To create a toolbar and set its general characteristics:

1. The Windows Common Controls have already been added to the project; create an instance of the toolbar on the MDI parent form. The toolbar appears across the top of the form by default.
2. Using the Properties window set the Name property to **tbrText.**
3. Activate the Property Pages for the control and make sure the **General** tab is active. Set the ImageList property to **ilsText.**

Defining the Toolbar's Buttons

Once the general characteristics of the toolbar have been defined, the individual buttons can be created. This is accomplished using the Buttons Property Page shown in Figure 7-10.

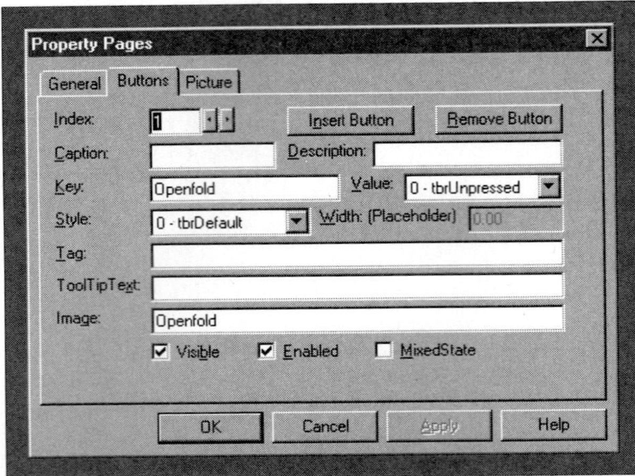

Figure 7-10: Buttons Property Page

As an ImageList control is made up of ListImage objects in the ListImages collection, the toolbar works similarly. Each button on a toolbar is implemented as a Button object in the Buttons collection and the Buttons Property Page is used to create, delete, and manipulate these Button objects. In addition to using the Property Page to create buttons, they can be added and deleted at run time by calling the methods of the Buttons collection. The following list describes the properties pertaining to each button:

- The **Index** property contains the numeric index of the Button object in the Buttons collection.
- The **Caption** property contains the text displayed on the button. This property usually is blank as buttons typically display an image.
- The **Key** property contains the string key that uniquely identifies the Button object in the Buttons collection.
- The **Style** property defines the behavior of the button. Button groups, checked buttons, placeholder buttons, and separator bars are defined with the Style property.
- The **Image** property is set either to the numeric index or string key of an image in the corresponding ImageList control.
- The **ToolTipText**, **Visible**, and **Enabled** properties have the same purpose as other controls you have used.

An instance of the ImageList control has already been created and contains the images for the toolbar. You now can proceed to create the buttons on the toolbar and display the images.

To create the images for the toolbar:

1. Activate the **Buttons Property Page** for the toolbar.
2. Click **Insert Button**. Set the Image property to **Openfold**. This is the name of the Key property for the image in the ImageList control. Insert a second button with the Image property set to **Clsdfold**. Set the Key property to the same value as the Image property for each button. The Key property represents the string key of the Button object in the Buttons collection. The Image property is used to locate the image in the ListImages collection identified by the ImageList control.
3. Insert a third button and set the Key property to **Drive** and the Image property to **Drive**.
4. Insert the fourth button and set the Style property to **3 - tbrSeparator**. This causes a separator bar to be inserted.
5. Insert the fifth button and set the Key and Image properties to **Print**. Create another separator bar for the sixth button.
6. The next three buttons will contain buttons to identify whether or not the selected text is bold, italicized, or underlined. These buttons correspond to the formatting commands on the toolbar. Use the Image and Key properties of **Bold, Italic**, and **Underline**. For each of these buttons, set the Style property to **1 - tbrCheck** because these buttons will be used to indicate whether or not the current text is formatted.
7. Create another separator bar and for the last three buttons, use the Image and Key properties of **Left, Center**, and **Right**. For each of these buttons, set the style to **2 - tbrButtonGroup**. These buttons will indicate the justification of the current line. Thus, it makes sense that only one button from the group can be selected at a time. Click **OK**.
8. When complete the toolbar should look like the one shown in Figure 7-11.

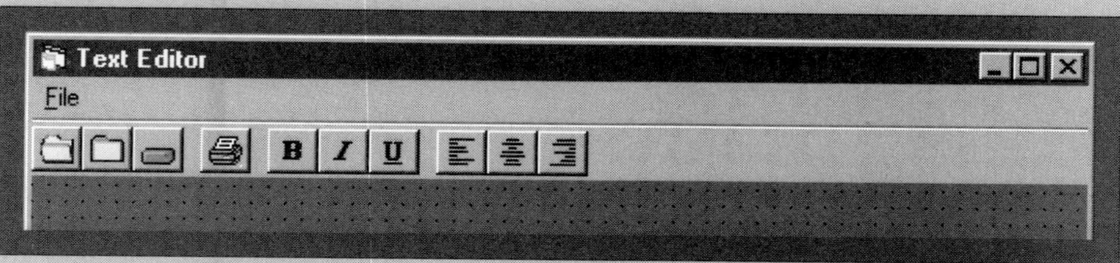

Figure 7-11: Completed toolbar

Once the toolbar has been created and its buttons assigned, the toolbar must be programmed to respond to events when clicked. Responding to toolbar events is quite different than responding to menu Click events because it is the toolbar in general that responds when a button is clicked rather than the specific button.

Programming the Toolbar

As you would expect, the toolbar responds to an event when clicked. Rather than each button responding to a different event, the toolbar responds to a ButtonClick event when clicked. This event takes one argument—a reference to the Button object that was clicked. It is the responsibility of the programmer to determine which button was clicked and perform the appropriate processing. Remember that each Button object supports a string key and a numeric index to identify uniquely the button in the Buttons collection. The value of these properties can be used to determine which button was clicked. This usually is performed with a Select Case statement. Consider the following ButtonClick event procedure:

```
Private Sub tbrText_ButtonClick(ByVal Button As _
    ComctlLib.Button)
    Select Case Button.Key
        Case "Openfold"
            OpenFile
        Case "Clsdfold"
            CloseFile
        ' Additional cases
    End Select
End Sub
```

These statements use the Key property of the button that was clicked to determine the correct button. Remember that the Key property contains the string key used to reference the Button object in the Buttons collection.

Typically, the Select Case statement is implemented such that there is one case for each button on the toolbar, excluding the separator bars and placeholder buttons. For each button, there is a case whose string value is the same as the button's string key. A general procedure then is executed that corresponds to a command. Either the procedure for the command can be called or the task can be implemented with a general procedure.

To program the ButtonClick event:

1. Locate the **tbrText_ButtonClick** event procedure in the Code window on the MDI parent form and enter the following statements:

```
Select Case Button.Key
    Case "Openfold"
        OpenFile
    Case "Clsdfold"
        CloseFile Screen.ActiveForm
    Case "Print"
        PrintFile Screen.ActiveForm
    Case "Drive"
        SaveFile Screen.ActiveForm
    Case "Bold"
        FormatBold Screen.ActiveForm
    Case "Italic"
        FormatItalic Screen.ActiveForm
    Case "Underline"
        FormatUnderline Screen.ActiveForm
    Case "Left"
        Justify "Left"
    Case "Center"
        Justify "Center"
    Case "Right"
        Justify "Right"
End Select
```

2. Remove the comments in the **BoldStatus**, **ItalicStatus**, and **UnderlineStatus** in the MDI parent form. The statements were commented because the toolbar did not yet exist and would have generated a syntax error.
3. Test the program. Click the different buttons on the toolbar to execute the general procedures corresponding to one of the commands.

This Select Case statement uses the string key of the selected button to determine which button was clicked and calls the appropriate general procedure. The numeric index also could be used, but the code is less readable as the numeric value provides no indication as to the purpose of the button. Buttons also support a Tag property that is ignored by Visual Basic. The tag also can be used as a way to identify the button uniquely.

Understanding the Windows Clipboard

As you have used programs like Microsoft Word, Excel, and other programs, you have undoubtedly used the Windows Clipboard to copy, cut, and paste text and other types of data within a document, between documents, and between different applications. Visual Basic provides support for the Windows Clipboard with the Clipboard object. In this chapter, you will learn how to copy text to and from the Clipboard.

Most programs support three operations that use the Clipboard.

- A cut operation deletes selected text from a document and places the deleted text on the Clipboard.
- A copy operation copies selected text from a document and places the copied text on the Clipboard.
- A paste operation copies the contents on the Clipboard to another object like a text box.

To perform these operations, the Clipboard object supports three methods.

Object	Clipboard
Methods	■ The **Clear** method removes the existing contents from the Clipboard. ■ The **SetText** method copies text to the Clipboard object. ■ The **GetText** method returns the text string currently stored on the Clipboard object. The text remains on the Clipboard after calling this method. Thus, repeated calls to the GetText method causes the same text to be retrieved from the Clipboard.

The GetText and SetText methods accept arguments to define the information copied on the Clipboard and the format of that information.

Syntax	**Clipboard.SetText** *data*, *format* **Clipboard.GetText** (*format*)
Dissection	■ The *data* argument pertains to the SetText method and contains the string identifying the text that is copied on the Clipboard. ■ Text on the Clipboard can be of different formats. Plain text or Rich Text Format is supported. The optional *format* argument contains the format of the text being copied on the Clipboard. If the constant **vbCFRTF** is used, the data is assumed to be in RTF format. If the constant **vbCFText** is used, the data is assumed to be in Text format. If no format is specified, vbCFText is assumed.

Code Example

```
Clipboard.Clear
Clipboard.SetText Text1.Text
Text1.Text = Clipboard.GetText
```

Before a copy or cut operation is performed, the contents on the Clipboard always should be cleared.

You have completed the programming for this chapter. You have seen how the CommonDialog control can improve the user interface dramatically by providing standard dialogs for common tasks. This dialog should be used whenever a program needs to open, save, or print files. It also is useful to set colors and fonts. In addition to the common dialog, you also have seen how a toolbar can augment the user interface by giving the user another way to execute common commands. These commands usually are equivalent to menu commands. You also have seen how the rich text box provides extensive capabilities to format and edit text.

This chapter has presented but one possible use of an MDI program. The MDI interface, however, is suitable for many other tasks. Any time an application manages like documents, an MDI interface is appropriate. Excel manages like documents (worksheets), and PowerPoint also manages like documents (presentations). Also, consider a process control or factory application. In a situation where a program is managing multiple machines or production lines that all work the same way, an MDI program also is suitable. In this situation, an instance of the MDI child form would be opened for each machine or production line.

SUMMARY

In this chapter, you have learned how to create MDI programs and the characteristics of MDI programming.

- An MDI program is made up of one MDI parent form, one or more MDI child forms, and possible standard forms typically used as modal dialogs. To create an MDI program, you add an MDI parent form to the project and set the MDI property for other desired forms to True causing them to behave as an MDI child form.
- A form module is considered a class and as such you can create multiple instances of the same class. This is particularly important because you can create multiple instances of the same MDI child form. Each form instance has a unique copy of its properties. Public variables declared in a form module are considered properties, and Public procedures are considered methods of the class.
- When unloading forms in an MDI program, the QueryUnload and Unload events occur for both the MDI parent and MDI child form instances. The QueryUnload event accepts two arguments. The *cancel* argument, if set to True, prevents subsequent Unload events from occurring. The other argument, UnloadMode, is used to determine what caused the event to occur.

- When working with multiple instances of the same form, the Forms collection is useful to examine all the loaded forms. The Forms collection works like the Controls collection. It contains a reference to all the loaded forms.
- The RichTextBox control is a superset of the intrinsic text box. It reads and writes formatted files, called Rich Text Files, using the LoadFile and SaveFile methods. The control supports properties to apply formatting attributes to selected text.
- The CommonDialog control is used to standardize the user interface of a program. It supports six methods corresponding to six different dialogs. Each method supports a unique set of flags that are used to change the behavior of the dialog. The common dialog does not actually perform the task identified by the dialog. Rather, it sets properties that your program then uses to perform the desired action.
- Another control used to improve the user interface is the Toolbar control. It contains buttons that the user can click to perform a specific action. Each button on the toolbar is represented as a Button object in the Buttons collection. You respond to a button being clicked using the ButtonClick event procedure that takes one argument—a reference to the button that was clicked.

QUESTIONS

1. An MDI program can contain ____________.
a. one MDI parent form
b. many MDI parent forms
c. one or more MDI child forms
d. both a and c
e. both b and c

2. What events are in the correct order?
a. QueryUnload, Unload.
b. Unload, QueryUnload.
c. Unload, Close.
d. Close, QueryUnload, Unload.
e. None of the above.

3. Which of the following statements is not true pertaining to an MDI program?
a. Menus appear just below the MDI parent form's title bar.
b. Every form in an MDI program may have a menu.
c. Standard forms can be used in an MDI program.
d. Message boxes and dialogs work as they do in other programs.
e. All of the above are true.

4. The following are valid methods of the CommonDialog control:
a. ShowOpen, ShowSaveFile, ShowPrint
b. ShowOpen, ShowSave, ShowFont
c. ShowPrinter, ShowColor
d. both a and b
e. both b and c

5. The __________________ and __________________ methods are used to read and write files using the rich text box.
   a. Input, Output
   b. LoadFile, SaveFile
   c. Load, Save
   d. Read, Write
   e. none of the above

6. If the CancelError property pertaining to the CommonDialog control is True, then __________________.
   a. a run-time error will be generated by the common dialog when the Cancel button is clicked
   b. the Cancel property will be set to true
   c. the event procedure will be cancelled automatically
   d. all of the above
   e. none of the above

7. The __________________ properties identify the typeface, name, and size of the selected text in a rich text box.
   a. SelBold, SelItalic, SelUnderline
   b. SelFontName, SelFontSize
   c. Bold, Italic, Underline
   d. both a and b
   e. both b and c

8. Before calling the ShowFont method of the common dialog, the Flags property must be set to __________________.
   a. cdlCFScreenFonts
   b. cdlCFPrinterFonts
   c. cdlCFBoth
   d. any of the above
   e. none of the above

9. Which of the following are valid styles for buttons on a toolbar?
   a. Checked.
   b. Placeholder.
   c. Separator bar.
   d. Button group.
   e. All of the above.

10. The __________________ event occurs when a button on the toolbar is clicked.
    a. Click
    b. Toolbar_Click
    c. ButtonClick
    d. Press
    e. Change

11. Declare an array named FormsArray. Write a For loop that will iterate 10 times. Each time through the loop, create a new instance of the form named **frmTest** and store a reference to the form in the array.

12. Using the Forms collection, create a For Each loop to unload all the forms of type frmDemo.
13. Assuming that an MDI parent form named MDIParent has been created, write the necessary statements to display a message box in the QueryUnload event procedure that will confirm that the user really wants to exit the program. If not, the event should be cancelled.
14. Assuming that an instance of the CommonDialog control named cdlOne has been created, write the code for the **cmdOpen_Click** event procedure that will display an Open dialog with an initial directory of **C:**, and a filter that will select a Jet database file having the extension **.mdb**. After setting the necessary properties, display the dialog.
15. Create an event procedure named **cmdColor**. The event procedure should display the Color dialog. Create an error handler to detect whether or not the user clicked the Cancel button. If the user did not click the Cancel button, set the background color of the form named Form1 to the selected color.
16. Write the necessary statements to set the typeface of the selected text in a rich text box named **rtfCurrent** to bold, underlined, and italicized.
17. Using the Screen object, write a statement to set the Caption property of the command button named cmdTest to **Test**. (*Hint:* Use the ActiveForm property of the Screen object.)
18. Using the Me keyword, write the necessary statements to print the caption of the form referenced by the Me keyword if the type of the form is frmDemo.
19. Write a For Each loop to print the Name property of each form in the Forms collection.
20. Assume that a toolbar has been created named **tbrDemo** with three buttons named **One, Two,** and **Three**. Write a Select Case statement in the ButtonClick event procedure that calls the general procedures PrintOne, PrintTwo, and PrintThree, respectively, when the corresponding button is clicked.

EXERCISES

1. In this exercise you will create an MDI program that will use a multiline text box to display ASCII files.
   a. Create a new project and set the Name property of the form to **frmExercise1**. Save the form using the name **Chapter.07\Exercise\frmExercise1.frm** and the project using the name **Chapter.07\Exercise\Exercise1.vbp**.
   b. Create an MDI parent form and make it the Startup object. Set the name of the MDI parent form to **MDIEdit**.
   c. Set the existing form to be an MDI child form. Create a multiline text box with both vertical and horizontal scroll bars.
   d. In this example, only the MDI parent form will have a menu. There should be a **File** menu with three commands named **Open**, **Close**, and **Exit**.
   e. The Open command should display a common dialog with the necessary filter to open text files with the extension ".txt." When clicked, the program should open the file, read each line, and display the information in the text box.

f. The Close command should close the current form.
g. The Exit command should exit the program by unloading the MDI parent form. Before exiting, the user should be prompted whether or not they really want to exit the program. If they do not, the Unload events should be cancelled.
h. Using the techniques presented in this chapter, the program should support an array to keep track of the different instances of the MDI child forms.
i. Test the program.

2. In this exercise you will use the different common dialogs to customize the fonts and color for all the text boxes on the form.

a. Create a new project and set the Name property of the form to **frmExercise2**. Save the form using the name **Chapter.07\Exercise\frmExercise2.frm** and the project using the name **Chapter.07\Exercise\Exercise2.vbp.**
b. Create an instance of the CommonDialog control on the form.
c. Create several text boxes on the form.
d. Using the Font dialog, allow the user to set the font for all the text boxes on the form. Use the Controls collection and a For Each loop to examine each of the controls. Inside the For Each loop, use the TypeOf keyword in an If statement to determine that the control is a text box before trying to set the fonts.
e. Inside the For Each loop, set the font size, font name, and typeface attributes.
f. Create two menu commands named Foreground and Background. Use these menu commands to set the foreground and background colors for the text boxes. The color should be set using the CommonDialog control.
g. Again, use the same For Each structure as you used in the previous steps to determine that the type of control is a text box.
h. Test the program by applying different colors and fonts to the text boxes.

3. In this exercise you will create a toolbar having each of the different types of button styles.

a. Create a new project and set the Name property of the form to **frmExercise3**. Save the form using the name **Chapter.07\Exercise\frmExercise3.frm** and the project using the name **Chapter.07\Exercise\Exercise3.vbp.**
b. Add the Windows Common Controls to the project.
c. Create an ImageList control and add the following images: **Trffc10a.ico, Trffc10b.ico, Trffc10c.ico, Trffc01.ico, Trffc02.ico, Trffc03.ico, Trffc04.ico**, and **Trffc14.ico**. The Images are located in the **Chapter.07\Exercise** folder. As you add the images, make sure to assign a string key for each one.
d. Create a toolbar on the form.
e. Create a button group made up of the following icons: **Trffc10a.ico, Trffc10b.ico**, and **Trffc10c.ico.**
f. Add a separator bar so it appears after the first button group.
g. Add the following buttons on the toolbar just after the separator bar: **Trffc01.ico, Trffc02.ico, Trffc03.ico**, and **Trffc04.ico.**
h. Create another separator bar and add a **Trffc14.ico** button.
i. Write the necessary code so when the **Trffc14.ico** button is clicked, the program will end.

4. In this exercise you will create an MDI program that serves a much different purpose than the one you created in this chapter. This program manages the output of machines in a production line. In this exercise you will record and accumulate the number of good and defective items manufactured on each production line.

a. Create a new project and set the Name property of the form to **frmExercise4**. Save the form using the name **Chapter.07\Exercise\frmExercise4.frm** and the project using the name **Chapter.07\Exercise\Exercise4.vbp**.

b. Add an MDI parent form to the project. Set **frmExercise4** as the child form.

c. On the MDI child form, create two text boxes in which the user will enter the number of good and defective manufactured items for a production run.

d. Create two output labels and a command button. When the command button is clicked, the program should add to the output labels the current contents of the text boxes. In other words, you are creating an accumulator.

e. On the MDI parent form, create two menu commands with the captions **Start** and **Stop**. When the Start command is clicked, a new instance of the MDI child form should be created. When the Stop command is clicked, the instance of the active MDI child form should be destroyed. Thus, when the machine is started, a new instance of the MDI child form will appear representing the newly started machine. When the machine is stopped, the corresponding form instance will be destroyed.

f. Create a command to display the production output of all machines. This procedure should iterate through the Forms collection and examine the totals for each machine and compute a grand total.

g. Create a third form to display the grand totals. This form should be implemented as a modal standard form.

h. Save and test the program.

CHAPTER

8

Reusing Code with Class Modules

Using an Event-Driven Visual Programming Language

case ▶ Marketing Research Incorporated (MRI) develops and sells software to help businesses analyze the surveys they conduct. Each survey consists of Multiple Choice and True/False questions. For each survey there may be a variable number of questions and responses to each question. MRI is developing a prototype package that will use object-oriented techniques to implement this software. More specifically, each question will be represented as an object. A developer will be able to access the methods of an object to store the responses to survey questions. The object will support other methods that will summarize and perform statistical analysis on the surveys.

SECTION A

objectives

In this section you will:

- Create your own class using a different type of module called a class module
- Create different types of properties for the class
- Create methods for the class
- Write code to create instances of the class and call its properties and methods

Fundamentals of a Class Module

Previewing the Completed Application

The completed application for this chapter differs from applications you have created previously. Instead of containing a form and standard modules, it contains a form module and multiple class modules. The form, as usual, provides the visual interface for the program. A second type of module, called a class module, contains the implementation of the Question objects. That is, it contains the necessary properties and methods to store and analyze the response to a question. This new type of module is stored in the Class Modules folder in the Project Explorer as shown in Figure 8-1.

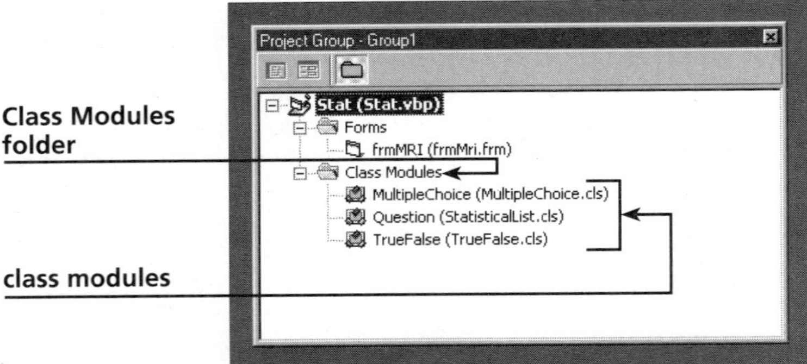

Figure 8-1: Class Modules folder in Project Explorer

The project contains two types of modules. It contains a form module and an additional type of module called a class module. In this example there are three class modules. The MultipleChoice and TrueFalse class modules provide the implementation for the Multiple Choice and True/False question types. The third class module, named Question, is called an abstract class. It defines the interface for all the types of questions supported by the class.

The completed form in this example contains a very simple user interface. In practice, the user interface for the program likely would be more sophisticated, but the focus of this chapter is to create and program class modules. Thus, the code in the form is intended only to demonstrate how to use the properties and methods defined in the various class modules.

To view the completed application:

1 Start **Visual Basic** and load the project named **Chapter.08\Complete\ MRI_C.vbp.** Print the code for the project.

2 Open the form module as shown in Figure 8-2.

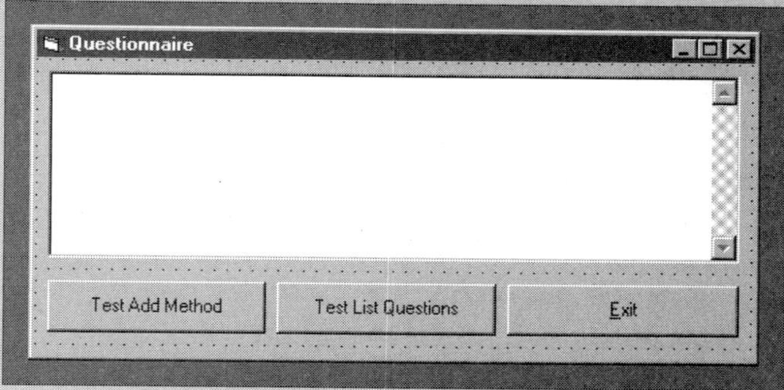

Figure 8-2: Completed form

As shown in Figure 8-2, the form contains a command button with the caption **Test Add Method** that is used to add responses to different questions. The **Test List Questions** command button is used to review the responses to the questions that were added. The **Exit** button simply unloads the current form causing the program to end. The instances of different questions are created in the Form_Load event procedure. If you analyze these procedures, you will see that the code looks much like the code you wrote to manipulate DAO, and other, objects in previous chapters.

3 Run the program. Click the **Test Add Method** command button. This command button executes the necessary code to add 10 simulated True/False questions and 10 Multiple Choice questions. Refer to the commented code in the Click event procedure for a more detailed analysis. This function does not produce any visible output.

4 Click the **Test List Questions** command button. The responses to the questions are displayed in the text box on the form.

5 End the program then exit Visual Basic.

The topics presented in this chapter, and the chapters that follow which describe the process of creating collections and ActiveX controls, either were supported minimally or not supported at all, prior to the release of Visual Basic 5.0. Visual Basic 5.0 brings to the Visual Basic programmer the capability to perform tasks previously only possible with languages like C++. The process of creating classes and ActiveX controls is much easier than it is using most other languages like C++.

The Requirements of an Object

One goal of object-oriented programming is to create reusable code. This is accomplished by creating objects from classes. You have created control instances like text boxes and used them to define the visual interface for a form, without needing to know how the text box is implemented. That is, the code that actually displays the characters, responds to events, and executes when you set properties and call the methods of the text box is transparent to you. You also have programmed objects like the recordset contained by the DAO hierarchy without having to know how the Jet database engine implements the Recordset object. You only need to understand how to use the methods and properties supported by the recordset. Writing programs that use objects created from classes has many benefits.

- Programmer productivity is shown to improve because complex tasks can be performed without having to worry how the object performs the task.
- Because an object performs a standard set of tasks, multiple programs can use the same object or objects. As you have seen, any Visual Basic program can use intrinsic and ActiveX controls, DAO objects, and other objects. This is what is meant by the term **reusable code**.
- The internal workings of an object can be changed so long as the interface (the object's properties, methods and events) do not change. Thus, the implementation of the code inside the object can be modified to improve performance without disturbing the interface of the object as seen by the programmers using it. Consider a sorted list box (the Sorted property is True). How the list box internally keeps the data sorted is the responsibility of the code in the list box. Thus, the type of sort algorithm used to organize the data could be changed without affecting the programs that use the list box.

The terms "class" and "object" have been used throughout this book. A class is a template or blueprint for an object, and by creating an instance of a class, an object is formed which you can access programmatically. In this chapter, you will learn how to create your own classes and then create objects based on those classes. The term "class" is used rather than the term "object." This is intentional, as in this chapter you will focus on the process of creating classes rather than the process of creating objects from classes that already have been created for you. Before creating a new class, there are a few key concepts and terms that form the core of object-oriented programming.

A class has a well-defined interface by which it communicates with the world. The **interface** is made up of data and processes that act on that data. This is referred to as **encapsulation**. In other words, the data and processes are encapsulated forming the class's interface. In Visual Basic, the interface of a class is made up of a defined set of properties, methods, and/or events. Collectively, these elements form the class's interface. The interface of a class commonly is called the **exposed part,** or the **public part,** of the class.

In addition to a public or exposed part, every class has a **private part** also known as the **hidden part**. The hidden part of a class is not visible to the programs that use the class. It does not matter how the hidden part of a class is implemented so long as the exposed part does not change. Thus, the term **implementation** commonly is used to describe the hidden part of a class. A class's interface defines the protocol by which it communicates with other programs, but it is not required that an interface has an implementation. In other words, the interface of a class defines its properties and methods but not what those properties and methods do. This is left to the implementation. This idea will be discussed later in the chapter.

It is possible for a class to have **multiple interfaces**. Consider the Recordset object as an example. Its interface consists of properties to determine the status of the current record pointer and methods to locate different records. Suppose you wanted to extend the functionality of the recordset by adding a new method that would locate the number of records in the recordset without having to locate the last record to obtain an accurate value. Additionally, suppose you have found a way to improve the performance of an existing method by modifying the code in the method (hidden part). To maintain compatibility with programs that use the original interface, one object can be created having the improved code in the original methods but with two separate interfaces. Older programs would use one interface, and programs that require the extended functionality could use the other interface. By creating two interfaces for one object, however, the enhanced methods will be used by any program that uses the object, regardless of which interface is used. Figure 8-3 illustrates a class with multiple interfaces.

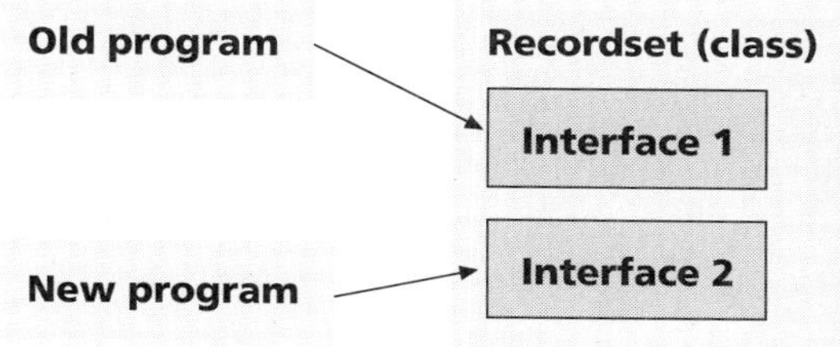

Figure 8-3: Multiple interfaces for a class

Another concept of object-oriented programming is called inheritance. **Inheritance** is the capability of an object to use the properties and methods of a class that already has been defined. Put in other terms, it is possible for classes to be derived from other classes. Again, consider the recordset example. You know that there are different types of recordsets, each of which has unique characteristics. For example, a **Dynaset-type** recordset allows data to be both read and written while a **Snapshot-type** recordset contains a static view of the data, which cannot be changed. Furthermore, a **Table-type** recordset has characteristics that differ from both the Dynaset-type and Snapshot-type recordsets. All three types of recordsets share certain characteristics, however. Using the concept of inheritance, a general class would be created to express the properties and methods common to all three classes. The specific details of the types of recordsets would be delegated to another class. In this case, there would be a separate class for each type of recordset. Each class would have properties and methods that may be unique to the class, and other properties and methods that are inherited from the general class. When talking about inheritance, the term **base class** commonly is used to identify the name of the class from which other classes inherit properties and methods. In addition to saying that a class can inherit properties and methods from a base class, you also can say that class is **derived** from a base class. Figure 8-4 illustrates the concept of inheritance.

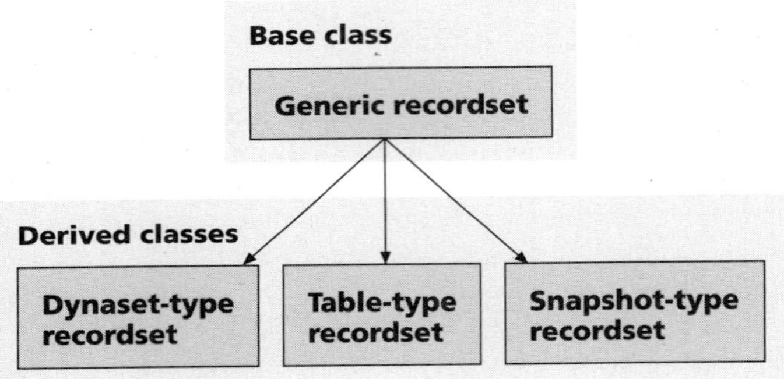

Figure 8-4: Inheritance

Visual Basic does not support inheritance in the same way as programming languages like C++. In Visual Basic, inheritance is accomplished by creating multiple interfaces for an object.

Closely related to the concept of inheritance is the notion of an abstract class. An **abstract class** contains no implementation. Rather, it only defines the interface for the class. This means that while an abstract class defines the properties and methods for a class, it does not define what those properties or methods do. Other classes that are derived from the abstract class supply the actual implementation for the abstract class.

In addition to inheritance, is the concept of polymorphism. **Polymorphism** is the capability for several functions (methods) to share the same name. Again, think of the recordset example where there are three types of recordsets. That is, even though there are three different interfaces, each executing different code, it still is possible to reference the recordset using the same object name, and the same name for its properties and methods. Most object-oriented programming languages like C++ implement polymorphism using inheritance. Visual Basic implements polymorphism using multiple interfaces for the class.

These terms pertain to object-oriented programming in general. That is, the concepts are applicable when programming in Visual Basic, C++, or other object-oriented programming languages. Having defined these terms, we now can proceed to describe how the process works with Visual Basic and Windows in general.

Component Object Modules

While intrinsic controls like the list box, ActiveX controls, and programmable objects like DAO may seem like disparate independent objects, they are not. The consistent look and feel of many Windows programs is not an accident. Consistency exists because Windows has defined a standard set of intrinsic objects like list boxes that can be used by many different development environments. Whether you use C++ or Visual Basic, you ultimately are referencing the same underlying Windows code that implements the list box.

Remember, the list box is an intrinsic control, so the code for the control is stored inside the executable file produced by Visual Basic. Visual Basic does not actually implement the list box itself, however. Rather, the list box actually is a control provided by the Windows operating system and available to programmers using other languages like Visual C++. Visual Basic merely provides an interface to the underlying ListBox control supported by Windows.

When you draw an ActiveX control like the DBGrid on a form, an instance of the control is created, but the code for the control is stored inside another file usually with the extension of .ocx. As we have mentioned, the .ocx file must be distributed with a Visual Basic application for the program to work properly on other computers. When you used the DAO hierarchy programmatically, you used the methods and properties of the various objects to navigate and perform operations on the data supported by those objects.

All these objects are derived from classes. Each of these classes has very different characteristics. For example, the list box has a visible interface while the Data Access Objects do not. ActiveX controls have Property Pages while intrinsic Visual Basic controls do not. All these classes, however, have one thing in common—they all can work together in the same program.

The concept of a class is not unique to Visual Basic. Rather, classes are integral to the way the Windows operating system supports object-oriented programming. When you create your own classes or ActiveX controls in Visual Basic, they are implemented internally using a standard technology known as **Component Object Modules** (**COM**). Simply put, COM defines the standard by which objects communicate with each other. Because all the Office 97 programs support COM technology, it is possible to access the interface of Word, Excel, and others from Visual Basic. It also is possible to create classes and ActiveX controls in Visual Basic that are usable by other programs and other programming languages. You most likely have used Word, and inserted graphics, PowerPoint slides, and other objects in a document. When one of these objects is inserted in a document, object communication between the different programs is possible because all the different types of objects have the same format and means of communication. It is the COM standards that define this format and means of communication. You may have heard the term OLE, OLE Automation, or Automation objects. The OLE technology relies on COM for communication. While a detailed explanation of the COM implementation is beyond the scope of this book, the basics of COM technology will help you understand why class modules work the way they do. As a result, you will find a brief discussion of COM technology interspersed with the Visual Basic class module presentation. This material is intended to help you better understand how the programs you are creating work.

Code Components

In Visual Basic, all class modules are created using ActiveX and COM technology. The class modules you will create in this chapter are but one type of ActiveX component supported by Visual Basic. This type of ActiveX component commonly is called a **code component**. This term is derived from the fact that class modules typically have no visual interface. The only way to access the properties and methods of the class is programmatically through code.

Author Versus Developer

Another distinction needs to be made before proceeding to create your first class module. In the previous chapters, the term programmer or developer meant the person developing a program. This definition is refined further in the context of class modules (code components). This terminology also is pertinent in the following chapters that show how to create collections and ActiveX controls.

- The person creating a code component (class module) or ActiveX control is considered the **author**.
- The person who writes a program that uses a code component or ActiveX control is referred to as the **developer**.

Anatomy of a Class Module

A class module is similar structurally and syntactically to a form module. As you saw in the previous chapter, a form is a class, and Public variables are considered properties of the Form class. Class modules also support Public variables and another way to implement properties using Property procedures. Private variables created in a form module are hidden inside the Form class. Furthermore, when a form is displayed or loaded, an instance of the form is created from the Form class. You can think of a class module as a form module with no visible interface. A class module has a general declarations section containing Public and Private variable declarations. Sub and Function procedures supply the functionality for the class just as they do for other types of modules. As in other modules, variables and procedures can be declared as either Public or Private. If a variable or procedure is declared as Public, then it is exposed; that is, other modules can use the variable or procedure. If a variable or procedure is declared as Private, then it cannot be used by other modules. Thus, Public variables and procedures form the exposed part of the class. Private variables and procedures form the hidden part of the class and are not part of its interface. Public variables are treated as properties of the class while Public procedures are treated as methods of the class. Figure 8-5 illustrates the logical components of a class module.

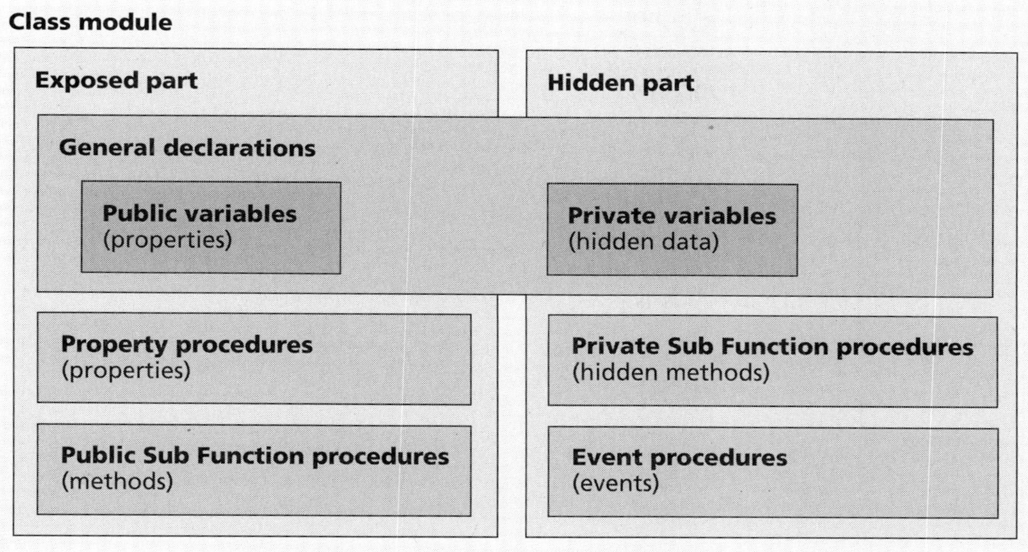

Figure 8-5: Anatomy of a class module

When creating class modules with several properties and methods, organize the properties and methods such that the Property procedures appear just after the general declarations, and such that the Sub and Function procedures appear after the Property procedures. Within these categories, keep the modules sorted by name. When viewing printed code listings, this will make locating a procedure much easier.

Proper naming of properties and methods will have a positive impact on the usability (interface) of the class module. The following list describes the conventions for naming properties and methods. The requirements for property and method names are the same as for other procedures.

- Property and method names cannot contain spaces.
- Use whole words with the first letter of each word capitalized.
- While subjective, if the name of a property or method seems too long, use the first syllable of a word rather than obscure abbreviations. Abbreviations are acceptable if they are well known. For example, “qty” and “amt” are common abbreviations for the words quantity and amount, respectively. If you abbreviate a word for a property or method, abbreviate that word for all properties and methods in the class for consistency.

- Use plural names for collections.
- When creating properties, use nouns such as AirplaneType.
- When creating methods, use a verb as the first word in the method's name, followed by a noun, such as AddAirplane.
- You cannot use the following names as property or method names: QueryInterface, AddRef, Release, GetTypeInfoCount, GetTypeInfo, GetIDsOfNames, or Invoke. If you try to use these names, a compilation error will occur. This is because the underlying COM objects use these names.

The interface for a class module takes careful design and planning. As the class's author, you should consider carefully the exposed properties and methods of the class. If the interface supports too many properties and methods, it may seem unwieldy to the developer using the class. You also need to decide whether to implement a specific function as either a property or a method. Consider the properties and methods of classes you already have used. As a general rule, if the procedure takes multiple arguments, it is implemented as a method rather than a property. When a perceived action is being performed like opening a recordset, the task also should be implemented as a method. A property implies a reference to data rather than performing a task. Thus, if you are reading or writing a data value, it generally should be implemented as a property.

In practice, because classes are independent of the programs that use them, they often are developed independently of the programs that use the class. In this chapter, you will create the properties and methods of the class, and then, using a form module, create object variables to reference the class. These object variables will in turn be used to reference the properties and methods of the class. This will better illustrate how class modules both are created and debugged. In the next chapter, you will see how to separate into multiple projects, the class modules developed by an author, and the form modules created by a developer, that uses the class.

Creating a Class Module

A new class module can be created, or an existing class module added to a project, just like any other module file. Clicking Project then Add Class Module will activate the Add Class Module dialog allowing you to create a new class module or add an existing class module to a project. Once added to a project, you write code in the Code window as with any other type of module. Because a class has no visible interface, however, there is no corresponding Form window. Class modules appear in the Project Explorer in the Class Modules folder. A project may contain zero, one, or many class modules. Like other module files, a class module is stored on the disk in a single text file. The file extension for class modules is ".cls."

Unlike a form, which supports several properties and events, a class module only has two predefined properties and two events. One property supported by all class modules is the Name property. The Name property for a class module has the same meaning and purpose as it does for a form module. It is the name by which you refer to the class when object variables are created from the class. This property is set using the Properties window. The other property supported by a class module is the Instancing property, which will be described in the next chapter.

In this example, first you will create the class to represent a Multiple Choice question. As such, the Name of the class will be MultipleChoice. The class name conforms to the naming conventions just mentioned. It consists of complete words with the first letter of each word capitalized.

To add a class module to the project:

1. Start **Visual Basic,** if necessary, then open the project named **Chapter.08\Startup\MRI_S1.vbp.**
2. On the menu bar, click **Project, Add Class Module.** Make sure the **New** tab is active. Click **Class Module** then the **Open** command button to create a new class module in the project. To open an existing class module, you can click the **Existing** tab, then use the Windows Explorer interface to locate and select the class module to use.
3. Opening the Properties window for the class module is accomplished by clicking the class in the Project Explorer, then right-clicking the mouse button and clicking **Properties** on the pop-up menu. Open the Properties window for the class module and set the Name property to **MultipleChoice.** This becomes the name of the class and will be used in Dim and Set statements when an object variable is used to create an instance of the class.
4. Save the class module on the disk by clicking **File, Save MultipleChoice As.** Use the name **Chapter.08\Startup\MultipleChoice.cls.**

One important point about class modules is that they have no visible interface. If you click the class module in the Project Explorer, the View Object button is disabled. Like the DAO objects you used in previous chapters, the only way to access the class is programmatically. Objects created from class modules work the same way. That is, the only way to create an instance of the class, set its properties, or call its methods is with code.

GUI Design ▶ tip

It is possible to display message boxes and input boxes from a class module, although the practice is not common. Rather, when an error occurs or information needs to be communicated outside the class, one of two options is more suitable. Either the procedure in the class module can raise an error, or the procedure can be implemented as a Function procedure and return a value to its caller. For example, if in a form module you tried to set a property to an invalid value, the procedure in the class module that was executing could raise an error. The procedure in the form module then should contain an error handler to determine the source of the error and what to do next.

At this point, you have created a class, so it is possible to declare object variables to reference the class and to create instances of the class. Consider the following statements:

```
Private Sub Form_Load( )
    Dim qmc As New MultipleChoice
    Dim qmc1 As MultipleChoice
    Set qmc = qmc1
End Sub
```

These statements assume that the class named MultipleChoice exists. This is the value stored in the Name property of the class itself. The first statement declares an object variable named qmc. Because the New keyword is used, an instance of the MultipleChoice class is created and a reference is stored in the object variable named qmc. The second statement creates a second object variable but no new object. Rather, the object variable points to Nothing. The final statement causes both object variables to reference the same underlying object. These statements work the same as those you have seen used to reference control instances, form instances, and other objects.

Programming tip

The previous statements used a three-character prefix to denote the object type. This is consistent with the naming conventions for the intrinsic controls and ActiveX components you have been using. As you create classes, adopting a standardized naming convention for objects created from a specific class will improve program readability.

Although a class has been created, it does not yet support any properties or methods. In other words, it neither has an interface nor an implementation. To create properties and methods for a class module, you must write the code for the class.

Creating the Properties of a Class

The simplest way to create a property is to declare a Public variable in a class module. A Public variable in a class module works like a Public variable in a form module. Because other modules can use the Public variable, it is exposed and part of the class's interface. Assume the following Public variable used to specify the name of the question has been declared in the MultipleChoice class:

```
Public Name As String
```

This variable creates a property in the MultipleChoice class having the name "Name." This variable name was chosen intentionally to illustrate that the variable "Name" is not the same as the class name (the value you assigned to the class using the Properties window). For example, given the previous variable declaration and the class named MultipleChoice, the following statements will create an instance of the class and set the Name property:

```
Dim qmc1 As New MultipleChoice
qmc1.Name = "How many children do you have?"
Debug.Print qmc1.Name
```

The first statement creates an object variable named qmc1 from the MultipleChoice class. Because the New keyword is used, a new instance of the object is created. Then, the second statement assigns a value to the Name property, which in this case is the name of the question that is being asked. The final statement reads the property and prints its value to the Immediate window. Imagine your survey had two questions instead of just one. Given this situation, you could create a second instance of the class. For example, consider the following statements:

```
Dim qmc2 As New MultipleChoice
qmc2.Name = "How many pets do you have?"
Debug.Print qmc2.Name
```

Combining these statements with the previous statements would cause two objects to be created from the MultipleChoice class. These objects are referenced using the object variables qmc1 and qmc2.

To demonstrate the use of a property implemented with a Public variable, you now will create the Name property for the class, create two instances of the class, and assign a value to the Name property for each instance.

To create two questions and set their Name property:

1. Locate the general declarations section of the class module named **MultipleChoice** and enter the following statement:

```
Public Name As String
```

2. In the form module, enter the following statements in the **cmdTestName_Click** event procedure:

```
Dim qmc1 As New MultipleChoice
Dim qmc2 As New MultipleChoice
qmc1.Name = "How many children do you have?"
qmc2.Name = "How many pets do you have?"
txtOut = ""
txtOut = qmc1.Name & vbCrLf & qmc2.Name
```

3. Test the program. Click the **Test Name Property** command button. The two question names should be displayed in the output text box.

The two Dim statements create two instances of the MultipleChoice class. In other words, the current survey now has two Multiple Choice questions. The two assignment statements set the Name property for each of the two questions. The final statements illustrate how to read the value of the two properties.

While implementing a property with a Public variable is suitable in some circumstances, it has serious limitations. Another way of creating a property is to create what are called Property procedures. The choice of whether to implement a property using a Public variable or Property procedures depends on the data stored in the property.

- When writing the property, it is not possible to execute code to verify that the value of the property is correct. Public variables are useful when the data cannot be validated and no code needs to be executed when the property is read or written. Property procedures commonly are used to validate input (the property is being set).
- There are times when writing a property should cause the value of another property to change, or a hidden variable to be updated. Property procedures also are useful to execute this type of code.

Hiding Data in the Class

In addition to creating exposed data with Public variables, it often is desirable to maintain data that only is visible inside the class. In other words, the author of the class can use the data, but not the developer using the class. Hiding data in a class is accomplished in the same manner as it is in form and standard modules. A variable is declared in the general declarations section of the class module as Private. Private variable names should use the standard prefixes for variable names rather than the property naming conventions, because they are not properties.

The class you are creating ultimately will store all the responses to a question, and the number of responses to any given question may vary. These requirements make a dynamic array the most suitable structure to store this data. How the responses are stored is the responsibility of the class rather than the program using the class. Thus, the array should be private to the class. The values for the array will be integers to denote the response. Thus, the chosen name for the array will be mintValues. The following declaration in the general declarations section of the class module will create the Private array:

```
Private mintValues( ) As Integer
```

To create a hidden variable:

1 Enter the following statement in the general declarations section of the **MultipleChoice** class module:

```
Private mintValues( ) As Integer
```

The Add method will use this variable to add responses to the question and the other methods that analyze the responses. The important point is that the dynamic array you just created is hidden in the class and can only be accessed using the properties and methods that you, as the author, expose.

Creating Properties with Property Procedures

Visual Basic allows you to execute code when a property is read or written by creating procedures inside a class module called **Property procedures**. Property procedures usually are written in pairs. One Property procedure is executed when the property is read, and the other procedure is executed when the property is written. As such, Property procedures often are referred to as **paired procedures**. In Visual Basic, the syntax of a Property procedure is much like the syntax of a Sub or Function procedure.

Each Property procedure contains a procedure declaration, which can have arguments, and some number of statements inside the procedure that execute when the property is read or written. Property procedures are implemented using the Property Let, Property Set, and Property Get statements.

The Property Get procedure is like a Function procedure; that is, it returns a value like a function. The Property Let and Property Set statements are used to write properties. They are much like Sub procedures because they do not return a value. When a Property procedure assigns a value to an ordinary variable, the Property Let statement is used. When a Property procedure is used to assign an object reference, the Property Set statement is used. Conceptually, this is analogous to the Set statement used to assign object references. The name you assign to a pair of Property procedures is significant. The name of the procedure is the same as the name of the property. The procedure name must be exactly the same for both the Property Let and Property Get procedure pair. This is an exception to the rule that procedure names must be unique. As you will see in a moment, if you create a pair of Property procedures with different names, two different properties are created—one for each name. Property procedures usually exist as a pair of procedures of the same name.

Syntax

[Public | Private | Friend][Static] Property Get *name* [(*argumentlist*)][**As** *type*]
    [*statements*]
    [*name* = *expression*]
    [Exit Property]
    [*statements*]
    [*name* = *expression*]
End Property

[Public | Private | Friend][Static] Property Let *name* [(*argumentlist*)]
    [*statements*]
    [*name* = *expression*]
    [Exit Property]
    [*statements*]
    [*name* = *expression*]
End Property

Dissection

- The **Property Get** and **Property Let** statements are used to declare procedures that read or write properties, respectively.
- If the optional **Public** keyword is used, then the Property procedure is visible to all other procedures in all other modules. If the optional **Private** keyword is used, then the Property procedure is visible only to the procedures in the class modules in the project.
- Optional **Friend** procedures are used to restrict the visibility of the property and are described in more detail in the following chapter.
- If the optional **Static** keyword is used, then the value of the local variables declared in the Property procedure will be preserved between calls to the procedure.
- The required *name* argument defines the name of the property and follows the standard naming conventions for property names.
- When setting a property requires arguments, the optional *argumentlist* allows you to pass one or more arguments used to set the property.
- Inside the Property procedure, there may be any number of *statements* that are executed when the property is set.
- The optional *expression* assigned to the name of the property is the value returned when the property is read. This is used in the Property Get procedure.
- The **Exit Property** statement works like the Exit Sub or Exit Function statements to cause the Property procedure to exit before the last statement in the procedure is reached.
- The **End Property** statement identifies the end of the Property procedure just like the End Sub statement identifies the end of a Sub procedure.

When Property procedures are used, the value of the property typically is stored in a hidden variable that, while global to the class, is not visible to the modules using the class. Thus, the variable is not part of the class's interface. When the property is written, the value is saved to this hidden variable. If the value of the property is read, the value of the hidden variable is read to determine the property's value. Figure 8-6 illustrates the Name property just created implemented as a pair of Property procedures.

As shown in Figure 8-6, when the Name property is set, the Property Let procedure executes, and stores the value of the property in the Private variable named mstrName. This variable is hidden and cannot be accessed outside the class. When the Name property is read, the Property Get procedure executes and the value stored in the hidden variable is stored in the Property procedure name. This syntax is identical to the syntax used to return a value from a function. In this case, the Property procedure does not execute any code other than manipulating the hidden variable. Thus, it could be implemented as a Public variable.

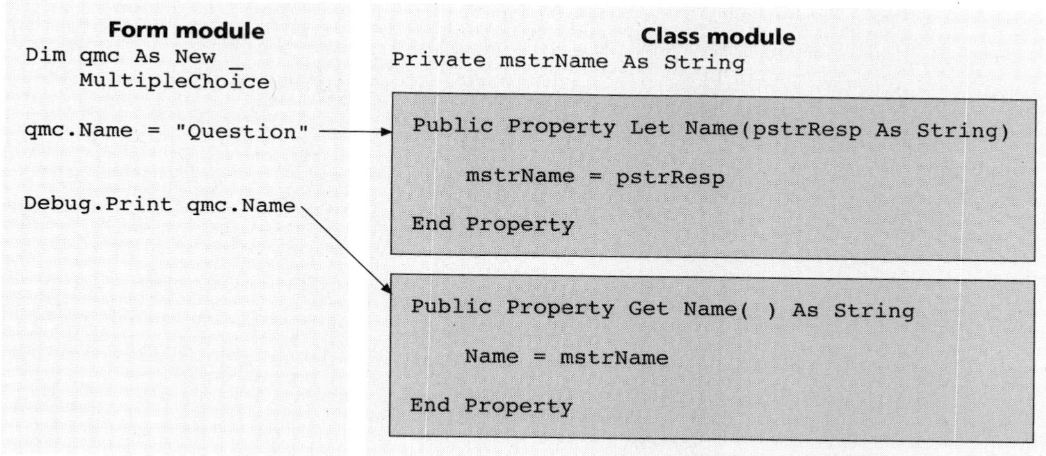
Form module
Dim qmc As New _
MultipleChoice
qmc.Name = "Question"
Debug.Print qmc.Name
Class module
Private mstrName As String
Public Property Let Name(pstrResp As String)
mstrName = pstrResp
End Property
Public Property Get Name( ) As String
Name = mstrName
End Property

Figure 8-6: Implementation of a Property procedure pair

Programming tip

You may think that a Property procedure will execute more slowly than a comparable Public variable because of the overhead to call a procedure. This is not the case, however. When the class is compiled and made into a COM object, all properties are implemented internally as a pair of Property procedures. Thus, there is really no difference between a Property procedure and a Public variable.

Consider another important point about Property procedures. Because a form module is considered a class, you also can create Property procedures in form modules.

Implementing Read-Write Properties with Property Procedures

A read-write property can be implemented by creating a Property Let, Property Get paired procedure, or creating a Property Set, Property Get paired procedure. The Property Let procedure assigns a value to a property and a Property Set procedure assigns a reference to an object. The Add procedure dialog is useful to create a pair of Property procedures. When the procedure type is set to Property, both a Property Get and Property Let procedure is created. Entering the code in the Code window for the desired class module also can be used to create Property procedures by hand.

Programming
tip

By default, the data type of the argument in the Property Let procedure is a Variant when Property procedures are created using the Add procedure dialog. This data type should be changed to a more specific type, if possible, to improve program performance if the type of data to be stored in the property can be determined.

Creating read-write properties with Property procedures is useful when you want to validate the value of the property that is being set, or perform some other operation when the property is read or written. In this example, you will use a pair of Property procedures to implement the question name. These Property procedures have the same effect as a Public variable but demonstrate the use of a hidden variable and paired Property procedures.

To create a read-write property with a pair of Property procedures:

1. Activate the Code window for the class module named **MultipleChoice**, then click **Tools, Add Procedure** to activate the Add procedure dialog.
2. Set the Name to **Name**, the type to **Property**, then click **OK**.
3. Enter the following statement in the general declarations section of the class module. This hidden variable will be used to store the value of the Name property used by the Property Let and Property Get procedures.

```
Private mstrName As String
```

4. Remove the following statement from the general declarations section of the class module:

```
Public Name As String
```

5. Create the Property Let procedure as follows:

```
Public Property Let Name(pstrResp As String)
    mstrName = pstrResp
End Property
```

6. Create the Property Get procedure as follows:

```
Public Property Get Name( ) As String
    Name = mstrName
End Property
```

7. Test the program. Click **Test Name Property**. It has exactly the same effect as the property implemented as a Public variable.

These statements illustrate the technique of using Property procedures and a hidden variable to implement a read-write property. The Property Let procedure, which is called when the property is written, stores the question name in the hidden variable mstrName. Conversely, when the property is read, the Property Get procedure executes. The value stored in mstrName is assigned to the property name (Name). This is analogous to returning a value from a function.

When you implement a property, either a Public variable or Property procedures are used, but not both. If you create a Public variable and Property procedures of the same name, Visual Basic will generate a compiler error indicating that an ambiguous name was detected.

Passing Arguments with Property Procedures

The arguments for Property procedures must adhere to certain characteristics. Remember that a Property Get procedure is a form of Function procedure that returns a value. The Property Let procedure is like a Sub procedure that accepts at least one argument used to set the property. Intuitively, these two values should have the same data type. Specifically, the return value of the Property Get procedure must be the same data type as the last argument in the Property Let procedure. Consider the following invalid pair of Property procedures:

```
Private mintThing As Integer
Property Get Thing( ) As Integer
    Thing = mintThing
End Property

Property Let Thing(New_Value As Double)
    mintThing = New_Value
End Property
```

These Property procedures will cause a compiler error to occur because the data type of the argument in the Property Let procedure is a Double, while the data type of the Property Get procedure is an Integer. In other words, these statements try to set the property to a Double when writing the property, but expect the value to be an Integer when reading the property. The data types of these two values must match exactly. You cannot use a Variant or Object data type for one procedure and a more specific data type for another. For example, the following statements also will fail:

```
Private mintThing As Variant
Property Get Thing( ) As Variant
    Thing = mintThing
End Property

Property Let Thing(New_Value As Double)
    mintThing = New_Value
End Property
```

If you make this type of mistake, Visual Basic will generate a compiler error saying that the definition of Property procedures for the same property is inconsistent.

Implementing Properties with Parameters

Each Multiple Choice question can have five different responses (the letters "a" through "e"). The meaning of a response will differ from question to question. For example, the letter "a" in one question may mean "very satisfied" while the letter "a" in another question may mean that a "family has no children." One improvement to the class module would be to store the five different descriptions in five different Public variables (properties). For example, you could create the following properties in the class module:

```
Public Response1 As String
Public Response2 As String
. . .
Public Response5 As String
```

Given that you have five variables of the same data type, you may be tempted to declare an array of five elements to store the responses and implement the property as an array as shown in the following declaration:

```
Public Responses(5) As String
```

If you attempt this, you will find that it does not work. Visual Basic does not support Public arrays in a class module. That is, you cannot create a property that is itself an array. There is a solution to the problem, however. Visual Basic allows you to specify multiple arguments in Property procedures. These arguments typically are used as an index in a Private array declared in a class module. This commonly is called a **parameterized property**. The hidden array has the same purpose as the hidden variable to store the Name property shown previously. Consider the following Private variable and Property procedures:

```
Private mstrListDescription(5) As String
Public Property Get ListDescription _
    (Index As Integer) As String
    ListDescription = mstrListDescription(Index)
End Property

Public Property Let ListDescription(Index As Integer, _
    ByVal New_Value As String)
    mstrListDescription(Index) = New_Value
End Property
```

Inside the class module, the Private variable mstrListDescription is an array that stores the five different response descriptions for the question. Because each Multiple Choice question has five responses, there are five elements in the array. When the property is set or retrieved, an additional argument is supplied to indicate which ListDescription to set.

Four points need to be made about these Property procedures.

1. The Property Let procedure has one more argument than the corresponding Property Get procedure. This is consistent with the previous discussion about the arguments of Property procedures.
2. In the Property Let procedure, the argument used to set the property appears last.
3. The position of the Index argument is the same for both Property procedures; that is, the Index argument appears first.
4. Finally, the name of the Index argument is the same for both procedures. This also is a requirement for the Property procedures to work.

In this example, you are implementing a one-dimensional array. Imagine that you wanted to implement a property that manages a two-dimensional array. In this case you would add additional parameters as shown in the following statements:

```
Public Property Get List( _
    Row As Integer, Col As Integer) As String

End Property

Public Property Let List( _
    Row As Integer, Col As Integer, _
    ByVal New_Value As String)

End Property
```

The previous statements implement a two-dimensional parameterized array. The order of the Row and Col arguments is the same for both the Property Let and Property Get procedures. Additionally, the name is the same for both arguments. This is another requirement of the parameters. If the Property Get procedure used the word Col as an argument and the Property Let procedure used the word Column, a compiler error would occur indicating that the arguments did not match.

In this example, you will implement the ListDescription property as a parameterized property. When reading or writing the value of the property, an Index value will be specified to indicate which element to use. You may find the implementation of this property to look much like the List property of a list box. In fact, the implementation is very similar as you will see when the property is read and written.

To create a parameterized property:

1. Create the following hidden variable declaration in the general declarations section of the **MultipleChoice** class module:

   ```
   Private mstrListDescription(5) As String
   ```

2. Enter the following Property procedures to read and write the **ListDescription** property:

   ```
   Public Property Get ListDescription(Index As Integer) _
       As String
       ListDescription = mstrListDescription(Index)
   End Property

   Public Property Let ListDescription(Index As Integer, _
       ByVal New_Value As String)
       mstrListDescription(Index) = New_Value
   End Property
   ```

3 Enter the following read-only property to identify how many items are in the list. This is an over simplification. In reality, there would be methods to add and delete the number of valid responses.

```
Public Property Get ListCount( ) As Integer
    ListCount = 5
End Property
```

4 Enter the following statements in the **cmdTestDescription_Click** event procedure in the form module to test the procedure:

```
Dim qmc1 As New MultipleChoice
Dim pintCount As Integer
qmc1.ListDescription(0) = "None"
qmc1.ListDescription(1) = "One"
qmc1.ListDescription(2) = "Two"
qmc1.ListDescription(3) = "Three to Five"
qmc1.ListDescription(4) = "More than Five"
txtOut = ""
For pintCount = 0 To qmc1.ListCount - 1
    txtOut = txtOut _
        & qmc1.ListDescription(pintCount) & vbCrLf
Next
```

5 Test the program. Click the **Test Description Property** command button on the form to execute the code you just wrote. The five descriptions should appear in the output text box.

The code for the ListDescription properties already has been described. You can compare the behavior of these procedures to the List property supported by a list box. The MultipleChoice class also supports the ListCount property to determine how many items are in the list. This behavior is reproduced by the read-only ListCount property. Because the list always supports five different responses, the ListCount property is set to five.

It would be reasonable to expand this class so the number of Multiple Choice responses could vary from question to question. In this scenario, the Add method may have an argument indicating the number of valid responses. This method likely would set the ListCount property to its correct value. Additionally, it also would be reasonable to create validation code to make sure that the index of the ListDescription property was inside a valid range, that is, from zero (0) to ListCount minus one (−1).

Using Object References in Property Procedures

In situations where reading or writing a property affects an object reference, a variation of the Property Get and Property Let procedures is used. When a Property procedure assigns an object reference, the Property Get and Property Set procedure pair is used. The Property Set procedure has the same syntax as the Property Let procedure except that an object reference is being set rather than a simple variable.

Syntax

[Public | Private | Friend][Static] Property Set *name* [(*argumentlist*)]
  [*statements*]
  [*name* = *expression*]
  [Exit Property]
  [*statements*]
  [*name* = *expression*]
End Property

Dissection

- The **Property Set** statement has exactly the same syntax as the Property Let statement. It is used, however, to write a property whose value is an object reference.

The importance of using Property procedures to assign object references will become apparent in the next chapter.

As you have seen with existing controls, some properties are read-write, others are read-only, and others are read-write but can be written only once. While the same Property procedures still are used to create these kinds of properties, Visual Basic supports techniques that allow read-only and write-once property types to be implemented.

As a rule, if the developer tries to perform an action that would cause an error, like setting the value of a write-once property twice or trying to write a value to a read-only property, the code in the class module should raise an error. When you raise an error in a class module, you should set the number of the error to a different value for each error you raise. This way the developer can use that value to determine the type of error and how to proceed. When setting the error number (code) in a class module, you should add the value of the constant vbObjectError to the error code.

Read-Only Properties

Visual Basic does not supply specific functions to implement read-only properties. Rather, the Property Let procedure can be omitted, or it can contain code to raise an error. In this example, you will create a read-only Count property that will return the number of responses to a question. Ultimately, its value will be calculated as responses are added to a question. Because the class computes the value, it does not make sense for the user to write a value to the property.

To create a read-only property:

1 Activate the Code window for the class module named **MultipleChoice** and insert the following statement into the general declarations section:

```
Private mintCount As Integer
```

2 Insert the following Property Get procedure. If you used the Add Procedure dialog, remove the Property Let procedure.

```
Public Property Get Count( ) As Integer
    Count = mintCount
End Property
```

The process of implementing a read-only property is similar to a read-write property but the Property Let procedure is omitted. You will see in a moment how the value of the hidden variable is set as questions are added so whenever the property is read, the hidden variable will contain the correct value. Assume that the code using the class module tried to set the value of the property using the following statement:

```
qmc1.Count = pintCurrentCount
```

This statement would cause a compiler error to occur indicating that you cannot set a value for a read-only property. This makes sense in this example, because the Count property, when read, will return the number of responses to a question. Because this value is computed, the developer using the class should never set it. If you chose the approach to implement the Property Let procedure and raise an error, the error would not occur at compile time as shown with the previous approach. Rather, the error would occur at run time only if the developer executed code that tried to set the property. Because this error pertains to the developer, the compile-time approach was chosen so the developer is notified immediately of the error when compiling.

Write-Once Properties

Sometimes, it is necessary to create a property that should be read-write but written only once. This is called a write-once property. In this example, you will create the Number property representing the question number so that once the value is set, it cannot be changed. Write-once properties are common when the value represents something like a unique index or key that should not be changed.

In this situation, both a Property Get and Property Let procedure are created, but the Property Let procedure contains code to raise an error if the developer tries to write the value of the property more than once. There is no way to detect this type of error at design time, because the task of reading and writing properties happens at run time. Thus, the Property Let procedure must be implemented and raise an error if a second attempt to set the property is made.

Consider the following statements:

```
Public Property Let Number(ByVal pintArg As Integer)
    Static pblnInitialized As Boolean
    If pblnInitialized Then
        Err.Raise 1024 + vbObjectError
    Else
        mintNumber = pintArg
        pblnInitialized = True
    End If
End Property
```

The Property Let procedure contains a static variable that is used to determine if the value of the property already has been written. If so, it will raise an error.

Programming tip

The error code 1024 was chosen for the error number. If a class module raises different errors for different reasons, the error number for each error should be unique. This way, the developer using your class can determine how to proceed based on the error that occurred.

To create a write-once property:

1. Activate the Code window for the class module named **MultipleChoice** and create the following hidden variable in the general declarations section to store the value of the property:

```
Private mintNumber As Integer
```

2. Create the following Property procedures in the **MultipleChoice** class module:

```
Public Property Get Number( ) As Integer
    Number = mintNumber
End Property

Public Property Let Number(ByVal pintArg As Integer)
    Static pblnInitialized As Boolean
    If pblnInitialized Then
        Err.Raise 1024 + vbObjectError
    Else
        mintNumber = pintArg
        pblnInitialized = True
    End If
End Property
```

3. To test the new property, enter the following statements in the **cmdTestNumber_Click** event procedure in the form module:

```
Dim qmc1 As New MultipleChoice
qmc1.Number = 1
qmc1.Number = 2
```

4 Test the program. Click the **Test Number Property** command button. The first statement that sets the number will execute normally. The second assignment statement, however, will cause a run-time error to occur. Usually, the form or standard module would contain an error handler for the procedure and determine the appropriate course of action.

The Property Get procedure works like the previous Property Get procedures you wrote. That is, the value of a hidden variable is assigned to the property name. The Property Let procedure is quite different. The technique to create a write-once property uses a hidden variable, in this case pblnInitialized. The first time the procedure is executed, the value of this variable is False so the value of the hidden variable is set. When the value of the hidden variable is set, the argument pblnInitialized is set to True. If this procedure is called again, the first part of the If statement is True, causing an error to be raised.

Notice that Visual Basic entered break mode and displayed the offending statement in the form module rather than in the class module where the error was raised. You will see in a moment how to change this behavior so a class module can be debugged.

Class Events

A class module responds to two events named Class_Initialize and Class_Terminate. These events are similar to the Form_Initialize and Form_Terminate events. This is logical because a form module is a type of class. The Class_Initialize event occurs when a new instance of the class is created and commonly is used to initialize variables. In this example, the Class_Initialize event will be used to initialize the array that stores the responses to a specific question. The Class_Terminate event occurs just before an instance of the class is destroyed. It commonly is used to save files or perform other housekeeping chores before destroying the class instance.

To program the Class_Initialize event:

1 Locate the **Class_Initialize** event procedure for the class module and enter the following statements:

```
ReDim mintValues(0)
mintCount = 0
```

The Class_Initialize event procedure is used in this example to give the array of responses an initial size. Remember that the variable mintCount is the hidden variable used to store the number of responses to a question. The value is assigned explicitly the value zero (0) indicating that no responses have been added. While this statement is redundant because the variable is initialized automatically to zero

(0) when the class is created, explicitly assigning a value to the property illustrates the desired initial value.

In addition to implementing properties for a class, it also is possible to create methods. Methods are implemented as Public, Function, and Sub procedures. Syntactically, there is no difference between these procedures in a class module and Function and Sub procedures implemented in other modules. The procedures are interpreted as methods instead of ordinary procedures. Private, Function, and Sub procedures also can be created in a class module. These procedures are not visible and are not part of the class's interface. Rather, they form the hidden part of the class's implementation. You also can create Private Property procedures. This causes properties to be created that are hidden in the class module.

Methods

Methods are implemented in a class module by creating Public, Function, and Sub procedures. Function methods return arguments and Sub methods do not. This is analogous to the behavior of Function and Sub procedures in standard modules.

In this example, you need to create a method to add Multiple Choice responses to each question. This method, named Add, will accept one argument—the value of the response. For brevity, assume that each Multiple Choice response has the same number of choices, in this case the letters "a" through "e." Thus, there are five possible responses. This is consistent with the behavior of the ListResponse property already created.

Consider the tasks to be performed by the Add method. Its purpose is to add one of five possible responses to a question. Logically, this value should be passed as an argument to the method. Each time a response is added, the array mintValues, which is hidden in the class, must be redimensioned to hold the new value, and the new value stored in the array. One other task could be performed to improve the robustness of the method. Because the value of a valid response is known, the method should validate the argument passed to it. If an invalid response is detected, this information should be communicated back to the procedure that called the method. There are two ways to inform the calling procedure of the error. One would be to use a Function procedure and return a value to the caller indicating whether or not the operation was successful. The other would be to raise an error in the procedure. The process to raise an error is the same as you saw with the Number Property procedure.

Another issue is the data type of the argument supplied to the Add method. While you could use a simple Integer value, it also is possible to use enumerated types in class modules. In this case, an enumerated type can be used to represent the letters "a" through "e." Remember that Visual Basic does not validate that the value assigned to an enumerated type is valid. As such, when the property is written, your code should verify that the value contains a valid enumeration.

Class Module Enumerations

The class module you have created could use the values zero (0) through four (4) to represent the five different letter responses to the questions. There are two ways that you can improve the robustness of the class module. First, the different responses can be represented by a Public enumeration. The developer using the class then can use the enumeration when adding a response to the Question object. It also is legal to create Private enumerations that are hidden in the class. Consider the following enumeration and statements to add a response to the current question:

```
Public Enum Letter
    letterA = 0
    letterB = 1
    letterC = 2
    letterD = 3
    letterE = 4
End Enum

Question1.Add(letterA)
```

This enumeration allows the programmer to use enumerated constants instead of Integer values to represent the response. This is only a partial solution to the problem, however. Consider what would happen if the developer added a response with an invalid value as shown in the following statement:

```
Question1.Add(99)
```

Unless the code in the Add method validates the response, it would be added to the question even though the response is invalid. As you have seen, enumerations are a programming convenience and the value is not validated by Visual Basic to determine that it contains a valid enumeration. So using an invalid Integer value will not cause an error, as the compiler does not check that the value is a valid enumeration. You can improve the interface of the class module further to verify that the argument supplied to the Add method contains a valid enumeration.

To create the enumeration and validate the arguments to the Add method:

1. Enter the following statements in the general declarations section of the **MultipleChoice** class module:

```
Public Enum Letter
    letterA = 0
    letterB = 1
    letterC = 2
    letterD = 3
    letterE = 4
End Enum
```

2 Create the **Add** method in the **MultipleChoice** class module using the following statements:

```
Public Sub Add(pintResp As Variant)
    Select Case pintResp
        Case Is = letterA, letterB, letterC, _
            letterD, letterE
            mintCount = mintCount + 1
            ReDim Preserve_
                mintValues(UBound(mintValues) + 1)
            mintValues(mintCount) = pintResp
            Exit Sub
    End Select
    Err.Raise vbObjectError + 1025, "MultipleChoice", _
        "Invalid Add argument."
End Sub
```

3 Enter the following statements in the **cmdTestAdd_Click** event procedure in the form module to test the method:

```
Dim qmc1 As New MultipleChoice
With qmc1
    .Add letterA
    .Add letterB
    .Add letterC
    .Add letterD
    .Add letterE
End With
```

4 Test the program. At this point, the program will not produce any output. The code you just wrote in the form module adds a question but it does not print the question to the output text box.

The response is passed as an argument to the method. The Add method performs two tasks. First, it determines whether or not the argument contains one of the valid enumerations. If so, then the second task is performed. This task is to redimension the array containing the responses and store the argument passed in the method in the correct array element.

One of the primary tasks to be performed by the class is to determine the percent of each response. This involves determining the count for a specific response and dividing that number by the total number of responses. Like most problems, there are different viable solutions for the implementation. Consider the following possible options:

- When the method is called, it could compute and return the percentage of all the different responses. This creates the options of returning an array or setting the values of other properties.

- When the method is called, it could be called with an argument indicating which response to compute. This creates a couple of options for the implementation of the procedure itself. In all cases, all the responses need to be examined. One solution, however, would be to maintain a single counter to count only the desired response. Determining if the response is the desired response would be accomplished with an If statement. Another approach would be to create a local array and accumulate all the responses regardless of which is selected. The performance impact of these two approaches is negligible because there is a tradeoff between executing the If statement and managing a five-element array.

In this example, you will implement the method by counting all the responses and returning only the desired response. Consider the ListDescription property you created earlier. It was implemented as a parameterized property much like the List property used by the ListBox control. The method to compute the percentage of a question works the same way. That is, the developer will specify an argument indicating which question to select from the list of questions. Thus, the name of the method is ListPercent to indicate clearly to the developer that the Property contains a list. It also makes the property name consistent with the ListDescription property.

To create the ListPercent method:

1 Enter the following Function procedure into the **MultipleChoice** class module:

```
Public Function ListPercent(pintResp As Integer) _
    As Single
    Dim pintCount As Integer
    Dim pintLetter(5) As Variant
    Dim pintTrue As Integer, pintFalse As Integer
    For pintCount = 1 To mintCount
        pintLetter(mintValues(pintCount)) = _
        pintLetter(mintValues(pintCount)) + 1
    Next
    ListPercent = pintLetter(pintResp) / mintCount
End Function
```

2 Enter the following statements in the **cmdTestPercent_Click** event procedure in the form module to test the method:

```
Dim qmc1 As New MultipleChoice
Dim pintCount As Integer
With qmc1
    .Add letterA
    .Add letterB
    .Add letterC
    .Add letterD
    .Add letterE
```

```
End With
txtOut = ""
For pintCount = 0 To qmc1.ListCount - 1
    txtOut = txtOut & qmc1.ListPercent(pintCount) & _
        vbCrLf
Next
```

3 Test the program. Click the **Test Percent Method** command button to test the method. The percentage of each response should be displayed in the text box. Because there are five distinct responses, the percentage of each response is 20 percent.

The ListPercent method is fairly simple. The table pintLetter contains five elements. Each element is used to count the response to the question. Thus, the count of letterA responses is stored in element zero (0), the letterB responses in element one (1), and so on. The For loop examines all the responses. The way the program is implemented, the first element in the array containing the responses (element zero (0)) is ignored. No value is ever stored in the array and the element is never referenced. The statements inside the array accumulate the counter for the corresponding response. Once all the responses have been examined, the method returns the percentage of the selected response by dividing the response by the total number of responses.

In reality, this method should contain the code to raise an error if an invalid response was supplied as the method's argument, but this code was omitted here for brevity.

You have completed the programming for this section. In the next section, you will learn more about the internals of class modules and how to create multiple interfaces for a class module.

SECTION B

objectives

In this lesson you will:

- Compare the code in a class module with a COM object project produced by Visual Basic
- Create an abstract class containing an interface but no implementation
- Use the Implements statement to derive classes from the abstract class
- Implement polymorphism using multiple ActiveX interfaces

Supporting Multiple Types of Questions

A Behind the Scenes Look at How Class Modules Work

Visual Basic hides most of the technical details of how classes work internally. In fact, you could create classes and ActiveX controls with little or no understanding of how COM works. A fundamental knowledge of COM, however, may help you better understand why a class module works the way it does. Remember that class modules are implemented by Visual Basic as COM objects. All COM objects have the following characteristics:

- Every COM object has one or more interfaces. Each interface contains a set of functions that define the class's implementation.
- Functions for a COM object are contained in a type of Dynamic Link Library (DLL). Any program that supports COM can access the library.
- Every COM object installed on a specific computer can be identified uniquely by an entry in the Windows Registry. This is called a Globally Unique Identifier (GUID).

The term interface was defined previously as it pertained to object-oriented programming, but the term has a much more specific meaning as it pertains to COM. We have said that every class supports at least one interface, but can support more than one interface. In fact, the classes you create in Visual Basic almost always support multiple COM interfaces. When you create classes in Visual Basic, the functions in the following interfaces are called for you automatically and transparently. Every class supports at least one interface named **IUnknown**. Notice the first character of the interface's name is I. By convention, interfaces begin with the letter "I." The IUnknown interface for a class contains three functions (methods). The first method is the **AddRef** method. It is called when an object is created from a class or an additional reference to an object is created. As you have seen in previous chapters, it is possible to create multiple references to the same object. Each time a reference to an object is created, the AddRef method is called to increment a counter defining the number of references to the object.

Thus, if two object variables currently referenced the same object, the reference counter for the object would be two. Consider the following statements:

```
Dim qmcRef1 As MultipleChoice, _
    qmcRef2 As MultipleChoice
Set qmcRef1 = New MultipleChoice
```

The Dim statements declare two object variables of type MultipleChoice. Because the New keyword is not used, an object is not created. Rather, two object variables are created that reference Nothing. The Set statement creates an instance of the MultipleChoice class and assigns a reference to the instance of the class in the variable qmcRef1. Thus, the reference counter for the object now is one.

```
Set qmcRef2 = qmcRef1
```

This statement assigns a second reference to the MultipleChoice object pointed to by qmcRef1. Thus, the AddRef method is called again and the reference counter is incremented to two. Remember that Visual Basic takes care of creating the IUnknown interface when you create a class, and then calling the AddRef method when assignment statements create additional references to an object. The following statement causes one of the references to the form to be destroyed:

```
Set qmcRef2 = Nothing
```

When the above statement is called, another method of the IUnknown interface is called. This method is known as the **Release** method. This method is called when a reference to an object is destroyed. If the reference count is greater than one, then the reference count is decremented by one. If the current reference count is one, then the memory and resources consumed by the object are destroyed, thus causing the object itself to be destroyed. In the preceding example, when qmcRef2 is set to Nothing, the reference count is decremented from two to one.

```
Set qmcRef1 = Nothing
```

The above Set statement causes the reference count to become zero causing the object itself to be destroyed. This fact is significant because objects are not destroyed until the reference count becomes zero; that is, there are no more references to the object.

When you are finished with an object, make sure to set all its references to Nothing. If you do not, the memory used by the object will not be released to the system. While not a problem with just a few objects, the performance impact can be significant in programs that manage many objects, or the object itself consumes large amounts of memory.

In addition to these two functions, the IUnknown interface supports one other function called **QueryInterface.** Remember that an object must have at least one, but can have many, interfaces. Classes would not be very useful if the only interface was IUnknown. You would be able to create references to objects, but the objects would not do anything. So the desired interface can be determined, the IUnknown interface supports a function named QueryInterface. QueryInterface is called with arguments that identify an interface. If the object supports the interface, QueryInterface returns a memory address containing the code for the interface. Carefully consider what happens when the following statements are executed:

```
Dim qmc1 As New MultipleChoice
Dim qmcRef As MultipleChoice
Set qmcRef = qmc1
```

In addition to IUnknown, another interface is supported named MultipleChoice. When qmc1 is declared, QueryInterface is called to obtain a reference to the MultipleChoice interface. It is by using this reference that the properties and methods of the object can be called. Additionally, the AddRef method also is called to increase the reference counter from zero to one. When the second Dim statement is called, QueryInterface again is called to obtain a reference to the MultipleChoice interface, and the reference counter is incremented to two.

In previous chapters, generic types like Object, Form, and Control were mentioned as a way to use a single object variable to reference different types of objects. Consider the following statements, which have the same effect as the previous statements, but are internally implemented much differently.

```
Dim qmc1 As New MultipleChoice
Dim qmcRef As Object
Set qmcRef = qmc1
```

In this example, the variable qmcRef is declared as a generic object variable capable of referencing any type of object. In the first set of statements, the interface used could be determined when the program was compiled, because the object variables specified a known interface. In this example, qmcRef can reference any type of object. Thus, Visual Basic cannot determine until run time the type of object that is being referenced, and thus the interface to use.

Windows supports yet another interface that is used to determine whether or not a class supports a specific interface. This interface is known as IDispatch and commonly is referred to as a **dispatch interface**. An object's dispatch interface serves no real purpose in and of itself. Rather, it is used to determine whether or not an object supports a specific interface, and the properties and methods that are supported by that interface.

When the Set statement is executed, QueryInterface is called as you have seen in the past. Instead of obtaining a reference to the MultipleChoice interface, QueryInterface is used to determine whether or not the object supports a dispatch interface (IDispatch).

Like the IUnknown interface, the IDispatch interface supports specific methods. Of particular interest are the **GetIDsOfNames** and **Invoke** methods. The GetIDsOfNames method is used to examine the interface for the properties and methods supported by the class. For each property or method, an integer is returned that represents the specific property or method. This value is called a **dispatch id**. Whenever a property is referenced or a method called, the Invoke method is called actually to execute the method or property. Using IDispatch or the dispatch interface is significant because of the impact on program performance. This is because IDispatch must determine if a given interface exists, and whether specific properties and/or methods are supported. More importantly, there is significant overhead involved in setting up the arguments to any methods or properties before calling the Invoke function.

There is much more to the internals of the inner workings of COM, but this introduction provides the foundation so you can understand what Visual Basic is doing when you create your own class modules. As you create class modules, we will refer to, and expand on, this information so you can visualize how Visual Basic converts the class modules you write in COM objects.

Debugging Class Modules

As you develop class modules and programs that use those modules, you need to be aware of different error trapping options supported by Visual Basic. These options control what happens when run-time errors occur in class modules and other parts of a program. Of particular importance in this chapter is the debugging of an ActiveX code component. It is possible for Visual Basic to enter break mode in a procedure even though there is an error handler active. It also is possible to have the error handler perform normally and return an error code to the caller of the ActiveX code component. Clicking Options on the Tools menu, and then clicking the General tab allows you to set the error trapping settings. The following option buttons on the General tab are used to change the debugging characteristics:

- If the **Break on All Errors** option button is selected, any error, whether or not there is an active error handler, will cause the project to enter break mode.
- If the **Break in Class Module** option button is selected, a handled error in a class module will cause the error to be trapped by the error handler and an error code to be returned to the caller. Unhandled errors in a class module will generate a run-time error and Visual Basic will enter break mode.
- If the **Break on Unhandled Errors** option button is selected, the error is trapped if there is an active error handler in any procedure. Break mode is entered only for unhandled errors. If an unhandled error occurs in a class module, Visual Basic will enter break mode and highlight the statement in the Code window that called the class module procedure where the error occurred, rather than in the class module itself.

To illustrate the effect of these settings, you again can click the Test Number Property command button. Remember, clicking this button will cause a run-time error because an error is raised when a second attempt is made to set the property.

To illustrate the effect of the error trapping options:

1. Click **Tools, Options**. Make sure the **General** tab is active. Click **Break in Class Module**. Click **OK** to close the dialog.

2 Test the program. Click **Test Number Property**. A dialog will appear indicating the nature of the error. Click the **Debug** button. The statement that raised the error in the class module is highlighted, because you said to enter break mode in the class module.

3 To see the effect of the Break on Unhandled Errors option, repeat Step 1, but click **Break on Unhandled Errors.**

4 Test the program again. Click **Test Number Property**. Instead of displaying the offending line in the class module, break mode is entered in the form module at the line that caused the error to occur.

Which debugging mode to use depends on whether you are debugging the class module or the form or standard modules that use the class module. If you suspect that the class module is producing incorrect results, use the Error Trapping option Break in Class Module, to help diagnose the specific cause of the error. Once you are convinced the class module is working correctly, set the option to Break on Unhandled Errors, to debug the form or standard module that uses the class. Refer to the Debugging Appendix for more information on this topic.

Enhancing the Class

Your class now supports the properties and methods to compute the percentage of responses to Multiple Choice questions. A Multiple Choice question is but one type of question that may be asked. In this example, you also need to support another type of question. The response to this other type of question will be True/False or Yes/No values. There are several ways to implement a solution to this problem.

- One solution is to create additional methods to store the different types of questions. For example, you could create an Add method for each type of question like AddTrueFalse and AddMultipleChoice. This solution would require that you create additional properties that correspond to these methods like CountTrueFalse and CountMultipleChoice. This solution is cumbersome because it doubles the number of properties and methods.
- A second solution is to create two distinct independent classes such that there is one class for each type of question. Using this solution, the methods and properties could all have the same name but there is no relationship between the classes.
- A third solution, and the one that will be implemented in this example, is to use an abstract class and polymorphism to create multiple interfaces for the class. To accomplish this, you will create three class modules. The first will be an abstract class. That is, it will define the interface for the other two classes but will contain no implementation. The other two classes will provide the implementation for the different types of questions. Figure 8-7 illustrates the relationship between the abstract class and the two other classes that provide the implementation.

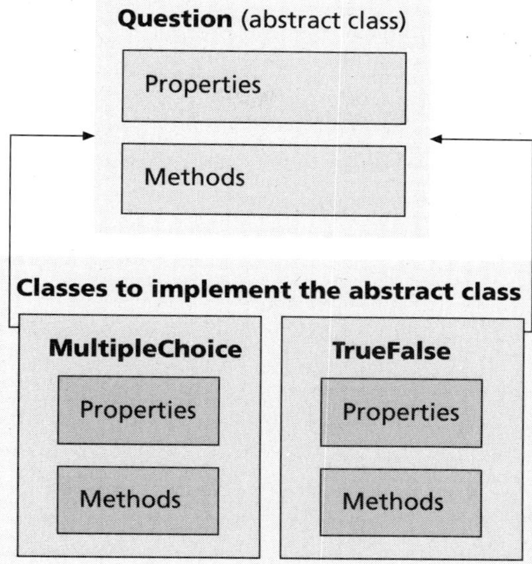

Figure 8-7: Abstract class

As shown in Figure 8-7, the Question class is an abstract class. It merely defines the interface that will be used by the other two classes. The MultipleChoice and TrueFalse classes implement the abstract class. This is accomplished by defining the same properties and methods as declared in the abstract class and writing the code to implement the properties.

Polymorphism Using the Implements Statement

At this point, your program supports a single class to support MultipleChoice questions. The class also should support questions that have two responses like Yes/No or True/False. Consider some of the possibilities for this implementation. It is possible to create additional methods and properties to support the different types of questions. That is, the interface could be modified and expanded. The following properties and methods could be used to implement the new class.

- The Name property would remain unchanged because each question has a Name regardless of the question type. The same is true for both the Number and Count properties.
- The Add method must be modified because it is important to know the type of response being added; that is, a True/False response or a Multiple Choice response. One possibility is to create two different Add methods, one for each type of question. Using this approach, there would be two Add methods each having a distinct name like AddTrueFalse and AddMultipleChoice.
- The names also would have to be changed for the ListPercent method.

This solution has several problems. Most importantly, the interface for the class now is more cumbersome because of the additional methods. It also is less generic. Another solution would be to create a second class module and implement the same methods and properties each having the same name. In other words, both classes would support the same interface. Using this solution, the MultipleChoice class would remain unchanged. A new TrueFalse class could be added having the same methods and properties. Thus, to create an instance of each class, the following statements could be used:

```
Dim qtf As New TrueFalse
Dim qmc As New MultipleChoice
```

This approach has the benefit of providing a consistent interface for both classes. You can think of this as a simple way to implement polymorphism. That is, two different methods of the same name execute entirely different functions. Using this approach, the two classes have nothing to do with each other. It is the responsibility of the programmer to make sure both classes implement the same functions. Another approach is to create what is called an abstract class.

The Abstract Class

There is another possibility to implement these two classes, but first a few words about how Visual Basic implements polymorphism. C++, a well known object-oriented programming language, supports polymorphism through inheritance. Consider this definition as it pertains to the Question classes you are creating. Using inheritance, it is possible to define a general class of questions having common properties and methods—in this case, properties like Name and Number. As you have seen, each type of question has unique characteristics. That is, the method to determine the percentage of a True or False response is different from the method to determine the percentage of a specific Multiple Choice response. Using inheritance, the classes for the specific question type would use the general characteristics of the Question class and override the methods of the general Question class. That is, the ListPercent method would have a different implementation for the TrueFalse and MultipleChoice class.

Visual Basic does not support polymorphism through inheritance. If you refer to the Help system, you will see that Visual Basic provides polymorphism through multiple ActiveX interfaces. This concept may best be described by an example.

In this section, you will implement two classes named MultipleChoice and TrueFalse. The MultipleChoice class will support exactly the same properties and methods as it did in the previous section. Another class named TrueFalse already has been created for you having the same properties and methods (interface) as the MultipleChoice class. The code for the methods of the same name differs between the classes because you are providing different implementations.

Given the two classes, TrueFalse and MultipleChoice, you now have two distinct and independent classes. Although these two classes support the same properties and methods, the two classes have nothing to do with each other. Assume that it is possible to create one interface for the class having two separate implementations, however. That is, assume you created a generic Question class that defined the interface for all the different types of questions. Then assume that there were two separate implementations for the two different types of questions. Given the classes you already have created, there would be a TrueFalse implementation and a MultipleChoice implementation. Consider the following statements:

```
Dim qArray(1 To 2) As Question

Dim qtf1 As New TrueFalse
Dim qmc1 As New MultipleChoice
Set qArray(1) = qtf1
Set qArray(2) = qmc1
qArray(1).Name = "Question 1"
qArray(1).Add True

qArray(1).Name = "Question 2"
qArray(2).Add letterB
```

These statements illustrate several important concepts. First the array named qArray is declared as the type of the abstract class (Question). It can store two types of questions (MultipleChoice and TrueFalse). The next two statements create an instance of a TrueFalse question and a MultipleChoice question, respectively. The Set statements create a second reference to each question via the array. Thus, the first element in qArray references the first TrueFalse question, and the second element references the MultipleChoice question.

The assignment statements following the Set statements illustrate the use of the abstract class as a vehicle to set properties and call methods. The abstract class knows which interface to use depending on the type of question. While the code is the same for the Name method, the Add methods work differently for the two different types of questions. The Add method for the MultipleChoice question has the possible values "a" through "e," while the possible values for the TrueFalse questions is True or False.

Having seen how an abstract class may be used with other classes, you now can examine how to create an abstract class and the classes that provide the implementation for the abstract class. Creating an abstract class in Visual Basic does not require a unique type of class module. Rather an abstract class is defined simply by creating the properties and methods of the class, but creating no code in the Property, Sub, or Function procedures. That is, the only purpose of the abstract class is to define the interface. Remember, properties and methods define a class' interface.

In addition to defining the properties and methods of the abstract class, the data types of any arguments supported by the properties and methods also must be declared.

To create the abstract class:

1 Start **Visual Basic**, if necessary, then create a new project.

2 Add a class module to the project, then set the Name property to **Question**. Save the class using the name **Chapter.08\Startup\Question.cls**.

3 Add the form named **Chapter.08\Startup\frmMRI_S2.frm** to the project. Using the Project Properties dialog make this form the Startup form.

4 Add the class named **Chapter.08\Startup\MultipleChoice.cls** to the project. This is the class you created in the previous section.

5 Add the class named **Chapter.08\Startup\TrueFalse.cls** to the project, then save the project using the name **Chapter.08\Exercise\MRI_S2.vbp**.

6 Enter the following statements in the **Question** class module to create the abstract type:

```
Public Property Get Name( ) As String

End Property

Public Property Let Name(pstrResp As String)

End Property

Public Property Get ListCount( ) As Integer

End Property

Public Property Get ListDescription(Index As Integer) _
    As String

End Property

Public Property Let ListDescription(Index As Integer, _
    ByVal New_Value As String)

End Property

Public Property Get Number( ) As Integer

End Property

Public Property Let Number(ByVal pintArg As Integer)

End Property

Public Sub Add(pintResp As Variant)

End Sub
```

```
Public Function ListPercent(pintResp As Integer) _
    As Single

End Function
```

The above code defines the interface for the abstract class. As you can see, the class supports exactly the same properties and methods supported by the MultipleChoice class you already created. Also, the names of the methods are identical as are the arguments and their data types.

As yet, only the interface has been defined. The next step is to define the implementation for the two different types of questions.

Implementing the Abstract Class

Once the abstract class has been created, adding another class module that implements the properties and methods of the abstract class creates each implementation. The class modules are added such that there is one class module for each implementation. The implementation must support all the methods and properties defined for the abstract class. Furthermore, the arguments of each property or method must be of exactly the same type. At this point you can modify the MultipleChoice class so it implements the abstract class. This requires that you make three changes to the class module as described in the following list:

- Each class that provides the implementation for the abstract class must contain the Implements statement followed by the abstract class that is being implemented.
- The names of the Property, Sub, and Function procedures that are used to implement the properties and methods of the abstract class must be modified so they have a prefix that is the same as the class being implemented.
- The Scope of the procedures that implement the properties and methods of the class should be changed from Public to Private. Remember that the class will be accessed through the abstract interface rather than the implemented class.

Having noted these changes, let's explain in more detail the mechanics of this process.

The Implements Statement

In this example, the TrueFalse class and MultipleChoice class will provide the implementation for the Question class. To tell Visual Basic that a class module provides the implementation for an abstract class you use the Implements statement in the general declarations section of the class module. The Implements statement contains the keyword, Implements, followed by the name of the abstract class being implemented. Thus, to tell Visual Basic that the MultipleChoice class provides the implementation for the abstract class named Question, you would use the following statement:

```
Implements Question
```

You now can add the Implements keyword to the MultipleChoice class to specify that this class implements the Question abstract class. The same statement already is included in the TrueFalse class.

To add the implementation for the interface:

1 Locate the general declarations section for the class module named **MultipleChoice** and enter the following statement just after the Option Explicit statement. This statement already has been added to the TrueFalse class.

```
Implements Question
```

Now that you have told Visual Basic that the MultipleChoice and TrueFalse classes provide the implementation for the Question class, you can proceed to the second step of the process—changing the procedure names in the class.

Setting Procedure Names for the Implemented Class

When a class implements an abstract class, the names of the procedures that declare the properties and methods of the implementing class must be changed. Visual Basic requires that the procedures be modified so the class being implemented is specified explicitly. This is accomplished by prefixing the property or method name with the abstract class name. The two names are separated by an underscore (_). The syntax looks much like the event procedure for a control instance. Assume that the following statements are declared in the Question abstract class.

```
Public Property Get Number( ) As Integer

End Property
```

The names of the Property procedures and methods are the names used by the developer accessing the class. Again, this is the interface for the class. Also, assume that the following implementation is declared and defined in the MultipleChoice class.

```
Private Property Get Question_Number( ) As Integer
    Question_Number = mintNumber
End Property

Private Property Let Question_Number( _
    ByVal pintArg As Integer)
    ' Code to validate that property has not been set.
    mintNumber = pintArg
End Property
```

The only change to these Property procedures is the addition of the abstract class name (Question) to the name of the Property procedures. Also, because the name of the Property Get procedure was changed, so was the statement that sets the property. This is consistent with the way a function's return value is set. This process must be repeated for every property and method in the class module. If you were trying to compile the program without implementing the entire interface defined by the abstract class, a compiler error will occur. Thus, this process must be performed before the class will compile. Next, you should convert the properties and methods of the **MultipleChoice** class so they implement the Question class.

To convert the properties and methods:

1. Insert the name of the abstract class before each of the Property, Sub, and Function procedure names. For example, the **Name** property should become the **Question_Name** property to indicate that the Question interface is being implemented.

   ```
   Question_
   ```

2. For each of the Function and Property Get procedures, make sure the name of the return value of the function or property is changed.

There is one task left to perform before the MultipleChoice implementation of the Question interface is complete. Each of the Property procedures and methods still is Public. As such, it is possible to access MultipleChoice questions without using the abstract Questions interface. That is, the following statement would be legal:

```
Dim qmc As New MultipleChoice,
qmc.Question_Name = "Do you have a car?"
```

This is not generally the desired effect as one of the goals of object-oriented programming is to make implementation details of the class completely transparent. Thus, the final step of the conversion process is to make the procedures in the MultipleChoice class visible only to the abstract Question class.

Setting the Scope of Implemented Procedures

Making the implementation details of the class completely transparent can be accomplished by making all the Property, Sub, and Function procedures that implement the methods Private.

This may seem a bit counterintuitive. We have said that a Private variable or procedure is visible only in the module in which it is declared. The abstract class, however, still can access the Private properties and methods of the implementing class even though the properties and methods are Private. A developer using the class cannot access these properties and methods. Thus, the final step in the process is to make the procedures in the MultipleChoice class visible only to the abstract class.

To hide the MultipleChoice class in the abstract Question class:

1. Open the Code window for the **MultipleChoice** class module.
2. For each of the Property, Function, and Sub procedures, change the scope of the procedure from Public to **Private.**
3. Test the program. Click the **Test Add Method** button then click the **Test List Questions** button. You are using a copy of the same form used in the completed case.

Abstract Class Initialization

Remember, the Class_Initialize event occurs when an instance of the class is created. In this example, however, there are two classes that implement the abstract class. Thus, the abstract Question class is implemented by the TrueFalse and MultipleChoice classes. A reasonable question to ask is, in which class do the Class_Initialize and Class_Terminate events occur? The answer is: "all of them." Given the fact that the Class_Initialize event occurs whenever an instance of the class is created, it makes sense that each class, even the abstract class, will raise these two events. Assume the following statements:

```
Dim q2 As New MultipleChoice
Dim q3 As New TrueFalse
Dim q1 As New Question
```

First, examine the first two declaration statements. Because the New keyword is used for both declarations, a new instance of each class is created. Consequently, the Class_Initialize and Class_Terminate events occur for each class. The event pertains to the individual class so different code can be placed in the event procedures to cause a different action to occur depending on the implementation.

You have completed the programming for this chapter. You have seen how to implement different types of classes, and different ways to create properties and methods for a class. As you will see in subsequent chapters, there are many other techniques to create more robust and more complex class modules.

SUMMARY

In this chapter, you have seen how to create class modules with properties and methods.

- A class module is like a form module without a visible interface. It has properties and methods.
- Properties in a class module can be created in one of two ways. You either can declare a Public variable in the class module or you create Property procedures.
- When you create Property Procedures, you generally create a Property Let and Property Get procedure. The Property Let procedure is executed when the property is written, and the Property Get procedure is executed when the property is read.
- To implement a read-only property, you create a Property Get procedure without a corresponding Property Let procedure.
- To implement a write-once property, you use a static Boolean variable in the Property Let procedure. This value is False the first time the Property procedure is executed. The code in the Property procedure sets this variable to True when executed. When executed, the code in the Property procedure should test the value of the Boolean variable to determine if it is True and if so, raise an error.
- The Property Set procedure works like a Property Let procedure except that it is used to assign object references.
- The arguments to Property Get and Property Let procedures must be of the same type. That is, the return value of a Property Get procedure must be of the exact same type as the argument to the Property Let procedure.
- Declaring Public, Function, or Sub procedures creates methods. Function methods return a value but Sub methods do not.
- Visual Basic implements inheritance using multiple interfaces. To create multiple interfaces, you create an abstract class that defines the interface for the class but no implementation. That is, you declare the Property, Function, and Sub procedures but place no code in those procedures.
- To create the classes that implement the abstract class, you declare the actual procedures containing the code. All the procedures declared in the abstract class must be implemented. Also, the data type of the procedures must be exactly the same.

QUESTIONS

1. Properties are created in a class module by ___________.
   a. declaring a Public variable
   b. creating a Property Let and Property Get procedure pair
   c. creating a Property Set and Property Get procedure pair
   d. none of the above
   e. all of the above
2. Methods are created in a class module by ___________.
   a. declaring Private, Function, and Sub procedures
   b. declaring Public, Function, and Sub procedures
   c. declaring a Method procedure
   d. both a and b
   e. all of the above
3. To create a read-only property you ___________.
   a. declare a Public variable in a class module
   b. declare a Property Let procedure without a corresponding Property Get procedure
   c. declare a Property Get procedure without a corresponding Property Let procedure
   d. declare a Property Read procedure
   e. both a and b
4. The ___________ event occurs when an object is created from a class and the ___________ event occurs when the object is destroyed.
   a. Class Load, Class Unload
   b. Class Load, Class QueryUnload
   c. Class Open, Class Close
   d. Class Begin, Class End
   e. Class Initialize, Class Terminate
5. A Public variable is ___________ while a Private variable is ___________.
   a. global, local
   b. local, global
   c. exposed, hidden
   d. hidden, exposed
   e. none of the above
6. Which of the following statements are True related to Property procedures?
   a. The last argument of the Property Set procedure must be the same as the return value for the Property Get procedure.
   b. Both the Property Get and Property Let procedures have the same name.
   c. The Property Let procedure can be omitted to implement a read-only property.
   d. All of the above.
   e. None of the above.

7. To create a write once property you ____________.
   a. omit the Property Let procedure
   b. omit the Property Get procedure
   c. raise an error in the Property Get procedure if the property already has been written
   d. raise an error in the Property Let procedure if the property already has been written
   e. none of the above

8. An abstract class ____________.
   a. defines an interface but no implementation
   b. is created using a class module
   c. can contain Property, Function, and Sub procedures
   d. has no code in the procedures
   e. all of the above

9. When you use the Implements statement ____________.
   a. the argument is the name of an abstract class
   b. the statement is placed in the abstract class
   c. the statement takes no arguments
   d. all of the above
   e. none of the above

10. What are the benefits of using Class modules?
    a. Code reuse.
    b. Programmer productivity is improved.
    c. Multiple programs can use the class.
    d. None of the above.
    e. All of the above.

11. The class module that implements an abstract class ____________.
    a. contains the Implements statement
    b. contains the same methods and properties as the abstract class
    c. has no code
    d. both a and b
    e. both a and c

12. Write the statements to declare an exposed variable (Property) named **Exposed** and a hidden variable named **mintHidden**. Both variables should be an Integer data type.

13. Assuming that a class module named Thing has exposed the Properties Name and Count having the String and Integer data type, respectively, write the statement to set the Name property to your name and the Count property to **1**. Also write the statement to read the value of both properties and display the value in the Immediate window.

14. Create the necessary Property procedures and Private variable named **mintCounter** to implement a property named **Counter** having an Integer data type.

15. Create the necessary Property procedure(s) to implement a read-only property named **Key**. The value of the read-only property should be determined using a hidden variable named **mintKey**.

16. Create a write-once property named **Index** that accepts one argument, a Long integer. If the property already has been written, raise an error.

17. Declare a Private array named **mintValues** with 10 elements as Integer. Then create a parameterized property named **Value** using property procedures. Each procedure should accept an argument to indicate the index to use in the table **mintValues.**

18. Create a method named **ElapsedMinutes**, that takes no arguments and returns a Long integer containing the number of minutes elapsed from midnight to the current time of day.

19. Create an abstract class having an interface consisting of two properties. The first property should store a string and have the name **LastName**. The second property should store a second property having the name **IDNumber**. The data type for this property should be an **Integer**.

20. Using the properties created in Problem 19, write the statements to implement the class specified in the problem. Assume the class name in Problem 19 is **Employee**. The properties should be implemented such that **LastName** is a read-write property and **IDNumber** is a read-write property.

EXERCISES

1. Using the scenario presented in this chapter, assume you wanted to create a class to support yet a different type of question. The responses to this type of question contain Integer values like a person's age, the number of years a person has lived at the same address, and so on. In other words, the valid responses to the question can be a discrete range of values. As such, there are different methods that would pertain to the class. For example, a **Sum** method could be used to get the total of all the responses, and an **Average** method could be used to determine the average of all the responses. The average is computed by dividing the count of the responses by the sum of the responses.
   a. Create a new project and a class module named **Range**.
   b. Using Property procedures, create a read-write property named **Name**, a write-once property called **Number**, and a read-only property called **Count.**
   c. Create a method named **Add** that will add a response to the question. This can be accomplished using a Private array and redimensioning the array as shown in this chapter. This method also should update the Count property using the same technique shown in this chapter.
   d. Create another method named **Sum** that will add the values of all the responses.
   e. Create another method named **Average** that will compute the average of all the responses.
   f. Using a form module, create an instance of the **Range** class. Set the Name and Number properties for the new class instance. Try to set the Number property again to see that the write-once property is working correctly.
   g. Add several responses with different Integer values to test the Add method.
   h. After adding the responses, use the **Count** method to test that it is counting the number of responses correctly.
   i. Finally, call the **Average** method to verify that the average is being computed correctly.
   j. Save the project using the name **Chapter.08\Exercise\Exercise1.vbp**, and the form using the name **Chapter.08\Exercise\frmRange.frm**. Use the name **Chapter.08\ Exercise\Range.cls** for the class module.

2. Many operating systems support a program that will count the number of characters, words, and lines in a file. A word is identified as a series of characters separated by spaces. A line is identified as a number of words terminated by a new line character. In this program, you will create a class that will determine the number of characters, words, and lines in a string.
   a. Create a new project and class module named **WordCount.**
   b. Create a read-write property to store a string. Use the Name **CharacterString** for the property name.
   c. Create three read-only properties named **Characters**, **Words**, and **Lines**. When read, these properties should return the number of characters, words, and lines in the character string.
   d. Consider carefully the implementation for the class. That is, use care to determine where to place the code to compute the number of characters, words, and lines. One solution is to compute each value when the property is read. Another solution is to compute the value for all the properties whenever the value of the CharacterString is written.
   e. Create a form with the following objects to test the class module. A multiline text box is needed to store the text that will be examined. Three output labels are needed to store the count of the characters, words, and lines in the text box. Finally, a command button is needed that, when clicked, will use the class module to calculate the number of characters, lines, and words in the text box.
   f. Save the project using the name **Chapter.08\Exercise\Exercise2.vbp**, the form using the name **Chapter.08\Exercise\frmWordCount.frm**, and the class using the name **Chapter.08\Exercise\WordCount.cls.**
3. In this exercise you will create an abstract class and three classes that implement the abstract class. A developer of residential track houses wants to create a class to represent the houses that are being built at a specific track. There are three different models of homes being built at the track. These models are named **Barcelona**, **Madrid**, and **Rio**.
   a. Create an abstract class named **House** with the following properties and methods: Name (String), GarageCount (Integer), Rooms (Integer), Price (Float).
   b. Create three classes to implement the abstract class. Name these classes **Barcelona**, **Madrid**, and **Rio**.
   c. Create the implementation for these three classes as follows. Each class should support a **Name** property to store the address of the house being built.
   d. Each class should support a **GarageCount** property. This will be used to store the size of the garage for the particular house. The Barcelona and Madrid houses can have either a two- or three-car garage but the Rio house only can have a two-car garage.
   e. Create another property named **Rooms** that will store configurations of the room. The Barcelona can have four bedrooms, or three bedrooms and a den. The same is true for the Madrid. The Rio can have four bedrooms, three bedrooms and a den, or two bedrooms, a den, and a master suite.

f. Create a method named **Price**; the price of the home is based on a formula derived from the model and the number of car garage. The base price of each home is $120,000, $130,000, and $140,000 for the Barcelona, Madrid, and Rio options. The three-car garage option costs an additional $1,500.
g. Save the class modules using the names **Chapter.08\Exercise\Barcelona.cls**, **Chapter.08\ Exercise\Madrid.cls**, and **Chapter.08\Exercise\Rio.cls**.
h. Create a form to add houses using the techniques in this chapter. Use your imagination to create a robust user interface to add houses and set their properties.
i. Save the form using the name **Chapter.08\Exercise\frmHouse.frm** and the project using the name **Chapter.08\Exercise\Exercise3.vbp**.

4. This exercise illustrates the concept of layering a class on top of another class. In this example, you will use the DAO hierarchy as you have done in the past. The interface for the class will expose only a few methods and properties, however. Create a method named **OpenDB** that takes one argument: a file name of a database to open. The method should return an instance of a database object. Create a second method named **OpenRS**. The method should take two arguments: the database object you returned in the previous section, and the name of the table. This method should return a recordset object. If the table is not found, raise an error. Create a form to test these two methods. Save the project using the name **Chapter.08\Exercise\Exercise4.vbp**.

CHAPTER

9

Creating a Collection Hierarchy

Implementing Multiple Class Modules

case▶ IGX Publishing is a small publisher of technical computer books. They need a program that will model part of the data they maintain. The program will keep track of the employees and writers that work for IGX. In addition, the program will keep track of the books created by each writer.

SECTION A

objectives

In this section you will:

- Create a collection
- Add, delete, and locate objects in the collection using the methods of the Collection object
- Create an object hierarchy using a Public collection
- Create an object hierarchy using a Private collection
- Create a type of class module called a Collection class
- Improve the robustness of classes with default properties and methods
- Use an object called an enumerator so a class module can support a For Each loop

Creating a Collection of Objects

Previewing the Completed Application

The implementation chosen for the completed application illustrates the use of an object hierarchy to manage data. The functionality of the object hierarchy is similar to other hierarchies you have used like DAO. From the developer's perspective, there is a defined set of objects pertaining to the organization as illustrated in Figure 9-1.

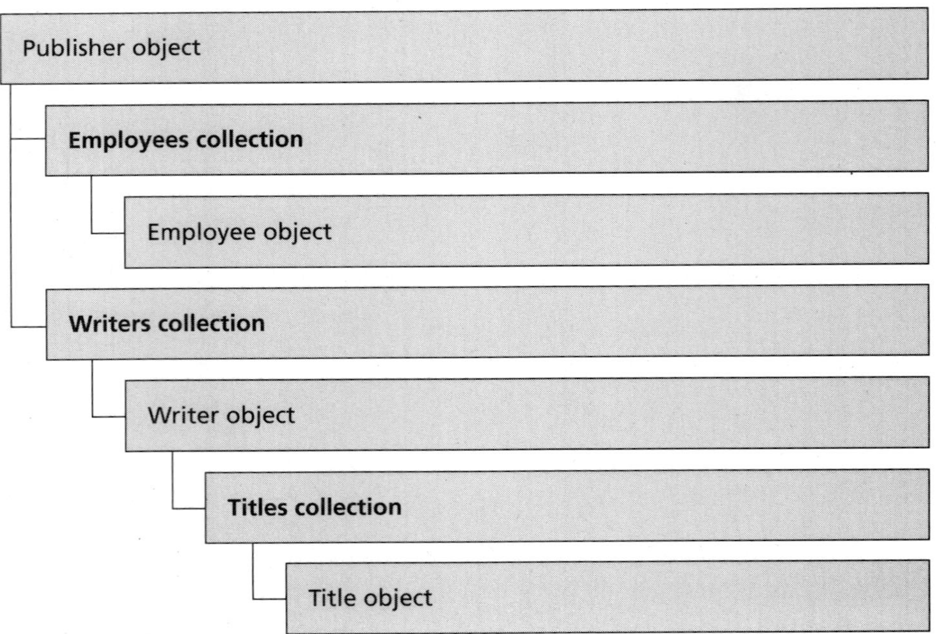

Figure 9-1: IGX object hierarchy

As shown in Figure 9-1, there is a root object called Publisher. This object supports two collections representing the employees that work for the publisher and the writers. Each of these collections contains a number of Employee and Writer objects. Each writer has written some number of books. The books created by a writer are stored in another collection called the Titles collection. There is one Titles collection for each writer. The Titles collection contains Title objects to store the individual titles written by a writer.

Each of these collections and objects is implemented as a distinct class module. The code in each collection is responsible for adding and removing its corresponding objects. For example, the methods in the Employees collection contain the code to add and remove Employee objects to and from the collection.

Another important concept in this application is the use of a project group. **Project groups** allow you to develop, test, and run multiple projects in a single instance of Visual Basic. In the IGX example, one project is used for the class modules and another project is used for the forms. Thus, the developer uses one project and the author uses the other project. The term "author" is used to define the person creating the collection hierarchy in the project and has the same meaning as it did in the last chapter pertaining to class modules. The term "author" also is typically used to identify the writer of a book. To reduce the confusion of using the same word in two different contexts, the word "writer" instead of "author" will be used to identify the person who writes books for the publisher. The term "author" will be used as it was in the previous chapter to identify the person creating the class modules. The project group combines these two projects so they both can be developed and tested in the same Visual Basic instance. Figure 9-2 shows the Project Explorer with two projects and the modules contained in those projects. Project groups are stored as individual files. The project group file stores references to the included project files. It has the file extension ".vbg."

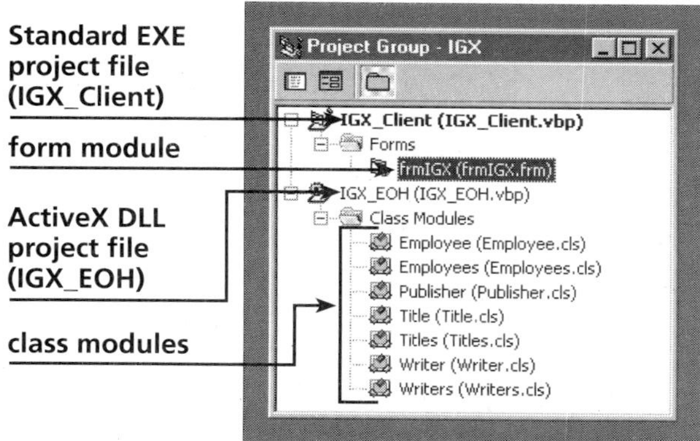

Figure 9-2: Project Explorer

As shown in Figure 9-2, the title bar of the Project Explorer contains the name of a project group rather than a specific project. Furthermore, there are two types of projects in the project group. The first project (IGX_Client) is a Standard EXE project and can be executed by the user just like any other project. The second project is an ActiveX .dll project. The project works just like the code component you created in the previous chapter. But instead of the project (form and class modules) being compiled into a single .exe file, the class modules are grouped into a second project. This project is compiled into a separate executable file that can be added to another project using the Project References dialog. The process is the same as you use to add a library like DAO.

There are class modules for the Employees, Writers, and Titles collections. These collections store Employee, Writer, and Title objects. These are implemented in the Employee, Writer, and Title classes, respectively. The final class is the Publisher class, which is the root class. In other words, the Publisher class is at the top of the object hierarchy.

To preview the completed application:

1. Open the project group named **Chapter.09\Complete\IGX_C.vbg.**
2. Activate the project named **IGX_Client** and print the code for the project. When you print the code, note that the code for the project named IGX_EOH is not printed. There is no way to print the code for all the projects at once. Click the project named **IGX_EOH** in the Project Explorer, then print the code for this project.
3. Run the program. The form should be displayed as shown in Figure 9-3.

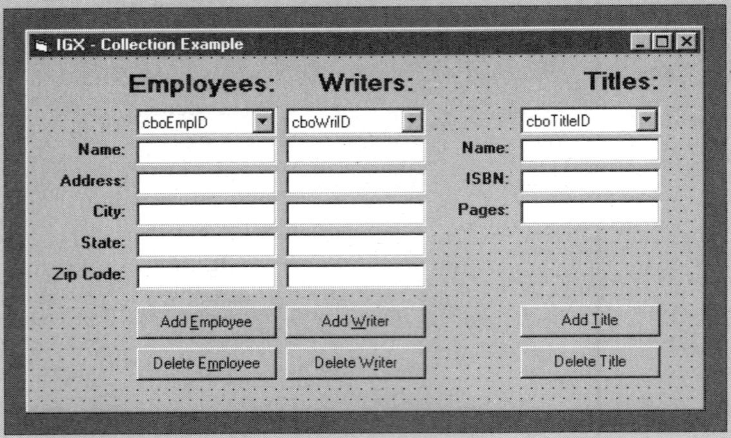

Figure 9-3: Completed form

As shown in Figure 9-3, the form contains control instances to manage the Employees, Writers, and Titles created by a writer. In practice, this data likely would be stored on different forms. The user interface, however, has been combined on a single form in this chapter for brevity.

4 Enter name, address, city, and state information into the text boxes below the Writers label and click the **Add Writer** command button. Repeat this process to add two more writers with different names.

5 Click the combo box below the writers label to select one of the writers you have added. Note that the program assigned a unique key for the writers you created.

6 Add titles corresponding to a writer. Select different writers and add more titles. Select different writers then titles. Only the titles pertaining to a specific writer are selected.

7 Click a title and remove it. Then click a writer and remove the entry. Notice that when the writer is removed, all the titles corresponding to the writer also are removed.

8 End the program then exit Visual Basic.

Designing an Object Hierarchy

Throughout this book, you have used several different collections. For example, you have used the collections and objects supported by the DAO hierarchy to navigate through a database. You have used various collections supported by Visual Basic like the Forms and Controls collections. Finally, you also have used collections that pertain to specific controls. For example, the ListImages collection contains ListImage objects for the ImageList control. Each of these predefined collections has similar characteristics. Specifically, they all support methods named Add and Remove to add and remove items. They also support a Count method or property to count the number of items in the collection. Finally, they all support the Item method, which is typically the default method, used to retrieve a specific object from the collection. Finally, the collections can be enumerated using a For Each loop. That is, you can write a For Each loop to examine each object in the collection rather than having to write a For loop.

In this chapter, you will see how to group objects, created from a class, into a collection. Collections you create are similar functionally to the collections used by different controls and the DAO hierarchy. That is, they typically support the same methods and properties to manage their objects—methods like Add and Remove. User-defined collections also are similar to arrays. Each is used to store multiple objects, usually of the same type. The number of objects stored in an array or collection can be changed dynamically at run time. User-defined collections supply functionality beyond that of conventional arrays. A collection contains methods to add and remove objects. Using an array, you must redimension manually the array to add new elements, and keep track of the elements in the array. User-defined collections typically support both a string key and numeric index to locate a specific item from within the collection. Using an array, it is necessary to code the routines to search for an element in the array. This additional functionality has a price, and that price is performance. The following list describes some of the disadvantages of using a collection instead of an array.

- By allocating and deallocating memory for objects, a collection may perform more slowly than a comparable array.
- Because each object in a user-defined collection is treated as a Variant data type, the performance suffers as with any variant reference.

When you create a collection in Visual Basic, it is created from a class just like any other object. This class is known as the Collection class, which supports the following properties and methods:

Object	**Collection**
Properties	■ The **Count** property returns the number of items in the collection. All collections created from the Collection class are one-based collections.
Methods	■ The **Add** method is used to add an item to the collection. Each item must have a unique numeric index and string key if a string key is used. ■ The **Item** method returns a Variant containing the value of the referenced item. An item in a collection can be referenced using either a numeric index or string key like most other collections. The Item method is the default method for the Collection class. ■ The **Remove** method is used to delete an item from a collection.

The Add and Remove methods have the following syntax:

Syntax	*object*.**Add** *item* [,*key*] [,*before*] [,*after*] *object*.**Remove** *index*
Dissection	■ The **Add** method adds a new *item* to the collection. ■ The **Remove** method removes an existing *item* from a collection. ■ The required *object* argument is an object expression that evaluates to an object in the Applies To list. ■ A required *item* in the collection always can be referenced by its numeric *index*. If the optional *key* is used, a string key also can be used to reference the *item* in the collection. The *key* must be unique. If an attempt is made to add an *item* with a duplicate string key, an error will occur. Like other collections, string keys are case-sensitive.

- The optional *before* and *after* arguments are used to add the *item* at a specific location in the collection. The value of the argument either can be the string key or the numeric index of an existing member of the collection. If *before* or *after* contains an index or key that does not exist, an error will occur. Either *before* or *after* can be used in the same statement but not both. If *before* is used, the *item* is added before the object referenced by the *before* argument. If *after* is used, the *item* is added after the object referenced by the *after* argument.
- The required *index* argument is used to identify the *item* in the collection to remove. It can contain an existing numeric index or string key of an *item* to remove. If no *item* exists having the specified *index*, an error will occur.

Code Example

```
Dim Employees As New Collection
Dim pempCurrent1 As New Employee
Dim pempCurrent2 As New Employee
Employees.Add pempCurrent1, "Emp1"
Employees.Add pempCurrent2, "Emp2", "Emp1"
Employees.Remove "Emp1"
```

Code Dissection

Assume that Employee is an existing class. The first Dim statement creates a new collection named Employees. Remember, collection names always should be plural. The other two Dim statements create two new object variables named pempCurrent1 and pempCurrent2. The first call to the Add method adds the object referenced by pempCurrent1 to the collection. By default, it has a numeric index of one (1). The item also can be referenced using the string key "Emp1." String keys are case-sensitive as with most collections. The second call to the Add method adds the second employee to the collection. This item is added before "Emp1" because the before argument was used. This item has a string key of "Emp2." The final statement removes "Emp1" from the collection.

Programming tip

Using string keys for all the items in a collection negates the need for the before and after arguments, as the developer no longer needs to be concerned with the positional placement of each item in the collection. When you implement a collection, always use a string key so the developer using the collection can locate items easily.

The singular name for a class and plural name for the collection that stores a reference to the instances of the class is a naming convention and is not required by Visual Basic. Visual Basic also does not require that the objects in a collection have the same underlying data type. For example, the following statements are legal assuming that Text1 has been declared:

```
Private colMisc As  New Collection
Private pempNew As New Employee
colMisc.Add Text1
colMisc.Add pempNew
```

Even though these statements are legal, they make little sense and their use is not recommended. There are limited times when it is desirable to store different types of objects in the same collection. The Controls collection is a good example. It stores references to different types of controls. Thus, the underlying type of each object is different.

In addition to the Add and Remove methods, the Collection class supports the Item method to locate a specific item in the collection.

Syntax *object*.**Item**(*index*)

Dissection

- The required *object* must contain a valid instance of the Collection class.
- The **Item** method returns an item from the specified collection and is the default method of the Collection class.
- The required *index* must contain either the numeric index or string key of an item in the collection. If an invalid index or key is used, an error will occur.

Code Example

```
Employees.Item("Emp1")
Employees.Item(1)
Employees("Emp1")
Employees(1)
```

Code Dissection The preceding statements illustrate the syntax of the Item method using both a string key and numeric index. The first two statements explicitly use the Item method. The second two statements have the same effect but take advantage of the fact that the Item method is the default method of the object. Like other objects, taking advantage of the default method or property improves performance.

Collections created from the Collection class support the For Each loop to iterate through the items in the collection. This is consistent with other collections you have used. Consider the following statements:

```
Dim Employees As Collection
Dim pempCurrent As Employee
' Code to add items to the Employees collection
For Each pempCurrent in Employees
    ' Code to reference pempCurrent
Next
```

Assuming that the Employees collection in the previous statements contains references to Employee objects, the For Each loop will iterate through the Employees collection. Each time through the loop, empCurrent will reference the next Employee object in the Employees collection.

Creating a First Collection

While you can use collections to store just about anything, a collection most commonly is used to store references to objects of the same type. For example, as you saw with the DAO hierarchy, the TableDefs collection stores references to TableDef objects, and the Recordsets collection stores a reference to zero (0) or more Recordset objects. If you create a collection and store different types of objects in the collection, you must write code to determine the object's type when it is retrieved from the collection. This can be accomplished with the TypeOf keyword in an If statement.

Suppose the program was to operate in two modes: browse mode and edit mode. In browse mode, the text boxes should be locked, and in edit mode they should be unlocked. One implementation solution is to create functions to lock and unlock the text boxes. These functions would set the Locked property of each text box to True or False, one at a time. Consider, however, another solution: it is possible to create a collection, and store in the collection a reference to each of the desired text boxes. Then, the function to lock or unlock the text boxes would iterate through the collection. Using this technique, you can create an object variable from the Collection class. Then, using the Add method, you can add references to the text boxes to the collection. Then, when setting the mode, you call a function to iterate through the collection.

To create a collection and add object references to it:

1 Start **Visual Basic** and open the project named **Chapter.09\Startup\IGX_S.vbp**. The form for this project is shown in Figure 9-4.

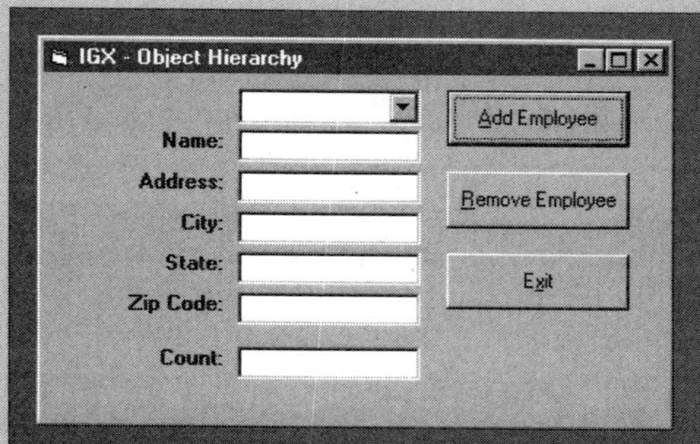

Figure 9-4: Startup form

2 Declare the following variable in the general declarations section of the form module named **frmHouses:**

```
Private mcolControls As New Collection
```

3 Enter the following statements in the **Form_Load** event procedure to add the text box references to the collection:

```
mcolControls.Add txtName
mcolControls.Add txtAddress
mcolControls.Add txtCity
mcolControls.Add txtState
mcolControls.Add txtZipCode
```

4 Create the following Sub procedure to iterate through the collection:

```
Private Sub Locked(pblnLocked As Boolean)
    Dim pctlCurrent As TextBox
    For Each pctlCurrent In mcolControls
        pctlCurrent.Locked = pblnLocked
    Next
End Sub
```

5 Create a command button named **cmdLock** and enter the following statement in the **cmdLock_Click** event procedure to lock the text boxes:

```
Locked True
```

6 Create a command button named **cmdUnlock** and enter the following statement in the **cmdUnlock_Click** event procedure to unlock the text boxes:

```
Locked False
```

7 Test the program. Enter values in each of the text boxes. Click the **Lock** command button to lock the text boxes. Try to change the contents of the text boxes. Notice that they are locked. Click the **Unlock** command button to unlock the text boxes, then verify that they are unlocked.

The code in the Locked function requires careful analysis. Like any other collection, a For Each loop is used to iterate through the individual objects in the collection.

```
Dim pctlCurrent As TextBox
```

The data type of the variable used to store the references to the individual collection members is TextBox, because all the objects in the collection are text boxes. If the collection were to store different types of controls like labels and text boxes, the object variable should have been declared as Control or Object. The For Each loop works just like the For Each loops you have used in the past. Each time through the loop, the object variable pctlCurrent stores a reference to the next text box in the collection.

```
pctlCurrent.Locked = pblnLocked
```

The properties and methods of the current text box can be accessed using the variable pctlCurrent because it references a text box. In this case, the Locked property is set to True or False for the current text box.

If different types of controls were added to the collection, each type of control must support the Locked property or an error would occur. In this situation, the TypeOf statement would be useful to verify the control's type.

Three Approaches to Creating a Collection Class

If you refer to the Microsoft documentation, you will find three different approaches described to create object hierarchies. These approaches are called the house of straw, house of sticks, and house of bricks. The differences between these three approaches lie in which properties and methods are exposed to the developer using the object hierarchy. Again, the term "author" is used to refer to the person creating the classes that make up the object hierarchy, and the "developer" is the person who uses the class modules. The following list summarizes the differences between the three approaches to implement the Employees collection and Employee class:

- In the house of straw approach, the management of the collection is performed in the form module. Because the developer has direct access to the Employees collection (form module), it is possible to add invalid objects to the collection.
- In the house of sticks approach, the Employees collection is hidden inside the Publisher class. Inside the Publisher class, there are methods to add and remove Employee objects from the collection. Because the collection is hidden from the developer, it is not possible to add invalid objects to the collection.
- In the house of bricks approach, a separate class is created to manage the collection. This has the effect of allowing polymorphism to be supported. That is, the methods of different collections can all share the same name.

Using the Collection object, you will begin to create the object hierarchy for IGX. The first step to create the hierarchy will consist of creating the root class named Publisher. This class will contain the Employees collection that will in turn contain zero (0) or more Employee objects. This object hierarchy is shown in Figure 9-5.

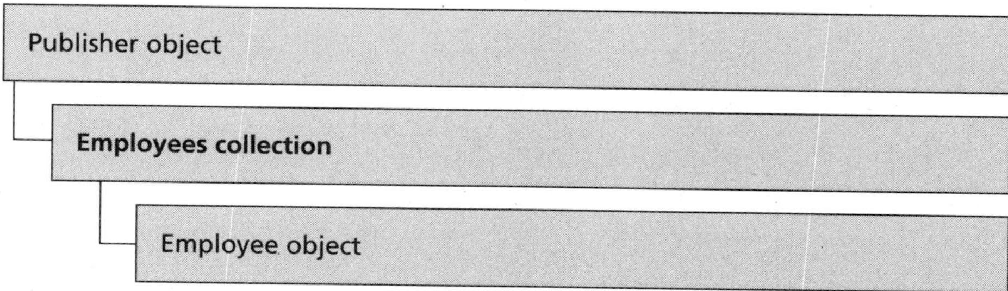

Figure 9-5: IGX object hierarchy

As shown in Figure 9-5, the Publisher object exposes a single public object—the collection named Employees. To create this public object, you use the same technique used in Chapter 8 to create a property in a class module. You create a Public variable. This Public variable is treated as a property of the class.

To create an instance of the Collection class:

1. Click **Add Class Module** on the **Project** menu to add a new class module to the project.
2. Using the Properties window, set the Name of the class to **Publisher.**
3. Enter the following statement in the class module:

```
Public Employees As New Collection
```

4. Save the class module using the name **Chapter.09\Startup\Publisher.cls.**

This code is very simple. It creates a property named Employees that is itself a collection. As such, the property is used to reference an object rather than an ordinary data type like an Integer. The name is plural to denote that the object property is a collection. The use of the term "object property" is intentional here. From the perspective of the developer, Employees is a property that references an object. As such, the term object property is used to indicate that the property does not contain an ordinary variable like an Integer or String. When an instance of the Publisher class is created, this declaration will cause a new instance of the Employees collection to be created because the New keyword is used. Consider the following statements in a form module:

```
Private mpubCurrent As New Publisher

Private Sub Form_Load( )
    Debug.Print mpubCurrent.Employees.Count
End Sub
```

When the new instance of the form module is created, the memory is allocated for the module-level variables—in this case the variable mpubCurrent. Because the New keyword is used in the declaration, an instance of the Publisher class is created. The argument to the Debug.Print statement references the Count property of the Employees collection. Of course, the value is zero (0) because no items have been added to the collection. As you can see, the Employees collection is a property of the Publisher class. It is, however, an object property.

The next step in the process is to create the class that will store each employee. Each employee will be represented by an instance of the Employee class and ultimately stored in the Employees collection. You need a mechanism to add and remove employees. Also, the Employee class will support properties to store the employee's name, address, city, state, and zip code.

To create the Employee class and its properties:

1. Click **Add Class Module** on the **Project** menu to add a new class module to the project.
2. Using the Properties window, set the Name of the class to **Employee.**
3. Save the class module using the name **Chapter.09\Startup\Employee.cls.**
4. In the general declarations section of the **Employee** class module, create the following properties to represent the data pertaining to the employee:

```
Public Name As String
Public Address As String
Public City As String
Public State As String
Public ZipCode As String
```

   Each employee will have an ID number. This will be implemented as a write-once property using the same technique presented in Chapter 8.

5. Enter the following statement in the general declarations section of the **Employee** class module. The property will correspond to the string key used to reference the employee in the Employees collection.

```
Private mstrID As String
```

6. Create the following Property procedures to implement the **ID** property:

```
Property Get ID( ) As String
    ID = mstrID
End Property

Property Let ID(pstrID As String)
    Static pblnWritten As Boolean
    If Not pblnWritten Then
        pblnWritten = True
        mstrID = pstrID
    End If
End Property
```

   Property procedures are Public by default so the Public keyword has been omitted for brevity.

The Name, Address, City, State, and ZipCode properties in the Employee class store the information for an employee. For brevity, Public variables are used. Property procedures to validate the data would be suitable for both the State and

ZipCode properties. Because the code component should not have any visible interface, the class module should raise an error if invalid data is detected. The ID property contains an identification number that is unique and cannot be changed so it is implemented as a write-once property. The technique is the same as you saw in Chapter 8.

Adding an Employee to the Employees Collection

Now that you have created the Employees collection and the Employee class, you can write the code to add Employee objects to the collection. Adding an employee to the collection can be divided into two steps. First, you need to create a new instance of the Employee class and set the properties. Then, you need to add a reference to the newly-created object to the Employees collection. In this house of straw implementation, all the remaining code is placed in the form module. This code will add new employees to the collection, remove an employee, and select a specific employee.

To add an employee:

1 Enter the following statements in the general declarations section of the **frmHouses** module to create an instance of the Publisher class:

```
Private mpubCurrent As New Publisher
```

2 Enter the following statements in the **cmdAdd_Click** event procedure in the form module:

```
Static pintID As Integer
Dim pempCurrent As New Employee
With pempCurrent
    pintID = pintID + 1
    .ID = "e" & Format(pintID, "000")
    .Name = txtName
    .Address = txtAddress
    .City = txtCity
    .State = txtState
    .ZipCode = txtZipCode
End With
mpubCurrent.Employees.Add pempCurrent, pempCurrent.ID
txtName = ""
txtAddress = ""
txtCity = ""
txtState = ""
txtZipCode = ""
cboID.AddItem pempCurrent.ID
```

3 Enter the following statements in the **cboID_Click** event procedure:

```
Dim pempCurrent As Employee
Set pempCurrent = mpubCurrent.Employees(cboID)
With pempCurrent
    txtName = .Name
    txtAddress = .Address
    txtCity = .City
    txtState = .State
    txtZipCode = .ZipCode
End With
```

4 Test the program. Enter name and address information in the text boxes, then click the **Add Employee** command button. Repeat the process to add two more employees.

5 Using the combo box, click any employee. The data pertaining to the employee is displayed.

The code for the Add Employee command button keeps track of the ID numbers for each employee in the static variable pintID. This counter is converted to a string and the character "e" is used as a prefix. Each time the procedure is executed, the value of the counter is incremented by one. The next statement creates a new instance of the Employee class. Thus, there will be one Employee object created each time this command button is clicked. Inside the With statement, the unique Employee ID is generated, and the values of the text boxes are stored in the properties of the Employee object.

```
mpubCurrent.Employees.Add pempCurrent, pempCurrent.ID
```

Remember, the Employees property has the type Collection and this collection is declared in the Publisher class. To add the current Employee object, a reference of which is stored in the object variable pempCurrent, the Add method is called with two arguments. The first is the pempCurrent object itself, and the second is the string key that uniquely identifies the object in the collection. Remember, a collection cannot contain a duplicate string key. Thus, if pempCurrent.ID contained a value that was the same as a string key already stored in the collection, an error would occur.

The final statements in the procedure clear the contents of the text boxes and add the Employee ID number to the combo box. This combo box is used to locate an employee in the collection.

```
Dim pempCurrent As Employee
Set pempCurrent = mpubCurrent.Employees(cboID)
```

The Dim statement creates an object variable to store a reference to an Employee object. When the Add method was called, the Employee ID was added to the combo box and is the same as the string key of the item in the Employees collection. Thus, cboID, when clicked, contains the string key of the employee in the Employees collection. That string key is used as the argument to the default Item method to locate an employee. Thus, the following statements are equivalent:

```
Set pempCurrent = mpubCurrent.Employees.Item(cboID)
Set pempCurrent = mpubCurrent.Employees(cboID)
```

The remaining statements use the reference to the employee stored in the object variable pempCurrent to read the values from the different properties and store those values in the text boxes.

Removing an Employee from the Collection

The process of removing an employee consists of selecting an employee using the combo box and then removing it from the Employees collection. Remember, the value in the combo box is the same as the string key for the employee in the Employees collection. Thus, it is used as the argument to the collection's Remove method.

To remove an employee from the collection:

1 Enter the following statements in the **cmdRemove_Click** event procedure for the form module:

```
If cboID.ListIndex > -1 Then
    mpubCurrent.Employees.Remove (cboID)
    cboID.RemoveItem cboID.ListIndex
    txtName = ""
    txtAddress = ""
    txtCity = ""
    txtState = ""
    txtZipCode = ""
End If
```

2 Test the program. Add an employee. Select the employee in the combo box, then click the **Remove Employee** command button.

3 Click the combo box again. The employee is removed from the combo box and from the collection. The text boxes are cleared indicating that the employee no longer exists.

The cmdRemove_Click event procedure first tests that an item is selected in the combo box. If so, the Remove method of the Employees collection is called. The Remove method takes one argument—the numeric index or string key of the object in the collection to remove. To synchronize the combo box with the collection, the item also is removed from the combo box, and the contents of the text boxes are cleared indicating that an employee is not selected.

Counting the Items in the Collection

The Count property supported by the Collection class returns the number of items in the collection. In the IGX example, you can use the Count property to display the current number of employees. This property needs to be read whenever an employee is added or removed from the Employees collection. You do not set explicitly the value of the Count property. Rather, the collection does this as items are added and removed.

To count the number of employees in the Employees collection:

1. Enter the following statement at the end of the **cmdAdd_Click** event procedure for the form module:

   ```
   lblCount = mpubCurrent.Employees.Count
   ```

2. Enter the following statement in the **cmdRemove_Click** event procedure for the form module:

   ```
   lblCount = mpubCurrent.Employees.Count
   ```

3. Test the program. Add and remove employees and notice the count of employees is displayed in the form's output label.

As the author of a class, you should create it such that the developer using the class cannot write code that will cause errors that would invalidate the object hierarchy. That is, the object hierarchy should protect itself from the developer as much as possible. As the class module presently exists, it has several deficiencies. First, and foremost, is the implementation of the Employees collection. Because the developer can reference the Employees collection directly, it is possible to add invalid objects to the collection. That is, there is no requirement that forces the developer to add Employee objects to the Employees collection. Furthermore, because the Employees collection can be referenced from anywhere in the project, any procedure can modify the collection directly. These problems are resolved using the second approach to creating an object hierarchy—the house of sticks.

Enhancing the Class—The House of Sticks

The simple object hierarchy you just created can be modified such that the robustness of the class is improved significantly. Robustness means that the developer cannot call methods or set properties that would allow invalid data to be stored in the object hierarchy. The basis of this improvement is to make the Employees collection private. Instead of the developer referencing the collection in the form module, the collection will be implemented and hidden inside the Publisher class. Hiding the collection in the Publisher class has significant implications. Because the developer no longer has access to the Employees collection, the Publisher class, which hides the collection, must contain methods to add, remove, locate, and list the items in the collection. By hiding the collection and implementing your own methods, you can hide the process of creating the Employee ID inside of the Add method, making the process transparent to the developer. More importantly, because the Publisher class is responsible for adding items to the Private collection, the possibility of the developer adding an invalid type of object is eliminated.

When hiding a collection and creating methods and properties to emulate the properties and methods of the underlying collection, you always should implement all the methods. That is, the methods you create should supply the same functionality as the Add, Remove, Item, and Count methods of the underlying collection. Of course, you also can create a more robust collection by supplying additional methods. In the IGX example, the implementation will consist of the following methods and properties:

- AddEmployee
- RemoveEmployee
- Employees
- CountEmployees

It is important to note that the method names are changed such that the Add, Remove, and Count methods all have the word Employees appended to them. In the IGX example, the Publisher class needs to support two collections. Instead of just supporting the Employees collection, it also supports the Writers collection. The Publisher class needs to support methods for both collections. Thus, the methods for the Writers collection will be AddWriter, RemoveWriter, and CountWriter. As you can see, a single method named Add would not work because there is no way to distinguish which collection to use.

The process of converting the house of straw implementation to the house of sticks implementation is relatively simple. First, the Employees collection, which was a Public collection, is converted to a Private variable causing it to be hidden in the Publisher class. Most of the code you wrote in the form module then is moved into the Publisher class to implement the methods for the Private collection.

To hide a collection from the developer:

1 Change the following statement in the Publisher class from

```
Public Employees As New Collection
```

to

```
Private mcolEmployees As New Collection
```

This creates the collection that replaces the Employees collection you created in the house of straw implementation. Instead of being publicly available to the developer, it is hidden inside the class module and no longer part of the interface.

2 Enter the following function into the Publisher class:

```
Public Function AddEmployee( ) As Employee
    Static pintID As Integer
    Dim pempCurrent As New Employee
    With pempCurrent
        pintID = pintID + 1
        .ID = "e" & Format(pintID, "000")
    End With
    mcolEmployees.Add pempCurrent, pempCurrent.ID
    Set AddEmployee = pempCurrent
End Function
```

This Function procedure will appear to the developer as a method. Remember, Public functions created in a class module are considered methods and are part of the class' interface. The code will add new employees to the collection and replaces most of the code contained in the Add Employee command button in the house of straw scenario. This code will not recycle deleted employee numbers. That is, if employee number e001 is deleted and a new employee is added, the number e001 will not be used again.

3 Enter the following Function procedure (method) in the Publisher class to remove items from the Employees collection:

```
Public Function RemoveEmployee(ByVal _
    pvntKey As Variant)
    mcolEmployees.Remove pvntKey
End Function
```

4 Enter the following Function procedure to return a reference to the collection. This has the effect of simulating the Item method.

```
Public Function Employees(ByVal pvntKey As Variant) _
    As Employee
    Set Employees = mcolEmployees.Item(pvntKey)
End Function
```

5 Enter the following Function procedure in the **Publisher** class to count the employees:

```
Public Function CountEmployee( ) As Long
    CountEmployee = mcolEmployees.Count
End Function
```

6 Modify the **cmdAdd_Click** event procedure for the form module so it contains only the following statements (changed words shown in bold):

```
Dim pempCurrent As Employee
Set pempCurrent = mpubCurrent.AddEmployee
With pempCurrent
    .Name = txtName
    .Address = txtAddress
    .City = txtCity
    .State = txtState
    .ZipCode = txtZipCode
End With
txtName = ""
txtAddress = ""
txtCity = ""
txtState = ""
txtZipCode = ""
cboID.AddItem pempCurrent.ID
lblCount = mpubCurrent.CountEmployee
```

7 Modify the **cmdRemove_Click** event procedure for the form module so it contains only the following statements (changed words shown in bold):

```
If cboID.ListIndex > -1 Then
    mpubCurrent.RemoveEmployee (cboID)
    cboID.RemoveItem cboID.ListIndex
End If
txtName = ""
txtAddress = ""
txtCity = ""
txtState = ""
txtZipCode = ""
lblCount = mpubCurrent.CountEmployee
```

8 Test the program. The program produces exactly the same results as the previous version. Instead of implementing the code to manage the Employees collection in the form, however, it is hidden in the Publisher class.

These modifications solve the primary deficiency of the previous implementation by hiding the Employees collection in the Publisher class, and creating methods to add, locate, and remove items from the collection explicitly. The developer only can reference the Employees collection through the methods you defined.

Most of the code that was in the Click event procedure for the Add Employee command button is moved into the AddEmployee method. This method takes care of assigning a unique Employee ID to the object, creating the object, then adding it to the Private collection. By computing the Employee ID in this way, the implementation is hidden from the developer. As a result, the developer cannot attempt to assign a duplicate Employee ID.

```
Set AddEmployee = pempCurrent
```

The previous statement in the AddEmployee method is not required, but improves the developer interface. After adding a new employee, the developer likely will want to set the properties for the newly-added employee. By returning a reference to the newly-added employee, the developer does not need to write any code then to locate the employee. Consider the following statements in the Add Employee command button:

```
Dim pempCurrent As Employee
Set pempCurrent = mpubCurrent.AddEmployee
pempCurrent.Name = txtName
. . .
```

These statements create an object variable named Employee to reference the Employee object that will be created. The Set statement assigns an object reference so pempCurrent contains a reference to the Employee object (returned by the AddEmployee method).

This technique is analogous to the one used when you created a new recordset. For example, consider the following statements:

```
Dim prstCurrent As Recordset
Set prstCurrent = dbCurrent.OpenRecordset("Demo.mdb")
prstCurrent.MoveFirst
```

Assume that dbCurrent referenced an existing database. The OpenRecordset and AddEmployee methods work similarly. That is, they create a new object, store a reference to the object in the corresponding collection, and return a reference to the newly-created object.

The RemoveEmployee method removes an Employee object from the Employees collection. It takes one argument—the index or string key of the item to remove. For brevity, this method does not validate that the index or key is valid, and will generate a run-time error if the key does not exist.

Because the collection actually is hidden inside the Publisher class, you must create explicitly a way for the programmer to reference a specific employee in the collection. That is, you must implement a method that will work like the Item method. The Employees method serves this purpose.

```
Public Function Employees(ByVal pvntKey As Variant) _
    As Employee
    Set Employees = mcolEmployees.Item(pvntKey)
End Function
```

This method has the effect of duplicating the Item method of a collection. This method takes one argument—the index or string key of the item in the collection to locate. This argument is passed to the mcolEmployees collection to locate the Employee in the Private collection. Again, for brevity, the error handling is omitted from this procedure. To reference this method, the following syntax is used:

```
Dim pempCurrent As Employee
Set pempCurrent = mpubCurrent.Employees(cboID)
```

While the house of sticks implementation is considerably more robust than the house of straw implementation, it has a couple of deficiencies. First, the method names must be unique so a particular collection can be identified. While this is not a drastic problem, it does not allow for the polymorphism concept of two methods having the same name. That is, if there was an Employees and a Writers collection contained by the Publisher class, it would be better to use a method named Add for both collections. Furthermore, because the Employees collection is hidden inside the Publisher class, there is no easy way to iterate through the elements in the collection using a For Each loop. Remember, to create a robust collection, you should provide a complete implementation.

Enhancing the Class—The House of Bricks

The final improvement to the object hierarchy is to implement the Employees collection in its own class module. This commonly is referred to as a **collection class.** All methods and properties to support the collection are encapsulated in a single class thereby improving the design. As indicated in the house of sticks solution, the method names would need to be unique if the Publisher class supported multiple collections. Using the house of bricks approach, however, two separate collection classes would be created. Because these exist as distinct classes, the same method names can be used. One other benefit of the house of bricks approach is that you can enable For Each support. That is, it is possible to enumerate the collection with a For Each loop.

The house of bricks implementation is very similar to the house of sticks implementation. Most of the changes pertain to creating the new Employees class and moving the code to implement the class from the Publisher class to the new Employees class.The code itself remains much the same.

To create the house of bricks:

1. Create a new class module named **Employees.** Set the Name property to **Employees** and save the class using the name **Chapter.09\Startup\Employees.cls.**
2. Declare the following variable in the **Employees** class module to hold the Private collection:

```
Private mcolEmployees As New Collection
```

3. Create the **Add** method in the class module named **Employees.**

```
Public Function Add( ) As Employee
    Static pintID As Integer
    Dim pempCurrent As New Employee
    With pempCurrent
        pintID = pintID + 1
        .ID = "e" & Format(pintID, "000")
    End With
    mcolEmployees.Add pempCurrent, pempCurrent.ID
    Set Add = pempCurrent
End Function
```

4. Create the **Remove** method in the **Employees** class module.

```
Public Function Remove(ByVal pvntKey As Variant)
    mcolEmployees.Remove pvntKey
End Function
```

5. Create the **Item** method in the **Employees** class module.

```
Public Function Item(ByVal pvntKey As Variant) _
    As Employee
    Set Item = mcolEmployees.Item(pvntKey)
End Function
```

6. Create the **Count** method in the **Employees** class module.

```
Public Function Count( ) As Integer
    Count = mcolEmployees.Count
End Function
```

7. Remove all code from the **Publisher** class module and enter the following declaration:

```
Public Employees As New Employees
```

8 Modify **cmdAdd_Click** so it contains only the following code (changes shown in bold):

```
Dim pempCurrent As Employee
Set pempCurrent = mPubCurrent.Employees.Add
With pempCurrent
    .Name = txtName
    .Address = txtAddress
    .City = txtCity
    .State = txtState
    .ZipCode = txtZipCode
End With
txtName = ""
txtAddress = ""
txtCity = ""
txtState = ""
txtZipCode = ""
cboID.AddItem pempCurrent.ID
lblCount = mPubCurrent.Employees.Count
```

9 Modify the **Remove** command button so it contains only the following code (changes shown in bold):

```
If cboID.ListIndex > -1 Then
    mPubCurrent.Employees.Remove (cboID)
    cboID.RemoveItem cboID.ListIndex
End If
txtName = ""
txtAddress = ""
txtCity = ""
txtState = ""
txtZipCode = ""
lblCount = mPubCurrent.Employees.Count
```

10 Modify the **cboID_Click** event procedure so it contains only the following code (changes shown in bold):

```
Dim pempCurrent As Employee
Set pempCurrent = mPubCurrent.Employees.Item(cboID)
With pempCurrent
    txtName = .Name
    txtAddress = .Address
    txtCity = .City
    txtState = .State
    txtZipCode = .ZipCode
End With
```

11 Test the program by adding, locating, and deleting employees. The functionality is the same as shown in the house of straw and house of sticks implementations.

The Publisher class contains the statement to create an instance of the Employees collection. Consider the following statement in the Publisher class:

```
Public Employees As New Employees
```

Whenever an instance of the Publisher class is created, the previous statement in the Publisher class creates an instance of the Employees collection. Suppose the Publisher class also supported a Writers collection. Assuming that this is the case, you would create Writers and Writer classes. The Writers class would be a collection class having the same methods as the Employees class you just created. The Writer class would resemble the Employee class. The Publisher class then would have the following declarations:

```
Public Employees As New Employees
Public Writers As New Writers
```

No matter how complex your collection hierarchy, this hierarchy of different class modules can be used. Another improvement can be made to the Publisher class. As the class currently exists, the Employees property is implemented as a Public variable. As a result, the developer can access the collection. For example, it would be legal to write the following statements in the form module:

```
Private mpubCurrent As Publishers
Set mpubCurrent.Employees = Nothing
```

Given the design principles presented in this chapter, however, it should not be possible for the developer to reference the collection directly. A simple solution to this problem is to implement the Employees property as a read-only property using a Property procedure. The technique is the same as the one presented in the previous chapter.

To implement the Employees collection as a read-only property:

1 Remove the following statement from the Publisher class:

```
Public Employees As New Employees
```

2 Enter the following statement in the general declarations section of the Publisher class module:

```
Private mempEmployees As New Employees
```

3 Create the following Property procedure in the class module:

```
Property Get Employees( ) As Employees
    Set Employees = mempEmployees
End Property
```

4 Test the program. Again, the results are the same but the developer is prevented from writing the Employees property.

Another improvement to the object hierarchy would be to define a default property for the different class modules.

Creating a Default Method or Property

Most collections use the Item method as their Default method as it is the most commonly used method. Your program as it currently exists, does not support a Default method or property, so to call the Item method, it must be referenced explicitly. Visual Basic allows a property or method in a class module to be the Default property or method. This is accomplished by activating the Code window for the desired class module, using the Procedure Attributes dialog, and selecting the property or method name.

To create a default method or property:

1. Activate the Code window for the **Employees** class.
2. Click **Procedure Attributes** on the **Tools** menu to open the dialog.
3. Click the procedure **Item** in the Name list box, then click **Advanced.** The Procedure Attributes dialog with the Advanced options is enabled as shown in Figure 9-6.

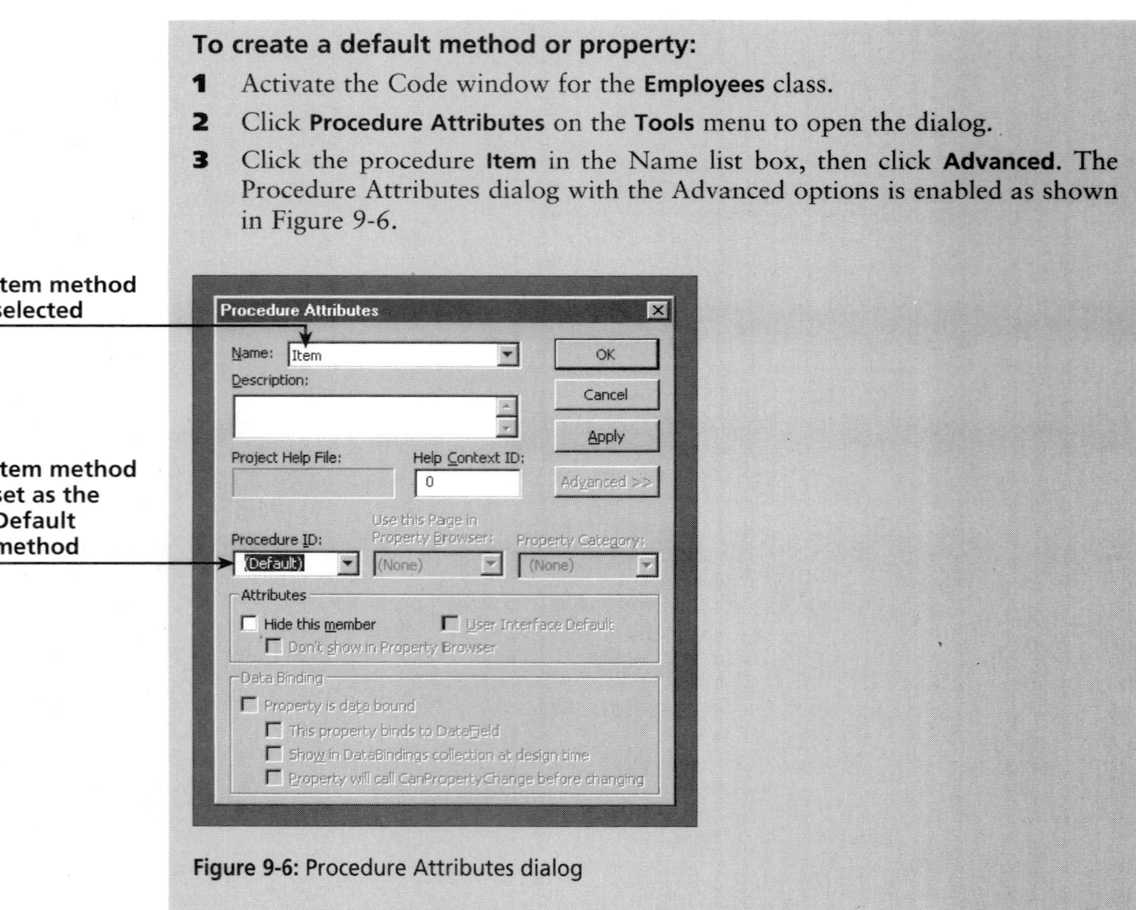

Figure 9-6: Procedure Attributes dialog

4. In the **Procedure ID** list box, click **(Default).**
5. Click **Apply** then **OK** to close the dialog.

The change you just made causes the Item method to be called if the property or method is not referenced explicitly. Consider the following statements:

```
Set pempCurrent = mpubCurrent.Employees.Item(cboID)
Set pempCurrent = mpubCurrent.Employees(cboID)
```

Prior to setting the Default property, the second of these two statements would have caused an error. Now, because Item is the Default method, no error will occur.

In addition to activating the Procedure Attributes dialog on the menu bar, it also is possible to accomplish the same task using the Object Browser. To do this, click the class in the Project/Library list box. In the Classes list, click the class you want to use. In the Members list, click the member you want, right-click the mouse button, and then click Properties. This opens the Procedure Attributes dialog.

Enabling "For Each" Support

The Employees collection class you have created supports all the methods and properties usually supported by a collection except one. Remember, collections can be iterated using a For Each loop as shown in the following statements:

```
Dim pempCurrent As Employee
For Each pempCurrent in Employees
    Debug.Print pempCurrent.Name
Next
```

If you try to include this code in your program, however, you will receive an error message indicating that the object does not support this property or method. Remember, Employees is just a class module and the actual collection named mcolEmployees is hidden inside the class. So you need a way for the developer to enumerate the Private collection declared in the class module.

The Collection class supports an object called an **enumerator**. It is by using this object that the For Each loop is able to enumerate the items in a collection. While you cannot create a method to work as an enumerator in Visual Basic, you can create a link between a method in your class module and the enumerator for the Private collection declared in the class module.

To explain how this works, we return again to the underlying COM objects. Remember, classes support at least one interface named IUnknown, but usually support multiple interfaces. Also remember, methods and properties are not called by name internally. Instead a unique number called a Procedure ID represents each method and property. The Collection class supports multiple interfaces and of course one of those interfaces is IUnknown. Furthermore, the procedure name for the enumerator is _NewEnum, and the Procedure ID is always minus four (-4). So you can expose the enumerator to the developer using your class, you must create a method for the class that will have the effect of calling the enumerator of the underlying collection named mcolEmployees. Consider the following function to define the enumerator:

```
Public Function NewEnum( ) As IUnknown
    Set NewEnum = mcolEmployees.[_NewEnum]
End Function
```

This function requires careful analysis. The function returns the enumerator of the IUnknown interface for the collection named mcolEmployees. The following statement fragment is used to reference the enumerator:

```
mcolEmployees.[_NewEnum]
```

The name requires a bit of explanation. While Visual Basic does not allow method or function names to begin with a leading underscore, you can reference the method name by surrounding it with square brackets ([ ]). The leading underscore is a convention to indicate that the member is hidden and not exposed in a type library.

Given the information presented so far, you may wonder how the For Each loop knows that the NewEnum method should be called to reference the enumerator. Remember from the discussion about COM objects in the last chapter, every property or method has a unique identification number, called a Procedure ID or Dispatch ID, and Visual Basic calls a property or method using this number. You can associate a specific Procedure ID with a method using the Procedure Attributes dialog. The process is similar to setting a Default property. The Procedure ID for the enumerator used by the For Each loop is minus four (-4). Thus, using the Procedure Attributes dialog and setting the Procedure ID to minus four (-4) is the final step to enable For Each support. It is by using the Procedure ID that Visual Basic calls the method rather than using the name. Thus, you could call the NewEnum function anything so long as the Procedure ID is set correctly.

To enable For Each Support for a collection:

1 Enter the following statements in the **Employees** class module:

```
Public Function NewEnum( ) As IUnknown
    Set NewEnum = mcolEmployees.[_NewEnum]
End Function
```

2 Click **Procedure Attributes** on the **Tools** menu, then click the **NewEnum** function. Click the **Advanced** button.

3 In the Procedure ID text box enter the value **–4**, then click **Apply**. Click **OK** to close the Procedure Attributes dialog.

4 To test the procedure, create a command button named **cmdTestEnum** with the caption **Test Enumerator**, then enter the following statements:

```
Dim pempCurrent As Employee
For Each pempCurrent In mpubCurrent.Employees
    Debug.Print pempCurrent.Name
Next
```

5 Test the program. Add several employees then click the **Test Enumerator** command button to execute the For Each loop. The name of each employee should appear in the Immediate window.

6 Exit Visual Basic.

As you can see, the process of using an enumerator with a Private collection is a rare instance where a basic knowledge of COM objects is not only helpful but necessary. In this case, you can see how both the IUnknown interface and the Procedure ID are used.

You have completed the programming for this section. As you have seen, there are three techniques that can be used to create an object hierarchy from multiple class modules. You also have seen how to improve the robustness of a class module by including support for a Default property and method, and proper use of hidden collections.

SECTION B

objectives

In this section you will:

- Expand the object hierarchy to include more classes and collections
- Use the Class Builder utility to create a template for an object hierarchy
- Work with multiple projects at the same time using a project group
- Understand the different types of servers supported by Visual Basic
- Change the properties of a class module to control how the class can be used from outside the project

Creating an ActiveX Server

Expanding the Object Hierarchy

The object hierarchy you created is much simpler than the one shown in the completed example. There are two significant differences between the completed application and the example you have created. First, the Publisher class supports two collections instead of just one. That is, the Publisher class supports both the Employees and Writers collections. Consider the following statements:

```
Private mempEmployees As New Employees
Private mwriWriters As New Writers

Property Get Employees( ) As Employees
    Set Employees = mempEmployees
End Property

Property Get Writers( ) As Writers
    Set Writers = mwriWriters
End Property
```

As you can see from the above statements, both the Writers and Employees collections are hidden inside the Publisher class module. Both are implemented as read-only properties. Second, the Writer object supports another collection called the Titles collection. This collection stores Title objects to identify the books pertaining to a writer. Consider the following declaration in the Writer class:

```
Private colTitles As New Titles
```

When an instance of the Writer class is created, an instance of the Titles collection is created for the writer. Thus, for each writer there will be a Titles collection. The Titles collection in turn contains the necessary methods to add, remove, and reference

Title objects in the Titles collection. The code in the Titles collection is nearly identical to the code in the Writers and Employees collections.

Using the techniques presented in this chapter, you now can see how to continue to expand the object hierarchy. Specifically, you can add multiple collections to an object as shown with the Publisher class containing the Writers and Employees collections. You also can expand the depth of the hierarchy as shown with the Titles collection.

Using the Class Builder Utility

As you can see, creating the collections and classes for an object hierarchy quickly can become a tedious process. Visual Basic supports a tool called the Class Builder that will help you to build a template for your object hierarchy. It creates methods for Collection classes automatically and can be used to create the function prototypes for the properties and methods supported by the individual class. Figure 9-7 shows the Class Builder utility with a simulated object hierarchy.

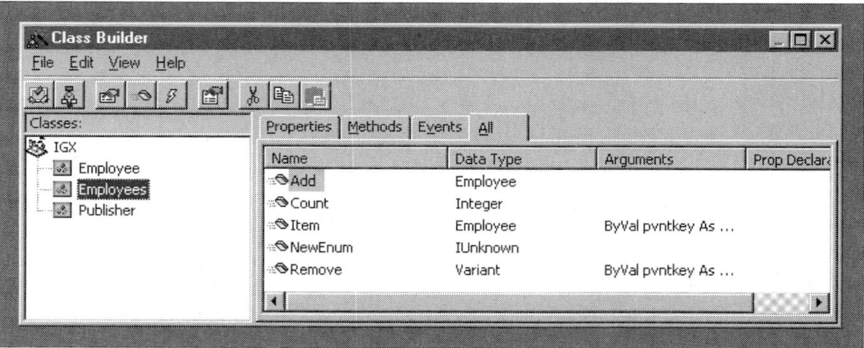

Figure 9-7: Class Builder utility

The Class Builder utility is most useful with a new project. If used with a project having existing classes, the Class Builder cannot place those classes in the object hierarchy. You must do this yourself by writing the code manually.

The File menu contains options to create new collections and classes. When a new collection is created, the Add, Remove, Item, Count, and NewEnum methods are created for you automatically. When you create a new class, you then can create the properties and methods of the class. The dialogs used to create properties and methods allow you to specify the data type of the property and whether to implement the property as a Property procedure or a Public variable.

Most automated development tools have limitations and the Class Builder is no exception. While very useful, it has limitations if you supply bad input data.

For example, if you try to create a property in a class and a collection of the same name in the same class, the utility may generate unpredictable results.

Whether or not to use the Class Builder utility is up to you. But once you have become familiar with its interface, the Class Builder can be an invaluable tool to prototype an object hierarchy and remove the tedium of its creation.

More About the Project

In the previous chapters, you have created a type of project called a Standard EXE project. This type of project usually has a visual interface (forms), although a visual interface is not required. Standard EXE projects are stand-alone projects. That is, they can be run directly from the command line, Start menu, shortcut, or other means. Windows supports executable files that, rather than being run from the command line, are executed from other programs. Consider a program like the Jet database engine. You do not execute the Jet database engine by executing it from the command line. Rather, the code executes when called by another program. This type of project is known by many names. Some common names include library or server. Visual Basic supports three other project types that are used to create servers designed to be used by other programs.

The type of project, and properties pertaining to the project, are used to determine the type of executable file that is created when a program is compiled. Consider the object hierarchy you have created. An object hierarchy like this provides a general set of services that could be useful to many programs. While a developer could add the class modules to the project to use them, it is possible to create a project containing only the class modules that pertain to the object hierarchy, and compile the modules into a server. The developer then can use the Components or References dialogs to add the server to the project.

When you create a server, you are creating a library that can be referenced by any program on the computer. Using the common ActiveX terminology, this library commonly is referred to as a **code component**.

When you use a code component like the DAO hierarchy, consider the relationship between your program and the code component. As your program runs, it occasionally calls the methods and properties supported by DAO. In other words, your program uses the services of DAO. This model of interaction between two programs commonly is referred to as a **client-server** model. Your program is considered the client, and the program that provides the DAO services is considered the server. When you create a class or group of classes, you can create an executable file that will behave as a server much like the DAO hierarchy. One characteristic of servers is the capability to support multiple clients at the same time. In the case of DAO, you can run multiple instances of Visual Basic and multiple programs that all rely on the DAO services.

As you develop a server, it is common to create a client to test the server as it is being created. This is what you did in the previous section. The server, in this case the Publisher class, can be implemented as a code component. In addition to creating the server, there is another task that is critical for the server to work correctly on the computer. As you probably are aware, the Windows Registry stores information about the programs residing on the computer. Again, consider what happens when you use the Components and References dialogs. The information about the different libraries and ActiveX controls actually is not stored inside Visual Basic. Rather, the information is stored in the Windows Registry. When you open these dialogs, the Windows Registry information is read and the component or controls registered on the system are displayed.

The object hierarchy can be compiled as a server, registered on the system, and accessed as a code component. To accomplish this, you must learn about two important concepts.

- Ultimately, the completed code component will be compiled into an executable library. From the development and testing perspective, however, it would be helpful to create two projects in one Visual Basic instance—one project containing the code component and another project to test the code component.
- The second key concept is to understand how servers are created, what happens on the computer when a server is created, and the different types of servers.

First, you will learn how to work with multiple projects at the same time. Second, you will learn more about project files, and the additional types of projects supported by Visual Basic.

Working with Project Groups

Previous versions of Visual Basic allowed one project to be open at a time. When developing a code component, however, it often is desirable to work with multiple projects at the same time. Consider the program you are creating for IGX. The class modules that implement the object hierarchy will be implemented as a code component. To make the code component easier to test and debug, you can create one project for the code component (class module), and a separate project for the form modules that use the code component. Visual Basic can load and run both projects at the same time using what is called a **project group**. A project group is really just a way to execute and debug the code contained in multiple projects at the same time. Project groups also are helpful when creating ActiveX controls, as you will see in subsequent chapters. Remember, a project contains form, class, and standard modules, and each module is stored in a separate text file. The project file in turn contains a reference to all the modules in a project. Also, the project group in turn contains a reference to all the projects in a project group. Figure 9-8 illustrates the relationship between these files.

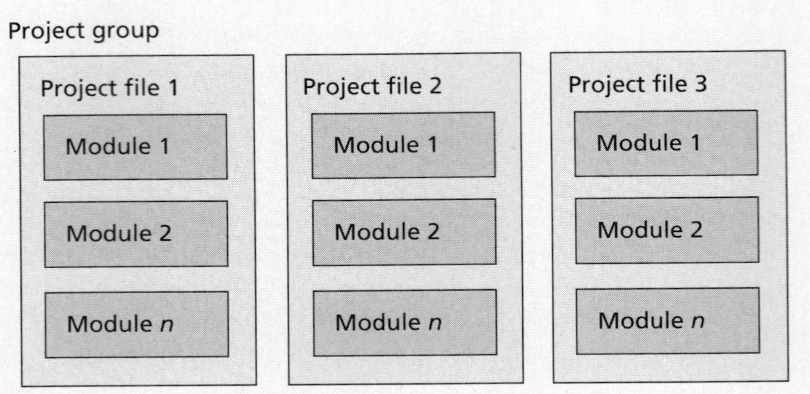

Figure 9-8: Project group

Before going into the details about the types of servers, and the implication of the server type on the performance of the program, you will learn how to create a project group, add and remove projects from the project group, and see how to debug two projects at the same time.

Adding a Project to a Project Group

Adding a project to a project group is accomplished by clicking Add Project on the File menu. The Add Project dialog appears allowing you to add an existing project or create a new project. When the second project is added, a project group automatically is created. Additional options appear on the File menu allowing you to save the project group. Project groups have a name much like projects. The name of the project group is the same as the file name on the disk. Project groups, by default, have the file extension ".vbg."

Creating a project group does not imply that the underlying projects cannot be opened and edited independently. In fact, the opposite is true. Creating a project group does nothing to the underlying project files. They can be opened, saved, and manipulated as if the project group did not even exist.

Projects can be removed from a project group by selecting the project in Project Explorer, then clicking Remove Project on the File menu. The project file is not removed from the disk. Rather, the project file is removed from the project group, which has the effect of disassociating the project file from the project group.

In the IGX example, you will create a project group with two projects. The first project will contain the form and user interface that uses the objects in the code component. The second project will contain the class modules that make up the code component. The significance of separating the two projects will become apparent in a moment when the code component is compiled into a server.

To create a project group:

1 Start **Visual Basic** and create a new Standard EXE project. Remove the form named **Form1**. Add the form named **Chapter.09\Startup\frmHouses.** Using the Project Properties window, set the Startup Object to **frmHouses.** Set the project name to **IGX_Client**, then save it using the name **Chapter.09\Startup\ IGX_Client.vbp.**

2 Create a second standard EXE project by clicking **Add Project** on the **File** menu. Remove the form from the project. Add the following class modules to this project. Use the class modules named **Publisher**, **Employees**, and **Employee** in the **Chapter.09\Startup** folder. These are the classes you created in the previous section. Be careful that you are adding the class modules to the correct project. Set the name of the second project to **IGX_EOH** and save the project using the name **IGX_EOH.vbp**. After adding the forms and class modules to the two projects, the Project Explorer should look like Figure 9-9.

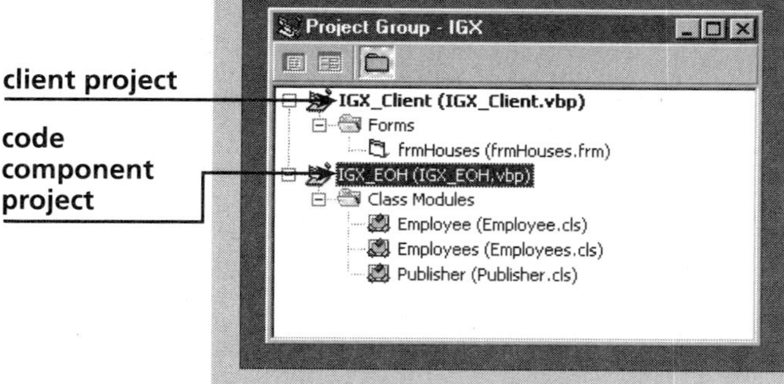

Figure 9-9: Project Explorer

3 Save the project group by clicking **Save Project Group** on the **File** menu. Set the name of the project group to **IGX.vbg**.

In the IGX example, the project group contains two projects. You certainly can have more than two projects in a project group, however. For example, if two code components were being developed concurrently, you could add both code components to the project group along with the client project and its forms that used the two code components. In fact, a project group can contain as many projects as you want.

Setting the Startup Project

In a single project application, you have set the Startup object either to a form or the Sub Main procedure in a standard module. But because a project group contains multiple projects, you must not only define the Startup object for a project, but which project is executed first when execution begins. (Visual Basic switches from design mode to run mode.) You select the startup project by right-clicking the mouse button on a project in Project Explorer and clicking the Set as Startup command.

To set the Startup project:

1. Open **Project Explorer** then click the project named **IGX_Client.**
2. Right-click the mouse button over the project then click the **Set as Startup** option.
3. Test the project group. You will receive a compile error indicating that the user-defined type is not defined, and the following line is highlighted in the Code window:

   ```
   Dim mpubCurrent As New Publisher
   ```

4. End the program.

The same form and class modules worked when used in the single project illustrated in the previous section. Suddenly, however, they do not work in a project group. The cause of this problem is rather interesting. In the previous section, the form was able to create objects from the Publisher class because they were in the same project. Now, however, the two projects are disconnected. To make the project group work as intended requires that you learn about the different types of servers supported by Visual Basic, type libraries, and the Windows Registry.

Creating a Client-Server Project Group

Getting the project group to work, and configuring the project named IGX_EOH so it is treated by Visual Basic as a code component (server) and compiled that way, requires that you understand three distinct but intertwined topics.

- Using the appropriate type of server—ActiveX DLL or ActiveX EXE
- Adding the code component to the client project
- Setting the Instancing property of the class modules

Remember, the client project can no longer locate the objects in the server project containing the class modules. The client program must add the server as a code component just as the DAO library must be added before it can be used. Again, a code component is added using the References dialog. If you try to add the code component, however you will find that it does not appear in the dialog. Before the Visual Basic run-time environment treats the code component as a server, its project type must be changed. By converting the project to a server, another property named Instancing must be set for each of the class modules. This property controls whether a class module is visible outside the code component and whether or not a client can create an instance of the class.

Types of Projects Supported by Visual Basic

In addition to Standard EXE projects, Visual Basic supports other types of projects used to create both servers and ActiveX controls. The following list describes the characteristics of the different project types.

- ActiveX DLL and ActiveX EXE servers are used to create programs that provide services to other programs. The servers typically, and often, cannot have a visual component, and both are considered code components. What happens when a client connects to a server depends on whether it is created as a DLL server or an EXE server. The difference between the two types of servers will be discussed in a moment.
- ActiveX control projects are used to create ActiveX controls that can be used in other projects and other computers. ActiveX controls you create have the same capabilities and characteristics of other controls you have used. That is, the Components dialog is used to add the control on the Toolbox. Once added on the Toolbox, it can be used in a project.
- ActiveX documents have a visual interface and code like a standard module. They combine code and data in a "document," and are suitable for use with other programs like Microsoft Binder and Web applications.

In this chapter, DLL and EXE servers will be discussed.

A Word About Executing Programs

When you run a standard EXE file created by Visual Basic, the program is read into memory from the disk and executed. This running instance of your program is called a **process**. Imagine what happens if you run a second copy of the same program at the same time. That is, two instances of the same standard EXE file. Windows loads a second copy of the program and creates a second process. Each process has its own private copy of its code and data. That is, assigning a value to a variable in one process will not affect the value of the same variable in the second process. Furthermore, each process can, and most likely will, be executing different statements. For example, assume that the program that is executing has a long running loop. Each instance of the program likely will be at a different point in the loop. In other words, each process has a unique execution point. This is called a **thread** or **thread of execution**.

Another important concept is that Windows is a **multitasking operating system**. That is, the operating system takes care of running multiple programs seemingly at the same time. How exactly Windows performs this task is beyond the scope of this book. In essence, Windows keeps a list of all the processes running on the computer. Processes are created from many sources. When you run a program, a process is created. You may have virus-checking software running in the background. These too are processes. As you access different libraries on the system, processes may be created. Each process can be in one of three different states. First, it can be running; the code in the process currently is executing. Second, it can be blocked. When a process is blocked, it is waiting for some external operation to complete, like reading data from the disk. Third, a process also can be idle. An idle process is runable but is waiting for the CPU. Windows allocates a fixed amount of CPU time to each runable process giving the user the illusion that multiple programs are executing at once. In reality, Windows only executes one program at a time, but switches back and forth between programs very quickly. This is not true for computers that have multiple CPUs. When a computer has multiple processors, each processor can be running a separate program.

We have said that Visual Basic supports ActiveX EXE servers and ActiveX DLL servers. These two types of servers are very different. Most notably, when an ActiveX EXE server is created, a new server process is created. When a standard EXE file calls a function in an ActiveX EXE server, two processes are created—one for the client program and another for the EXE server. This is called an **out of process** server. Figure 9-10 illustrates an out of process server.

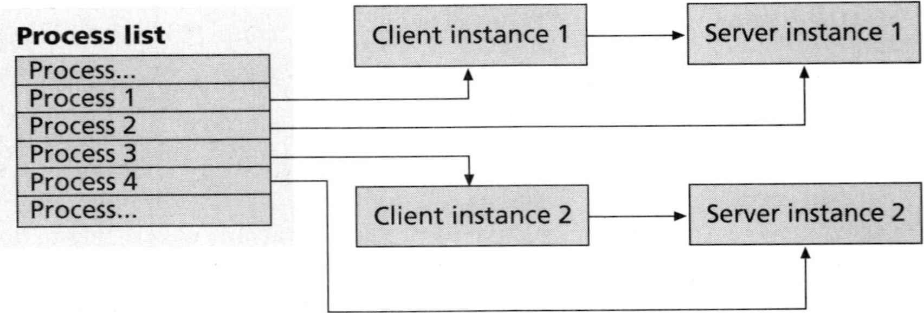

Figure 9-10: Out of process server

Assume that the code component was compiled as an EXE server, and assume that either of two separate client programs use the object hierarchy in the EXE server. Given this scenario, each client is considered a separate process. Additionally, a separate process is created for each of the servers. Conceptually, it is very similar to two copies of the same standard EXE program. Thus, four distinct processes are created and managed by Windows.

When the code in a DLL server is executed, a new process is not created. Rather, the code is executed in the process that called the DLL server. This is called an **in process** server. Figure 9-11 illustrates an in process DLL server.

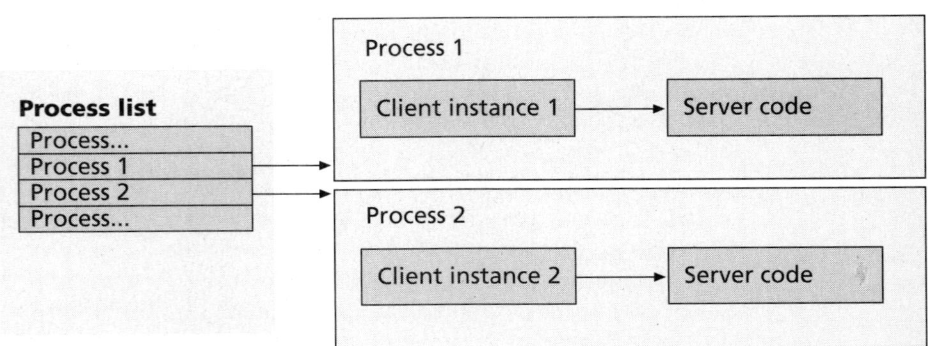

Figure 9-11: In process server

As shown in Figure 9-11 only two processes are created. One process is created for each client. An additional process is not created for the DLL server. The following list describes the pertinent characteristics of EXE and DLL servers:

- EXE servers always are run as out of process servers.
- DLL servers always are run as in process servers.
- When a client executes an EXE server, a process must be created and the EXE server loaded into memory. Thus, it takes considerably longer to execute an EXE server initially than a DLL server.
- When code in a DLL server is executed, a small amount of initialization code is loaded for the code component, rather than the entire module. When a method is called or a property read or written, the code for the property or method is loaded. Thus, in a large module where only a few of the properties or methods are used, a DLL server will provide better performance.

The Project Properties dialog is used to establish how a project is compiled and how the project is viewed in the Visual Basic IDE as part of a project group. When the project type is set to an ActiveX EXE or DLL server, it is enabled as a code component for the other projects in the project group. In other words, the project will appear in the References dialog. Several other pertinent pieces of information also are specified using this dialog. The Project Properties dialog is shown in Figure 9-12.

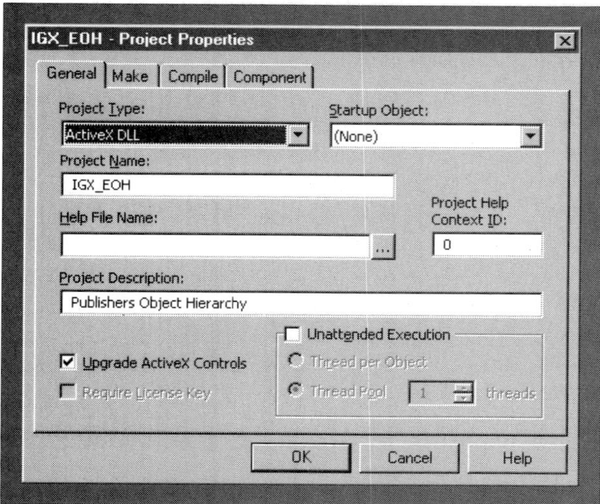

Figure 9-12: Project Properties dialog

The data specified in this dialog is vital to making a code component function properly. The following list identifies the different fields of this dialog and the field's significance:

- The Project Type list box identifies how Visual Basic compiles a program. Visual Basic can create standard EXE files, ActiveX EXE and DLL servers, ActiveX controls, and documents.

- The Project Name list box has two purposes. It is the name saved in the Windows Registry to identify the program. The name of the project also is displayed in the Object Browser.
- The Project description is used by the Object Browser for ActiveX controls and the Components dialog for ActiveX EXE and DLL servers. Thus, it is important to select a meaningful description for any components you create.
- The Unattended Execution check box is valid only for EXE servers. This option is used to create a type of server called a multithreaded server. Multithreaded servers are described later in the chapter.

While a detailed explanation of the Windows Registry is beyond the scope of this chapter, suffice it to say that code components, like the one you are creating, are made known to other programs on the system via the Windows Registry. When you compile an EXE or DLL server, Visual Basic adds your program to the Windows Registry automatically. In the IGX example, you will convert the project named IGX_EOH.vbp to a DLL server (code component).

To create the code component:

1. Click the project named **IGX_EOH.vbp**.
2. Click **IGX_EOH Properties** on the **Project** menu. Set the Project Type to **ActiveX DLL**, the Project Name to **IGX_EOH**, the Project Description to **Publishers Object Hierarchy**, then the Startup Object to **(None)**. Close the dialogs.
3. Select the project named **IGX_Client** in Project Explorer.
4. Click **References** on the **Project** menu. Using the scroll bars, locate the item named **IGX_EOH**. This is the description for the project you set using the Project Properties dialog. Check the check box to add a reference to the library to the project. Close the dialog.
5. Test the project group again. This time you will receive an error indicating that no publicly creatable class module is found. You will learn how to correct this problem in a moment.

At this point, if you were to compile the project named IGX_EOH, a DLL server would be created and saved on the system. Furthermore, the necessary information is written to the Windows Registry so the code component could be added to any project with or without a project group. Also, the information about the type library is saved to the Windows Registry. If the code component was distributed to another computer, the setup program must update the Windows Registry properly so the code component can be located.

If you tried to run the client project at this time, however, you still would produce an error. This is because of another concept called class instancing.

Class Instancing

In addition to the Name property, every class supports another property called **Instancing**. As the name implies, the value of the Instancing property controls whether or not an instance of a specific class can be created from outside a project. There are six possible values for the Instancing property.

1. The default **Private** option means when you create a Standard EXE project that uses class modules, it is not possible to create a code component that can be referenced by other projects. That is, the objects in the class module(s) are visible only to the project where the class module exists. In other words, the class module and modules that use the class module must exist in the same project file.
2. To explain the **PublicNotCreatable** option, consider the Recordset object and other DAO objects you have used. The recordset is public, meaning that it is exposed in the type library. This means it is visible in the Object Browser rather than being hidden in the class. NotCreatable means that you cannot create explicitly a new instance of the object. In other words, the following statement will generate an error, "Invalid use of New keyword," if the Instancing property of the class module is set to PublicNotCreatable.

   ```
   Dim prstCurrent As New Recordset
   ```

   Typically, calling the method(s) of another object creates an instance of the class. For example, calling the OpenRecordset method pertaining to the Database object creates a recordset.
3. The **SingleUse** option pertains only to ActiveX EXE servers and cannot be used by ActiveX DLL servers. When an object is created from a class that is declared as SingleUse, a new instance of the server is started for each class instance; that is, another process is created.
4. **GlobalSingleUse** is like the SingleUse option but it creates a global object. It is not necessary to declare an instance of the global object when the component is added to the client program. Rather, it is predefined. This is like the DBEngine object used by DAO. You do not need explicitly to create an instance of the DBEngine. Rather, it is predefined.
5. Both ActiveX EXE and DLL servers can use the **MultiUse** option. Like SingleUse, multiple instances of the class can be created, but in the case of an ActiveX EXE server, only one instance of the server is created and shared by all the processes using the server.
6. **GlobalMultiUse** is used to create global objects that can be referenced without being declared. This is similar to predefined objects supported by Visual Basic like the Printer, Clipboard, and Screen objects.

Consider the code component you are creating. A project that uses the code component should be able to create a new instance of the Publisher class. The MultiUse or GlobalMultiUse options would be suitable. If the MultiUse option were chosen, an instance of the Publisher class would need to be created explicitly.

This is the technique you have been using. If the GlobalMultiUse option were chosen, however, then a global object variable is created having the same name as the project name. Thus, the following statements would be legal to add an employee to the Employees collection:

```
Dim pempCurrent As Employee
Set pempCurrent = IGX_EOH.Employees.Add
```

Consider also the situation with the other two class modules. Both the Employees collection and Employee class should be thought of as dependent objects; that is, it should not be possible explicitly to create an instance of the objects. Thus, the following two statements should cause an error. This behavior is desirable because the Publisher class creates an instance of the Employees collection when the class is initialized. Furthermore, adding and removing employees from the collection should be performed by the methods you created in the Employees class module.

```
Dim pempNew As New Employee
Dim pempsNew As New Employees
```

As you have seen, however, it is useful to declare object variables to create an additional reference to an existing object. For example, the Add method of the Employees class creates a new instance of an Employee and returns a reference to that instance. Thus the following statements should be legal:

```
Dim pemp As Employee, pubCurrent As New Publisher
Set pemp = pubCurrent.Employees.Add
```

To achieve this behavior you can use the PublicNotCreatable value for the Instancing property. In the IGX example, the Employees and Employee classes should be PublicNotCreatable, and the Publisher class GlobalMultiUse.

To set the Instancing property for the class modules:

1. In Project Explorer, right-click the class module named **Employee**. Click **Properties** on the pop-up menu to activate the class module. Set the Instancing property to **PublicNotCreatable**.
2. For the Employees class module, set the Instancing property to **PublicNotCreatable**.
3. For the Publisher class module, set the Instancing property to **GlobalMultiUse**.
4. To test the Instancing property, run the project. It should work as before.

Just as creating default properties for classes and collections and enabling For Each support for collections, setting the Instancing property of the class module will improve further the developer interface.

An Introduction to Multithreading

We said in the previous section that a separate process is created for each ActiveX EXE server. An ActiveX EXE server, however, can be created with unique characteristics that allows a single server process to be created. Visual Basic does not support multithreaded clients (standard EXE files). Each process accessing the server can have a unique thread of execution. That is, each client that accesses the server has its own virtual copy of the object.

Visual Basic imposes a few restrictions on multithreaded servers. First and foremost, a multithreaded server cannot have any visual interface elements. This means that the server cannot display a form, message box, common dialog, or any other visual element. Creating a multithreaded server is accomplished by setting an option in the Project Properties dialog. If the Unattended Execution check box is checked, the server will be compiled as a multithreaded server.

In this section you have implemented only part of the object hierarchy illustrated in the completed program. The techniques to extend the object hierarchy are the same as those shown in the previous chapter. Consider reviewing the completed program to see how a single class can support multiple collections.

SECTION C

objectives

In this section you will:

- Use the GlobalMultiUse Instancing property setting to create a predefined object
- Use underlying DAO objects to create a persistent object hierarchy based on the Publisher class hierarchy

Creating a Persistent Collection Hierarchy

Creating an Object Hierarchy with Persistent Data

While the program as it presently exists illustrates how to create a hierarchy of objects, the data is not persistent. That is, the data is not stored on the disk and is not persistent from one invocation of the program to another. Conceptually, solving this problem is very simple. When an instance of the Publisher class is created, the data pertaining to the publisher must be read from the disk. Additionally, employees and writers that work for the publisher also must be loaded so the program can reference them. Furthermore, as new employees, writers, and titles are added, changed and deleted, that information also must be saved.

Consider first the implementation possibilities pertaining to the author of the class module. One option would be to read and write data to text or random files. The other would be to use a database and implement the object hierarchy in a manner similar to the DAO hierarchy. One possible implementation is to convert the house of bricks collection to read and write data from a database using the same hierarchy that was used in the first section. The developer interface for the code component also is a consideration. One possibility would be to implement the objects so they closely resemble the objects in the DAO hierarchy. That is, you would allow the developer to open recordsets and essentially mirror the functionality of DAO. One of the benefits of implementing a collection hierarchy like this, however, is to insulate the developer from the mechanical details of accessing the underlying data. As such, we will present in this chapter one possible implementation that will allow the developer to use persistent data that uses the same collections presented in the first section. This way, the developer can view the data as it pertains to the organization without having to know about the underlying details of opening recordsets or manipulating them. Furthermore, you could change the type of database used to manage the underlying data without the developer being affected because the data access methods are hidden inside the code component and not exposed to the developer.

To illustrate persistent data, the completed program from the chapter has been modified to read data from the database when the program is run. The database itself is named IGX.mdb. There are three tables in the database named tblEmployees, tblWriters, and tblTitles. These tables correspond to the Employees, Writers, and Titles collections. The records in the table are represented as objects in the respective collection. For example, each employee record in the tblEmployee table is stored as an Employee object in the Employees collection. The structure of the class modules is largely unchanged. The modifications involve reading the data from the database when the program is started.

To view the revised application:

1. Open the project group named **Chapter.09\Database\IGX.vbg.**
2. Print the code for both projects.
3. Run the program. Click the combo boxes to display the employees and writers.
4. After selecting a writer, click the **Titles** combo box. The titles pertaining to the writer are displayed.

The first change in the program is to read the contents of the database when the form is loaded. This involves calling a new procedure from the Form_Load event procedure. The procedure is declared in the Publisher class.

```
Set mpubCurrent = _
    pubEngine.OpenPublisher( _
    "A:\Chapter.09\Database\IGX.mdb")
For Each pempCurrent In mpubCurrent.Employees
    cboEmpID.AddItem pempCurrent.ID
Next
For Each pwriCurrent In mpubCurrent.Writers
    cboWriID.AddItem pwriCurrent.ID
Next
```

The preceding statements call the OpenPublisher method of the pubEngine object. The pubEngine class has its Instancing property set to GlobalMultiUse so the object variable is predefined. As you will see in a moment, this procedure loads the database records into the appropriate collections. The two For Each loops, using the data from the collection, load the contents of the Employees and Writers combo boxes.

At the heart of the changes, is the addition of the OpenPublisher method and modifications to the Add method for the various collections.

```
Public Function OpenPublisher(pstrDB As String) _
    As Publisher
    Dim pwriCurrent As Writer
    Dim pempCurrent As Employee
    Dim pttlCurrent As Title
    Dim prstCurrent As Recordset
    Dim prstTitles As Recordset
    Dim pstrSQL As String
    Set gdbPublisher = OpenDatabase(pstrDB)
    Set prstCurrent = gdbPublisher.OpenRecordset("tblWriters")
    Do Until prstCurrent.EOF
        Set pwriCurrent = _
            mwriWriters.Add(prstCurrent![fldID])
        pwriCurrent.ID = prstCurrent![fldID]
        pwriCurrent.Name = prstCurrent![fldName]
        pwriCurrent.Address = prstCurrent![fldAddress]
        pwriCurrent.City = prstCurrent![fldCity]
        pwriCurrent.State = prstCurrent![fldState]
        pwriCurrent.ZipCode = prstCurrent![fldZipCode]
        pstrSQL = "SELECT * FROM tblTitles" _
            " WHERE fldID = " & "'" & _
            pwriCurrent.ID & "'"
        Set prstTitles = _
            gdbPublisher.OpenRecordset(pstrSQL)
        Do Until prstTitles.EOF
            Set pttlCurrent = _
                pwriCurrent.Titles.Add( _
                prstTitles![fldISBN])
            pttlCurrent.ID = prstTitles![fldISBN]
            pttlCurrent.ISBN = prstTitles![fldISBN]
            pttlCurrent.Name = prstTitles![fldName]
            pttlCurrent.Pages = prstTitles![fldPages]
            prstTitles.MoveNext
        Loop
        prstCurrent.MoveNext
    Loop
    Set prstCurrent = _
        gdbPublisher.OpenRecordset("tblEmployees")
    Do Until prstCurrent.EOF
```

```
        Set pempCurrent = _
            mempEmployees.Add(prstCurrent![fldID])
        pempCurrent.ID = prstCurrent![fldID]
        pempCurrent.Name = prstCurrent![fldName]
        pempCurrent.Address = prstCurrent![fldAddress]
        pempCurrent.City = prstCurrent![fldCity]
        pempCurrent.State = prstCurrent![fldState]
        pempCurrent.ZipCode = prstCurrent![fldZipCode]
        prstCurrent.MoveNext
    Loop
    Set OpenPublisher = Me
End Function
```

The OpenPublisher method accepts one argument, the name of the database to open. The structure of the procedure is the same as other procedures you have created to process the records in a recordset. The recordset is created using the OpenRecordset method. Then, a Do loop is used to examine each of the records. First, the table named tblWriters is examined. For each record, an item is added to the Private collection named mriWriters. Remember, each writer can have one or more titles. As such, there is a Titles collection for each author. As each author is processed, the titles are added to the collection. Once all the authors and titles have been added, the employees are added using the same technique.

The Add method for each collection has been modified significantly. Instead of generating an ID number internally, the ID number is derived from a field in the database. As such, it is passed as an argument to the method. Consider the Add method for the Writers collection.

```
Public Function Add(pID As String) As Employee
    Dim pempCurrent As New Employee
    colEmployees.Add pempCurrent, pID
    Set Add = pempCurrent
End Function
```

This method creates a new Employee object. This object is added to the collection with a string key of pID. This is the same as the value of the Employee ID number. The method also returns a reference to the newly-added Employee object. This is done so the calling procedure can set the remaining properties for the new employee. It also would be reasonable to add optional arguments to the Add method to store values in the various properties like Name, Address, and so on. As it exists, the implementation is incomplete. There is no provision to add and remove records from the database. This task will be left for you to complete in

Exercise 4 at the end of the chapter. It will require that you synchronize the data in the collections with the data in the underlying database. That is, if an item is added to one of the collections, it also must be added to the corresponding database table. If an item is removed from one of the collections, the corresponding record also must be removed from the appropriate database table.

The Count and Item methods have not changed at all. The Item method locates an object in the collection and the Count method returns the number of objects in the collection. The Add method for both the Writers and Titles collections also is modified accordingly.

```
Public Function Add(pID As String) As Writer
    Dim pwriCurrent As New Writer
    colWriters.Add pwriCurrent, pID
    Set Add = pwriCurrent
End Function
```

As you can see, the structure of this method is identical to the method of the same name for the Employees collection. It creates a new Writer object and adds the object to the collection. The method then returns a reference to the newly-created object.

SUMMARY

In this chapter, you have learned how to test and debug multiple projects using a project group. You also have seen different techniques to create an object hierarchy and how to create servers.

- User-defined collections in Visual Basic are created from the Collection class. It supports the same methods as any other collection. These are the Add, Remove, Count, and Item methods. User-defined collections also can be enumerated with a For Each loop. They also support both a numeric index and string key.
- There are three approaches used to create an object hierarchy using a collection class. These are the house of straw, house of sticks, and house of bricks.

- The easiest of these implementations is the house of straw. Each of the collections in the hierarchy is exposed to the developer, giving the developer access to the properties and methods of the collection. Because of this, the collection does not protect itself against the developer adding invalid types of objects.
- The house of sticks implementation solves most of the deficiencies of the house of straw approach by hiding the collections from the developer. Using this technique, a collection is declared as a Private variable in a class module. Properties and methods are created that in turn call the methods and read and write properties of the Private collection. These methods then can validate data before any action is taken on the underlying Private collection.
- While the house of bricks implementation solves most of the deficiencies of the house of sticks approach, one major weakness remains. If an object supports more than one collection, the method names must be unique to identify a specific collection. Creating a separate class module for each Collection class can solve this problem.
- A Default property or method for a class module can be created by activating the Procedure Attributes dialog and selecting the property or method that is to become the default. Then, you click Advanced, and (Default) in the Procedure ID list box.
- For Each support for a collection is made possible because of another object called an enumerator. When a collection is hidden inside a class module, the enumerator can be exposed by creating a function with a Procedure ID of minus four (-4), and assigning to the return value of the function, the enumerator of the underlying collection as shown in the following statement:

  ```
  Set NewEnum = mcolEmployees.[_NewEnum]
  ```

- Visual Basic supports different project types in addition to a Standard EXE project. This chapter described the ActiveX DLL and ActiveX EXE servers. Both of these servers are considered code components. DLL servers run as in process servers and EXE servers run as out of process servers.

QUESTIONS

1. Which of the following methods does the Collection class support?
   a. Add.
   b. Remove.
   c. Item.
   d. Count.
   e. All of the above.
2. Items in a collection can be referenced using a __________.
   a. numeric index
   b. string key
   c. subscript
   d. both a and b
   e. all of the above
3. The __________ method is the Default method of the Collection class.
   a. Item
   b. Add
   c. Count
   d. Select
   e. Key
4. An enumerator __________.
   a. is supported by the Collection class
   b. has a Procedure ID of minus four (-4)
   c. can be declared in Visual Basic
   d. both a and b
   e. all of the above
5. A project group __________.
   a. replaces the project files
   b. allows multiple projects to be run in the same instance of Visual Basic
   c. is useful when developing client server programs
   d. both b and c
   e. all of the above
6. You can load __________ projects in a project group.
   a. 1
   b. 2
   c. 3
   d. 4
   e. any number of projects

7. Visual Basic supports ___________ project files.
   a. ActiveX EXE server
   b. ActiveX DLL server
   c. ActiveX control
   d. both a and c
   e. all of the above
8. A DLL is ___________ while an EXE server is ___________.
   a. in process, out of process
   b. out of process, in process
   c. a thread, not a thread
   d. both a and c
   e. both b and c
9. To create a class such that an instance of the class can be created from another project, the Instancing property should be set to ___________.
   a. MultiUse
   b. GlobalMultiUse
   c. PublicNotCreatable
   d. both a and b
   e. all of the above
10. To create a class such that an instance of the class cannot be created from another project, but an object reference can be created, the Instancing property should be set to ___________.
    a. MultiUse
    b. GlobalMultiUse
    c. PublicNotCreatable
    d. both a and b
    e. all of the above
11. Write the statement to create a collection named **colLabels**. Add the labels named **lbl1**, **lbl2**, and **lbl3** to the collection you just created. Use a string key for each item that is the same as the label name.
12. Assuming that a collection named **colButtons** has been declared and contains references to several command buttons, write a For Each loop to disable all the buttons in the collection.
13. Write the necessary statement to add an object named **Thing** to the collection named **Things** having a string key of **ABC**.
14. Write the necessary statement to remove an object from the collection named **Things** having the string key of **ABC**.

15. Write the statement to determine the number of items in the collection named **Things** and store the result in the variable named **pintCount**.
16. List the steps involved in creating a Default method or property.
17. Describe the steps involved in creating an enumerator for a Private collection.
18. Create a class module named **Thing** having the properties **Name** and **ID**. The ID property should be a write-once property.
19. Create a Collection class named **Things**. The Things class should implement a Private collection named **mcolThings**. Implement Add, Remove, Count, and Item methods for the Private collection. Also implement an enumerator for the collection. The methods should add, remove, and locate Thing objects.
20. Create a new ActiveX DLL project. Set the name of the class module to **Demo**, and set the Instancing property so other projects can create an instance of the class. Create a Name property for the class. Add a Standard EXE project thus creating a project group. In the Standard EXE project, create a reference to the project containing the Demo class. In the form for the Standard EXE project create an instance of the Demo class and set the Name property.

EXERCISES

Note: You may want to save each of the following exercises in a separate folder so that the individual class names will not be overwritten.

1. In this exercise you will develop part of the object hierarchy shown in Figure 9-13, and a form to test it using the house of straw approach presented in the chapter.

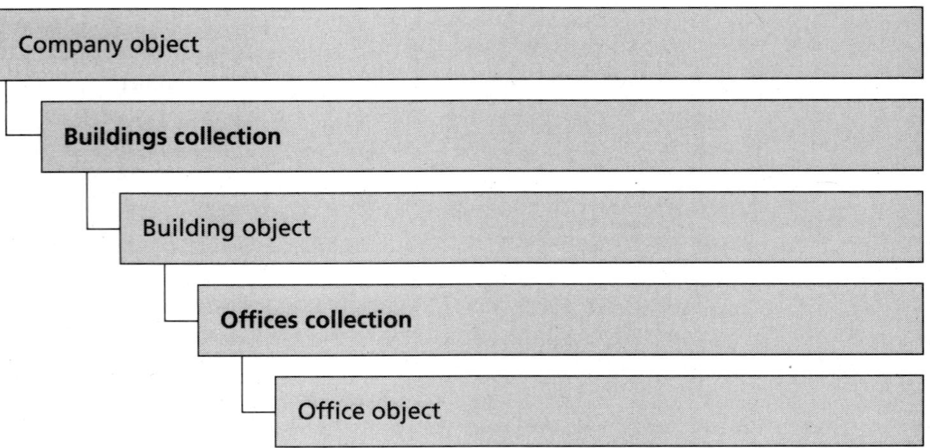

Figure 9-13: Object hierarchy

a. Create a new project.
b. Create a class named **Building**. Create properties for the class named **Name, MailStop**, and **Address.**
c. Create a root class named **Company**. In the class module, write the necessary statements to create a collection named **Buildings** of type Collection.
d. In the form module, create text boxes to store the properties of a building. Also, create a combo box to store a Building ID.
e. In the form module, create two command buttons—one to add Building objects to the collection and the other to remove existing Building objects.
f. The Add command button should contain the code to add a new Building object to the Buildings collection. Each building should have a unique string key assigned using the same techniques presented in the chapter. When a new building is added, append the string key of the Building ID to the combo box.
g. Using the selected item in the combo box, the Remove command button should remove the selected building from the collection.
h. Add the code to both the Add and Remove command buttons to display the count of the buildings in a Label control on the form.
i. Create a final command button that will iterate the Buildings collection. For each item in the collection, print the **Name** and **MailStop** properties in the Immediate window.
j. Save the class using the name **Chapter.09\Exercise\Building.cls**, the form using the name **Chapter.09\Exercise\frmStraw.frm**, and the project using the name **Chapter.09\Exercise\Straw.vbp**.

2. In this exercise you will extend the object hierarchy shown in Figure 9-13 and modify the implementation to use the house of sticks implementation presented in this chapter.
a. Create a new project, or copy and modify the project you created in Exercise 1.
b. In the **Company** class, create a Private collection to store the **Buildings** collection.
c. Create an **AddBuilding** method that has the same effect as the Add method in Exercise 1.
d. Create a **RemoveBuilding** method to remove a building from the collection.
e. Create a **CountBuilding** method to count the number of buildings in the collection.
f. Create a **Buildings** method to return a specific building from the collection.
g. Create the necessary text boxes and buttons on the form to add, remove, and locate buildings in the collection using the methods you created in the previous steps.
h. Save the form using the name **Chapter.09\Exercise\frmSticks.frm** and the project using the name **Chapter.09\Exercise\Sticks.vbp**.

3. In this exercise you will implement all of the object hierarchy shown in Figure 9-13 using the house of bricks approach, and create a project group to test the object hierarchy.
a. Create a new project.
b. Implement the **Buildings** and **Offices** collections as a Collection class.
c. Create **Add, Count, Remove**, and **Item** methods for both of the collections.
d. Enable the enumerator for both collections.
e. Create the **Building** and **Office** classes. The Building class should support the same properties used in Exercise 1. The Office class should support the following properties: **Name, Number**, and **Floor**. Both also should support a write-once ID property.
f. Set up the project so the project is implemented as a DLL server.

g. Set the instancing for the class modules and collections so the developer only can create an instance of the class named **Company**. The user should be able to reference the other classes but not create an instance of the classes.

h. Create the necessary text boxes and buttons on the form to add, remove, and locate buildings in the collection using the methods you created in the previous steps.

i. Save the form using the name **Chapter.09\Exercise\frmBricks.frm** and the project using the name **Chapter.09\Exercise\Bricks.vbp**.

4. In this exercise you will implement an object hierarchy that in turn will access the objects contained in the DAO hierarchy. In essence you are creating a layer of software that insulates the developer from the actual DAO hierarchy. Using the program in the Database folder as a template, you will round out the project by implementing the methods to add and delete records from the collections and synchronize the collections with the database.

a. Create a new project group with two projects. One project should be a Standard EXE project and the other should be an ActiveX DLL server.

b. Use the class modules in the **Chapter.09\Database** folder as a template for the object hierarchy in this problem.

c. In the Employees, Writers, and Titles collection, rename the Add method to the **Initialize** method. The reason for this is significant. The Initialize method will read the data from a database table and initialize the collections.

d. Create an **Add** method for each of the three collections. The Add method should create a new instance of the appropriate object (Employee, Writer, Title). In addition, it should insert the record in the corresponding database table.

e. Create a **Remove** method for each of the three collections. The Remove method should delete the desired item from the collection. It also must remove the record from the underlying table.

f. Save and test the program.

CHAPTER 10

Creating an ActiveX Control

Combining a Text Box and Label into One Control

case▶ Focus Management Company develops accounting applications using Visual Basic. Everyone creating Visual Basic programs uses intrinsic and ActiveX controls. The software development staff for Focus Management often creates the same code to enhance the behavior of some controls. Often, they want to use a text box so when it gets focus, all the characters in the text box are selected and the contents of the entire field are replaced easily. They also find that many text boxes are used in conjunction with a descriptive prompt stored in a label. They want to create a control that will perform both these tasks.

SECTION A

objectives

In this section you will:

- Use the UserControl object to create an ActiveX control
- Create a project group consisting of an ActiveX control and a Standard EXE project
- Add constituent controls to the User control
- Understand the difference between design time and run time as it pertains to ActiveX controls

The Basics of ActiveX Control Creation

Previewing the Completed Application

The completed application for this chapter is not an application in the sense of a form with a user interface. Rather, it is similar to the code component you created in the previous two chapters except that the ActiveX control has a visual interface. The user of the program does not use the code component. The developer does. The roles of author and developer are the same when creating and using ActiveX controls as they were when creating and using code components. The person creating an ActiveX control is the author and the person developing a program that uses the ActiveX control is the developer. In this chapter, you will assume the role of both author and developer. In this context, the **user** is the person who executes a program created by the developer. As the author, you will develop the visual interface for the control and define the properties and events that will be seen by the developer. As the developer, you will create instances of the ActiveX control on a form and test the control.

The completed application for this chapter contains an ActiveX control made up of two other controls called constituent controls. A **constituent control** is a control used to create other ActiveX controls. Intrinsic controls, like text boxes and existing ActiveX controls, can be used as constituent controls. As the author, you create the ActiveX control from one or more constituent controls and expose properties and methods to the developer. As the developer, you can access the properties of the ActiveX control, and respond to the events generated by the ActiveX control.

Before proceeding to create ActiveX controls, which may be based on one or more constituent controls, you need to be aware of the licensing restrictions placed on existing controls. Before creating your own ActiveX control that uses either Microsoft supplied or third-party supplied ActiveX controls, make sure to understand carefully the licensing agreement between you and the vendor of the control. Most license agreements allow you to distribute the .ocx file corresponding to the ActiveX control in your software. That is, if your program uses the Windows

Common Controls, like the TreeView or ListView controls, you may distribute that .ocx file with your program. If you create your own ActiveX control that is based on the TreeView control, however, your control must "add significant and primary functionality to any redistributable, such as (the) TreeView (control), in order to legally distribute it as part of the software you develop." You may have licenses for other controls that are much different. Some control vendors require you to purchase licenses for each .ocx file you distribute. You also must decide on the licensing restrictions that you want to place on the controls that you create. Chapter 11 discusses the details of creating a control that requires a license.

To preview the completed application:

1 Start **Visual Basic.** Load the project group named **Chapter.10\Complete\FMC_C.vbg.** Make sure to open the project group with the extension .vbg rather than the projects with the extension .vbp.

2 Open the **Project Explorer**. The Project Explorer for the completed application is shown in Figure 10-1.

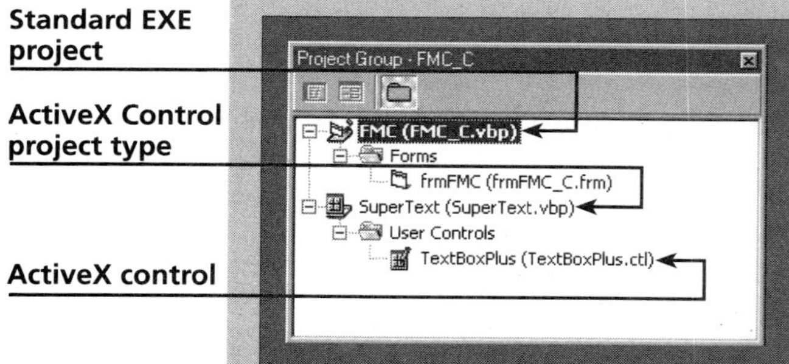

Figure 10-1: Project Explorer

The Project Explorer contains a new folder named User Controls. The UserControl object is the foundation of an ActiveX control.

This project is actually a project group, as in Chapter 9. A project group allows you to simultaneously create, test, and debug two or more projects so you can assume the role of both author and developer in the same instance of Visual Basic. The author uses one project to create the ActiveX component (in this case an ActiveX control). The developer uses the other project to test the ActiveX control.

3 Activate the Form window for the project named **FMC_C.vbp.**

4 Click the **TextBoxPlus** control and create a second instance of the control on the form as shown in Figure 10-2.

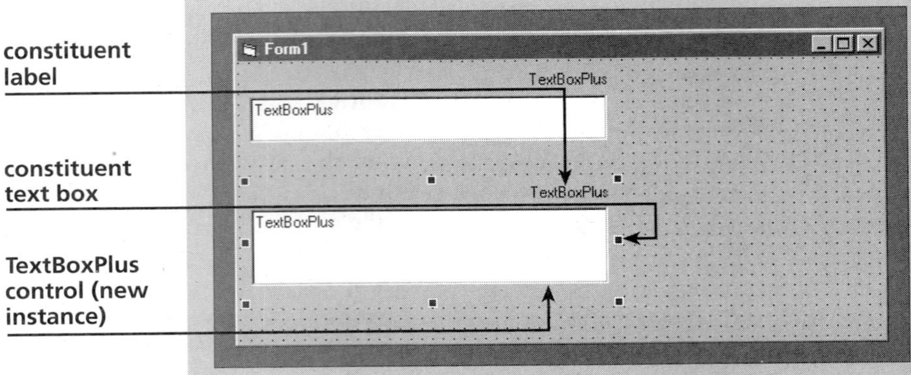

Figure 10-2: TextBoxPlus control

5 Activate the Properties window for the new TextBoxPlus control. The TextBoxPlus control has properties like any other control. Set the Name property to **tbpName**, the Caption property to **Name**, and remove the text from the Text property.

6 Activate the Code window for the form. In the Object list box, select the **tbpName** control. Activate the Procedure list box. The control responds to events like any other control.

7 Test the program. The TextBoxPlus control works like an ordinary text box. However, it consists of both a text box and a descriptive prompt. When the text box gets focus, all the characters are selected automatically.

8 End the program and exit Visual Basic. Do not save any of the changes.

A Brief History of ActiveX Technology

Before attempting to describe how to create an ActiveX control, a brief history lesson is in order about the evolution of the DOS and Windows operating systems. In the days of DOS, programs were islands, and each program operated independently of another. In other words, you would run a word processor. If you needed to insert data from the spreadsheet into the word processor, it was necessary to exit the word processor, start the spreadsheet, save the spreadsheet data in a format understood by both programs, exit the spreadsheet, restart the word processor, then insert the file into the word processor. This paradigm is considered application centered or **application-centric** computing. One disadvantage of this computing paradigm is the inherent difficulty of moving data from one program to another.

One step forward in the integration of data used by different programs was the original software suites. These suites combined a similar user interface for different applications like spreadsheet, word processing, and database tasks. The interaction of data between programs was accomplished using file converters to convert the data between one program and another. For example, to insert a spreadsheet into a word processing document, the spreadsheet file first was converted to a format understood by the word processor, then inserted in the document.

One of the shortcomings of the application-centric paradigm was that it did not always model the way people work or think. For example, consider the task of preparing a financial statement. The task involves obtaining raw financial data, then summarizing and performing computations on the data. The financial statement also contains a descriptive component with notes about the financial data, accounting methods, and business outlook. Using the application-centric paradigm, different applications likely would be necessary to produce the financial statement.

This has lead to a computing paradigm driven by data and the operations performed on the data called a **data-centric** paradigm. If this sounds like data represented as objects having properties and methods, it is. Using the data-centric paradigm, users see data as a document. Inside a document, the user can embed different objects. For example, it is possible to insert a spreadsheet or PowerPoint slide into a Word document. In essence, the user can focus on the data rather than the application that is providing the services to manipulate the data.

One of the first attempts to implement a data-centric paradigm was Dynamic Data Exchange (DDE). DDE worked by allowing one application to execute commands in another application. In addition to executing another application's commands, DDE applications could read and write data to and from different applications. Few applications support DDE today and those that do usually support it for backward compatibility.

After DDE, another technology called Object Linking and Embedding (OLE) was introduced to provide better interoperability between applications, improve performance, and generalize the communication between applications. A program that supports OLE makes available to other programs, a well-defined set of objects and defines how those objects communicate with each other.

OLE or COM

Precisely defining OLE and COM, and the exact relationship between the two, would be a lengthy task and would provide little help in creating ActiveX controls using Visual Basic. In fact, the technologies are so intertwined that you seldom use one without the other. The important thing to remember about OLE objects is that they allow you to embed an object inside another object and allow objects to communicate with each other. This is a fundamental concept that you need to understand about programs that support OLE and COM. We have said that when you create a control instance on a form, the form is the container for a control. Additionally, there are controls like the Frame control that can act as a container. Given the programs you have created thus far, the form is considered a container. The controls created on the form can be considered embedded objects. The important point to gather from this is that many programs can fulfill the role of a container and many programs also can be used as embedded objects.

Creating ActiveX Controls

Prior to Visual Basic 5.0, the creation of ActiveX controls required programming in C++. This, however, is no longer the case. You now can create ActiveX controls that work like the ActiveX controls you have used. For example, you can create controls that support events, properties, and methods. It also is possible to create Property Pages for your ActiveX controls. There are three ways to create an ActiveX control in Visual Basic.

- Enhance an existing control. When you enhance an existing control, you either use an existing intrinsic control, like a text box, or an ActiveX control, like the TreeView control. Then you can add additional properties or methods to the new control, or define additional events to which the control should respond. It also is possible to modify the behavior of existing events, properties, and methods.
- Create a control made up of multiple constituent controls. A control made from constituent controls is simply a control that is made up of other controls. Creating a constituent control is much like enhancing an existing control. To create a control made up of multiple constituent controls, you add multiple instances of the same control or different controls to your ActiveX control. That is, you could create an ActiveX control that is built upon the TextBox and TreeView controls.
- Create a control from scratch. Creating a control from scratch is much more difficult than creating a control based on an existing control. In this chapter, you will not create a control from scratch.

ActiveX Terminology

The term "container" has been used often in this book. Remember, a form is the default container for controls. In addition to the form, the Frame and PictureBox controls both can function as containers. The concept of a container is important for three reasons.

1. Many types of objects cannot exist by themselves. For example, if you created a simple program with a single visible object like a command button, an instance of the command button must be created on a form (container). The button cannot exist by itself.
2. Containers are not unique to Visual Basic. There is no reason why you cannot author an ActiveX control and create an instance of the control in a program like Internet Explorer or any other program that supports COM. The important point is that a form, or perhaps Internet Explorer, can act as a container for a control.
3. An object and its container interact with each other. For example, a container may suggest initial properties for your control instance like the foreground or background color. Additionally, your control may communicate information to its container. For example, an ActiveX control tells the container (form) to save the value of properties so the property settings will

persist from one invocation of Visual Basic to the next. The responsibility of saving the current values of specific properties belongs to the container not the control instance.

As you have seen, the visual interface for the form is created using the Form window, and the Code window is used to edit the code module for the form. A more generic and accurate term for the Form window is **visual designer**. A visual designer is a user interface that allows you to create the visual part of a form, ActiveX control, or other object. When the visual designer (Form window) is open, the object (form) is in design mode and you can create control instances on the form using controls on the Toolbox. Consider a standard form and an MDI parent form. You saw in Chapter 7 that these two types of forms have different properties and characteristics. In actuality, these are two, albeit minimally, different visual designers. When you create an ActiveX control, you also use a visual designer to create the visible part of the ActiveX control. The status of an object's visual designer is significant because it determines whether the object is in design mode or run mode.

ActiveX Control Objects

There are two types of modules related to the creation of ActiveX controls—User control modules and Property Page modules. Creating Property Page modules will be discussed in the next chapter. User control modules are similar to form modules in that both have a visual component and a code component. As a control's author, you interact with a User control module just like you do a form module. You use a visual designer to design the visual component of the ActiveX control or Property Page, and the Code window to develop the event and other procedures to determine the ActiveX control's actions. First, you will learn about the User control module. A User control module corresponds to the UserControl class just as a form module corresponds to the Form class. There are four predefined objects that are unique to the UserControl class.

The **UserControl** class is conceptually similar to a Form class. It has a visual designer to create the control's visual interface. The process of creating the visual interface is like the process of creating the visual interface for a form. Using the controls on the Toolbox, you create instances of constituent controls on the User control. The User control can respond to events like a form. For example, both the Form and UserControl classes respond to the Resize event. When the user resizes the form, the Resize event occurs for the form. When the developer resizes an instance of an ActiveX control created on a form, the Resize event occurs for the UserControl class. You also can create properties and methods for the User control that are used by the developer. You use the same techniques to create properties and methods as you used when you created code components. Specifically, to create a property you write paired Property procedures and to create a method you write Public, Function, or Sub procedures in the User control's code module.

Consider the process of the developer creating an instance of a control on a form. It is possible for the form to suggest default values for certain properties like colors and fonts. This information is communicated from the form (container) to a control instance using the **AmbientProperties** object. The term "form" in this context is not entirely accurate. Remember, a control instance can be created on a form, and the form acts as the container for the control. Other programs, like Internet Explorer, can be containers too.

There are several properties that are not defined by the control itself but rather by the container (form). You do not create these properties explicitly. Rather, the container (form) supplies them. These properties are communicated between your ActiveX control and its container through the **Extender** object. The Extender object is predefined by the UserControl object, much in the same way as Visual Basic predefines the Controls collection for a particular form. That is, you as the developer can access the Controls collection to reference the controls on a given form. As the author, you can access the properties of the Extender object to retrieve information from a container (in this case a Visual Basic form).

As the author of a control, you have the responsibility of loading initial properties for a control instance when it is created. Consider what happens when you create an instance of a text box. It has initial property values including font attributes and foreground and background colors. Furthermore, consider what happens when you set a design-time property for a control instance (i.e., the Text property of a text box). When you save the project file (or form containing the text box), the property settings are saved in the form module. When the project is loaded, these settings then are read and applied to the control instance. As the author of a control, you use the **PropertyBag** object to perform these tasks. The AmbientProperties, Extender, and PropertyBag objects are predefined by the User control. As such, you neither create an instance of these objects nor declare variables to reference these objects.

While not expressly part of the User control module type, there is another type of module used to create Property Pages. This type of module is used to implement a Property Page for the User control. Each module is considered a Property Page for the Property Pages supported by the User control. They function like the Property Pages you have used for other ActiveX controls. Property Pages are discussed in Chapter 11.

In addition to these three objects, your control may use other constituent controls. All these objects are combined together to create your own ActiveX control. Instead of discussing all the characteristics of the UserControl, AmbientProperties, and Extender objects, and how to create Property Pages and all the other intricacies of creating an ActiveX control, you will begin by creating a very simple ActiveX control to get a taste of the steps involved.

As you saw in Chapter 9, Visual Basic supports several different types of projects. One of these project types is the ActiveX Control project. As you saw in the previous chapters when you created an ActiveX DLL or EXE server, a project group is useful in debugging. That is, you can create the code component or ActiveX control in one project and create a program that uses the code component or ActiveX control in another project; all within the same instance of Visual Basic. This also is useful when creating ActiveX controls.

In this example, you will create a simple ActiveX control made from a constituent label and text box. The control will work just like the text box with a few extensions. Whenever the ActiveX control receives focus, it will select all the characters in the text box automatically. Also, the ActiveX control will display a descriptive prompt just above the text box. The ActiveX control you will create in this chapter will be called the TextBoxPlus control. In this chapter, we will refer to the ActiveX control that you are authoring as the TextBoxPlus control, the User control module that implements the TextBoxPlus control, or the ActiveX control. When referring to the constituent TextBox or Label controls, the word "constituent" will be used to help reduce any possible confusion.

The process of creating an ActiveX control is similar to the process of creating a form, especially when constituent controls are used to create an ActiveX control.

To create an ActiveX control:

1. Start **Visual Basic.** Open the project group named **Chapter.10\Startup\FMC_S.vbg.** Again, use caution to open the project group file (.vbg), rather than the project file (.vbp).
2. Click **Add Project** on the **File** menu to open the Add Project dialog, then double-click **ActiveX control.** This will cause a new project group to be created and a new ActiveX control to be added to the project.
3. Examine the Project Explorer. A new folder appears with the name **User Controls.** This folder contains the ActiveX controls pertaining to the project.
4. Save the UserControl module using the name **TextBoxPlus.ctl.** Save the project using the name **SuperText.vbp.** The process for saving an ActiveX Control project and its controls is identical to saving a project and form.

The disk files for an ActiveX control are similar structurally to the disk files pertaining to a form module. The code and visual component are stored in a single file with the suffix ".ctl," analogous to a form's ".frm" file. The ".ctl" file is a plain text file like an ".frm" file. If the ActiveX control contains graphical images, they are stored in a file with the suffix ".ctx." Again, this is analogous to a form's ".frx" file.

When you create an ActiveX Control project, the various controls in the project (each stored in a separate ".ctl" file), are compiled into an executable file with the extension ".ocx." This is the same file extension as the one used by other ActiveX controls. An ".ocx" file can contain one or many different ActiveX controls. For example, the Microsoft Data Bound List Controls are contained in a single ".ocx" file named DBLIST32.OCX. The one file supports both the DBList and DBCombo controls.

At the heart of every ActiveX control is the UserControl object. Every ActiveX control you create will have one UserControl object. In this program, you will create a single User control called a TextBoxPlus control. It also is possible to create a project consisting of multiple User controls hence multiple ActiveX controls in the same ".ocx" file. The User control module has a visual designer that works much like the Form window, and has properties which you can set using the

Properties window. It also supports properties, events, and methods in the same manner as a form module.

The UserControl object supports an exhaustive list of properties, events, and methods. Rather than presenting a complete list here, only the properties necessary to create a simple ActiveX control will be presented. Later in the chapter, and in subsequent chapters, additional properties, events, and methods will be presented as they are used.

Object	UserControl
Properties	The **CanGetFocus** property contains a Boolean value indicating whether or not the control can receive focus when the container (form) is running. Normally, it is desirable to display a border around the control or change the visual appearance in some way to indicate that the control has focus. This does not happen automatically but is the responsibility of the control's author. The **DefaultCancel** property allows the ActiveX control to act like a Default or Cancel button. That is, a UserControl object with the Default property set to True, will allow the ActiveX control to act as a Default button. If the Cancel property is set to True, the ActiveX control can act as a Cancel button. It is up to the developer to set the values of these properties if the ActiveX control should act as a Default or Cancel button. The **InvisibleAtRuntime** property, if True, causes the ActiveX control to be invisible, when the container (form) is running. In this case, the developer will not have access to the Visible property. Otherwise, the control will have a Visible property that can be set by the developer. Consider controls like CommonDialog or ImageList. These controls are not visible at run time. At design time, a fixed size icon is displayed so the developer is aware the control exists. The **Name** property defines the name of the control. From the developer's perspective, this is the class name of the ActiveX control. It is also the name used for the control's ToolTip on the Toolbox. Again, this is analogous to a form. Just as the Name property of a form is the class name, the Name property of a UserControl object becomes the class name of the ActiveX control as seen by the developer. The **Public** property is a Boolean value. It defines whether or not another application can create an instance of the control. The **ToolboxBitmap** property contains the bitmap that is displayed on the Toolbox. The **Top**, **Left**, **Height**, and **Width** properties define the size of the control on its container; in this chapter a form. The properties have the same meaning as the properties of the same name pertaining to other controls.

Creating the user interface for an ActiveX control is just like creating the interface for a form, especially when the control is built from constituent controls. You set the properties pertaining to the UserControl object with the Properties window just as you set a form's properties. While the process is the same as the process to set the properties pertaining to a form, you will notice that the list of properties differs. You create constituent controls on the User control including labels and text boxes to define its visual interface. From your perspective as the control's author, you can set the design-time properties of each constituent control using the Properties window in the same way as you do when creating controls on a form.

To identify the components of the UserControl module:

1. Click the UserControl named **UserControl1** in the Project window. The View Code and View Object buttons both are enabled. These buttons open the visual designer and Code window for the UserControl.
2. Click the **View Object** button to open the visual designer for the UserControl. The visual designer looks much like the Form window.
3. Right-click the visual designer and select **Properties** on the pop-up menu.

   The Properties window is opened and set to the UserControl1 object. Conceptually, this is analogous to opening the Properties window for the form. Just as a form, or any object for that matter, has a Name property, so does the UserControl object.
4. Set the Name property to **TextBoxPlus**.
5. Set the ToolboxBitmap property to **Chapter.10\Startup\tbp.bmp**. Set the drive designator as needed.
6. Close the visual designer and Code window. The icon appears on the Toolbox.

The UserControl is a much different class than a form and as such has different properties. At this point, your ActiveX control (user control) is like a blank form. There are no event procedures for the user control so it will not respond to any events. Because the user control has been created, however, you can create an instance of it on a form.

Design Time Versus Run Time

When you add a UserControl object to a project, an icon is added on the Toolbox. As the developer, you create an instance of the User control on a form just like any other control. If you leave the visual designer for the UserControl object open, however, the control instance will appear shaded on the Toolbox indicating the control is disabled.

Consider the notion of design time and run time as it pertains to a project with a single form. At design time, you can create an instance of a control on a form using the Form window (visual designer). At run time the visual designer is closed automatically by Visual Basic. In fact, the visual designer cannot be open.

When you create ActiveX controls, the concepts of design time and run time become much more complex. When you create an instance of a control on a form, like a text box or command button, you create an instance from the underlying class. This is accomplished by drawing an instance of the control on a form. Compare this to a code component. You create an instance of the class using the New keyword when declaring the object variable or with the Set statement. Even though the technique to create a class instance is very different from the technique to create an instance of an ActiveX control (user document), Visual Basic is doing the same thing. It is creating an instance from the class. After you create a class instance, you can set the properties of the object, and the object can respond to events. For a code component, the class instance is created at run time. For a control, creating a control instance occurs at design time. While this may seem to be a paradox, it is not.

When you create an instance of a control like a text box and set the Name to txtThing, it is as if the following statement had just been executed. Do not attempt to enter this statement. Text boxes are not externally creatable objects and as such cannot be created with the New keyword. The only way to create a TextBox control instance is using the Toolbox.

```
Dim txtThing As New TextBox
```

This implies that the control is running and in fact it is. When you set properties of a control instance at design time, the control itself actually is running. That is, it is responding to events, and executing code. Consider a control like the Data control. When you select the RecordSource property, the Data control must establish a connection with the database using the contents of the DatabaseName property. For the Data control to lookup the tables in a database, the Data control must be running. As such, when the developer is interacting with an instance of the ActiveX control you created by setting its properties, the control itself is in run mode, and the Form window (visual designer) is in design mode. Consider some of the ActiveX controls you have used. When you use the Property Pages for controls like the toolbar or status bar to define the buttons or panels, you are executing the code in the control, and as such, it is running.

ActiveX controls you create are no different. When you as the developer create an instance of the control in the Form window and set its properties, the control is running. When you as the author are creating the visual interface for the UserControl and the visual designer is open, the control itself is in design mode and cannot run. For this reason, the control is disabled (appears shaded) on the Toolbox. If you close the UserControl's visual designer, the control will be enabled. Additionally, if you have created an instance of the control on the form, those instances will appear with diagonal lines across the control instances indicating that the control itself is in design mode.

In summary, a Visual Basic project group containing an ActiveX Control project and a Standard EXE project can be in one of three different run states:

- If the visual designer for the user control is open, both the Standard EXE project and user control project are in design mode.

- If the visual designer for the user control is closed, and the form window is open, the Standard EXE project is in design mode but the User control itself is in run mode.
- If Visual Basic is in run mode, both the Standard EXE project and the control are in run mode.

From the point of view of the developer, your ActiveX control will work just like any other control. That is, the developer can create an instance of the control on the form. Properties are set using the Properties window and possibly Property Pages.

To create an instance of the ActiveX control:

1. Make sure the visual designer for the User control is closed and activate the Form window.
2. Click the **TextBoxPlus** control on the Toolbox and create an instance of the control on the form. At this point your control is running even though Visual Basic is in design mode. Nothing appears inside the region of the control as you have not yet defined any constituent controls to appear in the User control.
3. Press **F4** to open the Properties window if needed.

   You might expect that there would be no properties listed in the Properties window because you as the author have not created explicitly any properties yet. There are several properties listed that are common nearly to every other control you have created. For example, the Top, Left, Height, and Width properties are listed. The source of these properties is another object pertaining to the UserControl object called the Extender object. The Name property has been set automatically to TextBoxPlus1. This is consistent with other controls you have created. The default name for the control instance is the class name followed by a number.
4. Set the Name property to **tbpName**. A three-character prefix is used to identify the type of control. This is consistent with the practice of consistent object-naming conventions.
5. Activate the Code window for the Form module and select the object named **tbpName**. Only four events are supported. The Extender object defines the DragDrop, DragOver, GotFocus, and LostFocus events.
6. So you can see when the control is in design mode and in run mode, activate the Code window for the UserControl object and enter the following statement in the **UserControl_Resize** event:

   ```
   Debug.Print UserControl.Height, UserControl.Width
   ```
7. The previous statement will execute and print the height and width of the control whenever the TextBoxPlus control is resized. When the User control is in design mode, it is not processing events. Even though Visual Basic is in design mode, however, the control may be running. Make sure the Form window is open and the visual designer for the User control is closed. Resize

the control instance drawn on the form. As the form is resized, the Resize event occurs, and the current size is printed in the Immediate window. As you can see, the control is running and responding to events.

8 Open the visual designer for the User control, then activate the Form window. The control instance on the form appears shaded indicating that the control itself is not running. Resize the control again. The current size is not printed in the Immediate window because the control itself is in design mode and not responding to events.

At this point, your control does not support even simple events like Click. That is, the developer cannot write code to respond to the Click event. As the author, you must expose explicitly all properties, events, and methods to the developer by creating Property, Function, and Sub procedures except for those supplied by the Extender object.

The Extender Object

As mentioned, some properties and events are not defined by the User control, but are defined by its container. Although in this chapter the only container presented is a form, you will see in subsequent chapters that programs like Internet Explorer also can act as containers for your control. These properties and events are stored in the Extender object. This object is predefined and created automatically when the developer creates an instance of the User control. As the control's author, you do not create explicitly the Extender object. Many properties like Height and Width have exactly the same meaning as they do for other controls. The behavior of some of these properties varies depending on the settings of the UserControl object.

Object	Extender
Properties	The **Cancel** property appears only if the UserControl object's DefaultCancel property is True.
	The **Default** property indicates that the ActiveX control is the Default button for the container.
	The **Enabled** property is a read-only property that specifies whether or not the control itself supports an Enabled property.
	The **Name** property is a read-only property that contains the developer-defined name of the control.
	The **Parent** property is read-only at run time and contains a reference to the control's container, which typically is a form.
	The **TabStop** and **TabIndex** properties appear only if the CanGetFocus property for the UserControl object is True.

Events	The **GotFocus** and **LostFocus** events occur only if the UserControl object's CanGetFocus property is True.

Not all the properties listed in the Properties window come from the Extender object. There is another object called the **AmbientProperties** object. Both the AmbientProperties and Extender objects pertain to the container and in fact are very similar. Rather than being used by the developer, however, the AmbientProperties object is used by the author of the control. The AmbientProperties object contains properties of the container that are used to suggest default or initial values to your ActiveX control. Not all containers are created equally. Some containers support a more robust set of properties than others do.

Object	**AmbientProperties**
Properties	The **BackColor** property is a color that contains the suggested interior color of the contained control. The **DisplayAsDefault** property is a Boolean value that specifies whether or not the control is the default control. The **DisplayName** property is a string containing the name that the control should display for itself. The **Font** property is a Font object that contains the suggested font information of the contained control. If the container does not support this property, the Visual Basic supplied default is MS Sans Serif 8. The **ForeColor** property is a color that contains the suggested foreground color of the contained control. The **ScaleUnits** property is a String data type containing the name of the coordinate units being used by the container. The **ShowGrabHandles** property is a Boolean value that specifies if the container handles the showing of grab handles. If the container does not support this property, the Visual Basic supplied default is True. The **ShowHatching** property is a Boolean value that specifies if the container handles the showing of hatching. If the container does not support this property, the Visual Basic supplied default is True. The **SupportsMnemonics** property is a Boolean value that specifies if the container handles access keys for the control. If the container does not support this property, the Visual Basic supplied default is False. The **TextAlign** property is an enumeration that specifies how text is to be aligned. If the container does not support this property, the Visual Basic supplied default is 0 - General Align.

The **UserMode** property is a Boolean value that specifies if the environment is in design mode or end user mode. If the container does not support this property, the Visual Basic supplied default is True.

Constituent Controls

The easiest way to create an ActiveX control is to use other existing controls called constituent controls. In this example, you will implement a control made from two constituent controls. A constituent label will display a descriptive prompt. A constituent text box will have an additional feature to select all the text when the control gets focus. While you conceivably could create the ActiveX control from scratch, it is much easier to use the functionality of the label and text box and expand their features.

Before creating an instance of the ActiveX control on the form, you need to understand additional details pertaining to the role of author and developer. In this Focus Management example, there are two projects—one for the ActiveX control that you are creating in the role of the author and another that uses the ActiveX control in the role of the developer. Although these two projects are combined into a project group, when you are working with the project named FMC_S.vbp, you are assuming the role of the developer. When you are working with the project named SuperText.vbp, you are assuming the role of the author.

As the ActiveX control's author, you first must create the visual interface for the control. This process is very similar to creating the visual interface for a form. You open the UserControl's visual designer, which looks almost identical to the Form window. Then, using the Toolbox, you create instances of the constituent controls on the User control.

To create a constituent control:

1. Activate the visual designer for the **UserControl** object.
2. Create an instance of a text box on the User control designer as shown in Figure 10-3.

constituent text box

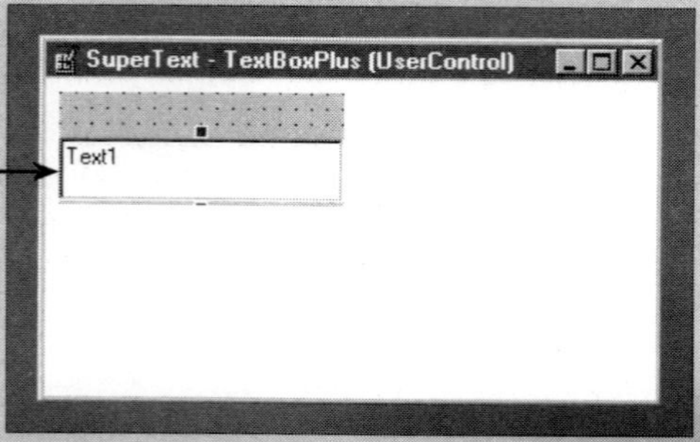

SuperText - TextBoxPlus (UserControl)

Text1

Figure 10-3: Creating the constituent text box

That's it! You have just created an ActiveX control made up of a single constituent control. To use the ActiveX control (assuming the role of the developer), you must close the visual designer for the control. Then, you can create a new instance of the control on your form. When creating a control instance from an ActiveX control or an intrinsic control, the role of developer does not change.

The events, properties, and methods of constituent controls, including the control you just created, are hidden inside the UserControl object. They are not available to the developer; that is, the developer does not have access to the events and properties supported by the underlying text box. To illustrate this concept, you will activate the Form window and view the properties and events supported by the TextBoxPlus control.

To confirm the hidden properties and events of the constituent control:

1. Close the visual designer for the TextBoxPlus object, then activate the **Form** window. The text box appears on the form.
2. Open the Code window for the form and select the **tbpName** object.
3. Click the **Procedure** list box. The events of the constituent text box are not listed. They are hidden from the developer.
4. Activate the **Properties** window for the control. Again, the properties of the constituent text box are hidden.
5. Close the Form window.

When the developer creates an instance of an ActiveX control, the developer does not directly interact with the properties of the constituent controls like text boxes or labels. Rather, the developer interacts with the ActiveX control using the properties, methods, and events you as the control's author expose explicitly. The developer does have access to the Extender properties, however. Conceptually, this is similar to the code component you created in the previous chapter. There were classes that were part of the code component's interface and other classes and objects that were not. This distinction is very important.

As the author of an ActiveX control, you have access to all the properties and methods of the constituent controls. Your ActiveX control also can respond to the events generated by the various constituent controls. For example, as the ActiveX control's author, you can set the Text property of the constituent text box and respond to events like Change and so on.

As the developer, however, the properties and methods of the constituent controls are hidden from you. As such, either to allow the developer to set the Text property of the constituent text box or to respond to an event like the Change event, as the author, you must expose explicitly the property or generate the event. Figure 10-4 illustrates this concept.

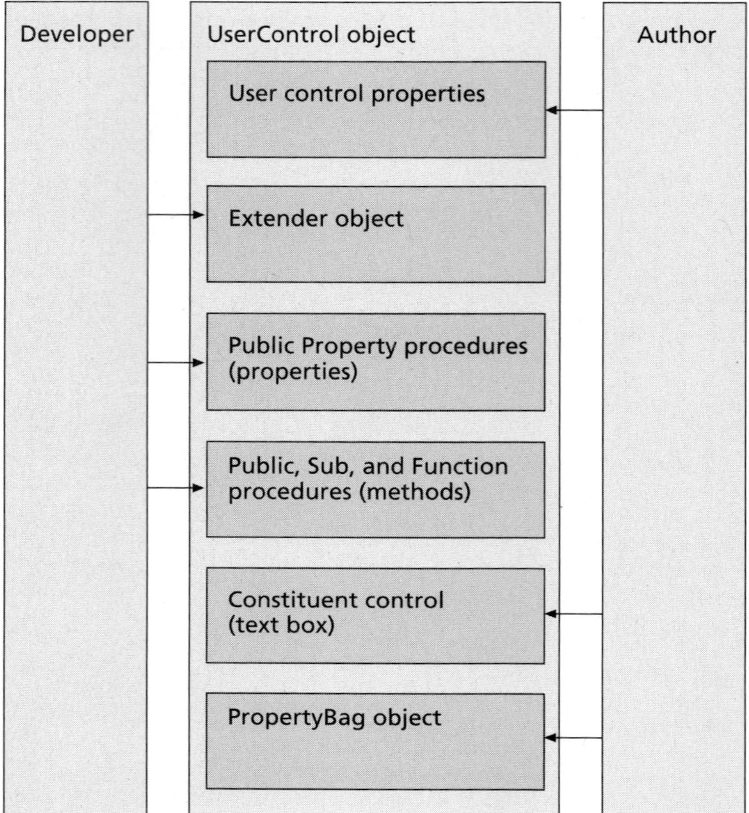

Figure 10-4: Interaction with the UserControl object

As shown in Figure 10-4, Property, Function, and Sub procedures are created in the User control to expose properties and methods to the developer. The properties and methods of the constituent controls, however, are available only to the author. Although not discussed yet, the PropertyBag object also is used by the ActiveX control's author.

Creating Multiple Constituent Controls

Throughout the programs in this book, text boxes have been created with a corresponding label used as a descriptive prompt. Additionally the name of the text box tends to be very similar to the contents of the prompt. For example, you may have a text box named txtAddress with a corresponding prompt of Address:. It is possible to create a constituent control made up of both a text box and a label.

To create a control with multiple constituent controls:

1 Activate the visual designer for the **TextBoxPlus** control.

2 Resize the control and create a label as shown in Figure 10-5.

constituent label

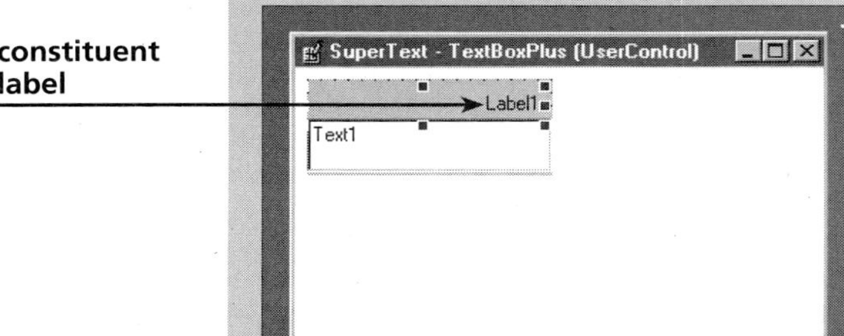

Figure 10-5: Creating the constituent label

3 Activate the Properties window and set the Alignment property to **1 - Right Justify**. Remember, as the author, you have access to the properties of the constituent controls; as the developer, you do not.

4 Close the visual designer for the User control, then open the **Form** window.

5 Delete the existing control instances, then create an instance of the control as shown in Figure 10-6.

constituent controls not resized

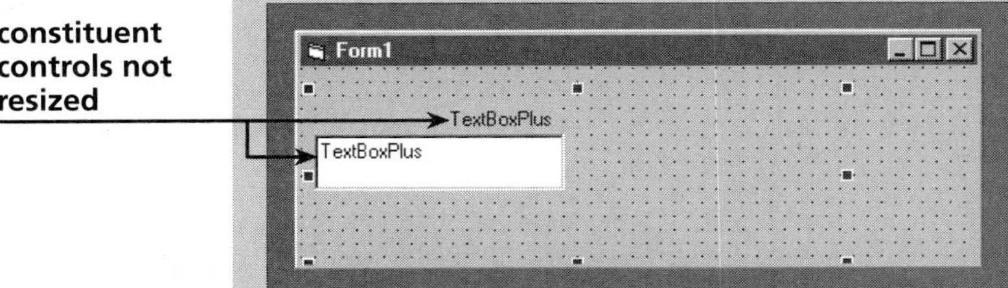

Figure 10-6: ActiveX control instance

6 Resize the control. The size of the constituent control does not change when the control is resized.

Programming tip

The names of the constituent text box and label have not been changed. In this example, the constituent label and text box have no inherent meaning. Furthermore, there is only one text box and label. As such, the names were not changed from their default values. You certainly could use names like lblPrompt and txtData. Remember, the developer can use the control for any purpose and the developer will never see the names of these constituent objects.

At this point, your control supports only a few properties. Those are the properties supported by the Extender object. Also, your control responds to only four events. The Extender object supports these events. For your control to be useful to the developer, it should respond to events like Click and Change. These are the same events that are supported by an ordinary text box. Also, the ActiveX control should support properties that allow the developer to set properties like the label's caption and the text of the text box. These are the subjects of the next section.

SECTION B

objectives

In this section you will:

- **Define event responses for ActiveX controls**
- **Generate events for use by the developer**
- **Create properties for an ActiveX control**
- **Save properties to a form file**
- **Read properties from a form file**

Events, Properties, and Methods

Properties, Events, and Methods

At this point, your control supports (from the developer's perspective) only those properties and events supplied by the Extender object. It does not respond to any other events. This poses an interesting question. Why can't the developer set the properties of the text box and respond to its events? The answer is that you, as the control's author, must expose explicitly the properties and methods of any constituent controls to the developer. You also must write the code that will respond to events and raise events for the developer.

The order in which you do this is somewhat arbitrary. In general, you need to define the properties, events, and methods pertaining to your control, and these activities are hopelessly interrelated. Consider the controls you have used. Changing the value of a text box causes a Change event. When you call the SetFocus method on a text box, the GotFocus event occurs, and so on. You will begin by exposing the events of your ActiveX control.

UserControl Events

As the author of an ActiveX control, the concept of responding to events takes on a whole new meaning. From the perspective of the developer, the behavior of a control is much different depending on whether Visual Basic is in design mode or run mode. Consider a command button. At design time clicking the command button will allow it to be resized or moved. You also can set its properties using the Properties window. At run time, the behavior of the same control is completely different. It generates a Click event. If the developer has written code to respond to the Click event, that code will be executed. While this may seem completely obvious, it defines the two parts to event processing that you, as the control's author, must supply.

As you may recall from the previous steps, the constituent controls that make up the TextBoxPlus control are not resized when the developer resizes the ActiveX control that you as the author created. From the developer's perspective, what happens when the TextBoxPlus control is resized should be automatic. The developer has no access to the underlying properties of the constituent controls. That is, the developer cannot directly set the height, width, or size of either of the two constituent controls.

As the author, you have two choices. You either can implement properties that will let the developer resize the controls individually or you can create an event procedure that will resize the two constituent controls when the TextBoxPlus control is resized.

Programming tip

In general, the specific behavior for any constituent controls should be transparent to the developer whenever possible. In the Focus Management example, when the developer resizes the TextBoxPlus control, the constituent controls will be resized automatically.

Remember, when the developer is interacting with your control, it is running and responding to events that are generated by the developer. One of the events supported by the UserControl object is the Resize event. This event occurs as the developer is resizing the control. This is not the same Resize event that pertains to the constituent text box or label. These events are hidden inside the control and are available only to the author.

When the developer resizes an instance of the TextBoxPlus control, as the author, you must write the code to resize the constituent label and text box whenever the UserControl object is resized.

On the surface, this task may seem trivial. There are several factors to consider as the control is resized, however.

- The width of both the constituent label and text box must be adjusted to fill the region of the control whenever it is resized.
- When the height of the TextBoxPlus control is changed, there are several implementation decisions to be made. One option would be to adjust the height of both the label and the text box. Another would be to use a fixed height for the label and adjust only the height of the text box.

The constituent control you are creating in this chapter takes several factors into account.

- The height of the label is fixed while the height of the text box will adjust to fill the height of the TextBoxPlus control instance created on a form.
- The width of the constituent control will adjust to fit inside the width of the TextBoxPlus control.
- A minimum control width will be defined, prohibiting the developer from designing a TextBoxPlus control that is so small that the constituent controls cannot be displayed.
- Interestingly, the recessed bottom and right borders of some three-dimensional controls will be obscured if the constituent control region is the same size as the UserControl. That is, if you set the width of the constituent text box to the same width as the UserControl, then the right recessed border will be obscured. To solve this problem, constants are used to define margins for the constituent control.

You now can resize the constituent controls.

To resize the constituent controls:

1 Active the Code window for the **TextBoxPlus** control and enter the following statements into the general declarations section of the module. These constants will be used as the margins for the TextBoxPlus control and the minimum height and width.

```
Private Const cTopMargin = 30
Private Const cLeftMargin = 20
Private Const cRightMargin = 80
Private Const cMinHeight = 615
Private Const cMinWidth = 1500
Private Const cBottomMargin = 80
```

2 Enter the following statements in the **UserControl_Resize** event procedure and remove the existing statement:

```
Dim pintWidth As Integer
Dim pintLabelHeight As Integer
Dim pintTextHeight As Integer
If UserControl.Height <= cMinHeight Or _
    UserControl.Width < cMinWidth Then
    UserControl.Height = cMinHeight
    UserControl.Width = cMinWidth
End If
pintWidth = UserControl.Width - cRightMargin
pintTextHeight = UserControl.Height - _
    Label1.Height - cBottomMargin
Text1.Move cLeftMargin, 280, pintWidth, pintTextHeight
Label1.Move cLeftMargin, 0, pintWidth, 255
```

3 Close the Code window and visual designer for the TextBoxPlus control, then open the **Form** window.

4 Activate an instance of the **TextBoxPlus** control, then change the size. Because the visual designer for the User control is closed, the User control is running and will execute the code you just wrote in response to the UserControl_Resize event. The constituent controls are resized to fill the visible region of the TextBoxPlus control.

5 Try to make the size of the control instance very small. The code in the Resize event prohibits the developer from making the control so small that the constituent controls are too small to hold text.

First, consider the constants just declared. As with other class modules, constants must be Private. Attempting to define a Public constant in a class module of any kind will cause a compiler error.

When the developer creates an instance of the TextBoxPlus control or resizes it, the Resize event will occur for the UserControl object. The event also will occur when the control instance first is placed on the form. The code in the event procedure uses the Height and Width properties of the UserControl object. These properties contain the current Height and Width after the TextBoxPlus control is resized and are used as the basis for resizing the constituent controls. First, the If statement verifies that the current height and width is greater than the minimum height and width. If not, the height and width are set to the minimum height and width. Next, the new size of the constituent controls is determined. Finally, the Move method is called to resize the controls.

Your control now responds to a design-time event as viewed by the developer. Consider the situation when the TextBoxPlus control is running from the developer's perspective. In this situation, your control needs to respond to events too. For example, the developer may execute code to resize a control at run time. If there were an instance of the TextBoxPlus control instance named tbpName on the form, the following statements could be used to resize the control when the form is loaded:

```
Private Sub Form_Load( )
    tbpName.Height = 1000
    tbpName.Width = 2000
    tbpName.Left = 100
    tbpName.Top = 100
End Sub
```

As you can see from the previous example, how your control is viewed by the developer is much different in run mode than in design mode. From your perspective as the control's author, the control is running.

Understanding the UserControl Events

Like most controls, the UserControl supports several events. The purpose of some of these events is similar to a form module's Load and Unload events. Remember, from the developer's perspective, a control exhibits very different behaviors at design time and at run time. That is, at run time, a command button will respond to a Click event when clicked, but at design time, clicking the same command button will make it the active object. Interestingly, when Visual Basic is toggled from design time to run time, the design-time control instances actually are destroyed and the run-time control instances are created. This is true for all controls, not just the ActiveX controls you create. Furthermore, when Visual Basic switches from run time to design time, the same process occurs in reverse. The run-time instances of all controls are destroyed and design-time instances of the controls are created.

There is a sequence of events that occurs to the UserControl object when Visual Basic is toggled between run time and design time. There also are events that occur when a control instance is created for the first time.

First, you will examine the events that occur as an instance of the ActiveX control is created, and the events that occur when Visual Basic switches from design mode to run mode and back. When the developer creates an instance of a control based on the UserControl, four events occur for the UserControl object in the following order:

1. The **Initialize** event is the first event to occur when an instance of your ActiveX control is drawn on the form. At this point, your ActiveX control is running and a design-time or run-time instance of the control is created depending on whether or not Visual Basic is in design mode or run mode. Typically, this event is used to initialize the values of the control's module-level variables.
2. The **InitProperties** event occurs just after the Initialize event. Typically, you set the initial values for persistent properties in this event. Persistent properties are discussed in the next section.
3. The **Resize** event occurs just after the InitProperties event occurs. In this event procedure, you should set the size of any constituent controls as needed.
4. Finally, the **Paint** event occurs.

When Visual Basic switches from design time to run time, several events also occur. These events are used to initialize variables pertaining to the User control at run time and to initialize run-time properties. These events occur in the following order. To understand these events, remember that Visual Basic destroys the design-time instance of the ActiveX control as it exists on the form module and creates a run-time instance.

1. The **Terminate** event occurs first when the design-time instance of the User control is destroyed.
2. The **Initialize** event occurs next when the run-time instance of the User control is created.
3. The **ReadProperties** event occurs allowing you to read any saved properties.
4. Finally, the **Resize** and **Paint** events occur as the run-time instance of the User control is drawn on the form.

Finally, a series of events occurs when Visual Basic switches from run mode to design mode. Again, remember that Visual Basic destroys the run-time instance of the control and creates a design-time instance.

1. The **Terminate** event occurs as the run-time instance of the User control is destroyed.
2. The **Initialize** event occurs as the design-time instance is created.
3. The **ReadProperties** event occurs next allowing the saved design-time properties to be read.
4. Then the **Resize** and **Paint** events occur as when the design-time instance of the control is created on the form.

Events also occur when the developer closes the Form window (container) where the instance of the UserControl has been created. In essence, when the Form window is closed, the design-time instance of the control is destroyed. The following events occur allowing you to save any necessary properties and perform housekeeping chores just before the control instance is destroyed.

1. The **WriteProperties** event occurs allowing you to save any changed properties to the form (container).
2. Next, the **Terminate** event occurs just before the design-time instance of the control is destroyed.

A developer usually does not use a control in a project group. Rather, the control is added on the Toolbox using the References dialog. That is, a reference to the .ocx file containing the code for the control is added to the project. This technique is the same as you have used for other ActiveX controls. Ultimately, the project with all the intrinsic and ActiveX controls are compiled into a Standard EXE file. The following events occur to an ActiveX control when the Standard EXE file is run and an instance of the control is created.

1. The **Initialize** event occurs first.
2. The **ReadProperties** event occurs next allowing you to set the initial values for the properties.
3. Finally, the **Resize** and **Paint** events occur when the control instance is created on the form.

Figure 10-7 illustrates the events that occur to the User control as Visual Basic switches from design mode to run mode. First, the design-time instance of the control is destroyed. Then Visual Basic enters run mode and a run-time instance of the User control is created.

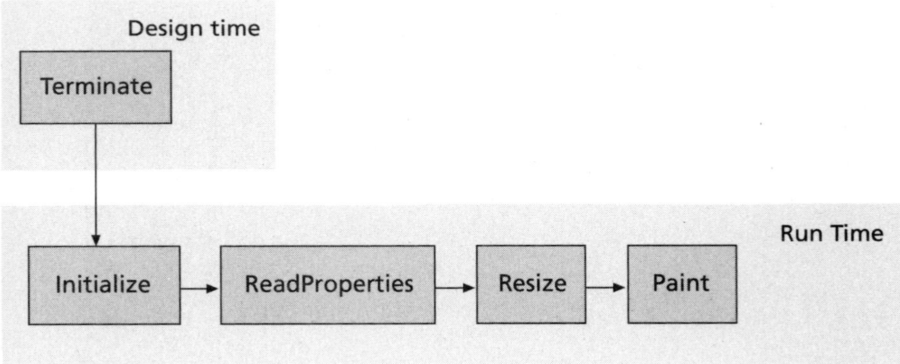

Figure 10-7: UserControl events

The code for these events will become more clear as you continue through the chapter. Specifically, the ReadProperties and WriteProperties events will be discussed in Section C that covers properties.

Object Focus

In addition to the Click event, consider two other events you have used—the GotFocus and LostFocus events. The reason for discussing the GotFocus and LostFocus events is quite intentional and should help distinguish between events that are predefined by the UserControl object, the Extender object, and events that you define inside the TextBoxPlus control. If you use the Help system to inspect the methods supported by the Extender object, you will find that the GotFocus and LostFocus events apply to the constituent text box, the Extender object, and the UserControl object. Given this, you may wonder which GotFocus event occurs to which object and when.

- One GotFocus event pertains to the Extender object. As such, the container (typically the form) raises the event at run time. As the author, you do not raise this event for the developer. Rather, the container raises it when a particular object receives focus.
- Another GotFocus event pertains to the UserControl object. This GotFocus event is intended for use only by the author of the control. The event occurs for the UserControl object only if there are no constituent controls that can receive focus.
- The final possibility is the GotFocus event for the constituent text box. This event is hidden completely from the developer. The author, however, can write code for the GotFocus event for a constituent control like a text box.

The concept of focus, when working with constituent controls, is slightly different than it is for controls you have used. Consider the control you just created. Does the control itself get focus or does the constituent text box get focus? There are four events pertaining to the UserControl object dealing with focus. These events pertain to the author of the control, not the developer.

- The **EnterFocus** event occurs first when the User control receives focus or a constituent control created in the UserControl receives focus.
- The **GotFocus** event occurs for the UserControl object after the EnterFocus event. It only occurs if there are no constituent controls on the UserControl that can get focus. Obviously, this is a different event than the GotFocus event that occurs for a constituent control like a text box.
- The **LostFocus** event occurs when the UserControl loses focus. Like the GotFocus event, it only occurs if there are no constituent controls on the UserControl that can get focus.
- The **ExitFocus** event happens last. It occurs whether or not there are any constituent controls on UserControl.

At this time, you will extend the functionality of your control so it will select all the text in the TextBoxPlus control whenever the control receives focus. There are two ways to accomplish this. Because the constituent text box can get focus, you could write the code in the text box's GotFocus event procedure. You cannot, however, write the code in the UserControl's GotFocus event procedure because the event is not generated when a constituent control can get focus. You can respond to the UserControl's EnterFocus event procedure however.

The code in the event procedure is very simple. The SelStart and SelLength of the constituent text box can be used to select all the text. To do this, SelStart is set to zero (0). SelLength is set to the size of the string. This causes all the characters in the string to be selected.

To define an event response:

1 Activate the Code window for the UserControl and enter the following statements into the **GotFocus** event procedure for the constituent text box, **Text1**:

```
Text1.SelStart = 0
Text1.SelLength = Len(Text1)
```

2 Enter the following statement in the **LostFocus** event procedure for **Text1**:

```
Text1.SelLength = 0
```

3 Close the visual designer and Code window for the User control if open. Activate the Form window then create a second TextBoxPlus instance.

4 Test the program. Enter text in the two text boxes and tab between them. The text is selected as the text box receives focus.

Remember, the GotFocus and LostFocus event procedures you just created pertain to the constituent text box and are hidden inside the ActiveX control. Furthermore, these are not the same events supplied by the Extender object and available to the developer. Assuming that the developer had created an instance of the TextBoxPlus control named tbpName, the following procedure would be valid in the form module:

```
Private Sub tbpName_GotFocus( )
    Debug.Print "tbpName GotFocus"
End Sub
```

At run time, the Extender object will raise a GotFocus event for the TextBoxPlus control. As the developer, you can write code to respond to this event.

Programming tip

When the program is run, the GotFocus event occurs first for the Extender object then for the constituent control. Again, the GotFocus event pertaining to the constituent text box and UserControl is hidden from the developer and available only to the author of the User control.

Remember, from the developer's perspective your ActiveX control only responds to the four events defined by the Extender object. A fully-functional control typically responds to a much more robust set of events. For example, a control that can receive focus typically responds to events like Click and Change. Assuming that the developer created an instance of the TextBoxPlus control and set the Name property to tbpName, then the following code should represent a valid event procedure. Furthermore, the event should be raised whenever the user clicks the constituent text box.

```
Private Sub tbpName_Click( )
    Debug.Print "Click"
End Sub
```

There are two parts involved in exposing an event to the developer. The first part involves declaring the event and the second part involves generating or raising the event. An event is declared using the Event statement as shown in the following syntax:

Syntax	[**Public**] **Event** *procedurename* [(*arglist*)]
Dissection	■ The **Public** keyword identifies the scope of the event. If declared as Public, then the event is visible throughout the project. ■ The **Event** keyword declares an event procedure. Syntactically, an event procedure is declared in the same way as it is for any other procedure like a Function or Sub. The developer does not call the event procedure explicitly. ■ The name of the event procedure is identified by *procedurename*. The *procedurename* must conform to the event names for other procedures. ■ The syntax for *arglist* is the same as it is for Function and Sub procedures. It defines the name of the arguments passed to the event and the data types of those arguments.
Notes	An event cannot return a value, nor can an event declaration exist in a standard module.
Code Example	`Public Event Click( )` `Public Event Change( )`
Code Dissection	The preceding statements declare two different events named Click and Change, respectively. The statements only declare the names of the events; they do not raise the events. Also, the events have no As Type clause because events cannot return a value.

An interesting point comes up when you consider the issue of focus. You have created an event procedure for the text box so it will select all the text in the constituent text box when the text box gets focus. Again, this event is hidden inside the text box itself and is therefore not available to the developer. Suppose, however, that as the author, you want the developer to have access to the GotFocus and LostFocus events. You may be tempted to create the following event declarations in your control:

```
Public Event GotFocus( )
Public Event LostFocus( )
```

If you place these two declarations inside the control's general declarations section, you will get the following syntax error as shown in Figure 10-8.

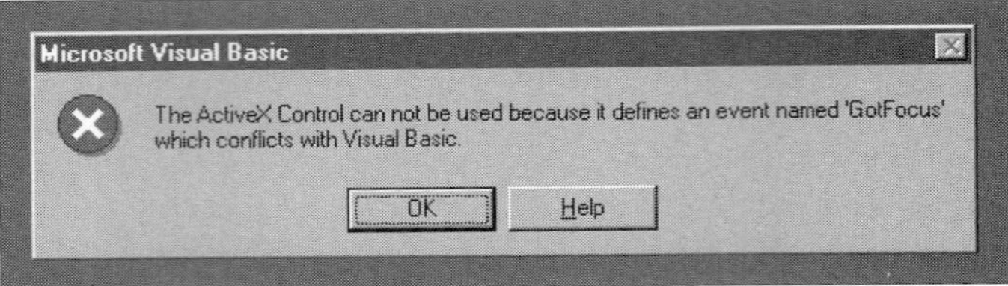

Figure 10-8: GotFocus event error message

The cause of the error is relatively straightforward. The Extender object predefines the GotFocus and LostFocus events for you. This becomes clear if, as the developer, you activate the Code window for a form module and select an instance of the control as the object. If you open the Procedure list box, you will see the GotFocus and LostFocus events already are defined.

Once an event has been declared, a mechanism is needed to generate the event. This commonly is referred to as **raising an event**. To raise an event, the RaiseEvent statement is used. The syntax is much like calling a procedure.

Syntax — **RaiseEvent** *eventname* [(*argumentlist*)]

Dissection

- The **RaiseEvent** statement generates the event identified by *eventname.*
- The required *eventname* is the name of the event to be generated. The *eventname* must have been declared already using an Event statement.
- The optional *argumentlist* contains a list of arguments passed to the event. In other words, the event procedure created by the developer will receive these values as arguments. Conceptually, this is the same as processing the events in any other procedure.

Code Example

```
Private Sub Text1_Click( )
    RaiseEvent Click
End Sub
```

Code Dissection — The previous code typically would exist in your ActiveX control. In this case, the text box named Text1 is a constituent control. When the user clicks the constituent text box, the Click event occurs. This causes the Click event to be raised as seen by the developer of your ActiveX control.

Conceptually, raising an event is the reverse of responding to one. Figure 10-9 illustrates the process of raising an event.

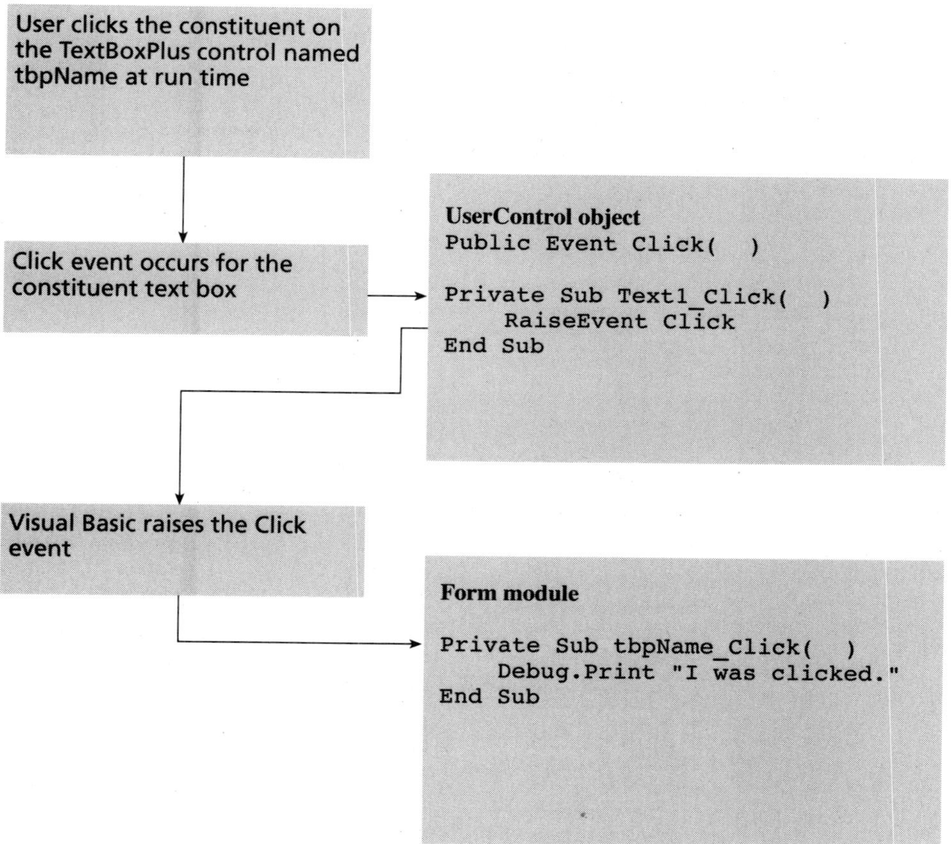

Figure 10-9: Raising an event

When the user clicks the constituent text box, the Click event occurs for the constituent text box. This event procedure raises the Click event for the developer. The code written by the developer then is executed. In other words, the Click event procedure in the form module is executed.

Given the previous event procedure, the developer now can respond to the Click event procedure for the TextBoxPlus control. Assuming that the developer had created an instance of the TextBoxPlus control named tbpName, the following event procedure could be used to respond to the Click event:

```
Private Sub tbpName_Click( )
    Debug.Print "I was clicked."
End Sub
```

You now have the tools to raise an event inside your User control.

To create the code to raise an event in a User control:

1. Create the following declaration in the general declarations section of the UserControl named **TextBoxPlus**:

```
Public Event Click( )
```

2. Create the following statement in the **Text1_Click** event procedure:

```
Private Sub Text1_Click( )
    RaiseEvent Click
End Sub
```

3. Enter the following statements in the form module:

```
Private Sub tbpName_Click( )
    Debug.Print "I was clicked."
End Sub
```

4. Test the program. Click the constituent text box part of the control instance named **tbpName** while Visual Basic is in run mode. The constituent text box raises the Click event procedure. The event procedure tbpName_Click then is raised and the text "I was clicked." is printed in the Immediate window.

At this point, your TextBoxPlus control can raise a Click event. The Extender object also will raise GotFocus and LostFocus events. In reality, TextBoxPlus controls should respond to many other events. For example, it would be reasonable to respond to events like Change, KeyDown, KeyUp, and KeyPress.

Exposing Properties to the Developer

To create a property that is available to the developer, you create Property procedures in the UserControl module in the same way you created Property procedures for class modules. Syntactically there is no difference. The way the properties are used by the developer, however, is much different from the way the developer uses properties defined in a code component. The developer can set the properties for your ActiveX control either using the Properties window at design time or with code at run time, just like any other control. There are roughly four strategies to create a property.

- **Delegation** is used to expose a property of a constituent control. This is common when a control is made from a single constituent control. For example, if you wanted the developer to be able to read and write the Text property of a constituent text box, you would create a pair of Property procedures in the User control that would in turn read and write the Text property of the constituent text box.

- **Aggregation** is used to group properties together when an ActiveX control is made from multiple constituent controls. Assume that you created a User control made from a constituent label and text box. Also assume that when the developer set the foreground color of the User control, the foreground color would be changed for both the constituent label and the text box. In this case, you can create a Property procedure named ForeColor. When the user reads or writes the property, the foreground color of both constituent controls are set. In other words, the properties of the constituent controls are aggregated into one property.
- It is possible to create **New** properties that are not supported by the constituent controls. For example, suppose you wanted to implement the User control with a Boolean property named SelectAll. When set to True, the User control should select all the characters when the control receives focus and not select the characters when the property is False.
- Technically, it is possible to modify the behavior of an existing property defined by a constituent control. That is, you could expose a property named Appearance that would change the appearance of a constituent text box but use constants that are different than the constants usually supported by the constituent text box. This technique is strongly discouraged because a developer is accustomed to a property of a specific name performing a specific task. For example, given a text box, it would be counterintuitive to redefine the behavior of the Text or Appearance properties.

For any given control, these strategies are not mutually exclusive. That is, you may aggregate properties by creating an Appearance property that would set the font attribute properties for multiple controls. You may delegate, however, the Text property of a constituent text box. Finally, you can create entirely new properties all in the same control.

Fundamentals of Properties

Remember, the control's container supports several properties through the Extender object. It is possible to expose other properties to the developer as needed. In the previous chapters, you learned two techniques to create properties. You either could use a Public variable or a pair of Property procedures. Syntactically, you expose properties for your ActiveX control in the same way. You can declare a Public variable or create Property procedures. As you will see in a moment, Public variables have severe limitations when used with ActiveX controls.

As a control's author, consider the following features that must be supported for use by the developer. These features are described from the perspective of the developer, not the author.

- Some properties may be available only at run time, others only at design time, and others at both design time and run time.
- Furthermore, properties may be read-only or read-write depending on whether or not the program's form module is in design mode or run mode.
- Design-time properties are edited using either the Properties window or Property Pages.

- Some properties should have default or initial values when a new instance of the ActiveX control is created. As a rule, any property that can be set at design time using the Properties window should have a default value.
- Properties can be persistent or not. For example, if the developer sets a design-time property using the Properties window or Property Pages, the value of the property should persist as the developer toggles Visual Basic between design time and run time. Also, the value of the property should persist after Visual Basic has exited. Other properties set at run time usually are not persistent.

The PropertyChanged Method

When the code in your control changes the value of an exposed property, the container must be notified of the change. This is so the container can update the Properties window or the control instance drawn on the form with the new value of the property. This notification is not automatic. Rather, when the code in your ActiveX control changes a property's value, you must call the PropertyChanged method of the UserControl object. This method notifies the container that a property has been changed so its value can be updated properly.

Syntax *object*.**PropertyChanged** *PropertyName*

Dissection

- The *object* must be a valid instance of the UserControl object.
- The **PropertyChanged** method notifies the container (usually a form) that the value of the property identified by *PropertyName* has changed.
- The *PropertyName* must be a property created with a Property procedure. This illustrates the limitations placed on Public variables as properties. When the developer reads or writes the value of a Public variable, there is no way to notify the container that the value of the property has changed.

Code Example

```
Public Property Let Enabled(ByVal New_Enabled _
    As Boolean)
    Text1.Enabled( ) = New_Enabled
    PropertyChanged "Enabled"
End Property
```

Code Dissection By calling the PropertyChanged method for the Enabled property, the container is notified whenever the value of the property changes.

It is not necessary to call the PropertyChanged method on properties that only can be used at run time.
Public variables should not be used to implement properties for ActiveX controls, as there is no way to notify the control's container that the value of the property has changed. Only Property procedures should be used.

You now have the necessary tools to create properties and communicate any changes back to the container (form). You now will proceed to define properties for your control using delegation, aggregation, and defining an entirely new property.

Delegating Properties

The constituent text box supports an Enabled property indicating whether or not the text box can get focus. You will implement the Enabled property using delegation. Remember, however, the properties and events of the text box are hidden from the developer. The only way the developer can access a property is for you as the control's author to create a Property procedure pair in the User control. The Property procedures must be Public, otherwise the property will be hidden from the developer.

Visual Basic is very intelligent with regard to the properties you create. Properties you create appear automatically in the Properties window. Furthermore, depending on the property's data type, Visual Basic will display list boxes as appropriate. For example, if you create a Boolean property, Visual Basic will display the values True and False in the value column of the Properties window. Properties with a well-defined set of values also appear in the code completion features in the Code window. You will see how this works in Section C of this chapter.

In this example, you will create a Property procedure pair named Enabled. These Property procedures will read or write the value of the Enabled property to the constituent text box. In other words, the Enabled property is delegated to the text box. You also will create Caption and Text properties so the developer can change the contents of the constituent controls. The properties are implemented by delegating the Caption property to the constituent label and the Text property to the constituent text box. These properties should be read-write both at design time and run time. Thus, you should create both Property Get and Property Let procedures.

To create properties using delegation:

1 Enter the following Property procedures in the **UserControl**:

```
Public Property Get Enabled( ) As Boolean
    Enabled = Text1.Enabled
End Property

Public Property Let Enabled(ByVal New_Enabled As _
    Boolean)
    Text1.Enabled( ) = New_Enabled
    PropertyChanged "Enabled"
End Property
```

```
Public Property Get Text( ) As String
    Text = Text1.Text
End Property

Public Property Let Text(ByVal New_Text As String)
    Text1.Text = New_Text
    PropertyChanged "Text"
End Property

Public Property Get Caption( ) As String
    Caption = Label1.Caption
End Property

Public Property Let Caption( _
    ByVal New_Caption As String)
    Label1.Caption = New_Caption
    PropertyChanged "Caption"
End Property
```

2. Close the visual designer and Code window for the UserControl. Open the Form window, then activate one of the **TextBoxPlus** objects.
3. Press **F4** to open the Properties window. If you select the TextBoxPlus control on the form, then right-click to activate the Properties window, the Properties command is not there. Three new properties named "Caption," "Enabled," and "Text" appear in the Properties window. Set the Enabled property to **True**. Because the property has a Boolean data type, the Properties window lists only the values True and False.
4. Set the value of the Caption and Text properties to **Testing**. When the value of the property is changed in the Properties window, the value is updated on the form.
5. These properties also are available at run time. Enter the following statements in the **Form_Load** event procedure:

```
tbpName.Enabled = True
tbpName.Caption = "Name"
tbpName.Text = ""
```

6. Test the program. The TextBoxPlus control instance should be enabled, have a caption of Name, and no text in the constituent text box.

These statements use delegation to implement the Caption, Enabled, and Text properties of the TextBoxPlus control. Remember, the properties of the constituent text box and label are hidden from the developer. Using this technique, the Caption, Enabled, and Text Property procedures pertaining to the User control simply set or read the property of the same name pertaining to the constituent text box or label.

Aggregating Properties

Aggregation is a technique very similar to delegation. Suppose you wanted to create a property named FontSize that is exposed to the developer. When the property is set, the FontSize property is set both for the constituent text box and the label. That is, you are aggregating the FontSize properties for the two constituent controls.

To create properties using aggregation:

1. Enter the following Property procedures in the **UserControl**:

```
Public Property Get FontSize( ) As Integer
    FontSize = Text1.FontSize
End Property

Public Property Let FontSize(ByVal New_Size As Integer)
    Label1.FontSize = New_Size
    Text1.FontSize = New_Size
End Property
```

2. Close the visual designer and Code window for the UserControl, open the Form window, then locate one of the **TextBoxPlus** objects.
3. In the Properties window, set the FontSize to **12**. The font size is updated for both the constituent labels and text boxes.

The preceding Property procedures are very similar to the Property procedures you created in the previous steps. Instead of delegating a property to a constituent control, the FontSize property is aggregated from the two constituent controls. When the developer sets the FontSize property, the value is changed for both constituent controls. The process of delegating or aggregating a read-only or write-once property is the same as the technique used in Chapter 8. To create a read-only property, the Property Let procedure is omitted. To implement a write-once property, the Property Let procedure contains a static Boolean variable to prevent the developer from setting the property's value more than once. Write-once and read-only properties most commonly are used with run-time properties.

Creating New Properties and Methods

New properties are defined using the same technique used to delegate and aggregate properties; that is, you create a pair of Property procedures. Again, to create read-write properties, you implement both Property Let and Property Get procedures. To implement a read-only property, the Property Let procedure either can be omitted or raise an error. Creating methods also is very simple. To create a method, you declare a Public, Sub, or Function procedure in the User control. This has the effect of creating a method just like the technique used to create a method in a class module.

Persistent Properties

Your control, as it presently exists, has a major flaw. If you set properties using the Properties window, the value will be updated on the form at design time. For example, if you as the developer set the Text property of the TextBoxPlus control, the value is reflected in the control instance drawn on the form. If you close the Form window, or switch from design time to run time, the changes you made to the Properties window are lost.

Remember, when Visual Basic switched from design time to run time, the design-time instance of the control was destroyed and a run-time instance of the control is created. Unless you explicitly tell the container (form), that the current value of a property should be maintained (persisted), the changes are lost. This is referred to as **property persistence.**

Properties set in the Properties window usually should persist between invocations of Visual Basic and between design time and run time. Consider what happens when the user saves a form file. Design-time property settings are saved to the form file. Also, consider what happens when you run a Standard EXE project. The current design-time settings for the form and its objects are set. These become the initial run-time values.

To understand persistent properties, you need to understand additional events that occur to your ActiveX control when an instance is created and when Visual Basic switches from design time to run time and back. First, not all properties should be persistent. For example, properties that have meaning only at run time are not generally persistent properties.

Before discussing persistent properties, consider the format of a form file. Figure 10-10 illustrates a segment of a form file with the property settings for a TextBoxPlus control instance.

```
Begin SuperText.TextBoxPlus TextBoxPlus1
      Height          =    1455
      Left            =    120
      TabIndex        =    0
      Top             =    240
      Width           =    4575
      _ExtentX        =    8070
      _ExtentY        =    2566
      ForeColor       =    16711680
      FontBold        =    0    'False
      ForeColor       =    16711680
   End
```

Figure 10-10: Form file segment

First, only the properties that differ from the default property values are listed. This helps to reduce the size of the form file and improve performance. Think of how long a form file would be and the time it would take to read the file if the value of every property for every control instance were listed in the form file.

The PropertyBag Object

Visual Basic neither saves design-time properties automatically when the form is closed or when Visual Basic switches from design time to run time, nor does it read the default values of properties when a control instance is created (either a design-time instance or a run-time instance). Persistent properties are saved and retrieved using an object called the PropertyBag. The PropertyBag object is predefined like the Extender object. Thus, you do not declare an instance of the PropertyBag object. Every UserControl object has one, and only one, property bag. The PropertyBag object supports two methods. The ReadProperty method reads a property from the property bag and returns the value for the property. The WriteProperty method writes the value of a property to the PropertyBag object. All defined properties are not saved automatically to the PropertyBag object. Rather, you must save explicitly each property whose value you want to persist.

Syntax

object.**ReadProperty**(*DataName*[, *DefaultValue*])
object.**WriteProperty**(*DataName*, *Value*[, *DefaultValue*])

Dissection

- The **ReadProperty** method reads a property from the property bag and the **WriteProperty** method writes a property to the property bag. This tells the container, in this case a form module, to save the value of the specified property.
- The *object* must be a valid PropertyBag object.
- The *DataName* contains the name by which the property is referenced in the property bag. It is a string key typically the same as the name for the property.
- The *DefaultValue*, when used with the ReadProperty method, causes this value to be returned if no value has been stored in the PropertyBag object. When used with the WriteProperty method, it contains the default value for the property.
- The *Value* is the data value that is saved to the property bag.

Code Example

```
Call PropBag.WriteProperty("Enabled", _
    Text1.Enabled, True)
Text1.Enabled = PropBag.ReadProperty("Enabled", True)
```

Code Dissection

The first statement calls the property bag's WriteProperty method. The property to be written is the Enabled property. The current value of the Text1.Enabled property is written to the property bag only if the value of the Enabled property differs from the default value which is True. The next statement reads the value of the Enabled property from the property bag if one exists. If there is no value stored in the property bag, then the Enabled property is set to True.

Saving properties to the property bag does not cause the properties to be saved to the form file on the disk. This happens when the developer saves the form or the project. In other words, it is the responsibility of the container (form), actually to save a persistent property to the disk.

When using the WriteProperty method, it is critical that you specify a default value. If you do not, the value of the property will be written to the form file no matter the current setting. For example, consider the following statements:

```
Call PropBag.WriteProperty("Enabled", _
    Text1.Enabled, True)
Call PropBag.WriteProperty("Enabled", Text1.Enabled)
```

Assuming that the value of Text1.Enabled is True, then the first statement will not cause the setting to be written to the form file because the value of the property is the same as the default value. The second statement, however, because no default value is specified will cause the property to be written to the form file because there is no default value.

The ReadProperty method needs to be called when the control is loaded and the WriteProperty method needs to be called when the control instance is unloaded. This can occur because the Form window is being closed or Visual Basic is switching from design time to run time. There are two events that occur to the UserControl object. In these event procedures, the ReadProperty and WriteProperty methods typically are called.

The ReadProperties event occurs whenever the ActiveX control is loaded. This can occur for several reasons. When you open the Form window containing an instance of the ActiveX control, a design-time instance of the ActiveX control is loaded causing the ReadProperties event to occur. Furthermore, whenever Visual Basic switches from design time to run time, the event also occurs. It is in this event procedure that you should read the values of persistent properties.

The WriteProperties event occurs whenever Visual Basic switches from design time to run time. It also occurs whenever the form containing the ActiveX control is saved. It is in this event procedure that you should write the necessary code to save the values of persistent properties. The PropertyBag object is passed as an argument to both the ReadProperties and WriteProperties events, which have the following syntax:

Syntax

Private Sub *object*_**ReadProperties(***pb* **As PropertyBag)**
Private Sub *object*_**WriteProperties(***pb* **As PropertyBag)**

Dissection

- The *pb* is an object of variable type PropertyBag. It is passed as an argument to both the ReadProperties and WriteProperties events.
- The *object* must be a valid instance of a UserControl.
- The **ReadProperties** event occurs when a User control instance is loaded, allowing you to read initial values for properties.
- The **WriteProperties** event occurs when an instance of the User control needs to be saved.

Code Example

```
Private Sub UserControl_ReadProperties( _
    PropBag As PropertyBag)
    Text1.Enabled = PropBag.ReadProperty( _
        "Enabled", True)
End Sub

Private Sub UserControl_WriteProperties( _
    PropBag As PropertyBag)
    Call PropBag.WriteProperty( _
        "Enabled", Text1.Enabled, True)
End Sub
```

Code Dissection

These two event procedures read and write the Enabled property to and from the property bag. The default value of the Enabled property is True.

In this example, the Caption, Enabled, and Text properties you have implemented should persist whenever Visual Basic switches from design time to run time, whenever the Form window is closed, and between invocations of Visual Basic.

To create persistent properties:

1 Enter the following statements in the **UserControl_InitProperties** event procedure. This procedure only will execute the first time the control is created. Thus, the code sets the initial value for the properties.

```
Text1.Text = UserControl.Name
Label1.Caption = UserControl.Name
```

2 Enter the following statements in the **UserControl_ReadProperties** event procedure. This event procedure will execute each time a control instance (either at design time or run time) is created.

```
Text1.Enabled = PropBag.ReadProperty( _
    "Enabled", True)
Label1.Caption = PropBag.ReadProperty("Caption", _
    UserControl.Name)
Text1.Text = PropBag.ReadProperty( _
    "Text", UserControl.Name)
```

3 Enter the following statements in the **UserControl_WriteProperties** event procedure:

```
Call PropBag.WriteProperty( _
    "Enabled", Text1.Enabled, True)
Call PropBag.WriteProperty("Text", Text1.Text, _
    UserControl.Name)
Call PropBag.WriteProperty("Caption", Label1.Caption, _
    UserControl.Name)
```

4 Remove the statements you wrote in the **Form_Load** event procedure.

5 Test the program. Close the visual designer and Code window for the User control. Open the Form window and set the value of the Enabled, Caption, and Text properties. Run the program then end it. The values of the properties are persistent.

The Enabled, Text, and Caption properties now are synchronized with the container. Furthermore, the properties will persist when Visual Basic switches between run time and design time. Furthermore, the property will persist between invocations of Visual Basic.

Read-Write and Read-Only Properties

As you have seen, properties can be read-only, read-write, or write-once properties. As the author, when creating ActiveX controls you also must determine the actions that can be performed on a property at both run time and design time. For example, some properties should be set only at design time and other properties set only at run time. Whether to create a run-time or design-time property depends on the needs of your particular control and property. To help you make this decision, consider other controls you have used. For example, it makes no sense to set the Data control's Recordset property at design time. This is because the Data control creates the recordset at run time. To accomplish this, you use Property procedures as you have done in the past. Before the property can be read or written, the Property procedure must determine whether or not the container (form) is in design time or run time.

Remember, the AmbientProperties object gets its information from the container, in this case the form. The AmbientProperties object supports a property called UserMode. The UserMode property contains a Boolean value indicating the state of the container. If True, then the container, in this case Visual Basic, is in run mode and if False, Visual Basic is in design mode.

Consider the following Property procedures that implement a property that is read-only at run time:

```
Private mEOF as Boolean

Property Get EOF As Boolean
    EOF = mEOF
End Property

Property Let EOF( )
    If AmbientProperties.UserMode then
        Err.Raise Number:=31013, _
            Description:= _
                "Cannot write property at run time."
```

```
        End If
        EOF = mEOF
        PropertyChanged EOF
End Property
```

These statements create a Boolean variable named mEOF. While not implemented in the above code, the property likely would be used to detect whether or not the state of the control was at the end of file. As an example, you might implement an ActiveX control consisting of a Data control and a set of bound text boxes. Developers then could add your control to their program without having to deal with the intricacies of the interaction between the Data control and bound controls. The Property procedures implement a property named EOF that is read-only at run time. The Property Let procedure tests the value of the AmbientProperties UserMode property. If Visual Basic is in run mode, then an error is raised. This Property procedure should not be available to the developer at design time either. You will see in Section C how to hide a property from the developer at design time, which has the effect of the hidden property not being displayed in the Properties window.

By creating the Property procedure pair, the property exists both at design time and run time. If the property only has meaning at run time, then it should not appear in the Properties window. This has the effect of hiding the property from the developer at design time. The Procedure Attributes dialog supports features pertaining to ActiveX controls that prevent the properties of your ActiveX control from appearing in the Properties window, or make a property or method the default property or method. As you know, the Properties window supports both an Alphabetic and Categorized tab. It also is possible to add properties so they appear in a specific, or new, category. Figure 10-11 shows the Procedure Attributes dialog and the settings to manipulate the appearance of properties in the Properties window.

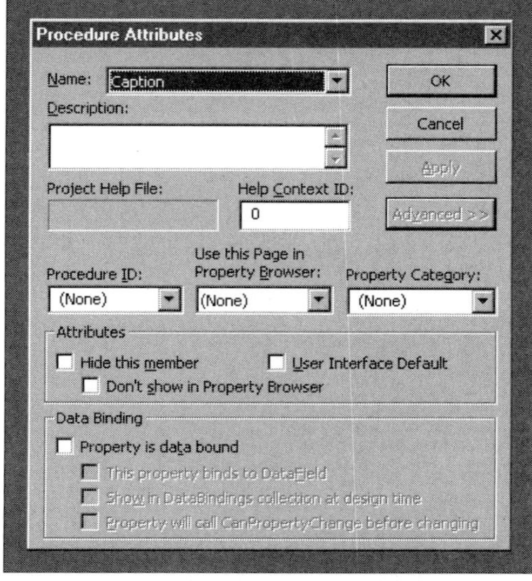

Figure 10-11: Procedure Attributes dialog

As shown in Figure 10-11, the Attributes section contains three check boxes.

- If the **Hide this member** check box is checked, the property or method will not appear in either the Object Browser or the Properties window. The properties can be accessed with code, however.
- If the **User Interface Default** check box is checked, the property is highlighted in the Properties window when it initially is opened. If the object is an event, then the Code window is set to the event by default when you double-click the control. There only can be one User Interface Default property and one User Interface Default event for a User control. The User Interface Default cannot be a method.
- If the **Don't show in Property Browser** check box is checked, then the property will not be shown in the Properties window. It will appear in the Object Browser and you can continue to write code to access it.

As you create the developer interface for your control, you should consider which property method or event will be the most commonly used and make it the default. Also, you should be careful to not display run-time only properties in the Properties window.

While you can hide properties and create default properties, the properties you have created have a deficiency. For example, some properties should display a list from which the developer selects a property. For other properties, a dialog should be displayed. This typically occurs when setting a font or color. This is the topic of the following section.

SECTION C

objectives

In this section you will:

- Create properties that activate dialogs
- Create enumerated properties
- Create default properties
- Make a control data aware so it can be used as a bound control with an instance of the Data control

Creating Better Properties

Improving the Behavior of the Properties Window

You undoubtedly have enjoyed the capability of the Properties window to display Properties buttons that activate dialogs to set colors and fonts. Colors usually are represented by hexadecimal numbers like &H80000008&. To force a developer, or user for that matter, to set a color in this way would be absurd. One of the features you can add to your control is support for Properties buttons that open a dialog and set the value for a specific property pertaining to your ActiveX control. In this example, you will aggregate the ForeColor property of the constituent label and text box controls. Instead of forcing the user to select a color by entering a hexadecimal number, a dialog will be displayed. This is accomplished using another data type supported by Visual Basic named OLE_COLOR. This data type is used for properties that return colors. Using this data type is as simple as declaring a Property Get procedure as the OLE_COLOR data type as shown in the following Property procedures:

```
Public Property Get ForeColor( ) As OLE_COLOR
    ForeColor = Text1.ForeColor
End Property

Public Property Let ForeColor _
    (ByVal New_ForeColor As OLE_COLOR)
    Label1.ForeColor = New_ForeColor
    Text1.ForeColor = New_ForeColor
    PropertyChanged "ForeColor"
End Property
```

In this example, the ForeColor Property Get procedure has a data type of OLE_COLOR. When executed, the Property procedure will display a dialog allowing the user to select a color. The color selected by the user will be returned by the Property procedure. The value actually is a long integer. To see how this works, you can create the BackColor and ForeColor properties.

To create properties using the OLE_COLOR data type:

1 Create the following four Property procedures in the UserControl object:

```
Public Property Get ForeColor( ) As OLE_COLOR
    ForeColor = Text1.ForeColor
End Property

Public Property Let ForeColor( _
    ByVal New_ForeColor As OLE_COLOR)
    Label1.ForeColor = New_ForeColor
    Text1.ForeColor = New_ForeColor
    PropertyChanged "ForeColor"
End Property

Public Property Get BackColor( ) As OLE_COLOR
    BackColor = Text1.BackColor
End Property

Public Property Let BackColor( _
    ByVal New_BackColor As OLE_COLOR)
    Label1.BackColor = New_BackColor
    Text1.BackColor = New_BackColor
    PropertyChanged "BackColor"
End Property
```

2 Enter the following statements in the **UserControl_WriteProperties** event procedure:

```
Call PropBag.WriteProperty("BackColor", _
    UserControl.BackColor, &H8000000F)
Call PropBag.WriteProperty("ForeColor", _
    Label1.ForeColor, &H80000012)
```

3 Enter the following statement in the **UserControl_ReadProperties** event procedure:

```
Text1.BackColor = PropBag.ReadProperty _
    ("BackColor", &H8000000F)
Label1.BackColor = PropBag.ReadProperty _
    ("BackColor", &H8000000F)
Text1.ForeColor = PropBag.ReadProperty _
    ("ForeColor", &H80000012)
Label1.ForeColor = PropBag.ReadProperty _
    ("ForeColor", &H80000012)
```

4 Test the program. Close the visual designer for the User control, then activate the Form window. Set the ForeColor and BackColor properties for an instance of the TextBoxPlus object. As you change the properties, the foreground and background color of the constituent controls are changed accordingly.

The code you just wrote uses the aggregation technique to implement the ForeColor and BackColor properties. The code is very similar to the code you wrote to aggregate the FontSize property in the previous section. The notable difference is that the OLE_COLOR data type is used to display a dialog to set the value. The values for the default property use the actual hexadecimal value for the property. The easiest way to determine this value is to create a control instance, set the value to the desired color, and copy the value to the event procedure.

Enumerated Properties

Many properties have a well-defined list of values. For example, a text box's Alignment property can be left-justified, right-justified, or centered. Trying to assign a different value would cause an error to occur. Another point to be made is that when a property has a defined set of values, those values are listed in the Properties window when the user clicks the Properties button.

In addition to using the OLE data types, you can use enumerations for properties. You can use two different types of enumerations for a property. You can use enumerations supported by an object's Type Library or you can create your own user-defined enumerations. To view the enumerations supported by the Type Library, you use the Object Browser. Visual Basic defines several enumerations for you. Each of these enumerations has the suffix "Constants" in the classes section of the Object Browser. If you click the enumerated constant in the Object Browser, the description window will indicate that the constant is an enumeration. Suppose you wanted to expose the text box's MousePointer property, which typically is represented by an enumeration in the Properties window. Consider the following statements:

```
Public Property Get MousePointer( ) _
    As MousePointerConstants
    ' Statements to change the mouse pointer.
End Property

Public Property Let MousePointer( _
    ByVal NewPointer As MousePointerConstants)
    ' Statements to change the mouse pointer.
End Property
```

These Property procedures have the enumerated type MousePointerConstants. As such, the applicable mouse pointer constants will be displayed automatically in the Properties window. Like all enumerated constants, Visual Basic does not prevent you from assigning an invalid value to the property. For example, consider the following statements:

```
Private Sub TextBoxPlus1_Click( )
    TextBoxPlus1.MousePointer = 999
End Sub
```

The statement in the event procedure will cause a run-time error because the property value is not valid. To prevent the run-time error, the Property Let procedure could validate the value to make sure the constant is not valid. This is an intricate situation. At design time, the developer will see the enumerated constant in the Properties window. At run time, however, the developer will be able to set the property using code. At this time it would be reasonable for the Property Let procedure to raise an error. If no error is raised, the developer will not know that the property was set to an invalid value. This could lead to a hard-to-find error.

To use the enumerated mouse pointers:

1 Create the following Property procedures for the **UserControl**:

```
Public Property Get MousePointer( ) _
    As MousePointerConstants
    MousePointer = Text1.MousePointer
End Property

Public Property Let MousePointer( _
    ByVal NewPointer As MousePointerConstants)
    Text1.MousePointer = NewPointer
    PropertyChanged "MousePointer"
End Property
```

2 Enter the following statement in the **UserControl_ReadProperties** event:

```
Text1.MousePointer = PropBag.ReadProperty( _
    "MousePointer", 0)
```

3 Enter the following statement in the **UserControl_WriteProperties** event:

```
Call PropBag.WriteProperty("MousePointer", _
    Text1.MousePointer, 0)
```

4 Test the program. Close the visual designer for the User control and activate the Form window. Activate the Properties window for the TextBoxPlus control instance and select the MousePointer property. The list of valid properties should be displayed in a list box.

User-Defined Enumerations

In addition to using predefined enumerations, it also is possible to create your own enumerations, expose them in a Type Library, and make them available in the Properties window. To accomplish this task, you can create a user-defined enumeration in the ActiveX control, then create the Property procedure pairs such that the Property Get procedure returns the enumerated type, and the Property Let procedure has an argument of the enumerated type.

Suppose that you wanted to supply two or three different formats that incorporated different font colors and attributes. This type of functionality would be suitable in situations where you wanted developers to use one of a few standardized styles.

To create a property having an enumerated type:

1 Enter the following statements in the general declarations section of the User control:

```
Enum tbpAttention
    tbpLight = 0
    tbpNormal = 1
    tbpDark = 2
End Enum

Private mAttention As tbpAttention
```

2 Create the following Property Get and Property Let procedures:

```
Public Property Get Attention( ) As tbpAttention
    Attention = mAttention
End Property

Public Property Let Attention( _
    New_Attention As tbpAttention)
    Select Case New_Attention
        Case tbpLight
            Text1.FontBold = False
            Text1.ForeColor = vbBlue
        Case tbpNormal
            Text1.FontBold = False
            Text1.ForeColor = vbBlack
        Case tbpDark
            Text1.FontBold = True
            Text1.ForeColor = vbBlack
    End Select
    mAttention = New_Attention
    PropertyChanged "Attention"
End Property
```

3 Enter the following statements in the **UserControl_ReadProperties** event:

```
Text1.FontBold = PropBag.ReadProperty( _
    "Attention", tbpNormal)
```

4 Enter the following statements in the **UserControl_WriteProperties** event:

```
Call PropBag.WriteProperty("Attention", tbpAttention)
```

5 Test the program. Activate the Code window for the **Form_Load** event procedure and enter the statement shown in Figure 10-12. The Auto List Members box displays the legal options for the setting.

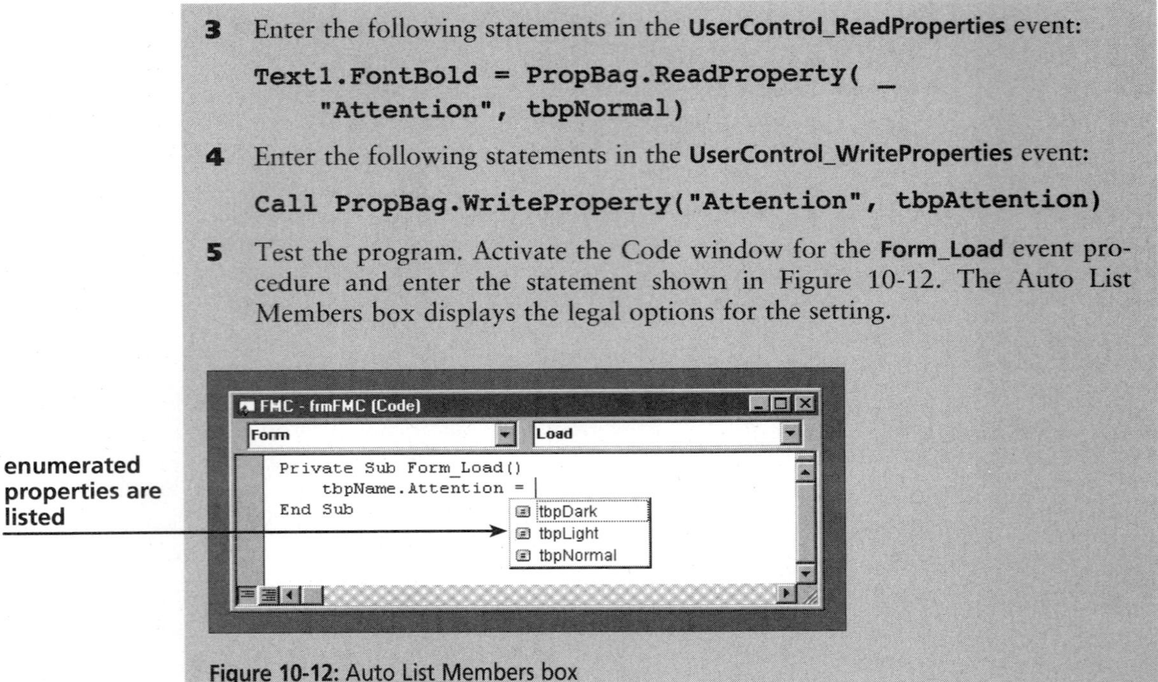

Figure 10-12: Auto List Members box

The code to create the Attention property is straightforward. The argument of the Property Let procedure has a data type of tbpAttention. This is the same data type as the return value of the Property Get procedure. The module-level variable mAttention is used to store the value of the property. So the property will persist, the properties are written to the property bag. This example exploits the concept of aggregating properties.

Creating Data-Aware Controls

As a superset of an ordinary text box, another capability that you can provide to the developer to round out the functionality of the control is to allow the control to be a data-aware control. Creating a data-aware control is quite simple. The following list summarizes the steps involved in making a control a data-aware control:

- The first step is to use the Procedure Attributes dialog to set the data-binding characteristics.
- Inside the Change event procedure of the constituent control, the PropertyChanged method must be called. This provides the linkage between your control and the Data control. This way, the Data control can update the database whenever the value of the control changes.

- The CanPropertyChange method pertains to the UserControl. It typically is used in a Property Let procedure of a constituent control to test that the value of the property can be changed.

To make a control a data-aware control:

1 Open the Code window for the **TextBoxPlus** control. Activate the **Procedure Attributes** dialog, then click the **Advanced** tab. Select **Text** from the Name drop-down list. Check the check boxes shown in Figure 10-13. Click **OK**.

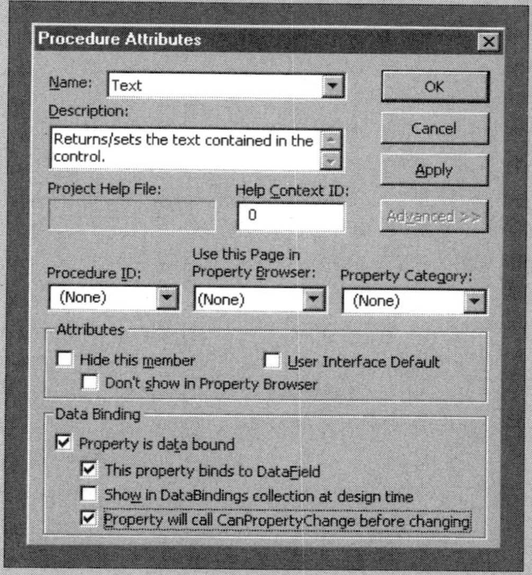

Figure 10-13: Procedure Attributes dialog

2 Activate the Code window for the **TextBoxPlus** control, then enter the following statement in the **Text1_Change** event:

```
PropertyChanged "Text"
```

3 If you consider a bound text box, it is the Text property that is bound to a Data control. As such, modify the following Property procedure to write the **Text** property:

```
Public Property Let Text(ByVal New_Text As String)
    If CanPropertyChange("Text") Then
        Text1.Text( ) = New_Text
        PropertyChanged "Text"
    End If
End Property
```

4 Test the program. Activate the Form window and select the instance of the TextBoxPlus object. The DataField and DataSource properties appear automatically in the Properties window. You can bind the control to a Data control just as you would any other bound control.

Using the ActiveX Control Interface Wizard

So far, you have exposed only a subset of the properties that the TextBoxPlus control should support. The developer cannot create a multiline text box, for example. Furthermore, the control supports only the Click and Change events. As such, your control cannot generate events to support a keyboard handler. A well-designed and implemented ActiveX control should support fully the properties and events of the constituent controls.

The process of delegating all the different properties usually supported by the text box is a tedious process. Fortunately, there is a Wizard supplied with Visual Basic that will help you to delegate and aggregate properties.

The Visual Basic ActiveX Control Interface Wizard helps you to expose the properties, methods, and events for a control. It can help aggregate and delegate properties. The Wizard consists of four dialogs.

- The Select Interface Members dialog is used to select a list of events, methods, and properties that you want to expose for your control.
- The Create Custom Interface Members dialog is used to create properties, events, and methods not listed in the previous dialog.
- The Set Mapping dialog is used to delegate properties to constituent controls.
- The Set Attributes dialog allows you to define the run-time and design-time behavior of properties (i.e., read-only, read-write). You also can assign default values to properties.

The code created by the Wizard utilizes the techniques presented in this chapter to delegate properties and create persistent properties. While it cannot write all the code for a control, it provides a great foundation from which to start. It relieves you of much of the tedium of mapping all the common properties manually. The completed program for this chapter was created using the Wizard and expanding on the code.

SUMMARY

This chapter has presented the fundamental topics of creating ActiveX controls.

- The UserControl object is the heart of an ActiveX control. It has properties to define the general characteristics of the control. It also supports several events that occur when the developer resizes the control, clicks it, and so on. Whenever the developer interacts with the UserControl, the control itself is running even though Visual Basic may be in design mode.
- The UserControl supports three predefined objects. The Extender object supports the container properties used by the developer. The AmbientProperties object supports properties used by the author. These properties are used to suggest default values for the control. The PropertyBag object communicates persistent properties to the container.
- ActiveX controls are created in Visual Basic by enhancing an existing control, creating a control based on multiple constituent controls, or creating a control from scratch.
- A control can raise events by declaring an event and then calling the RaiseEvent statement to generate the event.
- Properties are created using Property procedures, and methods are created using Public, Function, and Sub procedures. The techniques are the same as you used to create properties and methods in a class module.
- Events occur when a UserControl object is created on a form, when Visual Basic switches from design time to run time and back, and when the form is created.
- To create persistent properties, you call the WriteProperty and ReadProperty methods in the WriteProperties and ReadProperties events.
- Properties can have data types, like enumerated constants, and complex types, like OLE_COLOR. When enumerated types are used, the enumerated types are listed in the Properties window and in the Auto List Members box in the Code window.
- Setting the data-binding characteristics in the Procedure Attributes dialog creates data-aware controls.

QUESTIONS

1. Which of the following objects are used to make an ActiveX control?
   a. UserControl, Ambient, Extended, PropertyBag.
   b. UserControl, AmbientProperties, Extender, PropertyBag.
   c. Control, AmbientProperties, Extender, PropertyBag.
   d. Control, AmbientProperties, Extended, PropertyBag.
   e. None of the above.

2. Which of the following are true when the developer is setting properties for an ActiveX control?
   a. Visual Basic is in design mode.
   b. The control is in design mode.
   c. The control is in run mode.
   d. Both a and b
   e. Both a and c
3. An intrinsic or ActiveX control that is created on a UserControl object is called a ________________.
   a. Base control
   b. Visible control
   c. Constituent control
   d. text box
   e. label
4. Which of the following statements are true about constituent controls?
   a. Their properties and methods are hidden from the developer.
   b. Their properties and methods are visible to the developer.
   c. Their events are visible to the developer.
   d. Both a and c
   e. Both b and c
5. What is the correct order of events that occurs when a control is drawn on a form for the first time?
   a. Initialize, InitProperties, Resize, Paint.
   b. Initialize, InitProperties, Resize, Paint, Terminate.
   c. Terminate, Initialize, InitProperties, Resize, Paint.
   d. Initialize, ReadProperties, Resize, Paint.
   e. None of the above.
6. To generate an event in your control that is visible to the developer you must ________________.
   a. declare the event procedure using the Event keyword
   b. use the Declare statement
   c. raise the event procedure
   d. both a and b
   e. both a and c
7. Which method do you use to inform the container that the value of a property has been updated?
   a. Change.
   b. Changed.
   c. PropertyChange.
   d. PropertyChanged.
   e. Property.

8. What two methods do you call to read and write properties from the PropertyBag?
   a. ReadProperty, WriteProperty.
   b. ReadProperties, WriteProperties.
   c. ReadPropertyBag, WritePropertyBag.
   d. Property Let, Property Get.
   e. Public.
9. How do you prevent a property defined in a User control from appearing in the Properties window?
   a. Set the Visible property of the UserControl object to False.
   b. Set the Enabled property of the UserControl object to False.
   c. Use the Procedure Attributes dialog.
   d. Use the Tools Options menu.
   e. None of the above.
10. Which of the following steps are involved in creating a data-aware control?
    a. Setting the data-binding characteristics in the Procedure Attributes dialog.
    b. Calling the CanPropertyChange method.
    c. Calling the PropertyChanged method to notify the Data control.
    d. All of the above.
    e. None of the above.
11. The ________________ property is used by the control to determine whether Visual Basic is in run mode or design mode.
12. The ________________ event for the UserControl object, occurs once when the control instance is created on the form.
13. Write the statement to declare two event procedures named **DblClick** and **Click**. The event procedures should not accept any arguments.
14. Write the statements to raise the Click event you declared in the previous question when the constituent command button named **cmdButton** is clicked.
15. Create the necessary Property procedures to delegate the MultiLine property of a constituent text box named **txtLong** to the developer.
16. Create the Property procedures to aggregate the Min property for three constituent scroll bars named **hsb1**, **hsb2**, and **hsb3**.
17. Create the event procedure and statements in the procedure to save the value of the MultiLine property of the text box named **txtName** between invocations of Visual Basic. Use a default value of **False**.
18. Create the event procedure and statements in the procedure to load the value of the MultiLine property of the constituent text box named **txtName** between invocations of Visual Basic. The default value of the property should be **False**.
19. Create a Property procedure to set a property named **BackColor**. The property should aggregate the following properties: **txt1.BackColor**, **txt2.BackColor**, and **lbl1.BackColor**. Use the OLE_COLOR data type for the Property procedure's type.
20. Create a pair of Property procedures named **Month**. The procedures should use an enumerated data type containing the name of the month (January, February, March,…). Store the value in a module-level variable named **mStrMonth**.

EXERCISES

1. In this exercise you will create a control made from four constituent controls—a scroll bar and three labels. When the user changes the value of the scroll bar, the current value will be displayed in one of the labels. When the user changes the maximum or minimum properties of the control, the value of the two other labels should be updated.
   a. Create a new project and set the Name property of the form to **frmExercise1**. Save the form using the name **Chapter.10\Exercise\frmExercise1.frm** and the project using the name **Chapter.10\Exercise\Exercise1.vbp**. This form will be used to test the control.
   b. Add a second project (ActiveX control) and create a project group. Save the control with the name **ScrollBarPlus**.
   c. Add a constituent scroll bar and three labels to the ActiveX control. The three labels will display the maximum, minimum and current value of the scroll bar.
   d. Delegate the scroll bar's Max, Min, Value, SmallChange, and LargeChange properties.
   e. Make the properties you delegated in the previous step persistent.
   f. Expose the scroll bar's Click and Change events.
   g. Write the code in the ActiveX control to update the value label whenever the user changes the current value of the scroll bar.
   h. Write the code in the ActiveX control to update the maximum and minimum labels whenever the developer or user changes the Max and Min properties.
   i. Test the program. Create an instance of the ActiveX control on the form.
2. In this exercise you will create a control made from three constituent controls—two command buttons and a label. The label will display a number. The two command buttons will increment or decrement the number stored in the label.
   a. Create a new project and set the Name property of the form to **frmExercise2**. Save the form using the name **Chapter.10\Exercise\frmExercise2.frm** and the project using the name **Chapter.10\Exercise\Exercise2.vbp**.
   b. Add a second project and create a project group. Save the control with the name **UpDownBox**.
   c. Add a label and two command buttons to the form.
   d. Write the necessary code to increment the value of the label when the Up command button is clicked and decrement the label when the Down command button is clicked.
   e. Create two properties named **Min** and **Max**. The value of the label cannot exceed these values.
   f. Expose the necessary events so the user can click the buttons.
   g. Whenever the value of the label changes, a Change event should be generated. The Change event should pass one argument, an Integer, containing the value of the label.
   h. Test the program. Create an instance of the control on the form. Set the Min and Max properties.
   i. Test the program. Click the command buttons to make sure the value of the label is being updated correctly and that the Change event is working properly.

3. In this exercise you will create a control that will display one item in a list of items. Each time the control is clicked, it will display the next item in the list. If the last item in the list is the current item, then the first item in the list should be displayed.

a. Create a new project and set the Name property of the form to **frmExercise3**. Save the form using the name **Chapter.10\Exercise\frmExercise3.frm** and the project using the name **Chapter.10\Exercise\Exercise3.vbp**.

b. Add a second project and create a project group. Save the control with the name **CircularList**.

c. Add a Label control to the ActiveX control.

d. Create a method named **AddItem** that will add an item to the list. Internally, you should implement the list either as an array or a Private collection. Also implement the Remove and Item methods and a Count property.

e. Expose a Click event so that when the constituent label is clicked, the next item in the list is displayed. Again, if the last item in the list is selected, then display the first item.

f. Expose a Text property that returns the text of the currently selected list item. The property should be read-only at run time.

g. Expose the BackColor and ForeColor properties. Use the OLE_COLOR data type.

h. Test the program. Create an instance of the control. Call the AddItem method several times so the list is populated. Click the control at run time to make sure the list is being updated correctly.

4. In this exercise you will create an ActiveX control made from two constituent list boxes and four command buttons. Figure 10-14 shows the completed control.

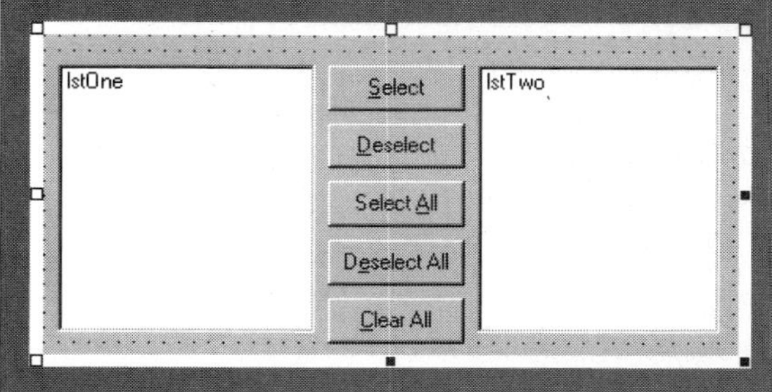

Figure 10-14

When the user clicks the Select command button, the currently selected item in the first list box should be moved to the second list box. When the Deselect command button is clicked, the selected item in the second list box should be moved to the first list box. The Select All command button should move all the items in the first list box to the second list box. The Deselect All command button should move all the items from the second list box to the first list box. This control would be useful for selecting fields in a database or names from a list.

a. Create a new project and set the Name property of the form to **frmExercise4**. Save the form using the name **Chapter.10\Exercise\frmExercise4.frm** and the project using the name **Chapter.10\Exercise\Exercise4.vbp**.

b. Add a second project (ActiveX control) and create a project group. Save the control with the name **SelectList**.

c. Create the list boxes and command buttons in the control.
d. Delegate the first list box's Add, Clear, and RemoveItem methods. Also delegate the List and Count properties.
e. Create a property named **SelectedList**. This property is really just the List property of the second list box.
f. Create a method named ClearAll to clear the contents of both list boxes.
g. Test the program. Create an instance of the ActiveX control on the form. Add items to the first list box. Test the control by selecting and deselecting items.

CHAPTER

11

Extending ActiveX Control Features

Adding Internet Support and Property Pages to an ActiveX Control

case▶ Extensive Controls is a software publisher that develops ActiveX controls used by software developers. Some controls they are developing are intended to be used by Visual Basic and also can be displayed on pages in a Web browser. One of the controls they are developing is a visual calendar. While the calendar already has been created, you will add Property Pages to the control and compile the control so it can be downloaded from the Internet and displayed in a Web browser.

SECTION A

objectives

In this section you will:

- Create ActiveX controls that support Property Pages
- Use standard Property Pages defined by Visual Basic
- Create user-defined Property Pages
- Synchronize Property Page settings with properties defined in the User control
- Debug an ActiveX control

Adding Property Pages to an ActiveX Control

Previewing the Completed Application

The completed application for this chapter is an ActiveX control that implements a visual calendar with several features. Figure 11-1 shows the visual interface for the calendar.

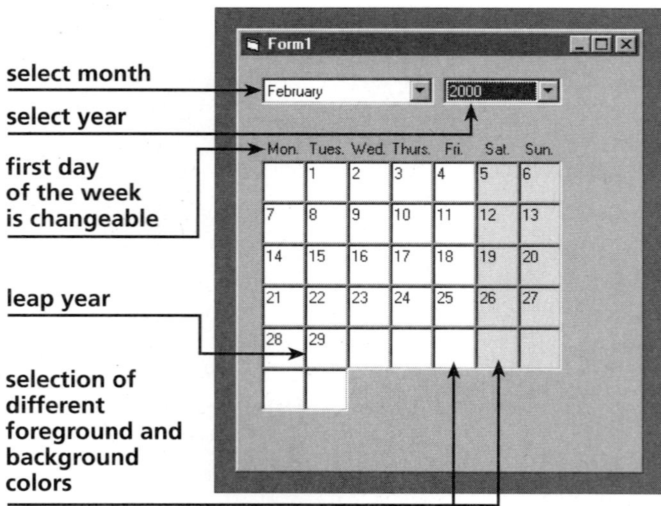

Figure 11-1: Calendar visual interface

As shown in Figure 11-1, the Calendar control contains two combo boxes. The user can select the month and the year with these combo boxes. Whenever the month or year is selected, the calendar will be updated accordingly. When the

Calendar control first is loaded, the selected month and year are the same as the current month and year. The calendar also contains labels to identify the day of the week. Below the labels is a control array of text boxes used to display the different dates. The Calendar control supports the following features:

- It displays dates such that the first day of the week either can be Sunday or Monday.
- When the user selects a month or year, the days in the calendar are updated accordingly.
- The foreground and background colors of both weekdays and weekend days can be changed.

You will not write the code to implement the Calendar control. This task already has been completed. In this chapter, you will write the code to implement Property Pages for the control, and enable the control so it can be displayed in a Web browser. The structure of the User control is the same as the User control you created in the previous chapter. The control used in this chapter, however, is more complex than the one you created in the previous chapter.

The roles of author and developer as they pertain to the Calendar control are the same as you have seen in the previous two chapters. That is, as the author, you will develop Property Pages for the Calendar control. As the developer, you will create an instance of the Calendar control on a form for testing purposes. As you may expect, you will assume the role of both author and developer and create two projects in a project group.

As shown in the previous chapter, the constituent text boxes, combo boxes, and labels are hidden from the developer and available only to the control's author. The exposed properties allow the developer to set the range of years in the combo box, define which day appears as the first day of the week, and set colors for weekdays and weekends. The following list describes the exposed properties of the Calendar control:

- The StartDay property is an enumerated type having the values Sunday and Monday. If set to Sunday, then Sunday appears as the first day of the week. If set to Monday, then Monday appears as the first day of the week and Sunday appears as the last day of the week.
- The StartYear property defines the first year displayed in the year combo box.
- The EndYear property defines the last year displayed in the year combo box.
- The WeekDayForeColor and WeekDayBackColor properties define the foreground and background colors for weekdays (Monday through Friday).
- The WeekEndForeColor and WeekEndBackColor properties define the foreground and background colors for weekends (Saturday and Sunday).

The code to implement the properties in the previous chapter was very simple. You either aggregated or delegated the properties of the various constituent controls. The Property procedures in this chapter are far more complex and interrelated. The text that follows is a summary of the code for the Calendar control. For a complete description of the Calendar control's implementation, refer to the commented code in the completed application.

The days of the month are stored in a control array of text boxes. The control array has a lower bound (the first index) of one (1) rather than zero (0). This simplifies the code to store the first day in the first text box. That is, the first day has a value of one (1) so the first element in the control array also has a value of one (1). Several events will cause the contents of the constituent text boxes to be updated. First, whenever the user selects a different month or year, the text box contents must be updated. Also, if the developer changes the StartDay property, the text boxes also must be updated so the calendar begins on the correct day. The procedure to reset the days in the Calendar control is called InitDayYears.

```
If IsNumeric(cboYear.Text) Then
    pintYear = CInt (cboYear.Text)
Else
    pintYear = Year(Date)
End If
pintMonth = cboMonth.ItemData(cboMonth.ListIndex)
pintDay = 1
pdatCurrent = DateSerial(pintYear, pintMonth, pintDay)
pintDaysInMonth = GetDaysInMonth(pintMonth)
If IsLeap(pintYear) And pintMonth = 2 Then
    pintDaysInMonth = 29
End If
```

The previous statements first determine the selected year. If a year has not yet been selected in the combo box, then the current year is used. The current month is found using the ItemData property of the month combo box. The first month (January) has an ItemData value of one (1), February an ItemData value of two (2), and so on. The day is set to one (1). This information is used to derive the date. This value is stored in the variable pdatCurrent.

The next step is to determine the number of days in the month. This is done in the Function procedure named GetDaysInMonth. The procedure takes one argument, the Integer number representing the selected month, and returns the number of days in the month. The code in the procedure is very simple. An enumerated type is used. The enumerated type contains a constant value for each month. The value is the number of days in the month. Refer to the commented code in the completed example for more detail on this function. Another function, named IsLeap, is a Boolean function that determines whether or not the selected year is a leap year. The function contains the following code:

```
Private Function IsLeap(y) As Boolean
    If (y Mod 4 = 0) And ((y Mod 100 <> 0) Or _
        (y Mod 400 = 0)) Then
        IsLeap = True
    Else
        IsLeap False
    End If
End Function
```

This is a well-known formula for determining whether or not a year is a leap year. If a year is divisible by 4, but not 100, then the year is a leap year. If the year is divisible by 400, however, it is not a leap year.

```
pintWeekDayOffset = WeekDay(pdatCurrent) - 1
```

The previous statement is very significant. The first day of the month may fall on any day. That is, the first day of the month can be Monday, Tuesday, and so on. Assuming that the first day of the month is Sunday, then the value (1) should be stored in the first text box in the control array. If the first day of the month is Monday, however, then the value (1) should be stored in the second text box and the first text box would be empty. The variable pintWeekDayOffset is used to adjust which text box is used to store the first day of the month. If pintWeekDayOffset is Sunday and the first day of the week is Sunday, then WeekDay(pdatCurrent) returns one (1). The value one (1) is subtracted from this value. Thus, if the first day is Sunday, then there is no offset. The use of this variable will become apparent in a moment.

At this point, all the information necessary to display the calendar has been computed. The final step is to display the values (dates) in the calendar's text boxes. This is accomplished using three For loops. The first For loop clears the contents of the initial text boxes. For example, if the first day of the month was Tuesday, the first two text boxes (Sunday, Monday) should be blank.

```
For pintCurrentText = 1 To pintWeekDayOffset
    txtDay(pintCurrentText) = ""
Next
```

The control array txtDay contains 37 elements numbered from 1 to 37. The reason there are 37 text boxes is that if a month contains 31 days and starts on a Saturday, then the first 6 text boxes would be blank, and the next 31 text boxes would contain the date values.

```
For pintCurrentText = (1 + pintWeekDayOffset) _
    To pintDaysInMonth + pintWeekDayOffset
    txtDay(pintCurrentText).Text = _
        pintCurrentText - pintWeekDayOffset
Next
```

The second For loop stores the day values in the text boxes. Again, the variable pintWeekDayOffset is used to adjust which control array element is used. If the first day of the week is Sunday, then the pintWeekDayOffset is zero (0). Thus, the value one (1) would be stored in the first element of the control array. pintDaysInMonth is added to the offset to determine how many values to store. pintDaysInMonth was computed by the GetDaysInMonth function.

```
For pintCurrentText = pintDaysInMonth + _
    pintWeekDayOffset + 1 To 37
    txtDay(pintCurrentText) = ""
Next
```

The last For loop performs the same task as the first For loop, but clears the contents of the last text boxes.

Setting the foreground and background colors is a difficult task. This is largely due to the fact that the first day of the week either can be Sunday or Monday. The code to set these properties must determine the first day of the week and set the color of the appropriate text boxes in the control array. Consider the following code to set the background color of the text boxes for weekend days:

```
Private Sub SetWeekEndBackColor(pColor As OLE_COLOR)
    Dim pintCurrent As Integer
    If mintStartDay = Sunday Then
        For pintCurrent = 1 To 36 Step 7
            txtDay(pintCurrent).BackColor = pColor
        Next
        For pintCurrent = 7 To 36 Step 7
            txtDay(pintCurrent).BackColor = pColor
        Next
    Else
        For pintCurrent = 6 To 36 Step 7
            txtDay(pintCurrent).BackColor = pColor
        Next
        For pintCurrent = 7 To 36 Step 7
            txtDay(pintCurrent).BackColor = pColor
        Next
        txtDay(36).BackColor = mWeekDayBackColor
    End If
End Sub
```

The If statement is used to determine if the variable mintStartDay (the first day of the week) is Sunday or Monday. If it is Sunday, then the first text box displays Sunday, the second Monday, and so on. If the first day is Monday, then Sunday appears as the last day of the week.

There are two For loops. The first For loop takes care of one weekend day and the other For loop the other weekend day. The For loops in either condition of the If statement are nearly identical. The only difference is the initial value. The implementation chosen for this program is but one of several possibilities.

Having reviewed the code for the control, you now can use the control on a form to see both the developer interface and the user interface.

To preview the completed application:

1. Start **Visual Basic** then load the project group named **Chapter.11\Complete\EC_C.vbg.**
2. Open the **Project Explorer.** The Project Explorer for the completed application is shown in Figure 11-2.

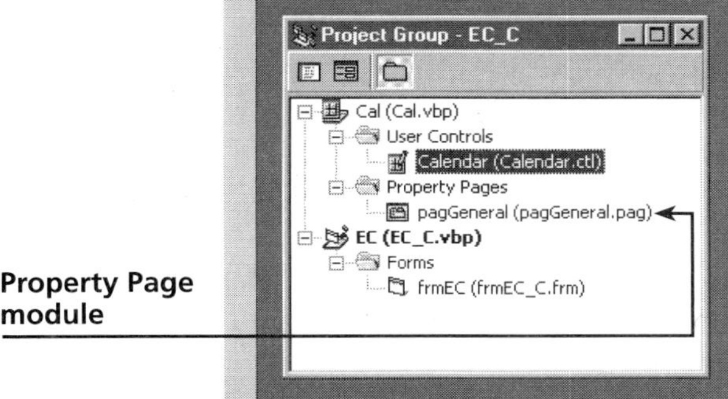

Figure 11-2: Project Explorer

As shown in Figure 11-2, the Project Explorer contains a new category of modules called Property Pages. This module type is used to create a Property Page for a control.

3 Open the **Form** window. Right-click the instance of the Calendar control drawn on the form and select **Properties**. This control supports Property Pages unlike the control you created in the previous chapter. The Property Pages for the control are shown in Figure 11-3.

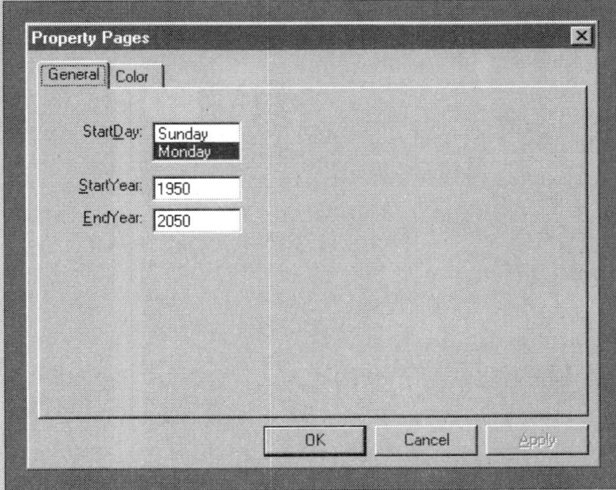

Figure 11-3: Property Pages

As shown in Figure 11-3, the Property Pages contain two tabs. The General tab is used to set common properties for the control. The Color Property Page is used to set the foreground and background colors of weekday and weekend days.

4 Select the **General** Property Page and set the StartDay to **Monday.** Set the StartYear to **1950** and the EndYear to **2050**. Click the **Apply** button on the Property Page to commit the changes.

5 Activate the **Color** Property Page. There are four properties related to colors named WeekDayForeColor, WeekDayBackColor, WeekEndForeColor, and WeekEndBackColor. Select each of these properties and change the colors. The colors are applied to the Calendar control instance on the form.

6 Close the Property Pages then test the program. Click different months and years. The calendar is updated accordingly.

This control also has been created such that it can be displayed on a Web page. As such, Visual Basic and the Form window are not the container for the control. Rather, Internet Explorer is acting as the control's container.

To display a control on a Web page:

1 Start **Internet Explorer.**

2 Select **Chapter.11\Dist\Cal.HTM** as the address. Make sure to include the letter of the drive where your data files are located. The calendar will appear in the Web browser as shown in Figure 11-4.

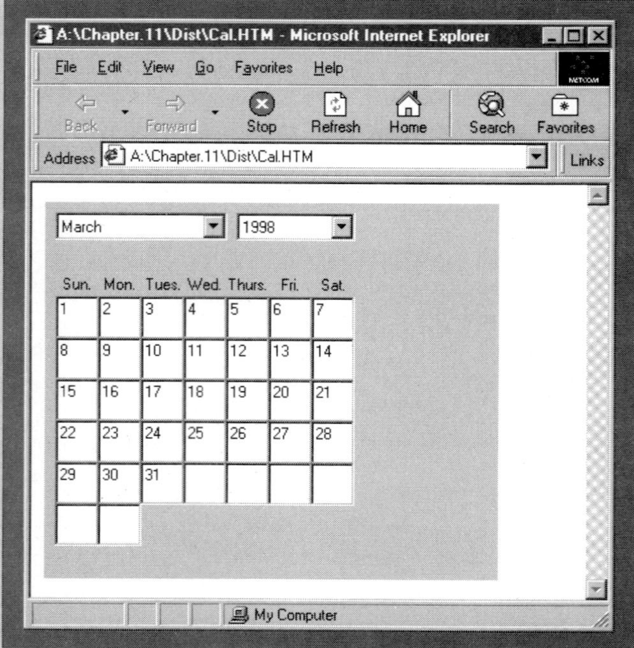

Figure 11-4: Calendar displayed in Internet Explorer

3 Select different years and months. The calendar is updated just as it was when displayed on a form.

The important point to note about this control is that multiple containers can use it. In this example, both Visual Basic and Internet Explorer are acting as containers for the Calendar control.

Creating Property Pages

As you have seen, ActiveX controls support Property Pages as a way for the developer to set the design-time properties of the control. Controls you create in Visual Basic also should provide support for Property Pages for two reasons. First, Property Pages allow for an infinitely customizable user interface for setting properties. Second, although Visual Basic allows you to set properties using the Properties window, not all containers support a mechanism to set properties. In these cases, the only way to set properties is using Property Pages.

Each tab in the set of Property Pages is considered a Property Page. A linguistic disaster would follow if the terms Property Pages and Property Page were used in the following discussion. Thus, the term Property Page tab, or just Page tab, will be used to identify a specific Property Page for a control's Property Pages.

Implementing Property Pages for a control does not preclude the developer from using the Properties window to set the same properties. This is consistent with other ActiveX controls you have used. Some properties, however, are too complex to be set using the Properties window. A good example of this is the ImageList control. As the developer, when you interact with the Images Property Page, the underlying code in the Property Page is creating the ListImage objects in the ListImages collection. There is no way to do this using the Properties window. As such, there is no entry in the Properties window for the ListImage object or the ListImages collection.

Another important point needs to be made when an ActiveX control supports Property Pages. Consider the method of creating a control's properties used in the previous chapter. You created paired Property procedures to define a specific property. You also used the PropertyBag object to make a specific property persistent. When using Property Pages, you define the properties for the ActiveX control in the same way as you did in Chapters 9 and 10. As you saw in those chapters, you can determine whether or not the property should appear in the Properties window by setting the procedure attributes for a particular Property procedure.

When you define a Property Page for a control, the code in the Property Page reads and writes the value of the properties defined in the User control. When an ActiveX control is built from one or more constituent controls, the properties, events, and methods of the constituent control are hidden from the developer and only are available to the author of the ActiveX control. These hidden properties and events are not visible to the Property Pages either. Only the Public properties declared in the

UserControl object are visible to the Property Pages. Figure 11-5 illustrates the relationship between the Property Pages and the control that uses them.

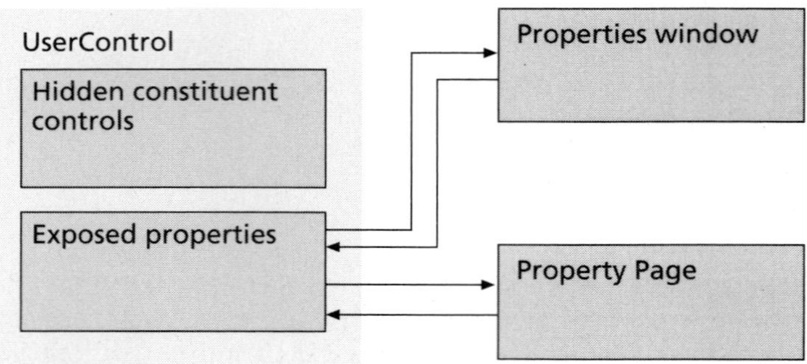

Figure 11-5: Property Page relationships

As shown in Figure 11-5, the exposed properties of the UserControl object can be set either using the Properties window or a Property Page. Neither has access to the hidden data stored in the constituent controls.

Visual Basic treats each Page tab as a single Property Page module file with the file extension ".pag." There is a visual designer for a Property Page and a corresponding code module. Any graphical images are stored in a corresponding file with the extension of ".pgx." This is consistent with other visible objects like Form and UserControl modules.

You may expect that a Property Page module would be used to define all the Page tabs that make up the Property Pages. This is not the case, however. Rather, each module corresponds to an individual tab on the control's Property Pages.

Like other components you have developed, Property Pages should have a standardized interface. In this case, we are referring to the developer interface rather than the user interface because the developer, rather than the user, uses the Property Pages. As a general rule, Property Pages should have the following general characteristics:

- When initially displayed, the focus should be set to the first tab.
- All the fields should support an access key. The letter "A" cannot be used as an access key because the Apply button uses it.
- Use a standard size for all Property Pages.
- When a label is used as a descriptive prompt, set the caption of the label to the property name. This will help the developer to identify the property when writing code.
- When a property is an enumerated type, use a list box or combo box for selection. Also, the value in the list box should be the same as the name of the enumerated type.
- When a control supports multiple Page tabs, as the author you must decide which tab will support which property. Properties that have a similar purpose or function should appear on the same tab.

- Standard Page tabs should appear as the last tab.
- Avoid displaying dialogs.
- Avoid graphics that serve no purpose. The pages should be as simple and fast as possible.

Most Property Pages consist of multiple Page tabs. When this occurs, there usually is one Page tab with the caption "General." Remember that an .ocx file can contain multiple ActiveX controls. Often, there is a Property Page that is used by all or most of the ActiveX controls in the .ocx file. The properties common to multiple ActiveX controls should be placed on the General tab. Furthermore, when the General tab is used, it should be the first tab on the Property Pages.

The process of creating the visual interface for a Property Page is just like the process used to create the visual interface for a User control or form. Intrinsic, and other ActiveX constituent controls, are drawn on the visual designer for the Property Page module. The events and methods of the constituent controls on a Property Page are hidden from the developer. When the developer opens the Property Pages for the ActiveX control, those Property Pages are in run mode. As the author, when you have the visual designer for a Property Page open, a Property Page is in design mode. This is consistent with the concept of run and design mode as it pertains to the UserControl object.

Standard Property Pages

There are two types of Page tabs—user-defined Page tabs and standard Page tabs. Standard Page tabs are used to set common attributes. There are three standard Page tabs.

- The StandardFont Page tab is used to set font attributes including the font name, font size, and effects like bold, italic, and underline.
- The StandardColor Page tab is used to set colors.
- The StandardPicture Page tab is used to assign pictures to properties.

In the previous chapter, you saw that you could create properties related to color using the OLE_COLOR data type. When this data type was used, the Properties window would activate a dialog to set the Color property. While a Long Integer number would be legal, the developer would have to set the property by entering a cryptic Long Integer number. Standard Page tabs are related to three data types. The StandardColor Page tab is used with properties having a data type of OLE_COLOR. The StandardFont Page tab is used with properties having a data type of Font, and the StandardPicture Page tab is used with properties having a data type of Picture.

A Property Page is not associated with a particular User control simply because it exists in the same project as the User control. Consider an ActiveX project with two or more ActiveX controls. Assume there are Page tabs that are common to all the ActiveX controls and tabs that are unique to a specific ActiveX control.

The UserControl object supports a property named PropertyPages. This property is an array of strings. Conceptually, this is much like the ListBox's List property, which also contains an array of strings. Each string in the array represents a specific

Property Page. The collective list of Property Page modules makes up the Property Pages for a particular ActiveX control. Figure 11-6 shows the relationship between a UserControl object and its Page tabs.

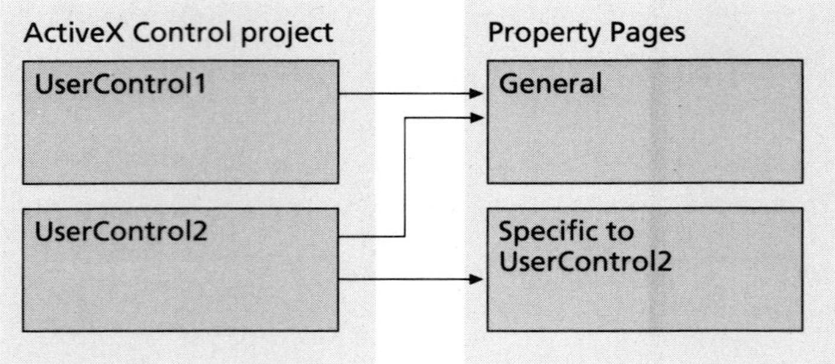

Figure 11-6: UserControl/Property Page relationship

As shown in Figure 11-6, there is an ActiveX control project with two separate UserControl objects. They both share a General Page tab. There also is a Property Page only used by the second UserControl.

When you set the UserControl's PropertyPages property, the Connect Property Pages dialog is displayed as shown in Figure 11-7.

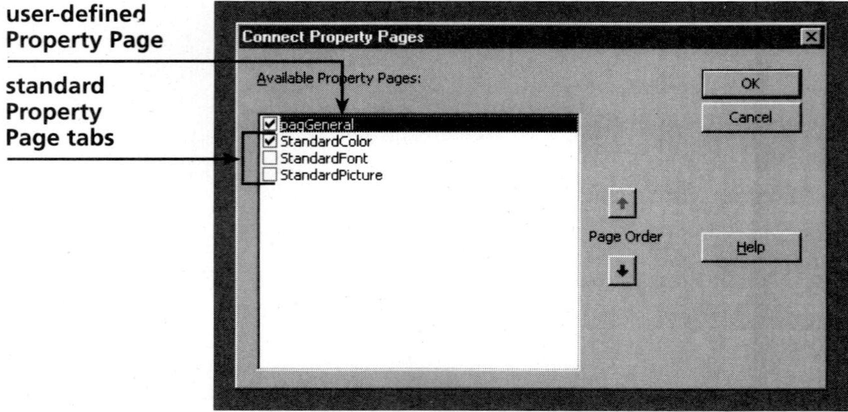

Figure 11-7: Connect Property Pages dialog

This dialog allows you to define which Property Page tabs are associated with a particular ActiveX control and the order in which each tab appears on the Property Pages. The three standard Page tabs always are listed in the dialog. Any other Property Page modules that are added to the project also will appear. To associate a particular Property Page with a control, you check the box to the left of the Property Page. The Page Order arrows on the dialog are used to set the order of the Page tabs. The order of the items displayed in the Available Property Pages list box defines the order of the tabs.

After the Property Pages have been associated with an ActiveX control, the developer can activate them in one of two ways. First, the Properties pop-up menu will appear when the developer right-clicks the mouse button of the ActiveX control. Second, the (Custom) property will appear in the Properties window.

To associate standard Property Pages with a control:

1 Start **Visual Basic** then load the project group named **Chapter.11\Startup\EC_S.vbg.**

2 Activate the **Properties** window for the User control. (Remember, you are now assuming the role of the control's author.)

3 Select the **PropertyPages** property, then click the **Properties** button to activate the **Connect Property Pages** dialog.

4 Check the check box of the **StandardColor** property, then click **OK**. At this point, the StandardColor Property Page is associated with the ActiveX Calendar control. As such, the developer can display the Property Pages.

5 Close the visual designer for the UserControl object, then open the **Form** window. (You now are assuming the role of developer rather than author.)

6 Right-click the **Calendar** object, then select **Properties.** The Property Pages appear as shown in Figure 11-8.

properties defined as OLE_COLOR

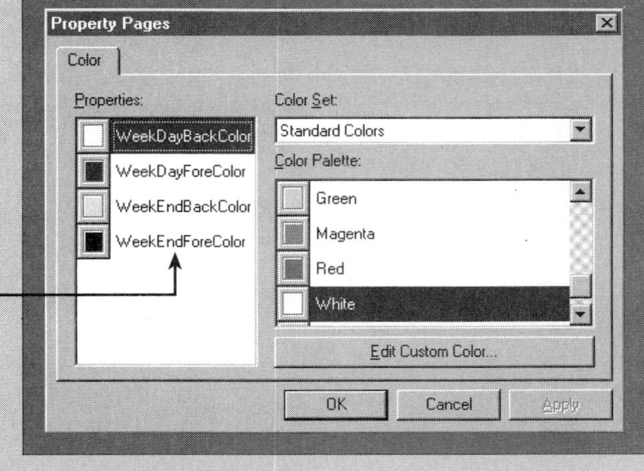

Figure 11-8: StandardColor Property Page

The four properties shown in Figure 11-8 appear in the StandardColor Property Page because these properties were declared as type OLE_COLOR. As the control's author, you do not add these properties explicitly. Rather, Visual Basic does this automatically.

7 Close the Property Pages.

When you displayed the Property Pages for the ActiveX control, you did not have to display the individual tabs explicitly. This functionality is built into the Property Pages themselves.

The Calendar control supports four properties related to color. These properties are named WeekDayForeColor, WeekDayBackColor, WeekEndForeColor, and WeekEndBackColor. The following Property procedures for the UserControl object already have been written to define these properties:

```
Property Let WeekDayForeColor(pColor As OLE_COLOR)
    mWeekDayForeColor = pColor
    SetWeekDayForeColor pColor
    PropertyChanged WeekDayForeColor
End Property

Property Get WeekDayForeColor( ) As OLE_COLOR
    WeekDayForeColor = mWeekDayForeColor
End Property

' The code for the other three color properties
' is nearly identical.
```

The important point about these properties is that they have the data type of OLE_COLOR. The data type of the StandardColor Property Page also is OLE_COLOR. When the developer opens the StandardColor Property Page, all the properties of the User control having the data type of OLE_COLOR are shown in the Properties section on the Property Page. These properties are named WeekDayForeColor, WeekDayBackColor, WeekEndForeColor, and WeekEndBackColor. Had you created a fifth property, named Shading of type OLE_COLOR, this property also would appear in the list.

The StandardFont Property Page works like the StandardColor Property Page, only it lists properties declared as type Font. The same is true for the StandardPicture Property Page. It displays all the properties of type Picture.

To see the effect of these Standard properties, you can test the Property Pages and see how to set colors.

To use the StandardColor Property Page:

1. Activate the **Form** window then activate the **Property Pages**. The four properties of type OLE_COLOR appear in the Properties section on the Property Page.
2. Select the **WeekDayForeColor** property then change the color. Repeat the process for the other three properties, apply the changes, and close the Property Pages. The colors you changed will appear in the ActiveX Calendar control.

The StandardColor Property Page is performing many tasks for you transparently. When the Property Pages are displayed, the Property Get procedure (in the UserControl module) is invoked for each of the four separate properties. The current setting (color) then is displayed to the left of the property. Whenever you click the Apply button or select a different property, the corresponding Property Let procedure is called with the new property setting. For a standard Page tab like Color, this process is automatic. When you create a user-defined Property Page, you must read explicitly the current value for a specific property in the Property Page, and save any changes explicitly.

User-Defined Property Pages

In addition to a standard Property Page, you also can add one or more user-defined Page tabs to a project. You add a Property Page to a project just like you add any other module. Once the Property Page has been added to the project, you can create constituent control instances on it in the same way that you used constituent controls to define the interface for a UserControl object. A project can have as many Property Page modules as needed.

Object	PropertyPage
Events	Property Pages are not modal. The effect of this is that the developer may change the number of selected controls at any time. Typically, the SelectedControls property should be read to determine which controls currently are selected and update the Property Pages accordingly whenever the **SelectionChanged** event occurs. This event occurs whenever the developer changes the selected controls and whenever the Property Page is opened. Every Property Page has an OK and an Apply button. The **ApplyChanges** event occurs when either the OK or Apply buttons are clicked. The ActiveX control's author should save the properties that were changed back to the User control in this situation. If the OK button is clicked, the Property Pages are closed when the ApplyChanges event procedure is complete. Clicking the Apply button does not cause the Property Pages to close. Every Property Page also has a Cancel button. When the Cancel button is clicked, the Property Pages are closed and the ApplyChanges event does not occur.

The **EditProperty** event is used to open a Property Page as a dialog when the developer clicks the Properties button in the Properties window.

The **Initialize** event occurs when the Property Page is displayed on the screen. It occurs before the SelectionChanged event.

Properties

The value of the **Caption** property is displayed on the tab for the Property Page.

The **StandardSize** property can be set to one of three values. If set to the default of zero (0), then the size of the Property Page is determined by the object. If set to one (1), small, then the Property Page is 101 pixels high by 375 pixels wide. If set to two (2), large, then the Property Page is 179 pixels high by 375 pixels wide.

The **Changed** property is a run-time property used to indicate that one of the properties on the Property Page has changed. Setting this property enables and disables the Apply button on the Property Page as needed.

The **SelectedControls** property is a collection containing a reference to all the controls currently selected by the developer. This property is updated as needed when the developer selects or deselects a control instance on the form.

A Property Page is similar to a User control in many ways. Like the User control, it supports events that occur when the Property Page is loaded. These events are hidden from the developer and exposed to the author. A Property Page is made up of constituent controls like a User control. The events and properties of these constituent controls also are hidden from the developer.

To create a user-defined Property Page:

1. Make sure the project named **Cal** is active. If the Standard EXE project is active, the Property Page will be added to the module containing the form.
2. Click **Project** then **Add Property Page**. The Add Property Page dialog may or may not appear depending on the settings on the Environment tab on the Options submenu. If the Add Property Page dialog appears, select the **New** tab, click **Property Page** then the **Open** button. The Property Page is added to the project and the visual designer is opened.

   Like all other module files, a Property Page has a disk file name and a Name property. As the author, it is the Name property you use to associate a Property Page with an ActiveX control (User control).
3. Open the **Properties** window for the Property Page you just added. Set the Name property to **pagGeneral**.
4. Set the Caption property to **General**. This caption will appear on the Page tab when the developer accesses the Calendar control's Property Pages.
5. Save the file using the name **pagGeneral.pag** in the **Chapter.11\Startup** folder.

6 At this point, the Property Page is like an empty form or User control. You now must add the control instances that the developer will use to set the properties. Create the control instances as shown in Figure 11-9.

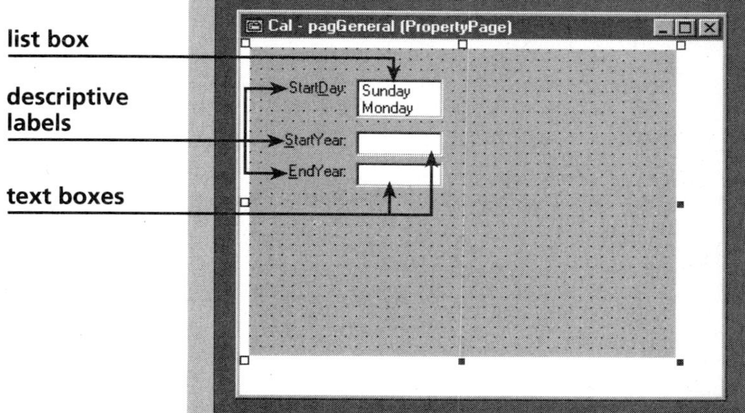

Figure 11-9: Creating the Property Page

As shown in Figure 11-9, there are three descriptive labels used as prompts. Each label has an access key. There are three constituent controls that can get focus—a list box and two text boxes. Set the Name property of the list box to **lstStartDay**, then store the values **Sunday** and **Monday** in the List property. Set the Name property of the two text boxes to **txtStartYear** and **txtEndYear**, respectively.

7 Close the visual designer for the Property Page. Activate the visual designer for the User control, then open the **Properties** window. Activate the PropertyPages property and click the button to activate the **Connect Property Pages** dialog.

8 Add the **General** Property Page named **pagGeneral** so it will appear on the Calendar control. Use the Page Order buttons so that the General Property Page appears before the StandardColor Property Page.

In this example, you have created a single user-defined Property Page. A control can support as many Property Page tabs as are needed. Each Property Page is a separate module. As such, each has its own code in the SelectedControls and ApplyChanges event procedure.

A word is in order about the access key defined for the three labels. As you know, a label cannot receive input focus. Interestingly, when an access key is used with a label like this, the next object in the Tab order is the object to receive focus. So the access keys will work properly, you must set the Tab order of both the labels and the corresponding list and text boxes.

To enable the access keys:

1. Activate the visual designer for the **General** Property Page, then open the **Properties** window.
2. Set the TabIndex property of the first label to **1**, then the TabIndex of the list box to **2**.
3. Set the TabIndex of the second label to **3**, then the txtStartYear text box to **4**.
4. Set the TabIndex of the last label to **5**, then the txtEndYear text box to **6**.
5. Test the Property Page. Verify the access keys are working properly.

As the developer, you can activate the user-defined Property Page for the Calendar control. There presently, however, is no communication between the Property Page and the User control instance. Remember, the actual properties are part of the User control (Calendar control). The Property Pages are only a means to set the underlying properties of the Calendar control. As such, you must write the necessary code to communicate property settings between the Calendar control instance and the Property Page. This communication runs in two directions.

As the developer, when you activate the Property Pages for an ActiveX control, the initial values should be loaded into the Property Page that has focus. Assuming that the User control has a Caption property, and that property currently has a value, then when the user activates the Property Pages for the control, the initial value of the caption on the Property Page should contain the same value. When the developer changes the value of a constituent control on a Page tab, as the author you must set explicitly the value of the actual property in the User control. First, you will see how to load the initial values for various properties. As the author, you can respond to two different events supported by a Property Page to copy property values from the User control to the Property Page and from the Property Page to the User control.

When a Property Page first is displayed, the SelectionChanged event occurs. In this event procedure, as the author you can write the necessary code to copy specific properties from the User control to the visible objects on the Property Page. When the Property Page is displayed, as the author you must save the current values of each supported property into the corresponding ActiveX control. This presents an interesting problem. It is possible for the developer to select several control instances before activating the Property Pages. It also is possible for the developer to change which controls are selected because Property Pages are modeless. If the developer selects multiple control instances, as the author you must determine the proper course of action when a specific property value differs between control instances. The SelectionChanged also occurs whenever the developer selects different controls.

To keep track of which controls are selected, a Property Page supports the SelectedControls property. This property contains a collection that works just like the Controls collection. Just as the Controls collection contains a reference to each of the controls on a form, the SelectedControls collection contains a reference to each of the ActiveX controls currently selected by the developer. If only one control is active, then there is one reference in the collection. The SelectedControls collection is a zero-based collection. Consider the code for the SelectionChanged event to read the StartYear property of an underlying User control.

```
Private Sub PropertyPage_SelectionChanged( )
    txtStartYear = SelectedControls(0).StartYear
End Sub
```

This event procedure occurs whenever the selected control or controls is changed. Consider the syntax to read the value of the StartYear property for the selected control. Remember, this Property Page is bound to a specific control; in this case, the Calendar control. As such, the only type of controls that can be stored in the SelectedControls collection are controls of type Calendar. Thus, the only properties you can read and write using the Property Page are those properties exposed by the Calendar control itself.

This example assumes that only one control can be selected. Thus, the following Code fragment references the currently selected User control:

```
txtStartYear = SelectedControls(0).StartYear
```

The Calendar User control supports the StartYear property. Thus, the SelectedControls(0).StartYear fragment refers to the StartYear property supported by the Calendar control. The value is stored in the Text property of the text box named txtStartYear on the Property Page. Again, note that the two constituent text boxes are hidden from the developer.

In the examples that follow, you will assume that only one control is selected at the same time. Later in the chapter, you will see how to work with multiple selected controls.

To load the initial property values:

1 Activate the Code window for the Property Page named **pagGeneral.**

2 Enter the following statements in the **PropertyPage_SelectionChanged** event procedure:

```
txtStartYear = SelectedControls(0).StartYear
txtEndYear = SelectedControls(0).EndYear
If SelectedControls(0).StartDay = Sunday Then
    lstStartDay.ListIndex = 0
Else
    lstStartDay.ListIndex = 1
End If
Changed = False
```

3 Close the Code window and the visual designer for the Property Page, then open the **Form** window.

4 Activate the Properties window for the **Calendar** object instance created on the Form window, then set the StartYear to **1995.**

5 Activate the Properties Pages, then select the **General** Property Page. The StartYear appears on the Property Page.

These statements set the initial values for the three properties supported by the Property Page. They also assume that only one Calendar control is selected. SelectedControls(0) references this control.

```
txtStartYear = SelectedControls(0).StartYear
txtEndYear = SelectedControls(0).EndYear
```

The previous statements are straightforward; the StartYear property of the User control is read and stored in the text box named txtStartYear. When the property is read, the StartYear Property Get procedure declared in the UserControl object is executed. The second statement performs the same task with the end year.

```
If SelectedControls(0).StartDay = Sunday Then
    lstStartDay.ListIndex = 0
Else
    lstStartDay.ListIndex = 1
End If
Changed = False
```

The previous statements to initialize the list box are a bit more interesting. The property StartDay is an enumerated type. When you used an enumerated type with the Properties window, the Properties window displayed a list of the valid enumerations. This is not the case with a Property Page, however. You loaded the valid enumerations at design time. You must set explicitly the selected item in the list box to the current value of the property.

The final statement in the procedure sets the Changed property to False. This causes the Property Page to be marked as clean. As such, the Apply button will be disabled.

At this point, the default properties are read when the Property Page is activated. The next step in the process is to determine when the value of a property has changed and write those properties back to the User control.

Remember, every Property Page has three buttons named OK, Cancel, and Apply. When the Property Page first is displayed, the Apply button is disabled because there have been no changes to any of the properties on the Properties Page. Saving the data on a Property Page to the selected control is a two-step process. First, you must keep track of which properties have changed, and actually save those properties back to the User control when the OK or Apply buttons are clicked. To advise the Property Page that a property has changed, you set the Changed property to True. This causes the Apply button to be enabled. When the user clicks the Apply button, the ApplyChanges event occurs allowing you to write the necessary code to save the changes back to the selected User control. After this event occurs, the Changed property is set to False and the Apply button is disabled again.

It is important to note that the Changed property identifies that one or more different properties have changed. It does not, however, keep track of which properties have changed. This is your responsibility as the control's author.

There are two implementation choices. First, you can create a module-level Boolean variable for each property. Whenever the value of a specific property changes, you set the Changed property to True, and set the value of the Boolean variable corresponding to the property to True. Then, in the ApplyChanges event, you can save only those properties that actually have changed by checking the value of the Boolean variable pertaining to a specific property.

The other option is not to keep track of which properties have changed and save all the properties back to the User control when the ApplyChanges event occurs. This option only should be used when the Property Page contains just a few properties.

To write the properties back to the User control:

1. Activate the Code window for the **General** Property Page and create the following event procedures:

```
Private Sub lstStartDay_Click( )
    Changed = True
End Sub

Private Sub txtEndYear_Change( )
    Changed = True
End Sub

Private Sub txtStartYear_Change( )
    Changed = True
End Sub
```

2. Enter the following code in the **PropertyPage_ApplyChanges** event procedure:

```
If IsNumeric(txtStartYear) And _
    IsNumeric(txtEndYear) Then
    SelectedControls(0).StartYear = txtStartYear
    SelectedControls(0).EndYear = txtEndYear
Else
    MsgBox "Start and End years must be numeric", _
        vbInformation & vbOKOnly
End If
If lstStartDay.ListIndex = 0 Then
    SelectedControls(0).StartDay = Sunday
Else
    SelectedControls(0).StartDay = Monday
End If
```

3 Close the visual designer then open the **Form** window.

4 Activate the **Property Pages** then change the value of the **StartYear, EndYear,** and **StartDay** properties. Click the **Apply** button to save the changes.

5 Test the program. The StartDay is updated. Select a year. The range of years in the combo box is bound by the start and end years you just defined.

Whenever the contents of either constituent text box changes, the Change event occurs for the constituent text box, and the Changed property (pertaining to the Property Page) is set to True. The Change events for the constituent controls are completely hidden from the developer.

When the developer clicks either the OK or Apply button, the ApplyChanges event occurs and the code in the ApplyChanges event procedure is executed. You do not have to set the Changed property to False. This is handled automatically by the event procedure itself.

```
If IsNumeric(txtStartYear) And IsNumeric(txtEndYear) Then
    SelectedControls(0).StartYear = txtStartYear
    SelectedControls(0).EndYear = txtEndYear
    . . .
```

The previous statements validate that the StartYear and EndYear both contain numeric values. If they do not, a message box is displayed advising the developer of the error condition. Just as you have validated user input in the past, you also should validate developer input. In this example, the validation could be extended easily to verify that the starting year was less than the ending year.

```
If lstStartDay.ListIndex = 0 Then
    SelectedControls(0).StartDay = Sunday
Else
    SelectedControls(0).StartDay = Monday
End If
```

These statements determine which item in the list box is selected and set the StartDay property accordingly. When the StartDay property is written from the Property Page, the Property Let procedure in the User control is executed. The code in the Property Let procedure actually updates the labels. After the ApplyChanges event completes, the Changed property is set to False causing the Apply button to be disabled.

In this example, there is no provision to determine which property has changed. As such, all the properties must be saved. Also, this example assumes there only is one selected control. If multiple controls were selected, then the property would be saved only for the first control in the collection.

This example is simplistic but it gives you the idea of the events that pertain to a Property Page and how to respond to them. Now lets expand the example to deal with multiple selected controls at the same time.

Multiple Selected Controls

When multiple controls can be selected, as the author you have several implementation choices to make.

How you set the properties for multiple selected controls depends largely on the purpose of the property. Consider the situation where you are setting the caption of multiple control instances. Assuming that multiple controls were selected, you must determine which initial caption, if any, should be displayed in the Property Page when it is loaded. If all the captions were the same, the choice is simple. Consider the situation when the selected controls have a different value for the Caption property. You could not display a caption at all, indicating no initial value. Another option would be to display the caption of the first selected control.

A more serious problem occurs when you must write the changed caption back to multiple selected controls. There are two logical implementation decisions in this situation. You can write the same caption back to all the selected controls. Using this implementation, you simply create a For Each loop to iterate through all the selected controls and write the appropriate property for each selected control as shown in the following statements:

```
Private Sub PropertyPage_ApplyChanges( )
    Dim pobjCurrent As Object
    For Each pobjCurrent In SelectedControls
        pobjCurrent.Caption = txtCaption
    Next
End Sub
```

These statements iterate through the SelectedControls collection. Each time through the For Each loop, pobjCurrent references one of the selected controls. The property is set to the contents of the text box on the Property Page. The variable is declared as type Object. Intuitively, you may think you could declare the variable as type Control. This is not the case, however, and will cause an error to occur.

Another option is to implement the Property Page so it allows the developer, inside the Property Page, to select a control instance and set properties for each selected control independently. This solution requires considerably more code than the other does. Conceptually, this behavior is much like the behavior of the standard Page tabs. Instead of selecting a property for a specific control, you would create a list box containing the selected controls. The developer then would select a control and apply the changes for a specific property.

Debugging ActiveX Controls

Debugging an ActiveX control is much like debugging a code component. ActiveX controls run as in-process components. Thus, debugging them is like debugging an ActiveX DLL. You can create a project group. One project is a test project used to test the control. The other project contains the ActiveX control(s) and associated Property Pages.

You can set breakpoints in the ActiveX control or Property Pages as needed to test them. When a breakpoint is reached, Visual Basic will enter break mode and the line in either the control or Property Page will be displayed.

To demonstrate this process, you will set breakpoints both in the User control and the Property Pages to see the events that occur as the developer sets the values of various properties.

To debug an ActiveX control:

1 Activate the **Code** window for the User control, then set a breakpoint at the first executable statement in the Property Let and Property Get procedures for the **StartDay** property.

2 Activate the Code window for the **General** Property Page and select the **1stStartDay_Click** event procedure, then set a breakpoint at the following statement. Refer to Appendix A if you are not familiar with setting breakpoints.

```
Changed = True
```

3 Close the visual designer for the property page. As the developer, open the **Form** window. Right-click the mouse button, then select properties to activate the Property Pages. The Property Pages are not displayed. Rather, the Code window for the User control is activated and the following statement is highlighted in the Property Get procedure:

```
StartDay = mintStartDay
```

This procedure is executed because the Property Page executed a statement that tried to read the property.

4 Test the program. The Code window is activated for the Property Page and the statement is highlighted in the lstStartDay_Click event procedure. This occurs because a statement in the Property Page set the initial value of the list box. Continue to click the Start button until the Property Page is displayed.

The important point to note is that as you click the Start button, Visual Basic is executing the code in either your ActiveX control or Property Page. You can debug this code, print values in the Immediate window, and perform other debugging tasks you as would do with a form.

SECTION B

objectives

In this section you will:

- Set up the Calendar control so it can be downloaded to a Web browser over the Internet
- License a control
- Deal with the issues surrounding control security

Enabling a Control for Use on the Internet

Using ActiveX Controls on the Web

You have seen that Visual Basic uses, and is part of, several intertwined technologies. ActiveX controls are not limited to running in Visual Basic. That is, an ActiveX control can run in containers other than Visual Basic. One of the exciting developments in Visual Basic is support for ActiveX controls that can be used by Web browsers like Internet Explorer. There is an edition of Visual Basic called VBScript. VBScript is a subset of the Visual Basic language used by Internet Explorer. This chapter presents several topics that are not related directly to Visual Basic. Rather, this section presents an overview of integrating ActiveX controls with the Web.

Before you begin this section, there are a few caveats you need to be aware of:

- Internet Explorer 4.0 must be installed on the system. If you have an older version of Internet Explorer, you can find the correct version on the resource CD accompanying this book. Other browsers like Netscape will not work in these examples.
- You do not need to have an Internet connection to complete the exercises in this chapter. Internet Explorer can display local documents without connecting the computer to the Internet.

The Web is made up of clients and servers. Web clients consist of browsers like Internet Explorer and Netscape. They are run on the client computer and display pages supplied by Web servers. There also are several companies that make Web servers. In this chapter, we neither will discuss the topics of how to get a connection to the Internet nor will we discuss how to create and support a Web server. This section will illustrate how to create a simple Web page, embed an ActiveX control on a Web page, and how to use an ActiveX control created in Visual Basic with Internet Explorer.

When you display a document in Internet Explorer, you are displaying a Web page. This page may exist on the local computer (the computer running Internet Explorer), or somewhere on the Internet. To identify a Web page you use a Uniform

Resource Locator (URL). If you have used the Web, you have undoubtedly seen that a URL looks like:

```
http://www.course.com
```

A URL really is made up of two parts. The first part defines the protocol to use and the second part identifies a location. Web documents are written in a language called the Hypertext Markup Language (HTML). The protocol used to transfer an HTML document from the server to the client is the Hypertext Transfer Protocol (HTTP). The second part of the URL is the file or location. A URL defines the protocol to use and the location of the server. Consider the following valid URLs:

```
http://www.course.com
ftp://ftp.course.com
file:\\A:\Chapter.11\Dist\Cal.htm
```

The first URL uses the HTTP protocol. The second uses the File Transfer Protocol (FTP). The last URL is more interesting and will be used in this example. A Web browser like Internet Explorer can display a Web page on a local computer in addition to a page on the Web. As far as Internet Explorer is concerned, they are the same. In this example, a Web page is assumed to be on the floppy drive in the folder A:\Chapter.11\Dist. To be more precise, a URL has the following syntax:

Syntax *method://server*[:port]/file[#anchor]

Dissection

- The term *method* in this context has a different meaning than it does pertaining to Visual Basic. The *method* indicates the protocol to use. Valid protocols include HTTP, FTP, News, and file.
- The *server* represents the Internet host that supports the method (protocol).
- Most methods communicate over a well-defined port. For testing purposes, however, a server can use a different port. To use that port, you specify the port address in the URL.
- The *file* argument contains the file to be transmitted.

This chapter only covers the HTTP protocol. The FTP protocol is discussed in Chapter 13.

Static and Dynamic Web Pages

Web pages can be divided roughly into two categories. Static Web pages can contain text and graphics and hyperlinks to other Web pages. They are very limited, in that the user cannot interact with them to perform common business tasks like looking up data in a database. You cannot create ActiveX controls or enter information in constituent controls like list boxes or text boxes either. Static Web pages do not execute any code. They just display information.

Dynamic Web pages offer a great deal more flexibility than static Web pages. Dynamic Web pages can display ActiveX controls that execute code inside the ActiveX control rather than inside the Web server. In this chapter, you will learn how to use an ActiveX control on a Web page. Thus, you are creating a dynamic Web page. To accomplish this, a brief introduction of the HTML programming language is in order.

A Very Brief Introduction to HTML

For all its capabilities, the HTML language itself is very simple. The HTML language is made up of two elements—tags and data. HTML documents are text files. They are made up of tags, which are like code and direct the browser to perform a task. Tags are embedded inside brackets (i.e., < *tag* >). Data, as the name implies, provides the information for the Web page. Data is not enclosed in brackets (< >). HTML is an interpreted language. You do not compile an HTML page in an executable file. Rather, the Web browser reads the text file, interprets the tags, and displays the Web page. The HTML language is not a case-sensitive language. Thus, all the following tags are the same: <HTML>, <Html>, and <html>. In this book, the convention of capitalizing the first character of the tag will be used. The following code segment shows part of an HTML document:

```
<Html>
This is a line of text
</Html>
```

As shown in the previous code segment, the <Html> and </Html> tags mark the beginning and end of the document. The document contains one line of text that will be displayed on the page. Another tag is the Title tag. This is used to specify the document title. The text in the Title tag will appear on the Internet Explorer title bar. For example, to add a title to the page, the following code would be used:

```
<Html>
<Title>
Calendar
</Title>
This is a line of text
</Html>
```

HTML supports extensive formatting capabilities. The following list summarizes some of the formatting tags:

- The <B> tag sets the text in a bold typeface.
- The <I> tag sets the text in an italic typeface.
- The <TT> tag specifies a monospaced courier font.
- The <P> tag specifies a paragraph boundary.
- The <Hr> tag draws a horizontal line on the page.

The following code segment illustrates the use of these tags:

```
<Html>
<B>This is a line of bold text</B>
<I>This is a line of italic text</I>
</Html>
```

Tags can be nested inside each other. Nesting tags is useful if you wanted to display a bold and italic font. The following statements display a line of text in a bold font. Embedded in that bold text is italicized bold text.

```
<B>This is a line of bold <I>Italic</I> text</B>
```

Documents also can have headers. Headers are used much like an outline. There are six levels of headers identified by header tags <H1> through <H6>. The following code segment illustrates the use of headers.

```
<H1>Heading1</H1>
<H2>Heading2</H2>
<H3>Heading3</H3>
```

One of the most commonly used tags is the anchor tag. The anchor tag is used to create links to other Web documents. The following statements illustrate the use of the anchor tag:

```
<a Href="http://www.course.com">"Jump to Course Technology"
```

The anchor tag contains a reference (Href) to another Web site (http://www.course.com).

These are but a few of the tags supported by the HTML language. There are other tags used to create tables and figures. There are many programs that will help you write HTML. In fact, Word 97 can save documents as HTML documents.

To create an HTML document:

1 Start **WordPad** or **Notepad** then enter the following text:

```
<Html>
<Title>Calendar</Title>
<H1>Sample HTML file</H1>
<p>This is a sample html file with a link to the Course
Technology Web site.
</p>
<a Href="http://www.course.com">"Jump to Course
Technology"
</Html>
```

2 Save the file as a text file using the name **Chapter.11\Startup\Demo.htm.**

3 Start **Windows Explorer** then locate the **Chapter.11\Startup** folder. Double-click the **Demo.htm** file. Internet Explorer starts then the Web page displays.

4 Click the underlined address (**www.course.com**). The link will not work unless your computer is connected to the Internet.

The HTML you just wrote contains a title that is displayed on the Internet Explorer title bar. It also contains one heading—a paragraph of text. The anchor is used to create a link to Course Technology's Web site.

There also are tags to manage images and lists. The point of this chapter's HTML discussion is to use an OBJECT tag to include an ActiveX control on a Web page. For more information on the HTML language, check the Microsoft Web site or any of the numerous books on the topic.

OBJECT Tags

Given the brief introduction to HTML, you now can proceed to learn how to insert ActiveX controls into an HTML document. Inserting an ActiveX control is accomplished using the OBJECT tag. The OBJECT tag is new to Version 3.0 of HTML and allows you to encapsulate an ActiveX control (or other type of object) inside a Web page (HTML document). When you insert an ActiveX control in a Web page, you insert only a reference to the control. The control is stored in a file separate from the Web page itself. The following example illustrates an OBJECT tag:

```
<HTML>
<OBJECT ID="Calendar"
    WIDTH=341
    HEIGHT=290
    CLASSID="CLSID:28B10CDB-97C8-11D1-ADD6-444553540000"
    CODEBASE="Calendar.CAB#version=1,0,0,0"
</OBJECT>
</HTML>
```

The OBJECT tag has many parts. The ID part contains the name of the control. The Height and Width parts are used to set the height and width of the control in the container (in this case Internet Explorer).

The CLASSID is very important. Remember, every control registered on the system is guaranteed to have a unique CLASSID. When an OBJECT tag is detected, Internet Explorer attempts to load the control on the local machine. Internet Explorer searches the Windows Registry for the CLASSID. If the control is found, it is loaded on the local machine. If it is not found, the control is downloaded from a remote server. Consider what would happen if a control already had been downloaded. After the user downloaded the control, assume that as the control's author, you upgraded the control. In this situation, the version of the control on the remote machine is out of date and should be downloaded again.

To determine whether or not the control is out of date, the CODEBASE parameter is used. The CODEBASE parameter contains the name of the file (control) to retrieve along with the version information pertaining to the control. Remember, you set the version information for a project using the Project Properties dialog. If the version of the control on the machine is older than the version specified in the CODEBASE argument, the control will be downloaded.

Preparing the Control for Downloading

Just creating an ActiveX control, and compiling it into an .ocx file, does not make the control available for downloading on the Web. The control must be compiled and converted into a special type of file known as a **Cabinet** or ".cab" file.

Consider the ActiveX controls you have created and used. Most of these controls have dependencies. These are support files that are necessary for the control to run. These support files are usually "DLL" files. The references are listed in a part of the .cab file called an ".inf" file or Information file. The .inf file has two purposes. First, it identifies the dependencies. Second, it contains a reference to a site where the dependent files can be downloaded. As the control's author, you have two choices for downloading dependent files. You can specify a site that you own for downloading. This requires that you have the necessary files on a server available for downloading. Fortunately, Microsoft allows dependent files to be downloaded from their site. This usually is the better choice as Microsoft keeps these files updated. Furthermore, it puts less strain on your Web server.

The Application Setup Wizard

The Application Setup Wizard is used to prepare applications for distribution. One of the types of distribution files is a downloadable control. The Application Setup Wizard is not run from inside the Visual Basic IDE. Rather, it is a stand-alone program that can be used to compile a project, if necessary, and create the necessary files for distribution.

In this chapter, you will use the following six dialogs supported by the Application Setup Wizard.

- The Select Project and Options dialog allows you to select a project for distribution. If the project has not been compiled, the Setup Wizard will compile the project for you. The Options section allows you to create a Setup file or an Internet Download Setup. In this chapter, only the Internet Download Setup is covered.
- The Internet Distribution Location is used to define where the downloadable files will be placed.

- The Internet Package dialog is used to specify where dependent files can be located. You either can choose to download files from Microsoft or specify your own site.
- Some controls may rely on additional ActiveX components to run. For example, you may have created a code component that is used by the ActiveX control. The ActiveX Server Components dialog is used to add these components.
- The File Summary dialog lists all the files and their locations necessary for the control to run.
- The Finished dialog allows you to create a template and/or complete the setup. If you will be building a project repeatedly, creating a template will save time.

When the Application Setup Wizard runs, it creates the .cab file so the control can be downloaded. It also creates a sample HTML document containing the necessary OBJECT tag to load the control.

You now have the necessary tools to create a control and prepare it for downloading.

To create a downloadable control:

1 Exit Visual Basic. If Visual Basic has files open, the Application Setup Wizard may not be able to save the necessary files or compile the program.

2 Start the **Application Setup Wizard.** This Wizard is run from the Start menu not Visual Basic. If the Introduction dialog appears, click the **Next** button. The Select Project and Options dialog appears as shown in Figure 11-10.

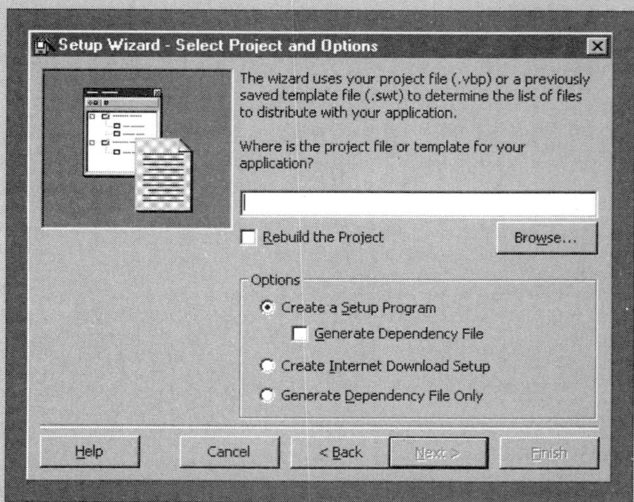

Figure 11-10: Select Project and Options dialog

3 Enter the file name **Chapter.11\Startup\Cal.vbp.** Use the appropriate drive designator depending on whether you are using the floppy or hard disk. In the Options section, click **Create Internet Download Setup**. Also, click the **Rebuild the Project** check box. Click the **Next** button to activate the Internet Distribution Location dialog, as shown in Figure 11-11. This step takes awhile because the Application Setup Wizard is recompiling the ActiveX control.

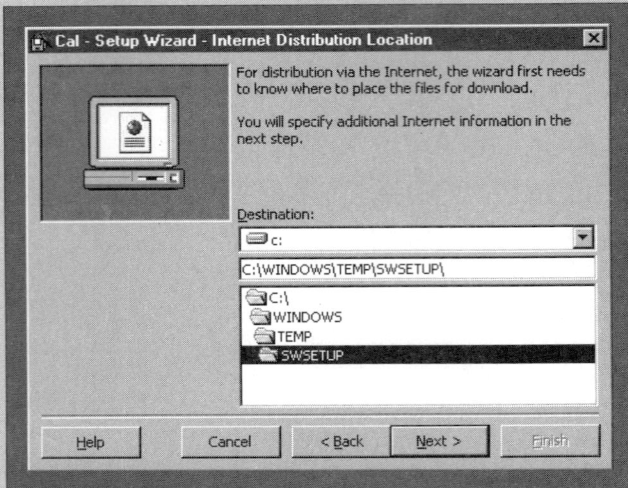

Figure 11-11: Internet Distribution Location dialog

4 Select the Destination **Chapter.11\Dist**. Use the appropriate drive designator depending on whether you are using the floppy or hard disk. If this folder did not exist, the Application Setup Wizard would have prompted you to create the folder. Respond **Yes**. If you repeat these steps, the folder will exist and you will see a dialog asking you whether or not to continue. Respond **Yes.**

5 In the Internet Package dialog, click the **Download from the Microsoft web site** option button. Click **Next**.

6 Because your control does not use any ActiveX servers, you do not need to complete the ActiveX Server Components dialog. Click the **Next** button.

7 The Application Setup Wizard will at this point display a dialog asking you if you want to use this control with a visual designer other than Visual Basic, and if so, whether or not to include the necessary DLL files. Respond **No.**

8 Click **Next** then click **Finish**. The Application Setup Wizard will create the necessary setup files for you.

The Application Setup Wizard creates both the .cab file and a sample HTML document containing the OBJECT tag. At this point, you now can run your ActiveX Calendar control inside a Web browser. Setting up an Internet Web server is beyond the scope of this book. You can see how your Calendar control will function inside a Web browser, however, by starting Internet Explorer and loading the HTML document created by the Application Setup Wizard. The following code segment shows the HTML document produced by the Application Setup Wizard as shown in Figure 11-12.

```
<HTML>
<!--  If any of the controls on this page require licensing, you must
      create a license package file.  Run LPK_TOOL.EXE to create the
      required LPK file.  LPK_TOOL.EXE can be found on the ActiveX SDK,
      http://www.microsoft.com/intdev/sdk/sdk.htm.  If you have the Visual
      Basic 5.0 CD, it can also be found in the \Tools\LPK_TOOL directory.

      The following is an example of the Object tag:

<OBJECT CLASSID="clsid:5220cb21-c88d-11cf-b347-00aa00a28331">
      <PARAM NAME="LPKPath" VALUE="LPKfilename.LPK">
</OBJECT>
-->

<OBJECT ID="Calendar" WIDTH=341 HEIGHT=290
CLASSID="CLSID:99477092-9895-11D1-ADD6-8C2B06C10000"
CODEBASE="Cal.CAB#version=1,0,0,0">
</OBJECT>
</HTML>
```

Figure 11-12: HTML produced by Application Setup Wizard

The HTML document is written in the Setup folder you specified. It contains a comment related to licensing. It also contains the necessary OBJECT tag to load the control.

To load an ActiveX control in a Web browser:

1 Locate the **Chapter.11\Dist** folder using Windows Explorer. The file named Cal.HTM should appear. Double-click **Cal.HTM**. The Internet Explorer should be activated, and the Calendar control will appear, as shown in Figure 11-13.

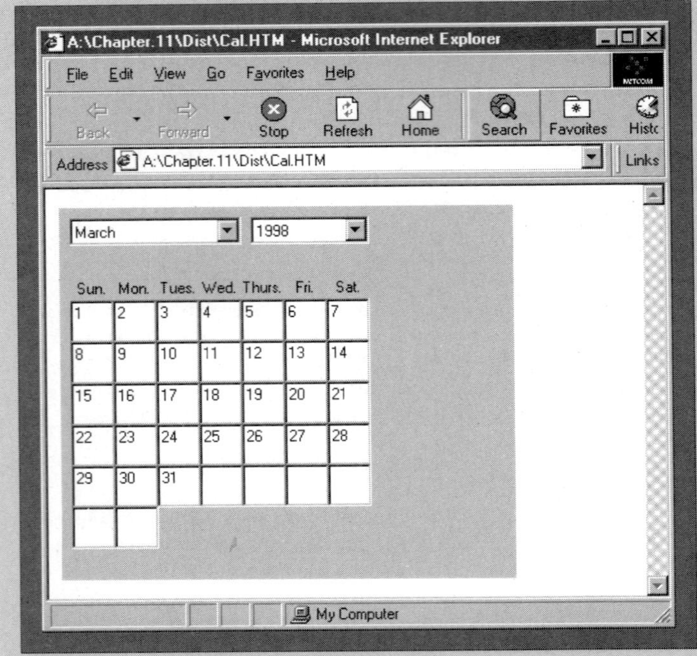

Figure 11-13: Control running in Internet Explorer

2 Click different months and years and note that the control works as it did in the Form window.

Control Security

You are no doubt aware of viruses and the importance of keeping them out of your computer. The first viruses were spread from computer to computer using floppy disks. People would share programs from unknown origins. When these programs were run, they generally would perform some malicious or at least irritating act on your computer. When the first personal computers were connected to the Internet, downloading a file and executing it also could contract a virus. The key point here is that executing the malicious code contracts the virus.

The first Web pages were not a source of viruses as they were static Web pages. These Web pages displayed information and possibly had links to other Web sites, but they did not execute any code. Like most technologies, however, the Web and Web browsers have become infinitely more sophisticated. Browsers now support scripting languages that allow a Web page to execute code. More importantly, it is possible to download a control that is executed inside the browser on the local computer. Thus, the same potential now exists for a computer to contract a virus by displaying a Web page.

When an ActiveX control is downloaded and executed on a computer, there is an implied security risk. Consider the possibility that a malicious control developer placed code in the control to remove all the files on your computer. If you were to download the control and execute it, then you would find your computer's data gone. Most computer users are very careful when downloading software and executing it on their computer. They make sure that the software comes from a reputable company and they avoid free programs whose origins are unknown. As an ActiveX control author, you must assure the user that a control is safe and free from viruses or other unexpected side effects.

There are two radically different approaches to solve this security dilemma. The first approach is used by the Java scripting language and often is called the **sandbox** approach. The term is coined because the code executes in a "sandbox" and cannot get out. Using this approach, the language itself prohibits a control from harming the computer. Using the sandbox approach, an intermediate language is used to execute the code in the control. The language itself prevents potential harmful activities like writing to the disk or calling operating system functions. The language also will not allow the control to access the memory of other procedures.

The second approach, and the one used by ActiveX controls, is called the **trust me** approach. Using this approach, a control is deemed safe because some authority has said the control is safe. The first step in this process is to create a control that is safe and free from harmful side effects. The second and more important part of the process is called **signing**. First, consider the issue of authority. You may think that there exists some organization that certifies controls as safe. This is not the case. Rather, you as the user, determine who is authoritative and who is not. For example, when you download supported software from Microsoft, you assume that the software is safe to use. Thus, you as the user have granted Microsoft authority. What about software from other companies? If you download software or controls from other companies like Seagate or IBM, you also assume that the control is safe to use. The key point is that you trust a company because you know them. You can be assured that if a company started distributing software that destroyed computers, nobody would trust them. You also could speculate that the company would be out of business in no time. Like friends, you trust them because you know them. The same is true for controls.

Obtaining a Digital Signature

A **digital signature** is a way for an end user to make sure about the identity of the software publisher and assured of the integrity of that software from the publisher to the end user. The goal of digital signing is to prevent software containing viruses from being released on the Internet. A digital signature neither prevents errors in code, nor does it prevent viruses themselves from occurring. Rather, it proves that the control's author is really the author. It is up to you to trust the author's integrity and credibility. As an analogy, consider going to the bank and writing a check. The bank authenticates you using certificates like a driver's license, credit cards, or other identification. Although the identification authenticates you, it does not necessarily cause the bank to trust you. The bank trusts you because of your reputation and credit history. The same applies to a digital signature. The digital signature authenticates the identity of the author, but it does not guarantee their credibility. The previous statement is true from a purely technical perspective. In reality, the grantors of digital signatures verify business and their financial worthiness. Furthermore, to have a digital signature you must make legal and binding promises to create virus free controls. Digital signatures work because of the integrity and accountability of the software publisher. Adding a digital signature to your control is a two-step process.

- First you must apply for a digital signature from a **certificate authority (CA)**.
- Once you have received a digital signature, you must sign your controls.

A certificate authority (CA) is an institution that grants certificates. One of these certificate authorities is Verisign. As a software publisher, you apply to Verisign for a certificate (digital signature). As part of the application, as the software publisher you must provide positive identification about your company. You must pledge that you cannot and will not distribute a program that is known to have viruses or contains code that would harm the user's machine. The CA will check the financial standing of your company using a Dun and Bradstreet rating. Once the CA has determined that your company is authentic, you will receive a digital signature.

A digital signature works using a technology called **public key cryptography**. A digital signature is made up of two separate keys known as a **public key** and a **private key**. Understanding the role of these two keys is best accomplished with an example. Suppose you have been granted a certificate containing a public and private key. As a control's author, you apply the private key to your control. In this model, the private key is secret and known only to the author. The only way to decode the private key is using the public key. In this example, the public key would be known to anyone who is using your control. The user of your control can be assured of the control's authenticity because the public key successfully decodes the private key.

From an implementation perspective, you sign a control using the ActiveX Software Development Kit. This kit can be downloaded from www.microsoft.com. To sign the files, you run the Signcode.exe program included in the SDK. Any type of file can be signed but digital signing most often is used with .cab files.

In addition to a control being safe, there is another issue to consider when scripting is used. Your control may have a digital signature and be free of bugs and malicious code. The control, however, may support features to remove and modify files. Imagine that you created a control that used features of a constituent CommonDialog control to manage and potentially remove files. In this example, your control is unsafe for scripting because an erroneous script potentially could damage the computer. Controls that are safe for scripting should not delete or modify files or change system settings. The control should not send unauthorized information to other computers.

There are two levels of safety you can apply to a control. By assigning a safety level to a control, you are making a legal guarantee that your control will not cause damage to the user's computer.

If a control is marked **safe for initialization**, then you guarantee that when a Web browser loads the control, it will not corrupt the end user's system. The control also must not corrupt the system when displayed by a Web page that you did not create. If a control is marked **safe for scripting**, a Web developer cannot write scripts using the control that will corrupt the end user's system. For the complete text of the legal guarantee pertaining to these safety levels, refer to the "Safety Dialog Box" Help topic.

Licensing a Control

As an ActiveX control's author, you likely will want to protect your controls from unauthorized use. You can prevent unauthorized use by including a license key with your control. License keys are used when a developer tries to create a design-time instance of a control you authored. If the control requires a license key, then the Windows Registry is used to make sure the license key exists and is correct. How you license a control depends on whether the control is built for standard distribution (an .ocx file), or for distribution over the Internet.

To license a control for standard distribution is very simple. The Project Properties dialog contains a check box on the General tab named Require License Key. If this box is checked, the developer must have a valid license key to create a design-time instance of the control. Creating a run-time instance of the control does not involve license keys.

Creating a license key for a control that will be distributed on the Internet is a two step process. The first step is to create a license package (.lpk) file. The second step is to create a reference to the licensing package file on the Web page. To require a license file, first you use the Project Properties dialog to require a license key and compile the project.

After licensing support is added to the control, the License Package Authoring tool is used to create the license package file. This file can be found in the Tools\Lpk_Tool folder on the Visual Basic CD-ROM. This tool allows you to select the controls that you want to license. Once the controls are selected, you save the license information to the .lpk file. Once you have created the license package file, you must modify the OBJECT tag in the Web page so the license package file can be located.

When the ActiveX control is created, the license information also is written to the Windows Registry. Because the license key is stored in the Windows Registry, the license package file is not needed or used. Thus, to test the license package file, you first must remove the key from the Windows Registry.

SUMMARY

In this chapter you have learned how to attach Property Pages to an ActiveX control and enable control downloading over the Internet.

- Property Pages are of two types. A standard Property Page is used with properties having a data type of Font, OLE_COLOR, or Picture. All properties having the same type as the standard Property Page are displayed on the Property Page. For example, if a User control exposed four properties of type OLE_COLOR, then those four properties would appear in the standard Color Property Page.
- User-defined Property Pages are added to a project by inserting a Property Page module. Once the module is inserted, you create control instances on the Property Page just like you do on a form. When you create a user-defined Property Page, you must respond to the SelectionChanged event to load the current property values in the controls on the Property Page. When the user changes the value of a property, you set the Changed property to True to indicate that there are changes that need to be saved back to the User control. When the user clicks the OK or Apply button, the ApplyChanges event occurs. Here, you write the necessary code to save the values back to the properties in the User control.
- ActiveX controls can be made available for downloading over the Internet using the Application Setup Wizard. The Application Setup Wizard creates a cabinet file, which is a compressed file containing the code for the control. In addition, the Application Setup Wizard creates an HTML document template that will load the control in a Web browser.
- When you create downloadable controls, you also must consider licensing and security. When you license a control, the developer must have a license key to create a design-time instance of the control. Run-time control instances can be created whether or not a license key is required.
- There are two approaches to control security. One approach, used by Java, is called the sandbox approach. Using the sandbox approach, the scripting language (Java) prevents the control from accessing system functions that could do any damage. The second approach, called the trust me approach, allows the control to access the functions of the operating system. Security is provided using a digital signature.

QUESTIONS

1. Which of the following statements are true pertaining to the style of a Property Page?
   a. All properties should have an access key
   b. The caption for a property should be the same as a property's name
   c. Properties should be groups on the same page based on their function
   d. None of the above
   e. All of the above

2. What are the data types supported by the three standard Property Pages?
   a. OLE_COLOR, Font, Picture
   b. OLE_COLOR, Fonts, Pictures
   c. Colors, Fonts, Pictures
   d. Color, Font, Picture
   e. None of the above
3. What are the names of the three standard Property Pages?
   a. OLE_COLOR, Font, Picture
   b. Color, Font, Picture
   c. StandardColor, StandardFont, StandardPicture
   d. None of the above
   e. All of the above
4. What event occurs in a Property Page module when the user selects a different control?
   a. SelectedControl
   b. SelectedControls
   c. Change
   d. Update
   e. Edit
5. Which event occurs when the user clicks the Apply or OK button on a Property Page?
   a. Change
   b. OK
   c. ApplyChanges
   d. Select
   e. Update
6. What property do you set to alert the Property Page that a value has been updated?
   a. Change
   b. Changed
   c. Updated
   d. Update
   e. None of the above
7. How do you associate a Property Page with a User control?
   a. Use the Object Browser
   b. Add a Property Page to the project
   c. Set the PropertyPages property for the form
   d. Set the PropertyPages property for the User control
   e. Use the Project Properties dialog
8. Which method do you use to inform the container that the value of a property has been updated?
   a. Change
   b. Changed
   c. PropertyChange
   d. PropertyChanged
   e. Property

9. When the developer selects different controls, the ______________ collection on the Property Page module contains a reference to the controls.
   a. Objects
   b. Control
   c. SelectedControl
   d. Controls
   e. SelectedControls

10. Which of the following is an invalid URL?
   a. http://www.microsoft.com
   b. ftp://ftp.microsoft.com
   c. file:\\A:\Demo.html
   d. None of the above are valid
   e. All of the above are valid

11. Which of the following statements are true regarding Web pages?
   a. Static Web pages do not execute code
   b. Dynamic Web pages do execute code
   c. Dynamic Web pages can execute ActiveX controls
   d. Both b and c are true
   e. All of the statements are true

12. Which of the following are valid HTML tags?
   a. <Html>
   b. <Object>
   c. <Title>
   d. Both a and b
   e. All of the above

13. Which tag is used in an HTML document to download a control?
   a. <Link>
   b. <Href>
   c. <Control>
   d. <Object>
   e. <ActiveX>

14. To create a downloadable control, you ______________.
   a. change the project type to Internet control
   b. use Internet Explorer
   c. use the Application Setup Wizard
   d. compile the program in Visual Basic
   e. none of the above

15. Which of the following statements are true regarding a digital signature?
   a. It guarantees the credibility of the control's author
   b. It authenticates that the control's author really is the author
   c. It uses a public key and private key
   d. Both b and c
   e. None of the above

16. Which of the following are valid safety options for a control?
    a. Safe for initialization
    b. Safe for scripting
    c. Safe for running
    d. Both a and b
    e. All of the above

For the following three questions, assume that a User control named SuperText exists and that the control has a Property Page named General.

17. Create the event procedure to load the first selected control in a text box on the Property Page named txtContents. Assume that you are reading the Contents property for the selected control.
18. Create the event procedure to save the property you read in the previous question.
19. Create the event procedure to notify the Property Page that the contents of the text box named txtContents have changed.
20. Assuming that several controls are selected, write a For Each loop to save the text in the text box named txtContents on the Property Pages to the Contents property of the User control.

EXERCISES

1. In this exercise you will create an ActiveX control and create Property Pages for the control.
    a. Create a new project and set the Name property of the form to **frmExercise1**. Save the form using the name **Chapter.11\Exercise\frmExercise1.frm** and the project using the name **Chapter.11\Exercise\Exercise1.vbp.**
    b. Using the TextBoxPlus control created in the previous chapter, add the ActiveX Control project and create a project group.
    c. Create a user-defined Property Page named **General**. Set the caption of the Property Page to **General**.
    d. Add to the General Property Page a check box. This check box should be used to support the Enabled property of the TextBoxPlus control.
    e. Add two text boxes to the Property Page. One text box should support the Caption property and the other should support the Text property.
    f. Create a list box to support the Attention property. Remember, this property is an enumerated type. The list box should display the valid enumerated types.
    g. Test the project group.

2. In this exercise you will expand on the Calendar control created in the chapter.
   a. Create a new project and set the Name property of the form to **frmExercise2**. Save the form using the name **Chapter.11\Exercise\frmExercise2.frm** and the project using the name **Chapter.11\Exercise\Exercise2.vbp**.
   b. Create a project group and add the Calendar control shown in this chapter to the project.
   c. Modify the control and the Property Page so the first day of the week can be any day instead of just Sunday or Monday.
   d. Validate the StartYear and EndYear properties on the Property Page so the starting year must be greater than the ending year. Display a message box if an error occurs.
   e. Test the program.
3. In this exercise you will use the control created in the previous exercise and make the control downloadable over the Internet.
   a. Using the Application Setup Wizard, complete the dialogs to create a downloadable control.
   b. Create or modify an HTML document as needed to display the control in a Web browser.
   c. Test the control.

CHAPTER

12

ActiveX Documents

case▶ Mid Pacific Bank originates several types of loans to customers across the United States. To better serve their customers and their branch offices, Mid Pacific Bank is exploring emerging technologies that will allow them to develop applications that can be used both over the Internet and on a stand-alone computer. They want a prototype created that will illustrate how a program like this might work.

SECTION A

objectives

In this section you will:

- Create an ActiveX document project
- Site the document in Internet Explorer used as a container
- Create persistent properties for an ActiveX document
- Create event procedures to navigate between different ActiveX documents

Creating an ActiveX Document Project

Previewing the Completed Application

Before you preview the completed application for this chapter, there are two caveats you need to be aware of. The applications in this chapter do not run as stand-alone programs. That is, you cannot view the visual interface at run time using Visual Basic. Rather, the project is viewed by another application called a **container** application. Two containers will be used in this chapter: Internet Explorer and Office Binder. For the completed application to work, you must have Internet Explorer installed on your system. To complete the exercises in this chapter, you must have both Internet Explorer and Office Binder installed on your computer. If you do not have Internet Explorer, you can find a copy of it on the CD-ROM accompanying this book. Office Binder is part of Microsoft Office. As such, you must have a licensed copy of Microsoft Office to use Office Binder. Internet Explorer can run without an actual connection to the Internet. Thus, you can complete these examples even if your computer is not connected to the Internet, as long as you have Office Binder and Internet Explorer.

To preview the completed application:

1. Start **Visual Basic** and load the project named **Chapter12\Complete\MPBLoan.vbp.**
2. Open **Project Explorer**, if necessary. The Project Explorer for the completed application is shown in Figure 12-1.

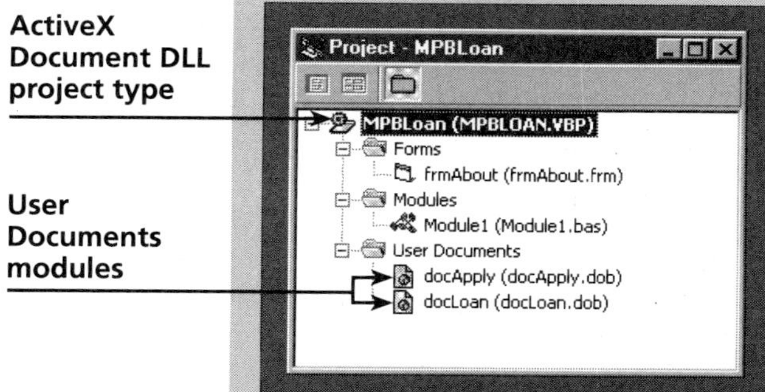

Figure 12-1: Project Explorer

As shown in Figure 12-1, the project contains a new type of module—an ActiveX document module. This project contains two separate documents named docApply and docLoan. Additionally, the project is of a different type than seen previously. The project is an ActiveX Document DLL.

3 Run the program. When you run the program, Visual Basic will enter run mode, but the ActiveX document will not appear, because the visual interface must be another container application.

4 Start **Internet Explorer.**

5 In the Address list box, enter the following address: **C:\Program Files\DevStudio\VB\docLoan.vbd.**

This address may be different depending on where on your computer Visual Basic is installed. This file name assumes that the default installation folder was chosen. The ActiveX document will appear in Internet Explorer as shown in Figure 12-2.

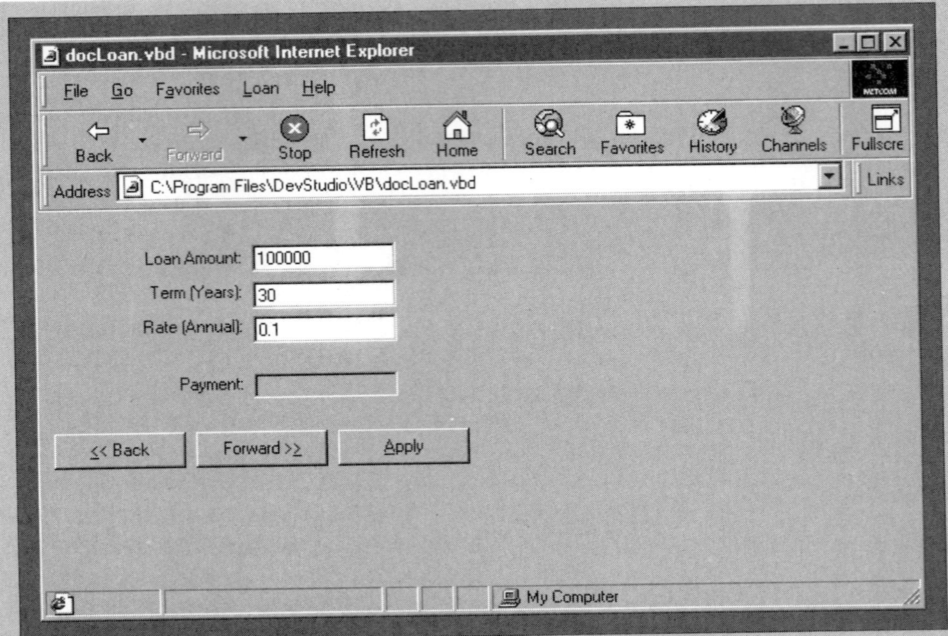

Figure 12-2: Completed program in Internet Explorer

The menus for the document are integrated with the menus for Internet Explorer.

6 Default values are supplied for the loan amount, term, and interest rate. Click **Calculate** on the **Loan** menu to calculate the payment of the loan.

The project consists of two document files. The loan form, which is shown on the screen, and a prototype for a form that ultimately will be used to submit a preliminary loan application.

7 Click the **Apply** command button to display the other form.

The Back and Forward command buttons are used to display the previous and next documents. The loan application document is very long so scroll bars appear in Internet Explorer. To make the buttons on this document visible, you must scroll to the bottom of the application form.

In actuality, these buttons display the previous and next Uniform Resource Locator (URL). A URL is a way to locate a file and the program that will operate on the file on a local computer or on the Internet transparently. If you are familiar with the Web, the term is likely well known to you.

8 Click **Back** to display the loan form then **Next** to display the prototype loan application form.

9 Exit Internet Explorer.

10 Exit Visual Basic.

The Role of ActiveX Documents

You have seen in the previous chapters that code components, and ActiveX controls, all rely on COM technology for communication. Additionally, when working with an ActiveX control, the term container was extended beyond the concept of a simple form. Specifically, you saw two different containers that could support an ActiveX control. These included a Visual Basic form and Internet Explorer. The important thing to remember is that an ActiveX control cannot exist by itself. Rather, it is run from a container. In this regard, ActiveX documents are very similar to ActiveX controls. ActiveX documents cannot run on their own. They too must be run from a container.

ActiveX document technology evolved from a proprietary Windows technology that initially was used by the Microsoft Office Binder application to collect and group the data from different Microsoft Office applications effectively. Internet Explorer also supports ActiveX document technology. As such, you can include ActiveX documents on a Web page just as you can an ActiveX control. The term **data-centric technology** was mentioned as a mechanism for users to work with information rather than concentrating on the programs that manipulated that information. ActiveX documents can be thought of as an implementation of that concept.

An ActiveX document project is not that much different from a project made up of multiple Visual Basic forms. A Visual Basic project made up of forms runs in a stand-alone mode. That is, the form is the container for the control instances but there is no container for the form. Users do not run ActiveX document projects directly. Rather, the project is loaded in another container. An ActiveX document project can have different types of modules like Standard EXE projects. For example, an ActiveX document project may have form, standard, and class modules.

ActiveX Containers

ActiveX document technology is rather new and as such is not adopted universally. Web browsers like Netscape do not support ActiveX document technology. Like any emerging technology, it is impossible to tell whether or not ActiveX documents will be a widely adopted way of presenting information. The concept, however, is promising and deserves discussion.

An ActiveX document only can be displayed inside a container. There are currently three, actually four, containers that support ActiveX documents: Internet Explorer, Office Binder, and the Visual Basic development environment. The reason for the numerical ambiguity stems from the fact that both Internet Explorer versions 3.0 and 4.0 support ActiveX documents. The notion of multiple containers is significant. Remember from Chapters 10 and 11, different containers may not support all the same characteristics. For example, when a project contains a User control, the container supports the Extender object and its properties as a way for the container to communicate information to the User control module. We also said that other containers might not support all these properties, and that some containers may support different properties. The visible area of the container application where the ActiveX document is displayed is called the Viewport. If the size of the ActiveX document will not fit in the Viewport, then the container will display scroll bars to allow the user to navigate to different parts of the document.

Another important consideration when working with ActiveX documents is menu negotiation. You saw a simple example of menu negotiation in Chapter 7 using the WindowList property with an MDI program. Containers typically have their own menus. This is true both for Internet Explorer and Office Binder. Your ActiveX document also may have a menu. When an ActiveX document is displayed in Internet Explorer, the menu of the document does not appear on the document itself. Rather, the menu is integrated on the menu of the container application (Internet Explorer).

An ActiveX document may be contained by other applications like Office Binder. As such, the user of your applications may not recognize the source or purpose of the application. So you should generally create an About menu command to display an About box that will identify your ActiveX document application to the user.

ActiveX Document Design Guidelines

When creating ActiveX documents, there are several design considerations you need to be aware of. Furthermore, there are a few limitations related to ActiveX documents. As mentioned, ActiveX documents must be hosted by a container application, and the capabilities of different containers will vary. As such, you should consider carefully the containers that may use your document. Your document must determine the container in which the document is being displayed, and execute the correct methods that pertain to the container. For example, the methods to navigate from one document to another are completely different in Office Binder and Internet Explorer.

Consider the techniques you have used to communicate data between modules in a Standard EXE project file. You can create procedures that accept arguments and return values. You also can declare global variables. To exchange data between multiple ActiveX documents, you must create global variables. You can create global (Public) variables in the ActiveX document. In this case, the variables are treated as properties. Global variables also can be declared in standard modules.

Because an ActiveX document project really is just a form of an ActiveX component, it can be created as an in-process component (DLL), or an out-of-process component (EXE). As a general rule, in-process components will perform better than out-of-process components. In-process components, however, have a limitation. You cannot display a modeless dialog (form) from an in-process component (DLL).

We have said that different types of containers support different properties and methods to manage the underlying ActiveX document. As such, instead of presenting all the information about an ActiveX document then discussing the implications of the container on that document, we will take a different tack. In this chapter, the presentation of the ActiveX document material will be coupled tightly with the container. The first section of this chapter will discuss using Internet Explorer as the container, and the second section will discuss using Office Binder as the container.

In this chapter, you will create ActiveX documents and display them in a container application on the same computer. In practice, however, it is likely that an ActiveX document would exist somewhere on the Web, and be downloaded across the Internet. When an ActiveX document is downloaded from a Web server, the document is executed on the client computer (the computer running the browser). This has the benefit of reducing the load on Web servers.

Creating an ActiveX Document

From Visual Basic's perspective, an ActiveX document is just another type of module. The module is stored in two files. The visual interface and code part of the document are stored in a file with the extension .dob and any graphical images are stored in a file with the extension .dox. This is analogous to .frm and .frx files. At the core of an ActiveX document module is the UserDocument object. This object is similar to the UserControl object pertaining to an ActiveX control. It supports events that occur when an instance of the UserDocument object is created. It also supports properties that can be made persistent by saving property values to the PropertyBag object.

Object	UserDocument
Events	■ Container applications download ActiveX documents asynchronously. When the downloading of a document is complete, the **AsyncReadComplete** event occurs. ■ The **Initialize** event occurs whenever an instance of an ActiveX document is created. ■ The **InitProperties** event occurs after the Initialize event when the document is sited on its container. ■ The **ReadProperties** event occurs after the Initialize event and only for a document that already has been saved. ■ The **Terminate** event occurs just before the ActiveX document instance is destroyed. ■ The **Show** event occurs when the user opens the ActiveX document that already has been sited. It also occurs when the user clicks the Forward or Back buttons on Internet Explorer. ■ The **Hide** event occurs before the Terminate event, when Internet Explorer is terminated, or when the user navigates to a different document.
Properties	■ The **Hyperlink** property returns a reference to a Hyperlink object. The Hyperlink object, discussed later in the chapter, is used when Internet Explorer is the container application. It contains methods to locate URLs.

- The **ContinuousScroll** property is used when the document will not fit in the visible region of the container. If False, the document only will be painted when the mouse button is released. If True, the document will be repainted as the scroll bar is moved.
- The **MinHeight** and **MinWidth** properties establish the minimum height and width for the document.
- The **ViewportHeight**, **ViewportLeft**, **ViewportTop**, and **ViewportWidth** properties return the position and size of the container's Viewport. These properties are read-only at run time.

Methods

- The **AsyncRead** method is used to begin an asynchronous read from a source. This can be a file or URL.
- The **CancelAsyncRead** method cancels a request made by the AsyncRead method.
- The **SetViewport** method sets the left and top coordinates of the UserDocument object that will be visible in the container's Viewport.

The process of creating an ActiveX document is almost the same as the process to create a form or other visible object. You use controls on the Toolbox to create control instances on the visual designer for the UserDocument object. In this example, you will create a program to compute the monthly payment for a loan. The user will supply input values to specify the amount, term, and interest rate for the loan. Admittedly the program is quite simple. The goal in this chapter, however, is to learn to display ActiveX documents in different containers and navigate between documents.

To create an ActiveX document project:

1. Start **Visual Basic** then double-click **New Project** on the **File** menu. On the **New Project** menu, click **ActiveX Document DLL**. The project is created and a new category of modules appears in Project Explorer. Just as the Standard EXE project is created with an empty form, an ActiveX Document DLL is created with an empty user document.
2. Open the visual designer for the UserDocument object and open the Properties window. Set the Name property to **docLoan.**
3. Save the document as **Chapter.12\Startup\docLoan.dob**, then the project as **Chapter.12\Startup\MPBLoan.vbp.**

At this point, the ActiveX document does nothing, and is like a form with no objects. An ActiveX document is like a form in many ways. The user interacts with the control instances created on the User document. The User document itself can display forms and dialogs. It also can have menus.

ActiveX Document Menus

ActiveX documents can have menus. These menus, however, appear on the menu bar of the container rather than the form. Most containers (Internet Explorer and Office Binder) have menus of their own. As such, the menu for an ActiveX document you create is integrated in the menu of the container application. The **NegotiatePosition** property is used to define how the menu of the ActiveX document will be integrated in the menu of the container application. Only menu titles are negotiable. That is, menus that appear indented in the Menu Editor only can have the NegotiatePosition property set to 0 – None (Default). If you attempt to set the NegotiatePosition property for a menu that is not a top-level menu, then the Menu Editor will display an error message. Menus can be negotiated in four different ways.

- **0 – None (Default).** The menu will not appear on the container's menu bar.
- **1 – Left.** The menu appears on the left-hand side of the container's menu bar. In the case of Internet Explorer, this menu will appear after the File menu defined by Internet Explorer.
- **2 – Middle.** The menu appears in the center of the container's menu bar.
- **3 – Right.** The menu appears on the right-hand side of the container's menu bar.

To illustrate menu negotiation between the ActiveX document and its container, you will create a menu for the UserDocument object. A menu responds to a Click event in exactly the same way as menus for forms. That is, when the user selects a menu command, a Click event is generated, and the code in the event procedure is executed.

To illustrate these concepts, you will create a simple menu that will negotiate with Internet Explorer's menu. One menu command will compute the results of the loan, another will save the current loan information, and another will display an About box. Remember, according to the design guidelines described earlier, all ActiveX documents should display an About box so the user can identify the origin of your program, and other pertinent information.

To create a menu for a UserDocument object:

1. Activate the **visual designer** for the UserDocument object. The visual designer looks like the visual designer for an ActiveX control.
2. Open the **Menu Editor** then create the menu shown in Figure 12-3.

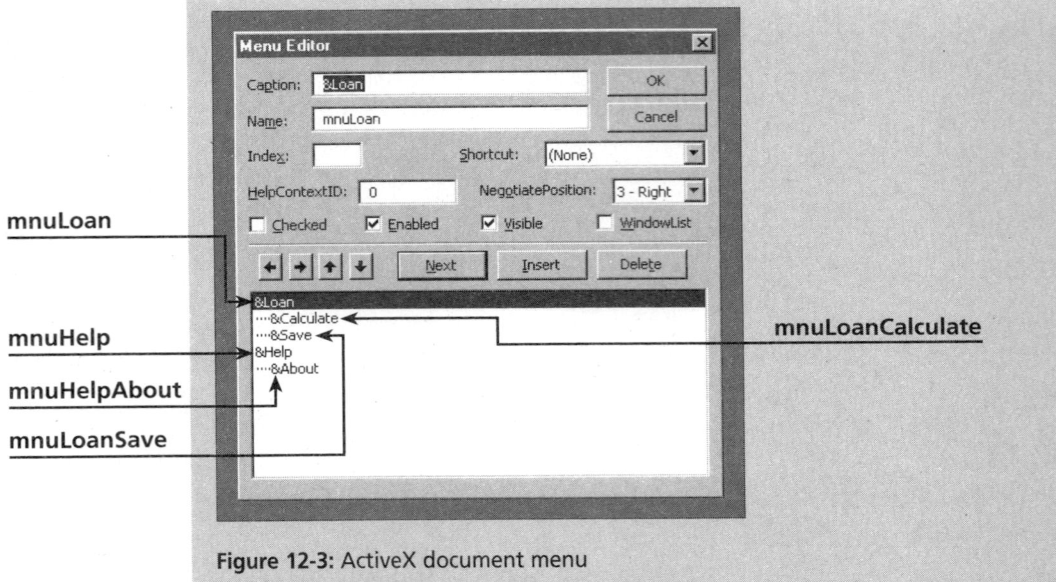

Figure 12-3: ActiveX document menu

3. As shown in Figure 12-3, there are two menu titles with the captions Loan and Help. Set the Name property of these titles to **mnuLoan** and **mnuHelp**, respectively. Set the NegotiatePosition property to **3 – Right** for both menu titles.
4. These menu titles contain menu commands with the captions **Calculate**, **Save**, and **About**. Set the Name property of these menus to **mnuLoanCalculate**, **mnuLoanSave**, and **mnuHelpAbout**.
5. Close the Menu Editor. The menu bar does not appear in the ActiveX document visual designer.
6. In the Code window for the ActiveX document, create the following event procedure to display the About form as a modal form:

```
Private Sub mnuHelpAbout_Click( )
    frmAbout.Show vbModal
End Sub
```

7. Click **Add Form** on the **Project** menu then add the form named **Chapter.12\Startup\frmAbout.**

This code is quite simple. It displays a modal form when the **About** command on the **Help** menu is clicked. While you have certainly used menus to display forms before, the appearance of the menu on the container is much different. As you will see in a moment, the Loan and Help menus will be integrated in the menu of the container.

As the next step in the process, you now will create the objects on the user document and write the code for the menu commands. The user interacts with controls created on a user document in the same way as they interact with the controls on a form.

To create the objects on the user document:

1 Create the necessary control instances on the user document as shown in Figure 12-4. These consist of four labels used as prompts, three text boxes to store the loan amount, term, and interest rate, and an output label to store the payment. Set the Name property of the text boxes to **txtLoanAmount**, **txtTerm**, and **txtRate**. Set the name of the output label to **lblPayment**.

2 For each of the text boxes, set the Text property to an empty string. For the label named lblPayment, set the BorderStyle property to **1 – Fixed Single**, and the caption property to an empty string.

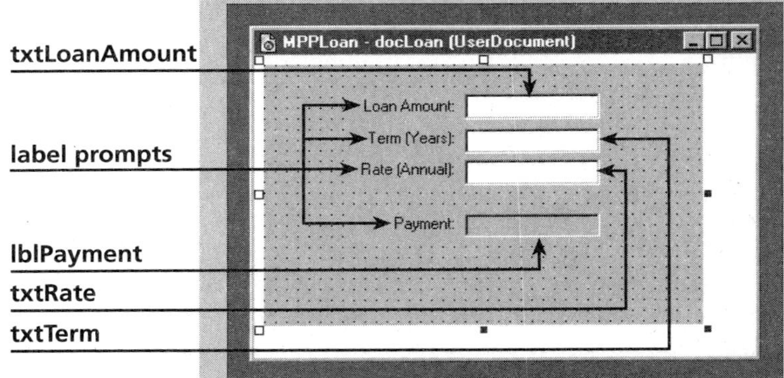

Figure 12-4: UserDocument visual designer

3 Declare the following variables in the general declarations of the user document code module:

```
Private msngLoanAmount As Single
Private mintTermYears As Integer
Private mintTermMonths As Integer
Private msngRateYears As Single
Private msngRateMonths As Single
```

4 Enter the following code in the event procedure named **mnuLoanCalculate_Click:**

```
Dim psngPayment As Single
If IsNumeric(txtLoanAmount) And IsNumeric(txtTerm) _
    And IsNumeric(txtRate) Then
    msngLoanAmount = CSng(txtLoanAmount)
    mintTermYears = CInt(txtTerm)
    msngRateYears = CSng(txtRate)
    mintTermMonths = mintTermYears * 12
    msngRateMonths = msngRateYears / 12
    psngPayment = Pmt(msngRateMonths, mintTermMonths, _
        txtLoanAmount)
```

```
        lblPayment = Format(psngPayment, "Currency")
    Else
        Call MsgBox("Invalid input", vbInformation + _
            vbOKOnly)
    End If
```

The variable declarations you just created serve two purposes. They will be used to store the validated input from the input text boxes. Another use, which will become apparent in a moment, is to create hidden variables that will be used by Property procedures. The implementation is the same as you used when you created your own ActiveX control and class modules.

The code to compute the loan payment is straightforward. First, the input fields are validated. If the data is valid, the loan payment is computed. The computations to calculate the payment involve converting the term of the loan and interest rate so the values are expressed in months instead of years. The converted values are stored in the variables mintTermMonths and msngRateMonths. Then the Pmt function is called to compute the loan payment amount.

If the input is invalid, a modal dialog (message box) is displayed. This brings up an important point. Whether you create DLL or EXE documents, you can display modal dialogs as necessary. These can consist of intrinsic dialogs like the message box and input box, or user-defined dialogs like the About box you created. You cannot, however, display modeless forms when the type of project is an ActiveX Document DLL project.

At this point, you have created a very basic ActiveX document. If you were to run the program, however, you would not see a visible window. In fact, you would see nothing happen at all. This is because ActiveX documents are not stand-alone applications. Rather, they are displayed from another program capable of acting as a container.

Executing an ActiveX Document

As you well know, a control instance cannot exist by itself. Rather, the control instance is drawn on a form, and the form acts as a container for the control. This process is called **siting**. When a control is sited on a form, the control's properties and methods become available to the container. In other words, you can set the properties of the control instance, and create code in the Code window to respond to the events.

The concept of siting extends beyond ActiveX controls. In Visual Basic, you create control instances on the user document. The user document does not become visible at run time until it is sited on a container. Several activities occur when an ActiveX document is sited on its container.

- The Parent property supported by the ActiveX document contains a reference to the container, usually a reference to Internet Explorer or Office Binder.

- The properties supported by the ActiveX document also become available to the container.
- ActiveX controls can have persistent properties. The InitProperties and ReadProperties events occur just as they do for ActiveX controls. You can use these events to read and write persistent properties to and from the PropertyBag object.

Testing an ActiveX document is very different than testing ActiveX controls and code components. While you create and edit the design time user document in Visual Basic, you cannot view the running document from Visual Basic. Rather, you must start an instance of a container application like Internet Explorer and load the document into the container's Viewport.

Before describing how to load an ActiveX document in a container application, a few words are in order about the files pertaining to the document itself. Ultimately, your ActiveX document project will be compiled into either a DLL or EXE server. The DLL or EXE server likely will contain many different user documents. There is an additional file called a Visual Basic document file (.vbd file) created for each ActiveX document in the project. This file has the extension ".vbd." The .vbd file is tightly coupled with the accompanying .dll or .exe file. The location of this file is significant. When you compile the document into a .dll or .exe file, the accompanying .vbd file is written to the same directory as the project.

When you run the ActiveX document project inside the Visual Basic IDE, however, Visual Basic creates the corresponding .vbd file in the directory where Visual Basic is installed, which may vary from computer to computer. A .vbd file is created for each ActiveX document in the project. Thus, if a project contained two UserDocument objects, two .vbd files would be created. In addition, when the project is running, Visual Basic creates a temporary entry in the Windows Registry so other programs like Office Binder can locate the document. When toggling from run mode to design mode, Visual Basic will destroy the temporary copy of the .vbd file.

If you have created an association for the file type, you can run the .vbd file by clicking it. Note that .vbd files only can be associated with Internet Explorer or Office Binder. When an ActiveX document project is run inside the Visual Basic development environment, the .vbd file is created in the root directory of the Visual Basic development environment. By default, the path name for Visual Basic is **C:\Program Files\DevStudio\VB**.

Testing the Document

Testing an ActiveX document is very different from testing standard .exe programs. Again, this is because displaying the document is performed by another application (containers). The following steps are required to display a document in a container and test it interactively with the Visual Basic run-time environment.

1. Run the Visual Basic document project. This causes the .vbd file to be written in the Visual Basic installation directory.
2. Start the container application if necessary.
3. Load the .vbd file in the container. For example, to load the .vbd file in Internet Explorer, you enter the file name in the Address list box.

There are significant differences between debugging an ActiveX document and a Standard EXE project. While you can set breakpoints at any executable statement and enter break mode, ending the program (Visual Basic is in design mode) typically will cause errors in the container application. When Visual Basic enters run mode, the .vbd file only is created temporarily. While switching between run mode and break mode, the contents of the .vbd file are persistent. When Visual Basic enters design mode, however, the corresponding .vbd file is destroyed along with the temporary entry in the Windows Registry. As such, it no longer can be located by the container application. Visual Basic can detect whether or not there is a container like Internet Explorer referencing the file and display a message to alert you to this, as shown in Figure 12-5.

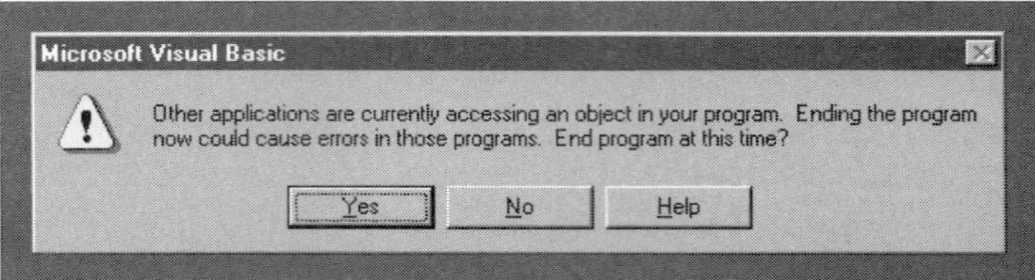

Figure 12-5: Warning error

Because Visual Basic will allow you to toggle back and forth between run and break mode, it is possible to set breakpoints, examine the values of variables and properties, and perform any other debugging tasks. You cannot, however, make changes that will require Visual Basic to enter design mode without affecting the container application. In this situation, you must rerun the program and reload the .vbd file from the container application.

To display (site) an ActiveX document in Internet Explorer:

1. Test the program. In Visual Basic, run the **MBPLoan** project.
2. Start **Internet Explorer.**
3. In the Address list box enter the file named **C:\Program Files\DevStudio\VB\docLoan.vbd.** (The path name of this file may differ depending on the installation location of Visual Basic on your computer. You do not load the project file in the container application. Rather, you load each user document individually.)
4. Enter the information in the text boxes. A loan amount of $100,000 for 30 years and 10 percent (.10), will have a payment of $877.57. Using the commands pertaining to the ActiveX document that are integrated on the menu bar for Internet Explorer, click **Calculate** on the **Loan** menu. The result should be calculated and displayed in the output label.

5 Activate **Visual Basic** then end the program. The warning message shown in Figure 12-5 is displayed indicating that a container presently is using the application. Click **No** to continue running the program.

6 Activate **Internet Explorer** then exit the program.

7 Activate **Visual Basic** then end the program. Because the container is no longer using your application, the warning message does not appear.

Had you ended the Visual Basic program without first closing the container application that was using the document, an error likely would have occurred in the container because it could no longer reference the .vbd file. The error may be severe enough that the container will exit. The behavior varies depending on the container.

Lifetime of an ActiveX Document

In ways, an ActiveX document is like a form, and in other ways it works much like the UserControl object used to create ActiveX controls. When looking at the lifetime of an ActiveX document, you must take into account the container application. When Internet Explorer loads an ActiveX document the first time, a set of events occurs pertaining to initialization. Because Internet Explorer maintains a cache of documents, however, these events do not occur as the user moves back and forth between one ActiveX document (or any other Web page), and another, so long as the document remains in the cache. There are, however, specific events that occur each time the document is displayed or hidden. As you will see later in the chapter, the Office Binder works much differently when it comes to document initialization. Consider the following sequence of events that occur as the user navigates between one document and another using Internet Explorer:

- When Internet Explorer loads a document for the first time, the Initialize and InitProperties events occur in that order. Then the Show event occurs.
- When Internet Explorer loads a document that has been saved, the Initialize and ReadProperties events occur in that order. Then the Show event occurs.
- When navigating between documents that are cached, only the Show event occurs.
- The Hide event occurs when the container navigates to another document.
- When the document is removed from the cache, the Terminate event occurs to the document.

To illustrate the use of the InitProperties event, you can set Initial values to the input text boxes, the first time Internet Explorer loads the .vbd file.

To initialize the UserDocument object:

1 Enter the following statements in the **UserDocument_InitProperties** event procedure:

```
txtLoanAmount = 100000
txtTerm = 30
txtRate = 0.1
```

2 Test the program. In Visual Basic, run the project. In Internet Explorer, load the .vbd file. (*Hint:* Rather than entering the page name in the Address list box again, use the list arrow to select the address from the saved list.) The settings for the text boxes have assumed initial values because of the statements in the InitProperties event.

At this point, the three text boxes have initial values. You can also make these values persistent between invocations of Internet Explorer.

Persistent Properties

An ActiveX document is much like an ActiveX control when working with properties. Properties are created using the Property Get and Property Let procedures. Properties can be initialized when an instance of the user document is created. Properties also can be made persistent. The technique is the same as the one you used to create persistent properties for an ActiveX control. You used the ReadProperties and WriteProperties events to store data in, and read data from, the PropertyBag object.

When you created an ActiveX control, the persistent properties were saved in the form file that used the control. The actual task of saving the form file to disk and reading the form file (module) was the responsibility of the container rather than the control itself. Your control told the container that a property should be persistent using the PropertyBag object, and informed the container that the value of a particular property had changed. The same process occurs when an ActiveX document is used inside a container like Internet Explorer.

The .vbd file is not an executable file. Rather, it is an OLE structured storage. This type of file is used by OLE to combine data with program information. Word documents also are an OLE structured storage. The important point is that a container can save information to this file using the PropertyBag object. To illustrate the use of persistent properties, you will allow the user to save the input parameters of the current loan to disk. When the file is reloaded, the values will be read and displayed in the appropriate document fields. This involves creating the three properties for the three different input values, writing those properties to the PropertyBag object, and reading them.

To create persistent properties:

1 Create the following Property procedures in the **UserDocument** object named docLoan:

```
Property Let LoanAmount(psngAmount As Single)
    msngLoanAmount = psngAmount
    LoanAmount = msngLoanAmount
End Property

Property Get LoanAmount() As Single
    LoanAmount = msngLoanAmount
End Property

Property Let TermYears(psngAmount As Single)
    mintTermYears = psngAmount
    TermYears = mintTermYears
End Property

Property Get TermYears() As Single
    TermYears = mintTermYears
End Property

Property Let RateYears(psngAmount As Single)
    msngRateYears = psngAmount
    RateYears = msngRateYears
End Property

Property Get RateYears() As Single
    RateYears = msngRateYears
End Property
```

2 Enter the following statements in the **ReadProperties** event for the User document named docLoan:

```
msngLoanAmount = PropBag.ReadProperty("LoanAmount")
mintTermYears = PropBag.ReadProperty("TermYears")
msngRateYears = PropBag.ReadProperty("RateYears")
txtLoanAmount = msngLoanAmount
txtTerm = mintTermYears
txtRate = msngRateYears
```

3 Enter the following statement in the **WriteProperties** event:

```
PropBag.WriteProperty "LoanAmount", CSng(txtLoanAmount)
PropBag.WriteProperty "TermYears", CInt(txtTerm)
PropBag.WriteProperty "RateYears", CSng(txtRate)
```

4 Enter the following statements in the **mnuLoanSave_Click** event procedures:

```
UserDocument.PropertyChanged "LoanAmount"
UserDocument.PropertyChanged "TermYears"
UserDocument.PropertyChanged "RateYears"
```

5 Test the program. Inside the Visual Basic IDE, run the project. Start **Internet Explorer** and load the .vbd file. Make changes to each of the three text boxes and click **Save** on the **Loan** menu. This notifies Internet Explorer that the properties have changed.

6 Try to exit Internet Explorer. The dialog shown in Figure 12-6 is displayed.

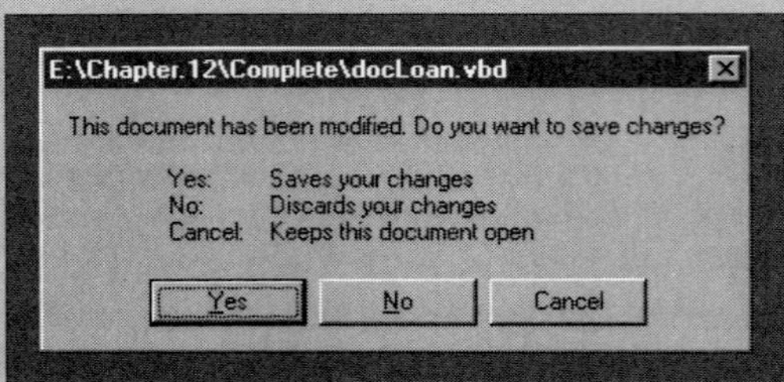

Figure 12-6: Save changes message

7 Click **Yes** to save the changes and Internet Explorer will exit. Start it again and reload the .vbd file. The changes are persistent from one invocation to the next.

As you can see from the interaction between Internet Explorer and your ActiveX document, Internet Explorer (the container) is responsible for saving the persistent properties rather than the User document itself. These changes are saved to the .vbd file. It also should be evident that once the document has been saved, the InitProperties event no longer occurs. The ReadProperties event occurs instead. Remember, the ReadProperties event contained code to set the initial input values for the document. The code in the ReadProperties event contains the code to read the values of the properties that had been saved. Had the InitProperties event occurred, the values of the input text boxes would have contained the initial values rather than the changed values.

The technique used to implement the three properties and make them persistent is the same as the one to persist ActiveX control properties used in Chapter 10. The Property procedures LoanAmount, TermYears, and RateYears implement the three read-write properties. To inform the container that a property has been changed, you call the PropertyChanged event with one argument—a string containing the name of the property. The ReadProperties and WriteProperties events occur for the document just as they did for an ActiveX control.

Programming tip

Not all containers support the PropertyBag object. Presently, only Internet Explorer and Office Binder do. To implement persistent properties without the use of the PropertyBag object, you would need to read and write text files.

Multiple ActiveX Document Applications

Just as many projects display and manage multiple forms, ActiveX document applications often consist of several user document modules. There are three significant differences between a Standard EXE project and an ActiveX document project, however.

- Standard EXE projects have a known beginning. That is, you as the developer can control which form appears first in an application.
- The user of a form-based application navigates from one form to another by clicking buttons that explicitly display different forms, typically by calling the Show method. As such, you as the developer can control which forms appear and when. The user of your ActiveX document project can display any document at any time. For example, consider the manner in which Web documents can be displayed. You can activate any document on the Web in any order by selecting the URL. Even if the document was intended to be displayed in a particular order with other documents.
- The methods you call to navigate between one document and another depend on the container in which the application is sited. For example, Internet Explorer uses the NavigateTo method of the Hyperlink object, while the Microsoft Office Binder application uses sections in a binder. Office Binder navigation will be explained in the next section.

Internet Explorer Navigation

We first will illustrate a multiple ActiveX document application that has buttons to navigate between the documents. These buttons do not prevent the user from explicitly referencing a document. They only provide an additional means of navigation. To locate another ActiveX document or other URL, you use the NavigateTo method pertaining to the Hyperlink object. The Hyperlink object supports three methods which have the following syntax:

Syntax

object.**GoBack**
object.**GoForward**
object.**NavigateTo** *Target* [, *Location* [, *FrameName*]]/

Dissection

- The **GoBack** method locates the previous URL.
- The **GoForward** method locates the next URL.
- The **NavigateTo** method locates the URL specified by *Target* and *Location*.
- The *object* must be a valid instance of the Hyperlink object.
- The *Target* must contain a valid URL to jump to. If the *Target* is invalid, then an error will occur which you can trap.
- The *Location* is the location within the *Target* URL to jump.
- If the URL contains frames, the *FrameName* argument specifies the frame within the URL.

Code Example

```
UserDocument.Hyperlink.GoBack
UserDocument.Hyperlink.GoForward
UserDocument.Hyperlink.NavigateTo _
    cstrPath & "docApply.vbd"
```

Code Dissection

The first two statements use the Hyperlink object to locate the previous and next URLs respectively. The final statement locates a specific URL. This is the ActiveX document stored in the .vbd file named docApply.vbd. This file name could be any valid URL. These statements assume that Internet Explorer is being used as the container application. It is assumed that the variable cstrPath contains the full path name of the document docApply.vbd.

To extend the example for Mid Pacific Bank, assume the payment calculation form is but one of the services that they want to make available to their customers. In addition, they would like the user to complete a preliminary loan application that ultimately will be sent to a customer services representative. (You will see how to send an electronic mail message in Chapter 13). In this example, you actually will not send a mail message. In this chapter, the goal is to understand how to navigate between one document and another. The process of navigation is the same, regardless of the contents of a specific document. In the example for Mid Pacific Bank, you will create a second user document that will contain a simple prototype for what would be expanded into a loan application form. You also will enhance the existing payment calculation form. The enhancements will include navigating from one document to another, and locating the previous and next documents in the container's cache. This involves calling the methods of the Hyperlink object.

ActiveX document projects support standard modules. You can create general procedures and declare variables in a standard module just as you have in the past. In the example for Mid Pacific Bank, you will be navigating to two different ActiveX documents stored on the local machine. The path name of the Visual Basic root directory will be stored as a constant in a standard module to reduce typing.

A second ActiveX document already has been created that contains a prototype for a loan application. In the example, nothing is done with any data entered by the user. The information could be collected and sent as a mail message to a loan representative, however, using the techniques presented in Chapter 13.

To perform document navigation using the Hyperlink object:

1 Add a standard module to the project. Save it as **Chapter.12\Startup\Standard.bas.** Enter the following statement in the module. Change the path name as necessary if you have installed Visual Basic in a different folder.

```
Public Const cstrPath = "C:\Program Files\DevStudio\VB\"
```

2 Save the standard module again. On the UserDocument form named **docLoan**, create three command buttons as shown in Figure 12-7.

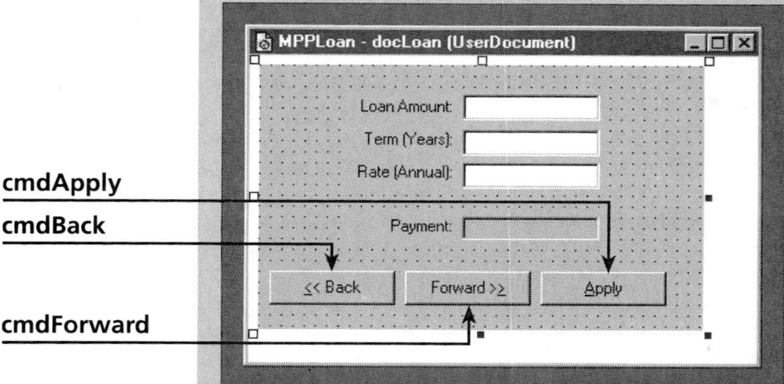

Figure 12-7: UserDocument command buttons

3 Set the captions as shown in Figure 12-7, then set the Name property of the buttons to **cmdBack**, **cmdForward**, and **cmdApply**, respectively.

4 Click **Add User Document** on the **Project** menu to add a second UserDocument object to the project. Select the existing UserDocument object named **docApply** from the **Chapter.12\Startup** folder. Figure 12-8 shows the completed document.

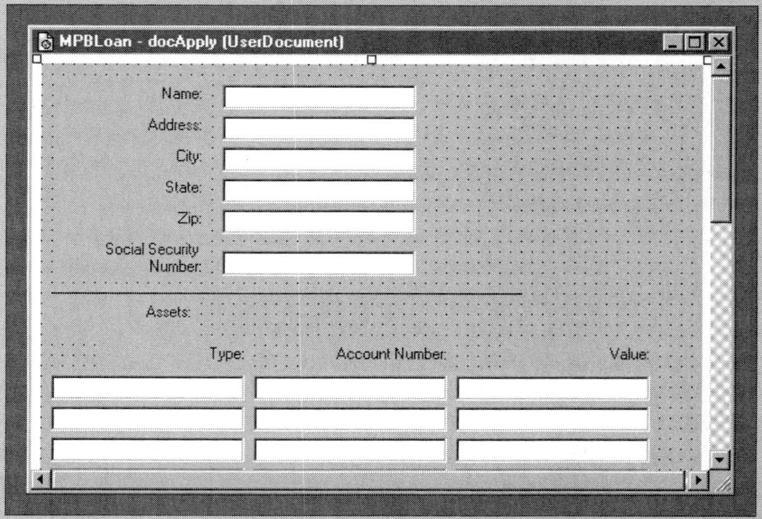

Figure 12-8: Completed document

5 Click **References** on the **Project** menu. Click **Microsoft Binder 8.0 Object Library**. These objects will be used in this project to allow you to reference the Office Binder and its objects. You will use the Office Binder objects in the next section of this chapter. Click **OK**.

6 On both UserDocument objects, create the **cmdBack_Click** and **cmdForward_Click** event procedures as follows:

```
Private Sub cmdBack_Click( )
On Error GoTo NoBack
    UserDocument.Hyperlink.GoBack
    Exit Sub
NoBack:
End Sub

Private Sub cmdForward_Click( )
On Error GoTo NoForward
    UserDocument.Hyperlink.GoForward
    Exit Sub
NoForward:
End Sub
```

7 On the UserDocument object named **docLoan**, enter the following statements in the **cmdApply_Click** event procedure:

```
UserDocument.Hyperlink.NavigateTo _
    cstrPath & "docApply.vbd"
```

8 On the UserDocument object named **docApply**, enter the following statements in the **cmdLoan_Click** event procedure:

```
UserDocument.Hyperlink.NavigateTo _
    cstrPath & "docLoan.vbd"
```

9 Test the program. Run the project inside the Visual Basic IDE and start Internet Explorer. Load the .vbd file named **docLoan**. Click **Apply.** This will cause the loan application document to be loaded and displayed. Click **Back** then **Forward** to locate the previous and next documents.

These statements illustrate the use of the methods supported by the Hyperlink object. The constant declaration makes the path name of the Visual Basic document files available to the rest of the program.

```
On Error GoTo NoBack
    UserDocument.Hyperlink.GoBack
    Exit Sub
NoBack:
```

The preceding statements are executed when the Back button is clicked. Syntactically, the UserDocument object's Hyperlink property contains a reference to a Hyperlink object. The GoBack method of the Hyperlink object locates the previous URL. An error handler is used in both the cmdBack_Click and cmdForward_Click event procedures. If there is no previous or next document in the document history, a run-time error will occur that you can trap.

The syntax of the NavigateTo method is straightforward.

```
UserDocument.Hyperlink.NavigateTo _
    cstrPath & "docApply.vbd"
```

The NavigateTo method accepts one argument—a URL to locate. This argument can contain a URL that specifics a local file or a document on the Internet. In this example, concatenating the path name of Visual Basic with the name of the document file defines the URL argument.

Controlling Navigation

The solution you just implemented allows the user to navigate from one document to another but it does not prevent the user from displaying a document without displaying the other document first. In some applications this is not a problem. Consider the situation where you want a user to navigate to a specific document first before displaying any other documents. There are a few reasons why you may want to create an implementation like this. For example, you may want to make sure that the user sees a disclaimer about the product or some type of copyright notice before proceeding. In the example for Mid Pacific Bank, assume they wanted to make sure the user read a disclaimer (UserDocument) before proceeding to the other documents to compute the loan payment or loan application. ActiveX documents themselves do not provide this functionality. There is a relatively simple coding technique you can use to create this type of behavior, however.

The key to the solution involves declaring a global object variable in a standard module. Assume the following declaration had been made in a standard module in the UserDocument project:

```
Public gdocInit As Object
```

Remember, a global variable references Nothing until an object has been assigned to it. When the startup or disclaimer document is displayed, an assignment statement is made to store a reference to the Startup object. This could be done in the Click event procedure as shown in the following statements:

```
Private Sub Command1_Click( )
    Set gdocInit = Me
    UserDocument.Hyperlink.NavigateTo _
        cstrPath & "docLoan.vbd"
End Sub
```

Each of the other user documents needs statements to determine whether or not the user has activated the Startup object. This can be achieved by checking whether the global variable references a valid object or nothing as shown in the following statements:

```
Private Sub UserDocument_Show( )
    If gdocInit Is Nothing Then
        UserDocument.Hyperlink.NavigateTo _
            cstrPath & "docInit.vbd"
    End If
End Sub
```

Understanding the Viewport

Because another application (container) is displaying an ActiveX document, the user arbitrarily can resize the container at any time. As mentioned, the Viewport is the visible area of the container application that displays the ActiveX document. By default, scroll bars will appear if the ActiveX document will not fit in the visible region of the Viewport.

In the example for Mid Pacific Bank, the loan application form will not fit in the region of the Viewport. Thus, a vertical scroll bar appears allowing the user to scroll up and down through the document. There is presently, however, a serious user interface design problem with the program. As the user enters data into the various text boxes, the user eventually will tab to a text box that is not visible in the Viewport. The problem is that the container will not necessarily scroll such that the text box that currently has focus is visible in the Viewport. This could be very confusing to the user of your program because the insertion point will seemingly disappear. Fortunately, there is a technique to assure that the object that has focus is visible in the Viewport. To accomplish this you can call the SetViewport method, which has the following syntax:

Syntax *object*.**SetViewport** *left, top*

Dissection

- The *object* must be an instance of the UserDocument object.
- The **SetViewport** method sets the left and top coordinates of the Viewport.
- The required *left* argument contains the left coordinate of the UserDocument object.
- The required *top* argument contains the top coordinate of the UserDocument object.

Code Example	`UserDocument.SetViewport 0, txtApply(Index).Top`
Code Dissection	This statement causes the ActiveX document to be positioned in the Viewport such that the top of the Viewport displays the text box that currently has focus. txtApply is assumed to be a control array of text boxes, and Index contains the text box that currently has focus.

You can use the previous statement in the GotFocus event for each of the text boxes on the application document, causing the text box that currently has focus to appear in the Viewport.

To control the Viewport:

1. Enter the following statement in the **txtApply_GotFocus** event procedure for the document named **docApply**:

   ```
   UserDocument.SetViewport 0, txtApply(Index).Top
   ```

2. Test the program. Run the project inside the Visual Basic IDE then start Internet Explorer. Load the .vbd file named **docApply**. Press the Tab key repeatedly and notice the text box that has focus appears in the Viewport.

In this section, you have seen how an ActiveX document interacts with Internet Explorer as a container. In the next section, you will see how to use the Office Binder application as a container.

SECTION B

objectives

In this section you will:

- Use the Microsoft Office Binder application
- Add documents to a binder
- Navigate between binder documents
- Modify an ActiveX document so it can support multiple containers

Using the Office Binder as an ActiveX Document Container

Office Binder as a Container

In the previous section, you saw how to display an ActiveX document using Internet Explorer as a container. In this example, you will see how to display the document using the Office Binder as a container. The Office Binder application is really just a container application used to display and organize other documents. Microsoft calls it an electronic paper clip. The Office Binder application is used to group together Microsoft Office data files. These include Word documents, Excel spreadsheets, PowerPoint presentations, and ActiveX documents created by Visual Basic. Figure 12-9 shows the Office Binder application with three documents—a Word document, an Excel spreadsheet, and a Visual Basic ActiveX document.

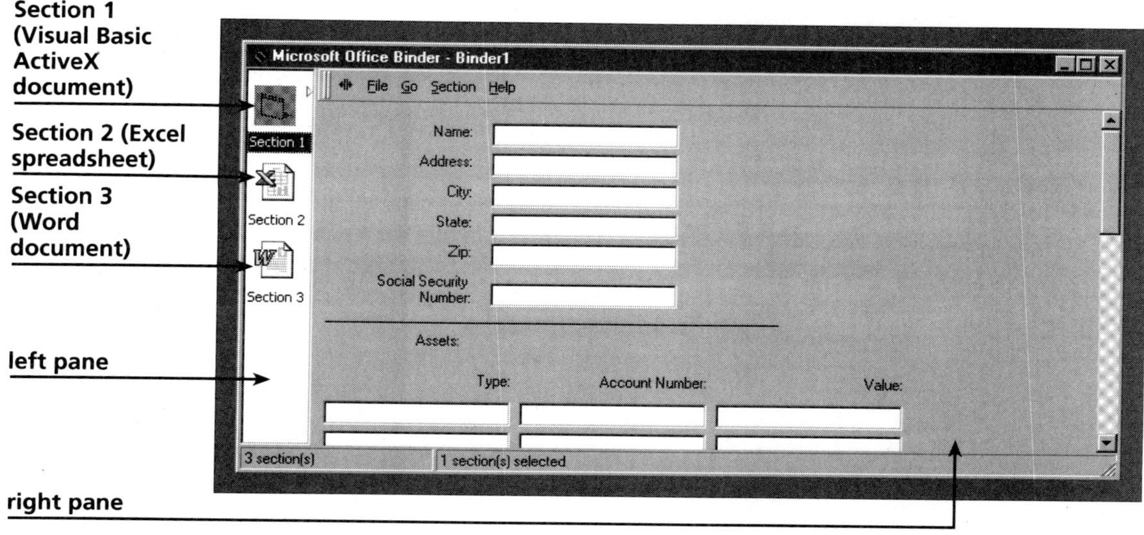

Figure 12-9: Microsoft Office Binder

As shown in Figure 12-9, Office Binder is divided into two panes. The left pane lists the documents that are part of the current binder. In the vernacular of Office Binder, each of these documents is called a section. Only one section can be visible and active at a time. Office Binder negotiates menus with the contained application in the same manner as Internet Explorer. That is, when a section is active, the Office Binder menu displays the menu of the contained application. For example, the Word 97 menus are displayed when a Word document is active.

While the appearance of ActiveX documents in Office Binder is the same as Internet Explorer, the two different containers manage the ActiveX documents much differently. When the container is Internet Explorer, document navigation is performed using the methods of the Hyperlink object. These are the methods you used in the previous section. The Hyperlink object, however, is not supported by Office Binder and cannot be used for navigation. As such, if multiple containers will display an ActiveX document, you must determine the container that is displaying the document, and call the appropriate methods supported by the individual container.

Introducing the Microsoft Office Binder

As the Microsoft Office Binder program is relatively new, it is likely that you have not used it to group together ActiveX documents. As such, a brief overview of the Office Binder application may be helpful. The key to understanding Office Binder is that each document, whether it be a Word document, an Excel spreadsheet, or an ActiveX document created with Visual Basic, is considered a section. Sections can be added and removed as needed.

To preview the Office Binder application:

1 Start **Microsoft Office Binder**. Depending on how the Microsoft Office software was installed, Office Binder may or may not be present on your system. Office Binder typically is located on the Start menu with the other Microsoft Office applications.

2 Click **Add** on the **Section** menu to add a new section to the current binder. The Add Section dialog appears as shown in Figure 12-10. The available document types and the tabs that will appear may vary depending upon the configuration of your system.

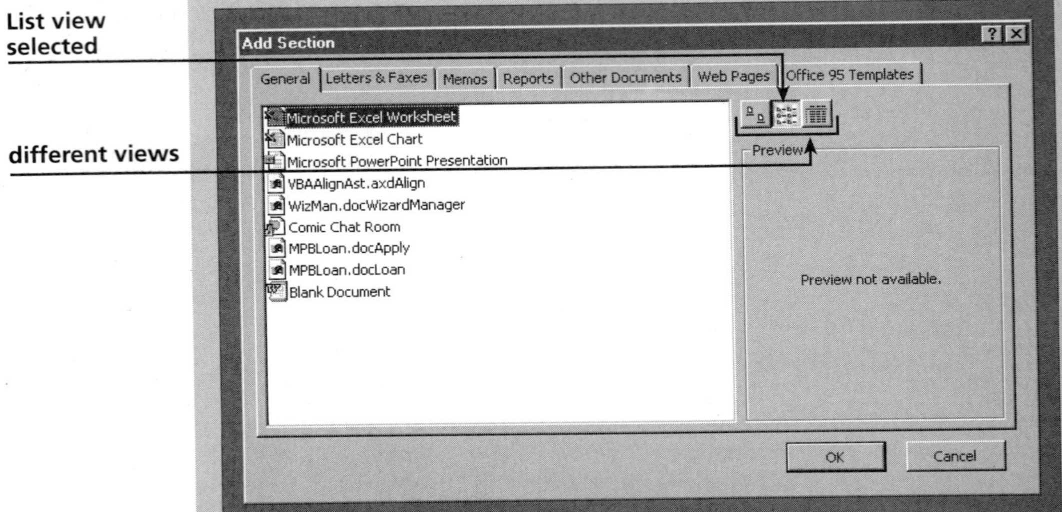

Figure 12-10: Add Section dialog

3 As shown in Figure 12-10, the dialog contains a list of the different types of documents that can be added to the current binder. The appearance of the items on the General tab will depend on which view is selected. The different views correspond to the different views supported by the ListView control. In Figure 12-10, List view is selected. Click **Blank Document** then click **OK**. A new Word document is inserted in the current binder.

4 Click **Add** on the **Section** menu to add a second section to the current binder. Click **Microsoft Excel Worksheet** then click **OK** to add a second section to the current binder.

5 To toggle between one section and another, you can click the section listed in the left pane of the current binder.

6 Click **Close** on the **File** menu to exit Office Binder. Office Binder will prompt you to save the current binder file. Click **No** in the dialog. There is no need to save it.

The previous steps provide a very brief introduction to the Microsoft Office Binder. In and of itself, Office Binder does very little. Its purpose is simply to manage other documents.

Determining the Container

As the code in your program presently exists, the only container supported is Internet Explorer. In this section, you will supply additional functionality so the user document also will support Office Binder as a container. The first step in the process is to determine the current container in which the document is running. This can be achieved using the Parent property of the UserDocument object. This property returns a string variable indicating the container. Consider the following statements:

```
Dim gstrContainer As String
gstrContainer = TypeName(UserDocument.Parent)
```

The statement fragment UserDocument.Parent returns a reference to the UserDocument object's container. Remember, the TypeName function returns a string that describes the type of a variable or object. The following list describes the strings returned by the TypeName function for various containers.

- Internet Explorer version 3.0 has a TypeName of **IWebBrowserApp**.
- Internet Explorer version 4.0 has a TypeName of **IWebBrowser2**.
- Office Binder has a TypeName of **Section**.

The code for all the navigational buttons will need to be modified to determine the type of container. Depending on the type of container, the code will call different methods. Consider the following Select Case statement:

```
Dim gstrContainer as String
Select Case gstrContainer
    Case "IWebBrowser2", "IWebBrowserApp"
        UserDocument.Hyperlink.GoBack
    Case "Section"
       ' Navigational code for the Binder
    Case Else
        Call MsgBox("Container not supported.")
End Select
```

The structure of this Select Case statement will be the same for all the navigational buttons on the two forms. If the container is a version of Internet Explorer, the methods of the Hyperlink object will be called. If the container is a version of Office Binder, different methods will be called to locate a specific section in the binder.

Accessing Office Binder Programmatically

The techniques to access the methods and properties of the Office Binder are similar to the techniques you used to manage DAO collections and objects. Figure 12-11 illustrates part of the Office Binder object hierarchy.

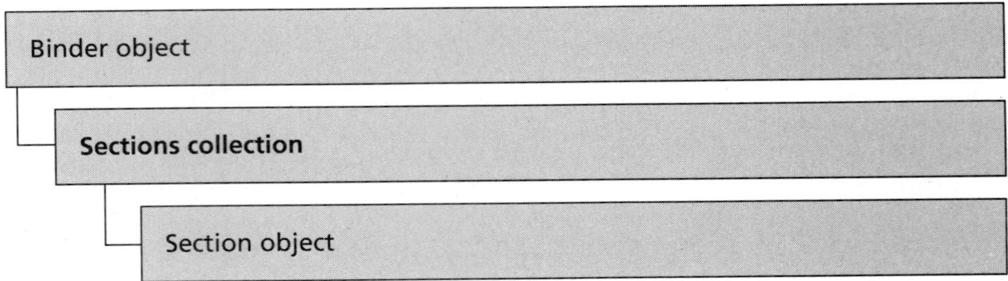

Figure 12-11: Office Binder object hierarchy

As shown in Figure 12-11, the Office Binder object is the root object. It contains a collection called the Sections collection. Every document, whether it be a Word document, an Excel spreadsheet, or an ActiveX document you created in Visual Basic, is considered a Section object in the Sections collection. The Sections collection is a one-based collection. Like other collections, a Section object can be referenced by a numeric index or string key. The Sections collection also supports methods to add and remove individual Section objects to and from the collection.

To access the objects pertaining to Office Binder, you must add a reference to the object library. The process is the same as the process to add a reference to the DAO objects or any other object library. You click References on the Project menu, and then add the Microsoft Binder 8.0 Object Library.

Unlike DAO objects, there is no predefined Office Binder object. The reference to an instance of the binder is made through the UserDocument object. Referencing the root Office Binder object from the Visual Basic ActiveX document is a bit contorted. Consider the following statements:

```
Dim secCurrent As Section
Set secCurrent = UserDocument.Parent
```

These statements return the section of the current object (in this case your ActiveX document), but it does not reference the Binder object itself. The Binder object is considered the parent of a section. Thus, to reference the Binder object, the following statements would be used:

```
Dim bndCurrent As Binder
Set bndCurrent = UserDocument.Parent.Parent
```

In the Mid Pacific Bank example, your goal is to create similar functionality for the navigational buttons regardless of whether the Office Binder or Internet Explorer is the container. As such, when Office Binder is the container, the Back button will locate the previous section in the list of sections, the Forward button will locate the Next section, and the Loan and Apply buttons will display the Loan and Apply documents, respectively. The behavior of these buttons when Internet Explorer is used as the container will not change. To learn how to create this functionality, you must learn about a few of the methods and properties supported by the Office Binder itself.

Object	**Binder**
Properties	■ The **ActiveSection** property identifies the Section object that currently has Focus. ■ The **Name** property is a string containing the name of the Section object. ■ The **Sections** property contains a reference to the Sections collection. This collection in turn contains a reference to the loaded Section objects.
Methods	■ The **Close** method closes the current binder. ■ The **Open** method opens a new binder. ■ The **Save** method saves the current binder.

Tightly coupled with the Office Binder object is the Section object. The Section object supports properties and methods that apply to the specific sections in the binder.

Object	**Section**
Properties	■ The **Name** property contains the name of the Section object excluding the path name. ■ The **Path** property contains the fully-qualified path name of the Section object. ■ The **Parent** property contains the Parent object of the Section object. This is typically the Office Binder object itself. ■ The **Type** property contains the OLE class name of the Section object.
Methods	■ The **Activate** method is used to activate a Section object. This causes the Section object to get focus. ■ The **Copy** method is used to duplicate a Section object. ■ The **Delete** method deletes a Section object.

In this example, the Back button will locate the previous Section object in the Selections collection. This requires that you determine the current Section object; then, activate the previous one. The following code illustrates one possible implementation to accomplish this:

```
With UserDocument.Parent.Parent
    For pintCurrent = 2 To .Sections.Count
        If .Sections(pintCurrent).Name = _
            .ActiveSection.Name Then
            Set secCurrent = .Sections(pintCurrent - 1)
            secCurrent.Activate
        End If
    Next
End With
```

As shown in the previous code segment, the binder is referenced with the code fragment UserDocument.Parent.Parent. The With statement is used to improve performance and reduce the number of characters you need to type. The For loop examines each of the Section objects in the Sections collection. The starting value in the For Loop is two instead of one (the first element in the collection). If the first Section object is active, then the statements in the For loop will never execute, so the Back button will do nothing. This is just one possible implementation, as it also would be reasonable to locate the last Section object if the first Section object were activated. That is, clicking the Back button would just loop around the Section objects indefinitely. Inside the If statement, the Name of the ActiveSection is compared with the current item in the collection. When they are the same, the previous Section object can be determined and activated by calling the Activate method on the Section object.

A similar loop can be written to program the Forward navigation button.

```
With UserDocument.Parent.Parent
    For pintCurrent = 1 To .Sections.Count - 1
        If .Sections(pintCurrent).Name = _
            .ActiveSection.Name Then
            Set secCurrent = .Sections(pintCurrent + 1)
            secCurrent.Activate
        End If
    Next
End With
```

As shown in the previous statements, the code differs little from the previous For loop. In this case, the last item in the collection is not examined. That is, if the last item is active, then the Forward button will do nothing.

You now can modify the code for the Forward and Back buttons to accommodate both Internet Explorer and Office Binder.

To create navigational code to support multiple containers:

1 Create the following global variable in the standard module for the project:

```
Public gstrContainer As String
```

2 Enter the following statements in the **UserDocument_Show** event procedure for both user documents. These statements determine the name of the container that is siting the document.

```
If gstrContainer = "" Then
    gstrContainer = TypeName(UserDocument.Parent)
End If
```

3 Modify the code in the **cmdForward_Click** event procedures for both user documents so they contain the following statements:

```
On Error GoTo NoForward
    Dim secCurrent As Section
    Dim pintCurrent As Integer

    Select Case gstrContainer
        Case "IWebBrowser2"
            UserDocument.Hyperlink.GoForward
        Case "Section"
            With UserDocument.Parent.Parent
                For pintCurrent = 1 To _
                   .Sections.Count - 1
                    If .Sections(pintCurrent).Name = _
                        .ActiveSection.Name Then
                        Set secCurrent = _
                            .Sections(pintCurrent + 1)
                            secCurrent.Activate
                    End If
                Next
            End With
        Case Else
            Call MsgBox("Container not supported.")
    End Select
    Exit Sub
NoForward:
```

4 Modify the code in the **cmdBack_Click** event procedures for both user documents so they contain the following statements:

```
Private Sub cmdBack_Click( )
On Error GoTo NoBack
    Dim secCurrent As Section
    Dim pintCurrent As Integer
    Select Case gstrContainer
```

```
            Case "IWebBrowser2"
                UserDocument.Hyperlink.GoBack
            Case "Section"
                With UserDocument.Parent.Parent
                    For pintCurrent = 2 To .Sections.Count
                        If .Sections(pintCurrent).Name = _
                            .ActiveSection.Name Then
                            Set secCurrent = _
                                .Sections(pintCurrent - 1)
                                secCurrent.Activate
                        End If
                    Next
                End With
            Case Else
                Call MsgBox("Container not supported. ")
        End Select
        Exit Sub
    NoBack:
```

The Code in the Show event procedure is the same for both modules.

```
If gstrContainer = "" Then
    gstrContainer = TypeName(UserDocument.Parent)
End If
```

If the string describing the container application has never been set, the container is determined by determining the type name of the UserDocument's Parent object. In the case of Office Binder, the result is the string "Section." The code is placed in the Show event rather than the Initialize event. If you placed the code in the Initialize event, the program would not work because the document is not yet sited on its container when the Initialize event occurs.

The code for both cmdBack_Click and cmdForward_Click event procedures is very similar. The variable gstrContainer stores the string describing the container application. If the container application is Internet Explorer, then the Hyperlink object is used as shown in the previous section of this chapter. If, however, the container is Office Binder, the Back button executes the following code to change the current Section object:

```
With UserDocument.Parent.Parent
    For pintCurrent = 2 To.Sections.Count
        If .Sections(pintCurrent).Name = _
            .ActiveSection.Name Then
            Set secCurrent = .Sections(pintCurrent - 1)
            secCurrent.Activate
        End If
    Next
End With
```

The With statement provides a reference to the Binder object. The For loop examines the second through the last Section objects. For each Section object examined, the name of the Section object is compared against the name of the active Section object (stored in the ActiveSection property of the Binder object.) If they are the same, the variable secCurrent is set to reference the previous Section object. Then the Activate method is called to activate the desired Section object.

The code to locate a different document is a bit more complicated. This is because the desired document may or may not be an active Section object in the binder. In the example for Mid Pacific Bank, the program will be implemented such that a new Section object will be added if the document type has not been added. If the document type already exists in the Sections collection, however, that document will be set to the active document. This requires that you learn how to determine the document type, and add new documents.

The Type property supported by the Section object contains a string that identifies the class name of the document. For ActiveX documents, this name contains the name of the project, followed by a period (.), followed by the name of the document. The following statement fragments contain the fully qualified names for the two ActiveX documents in this project:

```
MPBLoan.docApply
MPBLoan.docLoan
```

If a Section object is not loaded, it must be added to the Sections collection. This is accomplished by calling the Add method of the Sections collection, which has the following syntax:

Syntax	*expression*.**Add**(*Type*, *FileName*, *Before*, *After*)
Dissection	■ The *expression* must be a reference to the Sections collection. ■ The **Add** method adds a new Section object to the collection. ■ The *Type* argument contains the class name of the Section object to be created. For example, to create a Section object containing the Loan document, the *Type* argument would contain the value MPBLoan.docLoan. ■ The *FileName* contains the file name of the Section object to create. In the case of an ActiveX document, the file name can be the .vbd file on the disk. ■ The *Before* and *After* arguments can contain a reference to a Section object. If the *Before* argument is specified, the new Section object is added before the current Section object. If the *After* argument is specified, the new Section object is added after the current Section object. Either *Before* or *After* can be used in the same statement but not both.
Notes	Either the Type or FileName argument is required.

Code Example	`UserDocument.Parent.Parent.Sections.Add _` `    "MBPLoan.docApply"`
Code Dissection	The preceding statement adds the ActiveX document having the class name MPBLoan.docApply to the current binder.

You now have the tools to modify the Apply and Loan buttons so they will activate the desired document when either Office Binder or Internet Explorer is the container. This requires that you create a Select Case statement with the same structure as the one shown in the previous example.

To locate a specific document using the Office Binder as a container:

1. Replace the code in the **cmdApply_Click** event procedure for the **docLoan** UserDocument object with the following statements:

```
Dim secCurrent As Section
Select Case gstrContainer
    Case "IWebBrowser2"
        UserDocument.Hyperlink.NavigateTo _
        cstrPath & "docApply.vbd"
    Case "Section"
        With UserDocument.Parent.Parent
            For Each secCurrent In .Sections
                If secCurrent.Type = _
                    "MPBLoan.docApply" Then
                    secCurrent.Activate
                    Exit Sub
                End If
            Next
               .Sections.Add _
                    "MPBLoan.docApply"
        End With
    Case Else
        Call MsgBox("Container not supported.")
End Select
```

2. Replace the code in the **cmdLoan_Click** event procedure for the **docApply** UserDocument object with the following statements:

```
Dim secCurrent As Section
Select Case gstrContainer
    Case "IWebBrowser2"
        UserDocument.Hyperlink.NavigateTo _
        cstrPath & "docApply.vbd"
```

```
        Case "Section"
            With UserDocument.Parent.Parent
                For Each secCurrent In .Sections
                    If secCurrent.Type _
                        = "MPBLoan.docLoan" Then
                        secCurrent.Activate
                        Exit Sub
                    End If
                Next
                   .Sections.Add _
                        "MPBLoan.docLoan"
            End With
        Case Else
            Call MsgBox("Container not supported.")
    End Select
```

These two event procedures have a structure similar to the Back and Forward navigational event procedure. They both use a Select Case statement to determine the container and execute different statements, accordingly. The statements that are executed if the container is Internet Explorer have not changed. The statements to locate or add a new Section object, however, require careful examination.

```
With UserDocument.Parent.Parent
    For Each secCurrent In .Sections
        If secCurrent.Type = "MPBLoan.docLoan" Then
            secCurrent.Activate
            Exit Sub
        End If
    Next
       .Sections.Add _
            "MPBLoan.docLoan"
End With
```

The With statement provides the reference to the Office Binder object. The For loop examines each Section object in the Sections collection to determine if a Section object having the correct class has been loaded. If the Section object is found, the Section object is activated and the event procedure exits. If the Section object is not found, then it is added to the collection by calling the Add method.

Testing Office Binder

The easiest way to test the application you just wrote is to compile it into an Automation server so it is properly registered on the system. As you will see in a moment, Office Binder uses the information in the registry to determine the different types of documents it can load.

To compile the project:

1. Click **Project**, then **Properties.** On the General tab of the Project Properties dialog, set the Project Name to **MPBLoan.**
2. Close all the Visual Basic windows but Project Explorer.
3. Click **Make MPBLoan.DLL** on the **File** menu.
4. Save the DLL in the **Chapter.12\Startup** folder.

   These steps cause the DLL server to be registered on the system. You now can start the Office Binder application and load the different documents.
5. Start **Office Binder.**
6. Click **Add** on the **Section** menu to activate the Add Section dialog then click **List view.**
7. Click **MPBLoan.docApply** then click **OK** to add the Section object. The document will appear in Office Binder just as it appeared in Internet Explorer.
8. Scroll to the bottom of the document then click **Loan Payment.** The loan document will appear in a new Section object.
9. Click the **Forward** and **Back** buttons to navigate between the two documents.

As you can see, the documents appear in Office Binder just as they do in Internet Explorer. The only real difference is the methods used for navigation.

SUMMARY

- This chapter presented the fundamental techniques used to manage ActiveX documents with multiple containers.
- In some ways, an ActiveX document is like a form. It can have a menu. The user interacts with the ActiveX document in the same way as he or she does a form. The form, however, is displayed in a container application like Internet Explorer or Office Binder.
- In other ways, an ActiveX document is like an ActiveX control. Both the UserControl and UserDocument objects support events that occur when an instance of the object is created. There also are events that occur when the instance of the UserDocument object is destroyed.
- The Primary difference between an ActiveX document application and a form-based application is that an ActiveX document must be run inside another program called a container application.
- ActiveX documents support persistent properties in the same manner as ActiveX controls. The ReadProperties and WriteProperties events occur allowing you to read and write property values from and to the PropertyBag object.

- ActiveX documents support menus. Menus on an ActiveX document are negotiated with the menus of the container application. That is, the menus of both programs appear on the menu bar of the container application.
- Navigation between multiple ActiveX documents depends on the container application. If the container is Internet Explorer, then the Hyperlink object is used to navigate between one document and another. A reference to the Hyperlink object is stored in the Hyperlink property of the UserDocument object. The GoBack, GoForward, and NavigateTo methods locate the previous, next, and a specific, document.
- The Visible area of the container that displays ActiveX documents is called the Viewport. The user can resize the container at any time. Your document may need to adjust the portion of the ActiveX document when the user resizes the Viewport, or an object gets focus for an object that is not visible presently. This is achieved by calling the SetViewport method of the UserDocument object.
- Another container that supports ActiveX documents is Microsoft Office Binder. While it displays ActiveX documents, the methods to load and navigate between ActiveX documents differ considerably. Each document in the binder is considered a Section object in the Sections collection. Adding a Section object to the current binder can be accomplished by calling the Add method of the Sections collection.
- The ActivateSection method will set the focus to a specific Section object thus activating it.

QUESTIONS

1. Which of the following statements are true about menus as they pertain to ActiveX documents?

a. The menus for an ActiveX document appear on the menu for the container rather than the document itself.

b. Using the NegotiatePosition property controls how the menus are integrated with the container.

c. ActiveX documents do not support menus.

d. Both a and b.

e. All of the above.

2. Which of the following statements are true regarding ActiveX Document DLL projects?

a. They can display modal forms.

b. They can display modeless forms.

c. They can display dialog boxes.

d. Both a and c.

e. Both b and c.

3. The interaction between the menus on an ActiveX document and the container's program is referred to as ____________.
   a. combination menus
   b. integrated menus
   c. menu synchronization
   d. menu negotiation
   e. none of the above
4. Which are the valid file extensions for the files pertaining to an ActiveX document?
   a. .doc
   b. .dox
   c. .vbd
   d. Both a and b.
   e. All of the above.
5. The events pertaining to an ActiveX document occur in which order?
   a. Initialize, InitProperties, Show.
   b. Initialize, ReadProperties, Show.
   c. Initialize, Load, Show.
   d. Both a and b.
   e. Both b and c.
6. Which of the following methods are supported by the Hyperlink object?
   a. GoBack.
   b. GoForward.
   c. NavigateTo.
   d. Both a and b.
   e. All of the above.
7. Which of the following are valid container applications for ActiveX documents?
   a. Office Binder.
   b. Internet Explorer.
   c. Word.
   d. Both a and b.
   e. All of the above.
8. The individual documents stored in the binder are called ____________.
   a. Hyperlinks
   b. Page objects
   c. DAO objects
   d. Section objects
   e. Document objects
9. Office Binder can display and group together ____________.
   a. Word documents
   b. ActiveX documents
   c. Excel documents
   d. both a and b
   e. all of the above

10. The Type property as it pertains to a Section object contains ____________.
    a. the file name of the Section object
    b. an Integer
    c. the OLE class name of the Section object
    d. none of the above
    e. all of the above
11. What is the name of the method to set the position of an ActiveX document in the Viewport?
    a. SetViewport.
    b. Top.
    c. Left.
    d. Viewport.
    e. None of the above.
12. What are the valid strings for the Internet Explorer and Office Binder containers?
    a. IWebBrowser2.
    b. IWebBrowserApp.
    c. Section.
    d. Both a and b.
    e. All of the above.
13. Write the necessary statements to navigate forward to the next document. The statements you write should check that Internet Explorer is the current container.
14. Write the necessary statements to locate the URL named **Chapter.12\Question\docDemo**. Assume that Internet Explorer is the current container.
15. Create an event procedure that will set the Viewport to the top-left corner of an ActiveX document when the command button named **cmdHome** is clicked.
16. Write the necessary statement to determine the container of a UserDocument object. Store the string in the variable named gstrDemo.
17. With the UserDocument objects as a reference, write the necessary statement to reference an Office Binder object and store the reference in the object variable named bndCurrent.
18. Write a For Each loop to print the Type (class name) of all the Section objects in the binder. Again, use the UserDocument object to obtain a reference to the binder.
19. Write a statement to add a Section object to the binder. Again, use the UserDocument object to obtain a reference to the binder. Use the class named **ProjDemo.DocDemo** as the class name.
20. Write the necessary statement to set the active binder Section object to the Section object named **DemoSection**.

EXERCISES

1. In this exercise you will create an ActiveX document project that can be used by Internet Explorer.

a. Create a new project ActiveX Document DLL named **Chapter.12\Exercise\Exercise1.vbp.**

b. Create three ActiveX documents named **docIE1**, **docIE2**, and **docIE3**.

c. On each ActiveX document, create four command buttons. Two of the buttons should locate the previous and next document. Make sure to create an error handler in case there is no previous or next document.

d. The other two command buttons should locate the other two documents. That is, the two command buttons on the docIE2 should locate docIE1 and docIE3, respectively.

e. Test the program.

f. Start Internet Explorer and test the navigational methods of the three forms.

2. In this exercise you will create an ActiveX document project that can be used by Office Binder.

a. Create a new project ActiveX Document DLL named **Chapter.12\Exercise\Exercise2.vbp.**

b. Create three ActiveX documents named **docBind1**, **docBind2**, and **docBind3**.

c. On each ActiveX document, create four command buttons. Two of the buttons should locate the previous and next document in the Sections collection.

d. The other two command buttons should activate the other two documents. That is, the two command buttons on the docBind2 should activate docBind1 and docBind3, respectively.

e. Compile the project into an ActiveX DLL server.

f. Set the Project Name to **Exercise2**.

g. Start Office Binder. Add each of the three documents to the current binder and test the navigational command buttons.

3. In this exercise you will create an ActiveX document project that can be used by both Internet Explorer and Office Binder.

a. Create a new project ActiveX Document DLL named **Chapter.12\Exercise\Exercise3.vbp**.

b. Create three ActiveX documents named **docBind1**, **docBind2**, and **docBind3**.

c. On each ActiveX document, create four command buttons. Two of the buttons should locate the previous and next document. You must write the necessary code to determine the current container and based on that information, you must call the appropriate navigational methods.

d. Set the Project Name to **Exercise3**. Change the document named in step b to **docIEBind1**, **docIEBind2**, and **docIEBind3**.

e. The other two command buttons should activate the other two documents.

f. Test the program.

CHAPTER

13

Using Internet Controls

Working with SMTP and FTP

case MFD Productions wants to enable their applications for use on the Internet. Specifically, they want a program that will allow a user to send a mail message over the Internet without having to access or start another program. They also want a program that will allow users to transfer files using the File Transfer Protocol (FTP).

SECTION A

objectives

In this section you will:

- Use various Internet technologies
- Learn about the protocols used to communicate over the Internet
- Establish a connection to the Internet using the Winsock control
- Send an electronic mail message with the Simple Mail Transfer Protocol (SMTP)

Sending Mail Using the Winsock Control and the Simple Mail Transfer Protocol

Previewing the Completed Application

To use the completed program and complete the chapter and exercises, your computer must have a connection to the Internet, as the programs send electronic mail messages and download files from the Internet. You also must have a valid electronic mail address.

The completed application in this chapter is really two separate programs that share a common thread. They are both client applications that use the services of the Internet. The first application is used to send electronic mail and the second will transfer files using the File Transfer Protocol (FTP).

To preview the completed application:

1 Start **Visual Basic** and load the project named **Chapter.13\Complete\Inet_C.vbp**. The project consists of three forms. The first contains two command buttons that are used to display the other two forms. The second is used to send e-mail, and the third is used to display files available through FTP and download those files.

2 Run the program then click the **Winsock / Email** command button. The form to send an e-mail message appears. Figure 13-1 shows the Winsock form in design mode.

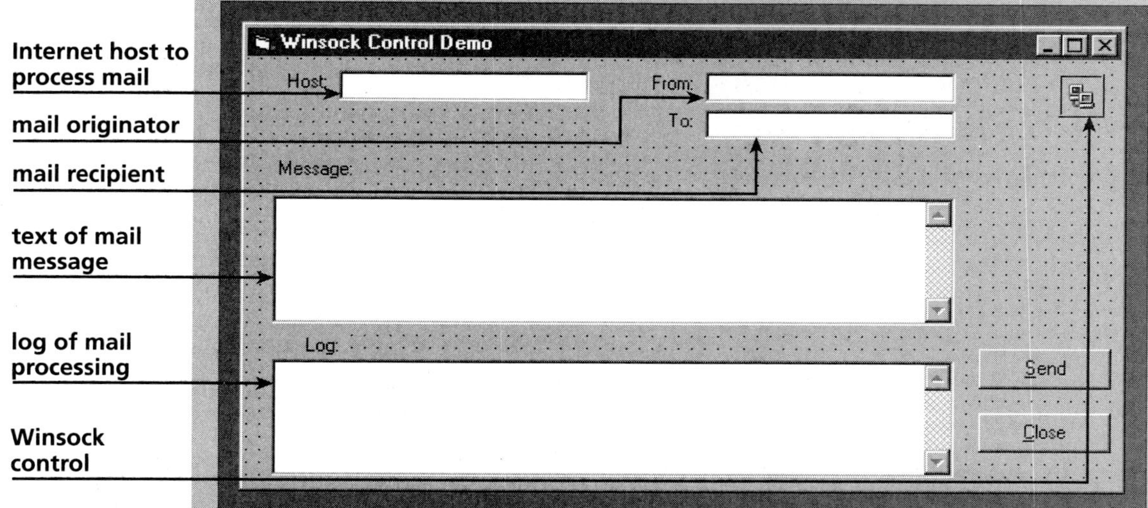

Figure 13-1: Completed Winsock form (design mode)

As shown in Figure 13-1, the form contains fields to enter both the sender and receiver e-mail addresses. It also contains a field to identify the computer that agrees to process your mail. While the sender and mail host usually are configured on a per computer basis, this solution allows the program to run generically without having to know about particulars related to your Internet provider. The form also contains a multiline text box to store the mail message itself, and a text box that displays a log of the commands exchanged between two computers as the mail message is being processed.

3 Establish a connection to your Internet provider. Obviously, the steps to accomplish this will vary depending upon how your computer is connected to the Internet.

4 Enter your e-mail address in the From and To text boxes. In the Host text box, enter the host name of the computer that accepts mail for you. If you do not know the name of the computer, check with your Internet provider or the administrator of your computer. You also can use the following address for the e-mail provider: **VBmail.AccessNV.com**. Access Nevada, an Internet provider, will provide electronic mail forwarding services for use in conjunction with this book. Before using this address, read the use restrictions imposed on this e-mail server found on the Copyright page in this book. In the Message text box, enter some text. This text is the body of the e-mail message. Click **Send**. As the program establishes the necessary connection and sends the message, a log of the messages sent and the responses received from the remote computer are displayed in the text box at the bottom of the form.

5 After a few minutes, check your e-mail to see if the message was delivered. The time it takes to deliver the message will vary depending on your Internet provider. Generally, the process takes less than a minute or two.

6 End the program.

The second part of the program implements an FTP client using the TreeView control. Programming the TreeView control was presented in Chapter 6. FTP servers have a hierarchical directory and file organization similar to both Windows and UNIX file systems. Because of this characteristic, the TreeView control is well-suited to displaying this information. Again, for this program to work, you must have a connection to the Internet.

To test the FTP client:

1 Start the program then make sure you are connected to the Internet.

2 Click the **Internet Transfer Control / FTP** button to activate the FTP form.

3 In the Address text box, enter the following FTP address: **ftp.microsoft.com**. This causes a request to be made to the FTP site and a list of the files in the root directory to be downloaded. Be patient. Depending on the speed of your Internet connection and the load on the remote site, the request may take a minute or two. The completed application changes the mouse pointer to an hourglass while the request is being processed. When complete, the files are listed in the TreeView control as shown in Figure 13-2.

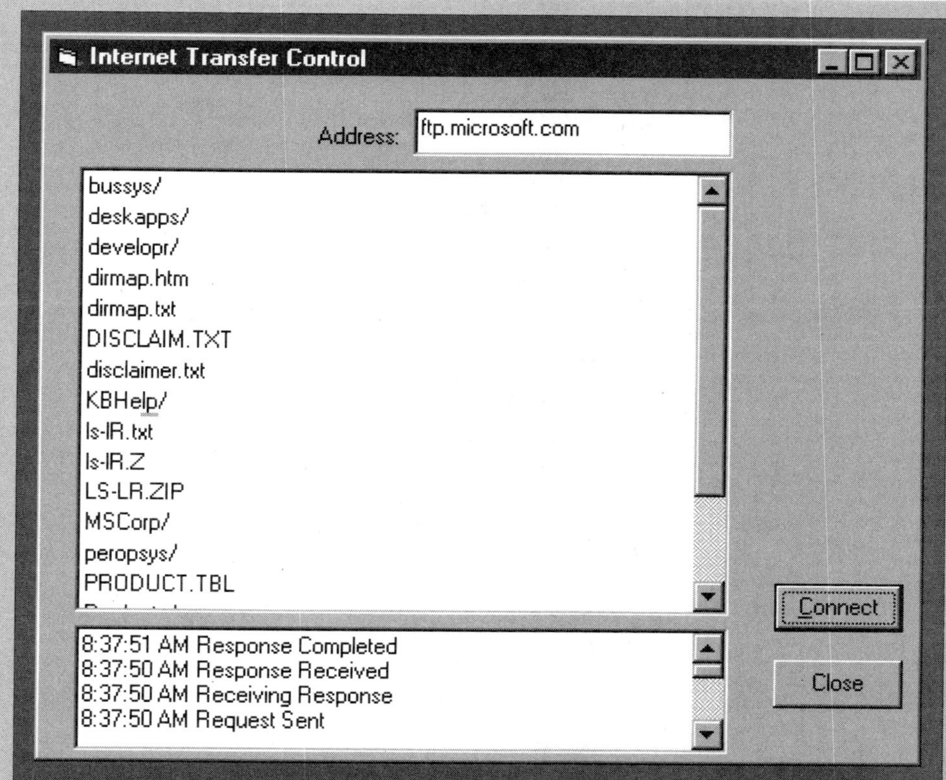

Figure 13-2: Completed FTP form

Some listings have a trailing forward slash (/). This indicates that the listing is a directory and not a file. Also, the contents of the remote computer are subject to change at any time. Thus, the list of files shown in Figure 13-2 may differ from the files listed when you run the program.

4 Click a directory. This causes another request to be made to display the contents of that directory. When the contents of the directory are received, they are displayed as children of the selected node. Thus, the organization of the files in the TreeView control is the same as the organization of the files on the FTP server. Note that if the directory is empty, nothing will happen.

5 To download a file, click a file that is not a directory.

This causes a dialog to be displayed asking you where the file should be saved. Many of the files are quite large; consider downloading the file named **Disclaim.txt.**

6 Specify the **Chapter.13\Complete** folder then click **Save.** Specify a drive designator as necessary.

7 End the program then exit Visual Basic.

If you are familiar with the Internet, an introduction to the Internet likely will be a review for you. The discussion on these pages is not intended to explain the details of how the Internet works, but to provide more of an executive overview of the Internet technologies and organization. The goal is to provide enough detail for you to create Visual Basic programs to access the various services that comprise the Internet and give you a general understanding of how those services work.

An Introduction to the Internet

The success of the Internet did not happen by accident. From the initial research funded by the Defense Advanced Research Projects Agency (DARPA), a set of network standards evolved that allowed heterogeneous and geographically distant computers to communicate. By heterogeneous, we mean that the computers are not required to have the same hardware or software. That is, some computers may run UNIX, others may run Windows, and others may run yet another operating system. By geographically distant, we mean the computers that communicate with each other can be located physically anywhere in the world. These network standards, or protocols as they often are called, commonly are referred to as the **Internet Protocol Suite**. Another word commonly used is **TCP/IP**. The importance of these protocols is that they hide the low-level details of the communication from computer to computer. These protocols are responsible for sending information from one computer to another. As an analogy, consider the process of sending a letter across the country. You put an address on a letter, put it in a mailbox, and it gets delivered. Neither you nor the intended recipient have to know how the message gets delivered. More specifically, you do not need to know the path the letter takes across the country, nor are you aware of the specific technologies used to deliver the letter.

Just as the postal service delivers a letter to a unique address, computers connected to the Internet each have a unique address to identify the computer. This address commonly is called an **Internet Number**, or an **IP number**. An Internet number is a 32-bit number divided into 4 octets. That is, a number like 131.216.39.3 is a valid Internet number. Because IP numbers are not intuitive, computers on the Internet also have a name. These names also are hierarchical and are organized into domains and subdomains. Most computers are categorized into the following primary domains:

- Commercial organizations are in the **com** domain.
- Governmental entities are in the **gov** domain.
- Educational institutions are in the **edu** domain.
- General organizations have a domain of **org**.
- Network organizations have a domain of **net**.
- Foreign countries have a two-character identifier to identify the country (e.g., the domain for the United Kingdom is **uk**).

Within these primary categories there are domains and subdomains that uniquely identify a host on the Internet. Names are written such that each domain or subdomain is separated by a dot (.). Names appear from the most specific to the most general as shown in the following list:

```
microsoft.com
ix.netcom.com
west.engineering.sun.com
West.Engineering.Sun.Com
```

An address can have any number of subdomains. These names are not case-sensitive. As such, the last two names are equivalent.

While you often hear TCP/IP as one acronym, TCP and IP are two very different protocols. This chapter does not attempt to define the mechanics of how TCP/IP works. Some background likely will be useful, however, as you develop programs that utilize the services provided by the Internet. Consider the following formal definitions of the Internet protocols:

- IP is defined as an unreliable, connectionless packet-delivery service.
- TCP is defined as a connected, reliable data-transport service.
- UDP is defined as an application-level, unreliable packet-delivery service.

A further explanation of these definitions is in order to provide more meaning as to the purpose of these protocols. Data sent across the Internet is sent in units called **packets**. It is the responsibility of IP to attempt to send a packet from the source computer to its destination. A unique IP number identifies each computer on the Internet and determines the source and destination. All IP does is send a packet of information. It does not actually establish any kind of connection with a remote computer; therefore, it is **connectionless**. It does not verify that the packet actually was received at the destination; therefore, it is **unreliable**. It also does not verify that messages made up of multiple packets were received in the correct order. All IP does is to send packets from one computer to another. IP packets commonly are referred to as **IP datagrams**. In the sentence above, the word "messages" refers to a group of IP datagrams and should not be confused with an e-mail message. To continue the post office analogy, when you send a letter, you do not get any acknowledgement that the letter got delivered. You just assume it does.

Given this, you may wonder why IP is of any use. If you cannot send a message from one computer to another and guarantee that it arrives, then what good is it? The answer lies in TCP. TCP is a higher-level protocol than IP. As IP packets arrive at a computer, TCP assembles the packets into their proper order and determines whether or not any packets were lost during transmission. If a packet was lost, then TCP automatically requests that the packet be resent. As such, the protocol is **reliable**. When communicating using TCP, both the sending and receiving computer have an established connection. Each computer receives the packets from IP and processes them. TCP also sends IP packets. As such, you can think of TCP layered on top of IP. To continue the post office analogy, if you sent the letter using TCP, it is analogous to sending a letter from the post office as "Return Receipt Requested." Imagine you sent a document that would not fit in one envelope. In this example, you will have several letters. If one of the letters was lost, the letter would be resent, although the whole document would not. Also, the recipient of the document will have to reassemble the parts of each document (contained in each letter) in their proper order.

Another closely related protocol is the User Datagram Protocol (UDP). UDP provides the mechanism for applications to send IP datagrams from a source to a destination. The UDP protocol is used for application programs that do not require that the receiver acknowledge the arrival of the datagram. Figure 13-3 illustrates the relationship between TCP, IP, and UDP.

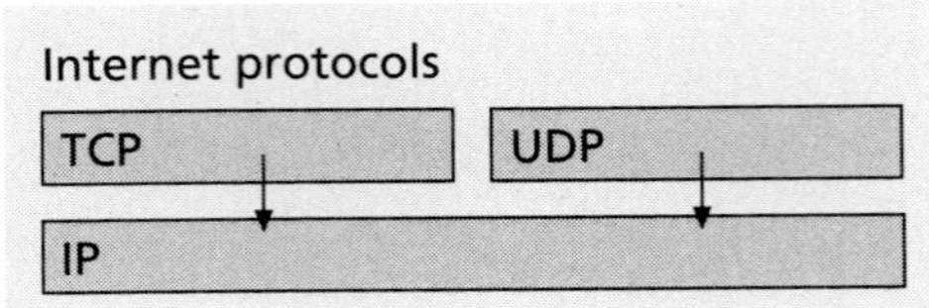

Figure 13-3: TCP, IP, and UDP relationships

As shown in Figure 13-3, TCP and UDP are independent protocols that both rely on the services of IP. The TCP/IP protocols do not care about the contents of the data inside a packet. That is, the data in a packet could well be a mail message, or the packet could contain parts of a file being downloaded using FTP or just a Web page transferred with HTTP. TCP/IP also does not care about the type of data that is being sent. That is, the data could contain ASCII characters or binary data.

Internet Services

Intertwined with TCP/IP, are several services that make up the suite of Internet services. If you have ever used the Internet, you have used these services. If you have read documents using the Web, you have used the HyperText Transfer Protocol (HTTP) to transfer Web pages from a remote computer to your computer. If you have downloaded a file, you have used the File Transfer Protocol (FTP) to transfer the file. If you have sent an electronic mail message, the program you used to send electronic mail relied on the Simple Mail Transfer Protocol (SMTP) to deliver the mail message. Web browsers, because of their sophisticated interface, cause these individual services to appear as a single application. They are not. Each of these three protocols is a distinct service as far as the Internet is concerned. Furthermore, these three protocols or services are but a few of the services provided by the Internet. Services on the Internet can be categorized roughly into low-level and high-level services. The following list summarizes a few of the more significant low-level services provided by the Internet:

- Nameservice—when you refer to a host by its name like ftp.course.com, that name is translated into an IP number like 35.17.12.128.
- Routing—routing is a low-level service that determines the path taken to deliver packets from the source to the destination. As a packet is transferred

between its source and destination, the packet may travel through many different hardware components to reach its final destination.

- Address resolution—while computers have an IP number, the devices have a physical address in addition to an IP address. The Address Resolution Protocol (ARP) maps IP addresses to physical addresses.
- Internet Control Message Protocol—sometimes packets may be corrupted during transmission. The Internet Control Message Protocol (ICMP) permits the sending of error and control messages between computers.

These low-level protocols are largely transparent to application developers. As you will see in a moment, you use Visual Basic to establish a connection to a remote host using either the name of the host or its IP number. As the application developer, you neither need to be concerned about how the host name gets translated into an IP number, nor do you need to be aware of the route (path) taken to deliver the information.

As an application developer, you can use the high-level services provided by the Internet to send mail, transfer files, and perform other tasks. The following list summarizes some of the high-level services provided on the Internet:

- E-mail uses SMTP to deliver a message from the source computer to its destination.
- File transfer uses FTP to upload and download files from one computer to another.
- Web pages are transferred using HTTP.
- Network News, commonly called News, is transferred between the client and the server using the Network News Transfer Protocol (NNTP).

Each of these high-level services also relies on TCP/IP to work. Figure 13-4 illustrates the relationship of these high-level services to the underlying TCP/IP protocols.

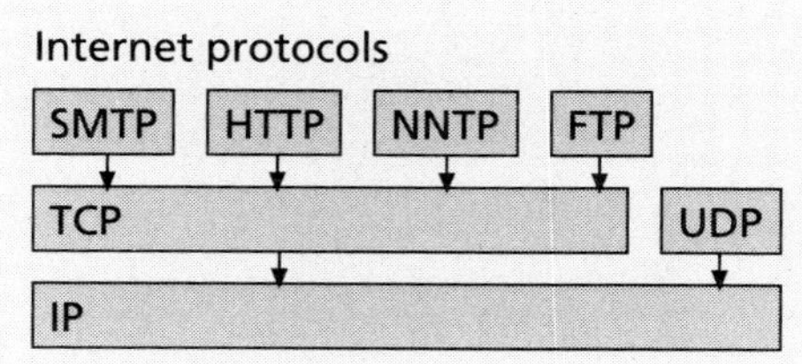

Figure 13-4: Internet services

As shown in Figure 13-4, the SMTP, FTP, HTTP, and NNTP services all rely on a TCP connection. TCP in turn relies on IP.

We have described the basic services that make the Internet work, and identified the terms used to describe those services. Next, you will see how these services are implemented.

Implementing Internet Services

Some of the first computers to use the Internet were UNIX-based computers. A program that wanted to make a connection to the Internet would do so using a socket. Briefly defined, a **socket** is an endpoint for communication. A more practical definition of a socket involves an analogy.

Imagine you write books for a publisher at home. You must communicate, however, with the publisher who is at one end of the country and your editor who is someplace else. In this case, there are three entities that need to communicate: you, the publisher, and the editor. Each has a physical address. This address is analogous to an Internet site. Assume that these three parties communicate in one of two ways: by telephone and by fax.

Assume that each office has two telephone lines—one for the telephone (voice), and the other for the fax machine. The important point to make is that if a fax is sent over the voice line, then the person sending the fax will hear an unintelligible garbled mess and the person receiving the telephone call will hear an almost deafening beep. If a voice connection is attempted on the fax line, then the fax machine will hear an unintelligible garbled mess. While each uses the same low-level protocol (the telephone line), the high level protocol is different for the two services as shown in Figure 13-5.

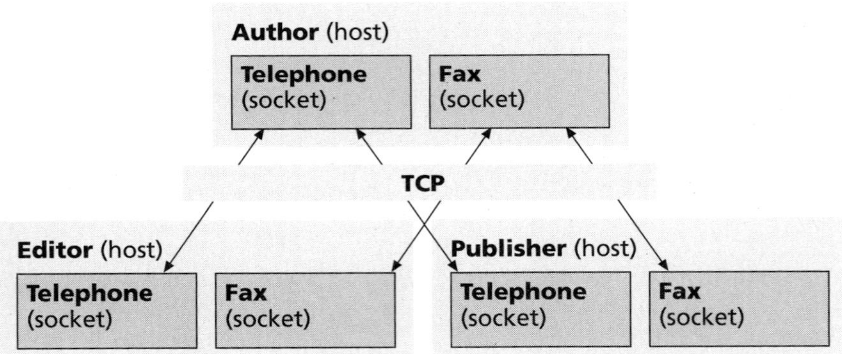

Figure 13-5: Sockets

As shown in Figure 13-5, each physical location is analogous to a host on the Internet. Each site has two different endpoints of communication—one for voice and the other for data. While they both use the same low-level protocol (the telephone line), the endpoints (sockets) use a completely different high-level protocol (voice, fax).

The same model can be extended to the Internet. Consider the two high-level protocols SMTP and FTP instead of a physical telephone line. The servers that process the incoming requests listen for requests at a specific port, and each port is identified by a distinct integer number. SMTP servers listen at port number 25, for example. If you try to send a mail message using SMTP to the FTP port, FTP will not understand the message. If you try to send an FTP request to the mail port (SMTP), SMTP will not understand the request.

One of the reasons that the Internet works is that these different services, like FTP and SMTP, all agree to communicate over the same well-defined and consistent port numbers. Referring back to the telephone example, the fax machine and voice lines have a different telephone number or port. If you were to switch the devices connected to the telephone line it would be like changing the port numbers.

The term socket has persisted as early personal computers used software known as Winsock (Windows socket) to connect to the Internet. Winsock supported the necessary protocols to establish TCP/IP connections. In Visual Basic, you use a control known as the Winsock control to make Internet connections.

All programs that work with sockets share the following common characteristics:

- They must have an IP address.
- They must identify a specific port.
- They must specify a connection type. In the context of Visual Basic, this means that you must specify whether to use the TCP or UDP protocols.

Now that you have a general idea how the Internet works in theory, you will see how it works in practice. The Internet protocols are available to you using the Winsock control. The Winsock control is an ActiveX control and as such must be added to the project. Like the CommonDialog control, it is invisible at run time. The user does not interact with the Winsock control. Rather, you as the programmer use its properties and methods by writing code. The standard prefix used for the Winsock control is "sok."

It is important to understand that the Winsock control itself neither sends a mail message nor transfers a file. All the Winsock control does is to establish a connection between two computers. It is the responsibility of your program to send the messages to the remote computer and process any responses from the remote computer.

When you access the services of the Internet, there often is a client-server relationship between two connected computers. For example, when you download a file from the Internet, your computer is considered the client. The client uses the services of another computer, which is considered the server. In this model, the server always is listening for requests from the clients. When a request for a connection is received, a connection with the client is established. This is referred to as accepting a connection. At this point, messages are exchanged between the client and server until the conversation is complete and then the connection is closed. After the connection is closed, the server begins waiting for another connection request from another client. This is somewhat of an oversimplification as most servers can accept several requests from different clients at the same time. The term message, in this context, simply means data sent from one computer to another. It does not imply a specific type of message. Thus, do not confuse the generic term message with a more specific use like an electronic mail message.

The Winsock Control

The Microsoft Winsock control implements both the TCP and UDP protocols. It is useful because the control handles many of the details necessary to communicate using TCP or UDP, inside its methods and properties.

Using the Winsock control consists of setting the necessary properties to establish a connection. Once established, the source and destination computers exchange messages. Once the exchange of messages is complete, the connection is closed. Consider plugging in a telephone jack. The telephone is an endpoint of communication. To make a telephone call, one endpoint (the source) tries to establish a connection with the destination (the other endpoint). Once the connection is established (you connect with someone at the other end of the telephone), the source and destination send messages (you talk back and forth). At some point, the connection is terminated and the socket awaits another incoming message; that is, you hang up the telephone and wait for it to ring again.

Object	Winsock
Properties	The read-only **LocalHostName** property contains the name of the local machine. The read-only **LocalIP** property contains the IP number of the local machine. The **LocalPort** property is a read-write property used to specify the local port to send data, or in the case of a server, the port where the server will listen for incoming connection requests. The **Protocol** property can be set to one of two constants. If set to 0 – sckTCPProtocol (the default), the TCP protocol is used for communication. If set to 1 – sckUDPProtocol, the UDP protocol is used. The Protocol property must be set to one of these constants to establish a connection or send a message. The **RemoteHost** property can contain either the Name of the remote host or its IP number. The **RemoteHostIP** property is a read-only property that contains the IP number of the remote host after a connection has been made. The **RemotePort** property contains the number of the port corresponding to the service you want to use (i.e., SMTP (25)). The **State** property is a read-only property that identifies the current state of the socket. There are unique states to indicate whether the socket is attempting a connection, the socket is connected, or the socket is closing a connection. Refer to the "State Property (Winsock Control)" Help page for a complete list of the constant values identifying the different states.

Events	The **Close** event occurs when the remote computer closes an established connection. Your program should respond to this event by calling the Close method. The **Connect** event occurs when a connection first is established between the client and server. This is different than the Connect method. The **ConnectionRequest** event is used when you are implementing a server program. This event occurs when a remote computer is requesting a connection from your computer. When new data arrives from the remote computer, it is stored in the input queue, and the **DataArrival** event occurs. Typically, you call the GetData method to move the data from the input queue into a string in your program. When you call a method like Connect, the request may fail for several reasons. For example, you may have specified an invalid host name. The **Error** event occurs whenever the request cannot be satisfied. When sending a message to a remote computer (typically using the SendData method), the **SendComplete** event occurs after the message has been sent. The **SendProgress** event is useful for sending large messages. The event contains arguments to identify the number of bytes already sent and the number of bytes that need to be sent.
Methods	The **Close** method closes an open socket. This has the effect of breaking an established connection. The **Connect** method is used to establish a connection to a remote computer. The RemoteHost, RemotePort, and Protocol properties must be set before calling this method. When the remote host sends data to the local computer, the data is stored in a buffer called the input queue. The **GetData** method moves data from this buffer into a variant or string variable. Used only for TCP connections, the **PeekData** method allows you to view the contents of the input queue without removing the existing contents. The **SendData** method is used to send a message to a remote computer. The contents of the message either can be text or binary data. The **Accept**, **Bind**, and **Listen** methods are used when the Winsock control is used to implement a server.

Using the Winsock control presents somewhat of a chicken and egg problem. On one hand, you need to know how to use the Winsock control to establish a connection. On the other hand, you need to understand the mechanics of the protocol you will be using so you can send and receive meaningful messages.

In this example, you first will establish a connection to a remote computer, and then you will expand the program to send a mail message. Thus, you will be using the SMTP service. Before a communication link can be established, you must define the computer you want to talk to. This involves setting the RemoteHost, Protocol, and RemotePort properties. Because the protocol used to send and receive mail messages relies on TCP rather than UDP, the protocol should be set to TCP. The remote host either can be set to the IP number or the name of the remote host. If a name is used, the Winsock control takes care of translating the name into an IP number. Finally, the port must be specified. The generally accepted port for SMTP is 25. As you may expect, a mail message consists of multiple parts. That is, you send each part of a message separately. You must send the e-mail address of the sender, the address of the recipient, and the body of the mail message. To keep track of where in the process the message is at any given time, you will use a variable named State to keep track of the current state of the mail transaction.

To establish a connection with a remote computer:

1. Start **Visual Basic** then load the project named **Chapter.13\Startup\InET_S.vbp.**
2. Using the Components dialog, make sure the **Microsoft Internet Controls** and the **Internet Transfer Control 5.0** have been added to the project. You will use the Internet Transfer Control in the next section of this chapter.
3. Create an instance of the Winsock control on the form named frmSok. Set the Name property of the control instance to **sokSMTP.**
4. Enter the following statements in the **cmdSend_Click** event procedure:

```
If mblnInProgress = True Then
    Exit Sub
End If
sokSMTP.Protocol = sckTCPProtocol
sokSMTP.RemoteHost = txtHost
sokSMTP.RemotePort = 25
sokSMTP.Connect
mblnInProgress = True
State = 0
```

5. Enter the following statement in the **sokSMTP_Connect** event procedure. This statement simply displays a message in the text box indicating that a connection has been established.

```
txtLog = "Connected"
```

6 Test the program. Make sure you have established a connection to the Internet.

Enter the name of the host that agrees to process your mail in the **Host** text box then click the **Send** command button. Again, you can use the address **VBMail.AccessNV.com** if you are not sure of the e-mail address of your Internet provider. When the Winsock control establishes a connection to the Internet, the message "Connected" should appear in the text box at the bottom of the form.

The statements in the cmdSend_Click event procedure attempt to establish a TCP connection with the remote host on port 25 (the SMTP port). This host is identified by the value stored in the text box named txtHost. If the connection is successful, the Connect event occurs. If the request is not successful, however, the Error event will occur indicating that a connection could not be established.

The module-level variable mblnInProgress is tested to see if the value is True. This variable is used to determine whether or not there is a mail message in progress and if there is, the procedure ends. Because establishing a connection is the first step in sending a message, the Boolean variable is set to True at the end of the procedure. Other procedures will set this variable as necessary to indicate when the sending of a message is complete.

The Error Event

The Winsock control can raise errors for many reasons. Your connection to the Internet either may be unavailable, or you may have specified an invalid host name. As such, you should write code to respond to the Error event so the user is aware that the connection could not be established.

Syntax

*object*_**Error(***number* **As Integer**, *Description* **As String**, *Scode* **As Long**, *Source* **As String**, *HelpFile* **As String**, *HelpContext* **As Long**, *CancelDisplay* **As Boolean)**

Dissection

- The *object* must contain an instance of the Winsock control.
- The **Error** event occurs whenever a TCP or IP error occurs.
- The *number* contains an integer to identify the source of the error. For a complete list of these values, refer to the "Error Event" Help page pertaining to the Winsock control.
- The *Description* argument contains a textual description of the error.
- The *Source* describes the source of the error. This value typically contains the project name that generated the error.
- The *HelpFile* and *HelpContext* arguments identify the help file contents of a Help page to be displayed.

- By default, Visual Basic will display a message box when the Error event occurs. Setting the *CancelDisplay* property to True will prevent the message box from being displayed.

One common cause of an error occurs when a host cannot be located. This can occur because a valid host is down or the user specified an invalid host name. In this example, you will display any error message in the Status text box.

To respond to the Error event:

1 Enter the following statements in the **sokSMTP_Error** event procedure:

```
Select Case Number
    Case sckHostNotFound, sckHostNotFoundTryAgain
        txtLog.Text = Number & " " & Description
End Select
sokSMTP.Close
mblnInProgress = False
```

2 Test the program. Enter the host named **notesgw.course.coz** (an invalid host name).

After a moment, a message will be displayed in the Status text box indicating the host could not be located. Another possible cause of an error is if you enter a host name that will not accept connections to process your mail.

The previous statements are very simple. When an error occurs pertaining to the Winsock control, the Error event is raised. This event contains arguments to identify the error number and its description. These values either can be used to inform the user as to the cause of the error, or to determine whether or not it makes sense to continue processing. This Select Case statement could be expanded easily to process the other possible errors. In addition to displaying the error message, the Close method is called in the Winsock control to close the connection. The final statement is:

```
mblnInProgress = False
```

The module-level variable is used to identify whether or not there is a mail transaction in progress. Checking the value of this variable in the cmdSend_Click event procedure will prevent the user from trying to send a mail message while a message is being sent. This variable will be set and its value tested throughout the program as you will see in a moment.

At this point, you can make a connection to a remote computer and detect whether or not an error occurred. It is important to note that by itself, the Winsock control does nothing. You can establish a connection with a remote computer, and send and receive messages. The Winsock control, however, does not interpret the contents of those messages. Again, the term message here refers to a general TCP message rather than an electronic mail message. This is the responsibility of your program. If you establish a connection to the FTP port, the messages contain information to send files back and forth between computers. If you establish a connection with the SMTP port, then the messages contain the information necessary to send and receive electronic mail. The important point is that the Winsock control itself does not care about the actual content of the messages. It merely delivers them. As such, before using the Winsock control to send and receive messages, you first must learn the basics of SMTP. Before discussing SMTP, however, a more general discussion of Internet services is in order.

Internet Standards (RFCs)

The Internet connects computers that utilize very different hardware and software. As a client, you can use computers from different manufacturers to access the Internet. These clients may run very different operating systems. For example, Windows, UNIX, and other operating systems all can connect to the Internet without knowing the hardware and software characteristics of the remote computer. One computer running Windows can send a message to another computer without knowing the type of hardware or software that is running on the remote computer. The Internet services, like SMTP, conform to a well-defined and well-adopted standard. Regardless of the computer hardware and software, every computer agrees to transfer mail using the SMTP service. As such, they all use exactly the same commands.

Other services like FTP and HTTP also use well-defined, well-adopted standards. These standards are specified in a type of document called a Request for Comments (RFC). The Internet Engineering Task Force (IETF) produces these documents. A unique number typically identifies an RFC. The RFC that defines SMTP is RFC 821. This document, and all RFCs for that matter, are widely available for downloading from the Internet. In this chapter, you also will use the FTP service. This service also is documented fully in RFC 959. (FTP has evolved significantly since it was created. As such, there are several other RFCs that describe FTP.)

For more specific information about these protocols, you can download the corresponding RFCs. There are hundreds of different RFCs that define the rules by which everyone on the Internet plays. As the Internet is a growing and evolving network, these standards too have evolved over time. Some RFCs are obsolete and are no longer applicable. Other RFCs have been superseded by revised documents. If you are interested in finding out more technical information on the Internet, you can peruse and download these documents from many sites including http://www.nexor.com/public/rfc/index/rfc.html.

SMTP

The SMTP model involves two-way connected communication between a sender and receiver. In this example, you are the sender. The receiver is the machine (Internet provider) who accepts your messages for delivery. The sender generates commands, which are sent to the receiver. For each command that is sent, the receiver acknowledges the command and whether or not it was successful. In this model, you as the sender, are the client and the receiver is the server. This section is not intended to be a complete discussion of SMTP, but rather SMTP is used as a vehicle to illustrate the use of the Winsock control. Thus, only the most fundamental commands pertaining to the creation of an SMTP client will be presented.

Consider the process of sending an e-mail message as a transaction having the following four steps:

1. The first step is an acknowledgment between the sender and receiver.
2. The second step identifies the sender.
3. The third step identifies the receiver.
4. The final step is to send the contents or body of the message.

SMTP commands all use the same generic syntax. A command consists of a three- or four-character command name, which is followed by data and must be terminated with a carriage return (vbCrLf). SMTP commands are not case-sensitive. As such, you can use any combination of uppercase and lowercase letters to specify an SMTP command. This book will use the convention of capitalizing all SMTP commands. Another important point is that e-mail addresses are not case-sensitive either. All the following e-mail addresses are equivalent:

```
ekedahl@course.com
Ekedahl@Course.Com
EKEDAHL@COURSE.COM
```

As commands are executed to move through the previously listed steps, an SMTP server (the remote computer in this case), keeps track of the transaction's state. This is significant because if you do not send the commands in the proper order, errors will occur. The notion of SMTP errors brings up an important point. If you send an offending command to an SMTP server, it will send a message indicating that it cannot successfully process the command. You may expect this to cause Visual Basic, or more specifically the Winsock control, to raise an error but this is not the case. The Error event pertaining to the Winsock control only is raised when a TCP error is detected. A TCP error occurs because a connection with the SMTP server cannot be established or because the connection has been lost. An SMTP error, however, is just a textual message indicating that the SMTP server cannot process the command. There is no error as far as TCP is concerned. As such, as you send messages to SMTP and receive responses, it is your responsibility as the programmer to write code to interpret these messages, determine whether or not an error has occurred, and whether or not it makes sense to continue.

Each time you send a command to an SMTP server, it processes the command and generates a response. This response is in the form of a textual message containing two parts—a three-digit number that identifies the response and a textual description.

After a connection is established with an SMTP server, the first step in sending a mail message is to send the HELO command. The HELO command identifies the sender and receiver. It sets the initial state indicating that there is no transaction in progress. If the HELO command is successful, the SMTP server sends a return code of 250. After the HELO command, the MAIL FROM command must be sent.

The MAIL FROM command identifies the sender and has the syntax as shown in the following statement fragment:

```
MAIL FROM: <Ekedahl@Course.com>
```

This statement tells the SMTP server (receiver) that a mail transaction is beginning and identifies the sender of the mail message. The sender of the mail message is enclosed in angled brackets (< >). In this sample statement, the sender has an e-mail address of Ekedahl@Course.com. The RCPT TO command is the next step in the transaction and has the following syntax:

```
RCPT TO: <Kate@Course.com>
```

This statement tells the receiver (SMTP server) the intended recipient of the mail. If the name of the recipient is valid, then the SMTP server sends a return code of 250. A return code of 550 indicates that the request failed. The syntax is the same as the MAIL FROM command. The e-mail address of the recipient is enclosed in angled brackets.

An important point needs to be made about this command. Some mail servers may perform forwarding. That is, you may specify a recipient who is not on the receiving machine. For example, you send a message to "Joe@beets.com" to the server at Course.com. It is up to the server at Course.com to determine whether it will forward the mail to beets.com. This configuration will vary between SMTP servers. The SMTP server at VBMail@AccessNV.com has agreed to forward mail for use with the exercises in this book. You should refer to the copyright page for restrictions pertaining to the use of this SMTP server for the purposes of e-mail forwarding. Another important point is that a mail message may have multiple recipients. In this case, you send multiple RCPT TO commands—one for each intended recipient.

The third step is to send the body of the message. This is accomplished using the DATA command. The DATA command takes no arguments. If this statement is completed successfully, then the SMTP server sends a return code of 354. Following the DATA command, you send the text of the message. After the text of the message has been sent, the DATA command is terminated by a carriage return followed by a period (.) followed by another carriage return. The following statements illustrate a complete mail transaction. In the transaction that follows, the "S" in the first column indicates the sender's message and the "R" indicates the response from the receiver.

```
S HELO
R GREETINGS

S MAIL FROM:<Ekedahl@Course.com>
R 250 OK

S RCPT TO: <Kate@Course.com>
R 250 OK

S DATA
R 354 Start mail input; end with <CrLf>.<CrLf>

S A first mail message
S Michael V. Ekedahl
S <CrLf>.<CrLf>
R 250 OK
```

This completed transaction sends a mail message from Ekedahl@Course.com to Kate@Course.com. The data of the message contains two lines—"A first mail message," and the name "Michael V. Ekedahl." The message is terminated with a period (.) on a line by itself.

The process of communication when sending a mail message involves two-way communication between the sender (your computer) and the receiver (the remote computer). The first step is to send a message to acknowledge yourself. The receiver gets this message and replies to you with an acknowledgment. Then you proceed through the remaining steps in the transaction to identify the sender of the message, the receiver of the message, and the data contained in the message.

To keep track of the current state of the transaction, an enumerated type is implemented containing the possible states of this simple form of a mail message. The following code segment illustrates the enumerated type used to identify the states of a mail transaction. The way this program is implemented, the states proceed from the first to the last member of the enumerated type. This enumerated type already has been declared.

```
Private Enum EState
    Connect
    Helo
    MailFrom
    SendTo
    Data
    MessageData
    EndMessage
End Enum
```

As shown in the previous code, the initial state is the Connect state indicating that the program has connected to the server, but a mail transaction is not in progress. The next states are used for the HELO initialization state, and to indicate the MAIL FROM and RCPT TO commands have been sent. The Data and

MessageData states are used to denote when the DATA command has started and when the sending of data is complete. The final state, EndMessage, is used to indicate that the mail message transaction has been completed.

In this example, you will print a log of the server requests and the server's acknowledgments in a multiline text box. To send a TCP message to a receiver, you call the SendData method of the Winsock control.

Syntax *object*.**SendData** *data*

Dissection

- The *object* must be a valid instance of the Winsock control.
- The **SendData** method sends a message to the connected host. If there is no established connection the Winsock control will raise the Error event.
- The SendData method either can send textual or binary *data*. If textual data is being sent, then a string should be used. If binary data is being sent, then a byte array should be used.

Code Example

```
sokSMTP.SendData "HELO VBMail.AccessNV.com" & vbCrLf
```

Code Dissection This code sends the HELO message and identifies the local host as VBMail.AccessNV.com. Again, this assumes that a connection already has been established. The string is terminated explicitly with a carriage return. If this character is omitted, then SMTP will not recognize the string as a complete command.

In this example, your program needs to send the HELO command to the SMTP server when a connection is made. As such, the code needs to be added to the Connect event procedure.

To send an SMTP HELO command:

1 Enter the following statements (shown in bold) in the **sokSMTP_Connect** event procedure:

```
txtLog = "Connected"
State = Connect
sokSMTP.SendData "HELO " & txtHost & vbCrLf
mblnInProgress = True
```

These statements reset the state of the mail transaction to indicate that there is a transaction in progress. The SendData method sends a HELO command to the server. The server name is contained in the text box named txtHost. If the host does not exist, the Winsock control will raise an Error event.

Processing Incoming Data

When a message is received from the remote site, the Winsock control generates the DataArrival event. Your client program needs to respond to this event to determine the receiver's response. Remember, the Winsock control does not interpret the contents of any TCP messages sent by the server (remote computer). It merely passes them on to your program, and it is the responsibility of the code in your program to process the contents of any TCP messages received by the server. In this example, the TCP messages consist of SMTP commands and responses. As far as the Winsock control is concerned, however, those messages could be FTP messages or some other high-level protocol.

Syntax *object*_**DataArrival** (*bytesTotal* **As Long**)

Dissection

- The *object* must be a valid instance of the Winsock control.
- Each time data arrives from the remote host, the **DataArrival** event occurs.
- The *bytesTotal* argument indicates the number of bytes that have been received from the remote host.

When data arrives from the remote host (SMTP server) and the DataArrival event occurs, the data is stored in an input queue. This is a temporary storage area from which your program must move the data. Data is moved from the input queue into a variable in your program using the GetData method pertaining to the Winsock control.

Syntax *object*.**GetData** *data*, [*type*,] [*maxLen*]

Dissection

- The *object* must be an instance of the Winsock control.
- The **GetData** method reads a fixed number of bytes from the input queue into a program variable.
- The *data* argument contains a variable where the data moved from the input queue is stored. The data type of this variable will depend on the value of the *type* argument.
- The optional *type* argument identifies how the data in the input queue is interpreted. Using SMTP, all the data will be interpreted as strings. Data also can be interpreted as Numeric or Date data types. For a complete list of the valid types, refer to the "GetData Method (Winsock Control)" Help page.
- The optional *MaxLen* argument identifies the maximum number of bytes to read. If this argument is less than the total number of bytes in the input queue, the method will return the error code 10040.

Code Example	`sokSMTP.GetData strBuffer, vbString`
Code Dissection	This statement gets the data stored in the input buffer and stores it in the string variable strBuffer. The data is interpreted as a String data type.

In this example, you already sent the HELO command when the connection to the remote host was established. This will cause the SMTP server to receive the message. The server then will generate a reply. You can read this reply by calling the GetData method in the DataArrival event. Pay attention to the sequence of events that is occurring. You send a message to the server and wait for a reply. When you receive a reply, you get the data from the input queue, process it, and then send another message. This process continues until the conversation is complete. Consider this process as the **message loop**.

To program a message loop:

1 Enter the following statements in the **sokSMTP_DataArrival** event procedure to read the data from the input queue and reset the current state:

```
Dim pblnStatus As Boolean
Dim pstrBuffer as String
Select Case State
    Case Connect
        sokSMTP.GetData pstrBuffer, vbString
        pblnStatus = CheckResponse(pstrBuffer, "220")
        If pblnStatus = True Then
            txtLog = Time & " " & pstrBuffer & _
                vbCrLf & txtLog.Text
            State = State + 1
        Else
            sokSMTP.Close
            State = 0
        End If
End Select
```

2 Test the program. When the data is received, the response from the HELO message is stored in the Log text box.

The statements in the sokSMTP_DataArrival event procedure process the data sent by the remote server because of the SendData command. The data retrieved is stored in the variable named pstrBuffer. This value is appended to the text box representing the log of messages sent from the remote SMTP server. The following statement increments the State variable:

```
State = State + 1
```

This statement updates the current state of the mail transaction. That is, the initial state was Connect. After incrementing the variable, the state now has the value of Helo indicating that the HELO command has been processed.

The procedure also calls the CheckResponse function. This function takes two arguments—the expected response and the actual response returned by the server. The procedure already has been created and is shown in the following code:

```
Private Function CheckResponse(pstrGot, pstrExpect) _
    As Boolean
    Dim pstrResp As String
    pstrResp = Mid(pstrGot, 1, 3)
    If StrComp(pstrResp, pstrExpect) = 0 Then
        CheckResponse = True
    Else
        CheckResponse = False
    End If
End Function
```

As shown in the preceding code segment, the procedure compares the first three characters of the SMTP response with the expected response. If they are the same, the function returns True. Otherwise the function returns False. If the function returned True, the state is incremented and the response is added to the Log text box. If there was an error, the function returns False. If this occurs, then the connection is closed and the state is reset to zero (0).

Completing the transaction, or in other words sending the remaining parts of the mail message, involves sending the MAIL FROM and RCPT TO commands, sending the body of the message, and then closing the connection. This can be accomplished by sending the necessary data, processing the response, and updating the state by incrementing the State variable.

To complete the mail transaction:

1 Enter the following statements (shown in bold) in the **sokSMTP_DataArrival** event procedure:

```
Select Case State
    Case Connect
        sokSMTP.GetData pstrBuffer, vbString
        pblnStatus = CheckResponse(pstrBuffer, "220")
        If pblnStatus = True Then
            txtLog = Time & " " & pstrBuffer & _
                vbCrLf & txtLog.Text
            State = State + 1
        Else
            sokSMTP.Close
            State = 0
        End If
```

```
        Case Helo
            sokSMTP.GetData pstrBuffer, vbString
            pblnStatus = CheckResponse(pstrBuffer, "250")
            If pblnStatus = True Then
                txtLog = Time & " " & pstrBuffer & _
                    vbCrLf & txtLog.Text
                sokSMTP.SendData "MAIL FROM:" & _
                    txtMailFrom & vbCrLf
                State = State + 1
            Else
                sokSMTP.Close
                State = 0
                mblnInProgress = False
                Exit Sub
            End If
        Case MailFrom
            sokSMTP.GetData pstrBuffer, vbString
            pblnStatus = CheckResponse(pstrBuffer, "250")
            If pblnStatus = True Then
                txtLog = Time & " " & pstrBuffer & _
                    vbCrLf & txtLog.Text
                sokSMTP.SendData "RCPT TO:" & _
                    txtRecvTo & vbCrLf
                State = State + 1
            Else
                sokSMTP.Close
                State = 0
                mblnInProgress = False
                Exit Sub
            End If
        Case SendTo
            sokSMTP.GetData pstrBuffer, vbString
            txtLog = Time & " " & pstrBuffer & vbCrLf & _
                txtLog.Text
            sokSMTP.SendData "DATA" & vbCrLf
            State = State + 1
        Case Data
            sokSMTP.GetData pstrBuffer, vbString
            txtLog = Time & " " & pstrBuffer & _
                vbCrLf & txtLog.Text
            sokSMTP.SendData txtMessage & vbCrLf & _
                "." & vbCrLf
            State = State + 1
        Case MessageData
```

```
            sokSMTP.GetData pstrBuffer, vbString
            txtLog = Time & " " & pstrBuffer & _
                vbCrLf & txtLog.Text
            sokSMTP.Close
            State = State + 1
            mblnInProgress = False
    End Select
```

2 Test the program. Enter the host name of your Internet provider, then click the **Send** command button. The program will connect to the server and send the HELO command, then continue to send the remaining messages until the mail message is delivered.

These statements involve processing each of the transactions generated by the remote server. While you could implement this program in different ways, the implementation chosen here is to respond to the DataArrival event by processing the data received by the server and sending a message representing the next part of the transaction. Each of these transaction components is examined in detail in the syntax presentation that follows:

```
Case Helo
    sokSMTP.GetData pstrBuffer, vbString
    pblnStatus = CheckResponse(pstrBuffer, "250")
    If pblnStatus = True Then
        txtLog = Time & " " & pstrBuffer & _
            vbCrLf & txtLog.Text
        sokSMTP.SendData "MAIL FROM:" & _
            txtMailFrom & vbCrLf
        State = State + 1
    Else
        sokSMTP.Close
        State = 0
        mblnInProgress = False
        Exit Sub
    End If
```

After the Connect state, the program enters the Helo state. The response of the HELO command is retrieved and verified. If the expected response is received, then the Log text box is updated, the MAIL FROM command is sent, and the state is updated. If an unexpected response is received, then the connection is closed.

After the Helo state, the MailFrom state is entered. The code for this case is nearly identical to the code for the Helo case. The response is validated. If okay, then the RCPT TO command is sent.

The remaining states are used to send the DATA command and the message data itself.

Other Uses of the Winsock Control

This example demonstrated the use of the Winsock control to send a mail message. The techniques you used to communicate requests and responses to those requests back and forth between the client and server, however, can be used to implement just about any other application-level service (protocol). Usenet or Network News use a similar mechanism to exchange messages. As the client, you send requests to a server. The server in turn responds to those requests, which your program then must process. The difference is that the protocol used is usually the Network News Transfer Protocol (NNTP). While NNTP has a completely different set of commands, the concept of sending commands and processing responses is the same.

The key is to understand the commands that make up the protocol that you are implementing. Understanding the protocol is a matter of downloading the appropriate RFC, and implementing the standard laid forth in the document.

The Winsock control is not limited to exchanging information using SMTP. Using the techniques you just learned, you could use Winsock to implement an FTP client or server. In this situation, you set the host and port as you did previously. Instead of processing SMTP commands, however, you process FTP commands. They work the same way. The commands and responses, however, are different. Fortunately, you do not have to implement an FTP client yourself. The Internet Transfer control implements this protocol for you.

Creating a Winsock Server

In this example, you have created an Internet client application that makes a connection to a server on the Internet. It also is possible to create a program that behaves as an Internet server. In this situation, you create a socket. Instead of sending data, however, the socket listens for incoming requests. When a request is received, you accept the connection. Then your program enters a two-way dialog like the one just used. Your program is processing requests sent to you by a client computer however. Processing a request as an Internet server requires that you perform the following steps:

1. The **Bind** method is used to associate a particular port with a protocol (socket).
2. The server must be started and the **Listen** method called. By calling this method, the server is awaiting incoming requests.
3. When a request arrives, the **Accept** method is called to establish a connection as a result of the incoming request.
4. At this point the port can communicate with the client. The technique to exchange information between the client and server is the same as you saw in this chapter. The process is reversed, however. In this situation, as the server your program is processing client requests and responding to them.

SECTION B

objectives

In this section you will:

- Communicate with the Internet using the Internet Transfer control
- Create an FTP client capable of navigating through the files on an Internet server and download files from that server

Transferring Files with the Internet Transfer Control

The Internet Transfer Control

In the previous section, you used the Winsock control to establish a connection to the Internet and process a transaction between a client and a server. In this case, the transaction was an electronic mail message. While you also could use the Winsock control to establish a connection with an FTP server for downloading files, there is another control, the Internet Transfer control, which will simplify the process.

As you saw in the previous section, TCP is layered on top of IP. The various Internet services are layered on top of TCP. You can think of the Internet Transfer control as being layered on top of the Winsock control. Using the Internet Transfer control, you do not have to be concerned with explicitly specifying the host name and service (port) that you want to use. Rather, you specify a Uniform Resource Locator (URL). From the information specified in the URL, the Internet Transfer control will establish the connection. In this example, you will use the Internet Transfer control to create an FTP client. Like every other object, the Internet Transfer control supports properties, methods, and events to establish a connection, and move files between the source and destination computer.

Object	Internet Transfer
Events	As the server processes requests, the **StateChanged** event occurs to indicate the current state of the connection. The state is identified by a constant value. See the "StateChanged Event" Help page for a complete list of these constant values.
Methods	The **Cancel** method will cancel any pending request and close the open connection.

When data is sent from the server, the Internet Transfer control places the data into a buffer (input queue) much like the Winsock control. The data is moved out of this buffer using the **GetChunk** method.

The **GetHeader** method only is used with HTTP and retrieves the header text from an HTTP file.

The **Execute** method requests a service from the remote computer. For example, the Execute method can be used to initiate an FTP session or download a file.

The **OpenURL** method opens an HTML document.

Properties

The **Password** property contains the password that will be sent to log on to a remote computer.

The **Protocol** property specifies which Internet protocol to use. If set to icFTP, the File Transfer Protocol is used. If set to icHTTP, the HyperText Transfer Protocol is used. To establish a secure Internet connection, the icHTTPS protocol should be used. Both the OpenURL and Execute methods modify the value of this property.

The **RemoteHost** property contains either the name or the IP address of the remote host. You do not set the port explicitly like you do when using the Winsock control. This is handled automatically by the Internet Transfer control itself.

The **RequestTimeout** property is used to indicate the number of seconds allowed for a request to complete. If the Execute method is used to make a request, then a timeout will cause the StateChanged event to occur with an icError error code. If the OpenURL method is used, an error will be raised.

The **ResponseCode** property is set whenever the StateChanged event occurs. It contains the numeric value of the response from the remote server.

The **ResponseInfo** property contains the textual description corresponding to the response identified by the ResponseCode property.

The **StillExecuting** property contains a Boolean value indicating whether or not the Internet Transfer control is busy. In other words, there is a server request in process. The Internet Transfer control does not respond to events while the StillExecuting property is True.

The **URL** property contains the Uniform Resource Locator that is used by the Execute and OpenURL methods.

The **UserName** property is used in conjunction with the Password property and is used to specify the user name on the remote host.

The Internet Transfer control is useful for two different Internet protocols (services). It can send requests to an FTP server or an HTTP server. When you are accessing these two services, the Internet Transfer control is the logical choice as the control itself takes care of several details concerning the underlying FTP or HTTP protocols. If you are using a different service like SMTP or NNTP, however, the Internet Transfer control is not a suitable choice, as it does not support these protocols. In these situations, the Winsock control is the only solution to the problem.

Synchronous Versus Asynchronous Transmission

Before trying to use the Internet Transfer control, a word about two different transmission modes is in order. In fact, the term transmission mode is too specific. The following terms can be used to describe how any command is executed:

- A command can be executed **synchronously**. This means that execution of the command must be completed before the next command is executed. From the perspective of executing a Visual Basic statement that calls a Function procedure, the Function procedure must execute and return a value before the next statement is executed. From the perspective of the Internet Transfer control, a request to download a file from the Internet must be completed before another file download request can be made.
- A command can be executed **asynchronously**. This means that a statement will start executing a command, and then begin executing other commands regardless of whether or not the first command has finished executing. From the perspective of executing a Visual Basic command, you may execute several commands that affect the appearance of the form and its controls as they are seen on the screen. You can continue to execute statements while Windows processes tasks that you already have requested. From the perspective of the Internet Transfer control, you may execute a statement that makes a request from a server. Visual Basic will continue to execute other statements in your program although the first request for service from the Internet has not yet been completed.

The Internet Transfer control uses the synchronous and asynchronous transmission modes depending on whether the OpenURL or Execute method is used. If the OpenURL method is used, transmission is synchronous. This means that the request must be completed before the next statement will execute. The Execute method is asynchronous meaning that a statement that requests FTP services does not need to complete before the next statement is executed. To illustrate this, consider the following statements:

```
itt1.Execute "FTP://" & txtAddress, _
    "DIR /*"
itt1.Execute "FTP://" & txtAddress, _
    "Get localfile remotefile"
```

The preceding statements make two requests. The first statement attempts to establish a connection with an FTP server, and the next statement tries to download a specific file. If you execute these statements, your program likely will generate a run-time error because the second statement will try to get the file before the first statement that is responsible for establishing the connection has had the opportunity to complete. Figure 13-6 shows the common error that is generated.

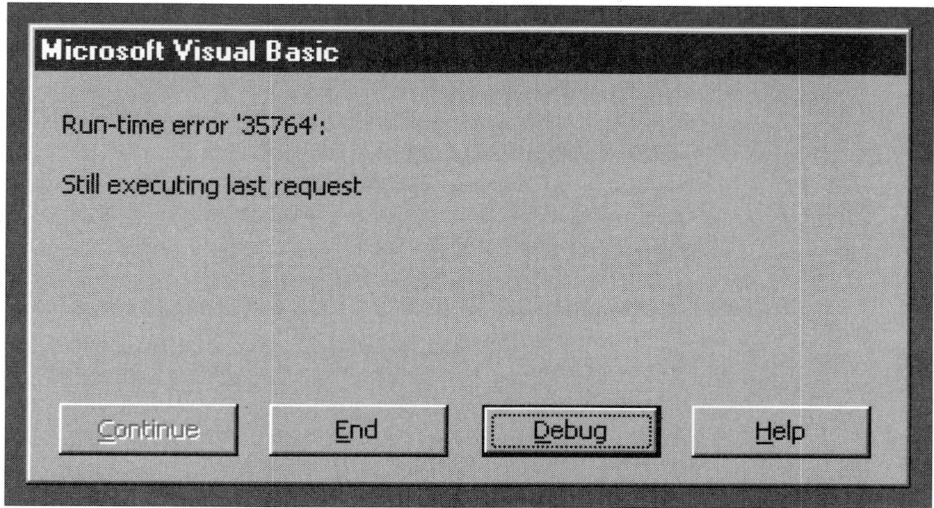

Figure 13-6: Error message

Because of this situation, when using the FTP service, your program must be careful not to make requests while there is another request pending or an error will occur.

Implementing an FTP Client

The File Transfer Protocol or FTP has existed since the beginning of the Internet; far longer than the World Wide Web and HTTP. The purpose of FTP is to transfer files across the Internet from one computer to another. In the examples that follow, we will assume that you already have established a connection to the Internet. Perhaps you are working on a computer with a high-speed connection or you are using a modem to call an Internet provider for service. The speed of the connection is not an issue. Your computer must be connected to the Internet for these examples to function, however.

Before trying to use the Internet Transfer control to move files across the Internet, a few words about FTP itself are in order. First, FTP is a client/server-based protocol much like SMTP is a client/server-based protocol. Whenever you download a file from a remote computer to your computer, the remote computer is considered the FTP server and your computer is considered the FTP client. The remote computer (server), listens for requests coming from various client computers. The first step in an FTP request is authentication. To download a file from an

FTP server, the FTP server usually requires that you specify both a login and a password. By convention, most publicly accessible FTP servers allow access using a well-known login and password. The login name is "anonymous" (hence the name anonymous FTP). The agreed upon password is the electronic mail address of the client user.

When using anonymous FTP, there are many restrictions on what you, as the client, can do. Because you are not a privileged user, you can look at and download files. It is not permissible, however, for you to write files to the server or change the contents of existing files.

Implementing the File Transfer Protocol

There are several issues involved in creating an FTP client to transfer files across the Internet. Files can be of different types. The default file type is ASCII and is supported by all FTP implementations. Most FTP implementations also support image, or binary files. Binary files are transferred as a series of contiguous bytes. Like SMTP, FTP uses a connected server to process requests. Requests are sent from the client to the server in the form of commands, much like commands are sent to an SMTP server. The notion of a transaction does not exist in the same sense as it does with an SMTP server as each command is treated as a distinct unit.

When you use the Internet Transfer control as a way to access FTP, you can think of the Internet Transfer control as being layered on top of FTP. On one hand, it makes the process of transferring a file simpler. You do not have access to all the underlying commands supported by FTP itself, however. To access these commands, you would need to use the Winsock control, and send requests and process the responses using the same techniques as you saw with SMTP. The following list summarizes some of the FTP commands supported by the Internet Transfer control:

- The CD command changes the current working directory.
- The DIR command lists files on a remote computer.
- The GET and RECV commands are equivalent. They retrieve a file from the remote computer.
- The LS command lists files on the remote computer.

The preceding commands can be used when you are an authenticated user or when anonymous FTP is used. Some commands only can be executed if the user has the necessary privileges on the remote computer. These privileges are not usually granted through anonymous FTP.

- The DELETE command removes a file from the remote computer.
- The MKDIR command creates a new directory on the remote computer.
- The SEND and PUT commands send a file from the local computer to the remote computer.
- The RENAME command changes the name of a file on the remote computer.

To execute FTP commands using the Internet Transfer control, you embed the command and its arguments inside the operation argument of the Execute method. This is accomplished by calling the Execute method of the Internet Transfer control.

Syntax *object*.**Execute** *url, operation, data, requestHeaders*

Dissection

- The *object* must be a valid instance of the Internet Transfer control.
- The **Execute** method sends the command stored in *operation* to the specified *url.*
- The optional *url* specifies the Internet address of the remote server where the request will be executed.
- The optional *operation*, when used with FTP, specifies what to do. These operations include downloading or uploading files and changing or listing directories.
- The optional *data* argument is used for certain operations that take arguments. For example, the CD command takes one argument—a directory name. In this case, the directory name is specified in the *data* argument.
- The optional *requestHeaders* argument sends additional header information to the remote server.

Code Example

```
itt1.Execute "ftp://ftp.course.com" "DIR"
```

Code Dissection This statement establishes a connection with the host named ftp.course.com using FTP. Using the *operation* argument it executes the DIR command on the remote server. The response from this request is stored in the input queue until retrieved by the GetChunk method.

If you have used FTP for any length of time, you will find the syntax of the previous statement interesting. If you have used the UNIX or DOS shell to perform FTP, you probably have typed a statement like the following:

```
ftp ftp.course.com
```

This statement establishes an interactive FTP connection with the host ftp.course.com. The syntax of the Execute method is much different, however. It uses the form of a URL. The first part of the URL (ftp://) specifies the protocol to use and the second part specifies the location (host). The Internet Transfer control is designed to download HTML documents in addition to providing FTP services. As such, the Execute method uses a URL syntax to specify a Web site.

Once a connection has been established, you can execute FTP commands to look at the directories on a remote computer, move files back and forth, and set various options. These FTP commands are executed by calling the Execute method of the Internet Transfer control.

Remember, the Execute method runs asynchronously. This means that your program will continue to execute statements while an FTP request is pending. This poses an interesting problem. If you call the Execute method to make another request while a request is pending, the Internet Transfer control will generate an error indicating that a request still is being executed. This is because each request must be completed before the next request can be executed. In this example, the user will enter an Internet address in the Address text box and click the Connect command button to establish a connection with the remote FTP server. The user must be prevented from making another request, however, until the last request has been executed. To prevent this error, the StillExecuting property, which is True if there is a pending request and False otherwise, should be checked before attempting to execute another FTP request. You now can write the code to request a connection with a remote FTP server.

To establish an FTP connection using the Internet Transfer control:

1. Using the Components dialog, make sure that the **Internet Transfer control 5.0** has been added to the project.
2. Create an instance of the Internet Transfer control on the form named **frmITC**, then set the Name property to **itt1**.
3. Enter the following statements in the **cmdConnect_Click** event procedure:

```
On Error Resume Next
    If itt1.StillExecuting Then
        Exit Sub
    Else
        itt1.Execute "FTP://" & txtAddress, _
            "DIR /*"
    End If
```

These statements test that there is no pending request by checking the value of the StillExecuting property. If there is not a pending request, the Execute method is called. The operation argument tells the FTP server to get a directory listing of the root directory. At this point, you have written the necessary code to get a directory listing from the remote computer. You have as yet not written the necessary code to display the information returned from the FTP server. To accomplish this, you need first to be able to detect when the request is complete, and second you need to process the data returned by the request.

As you send requests to the Internet Transfer control using the Execute method, the control keeps track of the progress of that request. Every time the status of the request changes, the StateChanged event occurs. This event is the only event supported by the Internet Transfer control but knowledge of its use is imperative to use the control effectively. The StateChanged event takes one argument, an integer containing the current state of the request. In this example, you will write code for the following states:

- When a request is being sent, the state is set to the constant icRequesting.
- If the request causes a response that returns data like a DIR or LS command, then the state is set to icResponseCompleted.
- Some requests do not return any data. For example, if you try to retrieve the contents of an empty directory, the state is set to icResponseReceived rather than icResponseCompleted.

In addition to executing a command asynchronously with the Execute method, you can use the Open URL method to execute a command synchronously. The purpose of the Execute and OpenURL methods is nearly the same. The primary difference lies in the mode of transmission.

Syntax *object*.**OpenUrl** *url* [,*datatype*]

Dissection

- The *object* must be a valid instance of the Internet Transfer control.
- The **OpenURL** method opens a URL synchronously.
- The required *url* argument contains the name of the URL.
- The optional *datatype* argument identifies the type of data to be retrieved. If retrieving binary data, then the value should be set to the constant 1 – icByteArray. If retrieving string data, then the constant value should be set to 0 – icString (the default).

Notes The OpenURL method returns a String or Byte array. Using the OpenURL method, there is no need to copy data from the input queue. Instead, the method returns the characters in an array.

Code Example

```
Dim pbytBuf( ) As Byte
pbytBuf( ) = _
    itt1.OpenURL( _
    "FTP://ftp.microsoft.com/disclaimer.txt", _
    icByteArray)
Open "C:\Disclaim.htm" For Binary Access _
    Write As #1
Put #1, , pbytBuf
Close #1
```

Code Dissection The preceding statements open the URL disclaimer.txt from the site ftp.microsoft.com. When the command completes, the HTML page will be stored in the variable named pbytBuf. This byte array then is saved using the file named C:\Disclaim.htm.

Data returned from the OpenURL method is returned in the form of an HTML document. As such, a document downloaded using this method can be viewed with a Web browser like Internet Explorer.

Processing Responses from the Internet Transfer Control

Processing data sent from the server using the Internet Transfer control is similar to the technique used with the Winsock control; that is, the data is read into an input queue. You then must copy the data from the input queue and store it in your program. In this example, when the DIR statement reads the directory, the data must be copied from the input queue into a program string. The program as needed then can process this string. Data read because of calling the Execute method is retrieved into the program by calling the GetChunk method.

Syntax *object*.**GetChunk**(*size* [,*datatype*])

Dissection

- The *object* must be an instance of the Internet Transfer control.
- The **GetChunk** method reads the number of bytes from the input queue.
- The required *size* argument determines the number of bytes to read.
- The optional *datatype* argument determines whether the data is interpreted as a string or an array of bytes.

Code Example

```
Dim pstrRecv as String
pstrRecv = itt1.GetChunk(1024, icString)
```

Code Dissection These statements read at most 1024 characters from the input queue into the string named pstrRecv.

In this example, you can use the StateChanged event to advise the user of the program's progress and change the insertion point so that the user will be aware that a request currently is executing.

To program the StateChanged event:

1 Enter the following statement in the **itt1_StateChanged** event procedure:

```
On Error Resume Next
    Dim pstrRecv As String
    Dim pstrTemp As String
    Select Case State
        Case icNone
        ' Case icHostResolving
        Case icHostResolved
```

```
        Case icConnecting
        Case icConnected
        Case icRequesting
            Screen.MousePointer = vbHourglass
        Case icRequestSent
        Case icReceivingResponse
        Case icResponseReceived
            Screen.MousePointer = vbNormal
        Case icDisconnecting
        Case icDisconnected
        Case icError
            PrintLog icError
        Case icResponseCompleted
            pstrRecv = itt1.GetChunk(1024, icString)
            LoadNodes pstrRecv
            Screen.MousePointer = vbNormal
    End Select
    PrintLog State
```

2 Test the program. Make sure you have established a connection with your Internet provider. Use the default address (ftp.microsoft.com) shown in the Address text box and click **Connect**. As the request is executed, the Internet Transfer control moves through various states. These state transitions are displayed in the Log text box at the bottom of the form as shown in Figure 13-7.

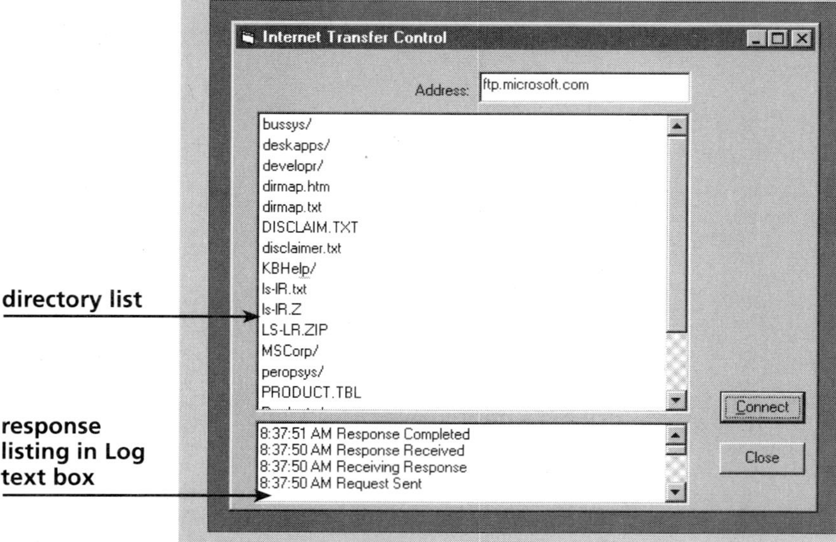

Figure 13-7: FTP listing

These statements change the mouse pointer to an hourglass while a request currently is pending, and return the mouse pointer to normal when the request is complete. When the state is changed, the PrintLog Sub procedure is called to write a log message into the multiline text box at the bottom of the form. This level of detail is overkill for most users. The log messages may help you, as the programmer, to visualize the events that are occurring and the different state transitions that are occurring as requests are made and then satisfied.

The important code in this procedure is contained in the icResponseCompleted state.

```
pstrRecv = itt1.GetChunk(1024, icString)
LoadNodes pstrRecv
Screen.MousePointer = vbNormal
```

The GetChunk method is called to read the data from the input queue. At most 1024 characters are read. If the input queue contains more that 1024 characters, the remaining data will be ignored and will remain in the input queue. This procedure could be improved by writing a For loop and examining the length of the string returned. If the length of the string is less than the number of bytes requested, then all the data has been read.

The string contains a directory listing of the FTP server's root directory. Almost all FTP servers return the directory listing in a well-defined format. Each directory has a trailing forward slash (/). Ordinary files do not. Each directory or file is separated by a carriage return and line feed sequence. This information is used to store each directory or file into a node in the TreeView control. Consider the following statements in the LoadNodes general procedure. This procedure already has been created.

```
Private Sub LoadNodes(pstr As String)
    Dim pstrTemp As String
    Dim pintCurrent As Integer
    Dim pintLast As Integer
    Static pblnInit As Integer
    pintLast = 1
    For pintCurrent = 1 To Len(pstr) - 2
        Debug.Print (Asc(Mid(pstr, pintCurrent, 1)))
        If Asc(Mid(pstr, pintCurrent, 1)) = 13 Then
            pstrTemp = Mid(pstr, pintLast, _
                pintCurrent - pintLast)
            If Not pblnInit Then
                tvwFTP.Nodes.Add , , , pstrTemp
            Else
                tvwFTP.Nodes.Add mnodCurrent, _
                    tvwChild, , pstrTemp
                mnodCurrent.Expanded = True
            End If
            pintLast = pintCurrent + 2
```

```
        End If
    Next
    pblnInit = True
End Sub
```

The procedure examines the input string and breaks it into the individual directory and file entries. It does this by locating the carriage return characters in the string. Each time a carriage return is detected, the Mid function is used to copy a part of the string. This substring is added to the text of a new node. The static variable pblnInit is used to determine if this is the first time the procedure is called. In other words, it is used to see if the root directory is being examined. If the root-level directory is examined, the nodes are added as top-level nodes. If a child node was clicked, this node is referenced in the module-level variable mnodCurrent. The new nodes then are added as children of the node that was clicked.

In addition to this code, the following code already has been written in the PrintLog procedure:

```
Private Sub PrintLog(pintState As Integer)
    Dim pstrState As String
    Select Case pintState
        Case icNone
            pstrState = "None"
        Case icHostResolved
            pstrState = "Host Resolved"
        Case icConnecting
            pstrState = "Connecting"
        Case icConnected
            pstrState = "Connected"
        Case icRequesting
            pstrState = "Requesting"
        Case icRequestSent
            pstrState = "Request Sent"
        Case icReceivingResponse
            pstrState = "Receiving Response"
        Case icResponseReceived
            pstrState = "Response Received"
        Case icDisconnecting
            pstrState = "Disconnecting"
        Case icDisconnected
            pstrState = "Disconnected"
        Case icError
            pstrState = "Cannot process request"
        Case icResponseCompleted
            pstrState = "Response completed"
    End Select
    txtLog = Time & " " & pstrState & vbCrLf & txtLog
End Sub
```

This procedure is very simple. It takes one argument, the state of the Internet Transfer control. This value is used to insert a message in the Log text box containing the current time and the state of the control. In reality, this level of logging detail likely would be overkill. It is included here to help illustrate the state transitions that occur to the control.

At this point, your program will display the files and directories in the FTP server's root directory. Most servers have many levels of directories, however. Presently, these directories are displayed as nodes in the TreeView control. When the user clicks one of these nodes, one of two actions should occur.

- If the node is a directory, then another request should be made to the FTP server, and the directories and files in that directory should be displayed in the TreeView control as children of the TreeView control.
- If the node is a file, then the file should be downloaded from the FTP server to the local computer.

You may have noticed from Figure 13-7 that some files have a forward slash as the last character of the file and others do not. This character is used to identify that the file is a directory rather than an ordinary file. Thus, when a node is clicked, your code needs to check the last character in the node's Text property. If it is a file, then the file should be downloaded. Otherwise, the files in that directory should be listed and added as children of the current node.

To determine the file type:

1 Enter the following statements in the **tvwFTP_NodeClick** event procedure:

```
Dim pstrFile As String
Set mnodCurrent = Node
pstrFile = mnodCurrent.Text
If Mid(pstrFile, Len(pstrFile), 1) = "/" Then
    GetDir Node
Else
    GetFile Node
End If
```

This procedure is based on the assumption that the last character of a directory name contains a forward slash. If this is True, then the GetDir procedure is called. If not, then the entry is an ordinary file and the GetFile procedure is called. Remember, you tested the StillExecuting property when the Connect command button was clicked to prevent another request from being made while one was still pending. Both the GetDir and GetFile procedures should perform the same check. This is because the user could click a directory causing the GetDir procedure to execute. While the request is being satisfied, the user could click another directory or file name. This would cause an error. Another solution to this problem would be to lock specific controls while there is a pending request by adding the following statements in the GetDir function:

```
If mnodCurrent.Children = 0 Then
    ittl.Execute "FTP://" & txtAddress, _
    "dir " & pnod.FullPath & "/*"
End If
```

The If statement checks the value of the current node's Children property to see if the node presently has children or not. Interestingly, if the node has children, then the directory already has been read from the server and should not be read again. The other option would be to delete all the child nodes, and make the request again. While this would have the effect of refreshing the server directory, it is likely that the request is not necessary and will just delay the user from getting a response.

The GetFile procedure is more interesting. It uses a different operation (the *operation* argument) for the Execute method. This time, a GET operation is performed.

```
ittl.Execute "FTP://" & txtAddress, _
   "GET " & pnod.FullPath & " " & cdlInet.filename
```

The GET operation takes two arguments instead of just one. The first is the name of the remote file. This file name can be found by obtaining the full path of the node in the TreeView control. For this to work, note that the path separator is set to an empty string "". This is because the paths already are embedded in the file names as displayed in the nodes.

To download a file:

1 Create the **GetDir** procedure and insert the following statements:

```
Private Sub GetDir(pnod As Node)
    If ittl.StillExecuting Then
        Exit Sub
    Else
        If mnodCurrent.Children = 0 Then
            ittl.Execute "FTP://" & txtAddress, _
            "dir " & pnod.FullPath & "/*"
        End If
    End If
End Sub
```

2 Create the **GetFile** procedure and insert the following statements:

```
Private Sub GetFile(pnod As Node)
On Error GoTo CancelError
    If ittl.StillExecuting Then
        Exit Sub
    Else
        cdlInet.filename = pnod.Text
        cdlInet.ShowSave

        ittl.Execute "FTP://" & txtAddress, _
        "GET " & pnod.FullPath & " " & cdlInet.filename
    End If
    Exit Sub
CancelError:
End Sub
```

3 Test the program. Establish an FTP connection to **ftp.microsoft.com** then wait for the root directory to be downloaded. Click a directory (an entry with a trailing slash). This causes another request to be made from the server and the contents of that directory to be downloaded.

Click a file that is not a directory. The CommonDialog control will be activated allowing you to download a file. Enter a file name then click **Save** to begin the download process. (Again, consider downloading Disclaim.txt.)

The GetDir general procedure first tests to determine whether the current node has any children. If the current node has children, then the program should not reread the child directory because this already has been done. Otherwise, the child directory is read. The general procedure does not deal with the response from the FTP server. The StateChanged event procedure that gets the data returned handles this.

If the current node is a file rather than a directory, the code in the GetFile procedure is executed. This code calls the Execute method to make an FTP request just like the other procedures you have called. This request is a request to download a file, however. This code calls the Execute method as you have seen before. The operation argument is much different. This time a GET operation is performed to download data from the remote server. The GET operation takes two arguments—the file to be downloaded from the remote server, and the name of the file to be stored on the local disk.

Network Timeouts

One of the problems that can occur with programs that access the network is **network timeout**. That is, you send a request to the server but a response is never received. You can control how long your program will wait for a server response by setting the RequestTimeout property of the Internet Transfer control. As the developer, you need to decide what is a reasonable amount of time to wait for a server response. Determining this value is subjective. If the value is too small, the program may not behave as desired when the Internet or your network provider is busy. If the interval is too long, then the user may not be aware that the server is no longer available and continue waiting. One option is to allow the user to configure this parameter.

The RequestTimeout property contains an Integer value indicating the number of seconds to wait before either raising an error, in the case of the OpenURL method, or raising the StateChanged event, as in the case of the Execute method. By default, the value of the RequestTimeout property is 60 (60 seconds or 1 minute).

SUMMARY

In this chapter, you have seen how to implement an Internet client that accesses the services supplied by Internet servers. While you saw the basics of two services (SMTP and FTP), there are many more commands that apply to these services. Furthermore, there are many more services than the two presented here. The techniques used to exchange messages between a client and server are very similar, however.

- The Internet is made up of several (layered) protocols. At the bottom layer is the Internet Protocol (IP). Two other protocols, the Transmission Control Protocol (TCP) and the User Datagram Protocol (UDP), rely on IP for communication. Layered on top of these protocols are various services including the File Transfer Protocol (FTP) and the Simple Mail Transfer Protocol (SMTP).
- The Winsock control implements both TCP and UDP. The most common use of the Winsock control is to tap into the various services that rely on either TCP or UDP. These services include FTP, SMTP, and NNTP to name a few. Communication using the Winsock control usually is a two-way connection between a client and server. In this situation, the client sends a request to the server using the SendData method, and then processes the response using the GetData method. The GetData method usually is called in response to the DataArrival event.
- Care must be taken when processing the asynchronous commands pertaining to both the Winsock control and the Internet Transfer control. That is, when a request is sent, other commands can execute although no response has been returned from the server. As such, you as the programmer, often must keep track of the state of a request and disallow other requests (SendData) from being executed until the last request has been completed. Otherwise, a run-time error likely will occur.
- The Winsock control can be used to implement any of the Internet services. If the FTP or HTTP service is being used, however, the Internet Transfer control may be a more feasible control as it insulates you, as the developer, from some of the intricacies of TCP/IP processing. The Internet Transfer control can be thought of as a layer of software residing on top of the Winsock control.
- The Internet Transfer control supports two protocols—HTTP and FTP. To utilize these protocols, either the Execute or OpenURL methods can be used. The Execute method is asynchronous while the OpenURL method is synchronous. The OpenURL method returns a URL (an HTTP document) that can be viewed by a Web browser. The Execute method makes a request to a server. It is the responsibility of the programmer to process the server's response using the GetChunk method.
- When using the Internet Transfer control to process FTP requests, the operation argument of the Execute method contains the FTP request. The valid operations can be thought of as layered on the underlying FTP protocol.
- As requests are being made and processed, the Internet Transfer control generates the StateChanged event so you either can display messages to the user or can maintain state information necessary for your program.

QUESTIONS

1. Which of the following protocols are supported by the Winsock control?
   a. IP / UDP.
   b. TCP / IP.
   c. TCP / UDP.
   d. All of the above.
   e. None of the above.
2. What is the well-defined port number used by SMTP?
   a. 10.
   b. 25.
   c. 30.
   d. 35.
   e. 40.
3. Which of the following statement(s) are true about SMTP?
   a. Commands are not case-sensitive.
   b. Mail addresses are not case-sensitive.
   c. Commands are terminated with a carriage return / line feed sequence.
   d. All of the above.
   e. None of the above.
4. Which of the following are valid SMTP commands?
   a. MAIL TO.
   b. RECV FROM.
   c. MAIL FROM.
   d. SEND.
   e. RECEIVE.
5. The ____________ method is used to transmit data to a remote host and the ____________ method is used to retrieve data from the input queue.
   a. DataSend, DataGet
   b. Write, Read
   c. SendData, GetData
   d. Output, Input
   e. None of the above
6. Which of the following protocols are supported by the Internet Transfer control?
   a. TCP / IP.
   b. TCP / UDP.
   c. FTP / HTTP.
   d. FTP / TCP.
   e. FTP / IP.

7. Which of the following are valid anonymous FTP commands?
   a. LS.
   b. LIST.
   c. DIRECTORY.
   d. WRITE.
   e. READ.
8. Which of the following are valid privileged FTP commands?
   a. RMDIR.
   b. RENAME.
   c. PUT.
   d. None of the above.
   e. All of the above.
9. Which of the following are true statements about the Internet Transfer control's StateChanged event?
   a. The StateChanged event occurs as a request is made and then completed.
   b. The StateChanged event raises the Error event.
   c. When a request is made, the current state is Requested.
   d. All of the above.
   e. None of the above.
10. To send an FTP command using the Internet Transfer control, the ____________ method should be used.
    a. FTP
    b. Execute
    c. Write
    d. SendData
    e. SendMessage
11. Which of the following statements are true about transmission modes?
    a. Synchronous transmission means that the execution of a command must be completed before the next command is executed.
    b. Asynchronous transmission means that the execution of commands can continue although the execution of a previous command has not been completed.
    c. Synchronous transmission is used by the Execute method of the Internet Transfer control.
    d. Both a and b.
    e. All of the above.
12. To copy data from the input queue to a variable in your program using the Internet Transfer control, the ____________ method is used.
    a. GetData
    b. Read
    c. GetChunk
    d. GetInfo
    e. Input

13. Write the necessary statements to connect to the host named mail.microsoft.com using a Winsock control named **sokMail**. Use the SMTP port.
14. Write the necessary statement to send the HELO SMTP command to the host named mail.microsoft.com using the Winsock control named sokSMTP.
15. Create the necessary event procedure to store incoming data from the Winsock control named **sokSMTP**. Store the incoming data in the string variable named **pstrBuffer**.
16. Assuming an Internet Transfer control named **ittFTP** has been created, write the statements to execute the URL to connect to the FTP site named **ftp.microsoft.com**, and then list the files in the root directory. Make sure that a request currently is not being executed.
17. Again, assuming that an Internet Transfer control named **ittFTP** has been created, write the statements to download the file named **ls.txt** from the FTP server named **ftp.microsoft.com**. Save the file in the folder named **A:\ls.txt**.
18. Write the necessary statement(s) to retrieve the response from the Internet Transfer control named **ittFTP**, and store the response in the string variable named **pstrFTP**.
19. Write the statement to change the timeout of an Internet Transfer control named **ittFTP** to two minutes in a program's Form_Load event procedure.
20. Write a case statement to print in the Immediate window the different states that can occur during the StateChanged event.

EXERCISES

1. In this exercise you will create a program to send mail messages. Instead of sending a message to a single recipient, however, the program will send messages to multiple recipients.
   a. Create a new project and set the Name property of the form to **frmExercise1**. Save the form using the name **Chapter.13\Exercise\frmExercise1.frm** and the project using the name **Chapter.13\Exercise\Exercise1.vbp**.
   b. Create an instance of the Winsock control on the form.
   c. Create text boxes to store the host name (of the mail server) and the return address of the mail message. Also create a text box to store the message itself.
   d. Create a checked list box (the Style property of the list box is set to CheckBox). Add to that list box e-mail addresses of people you know.
   e. Create a command button named **Send**. When clicked, the program should try to send an e-mail message to each of the recipients. The process is identical to the one presented in this chapter with one exception. Instead of using the RCPT TO command once, it must be called for each selected person in the list box. Thus, you need to create a For loop to examine all the elements in the list box, determine if the item is selected, and then add the recipient.
   f. Test the program.

2. In this exercise you will use the techniques presented in this chapter to create an FTP client. This program will use both the ListView and TreeView controls. Directories will be displayed in the TreeView control and ordinary files will be displayed in the ListView control.
   a. Create a new project and set the Name property of the form to **frmExercise2**. Save the form using the name **Chapter.13\Exercise\frmExercise2.frm** and the project using the name **Chapter.13\Exercise\Exercise2.vbp**.
   b. Create a ListView, TreeView, and Internet Transfer control on the form.
   c. Create a text box so the user can enter an FTP address. Create a command button that when clicked will establish a connection with the server.
   d. Instead of displaying all the entries in a TreeView control as shown in this chapter, display directory entries in the TreeView control, and display file names in the ListView control.
   e. When the user clicks a node in the TreeView control, connect to the server and download the directory. Directories should appear as children of the node that was clicked. Regular files should appear in the ListView control.
   f. Save and test the program.
3. In this exercise you will use the OpenURL method to download a Web page and display it in Internet Explorer.
   a. Create a new project and set the Name property of the form to **frmExercise3**. Save the form using the name **Chapter.13\Exercise\frmExercise3.frm** and the project using the name **Chapter.13\Exercise\Exercise3.vbp**.
   b. Create an instance of the Internet Transfer control on the form.
   c. Create a text box to store a URL and a command button that when clicked will execute the URL and save it on a file on the disk.
   d. Test the program. Download a file from the Internet. Start Internet Explorer and view the URL you just downloaded.

CHAPTER

14

The Windows Application Programming Interface

Expanding the Power of Visual Basic by Calling DLL Functions

case▶ Geological Services Corporation (GSC) is developing programs in Visual Basic. They have found some inherent limitations in Visual Basic. First, they want to be able to save current program configuration information so it can be reloaded the next time the program is started. They want to save a list of recently opened files so when a program is restarted, the list of files is displayed on the File menu. Conceptually, this is similar to the behavior of other Windows-based programs that manage a list of recently opened files.

Second, they require capabilities not supported by Visual Basic. These include functions to cause a specific form to always appear as the topmost form, create temporary files, and copy files. This problem can be resolved by calling various functions supported by the Windows operating system.

SECTION A

objectives

In this section you will:

- Save the current configuration of a program in the Windows Registry
- Read specific Windows Registry settings to configure a program
- Manipulate the Windows Registry using the RegEdit program

Programming the Windows Registry

Previewing the Completed Application

In this chapter, the focus of the material is to provide a brief introduction of how to read and write information to and from the Windows Registry and call specific functions of the Windows operating system. Presenting all the functions supported by Windows most certainly is beyond the scope of this book. We will present only a few Windows functions that a typical Visual Basic programmer may find useful. The completed application for this chapter calls these DLL functions. As such, the completed application is not a fully-functional application in the true sense of the word. Rather, the functions that are implemented in the completed application appear so you can see how they call the underlying Windows DLL functions.

To preview the completed application:

1 Start **Visual Basic** then load the project named **Chapter.14\Complete\GSC_C.vbp.** The main form for the project is shown in Figure 14-1.

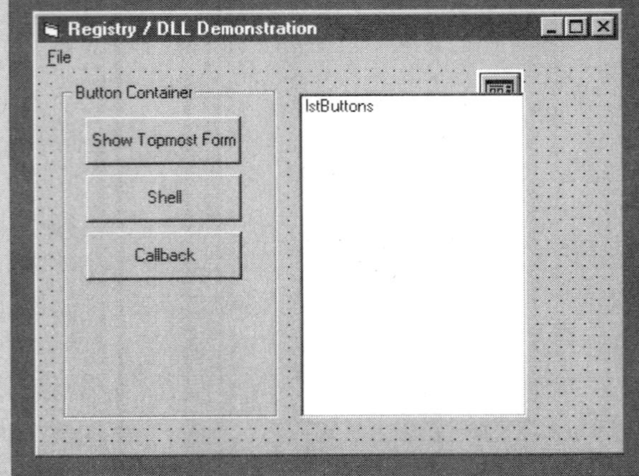

Figure 14-1: Completed application

2 Print the code for the project.

3 Run the program then click the **Show Topmost Form** command button. This causes the form shown in Figure 14-2 to be displayed as a modal form that cannot be obscured. Try to obscure the form by activating another window and moving that window over the region of the form shown in Figure 14-2. The window shown in Figure 14-2 always will appear as the topmost window. This is accomplished by calling a Windows DLL that changes the characteristics of a particular form.

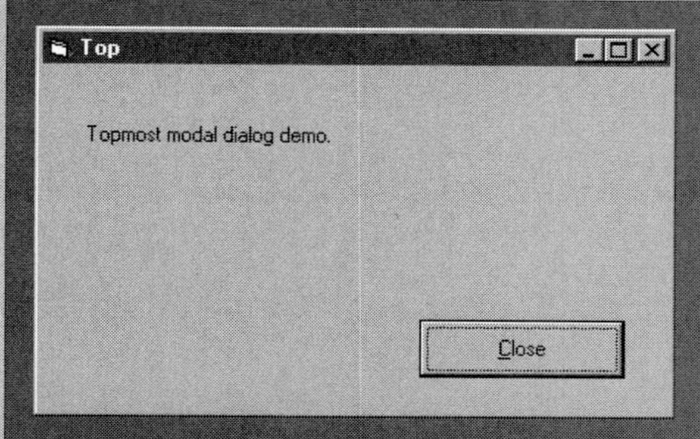

Figure 14-2: Topmost dialog

4 Close the form by clicking the **Close** button.

5 Click **Open** on the **File** menu, then select a file name in the common dialog and click **Open**. The prototype program does not actually open the files so it does not matter which file you select. Repeat the process four times opening a different file each time. Click **Exit** on the **File** menu to exit the program. This causes the Form_Unload event procedure to be executed and the list of recently opened files to be written to the Windows Registry.

6 Run the program again and click **File**. The list of files is read from the Windows Registry then displayed on the File menu.

7 Exit Visual Basic.

While the actions of the completed program are quite trivial, they cannot be readily accomplished by calling Visual Basic statements or intrinsic functions. Instead, these commands interact with the Windows Registry and call functions that are part of the Windows Application Programming Interface.

Introducing the Windows Registry

Before beginning to program the Windows Registry, a strong word of caution is in order. The Windows Registry maintains information vital for your computer to run properly. If you accidentally delete critical Windows Registry information, your system may become corrupted and will not boot or existing programs you have been using will not work properly. As such, you should consider preparing a Windows emergency disk, or backing up your system so you can recover easily from accidental system corruption. Also, use caution when performing the steps in this section, especially when using the RegEdit program. Finally, depending on the configuration of your system, you may not be able to write to the Windows Registry directly. If this occurs, contact your system administrator.

One of the important capabilities of a robust program is the capability to save information about itself when the program exits. Common configuration data may include a recent list of files that were last opened, or the position of various windows on the screen. This data is read when the program is run and saved when the program exits. Furthermore, programs also must make themselves known to the system. As you have seen in previous chapters, ActiveX controls and DLL components are registered on the system using the Windows Registry. In previous chapters, the information stored in the Windows Registry was put there by Visual Basic. In this section, you will see how to store information of your choosing in the Windows Registry.

In Windows 3.1, information about an application was saved using initialization files. Initialization files commonly are called ".ini" files. When a program was started, one or more initialization files were read and the program configured based on the information contained in each file. The program then would save information to the .ini file(s) when the current configuration changed or just before exiting the program. As programs and Windows itself have become much more complex, the number and size of the .ini files resident on a system became cumbersome and difficult to manage.

The .ini files pertaining to an application largely have been replaced by another piece of software called the Windows Registry, also known as the System Registry or just Registry. In this chapter, the term Registry will be used for brevity. The Registry stores the configuration information for specific programs in a hierarchical database. The information you store combines the information from the different .ini files pertaining to a specific application into one central location. The Registry also contains the current configuration of the computer. It identifies all the installed hardware and peripherals. It identifies all the software currently installed on the computer. It also maintains information pertaining to particular programs.

The Registry is sorted into two files. **System.dat** contains the Registry itself. **User.dat** contains the information pertaining to the users on the system. There are backup copies of these files stored in **System.da0** and **User.da0**. If the Registry becomes corrupted, Windows will recreate the Registry information from the backup files. The Registry is hierarchical, much like the Windows file system is hierarchical. In fact, the program used to edit the Registry, called RegEdit, has an interface very similar to the Windows Explorer program. There are trees and subtrees to organize Registry information. A tree or subtree is analogous roughly to a folder in Windows Explorer. Inside a tree or subtree, there are keys that contain data. The keys and their corresponding data are analogous roughly to the files displayed by Windows Explorer. Figure 14-3 shows the RegEdit program displaying the primary trees in the Registry.

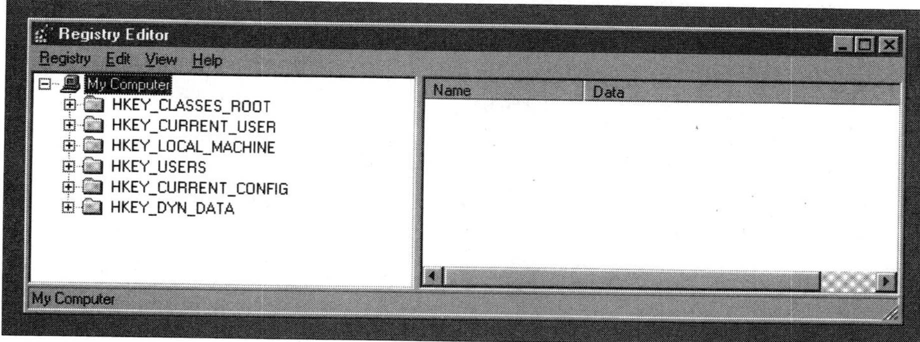

Figure 14-3: Registry Editor - trees

As shown in Figure 14-3 the Registry is divided into the following six trees. In this chapter, the capitalization for Registry tree and subtree entries will be presented in a manner consistent with RegEdit. If you view different books on the Registry, you soon will discover that texts differ on their capitalization conventions.

- **HKEY_CLASSES_ROOT** points to a subtree of HKEY_LOCAL_MACHINE and is used to define software settings.
- **HKEY_CURRENT_USER** contains the user profile for the user that currently is logged on the system.
- **HKEY_LOCAL_MACHINE** contains the configuration of the local computer. It has subtrees to list the hardware and software installed on the computer.
- **HKEY_USERS** is used to maintain user profile information about the various users on the system.
- **HKEY_CURRENT_CONFIG** points to the current system configuration in the collection of configurations stored in HKEY_LOCAL_MACHINE\Config.
- **HKEY_DYN_DATA** is used to store information in RAM, which requires fast modification and retrieval that would be too slow if the data had to be read and written from the disk.

These six trees look much like folders in Windows Explorer. Each folder may contain other folders and a folder also may contain files. Using Registry terminology, the term folder is replaced by the terms **tree** and **subtree**. This is because a tree or subtree is not really a physical file. It is merely a way of organizing information in the Registry. A tree can contain one or more subtrees, which in turn can contain zero or more subtrees and so on. The data in the Registry are not called files. Rather, a key/value pair is used to represent data. The **key** is used to identify a particular item of data in a subtree. The **value** contains the data pertaining to that key. The concept of a data type does not really exist as it pertains to Registry information. Conceptually, you can think of keys as strings and data values as variants. Any type of information can be stored as the value associated with a key.

Registry Functions

There are two Visual Basic functions that operate on the Registry. The **GetSetting** function returns a string containing the value of a specific Registry entry and the **SaveSetting** function is used to save a key and its value to the Registry. These two functions have limitations on where information in the Registry is stored. That is, the GetSetting and SaveSetting functions are limited to saving data in the following Registry section: "HKEY_USERS\Default\Software\VB and VBA Program Settings." To read and write data from and to other Registry locations, you must revert to DLL functions.

Syntax

GetSetting(*appname*, *section*, *key*[, *default*])

SaveSetting *appname*, *section*, *key*, *setting*

Dissection

- The **GetSetting** function reads a setting from the Registry. This setting is a unique combination of an application name, section, and key. If there is no valid entry for the *appname*, *section,* and *key*, and a *default* value is not specified, GetSetting returns an empty string. It returns the value for the unique key if a value is found or the *default* value if no value is found.
- The **SaveSetting** function writes a setting to the Registry. If a value already exists for the *appname*, *section,* and *key*, the value is overwritten. If the *key* does not yet exist, the *key*, corresponding *section*, and *appname* are added as necessary.
- The required *appname* argument contains the name of the application. This value must be a string and should contain the name of the application or project.
- The required *section* refers to a subtree of *appname*.
- The required *key* contains the unique key used to look up the value in the Registry. If there is no value for the specific key, the value of *default* is returned in the case of GetSetting. Otherwise, an empty string is returned.

Code Example

```
mintFiles = GetSetting(App.Title, "Files", "FileCount", 10)
SaveSetting App.Title, "Files", "FileCount", "10"
```

Code Dissection

The GetSetting function attempts to read the FileCount key in the section named Files for the application specified by App.Title. If there is a value, it is returned in mintFiles. If there is not an existing value, the default value 10 is returned. The SaveSetting function stores the value 10 for the same setting specified by the GetSetting function.

One common piece of information that can be stored in the Registry is a list of the last few files that were opened by a program. These files then are displayed on the File menu. This is common for most well-designed Windows programs like Word and Visual Basic itself. The process used in this example is fairly simple.

When the form is loaded, a list of the last few files (in this example 5), are read from the Registry and added to a control array of menu commands. When files are opened, the most recent file appears first on the menu and the least recently used file appears last. If there already are five files in the list of files, then the least recently opened file should disappear from the list. That is, the list of recent files will not grow indefinitely. Again, this is a common practice as a list of the last 100 files would be of little use. When the program is closed, the current list of files is saved to the Registry so the list can be reloaded the next time the program is run.

In the GSC example, you will maintain a list of recently opened files using the Registry. Of course, an .ini file or text file also would work. The Registry, however, is the preferred technique for saving persistent program information. This example is a prototype, however, in that the program does not actually process any of the open files. That is, the common dialog is used to select a file to open, but the program does nothing with the selected file. Opening multiple files at the same time is not the intent of this chapter. The concept already has been presented in Chapter 12 in relation to MDI programming.

To read and write information from and to the Registry:

1. Start **Visual Basic** then load the project named **Chapter.14\Startup\GSC_S.vbp.**
2. Activate the Code window for the **Form_Load** event procedure for the form named **frmGSC**, then enter the following statements:

```
Dim pintCount As Integer
Dim pstrFile As String
For pintCount = 1 To cMaxMenu
    pstrFile = GetSetting(App.Title, _
        "Files", "File" & CStr(pintCount))
    If pstrFile = "" Then
        Exit Sub
    End If
    Load mnuFileList(mnuFileList.UBound + 1)
    mnuFileList(mnuFileList.UBound).Caption = pstrFile
    mnuFileList(mnuFileList.UBound).Visible = True
Next
```

3. For the same form, activate the Code window for the **Form_Unload** event procedure, then enter the following statements:

```
Dim pintMax As Integer
Dim pintCurrent As Integer
pintMax = mnuFileList.UBound
For pintCurrent = 1 To pintMax
    SaveSetting App.Title, "Files", "File" & _
        CStr(pintCurrent), _
        mnuFileList(pintCurrent).Caption
Next
```

4 On the same form, enter the following statements in the **mnuFileOpen_Click** event procedure:

```
On Error GoTo CancelError
    Dim pintMax As Integer, pintCurrent As Integer
    Dim pintPrevious As Integer
    cdl1.ShowOpen
    pintMax = mnuFileList.UBound
    If pintMax < cMaxMenu Then
        pintMax = pintMax + 1
        Load mnuFileList(pintMax)
        mnuFileList(pintMax).Caption = _
            mnuFileList(pintMax - 1).Caption
    End If
    pintCurrent = pintMax
    pintPrevious = pintMax - 1
    Do While pintPrevious >= 0
        mnuFileList(pintCurrent).Caption = _
            mnuFileList(pintPrevious).Caption
        pintCurrent = pintCurrent - 1
        pintPrevious = pintPrevious - 1
    Loop
    mnuFileList(1).Caption = cdl1.filename
    Exit Sub
CancelError:
```

5 Test the program. Click **Open** on the **File** menu to display the CommonDialog control to open a file. Click **Open** on the **File** menu repeatedly to continue to open files. Remember, this code does not actually open the file. It merely demonstrates how to store a list of current files in the Registry.

6 Click **Exit** on the **File** menu. Do not click the End button on the Visual Basic toolbar. If you do, the Form_Unload event will not occur and the current file list will not be written to the Registry.

7 Run the program again then click **Open** on the **File** menu. The file list should appear containing the files you last opened.

The preceding code requires careful analysis. When the program is run, the Form_Load event occurs. In this event procedure, an attempt is made to read the most recently opened files from the Registry. When the form is unloaded, the most recently opened files are written back to the Registry. First, we will examine the code in the Form_Load event procedure. The difficult part of this procedure is to understand that it may be possible that this is the first time the user has run the program. In this case, there may be no recent files in the Registry to list on the menu. The constant cMaxMenu contains the constant value five (5), which is the maximum number of files to list. The statements inside the For loop attempt to load the full path of the last five files opened.

```
pstrFile = GetSetting(App.Title, _
    "Files", "File" & CStr(pintCount))
```

The GetSetting function uses App.Title (the Title property of the App object) to specify the application. In this example, the literal value "Files" is used for the section. Remember, this statement is executing inside a For loop. As such, pintCount contains an integer from one (1) to five (5). This value is converted to a string and concatenated to the literal value "File" to define the keys. Thus, the keys are File1, File2, File3, and so on. If the call to GetSetting succeeds, the key, section, and title all exist and the value is stored in pstrFile.

```
If pstrFile = "" Then
    Exit Sub
End If
```

If the call fails, then an empty string is stored in pstrFile. If no file is found, the procedure exits as shown in the preceding statements. If a file is found, the following statements are executed:

```
Load mnuFileList(mnuFileList.UBound + 1)
mnuFileList(mnuFileList.UBound).Caption = pstrFile
mnuFileList(mnuFileList.UBound).Visible = True
```

Remember, the Load statement can be used to increase the number of elements in a control array. The implementation chosen in this example is a bit tricky. The menu named mnuFileList was created as a control array using the Menu Editor. The control array has one element, having a separator bar as its caption. When a recent file is found in the Registry, the Load statement is called to increase the size of the mnuFileList control array by one (1), set the caption of the new element to the file name returned by GetSetting, and set the Visible property to True. This technique is common to manage a recent file list.

The Form_Unload event procedure is responsible for saving the list of current files back to the Registry. The first statement determines the number of elements in the control array. Element 0 contains the separator bar. Elements 1 through 5, if they exist, contain the list of files. Thus, the For loop iterates between one (1) and the number of current files. The call to the SaveSetting function writes the contents of the current control array element (current file) to the same section of the Registry used for the GetSetting function.

```
SaveSetting App.Title, "Files", "File" & _
    CStr(pintCurrent), _
    mnuFileList(pintCurrent).Caption
```

App.Title and "Files" identify the application and section in the Registry. Determining the file number (Registry key) is accomplished by concatenating an Integer value to the literal "File." This value is stored in the caption of the current element in the control array.

The Open command does nothing with the Registry itself. It merely manages the control array containing the recent list of files. Managing a dynamic control array was discussed in Chapter 3. For further information about this function, refer to the completed code for this example.

Viewing the Registry Using RegEdit

At this point, it would be very difficult to look at the values in the Registry to see if the calls to the SaveSetting and GetSetting functions are working correctly. Fortunately, there is a program called RegEdit, short for Registry Editor that will allow you to add, change, and delete entries in the Registry manually. The Registry Editor is very simple to use. It displays the hierarchy of Registry entries in a hierarchical fashion just like Windows Explorer. In fact, the interface is nearly identical. Figure 14-4 shows the Registry Editor with selected trees and subtrees open.

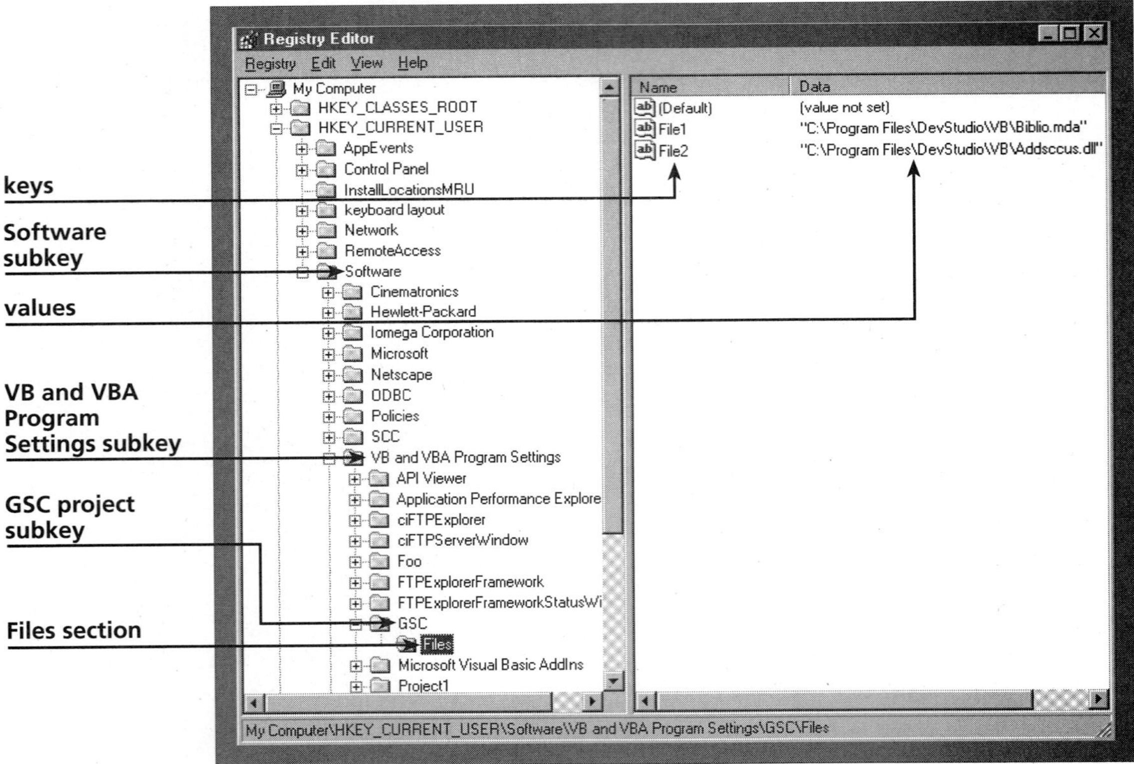

Figure 14-4: Registry Editor - subtrees

As shown in Figure 14-4, the interface for the Registry Editor looks like the interface for Windows Explorer or the interface you created using the TreeView and ListView controls. Although the interface is the same, the meaning and purpose of the data is much different. As shown in Figure 14-4, there is a Software subkey. Inside the Software subkey, there is another subkey named VB and VBA Program Settings. Inside that subkey, there is a subkey for the GSC project. That subkey in turn contains a Files subkey listing the recently saved files. The list portion of the Registry Editor displays the keys for the recently opened files and the values corresponding to those keys. In Figure 14-4, there are only two recently opened files. When you activate the Registry Editor on your computer, the number of subtrees likely will differ as you will have different software installed on your computer. Rather than explaining the details of each and every Registry entry, you first will see how to view the Registry settings you saved in the previous steps.

To locate an entry in the Registry:

1 Click **Run** on the **Start** menu, then enter the file name **RegEdit** to start the Registry Editor. (RegEdit usually is not available on the Start menu as it is intended to be hidden from general users.) The Registry Editor starts.

2 Click **Find** on the **Edit** menu to display the Find dialog shown in Figure 14-5.

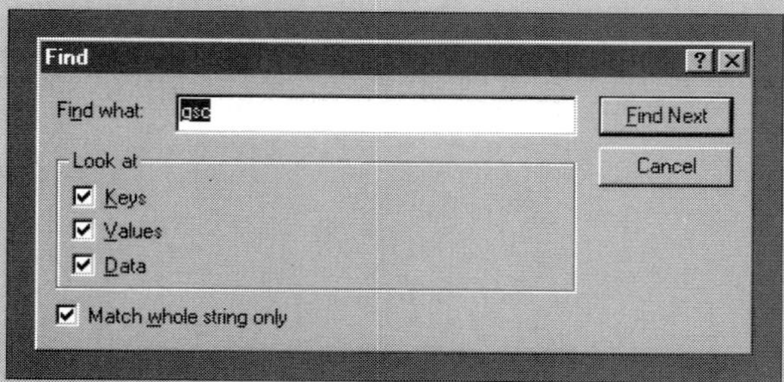

Figure 14-5: Find dialog

3 Click the check box options as shown in Figure 14-5. Enter the text **GSC** in the Find what text box, then click **Find Next.**

4 In the Registry Editor, open the folder named **GSC**, then double-click **Files.** The keys and data files for the files you last opened should appear in the Registry Editor.

RegEdit also will allow you to add new keys, modify existing keys, and delete keys. To change the value of a key, you select a key name. The Edit menu contains a Modify option that allows you to change the value of the selected key. To remove a key or section, you can select the key or section name and then click Remove on the Edit menu.

To edit and remove keys from the Registry:

1 Click the key named **File1**, then click **Modify** on the **Edit** menu to activate the Edit String dialog shown in Figure 14-6.

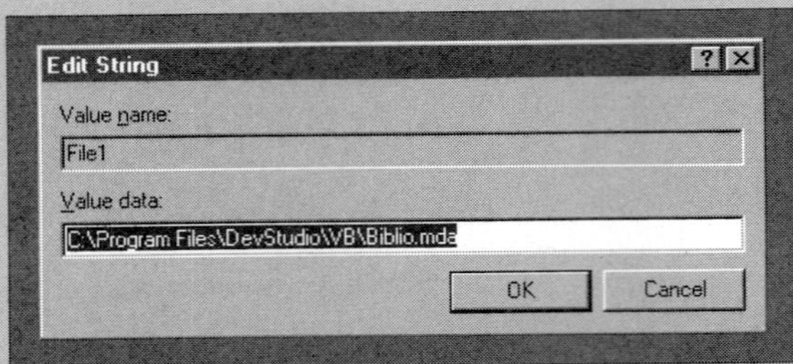

Figure 14-6: Edit String dialog

2 Change the name of the file to any name of your choosing. Click **OK** to close the dialog.

3 Test the program. Click the **File** menu. The changes you made to the Registry should appear in the listing on the File menu. Exit the program.

4 Click the **Files** subtree in the Registry Editor, then delete it.

5 Test the program. No files appear in the listing on the File menu because the entries were removed from the Registry.

In addition to deleting Registry entries using RegEdit, you also can delete them from Visual Basic.

Deleting Registry Entries

The DeleteSetting function is used to remove a specific key and value pair from the Registry. It also can be used to delete the key/value pairs for an entire section or all the Registry settings for an application.

Syntax **DeleteSetting** *appname*, *section*[, *key*]

Dissection

- The required *appname* argument contains the name of the application stored in the Registry.
- The required *section* argument identifies a section of the application.
- The optional *key* argument specifies a specific key value in the *section*. If the *key* is omitted, the entire section is removed.

Code Example	`DeleteSetting App.Title, "Files", "File1"`
	`DeleteSetting App.Title, "Files"`
	`DeleteSetting App.Title`

Code Dissection	The first call to the DeleteSetting function removes the key and value for the File1 key in the Files section of the application "App.Title." The second removes the entire Files section, and the third removes all the settings for the application.

Using these Visual Basic functions to manipulate the Registry has limitations. Although not usually a problem, these functions only can access a small part of the Registry. One benefit of this is that Visual Basic prevents you from changing a Registry entry that would cause other programs on the system to stop working. If you need to work with other parts of the Registry, however, you must use the DLL functions pertaining to Registry information. DLL functions are described in the next section.

Registering a Server

Remember, when you created ActiveX controls and ActiveX DLL servers, the necessary information pertaining to those servers was added to the Registry. This allowed you to create project groups to debug and test your DLLs and ActiveX control projects. When a project is run from the Visual Basic IDE, the program temporarily is registered by Visual Basic. There are times, however, when you may need to register a server manually. This can be accomplished by a simple utility called RegSvr32.exe. There is usually a copy of this utility in the Windows or Windows\System folder. If there is not, a copy of the RegSvr32 can be found on the Visual Basic CD-ROM. The RegSvr32.exe program is not run from Visual Basic. Rather, it can be called from the MS-DOS prompt or the Run dialog on the Start menu. The command has a very simple syntax. Consider the following commands:

```
RegSvr32 Demo.dll
RegSvr32 /u Demo.dll
```

The first statement registers the component named Demo.dll, and the second statement removes the program named Demo.dll from the Registry.

Remote Component Registration

In addition to accessing COM modules (code components) on a local machine, Visual Basic supports two facilities to work with components on a remote machine. The facilities are known as a Distributed COM (DCOM) and Remote Automation. When a program is operating with code components on remote machines, registering those components is accomplished using a tool called the Remote Automation Connection Manager (RACM). RACM is a stand-alone program typically found in the VB\Clisvr folder. Note that this facility is only included in the Enterprise Version of Visual Basic.

SECTION B

objectives

In this section you will:

- Learn about the characteristics of Windows Dynamic Link Libraries
- Expose a function declared in a DLL to your Visual Basic program
- Call a DLL function
- Understand the implications passing different data types to DLL functions

The Basics of Windows Dynamic Link Libraries

A Dynamic Link Library Defined

Throughout this book, you have written programs consisting entirely of Visual Basic statements. We, however, have said that Visual Basic, and the objects supported by Visual Basic, are not an island independent of Windows. Rather, Visual Basic is a software component that simplifies the development of programs by encapsulating the functionality of various Windows objects into an integrated development environment.

Much of the functionality supported by Windows is available to other programming languages using a facility known as the Application Programming Interface (API). Another common term is the Windows API, or just API. In Chapter 9, you created an ActiveX DLL server that implemented a set of collections and objects to store and manipulate the database records pertaining to a particular database. This ActiveX DLL server was a library that could be called from another program by providing Visual Basic a reference to the library (using the Project References dialog).

In the case of the DLLs you created, a developer could reference the objects in the DLL by calling its methods and setting properties. Conceptually, calling the functions in a Windows DLL is very similar to calling a Visual Basic function or method contained in an object library like DAO. In each case, you really are just calling a function supported by a library, be it a DLL or object library. The process of preparing to call a function in a DLL is much different than the process of establishing a reference to a particular object library and calling the methods of that library.

Before discussing the implementation details of how to access a Windows DLL, a word about program compilation and linking may be helpful in understanding how Windows DLLs work. The sophistication of both operating system software and programming languages has improved considerably over the past several years. The early programs on the first personal computers had to do everything themselves.

That is, the program itself had to take care of trivial details like reading input and formatting output. There were no equivalent intrinsic functions like Format, or Input#, and so on.

Over time, operating systems and programming languages evolved to free the programmer from the trivial details of reading input or formatting output. Imagine having to write programs without having access to common mathematical functions, string conversion functions, type classification functions, or any of the other tools you have become accustomed to using. To improve programmer productivity, common functions were encapsulated into what is called a **library**. When a program is compiled, the language statements are translated into some form of executable file. The first step of the process is **compilation**. In this stage, the source language statements are translated into a form understood by the actual computer hardware. These statements likely will make references to library routines stored in another file. A second step in the process is to copy those library routines from the library into the executable file itself. The process of establishing a reference to a procedure in a library is called **linking**. One technique to link programs was called static linking. When static linking is used, the necessary code to execute a specific library function is copied from the library into the executable file. For example, if you called the Format function, all the code written to implement that function was copied into your executable program. Figure 14-7 illustrates the process of static linking.

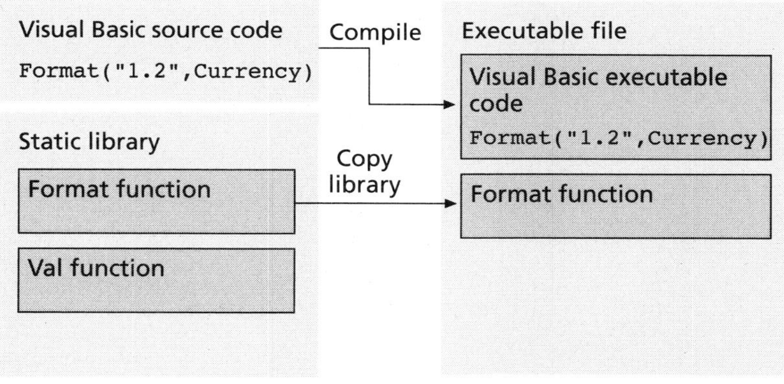

Figure 14-7: Static linking

The technique of static linking had a serious flaw. As you may expect, most programs written likely would utilize the same functions. For example, nearly every Visual Basic program you write will use the Format function, the string conversion functions, and many others. Thus, every program written likely would have a copy of these same functions stored in its executable file on the disk. This makes each program much larger than it would be if the program itself just could call a function that existed in a common library. Furthermore, by storing several copies of the same function, disk space is wasted. Another form of linking, called **dynamic linking**, was introduced to overcome the flaws of static linking. Using dynamic linking, one copy of a particular library procedure is stored in a single file. Conceptually, this is analogous to there being one copy of the code that contains the Format function resident on the system. Consider what happens when you run a program that uses a function (like Format) in a dynamically-linked library. Instead of the code for the Format statement being copied into the executable file that is your program, a reference is created in your program that allows the executable file to find the file and function in the library containing the code for the Format statement. The term dynamic linking comes from the fact that programs are linked to various libraries dynamically at run time. Figure 14-8 illustrates a program that is dynamically linked.

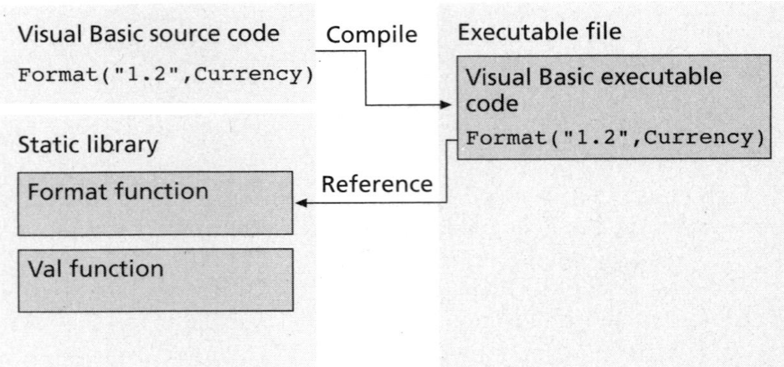

Figure 14-8: Dynamic linking

As you can see, the term dynamic link library makes perfect sense. A dynamic link library contains a set of functions that are dynamically linked to other programs at run time. While this discussion of static and dynamic linking may seem rather academic, it is not. Windows DLLs, as the name implies, are dynamically linked. To call one of these procedures from a Visual Basic program, you tell Visual Basic the name of the library and the name of the function you want to call. The code for this function is not copied into the Visual Basic program. Rather, your program stores a reference to the actual library and function in that library.

Referencing a Dynamic-Link Library

In Chapter 9, you saw how to compile an ActiveX component to a DLL server. In addition to creating your own DLL servers, you can from Visual Basic, access the hundreds of procedures stored in the DLL libraries already defined by Windows. There are several reasons to use Windows DLL functions.

- Some tasks are difficult, if not impossible, to perform using Visual Basic. In these circumstances, a DLL can be useful.
- While you are all too familiar with the capabilities supported by Visual Basic controls, the functionality of many controls can be expanded using DLL procedures. In this case, DLL procedures can extend the functionality of a control as exposed by Visual Basic.

- The procedures in a DLL typically are optimized for performance. As such, executing a procedure in a DLL can impact positively on your program's performance.

There are many dynamic-link libraries (DLL) that are components of the Windows operating system. Each DLL contains a set of procedures you can call at run time. These procedures perform tasks like updating windows, reading and writing information to and from the disk, and so on. You can call DLL procedures much like you can call intrinsic Visual Basic procedures. Using a DLL procedure in a Visual Basic program consists of the following two steps:

1. The name and arguments of the DLL procedure must be made known to the Visual Basic program.
2. The DLL procedure can be called as needed.

There are many DLLs defined by the Windows operating system. There are a few DLLs, however, defined by Windows that are of particular importance.

- **Comdlg32.dll** contains the actual library functions for the CommonDialog control. These are the functions that ultimately are called by the Visual Basic CommonDialog control.
- **GDI32.dll** is used to perform graphical and drawing operations.
- **Kernel32.dll** is used to perform tasks closely related to the operating system.
- **Shell32.dll** contains functions to access the Windows shell.
- **User32.dll** contains functions to manage windows. You also can access the actual functions of intrinsic controls like text boxes. Remember, an intrinsic control, like a text box, is not specific to Visual Basic but common to the Windows operating system.

Exploring the complete set of DLL procedures is far beyond the scope of this chapter. The intent of this chapter is to explain the mechanics of calling a DLL procedure and getting it to work with your program. If you are interested in expanding your DLL knowledge, and you have Visual C++ installed on your computer, the Help system for Visual C++ can be an invaluable tool as it provides extensive documentation for each of the DLL calls. Furthermore, there are several books published by Microsoft Press and others that fully document the myriad of DLL calls supported by Windows.

Declaring a DLL Procedure

The process of exposing a DLL procedure to a Visual Basic program is much different than the process of making an object library available. Before a DLL procedure can be used in a program, the name of the Windows library, the procedure name, and the arguments required by the procedure, must be declared so the Visual Basic program can locate the Windows library at run time. This is accomplished using the Declare statement.

Syntax

[**Public** | **Private**] **Declare Sub** *name* **Lib** "*libname*" [**Alias** "*aliasname*"] [([*arglist*])]

[**Public** | **Private**] **Declare Function** *name* **Lib** "*libname*" [**Alias** "*aliasname*"] [([*arglist*])] [**As** *type*]

Dissection

- The optional **Public** and **Private** statements are used to declare procedures that are visible to all other procedures in all modules, or in the module where the procedure is declared, respectively. Their meaning is the same as when you are declaring Visual Basic functions and procedures. Declared procedures are Public by default. A Declare statement with the Public keyword can only be used in a standard .bas module. DLLs declared in a form or any type of class module must be Private.
- The **Declare** statement defines a DLL procedure so a Visual Basic program can use it.
- The **Sub** keyword indicates that the DLL procedure does not return a value. The **Function** keyword indicates that the DLL procedure does return a value. Either the Function or Sub keyword must exist.
- The meaning of the required *name* argument depends on whether or not the Alias keyword is used. If the Alias keyword is not used, then *name* represents both the name of the procedure within the DLL and the name of the procedure as it is known to your Visual Basic program. DLL procedure names are case-sensitive unlike ordinary Visual Basic procedure names.
- The required **Lib** and *libname* arguments define the library containing the DLL procedure.
- The **Alias** keyword indicates that the procedure being called has another name in the DLL. This is useful when the DLL procedure name has the same name as a Visual Basic keyword. You also can use the Alias keyword when a DLL procedure has the same name as a Public variable, constant, or any other procedure in the same scope. An Alias also is useful if any characters in the DLL procedure name are not allowed by the Visual Basic naming conventions.
- The optional *aliasname* contains the name of the procedure in the DLL or code resource. If the first character is not a number sign (#), *aliasname* is the name of the procedure's entry point in the DLL. If (#) is the first character, all characters that follow must indicate the ordinal number of the procedure's entry point.
- The optional *arglist* contains a list of variables representing arguments that are passed to the procedure when it is called.
- The optional *type* argument contains the data type of the value returned by a Function procedure. The value may be a Byte, Boolean, Integer, Long, Currency, Single, Double, Date, String (variable length only), or Variant, a user-defined type, or an object type.

Code Example

```
Declare Function SetWindowPos Lib "user32" _
    (ByVal hwnd As Long, _
    ByVal hWndInsertAfter As Long, _
    ByVal x As Long, _
    ByVal y As Long, _
    ByVal cx As Long, _
    ByVal cy As Long, _
    ByVal wFlags As Long) As Long
```

Code Dissection

The previous statement declares the Windows DLL procedure named SetWindowPos so it can be used by your Visual Basic program. The DLL procedure is in the User32.dll library. The Function procedure takes seven arguments, all passed by value, and returns a Long Integer data type. The purpose of this DLL function and the meaning of the various arguments will be discussed later in the chapter. Note the case of the User32 library name and the case of the hwnd argument. In the above syntax, both words were lower case even though the file name on the disk is really User32.dll and most objects refer to the hwnd property as hWnd. This declaration was extracted from the API text viewer which will be shown in a moment. We have not changed the case of the declarations of the API viewer.

A word about the formatting of the DLL procedure in the previous syntax code dissection is in order. As you can see, a Declare statement can become quite long as many DLL procedures accept a long list of arguments. As such, this book will take the approach of using continuation lines to declare a DLL procedure. Each argument will appear on its own continuation line. The intent is to improve readability.

Programming tip

A strong word of caution about DLL programming is in order. When you are programming entirely inside the Visual Basic programming environment, Visual Basic prevents you from writing statements that may cause Visual Basic or Windows to crash. Calling DLLs with improper function arguments, however, most likely will cause Visual Basic to crash. It also can corrupt important data needed by the operating system causing Windows to crash, or possibly to corrupt the data of other programs. As such, you should use great care and caution when developing programs that access DLLs. Any time you write code to call DLL functions, you should save all the files pertaining to the active project or project group before attempting to test the program. That way, if Visual Basic crashes because of invalid data being passed to a DLL procedure, any changes you have made will not be lost.

Creating Aliases

As shown in the syntax for the Declare statement, a DLL procedure may contain the Alias keyword. An alias is used to define a name for a DLL procedure, as it is seen by your Visual Basic program, which is different from the actual name of the DLL procedure. Aliases are necessary for some DLL procedures because some DLL procedures have names that are not legal Visual Basic names. For example, many DLL procedures contain a leading underscore or a hyphen embedded in the procedure name. Aliases also are useful when a DLL procedure has the same name as a Visual Basic intrinsic function. Aliases also can be used to provide shorthand names for procedures. Consider the following Declare statement that uses an alias:

```
Private Declare Function GetTempFileName _
    Lib "kernel32" Alias "GetTempFileNameA" _
    (ByVal lpszPath As String, _
    ByVal lpPrefixString As String, _
    ByVal wUnique As Long, _
    ByVal lpTempFileName As String) As Long
```

The previous Declare statement uses an alias. The GetTempFileNameA DLL function contained in the kernel32.dll file is used to create unique temporary files for use by your Visual Basic program. The function name as it will be used in your program, however, will be known as GetTempFileName.

Another common use for aliases is to redefine a DLL procedure name because its name conflicts with a Visual Basic statement or function. For example, Visual Basic supports a function named Beep that will generate an audible beep. There also is a Windows DLL procedure named Beep that you can use in your program. Consider the following statements:

```
Private Declare Function Beep Lib "kernel32" _
    (ByVal dwFreq As Long, _
    ByVal dwDuration As Long) As Long

Private Sub Command1_Click( )
    Beep
End Sub
```

There is a problem with the previous statements. The Declare statement makes the Windows DLL Beep function available to your program. Assume that the code in the command button's Click event procedure intended to call the Visual Basic Beep statement. These statements will cause a compiler error. The name of the DLL procedure Beep overrides the Visual Basic Beep function as far as the compiler is concerned. As such, the number of arguments in the Visual Basic Beep function does not match the expected number of arguments in the DLL procedure. To solve this problem, you can create an alias for the DLL Beep procedure as shown in the following statements:

```
Private Declare Function BeepWin32 Lib "kernel32" _
    Alias "Beep" _
    (ByVal dwFreq As Long, _
    ByVal dwDuration As Long) As Long

Private Sub Command1_Click( )
    Dim pLng As Long
    pLng = BeepWin32(0, 0)
End Sub
```

The preceding statements resolve the problem by creating an alias named BeepWin32 for the actual DLL Beep function. Because the function is known to your Visual Basic program as BeepWin32, the code in the command button has been changed to call the DLL Beep function and the function has been changed to contain the necessary arguments. Using Windows 95, there really is no reason to redefine the DLL Beep function. Using Windows NT, however, you can enhance the DLL Beep function by passing arguments to define the frequency, and the duration, of the beep. Windows 95 ignores these arguments.

Locating a DLL Procedure

The first step in beginning to use DLL procedures is to learn which DLL procedures exist, the return value of those procedures, and the arguments required by a DLL procedure. Conceptually, this is just like defining the return value and arguments for the Visual Basic functions that you create. DLLs and Windows, however, are much more particular about the accuracy of the data types used by both DLL arguments and the return value of a DLL function.

Starting to work with Windows DLLs can be a daunting task at first, simply because of the sheer number of DLL functions supported by Windows. There literally are thousands of Windows DLL procedures, each of which requires specific arguments. Many of these arguments are represented by constant values.

Before beginning to declare and call DLL procedures, another word about how those DLLs were created is in order. Much of the Windows operating system is written in the C or C++ programming languages. That is, the DLL functions you are calling were written in C. The two languages—C (C++) and Visual Basic—do not share the same data types. Figure 14-9 describes some of the C data types and the equivalent Visual Basic data types that should be used as the arguments to a DLL procedure.

C data type	Visual Basic data type
ATOM	ByVal *variable* As Integer
BOOL	ByVal *variable* As Long
CHAR	ByVal *variable* As Byte
LONG	ByVal *variable* As Long
LPSTR, LPCSTR	ByVal *variable* As String
NULL	ByVal *variable* As Long
SHORT	ByVal *variable* As Integer

Figure 14-9: C data types

Given the number of DLL procedures that exist, and that each procedure may have several arguments that use various constants, you may expect that the process of declaring each of the API functions would be a tedious task. To some degree it is. Visual Basic, however, supports a rudimentary tool to help you declare Windows API procedures. This tool is called the API Viewer or API Text Viewer. The term API Viewer will be used in this book. It is shown in Figure 14-10.

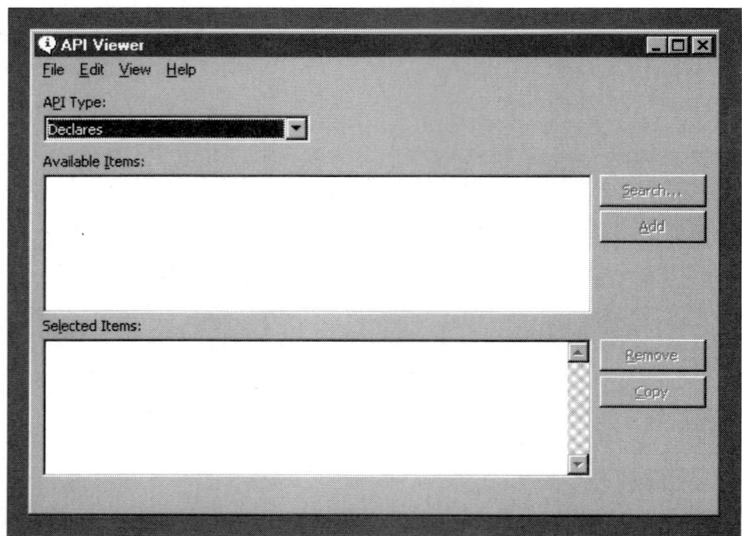

Figure 14-10: API Viewer

The purpose of the API Viewer is to provide the constants, function declarations, and types needed to call a particular DLL. The process of using the API Viewer is simple. In general, you select items from the Available Items list box, causing them to appear in the Selected Items list box. Once you have selected all the constants, function declarations, and types you want to use, you click the Copy button causing the selected items to be copied to the Windows clipboard. The data then can be pasted in a module in your program. If, as you develop your program, you determine that you forgot to add a particular DLL procedure, you can reactivate the API Viewer, and select any additional items you want to use, copy them to the clipboard, and add them to the desired module file.

The API information usually is stored in the file named Win32API.txt, which usually is located in the WinAPI folder in the Visual Basic root directory. This file may not exist depending on the Visual Basic installation options chosen. Before you can select items, you first must load the text file in the API Viewer.

Programming ▶ tip

If you frequently use DLLs in your programs, the Win32API.txt file can be converted into a database file readable by the Jet Database Engine. The default file name is Win32API.mdb, and generally is written to the same folder as the file Win32API.txt. Converting the text file to a database file can be accomplished by clicking Load Text File on the File menu and then clicking Convert Text to Database on the File menu. Once converted to a database file, the database file can be opened by clicking Load Database File on the File menu.

In this example, you will call the following DLL functions:

- CopyFileA
- EnumChildWindows
- GetTempFileNameA
- GetTempPathA
- GetWindowText
- SetWindowPos

You now can use the API Viewer to add the necessary constants and Declare statements to your program.

To view the Win32API.txt file:

1. Start the **API Viewer** either on the Start menu or the Tools Add-Ins menu.
2. Click **Load Text File** on the **File** menu.
3. Click the file **VB\WinAPI\Win32API.txt**, then click the **Open** button. The root VB directory usually is found in the folder \Program Files\DevStudio. (The full path on your machine may differ depending on your installation.)

   The text file loads.
4. Click **File** again. If the option **Convert Text to Database** is active, click it. Save the output file in the same directory as the file Win32API.txt.

   In the future, you can click Open Database File to read the equivalent database file in the API Viewer. The database file will perform much faster than if an ordinary text file were used.
5. In the API Type list box, click **Declares**. The Declare statements for all the DLL functions will appear in the Available Items list box.
6. In the Available Items list box, click the DLLs named **GetTempFileName** and **GetTempPath**. Click **Add** after clicking each item. The items should appear as shown in Figure 14-11.

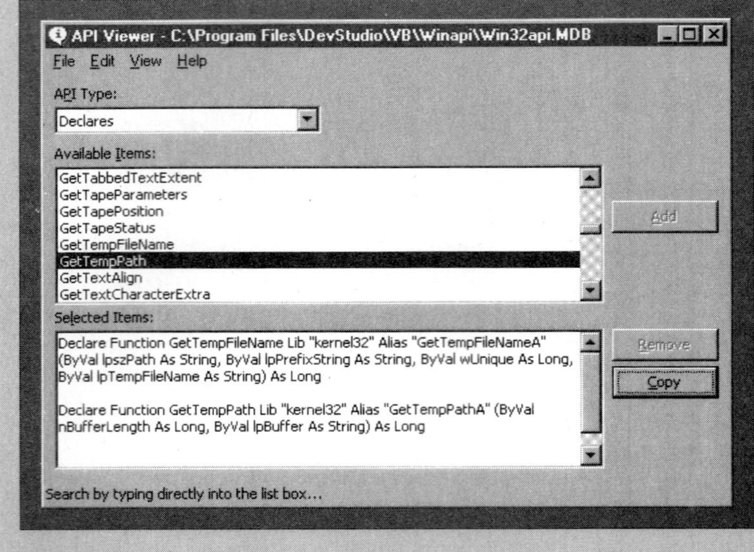

Figure 14-11: API Viewer

7 Click **Copy** to copy the items on the Windows clipboard.

8 These items could be pasted to any Visual Basic module. This is not necessary, however, as all the DLL declarations already have been made in the standard module named API.bas.

Before calling these DLL procedures, you should consider program design. Imagine that you had created a large program with several forms. Assume that many of these forms required the services of several common DLL procedures. Given a scenario like this, you have several implementation options to choose from.

- A Declare statement with the Private keyword could be created in each form that used the DLL procedure. The code in the form module then would call the DLL directly.
- Each DLL procedure could be declared as Public in a standard module. This allows the DLL procedure to be declared only once. Each form or other module then could call the DLL procedure directly.
- The third, and best, approach is to create what is called a wrapper procedure. Using this technique, a standard module is created. Each of the DLL procedures used by the program is declared in the standard module. Instead of calling the DLL procedures directly from other forms and modules, another procedure is created in the standard module called a wrapper procedure. The wrapper procedure in turn calls the DLL procedure or procedures. This technique frees the developer from having to worry about the technical details of calling the various DLL procedures, or that they even exist.

Programming DLLs requires much more than just learning a list of DLL functions and their arguments. As DLLs are used to access the fundamental functions of the Windows operating system, it follows that to effectively use the various DLL procedures, you must understand the underlying Windows concepts related to different types of DLL procedures. One of the fundamental concepts of Windows, obviously, is the concept of a window. In the discussion that follows, the term operating system will be used to refer to the Windows operating system. The intent is to improve readability as the following discussion focuses on the windows managed by Windows. As far as the operating system is concerned, every form, and nearly every control instance, is considered a unique window. Each window is assigned a unique Long Integer number, which is stored in the hWnd property of a particular form or control. This commonly is called a **window handle**. Labels, lines, and shapes actually are not windows and as such have no hWnd property.

Many of the operating system functions (DLL procedures) require that you pass, as an argument, the window you are referring to. To illustrate how this works, suppose that you wanted to create a dialog that always would appear on top of all other windows, even if the window did not have focus. This may be useful to display a dialog notifying the user of a very important error condition that should not be overlooked. It also may be useful to display a floating toolbar that should never be hidden (obscured by another window). Rather than explaining all the details about calling the DLL to accomplish this task, we will begin by introducing a few key concepts and demonstrating the basic mechanics of calling a simple DLL.

Using ByVal and ByRef Arguments in DLL Procedures

Remember, in Visual Basic all function arguments are passed either by reference or by value, and Visual Basic passes arguments by reference unless otherwise specified. For data types like Integer, Float, and Boolean, passing an argument by reference means that the memory address of the variable is passed to the procedure rather than the data to itself. Many DLL procedures expect their arguments to be passed by value. Thus, the Declare statement always should contain the ByVal or ByRef keyword for each argument so the arguments are passed to the DLL correctly.

While the data types Long, Integer, and Single pass a memory address when the argument is declared with the ByRef keyword, and the data is passed when the ByVal keyword is used, strings work much differently. When a string variable is passed by value (the ByVal keyword is used), the memory address of the first data byte is passed in the argument. When a string variable is passed by reference, the value passed contains a memory address where another memory address is stored. In Visual Basic, you nearly always pass strings by value to DLL functions.

When declaring DLL procedures, care must be taken to make sure that the declaration correctly defines how each argument is passed. If a DLL expects an argument to be passed ByVal and it is passed ByRef, the DLL will receive incorrect information and errors will occur.

Calling the First DLL

There is a DLL called SetWindowPos, which is used to change the size of a window, its position, or its ZOrder relative to other windows. This function has the following type declaration in Win32API.txt:

Syntax

Declare Function SetWindowPos Lib "user32" Alias "SetWindowPos"
(ByVal *hWnd* **As Long, _**
ByVal *hWndInsertAfter* **As Long, _**
ByVal *x* **As Long, _**
ByVal *y* **As Long, _**
ByVal *cx* **As Long, _**
ByVal *cy* **As Long, _**
ByVal *wFlags* **As Long) As Long**

Dissection

- The **SetWindowPos** DLL function is contained in the DLL named User32.dll. The function is used to change the size, position, and ZOrder of a window.
- The *hWnd* argument contains a Long Integer data type representing a window handle. This value typically is obtained by reading the hWnd property of a form or control instance.
- The *hWndInsertAfter* argument specifies the window that will precede the window referenced by hWnd in the ZOrder. There are several valid constants for this argument. HWND_BOTTOM causes the window to appear at the bottom of the ZOrder. HWND_NOTOPMOST causes the window to appear above all the non-topmost windows. HWND_TOP places the window at the top of the ZOrder.
- The *x* and *y* properties specify the left-hand side and top of the window.
- The *cx* and *cy* arguments specify the new width and height of the window.
- The *wFlags* argument contains the flags that are used to determine various sizing and positioning characteristics of the window. While several more flags are declared than are discussed in this chapter, there are two flags of particular importance. The flag SWP_NOMOVE retains the current position of the window. The flag SWP_NOSIZE retains the current size of the window.

In this example, you will create a function that will cause a form to appear as the topmost window when the form is displayed.

To make a window appear as the topmost window:

1 Create the following wrapper procedure in the standard module named **API.bas** to hide the DLL from the programmer. The Declare statement for the SetWindowPos function already has been placed in the standard module.

```
Public Sub SetTop(frm As Form)
    Dim plngFlags As Long, plngResult As Long
    plngFlags = SWP_NOSIZE Or SWP_NOMOVE
    frm.Show
    plngResult = SetWindowPos(frm.hWnd, _
        HWND_TOPMOST, 0, 0, 0, 0, plngFlags)
End Sub
```

2 In the form named **frmGSC**, enter the following statement in the **cmdShowTop_Click** event procedure:

```
SetTop frmTop
```

3 Test the program. Click the **Show Topmost Form** command button. The dialog will appear with the caption Top. Try to obscure the window. It always will appear as the topmost window.

4 Click the **Close** button to close the form then exit the program.

A careful analysis of the SetTop Sub procedure is in order. First, the procedure accepts one argument—a reference to a form. The following statement uses the necessary flags so the size and position arguments will be ignored. Thus, the settings of the form's Height, Width, and positioning properties will be used to determine the size and position of the form on the string.

```
plngFlags = SWP_NOSIZE Or SWP_NOMOVE
```

The form is shown as a modeless form, and finally the DLL function procedure is called as shown in the following statement:

```
plngResult = SetWindowPos(frm.hWnd, _
    HWND_TOPMOST, 0, 0, 0, 0, plngFlags)
```

This statement uses the window handle of the form (stored in the hWnd property of the form) as the first argument. The second argument contains the constant value HWND_TOPMOST, causing the form to appear as the topmost form. Because the flags are set to SWP_NOSIZE and SWP_NOMOVE, the form's positional properties are used to determine the size and position of the form on the screen.

The technique used to display a form as a topmost form illustrates the use of a wrapper procedure. A programmer can call the SetTop procedure without having to worry about the details of calling the SetWindowPos DLL.

Managing Temporary Files

A common requirement of many applications is a need to create and destroy temporary files. These files typically are transparent to the user of your program. As an example, consider what happens when you open a Word document. Word creates a temporary file associated with that document. The user never sees this file, unless for some reason the temporary file was not destroyed when Word was closed and it is found using a program like Windows Explorer. Consider another situation where you wanted to save data for a short time while a program is running.

While you just could create an arbitrary empty file, your program should make sure that the file name already does not exist. Fortunately, Windows supports a set of DLL procedures that allow you to control where temporary files are stored, and to obtain a file name for the temporary file that is guaranteed to be unique. These two functions are named GetTempPath and GetTempFileName. Both of these DLL procedures use strings as arguments. As a Visual Basic programmer, passing string arguments to a Windows DLL procedure requires that you be very careful.

Passing Strings to DLL Procedures

Passing strings as arguments to a DLL procedure also requires that you understand: how string arguments work, the difference between the Visual Basic representation of a string and the C representation of a string, and the concept of a pointer. The concepts of passing arguments by reference and passing them by value also is important.

In general, strings are represented in one of two ways. Internally, Windows 95 DLLs process strings using the LPSTR C data type. This value is a 32-bit pointer to an ASCII character string. Windows NT internally supports two character sets. Windows NT can store strings internally in a format called UNICODE, which requires two bytes for each character instead of just one or in ASCII which requires one byte for each character. The difficulty arises in that Visual Basic internally manipulates strings as UNICODE. To resolve this discrepancy, Windows DLL procedures that manipulate strings likely will exist in two versions. Consider the following two possible Declare statements for the GetTempPath function:

```
Declare Function GetTempPath Lib "kernel32" _
    Alias "GetTempPathA" _
    (ByVal nBufferLength As Long, _
    ByVal lpBuffer As String) As Long
Declare Function GetTempPath Lib "kernel32" _
    Alias "GetTempPathW" _
    (ByVal nBufferLength As Long, _
    ByVal lpBuffer As String) As Long
```

These two Declare statements are identical with one exception—they have a different value for the Alias argument. When you call the DLL from Visual Basic, the function name GetTempPath will be used. In the first Declare statement, however, the actual function name in Windows DLL is GetTempPathA. In the second Declare statement, the function name is GetTempPathW. GetTempPathA specifies the ASCII version of the function, while GetTempPathW specifies the UNICODE version of the function. The character "W" as the suffix stems from the word "Wide."

Programming ▶ tip

In Visual Basic, you generally should use the ASCII version of string functions rather than the UNICODE version, as Windows 95 supports only the ASCII versions. Both the ASCII and UNICODE versions are supported by Windows NT. Thus, only use the UNICODE version if you are completely confident that your program only will be run on the Windows NT platform.

Internally, Visual Basic stores a string with a header. This header contains information pertinent to the string including the size of the string. Following the header are the characters that make up the string. Finally, the string is terminated with a null byte. A null byte is a character with the value zero Chr(0). This is different from the number zero (0).

Most DLL procedures expect a different type of string. This type of string does not have the embedded header information built into the string. Rather, it simply consists of the string followed by a null byte. This type of string is called an LPSTR.

When strings are passed to a DLL procedure, the string always is passed ByVal rather than ByRef. What this means is that when you pass a string to a DLL, you are not passing the string itself but rather the memory address of the string. One of the problems that can arise when passing strings to a DLL procedure occurs when the DLL procedure itself modifies the contents of the string. Consider the following simple Visual Basic function and function call:

```
Public Sub GetDateString(ByRef pstrValue As String)
    pstrValue = Date( )
End Sub

Dim pstrDateString As String
Call GetDateString(pstrDateString)
```

While nonsensical, this Sub procedure and the call to the Sub procedure, illustrates a very important point. When pstrDateString is declared, it contains no characters. This empty string then is passed to the Sub procedure GetDateString. Inside that procedure, the size of the string is increased to store the string representation of the current date.

When you pass a string to a DLL procedure, this technique will not work. DLL procedures cannot increase the size of a string argument. If there is not enough space to store the data in the string, the DLL procedure will not increase the size of the string. Rather, it will overwrite memory that is used by another variable. This likely will cause the data in your program to be corrupted or Visual Basic to crash. There are two solutions to this problem.

- The first solution is to use variable-length strings. When this solution is used, it is necessary that the string passed to the DLL be large enough to hold the string returned by the DLL. The Visual Basic String function can be used to store a repeating character in the string. This has the effect of defining an explicit size for the string.
- The second solution is to use fixed-length strings. When using a fixed-length string, make sure the size of the string is large enough to store the result created by the DLL.

To illustrate these two techniques, consider the following string declarations and statements.

```
Dim pstrFixed As String * 255
Dim pstrVariable As String
pstrVariable = String(255, Chr(0))
```

The first statement declares a fixed-length string 255 characters in length. The second and third statements create a variable-length string and store 255 null bytes in the string. Thus, both strings are 255 characters in length. Both strings can be passed to a DLL procedure. That DLL procedure can store up to 255 characters in the string without causing an error.

Another important consideration is the way Visual Basic stores strings and the way Visual C and C++ store them. In C, strings are stored as consecutive ASCII characters. A special character called a null byte always terminates the string. The constant vbNullString can be used to represent a null byte. Another way to store a null byte in a string is to use the Chr function with the argument zero (0). The following statements create a string containing only a null byte:

```
Dim pstrNull As String*255
pstrNull = Chr(0)
```

When a DLL expects a string as an argument, it may be necessary to pass a null string (a string containing only a null byte). This requires you to store only a null byte in the string and pass it as an argument. The easiest way to accomplish this is to use the constant vbNullString when passing the argument. You cannot use an empty string identified by the following statements:

```
Dim pstrEmpty As String
pstrEmpty = ""
```

Having explained the basic mechanics of passing string arguments to a DLL procedure, you now will see how to use string arguments in the GetTempPathA and GetTempFileNameA functions.

Syntax

```
Declare Function GetTempPath Lib "kernel32" Alias "GetTempPathA" _
    (ByVal nBufferLength As Long, _
    ByVal lpBuffer As String) As Long
```

Dissection

- The DLL function **GetTempPathA** will retrieve the full path, including the drive designator of the directory where Windows creates temporary files.
- The *nBufferLenth* contains a Long Integer data type that defines the length of the character buffer (*lpBuffer*) used to store the temporary file path.
- The *lpBuffer* argument contains the address of the string variable where the path of the temporary directory is stored.
- If the function is successful, the value returned is the number of characters copied to the string named *lpBuffer*. If the function fails for any reason, the value zero (0) is returned.

Notes

The TMP and TEMP environment variables determine the setting of lpBuffer. If TMP is defined, *lpBuffer* contains the value of TMP. If TMP is not defined and TEMP is defined, then *lpBuffer* contains the value of TEMP. If neither is defined, then the full path of the current directory is returned.

The GetTempFileNameA function has the following syntax:

Syntax

```
Declare Function GetTempFileName Lib "kernel32" Alias _
    "GetTempFileNameA" _
    (ByVal lpszPath As String, _
    ByVal lpPrefixString As String, _
    ByVal wUnique As Long, _
    ByVal lpTempFileName As String) As Long
```

Dissection

- The **GetTempFileNameA** function either creates a temporary file or creates a name for a temporary file.
- The argument *lpszPath* contains the full path where the temporary file will be created. Usually, this value is determined by calling the GetTempPathA function.
- The *lpPrefixString* contains a string-character prefix. GetTempFileNameA uses the first three characters of the string as the prefix of the file name. This string must be a null terminated string.
- The *wUnique* flag is an integer. The GetTempFileNameA function converts this value to a hexadecimal number that is used to derive a file name. If the value is zero (0), the hexadecimal string is derived from the system date. Windows guarantees that the file name already does not exist on the system. If this value is not zero (0), the value is converted to a hexadecimal string and is used as the basis for the temporary file name. Windows does not test whether or not the file exists.

- The *lpTempFileName* argument contains the memory address of the string where the temporary file name is stored.
- If successful, GetTempFileNameA returns a unique numeric value used in the temporary file name. If the function fails, the value zero (0) is returned.

To illustrate the use of these two functions and the dangers of processing strings with DLL arguments, you will create a Public function procedure in the standard module named API.bas that ultimately will call these two DLL procedures. Again, this procedure is a wrapper procedure. This will allow a developer to call a Visual Basic function that will create a temporary file name without having to worry about the details of calling a DLL procedure. Again, this illustrates the technique of creating a wrapper procedure. These two DLLs have already been declared in the standard module. The next step is to create a Public general procedure that will call these DLLs. Consider the following statements:

```
Public Function GetTempFileA( ) As String
    Dim pstrPrefix As String * 4
    Dim pstrPath As String * 255
    Dim pstrFileName As String * 1024
    Dim pintSize As Integer
    Dim plngSize As Long
    pstrPrefix = "VBT" & Chr(0)
    pintSize = GetTempPathA(255, pstrPath)
    plngSize = GetTempFileNameA(pstrPath, _
        pstrPrefix, 0, pstrFileName)
    GetTempFileA = pstrFileName
End Function
```

This function requires careful analysis. First, consider the following statements to declare the variable pstrPath used to store the path of the temporary directory and the syntax of the GetTempPathA function:

```
Dim pintSize As Integer
Dim pstrPath As String * 255
pintSize = GetTempPathA(255, pstrPath)
```

The first important point to consider is that pstrPath is declared as a fixed-length string 255 characters in size. As such, the memory is allocated for a 255-character string when the variable is declared. Remember, the DLL procedure will not increase the size of the string passed as an argument. As such, the following statement most certainly would generate an error:

```
Dim pintSize As Integer
Dim pstrPath As String
pintSize = GetTempPathA(255, pstrPath)
```

In the preceding statements, a variable-length string is used. When variable-length strings are used, however, memory is allocated and deallocated by Visual Basic as characters are stored in the string. Because nothing has been stored in the string, there is no memory allocated in the string to store the path returned by GetTempPathA. As such, the DLL procedure will overwrite the memory used by another variable and cause errors.

One common task is to copy data from an original file that is opened in a temporary file. This way, the original contents of the original file can be restored if the file becomes corrupted or the user makes some error from which they cannot recover. For example, in a data processing example, you may want to copy a particular database file to a temporary file before opening the database. This requires that you learn how to call another DLL procedure to copy files.

Syntax

Declare Function CopyFile Lib "kernel32" Alias _
"CopyFileA" _
(ByVal *lpExistingFileName* **As String, _**
ByVal *lpNewFileName* **As String, _**
ByVal *bFailIfExists* **As Long) As Long**

Declare Function DeleteFile Lib "kernel32" Alias _
"DeleteFileA" _
(ByVal *lpFileName* **As String) As Long**

Dissection

- The **CopyFileA** function is located in the kernel32 library and makes a copy of an existing file.
- The **DeleteFileA** function is located in the kernel32 library and removes an existing file from the disk.
- The *lpExistingFileName* argument is a null-terminated string containing the file to be copied. You can think of this as the source file.
- The *lpNewFileName* is a null-terminated string containing the destination file.
- *bFailIfExists* actually is a Boolean variable that can be True or False. If True, the destination file will be overwritten if it already exists. If False, the file will not be overwritten.

In this example, you will modify the mnuFileOpen_Click event procedure you created in the first section to make a copy of the file that is opened to a temporary directory. This example is intended to illustrate the use of the Windows DLL functions that create and copy temporary files. Part of the implementation is notably absent. The program does not keep track of temporary files once created. This could be implemented easily by creating an array containing the temporary files corresponding to a particular open file. It also does not have a mechanism to copy temporary files back to the original files. Finally, there is not a provision to delete temporary files.

To create and copy temporary files:

1. Create the following general procedures in the standard module named **API.bas**:

```
Public Sub Copy(pstrSource As String, pstrDest _
    As String)
    Dim pblnReturn As Boolean
    pstrSource = pstrSource & Chr(0)
    pblnReturn = CopyFile(pstrSource, pstrDest, False)
End Sub

Public Function GetTempFile( ) As String
    Dim pstrPrefix As String * 4
    Dim pstrPath As String * 255
    Dim pstrFileName As String * 1024
    Dim pintSize As Integer
    Dim plngSize As Long
    pstrPrefix = "VBT" & Chr(0)
    pintSize = GetTempPath(255, pstrPath)
    plngSize = GetTempFileName(pstrPath, _
        pstrPrefix, 0, pstrFileName)
    GetTempFile = pstrFileName
End Function
```

2. Modify the **mnuFileOpen_Click** event procedure in the form named **frmGSC** so it calls the following general procedure:

```
    mnuFileList(1).Caption = cdl1.filename
    pstrTemp = GetTempFile
    Call Copy(cdl1.filename, pstrTemp)
    Exit Sub
CancelError:
```

3. Test the program. A temporary file will be created in the appropriate folder depending on the configuration of your system.

Passing Properties

Passing property values to a DLL procedure is very similar to passing variables. When passing properties that contain strings, however, you cannot pass the property directly in a DLL argument. For example, suppose you wanted to store the path of the Windows temporary directory in another object like a text box. As such, you may be tempted to enter the following statements:

```
Dim pstrTempPath As String * 255
pintSize = GetTempPath(255, Text1.Text)
```

This will not work. Instead, you must use another technique. Remember, strings must be passed to a DLL procedure by value. This causes a pointer to be passed containing an address of the first character of the string. To use a string property as an argument in a DLL call, you must create a temporary variable to hold the string, and read and write the variable.

```
Dim pstrTempPath As String * 255
pstrTempPath = Text1.Text
pintSize = GetTempPath(255, pstrTempPath)
```

Passing Null Pointers

Another special case arises when a DLL procedure expects a null pointer. Conceptually, a null pointer is something like an object variable that references Nothing. A null pointer typically is used to pass a string that contains no data. A null pointer and an empty string are not the same. For example, the following statement creates an empty string, but is not a null pointer:

```
Dim pstrDemo As String 255
pstrDemo = ""
```

Passing a null pointer to a Windows DLL can be accomplished using two different techniques. One technique is to use the constant value vbNullString. A second method is to pass a Long Integer argument to the string where the Long Integer argument has the value of zero (0).

Windows Messaging

The concept of a window is fundamental to the Windows operating system. Every window is derived from a class; or in other words, every window belongs to a class. An intrinsic command button or list box is derived from a specific class. Command buttons are derived from the BUTTON class and list boxes are derived from the LISTBOX class. ActiveX controls belonging to the set of Windows common controls also are derived from a WINDOW class. For example, the ListView and TreeView controls are derived from the WC_LISTVIEW and WC_TREEVIEW classes, respectively.

The operating system communicates with different windows by sending messages to them. The window then can respond to the message or ignore it. Conceptually, this is like an event. For example, when you create a command button (a window), the operating system sends a message to the button causing it to execute code (typically a Click event). Understanding the details of Windows messaging is beyond the scope of this book. The important point to note is that Visual Basic events really are nothing more than messages sent by the Windows operating system.

Callback Functions

If you are familiar with the C programming language, the discussion that follows likely will be familiar to you. If you have not seen the capabilities of C pointers before, however, the concept of a callback function will be less intuitive. To introduce the concept of a callback function, consider the ways you know how to call a Function or Sub procedure in Visual Basic.

- You can call a Function or Sub procedure explicitly by writing a statement to call it. While the syntax differs slightly between standard and class modules, the ultimate action is the same. The Function or Sub procedure is executed in direct response to being called from a statement that you wrote.
- An event procedure can be executed in response to some event. The important point here is that an event is generated that in turn causes the code in the event procedure to be executed. In this situation, you do not call the event procedure explicitly. Rather, it is executed automatically in response to some event generated by Windows.
- When you created an ActiveX control, as the author you could raise an event. This would cause Visual Basic to respond to an event procedure written by a developer.

With the release of Visual Basic 5.0, you now can execute procedures in a different way. You now can call Windows DLL functions that will examine certain system objects, like the open windows on the system. For each object examined, Windows will execute a specific Visual Basic function. This mode of execution is referred to as a callback function. Creating a callback function in Visual Basic is no different than creating any other Visual Basic function. How that function gets called is a completely different matter. You saw in Chapter 11 how to raise events from Visual Basic thereby causing a procedure you declared to be executed. In this case, the process was rather automatic. A callback function is a variation of this technique. You register a procedure to a Windows function. When a Windows event is fired, Windows will execute the callback procedure you registered.

Understanding the mechanics of a callback function may be best understood by looking at a specific example, then explaining the syntax and mechanics in more detail. There are two phases to implementing a callback function. First, you must register your callback function with Windows. You do this by calling a Windows function with an argument that indicates the name of the Visual Basic function to be called when a specific Windows event occurs. Second, you write the Visual Basic function that Windows will call. This function is called by Windows and works much like any other event. The difference is that the Visual Basic function does not correspond to an actual control event.

In this example, you will create a simple callback function that illustrates a completely new technique to implement a well-known task. You have used the Controls collection to iterate through the controls on a form. You now will see a very different technique to do nearly the same thing. Imagine that you have a form with many different frames that divide the form into functional areas. Imagine also that the frame contains the controls on the form. In this example, you will see another way to manipulate multiple command buttons created on a frame as a group. This example is very simple but it does illustrate the use of a callback function.

There is a Windows DLL function named EnumChildWindows that will enumerate the windows in your program, or any program for that matter. Remember, a form is a window and the form contains the control instances created on it. As such, the control instances are considered child windows of the form. A frame also can be used as a container for controls. When a frame contains a control, the control is considered a child of the frame, which is in turn a child of the form.

Syntax

Declare Function EnumChildWindows Lib "user32" _
(ByVal *hWndParent* **As Long, _**
ByVal *lpEnumFunc* **As Long, _**
ByVal *lparam* **As Long) As Boolean**

Dissection

- The **EnumChildWindows** function is in the user32.dll library. It will execute a callback function for each window that is enumerated.
- *hWndParent* contains the handle to the parent window.
- *lpEnumFunc* contains the memory address of the callback function to be executed.
- *lparam* contains an application-defined value that will be passed to the callback function.

To call the EnumChildWindows DLL, you must learn about another Visual Basic operator called the AddressOf keyword. The AddressOf keyword is used to pass the address of a callback procedure to a Windows DLL function. To illustrate the use of the AddressOf keyword, assume that the Visual Basic callback procedure named SaveButtons has been declared and that the frame named fraContainer exists.

```
Dim pblnOK As Boolean
pblnOK = EnumChildWindows(fraContainer.hWnd, _
    AddressOf SaveButtons, 0)
```

The preceding statements call the Windows DLL named EnumChildWindows to enumerate all the child windows of fraContainer. For each window enumerated, the SaveButtons function will be called.

To create a callback function:

1 Enter the following statements in the **cmdCallback_Click** event procedure of frmGSC:

```
Dim pblnOK As Boolean
pblnOK = EnumChildWindows(fraContainer.hWnd, _
    AddressOf SaveButtons, 0)
```

2 Create the following callback procedure in the standard module named **API.bas**. The callback procedure must be in a standard module. They will not work in form or class modules.

```
Public Function SaveButtons(ByVal hWnd As Long, _
    ByVal lparam As Long) As Boolean
    Dim pintSize As Integer
    Dim pstrText As String
    pstrText = String(255, 0)
    pintSize = GetWindowText(hWnd, pstrText, _
        Len(pstrText))
    frmGSC.lstButtons.AddItem Trim(pstrText)
    SaveButtons = True
End Function
```

3 Test the program. Click the **Callback** command button. The caption of the command buttons is displayed in the list box.

Executing Other Programs

There are circumstances when a program needs to call another executable program. For example, suppose you had created a complex program consisting of several executable files. Each of these .exe files was a stand-alone executable. You could create another program consisting of only a toolbar. Each button on the toolbar then would be used to start one of the different executable programs. Conceptually, this is similar to having the Microsoft Office toolbar visible on the screen. The buttons on the toolbar are used to execute the individual Microsoft Office programs. Executing a program from Visual Basic is accomplished using the Shell function.

Syntax **Shell**(*pathname*[,*windowstyle*])

Dissection

- The *pathname* argument must contain the full path, including the drive designator, of the file to be executed.
- The optional *windowstyle* argument can contain a constant value indicating how the window will appear to the user when it is opened. If set to the constant vbHide, the window is hidden. If set to vbNormalFocus, the new window has focus and is displayed with its original size and position. The constants vbMinimizedFocus and vbMaximizedFocus cause the window to be displayed as an icon or maximized, respectively. The constants vbNormalNoFocus and vbMinimizedNoFocus cause the active window to remain active and the new window not to receive focus.

Code Example	`Dim pintID As Long` `pintID = Shell("C:\demo.exe", vbNormalFocus)`
Code Dissection	The previous statement attempts to execute the executable file named Demo.exe located in the root directory of drive C. If the file does not exist, an error will be returned. The window displayed by the executable program will be displayed using normal focus.

The Shell command has many uses. In this example, you will create a general-purpose application of the Shell function where the user can select an .exe file using the CommonDialog control. The file selected then is executed.

To execute a program with the Shell function:

1. On the form named **frmGSC**, enter the following statements in the **cmdShell_Click** event procedure:

```
On Error Resume Next
    Dim pintID As Long
    cdl1.Filter = "Executable files (*.exe)|*.exe"
    cdl1.ShowOpen
    pintID = Shell(cdl1.filename, vbNormalFocus)
```

2. Test the program. Click the **Shell** command button, then select an executable file. Open the file then the Shell statement will execute the selected file.

These statements are very simple. The user using the CommonDialog control selects a file name. The FileName argument is passed to the Shell function for execution. The constant vbNormalFocus is used so the window will get focus and will be restored to its normal size and position.

SUMMARY

Two significant topics were presented in this chapter that pertain more to programming in the Windows environment than to Visual Basic. These topics included reading and writing data to the Registry and calling Windows operating system functions contained in dynamic link libraries (DLLs).

- The Registry is contained in two files named System.dat and User.dat. The first file contains information pertaining to the system in general and the second contains information pertaining to the users on the system. Information in the Registry is organized hierarchically into trees and subtrees. Subtrees in turn can contain additional subtrees or data.
- The Registry can be edited manually using a program called RegEdit. The interface for RegEdit is very similar to the Windows Explorer program. The left-hand pane is used to navigate through the trees and subtrees. The right-hand pane displays the keys and associated data values.
- Visual Basic supports functions that provide limited Registry editing capabilities. The GetSetting function reads a value from the Registry and the SaveSetting function writes a value to the Registry. The DeleteSetting function removes a Registry value. Using these functions, all Registry entries are read and written from and to the folder named HKEY_USERS\Default\Software\VB and VBA Program Settings. To manipulate Registry information in other sections, DLL functions must be used.
- Servers usually must be registered on the system before they can be used. Manual registration can be accomplished using the RegSvr32.exe program.

Windows DLLs allow you to expand the power and flexibility of Visual Basic by accessing the exposed functions of the Windows operating system itself. The process of using DLLs in a Visual Basic program consists of declaring the DLL and then calling it.

- Declaring a DLL procedure in a Visual Basic program is accomplished using the Declare statement. The Declare statement has options to specify a specific Windows library, the arguments required by the function, and optionally an alias for the function.
- Once declared, the syntax to call a DLL procedure is the same as calling any other Visual Basic Function or Sub procedure.
- The API Viewer typically is used as a tool to help you add the correct DLL declarations to a Visual Basic program.
- The difficulty in calling DLL procedures involves determining whether or not the arguments are passed by reference or by value. Passing arguments improperly most likely will result in the program, and Visual Basic for that matter, crashing.

The Visual Basic Shell function provides your Visual Basic program with the capability to execute other programs. Any .exe file typically run from the command line can be run from Visual Basic using the Shell function.

QUESTIONS

1. Which of the following are valid trees in the Registry?
   a. HKEY_LOCAL_MACHINE.
   b. HKEY_USERS.
   c. HKEY_CURRENT_CONFIG.
   d. Both a and b.
   e. All of the above.
2. The ___________ function will read a setting from the Registry and the ___________ function will write a value.
   a. ReadSetting, WriteSetting
   b. GetSetting, SaveSetting
   c. GetRegEnt, SaveRegEnt
   d. Read, Write
   e. none of the above
3. The Visual Basic statements to manipulate the Registry store information in which subtree?
   a. VB and VBA Program Settings.
   b. Visual Basic.
   c. Settings.
   d. Program Files.
   e. Program Settings.
4. You can use the Registry Editor to ___________.
   a. add entries to the Registry
   b. change the values corresponding to a particular Registry key
   c. delete entries from the Registry
   d. both a and c
   e. all of the above
5. Which are valid types of linking?
   a. Common linking.
   b. Static linking.
   c. Dynamic linking.
   d. Both a and b.
   e. Both b and c.
6. Which of the following statements is false regarding the declaration of DLL procedures?
   a. A Declare statement can exist in a standard module.
   b. A Declare statement can exist in a form module.
   c. The Alias keyword is used to call a DLL by a different name.
   d. The Lib keyword contains the name of the Windows library.
   e. All DLL procedures are Sub procedures.

7. Which of the following elements does the API Viewer list?
   a. Constants.
   b. Function Declarations.
   c. Types.
   d. Both a and b.
   e. All of the above.
8. What is the name of the DLL function used to set a window's position?
   a. WindowPosition.
   b. Set.
   c. SetWindowPosition.
   d. SetWindowPos.
   e. SetPosition.
9. What are the names of the two DLL procedures used to obtain the temporary directory and create a temporary file?
   a. GetTempPathA, GetTempFileNameA.
   b. GetTmpPathA, GetTmpFileNameA.
   c. GetTempDirA, GetTempFileA.
   d. GetTempDir, GetTempFile.
   e. None of the above.
10. What are the names of the DLL procedures to copy and delete files?
    a. WinCopy, WinDelete.
    b. Copy, Delete.
    c. CopyFile, DeleteFile.
    d. WinCopyFile, WinDeleteFile.
    e. CopyFileA, DeleteFileA.
11. When passing string properties to a DLL procedure, you must ____________.
    a. use the AddressOf keyword
    b. use a temporary variable to store the property
    c. use the string function
    d. both a and b
    e. both a and c
12. A callback function is ____________.
    a. written in Visual Basic
    b. called by a Windows DLL
    c. not possible using Visual Basic
    d. all of the above
    e. none of the above
13. Write the necessary statement to read the Registry value for the application named **Demo**, the section named **Position**, and the key named **Top**.
14. Write the necessary statement to write the value 150 to the Registry setting defined in the previous section.
15. Write the necessary statement to delete the Registry setting having an application name of **Demo**, the section named **Position**, and a key named **Left**.
16. Write the necessary statement to call the executable file named **Demo.exe** in the root directory of the drive C.

EXERCISES

1. In this exercise you will save information to the Registry when a program exits and read information when the program starts. Many programs save the current condition of open windows when a program is closed and restore the window to the same condition when the program starts.

a. Create a new project and set the Name property of the form to **frmEx1Main**. Save the form using the name **Chapter.14\Exercise\frmEx1Main.frm** and the project using the name **Chapter.14\Exercise\Exercise1.vbp**. This should be the Startup form for the program.

b. Create two additional forms named **frmEx1Sub1** and **frmEx1Sub2**. On each form, create three command buttons. Two of the command buttons set the focus to the other two forms. Thus, on frmEx1Main, one command button should display frmEx1Sub1, and the other should display frmEx1Sub2.

c. One of the command buttons should exit the program.

d. Whenever the program is exited (by calling the Exit command button on one of the forms), a general procedure should be called to write the current condition of the open forms. Consider the following implementation. Delete the information pertaining to the current state of the program from the Registry. Create a For Each loop in this general procedure to examine the Forms collection. For each form, save the size and position related properties to a section in the Registry.

e. When the program is started, a procedure needs to be executed that will read the contents of the Registry to restore the contents of the program to the state it was in when the program was closed.

f. Test the program.

2. In this exercise you will use the Registry and Shell function to execute programs and keep a list of the programs that were recently executed.

a. Create a new project and set the Name property of the form to **frmExercise2**. Save the form using the name **Chapter.14\Exercise\frmExercise2.frm** and the project using the name **Chapter.14\Exercise\Exercise2.vbp**.

b. On the form, create a menu named **File**.

c. On the File menu, create a menu named **Execute**, that when clicked will display a CommonDialog control.

d. Using the file returned by the CommonDialog, execute the Shell command to execute the file.

e. Using the technique presented in the chapter, create a menu control array with the first element having a separator bar as its caption. This control array should appear at the end of the File menu.

f. When the **Execute** menu is clicked and just before executing the command, add the command to the control array.

g. When the form is unloaded, write the list of recently executed files to the Registry.

h. When the form is loaded, read the list of recently executed files from the registry. Note that the program should list at most 10 files.

i. Test the program.

3. In this exercise you will call DLLs to copy files.

a. Create a new project and set the Name property of the form to **frmExercise3.** Save the form using the name **Chapter.14\Exercise\frmExercise3.frm** and the project using the name **Chapter.14\Exercise\Exercise3.vbp.**

b. On the form create two text boxes. These will be used to specify the source file and destination file.

c. Create a command button with the caption **Set Source** that will display a common dialog to locate an existing file. This file should be displayed in the source text box.

d. Create another button named **Set Destination** that will display a common dialog control to create a new file. This file should be displayed in the destination text box.

e. Create another button that will copy the source file to the destination file. You will need to declare the necessary DLL procedure and call it to copy the file.

f. Test the program.

CHAPTER

Creating Visual Basic Programs for Distribution

15

Understanding the Visual Basic Setup Wizard

case▶ Software Sales Incorporated sells commercial software. As such, their software must be distributed to their customers on either floppy disk or CD-ROM. The end user of the software then runs a setup program to install the software. The software they sell must be compiled so it is optimized for performance. This software also must be able to display help for the user.

SECTION A

objectives

In this section you will:

- Compile programs into executable files
- Understand the types of executable files supported by Visual Basic
- Understand the different options available to optimize a program
- Conditionally compile code into a program

The Visual Basic Compiler

Previewing the Completed Application

The focus of this chapter is not on the application itself. Rather, the chapter discusses three separate topics related to creating distributable programs.

- How to compile an application to achieve peak performance—the completed application for the chapter was created specifically to be computationally intensive so the performance effects of different program compilation options are noticeable. The completed application determines whether or not a number is a prime number. As you probably are well aware, a prime number is a number that is divisible only by one (1), and itself.
- How to prepare a program for distribution—most programs that are developed must be distributed to other computers, and there are several physical media used to distribute a program. Common media include floppy disks, CD-ROMs, and distribution over the Internet.
- How to implement help for an application—any robust application likely will have a Help system to guide the user through the program's usage.

The steps that follow assume you are familiar with installing programs using a Setup program and uninstalling programs using the Add/Remove Properties dialog on the Control Panel. Completion of the following steps requires that you have permission to write to the system disk and update the Windows Registry. If you do not, you will not be able to complete the following steps.

To preview the completed application:

1 The file **Chapter.15\Complete\Setup\Setup.exe** contains the necessary code to install the example program for this chapter on your system. Make sure to set the drive designator as necessary depending on your system. Using Windows Explorer, examine the files in this folder.

You will see several files in this folder. The file named **Setup.exe** is the executable file that the user (you, in this case) will run to install the application. The file named **Setup.lst** contains configuration information used by the Setup.exe program to install the program. The remaining files all appear with an underscore as the last character of the three-character suffix. These files represent all the additional files necessary for your Visual Basic program to execute. They have been compressed to minimize the disk space used for the distribution files. Executing the Setup.exe file has the same effect as running a Setup program used to install just about any application. This Setup executable was created using a tool supplied with Visual Basic called the Setup Wizard. In this chapter, the term Setup Kit will be used to refer to all the files necessary to install a particular Visual Basic program.

2 In Windows Explorer, double-click **Setup.exe** to execute the file. The Setup window will appear as shown in Figure 15-1.

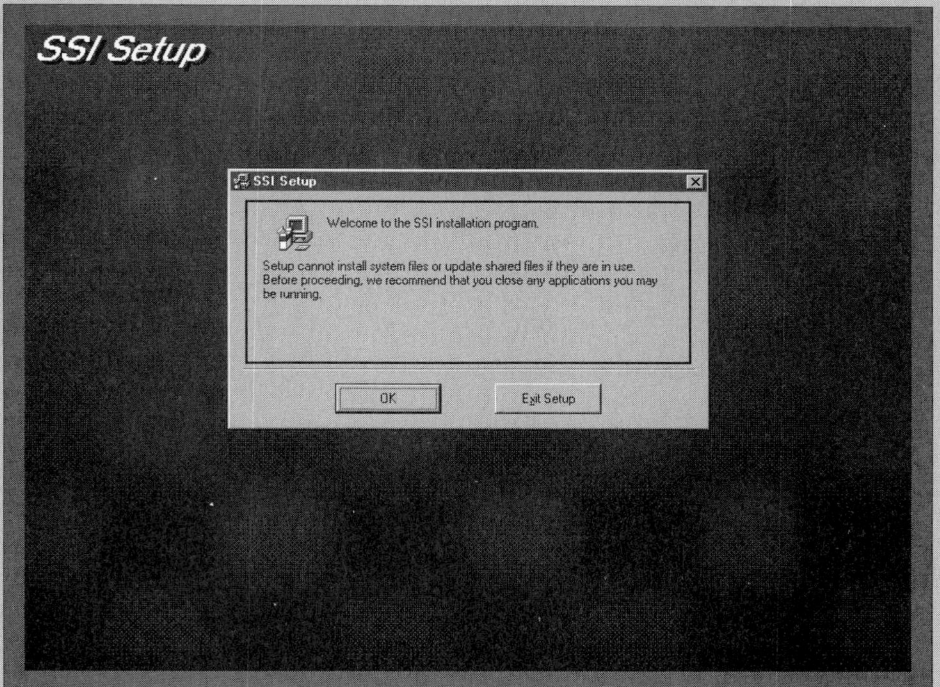

Figure 15-1: Running Setup

As shown in Figure 15-1, Setup will warn you to close other programs before attempting to install the software. You should do so before proceeding. Setup will uncompress and install any DLLs and other necessary files for the program to run. If another application currently is using these files, then an error will occur because Setup will not be able to overwrite a file that presently is open.

3 The next dialog displayed by Setup contains a button to install the application. After closing any other running applications, click this button. The Setup program will install the executable file named **SSI.exe**, then other necessary files for the program to run. It also will add an entry to the Start menu so the program can be located easily. It also will register the program on the system.

When you click the button to install the SSI program, Setup is performing several tasks for you. It copies the executable file (the program run by the user) to the hard disk. It also copies any support files necessary for the program to run properly. These files include the .ocx files corresponding to a particular ActiveX control used by your program, or other DLLs that may be used by the program or component ActiveX control. One of the DLLs usually is the Visual Basic run-time library. This library is required to run any Visual Basic executable.

We have played an interesting trick with regard to this Setup file so all the necessary files would fit on a single floppy disk. One of the files required for a program to run is the Visual Basic run-time library. This file is named Msvbvm50.dll and is not included in the Setup Kit. If Visual Basic is not already installed on your computer, this file will not exist and Visual Basic programs will not run. Because we assume that the computer you are using will have Visual Basic installed, and consequently this file, the Setup kit does not contain this file.

4 Execute the **SSI** program on the **Start** menu. By default, the SSI entry will appear on the Programs menu. The main form for the SSI program is shown in Figure 15-2.

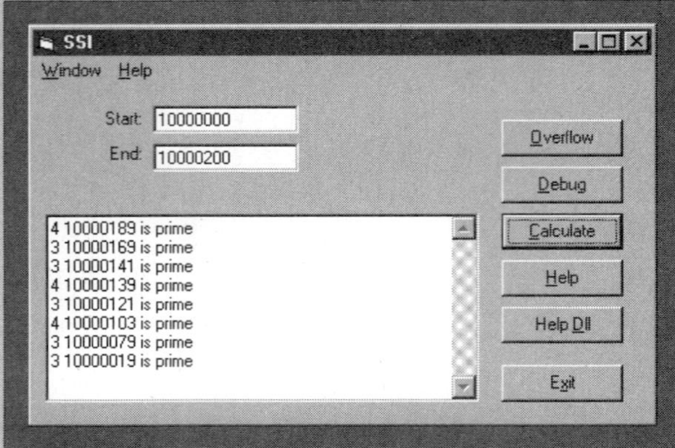

Figure 15-2: Main form

As shown in Figure 15-2, the program contains two text boxes having a caption of Start and End. These values represent the lower and upper bound of a range of numbers. For each Long Integer data type within this range, the program will determine whether or not the number is a prime number. If it is, the number will be printed. In the example shown in Figure 15-2, the range of numbers specified was between 10,000,000 and 10,000,200. For each number in the range, the number was tested to determine if it was a prime number. If the number was prime, it was displayed in the multiline text box at the bottom of the form. The number in the left-hand column of the text box is the elapsed seconds it took to determine that a specific number was prime.

5 The task of computing prime numbers is not the focus of this chapter. The program was created because it is computationally intensive and can be used to illustrate how compiling a Visual Basic program in different ways can effect program performance. Enter the value **10,000,000** in the Start text box, then the value **10,000,200** in the End text box, then click the **Calculate** button. The prime numbers between the above range will be printed as shown in Figure 15-2. Do not enter the comma separators in the text boxes. They are shown here to improve readability.

6 Exit the program by clicking the **Exit** button.

In addition to installing software, it often needs to be uninstalled. The Setup program supplied with Visual Basic contains the necessary helper applications to remove an application. To remove an application, you use the Add/Remove Programs dialog on the Control Panel. You now will remove the program you just installed.

To remove an application:

1 Click the **Settings** option on the **Start** menu, then select **Control Panel.**

2 On the Control Panel, double-click **Add/Remove Programs.**

3 On the Add/Remove Programs dialog, locate the program named **SSI** in the list box and click **Add/Remove** to remove the program. Windows will prompt you warning that you are about to remove software from the system. Continue to remove the program.

4 Note that the program has been removed from the system and the Start menu.

Almost all the code for the program has been written. In this chapter, you will compile the program in different ways to see the effect on program performance, create the Setup file for the program, and write the few lines of code necessary to display Help topics.

The Visual Basic Compiler

As you know, the process of translating language statements (in this case, Visual Basic statements) into an executable program is called **compilation**. Visual Basic can compile a program into two types of executable files.

The first type of file is called **p-code**. When you compile a program into p-code, the p-code file that is produced by Visual Basic cannot run on its own. Rather, a p-code file is an **interpreted file**. When a p-code file is executed, the statements in the file are interpreted by the Visual Basic run-time library, translated to an executable form, then executed.

The other type of executable file produced by Visual Basic is called **native code**. A native code executable file does not require the Visual Basic run-time library. In general, executing Visual Basic statements that are compiled to native code is faster than executing the same statements compiled into p-code.

Whether to compile a program into p-code or native code depends on the nature of the program itself. In general, native code will run faster than p-code. Depending on several factors, however, like whether your program is computationally intensive, the difference in performance may be minimal. The following list summarizes the circumstances where a program will not benefit by being compiled into native code instead of p-code:

- Programs that spend most of their time inside form modules performing tasks like responding to events, and processing character input and output will benefit very little by compiling a program to native code.
- Programs that manipulate objects extensively will not benefit from native code. For example, if the bulk of the program statements are reading and writing object properties, or calling methods, program performance will improve very little by compiling a program to native code.
- Calling DLL functions. The performance of p-code and native code is about the same. This is because most of the execution time is spent inside the DLL, and the overhead to call a DLL function is about the same for both native code and p-code.

The Compile tab on the Project Properties dialog contains several options to define how Visual Basic will compile a project. Figure 15-3 shows the Compile tab.

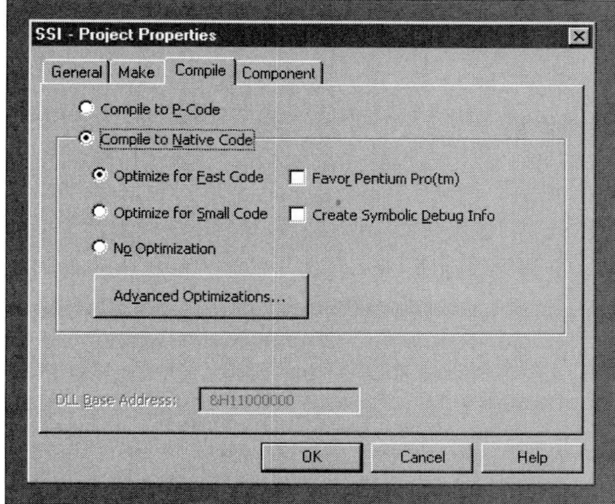

Figure 15-3: Compile tab

As shown in Figure 15-3, a program can be compiled into either p-code or native code. When a program is compiled into native code, there are several optimizations that Visual Basic can perform.

- In general, there is a tradeoff between code size (the size of the executable file produced) and the speed of the executable file. If **Optimize for Fast Code** is selected, the compiler will optimize the executable file for speed over size. If **Optimize for Small Code** is selected, the compiler will optimize the executable for size over speed.
- The **No Optimization** option causes Visual Basic to perform no optimization on the executable file.
- The **Favor Pentium Pro(tm)** option causes programs that are executed on a Pentium Pro processor to run faster if this option is selected. If the program is run on other types of processors, however, degradation in performance will be seen.
- The **Create Symbolic Debug Info** option is used when the executable file will be debugged by another program like Visual C++. This chapter does not discuss how to debug Visual Basic programs in other languages like C++.

While there are no hard and fast rules that apply to every program you create, the following characteristics apply to most programs. Most systems today have large disks. As such, most users likely will prefer a faster program to a smaller program that runs slower. Furthermore, compiling a program to native code almost always will run faster than a program compiled to p-code. In some cases, however, the performance improvement will be minimal.

As shown in Figure 15-3, there is a button having a caption of Advanced Optimizations. Clicking the Advanced Optimizations button activates the Advanced Optimizations dialog. This dialog contains an additional set of options that can improve the performance of a computationally intensive program considerably.

Programming tip

The options on the Advanced Optimizations dialog contain optimization options that should be used with great caution. Checking any of these options will cause the executable file to ignore common tests to make sure that both array references and arithmetic operations are correct. Omitting these "sanity checks" may cause programs to crash, or worse, produce incorrect results.

The Assume No Aliasing check box tells the compiler that the program does not use aliases. Aliasing occurs when a program uses multiple names to refer to the same variable or memory location. It commonly occurs when using arguments that are passed by reference as shown in the following code segment:

```
Dim gintY As Integer
Sub Foo(ByRef pintX As Integer)
    pintX=5
    gintY=6
End Sub
Sub Main
    Foo gintY
End Sub
```

The global variable named gintY is being referenced by two different names. Inside the Sub procedure, the argument pintX points to the same memory used by the global variable named gintY. In this case, pintX and gintY are aliases to the same memory location. In this circumstance, if the Assume No Aliasing check box is checked, the program will produce incorrect results.

Each time you write a statement that reads or writes data from or to an array, Visual Basic checks that a valid element is referenced (subscript is valid). That is, Visual Basic checks that the subscript(s) used is(are) between the lower and upper bound of the array dimension. If the array subscript is not within the bounds of the array dimension, Visual Basic will, by default, generate a run-time error. Checking the Remove Array Bounds Checks check box causes these array bound checks not to be performed. While this has the effect of improving program performance, a reference to an invalid array element can cause invalid results to be generated or the program may crash. Consider an array that has been declared with 10 elements. Assume also that you have written a statement to store a value in the 11th array element that does not exist. If you have removed the array bound checking, then Visual Basic will compute a memory address for this nonexistent element and store a value in that memory address. This memory address likely is used by another variable, or may contain a reference (pointer) to an object. Because the contents of the memory address have been corrupted, the variable likely would contain an incorrect value, or the object reference would no longer point to a valid object. Rather, it would point to some arbitrary memory location.

Each time you perform integer arithmetic on a value, Visual Basic checks that the value is within the range of the underlying data type and will generate a run-time error in the event of numeric overflow or underflow. For example, the largest positive number that can be stored in an Integer data type is 32767 and the largest negative number that can be stored in an Integer data type is –32768. Attempting to store a number outside of this range will cause an overflow or underflow condition. Adding one (1) to 32767 will cause an overflow condition and subtracting one (1) from –32768 will cause an underflow condition. By default, a run-time error will occur in these circumstances because of checking for underflow or overflow. If the Remove Integer Overflow Checks check box is marked, Visual Basic will not perform these checks. As an example, consider the following statements:

```
On Error Resume Next
    Dim pintBad As Integer
    pintBad = 32767
    pintBad = pintBad + 1
    txtBad = pintBad
```

The Integer variable pintBad contains the maximum valid value for an Integer number (32767). By default, adding one (1) to this number will cause a run-time error to occur. If the Remove Integer Overflow Checks check box is checked, the run-time error will not occur, and the value –32768 will be stored in the text box named txtBad. The reason –32768 is stored in the variable stems from the way that integer arithmetic is performed.

In addition to overflow and underflow checks on Integer values, similar checks are made on floating point values. By default, if a numeric overflow or underflow condition occurs when evaluating a floating point expression, then Visual Basic will generate a run-time error. If the Remove Floating Point Error Checks check box is marked, then no run-time error will occur and the program likely will produce incorrect results. The situation is very similar to the one you saw with the integer overflow.

The Allow Unrounded Floating Point Operations check box causes floating point operations not to be rounded. While this may improve the performance of the program, the result of arithmetic expressions is maintained to a much higher precision. This is significant when comparing two floating point numbers in an If statement. Because of the extended precision, and the way floating point arithmetic is performed, two values you may expect to be the same will differ by a very small amount.

The final option is the Remove Safe Pentium(tm) FDIV Checks. This option pertains to some of the first Pentium processors created. These processors had a bug, known as the FDIV bug, which would, in very limited situations, produce incorrect results. The Visual Basic compiler, by default, will produce code that will avoid this bug. If this check box is checked, then this code will not be generated and certain Pentium processors may produce incorrect results in rare situations.

To illustrate the effect of performance based on different compiler options, you will compile the prime number calculator using different compilation options. The prime number calculator contains the following code to determine whether a number is a prime number. This code is by no means the most efficient way to determine whether a number is a prime number. Its purpose is to create a computationally intensive routine that will take more than a few seconds to run.

```
Dim plngPrime As Long, plngCheck As Long
Dim plngMax As Long, ptmpCheck As Long
Dim ptmpPrime As Long, pblnPrime As Boolean
Dim pdatStart As Date, pdatEnd As Date
Dim plngElapsed As Long, plngMin As Long
plngMin = CLng(txtMin)
plngMax = CLng(txtMax)
For plngPrime = plngMin To plngMax
    ptmpPrime = plngPrime
    pdatStart = Time
    For plngCheck = 2 To plngPrime - 1
        ptmpCheck = plngCheck
        If (ptmpPrime Mod (ptmpCheck)) = 0 Then
            pblnPrime = False
            Exit For
        Else
            pblnPrime = True
        End If
    Next
    pdatEnd = Time
    plngElapsed = DateDiff("s", pdatStart, pdatEnd)
    If pblnPrime Then
       txtOut = plngElapsed & " " & _
           plngPrime & " is prime " & vbCrLf & txtOut
    End If
    txtOut.Refresh
    DoEvents
    pblnPrime = False
Next
```

A few words are in order about how the procedure works. First, the procedure tries to determine if a range of numbers is prime. This range of numbers is specified using the text boxes named txtMin and txtMax. The outer For loop examines all the numbers in this range. A prime number is defined as a number that is divisible evenly by the number one (1) and the number itself. Thus, the inner For loop tries to divide the current number by two (2), three (3), four (4), and so on up to the current number. The first time the division does not produce a remainder, the number is not prime and the next number is examined. If a number is determined to be prime, it is printed in the output text box. The start and end time values are used to compute the number of elapsed seconds that were required to determine that a specific number is a prime number.

As this procedure is computationally intensive, compiling the program to native code should be considerably faster than compiling the same program to p-code. You should also note that the executable files also will run faster than running the same program inside the Visual Basic IDE.

To test the different compilation options:

1. Start **Visual Basic.** Load the project group named **Chapter15\Complete\SSI_C.vbp.** Print the code for the project, then exit Visual Basic.
2. Compile the program to p-code and save the executable file as **Chapter.15\Startup\SSI_P.exe.** Use the **Compile** tab in the Project Properties dialog, then select the **Compile to P-Code** option.
3. Compile the program again to native code. Optimize the program for speed, and save the executable file as **Chapter.15\Startup\SSI_N.exe.** Again, use the **Compile** tab in the Project Properties dialog, then select the **Compile to Native Code** option.
4. Run each of the programs outside the Visual Basic IDE. Because the program is computationally intensive, you should see the native code version run much faster than the p-code version. Figure 15-4 shows the times when the program was compiled on a 166 MHz Pentium with adequate memory that the program did not have to be swapped to disk. While your timings may differ depending on the speed of your computer, the relative performance between native code and interpreted code should be similar.

Number	Elapsed seconds (native code)	Elapsed seconds (p-code)
10000189	3	12
10000169	4	12
10000141	3	12
10000139	3	12
10000121	4	12
...		

Figure 15-4: Execution speed

As shown in Figure 15-4, the native code performs between three and four times faster than the compiled p-code. Because this program is computationally intensive, the benefit of compiling to native code is maximized. As mentioned, code that consists mostly of DLL calls or form management will benefit much less from compiling a program to native code.

In summary, the best way to determine the best compiler options for your program is to experiment. Try different options and examine the performance impact of those options. Again there is no hard and fast rule that applies in all cases.

Conditional Compilation

This topic has nothing to do with program compilation from the perspective of optimization. It does relate to program compilation, however, in that conditional compilation allows specific statements to be included or excluded from an executable file.

Just as you can use an If statement to execute different code depending on some condition, you can use another form of an If statement to determine whether or not specific statements in a program are compiled into the executable program. This commonly is called **conditional compilation**. Conditional compilation uses constants and the following form of an If statement:

Syntax

#If *expression* **Then**
statements
[**#ElseIf** *expression-n* **Then**
[*elseifstatements*]]
[#Else
[*elsestatements*]]
#End If

Dissection

- The required *expression* can contain constants, literal values, and operators. The *expression* must evaluate to True or False as in other If statements.
- The required *statements* contain the Visual Basic statements that are included in the executable file if the *expression* is True.
- Like an ordinary If statement, the **#If** statement can contain zero or more **#ElseIf** clauses and an optional **#Else** clause.
- The **#End If** statement marks the end of the **#If** block.

Code Example

```
#If (cDebugLevel = 1) Then
    Debug.Print "Basic Debugging"
#ElseIf (cDebugLevel = 2) Then
    Debug.Print "Extended Debugging"
#End If
```

Code Dissection

The previous statements test the constant value cDebugLevel to determine if its value is one (1) or two (2). If the value is one, the value "Basic Debugging" is printed in the Immediate window. If the value is two (2), then the value "Extended Debugging" is printed in the Immediate window. If the constant is set to a different value, then nothing is printed in the Immediate window. In reality, the values of pertinent program variables likely would be printed in the Immediate window.

There are several reasons to use conditional compilation.

- Debugging—as you develop large programs, you commonly may insert Debug.Print statements into a program to trace the flow of execution and examine the value of variables. After the program is working correctly, you may have removed these statements from the final product. Rather than removing these statements, you can conditionally compile the debugging code into the completed executable and exclude it from the finished product. This way, if you detect a bug in your code, you can enable the debugging code without having to recreate it.
- Multiple configurations—in another scenario, assume that you are developing a software product where the user obtains a license to specific parts of the program; something analogous to the Visual Basic Learning Edition, Professional Edition, or Enterprise Edition. In a situation like this, you can conditionally compile code in modules to enable or disable specific functions.
- Custom configurations—in a final scenario, suppose you have developed a Visual Basic program, but there are a few customizations for specific customers. Rather than maintaining different programs for each customer, you can conditionally compile specific customized code for the customers that need it and omit the customizations for others. This way, you as the developer only need to maintain a single copy of the source code for a program.

To define the values for the constants used in conditional compilation, you use the Conditional Compilation Argument on the Make tab in the Project Properties dialog. To define a constant, you specify the constant name followed by an equals sign (=) followed by a value. Separating each declaration by a full colon (:) can be used to specify multiple constants.

```
cDebugLevel = 1
cDebugLevel = 1 : cOther = 3
```

The first statement declares a constant named cDebugLevel having a value of one (1). The second statement declares two constants named cDebugLevel and cOther, respectively. The first has a value of one (1), and the second a value of three (3). You now can proceed to see how to compile conditionally different statements into a program. While the following example is a simple illustration, it does show how conditional compilation can be used in a program.

To compile code conditionally:

1 Start Visual Basic if necessary and open the project file named **Chapter.15\Startup\SSI_5.vbp.**

2 Enter the following statements into the **cmdDebug_Click** event procedure on the form named **frmSSI**:

```
#If (cDebugLevel = 1) Then
    Debug.Print "Basic Debugging."
#ElseIf (cDebugLevel = 2) Then
    Debug.Print "Extended Debugging."
#End If
```

3 Activate the Project Properties dialog then click the **Make** tab.

4 In the Conditional Compilation Argument text box, enter the following line:

```
cDebugLevel = 1
```

Click **OK**.

5 Test the program. Click the **Debug** command button. The text string "Basic Debugging." is printed in the Immediate window.

6 Change the Conditional Compilation argument to the following:

```
cDebugLevel = 2
```

7 Test the program again. Click the **Debug** command button. The text string "Extended Debugging." is printed in the Immediate window.

These statements illustrate a simple use of conditional compilation. As programs become more complex, you may define several different conditional compilation constants to control the statements included in an executable file.

There are two predefined constants supported by Visual Basic. The #Win16 constant has a value of True on 16 bit systems (Windows 3.1) and a value of False on 32 bit systems. The #Win32 constant has a value of False on 16 bit systems (Windows 3.1) and a value of True on 32 bit systems. Trying to define these constants will cause an error to occur.

SECTION B

objectives

In this section you will:

- **Understand the purpose of the Setup Wizard to create distributable Visual Basic programs**
- **Identify the different files that make up a software distribution**
- **Create a Setup program that will be run by the end user to install an application on a different computer than the computer where the software was developed**
- **Customize the behavior of the Setup program**

Distributing Programs Using the Setup Wizard

Understanding the Visual Basic Setup Wizard

In Chapter 11, you saw how to use the Setup Wizard to create an ActiveX control that was downloadable over the Internet. This topic was included in Chapter 11 because it was specific to ActiveX controls and the Internet. Most of the programs that you create must be distributed to a remote computer. The Internet is but one mechanism for program distribution. It is unlikely that the computer you are using as the developer will be the same computer used by the end user of your program. It also is possible that the user of a program will not be connected to the Internet and will require that software be distributed via floppy disk or CD-ROM. Most often, you as the author of an ActiveX control or the developer of a particular piece of software, will need to distribute your application in a manner convenient to the developer of your ActiveX control or the end user of your application.

Consider the process you go through when you install a software component. Most often it is a simple matter of running a Setup program that exists on a floppy or CD-ROM distribution. Visual Basic supports a wizard that allows you to create a Setup program and distribute the software you create.

The Application Setup Wizard, or just Setup Wizard, has the same characteristics of any other wizard. You complete a series of dialogs. Based on the information you specify in the various dialogs, the Setup Wizard will create the necessary Setup executable file that will be run by the end user. This file will in turn read other files and install them on a remote computer. The Setup Wizard is the easiest way to create a software distribution. Instead of describing all the features of the Setup Wizard, you will see the mechanics first hand of how to create a simple setup distribution.

The Setup Wizard is not part of Visual Basic, but rather is a stand-alone application solely used to distribute programs. The Setup Wizard contains a series of dialogs that lead you through the process of preparing an application for distribution. The first dialog of interest is the Select Project and Options dialog shown in Figure 15-5.

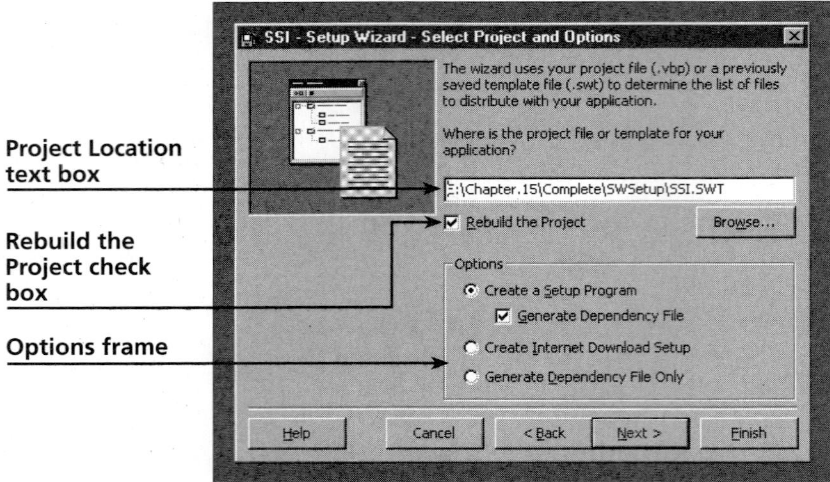

Figure 15-5: Select Project and Options dialog

As shown in Figure 15-5, there are several fields that can be completed. The following list describes those fields:

- The Project Location text box allows you to specify the Visual Basic project file you want to distribute, and the location of that file. Generally, you should not have the project open in Visual Basic when creating the distribution. If the Setup Wizard tries to read the project file while it is open, the Setup Wizard will be unable to build the distribution.
- The Rebuild the Project check box forces the executable project in the Project Location text box to be rebuilt (recompiled). That is, the .exe or .dll file will be recreated from the current module files referenced in the project file. Note that the Setup Wizard does not distribute the source code (module files) that make up a program. It only distributes the executable file(s) necessary for that executable file to run.
- There are several option buttons in the Options frame that control how the software distribution is created. The Create a Setup Program option button will cause a Setup executable to be created.
- The Generate Dependency File check box causes a file to be created that identifies all the .ocx, .dll, or .exe files necessary for your program to run properly. Remember, a project file may include one or more ActiveX controls or reference a particular object library. In these situations, the Visual Basic program is dependent on these necessary support files for the program to run. As such, these files must be distributed to the remote computer. An .ocx file may in turn reference another .dll or other file. Again the Setup Wizard

will analyze the .ocx file so any dlls or other files also will be distributed with the program. The dependency file lists the dependent files and adds them to the software distribution.

- The Generate Dependency File Only option button generates the dependency file but does not cause the entire setup distribution to be created.
- The Create Internet Download Setup option button was covered in the chapters that discussed ActiveX controls.

The second dialog that is of significance is the Distribution Method dialog. It allows you to define whether your software distribution is intended for a CD-ROM device or a floppy disk. There are three option buttons in this dialog as shown in Figure 15-6.

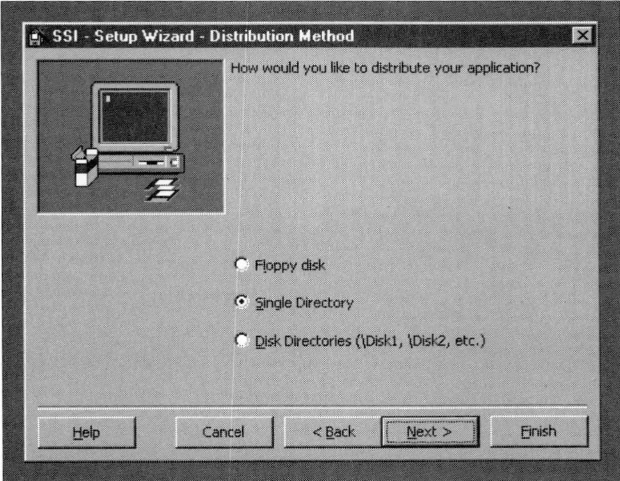

Figure 15-6: Distribution Method dialog

As shown in Figure 15-6, there are three option buttons. The following list describes the purpose of each button:

- The Floppy disk option button will create the actual distribution on floppy disks. If the software distribution will not fit on a single floppy disk, the Setup Wizard will prompt for additional floppy disks as necessary. Note that the Setup Wizard will work with floppy disks having different capacities. For example, you can create a floppy disk distribution for regular or high density 3½-inch floppy disks. After creating the master floppy disks for the distribution, you then can use a disk duplication program like Diskcopy, or some other third party utility, to make duplicate copies of the software distribution. Note that if you are making more than a few duplicate software distribution disks, creating the floppy disks can be a tedious process. There are high-speed disk duplicating machines commercially available to perform this task.
- The Single Directory option button is intended primarily for use when an application will be distributed on a CD-ROM that can hold the entire software

distribution. In this situation, all the distribution files are written to a single directory, which then can be written to a CD-ROM.

- The Disk Directories (\Disk1, \Disk2, etc.) option button commonly is used with floppy disk distributions. Instead of creating the distribution files on individual floppy disks, the distribution files are written to disk directories on the hard disk such that each hard disk directory is intended to be copied to a floppy disk. This option is helpful for testing as it eliminates the need to repeatedly create several floppy disks.

The next dialog of significance depends on which option was chosen in the Distribution Method dialog.

- If the Floppy disk option button was chosen, then the next dialog will ask you to select the name of the floppy disk and the capacity of the disk. Specifying the capacity is necessary so the Setup Wizard can compute the number of files that will fit on a single disk.
- If the Single Directory option button was chosen, then all the files are written to the specified directory. Note that if there are files in the chosen directory, those files will not be deleted. Generally, you should make sure that the directory you choose has no files in it.
- If the Disk Directories (\Disk1, \Disk2, etc.) option button was chosen, then you must select the hard disk directory where the setup files will be created. Folders in this directory will be created and named Disk1, Disk2, Disk3, and so on corresponding to the floppy disks that ultimately will be created.

If your program relies on specific ActiveX controls or other libraries to run, then the program is said to be dependent on those files. For the most part, the Setup Wizard will be able to detect the dependencies from the information contained in the project file. The Confirm Dependencies dialog, shown in Figure 15-7, allows you to modify those dependencies.

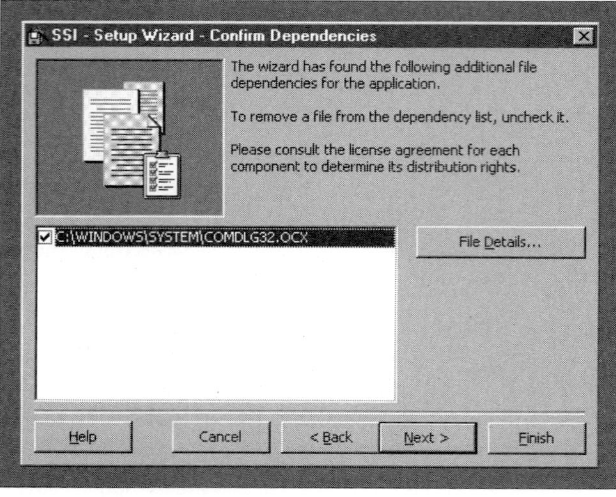

Figure 15-7: Confirm Dependencies dialog

As shown in Figure 15-7, the program is dependent on a single file named COMDLG32.OCX. This file contains the code for the CommonDialog control—the only ActiveX control used in this project. You can remove the dependencies by removing the check from the check box to the left of the dependency entry.

After completing this dialog, the Setup Wizard will proceed to create the software distribution files in the specified directory. It also will display a summary of the files that comprise the distribution as shown in Figure 15-8.

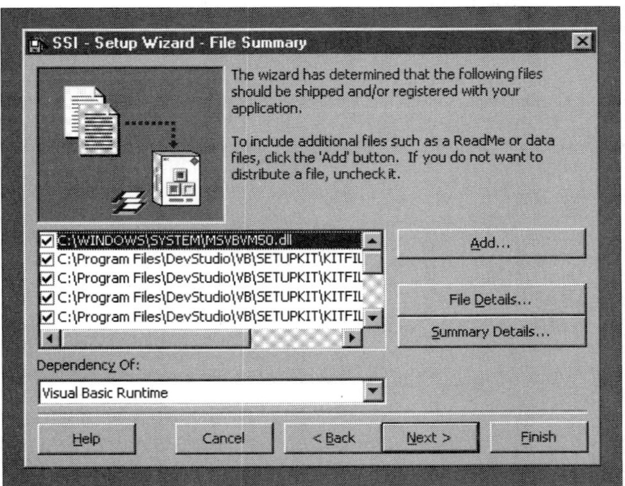

Figure 15-8: File Summary dialog

As shown in Figure 15-8, you can add additional files needed for the distribution, or examine the files that make up the distribution. The final dialog is the Finished dialog. Clicking this button completes the process of building the software distribution.

To illustrate the use of the Setup Wizard, you will create a software distribution in a single directory and then run the Setup program created by the Setup Wizard.

To create a single directory software distribution:

1. Exit **Visual Basic** if it is open.
2. Run the **Application Setup Wizard**. The Setup Wizard can be executed from the Visual Basic Start menu. When started, an Introductory dialog may appear. Click **Next**. The Select Project and Options dialog will appear as shown in Figure 15-9.

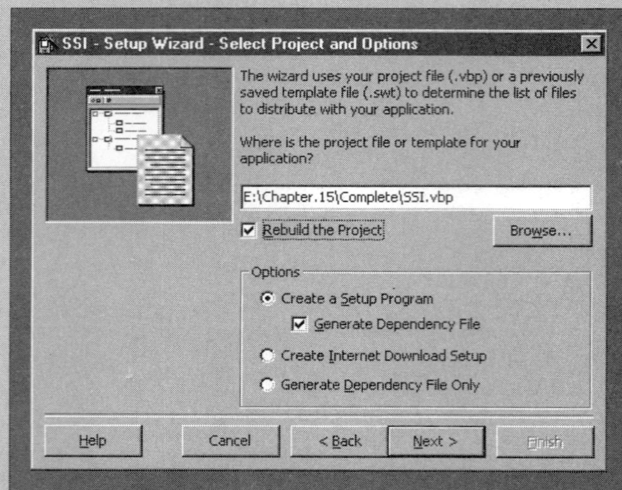

Figure 15-9: Select Project and Options dialog

3 Click the options shown in Figure 15-9. Make sure to replace the drive designator with the current disk drive you are using. These options cause the project to be recompiled and a dependency file to be built. Click the **Next** button to rebuild the project, generate the dependency file, then activate the **Distribution Method** dialog.

4 The Distribution Method dialog describes whether the files will be written to floppy disk, to multiple disk directories intended to be copied to floppy disks later, or to a single directory copied to CD-ROM. Click the **Single Directory** option button then click **Next.** The Single Directory dialog will appear.

5 The purpose of this dialog is to define where the distribution files will be copied. The default directory is C:\WINDOWS\TEMP\SWSETUP\. Change this directory to the folder you want to use. You likely will not be able to select a floppy disk for this directory as the files will not fit on a single floppy. Make sure the directory you specify contains no files.

6 Click the **Next** Button to activate the next dialog. This dialog is the ActiveX Server Components dialog and is necessary when your program uses one or more ActiveX servers. Because this program does not use any ActiveX servers, you can skip this dialog. Click the **Next** button to display the File Dependencies dialog.

7 The File Dependencies dialog lists the dependencies found in your program. You can verify that this list is complete and add other files as necessary. In this example, the program uses the CommonDialog control. The code for this control is stored in the file named COMDLG32.OCX. This .ocx file will be distributed with the application.

8 Click **Next** again. The Setup Wizard now will create the actual software distribution. As the Setup Wizard moves through the steps in this process, the current state will be displayed in the dialog. When complete, the File Summary dialog is displayed. The dialog lists the various dependent files used by the project.

In the File Summary dialog, notice there are several files that are part of the distribution in addition to the executable program itself and the .ocx file corresponding to the CommonDialog control. These files include the Visual Basic run-time library and other .dll files necessary to run the program. Again, remember the Setup Wizard detects these dependencies for you.

9 Click **Next**, then click the **Finish** button to complete the distribution.

At this point, you can use Windows Explorer to navigate through the folders and files created by the Setup Wizard. If you examine the folder named C:\WINDOWS\TEMP\SWSETUP\, you will see that a file has been placed in that folder named Setup.exe. The user will execute this Setup program. Note that many of the files have a file extension ending in an underscore (_). These files will be installed when the Setup.exe program is run. The underscore suffix indicates that the files are compressed. The Setup Wizard compresses files to save space on the distribution media. When the Setup.exe file is run, these files will be uncompressed and installed as necessary.

Before proceeding, a word about the Setup Wizard is in order. The Setup Wizard is stored in the file named SetupWiz.exe and is used to build the software distribution. The program Setup.exe reads a configuration file and installs the software distribution. The program Setup.exe is just a Visual Basic program with the source code provided. As such, you can examine the program to see how Setup.exe installs software. You also can modify this program, if desired, to customize the behavior of Setup.exe. The source code for the Setup.exe program is in the folder VB\SetupKit\Setup1\Setup1.vbp.

Setup Files

As the Setup Wizard produces the distribution files, it also creates a configuration file named Setup.lst. The Setup.exe program reads this file to determine the files that make up the distribution and the location of those files. It also contains the information that Setup.exe uses to determine where each of the distribution files will be installed.

You can edit this file to change the locations where the Setup.exe program will look for the distribution files and where it will install the files. The following code segment shows the Setup.lst file pertaining to this application:

```
[BootStrap]

File1=1,,setup1.ex_,setup1.exe,$(WinPath),,,1/16/1997 0:00:
00,164864,5.0.0.3716,"","",""
```

```
File2=1,,VB5StKit.dl_,VB5StKit.dll,$(WinSysPath),,$(Shared)
,1/16/1997 0:00:00,29696,5.0.37.16,"","",""
File3=1,,MSVBVM50.dl_,MSVBVM50.dll,$(WinSysPathSysFile),$(D
LLSelfRegister),,7/19/1997 16:55:40,1347344,5.1.43.19,"",""
,""
File4=1,,StdOle2.tl_,StdOle2.tlb,$(WinSysPathSysFile),$(TLB
Register),,1/15/1997 0:00:00,16896,2.20.4054.1,"","",""
File5=1,,OleAut32.dl_,OleAut32.dll,$(WinSysPathSysFile),$(D
LLSelfRegister),,1/15/1997 0:00:00,491792,2.20.4054.1,"",""
,""
File6=1,,OlePro32.dl_,OlePro32.dll,$(WinSysPathSysFile),$(D
LLSelfRegister),,1/15/1997 0:00:00,32528,5.0.4055.1,"","","
"
File7=1,,AsycFilt.dl_,AsycFilt.dll,$(WinSysPathSysFile),,,1
/15/1997 0:00:00,120592,2.20.4056.1,"","",""
File8=1,,Ctl3d32.dl_,Ctl3d32.dll,$(WinSysPathSysFile),,,8/2
1/1996 0:00:00,27136,2.31.0.0,"","",""
File9=1,,ComCat.dl_,ComCat.dll,$(WinSysPathSysFile),$(DLLSe
lfRegister),,10/31/1996 0:00:00,22288,4.71.1441.1,"","",""

[Files]
File1=1,,COMDLG32.OC_,COMDLG32.OCX,$(WinSysPath),$(DLLSelfR
egister),$(Shared),7/19/1997 16:00:32,129808,5.1.43.19,"","
",""
File2=1,,SSI.ex_,SSI.exe,$(AppPath),,,3/15/1998 20:29:48,16
384,1.0.0.0,"","SSI","$(AppPath)\SSI.exe"
File3=1,,SSI.DE_,SSI.DEP,$(AppPath),,,3/15/1998 20:37:42,27
57,1.0.0.0,"","",""

[Setup]
Title=SSI
DefProgramGroup=SSI
DefaultDir=$(ProgramFiles)\SSI
Setup=setup1.exe
AppExe=SSI.exe
AppToUninstall=SSI.exe
AppPath=
```

As shown in the previous code segment, the file has the same format as an .ini file. It contains three sections named BootStrap, Files, and Setup. The Bootstrap section contains the names of the distribution files that are necessary for the Setup.exe program itself to execute. The Files section contains the names of the files pertaining to your program that will be installed. You can modify the contents of this section, if necessary, to customize the installation of the program.

```
File2=1,,SSI.ex_,SSI.exe,$(AppPath),,,3/15/1998 20:29:48,16
384,1.0.0.0,"","SSI","$(AppPath)\SSI.exe"
```

Note that the preceding statement is one of three statements in the Files section. Each statement identifies a file that will be installed on the target computer. Thus, three files will be installed. The format of each statement consists of a set of directives separated by commas. This line is read and stored in the following user-defined type. This type is declared in the module named basSetup1.bas in the source code for Setup.exe.

```
Type FILEINFO format
    intDiskNum As Integer   ' disk number
    fSplit As Integer       ' split flag
    strSrcName As String    ' name of source file
    strDestName As String   ' name of destination file
    strDestDir As String    ' destination directory
    strRegister As String   ' registration info
    fShared As Boolean      ' shared or private
    fSystem As Boolean      ' system file
    varDate As Variant      ' file date
    lFileSize As Long       ' file size
    sVerInfo As VERINFO     ' file version number
    strReserved As String   ' Reserved
    strProgramIconTitle As String
    strProgramIconCmdLine As String
End Type
```

As you may have noticed, the format of the statements in the Files section corresponds to the above user-defined type. For example, the source file of the above statement is SSI.ex_, and the destination file is SSI.exe.

The destination directory syntax is a bit more interesting. In this case, the destination directory is $(AppPath). This actually is a macro used by Setup.exe. Setup.exe replaces this text with a value either stored in the Setup program itself, or obtained from the Windows Registry. Other values include the date the file was created and the size of the file. It also contains version information and any icons that may need to be installed.

The final section, Setup, contains other information about how the program will be installed. Here you either can change the program name or the directory where the program will be installed.

The other important file pertaining to the Setup Wizard is the Vb5Dep.ini file. This file contains the general dependencies for the Setup Wizard and Visual Basic. Note that the Setup Wizard not the Setup.exe program uses this file. This file typically is stored in the folder named VB\SetupKit\KitFil32\Vb5Dep.ini. Consider the following segment of this file:

```
[SetupWiz]
Drive1=1.44 MB,1457664,512
Drive2=2.88 MB,2915328,1024
Drive3=1.2 MB,1213952,512
Drive4=720 KB,730112,1024
Drive5=360 KB,362496,1024
```

This segment defines the different possibilities for distribution disk drives. If you had a different type of drive, like a Zip drive, you could add the drive, and the size of the disk, to this file. This way, the Setup Wizard could create distribution files on media different from the usual floppy disks or CD-ROMs.

```
BootStrap=C:\Program
Files\DevStudio\VB\SETUPKIT\KITFIL32\SETUP.EXE
VBExe=C:\Program Files\DevStudio\VB\VB5.EXE
RemoveInstallEXE=C:\Program
Files\DevStudio\VB\SETUPKIT\KITFIL32\ST5UNST.EXE
Last Project=A:\Chapter.15\Complete\SSI.vbp
MakeCab=C:\Program
Files\DevStudio\VB\SETUPKIT\KITFIL32\MAKECAB.EXE
Setup1Exe=C:\Program
Files\DevStudio\VB\SETUPKIT\SETUP1\setup1.exe
Setup1Proj=C:\Program
Files\DevStudio\VB\SETUPKIT\SETUP1\SETUP1.VBP
```

The above statements tell the Setup Wizard the location of various files it needs to create the Setup program. This includes the location of Visual Basic, the program that will be used to uninstall a program, and the location of the Setup.exe file. Again, these locations can be changed depending on the configuration of your system.

A final word about the Setup Wizard and the Setup.exe program is in order. The Setup Wizard is but one way to create distributable programs. In addition to the Setup Wizard, several third party programs perform essentially the same task. These programs offer additional flexibility beyond the capabilities provided by the Setup Wizard. Again, which to use is a matter of personal preference.

A Word About Creating and Distributing DLL Applications

This topic could have been presented in the chapter that talked about creating DLL servers. It is covered here, however, because the topic also is related to creating DLL servers for distribution. If you look at the Compile tab in the Project Properties dialog, you will see that there is a field named DLL Base Address in the dialog. This field only is enabled when the project type is an ActiveX DLL server. This is because the DLL Base Address setting pertains only to DLL server components. This setting often is neglected and failing to set this value properly can have a negative impact on the performance of your DLL server. To understand the purpose of this setting, a brief explanation about how Windows manages memory is in order. As you are well aware, programs are loaded into memory and executed. In the days of DOS, memory management was simple as only one program could run at a time. As you know, however, Windows loads and seemingly runs several programs concurrently. It is also possible for many different programs to use the same physical DLL concurrently. For example, you may have several programs on the system that all use the DAO library concurrently. In general, Windows tries to share the code in a single DLL between the different processes that use the DLL. The following list illustrates what happens when Windows tries to load a DLL into memory:

1. First, an attempt is made to load the DLL component at the default base address. This is the memory address specified in the DLL Base Address setting in the Project Properties dialog.
2. If that address is being used by another DLL, the component (DLL) must be relocated to a memory address that is not in use. This activity is performed by Windows rather than by you as the developer. This is called **rebasing**.

Rebasing a DLL can have a significant impact on the performance of the program for two reasons. First, the code for the rebased DLL cannot be shared. Also, there is considerable overhead to relocate the DLL.

The default value of the DLL base address is &H11000000. If you create several programs all having the same DLL base address, then there is a high probability that two or more DLLs will try to use the same base address resulting in a conflict. Imagine that you have created several DLLs that likely will be accessed by multiple programs that likely will be run concurrently and assume that you did not change the DLL Base Address setting. Assume also that other developers have been using Visual Basic but did not change the DLL Base Address setting either. In this set of circumstances, a computer would have several DLLs all with the same base address. As such, the probability of conflicts would be great. This would require that the DLLs be relocated.

Consider the following guidelines when setting the default base address for your programs:

- The base address must be between 16,777,216 and 2,147,483,648.
- The value should be a multiple of 64K. When using hexadecimal representation, the last four digits should all be zero (0).
- Consider randomly calculating the base address of your DLL programs. This will minimize the possibility that two DLLs will attempt to use the same base address.

SECTION C

objectives

In this section you will:

- Review the fundamental techniques and ways to create Help files
- Modify a Visual Basic program to display a Help window
- Display context-sensitive help from a Visual Basic program

Adding Help to a Program

The Two Views of Help

Consider the user's view of the Help system. It usually is possible to display different Help files from inside an application, display a Help file with the extension .hlp by selecting it from Windows Explorer, or by pressing the F1 key, and so on. While the Help pages for some programs are infinitely more sophisticated than those found in others, they all consist of very similar features. Most support a tabbed dialog like the one shown in Figure 15-10 to display a table of contents.

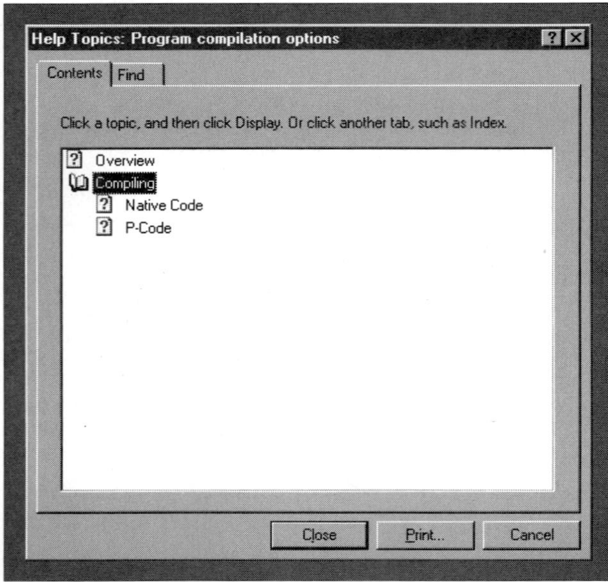

Figure 15-10: Help table of contents

In this chapter, you will edit a Help file using the table of contents shown in Figure 15-10. This Help file supports the following features:

- There is a **table of contents** so the user can navigate through the contents to select a particular page.
- There are **popups** associated with certain words on a Help page. When the word or phrase is clicked, a popup, which is visually much like a ToolTip, appears. WinHelp automatically formats the popup to an optimal size.
- There are **jumps** associated with certain words on a Help page. When the user clicks a jump, a specific Help page (topic) is displayed pertaining to the jump.
- The user also will be able to display specific Help topics using **context-sensitive help**.

The functionality of the Windows Help system is provided by Windows itself rather than by Visual Basic. Conceptually, Help is just a collection of data files that are read by a program that displays the Help pages in the Help file. This program is known as WinHelp.exe. It reads the data files, typically a single file with the extension .hlp, associated with a program's Help system and displays it. When the user navigates through the different topics in the Help system, the user is interacting with the WinHelp program rather than Visual Basic.

From your perspective as a Visual Basic developer, you have the task of developing Help files, and displaying the data contained in those Help files from your Visual Basic program. Help files, as they are tightly coupled with the Windows operating system, are not created inside Visual Basic. Rather, they can be created using various tools supplied both by Microsoft and third party vendors. Windows supports a tool to create Help files called Help Workshop. Other tools can be purchased from third party vendors to create Help files. Which to use is a matter of personal preference, although some of the commercially available products supply an interface that is considerably easier to use than Help Workshop. Some of these tools cost more than Visual Basic itself, however.

By default, Help Workshop is not installed when Visual Basic is installed. The Setup program and necessary support files can be found in the Tools\HCW folder on the Visual Basic CD-ROM. Running the Setup program in this folder will install Help Workshop and add an entry on the Start menu. Help Workshop only performs part of the task of creating Help files. The Help pages that you see actually are created in Word.

Programming ▶ tip

There is an incompatibility between the version of Help Workshop found on the Visual Basic distribution CD-ROM and Word 97. If you are using Word 97, you can download a more current version of Help Workshop from microsoft.com. The file name is Hcwsetup.exe and can be found using the Support Online Web pages.

The discussion that follows contains a brief introduction to creating the fundamental elements of a Help file for an application using Help Workshop and Microsoft Word. It is not intended to show all the intricacies of creating Help files. For example, the Help file you are working with neither supports indexes or keyword searches nor displays graphics. For more extensive information on how to create these elements, refer to the Help pages pertaining to Help Workshop. Help files usually are created on a per application basis. Creating a Help file is similar to developing a program. Source files are created using Word and Help Workshop. These source files are interpreted by Help Workshop and translated into a file with the extension .hlp that can be read by WinHelp.exe. Many source files often will be used to create the .hlp file pertaining to an application.

As mentioned, creating a Help file for an application requires that you use Word and Help Workshop. Before discussing Help Workshop, a brief discussion about the role of Word in the creation of Help files is in order. The textual Help pages seen by the user and the graphics on those pages are created as rich text files (RTF). RTF files were discussed in Chapter 7. Any editor that fully supports the RTF format can be used to create these data files. As most people have some familiarity with Word, however, it will be used to create and edit the RTF files. After the RTF files are created, Help Workshop is used to define the general characteristics of the Help file, the interface that the user has access to for displaying the various pages in the Help file, and the RTF files that will make up the Help file.

The order of whether to present the Help Workshop or how to create the RTF files in Word presents somewhat of a chicken and egg problem, as both programs are dependent on the files created by the other. We will discuss the Word component first although the order is somewhat arbitrary.

Every page the user sees in Help is considered a **topic**. As you know, most Help topics allow you to jump to other topics. The document you create in Word is more than just a document. The formatting characteristics you apply, like underlining words and inserting hard page breaks, have a very special meaning when the file is read by Help Workshop. Hard page breaks are used to separate topics and underlined words (along with hidden text) are used to display popups. Figure 15-11 shows part of an RTF file loaded in Microsoft Word.

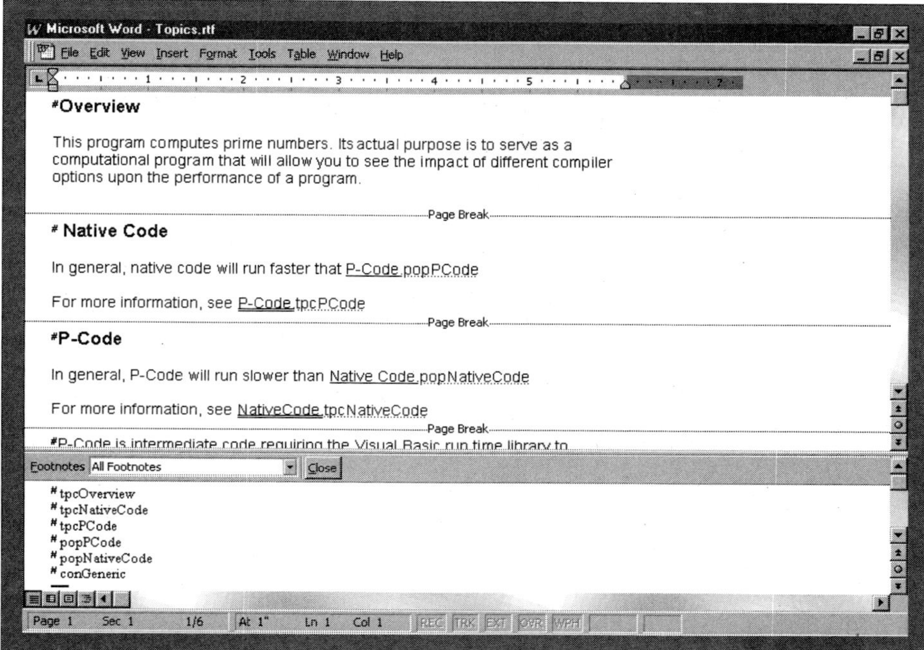

Figure 15-11: Help Topics RTF file

As shown in Figure 15-11, the first Help topic begins with the text Overview, and ends with a page break. The size and font of the text are important. This information is stored in the RTF file and will be used by WinHelp to format the Help topic when displayed. Note that the first character contains a pound sign and is associated with a footnote. Every topic you create must have an associated footnote. The footnote is used by WinHelp to identify a particular Help topic. The name of the footnote must begin with the pound sign (#) as a special symbol. The text that follows the pound sign in the footnote is called the **topicID**. The topicID is a character string that uniquely identifies a particular Help topic. Each topicID must be unique. As shown in Figure 15-11, the Overview topic has a topicID of tpcOverview. The following steps can be used to create a new Help topic and a topicID for that topic:

1. Enter the text to be used as a topic.
2. Apply formatting including specific fonts, font sizes, and italicized text as desired. These formatting attributes will appear in the Help topic.
3. Press Ctrl+Enter to insert a hard page break in the RTF file. Consider changing the Word 97 options to display hidden text so you easily can see the page breaks. The hard page break marks the end of a particular Help topic.
4. Set the insertion point so it precedes the first character of the Help topic.
5. Click Footnote on the Insert menu to activate the Footnote and Endnote dialog as shown in Figure 15-12.

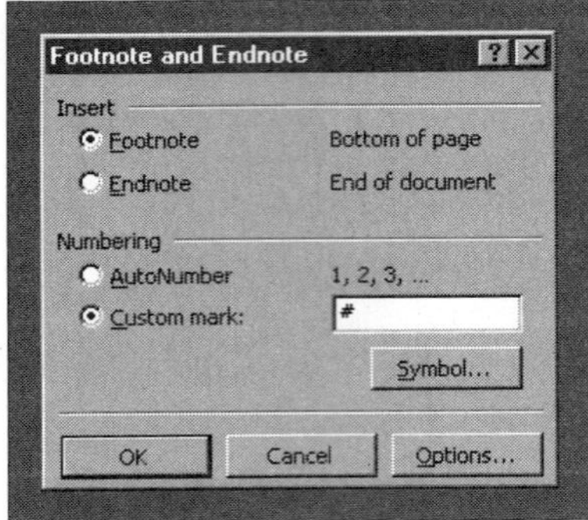

Figure 15-12: Footnote and Endnote dialog

6. Make sure the Insert and Numbering options are set to the values shown in Figure 15-12.
7. Word will split the window. The document window will split horizontally and the footnote pane will appear on the bottom.
8. Enter the topicID as the text for the footnote.

This topic is very simple and lacks many of the elements that make up a robust Help system. One of the elements that is missing is the capability to click a word or phrase to display another topic. Using Help terminology, this is called a **jump.** When the user clicks a word or phrase defined as a jump, a specific Help page defined by the jump is activated. Defining a jump inside of a topic also is accomplished using Word. Again, referring to Figure 15-11, for the topic "Native Code," the underlined character string is P-Code. The user will see the jump characters as underlined characters. When clicking any part of the underlined string, WinHelp will jump to another topic. Note the hidden text following the underlined text. For the jump to P-Code, the hidden text contains the string "tpcPCode." This is the name of the topicID for another topic.

The following steps can be used to define a jump:

1. If the jump topic has not been created, create the topic and the topicID, using the previous steps. Again, the topic must be separated by hard page breaks.
2. Highlight a word or phrase. Click Font on the Format menu to activate the Font dialog. In the Underline list box, click Double Underline. This text will appear underlined to the user and when clicked will cause WinHelp to jump to the specified topic.
3. Immediately following the text you just underlined, enter the topicID corresponding to the desired Help topic that WinHelp will jump to.
4. Select the text and click Font on the Format menu to activate the Font dialog. In the Effects section, check the Hidden check box. Again, you may find it helpful to set the Word options to display hidden text.

Closely related to the concept of a jump is a popup. A popup displays a popup window containing text that is similar in appearance to a ToolTip. You define text seen by the user by underlining it. Following the underlined text, you create hidden text containing the topicID of a specific topic. The use of the word topic in this context is intentional. The text displayed in a popup is a topic and thus is a Help page just as any other Help page is a topic. As such, you create the topic for a popup using the same techniques as you used to create other Help topics. As shown in Figure 15-11, the text P-Code is underlined indicating that it is popup text. Following the popup text, is a hidden text string, popPCode, which is the topicID. The topic popPCode is shown at the bottom of the top pane in Word, also shown in Figure 15-11. The following steps can be used to create a popup:

1. If the popup topic has not been created, create the topic and the topicID using the previous steps.
2. Highlight a word or phrase. Click Font on the Format menu to activate the Font dialog. In the Underline list box, click Underline. This text will appear underlined to the user, and when clicked, will jump to the specified topic.
3. Immediately following the text you just underlined, enter the topicID corresponding to the desired Help topic that WinHelp will pop up.
4. Select the text and click Font on the Format menu to activate the Font dialog. In the Effects section, check the Hidden check box. Again, you may find it helpful to set the Word options to display hidden text.

This section has presented the most basic of Help capabilities. It also is possible to display graphics, and perform much more complex formatting. For more information on creating more complex Help files, refer to the Help pages for Help Workshop. You may find the documentation for Help Workshop rather terse. As an additional resource, consider searching the Microsoft Support Online database for further examples and details related to creating Help files using Word.

The topics file for this Help system already has been created. You can view the elements of the file using Word to see how the file works.

To edit a topics file:

1 Start **Word 97** then open the file named **Chapter.15\Help\Topics.rtf.** Note that the file is an RTF file rather than a Word document file.

2 Set the Word options to view hidden text.

3 Click **Footnotes** on the **View** menu to view the footnotes that define the topicIDs for each of the Help topics.

4 Exit Word.

As mentioned, you can use Word to create the Help topics themselves. To link the various topics together and create the actual Help system, however, you must learn how to use Help Workshop.

Building the Help File

The other software component used to create a Help system is Help Workshop. Help Workshop is an MDI application that displays two types of child windows. One window is called a Project window and the other is called the Contents window. The Project window is used to display and edit project files and is shown in Figure 15-13. Conceptually, a Help Workshop project file is similar to a Visual Basic project file. It is used to define the general characteristics of the Help system. The format of a Help Workshop project file, however, is much different than the one used by Visual Basic.

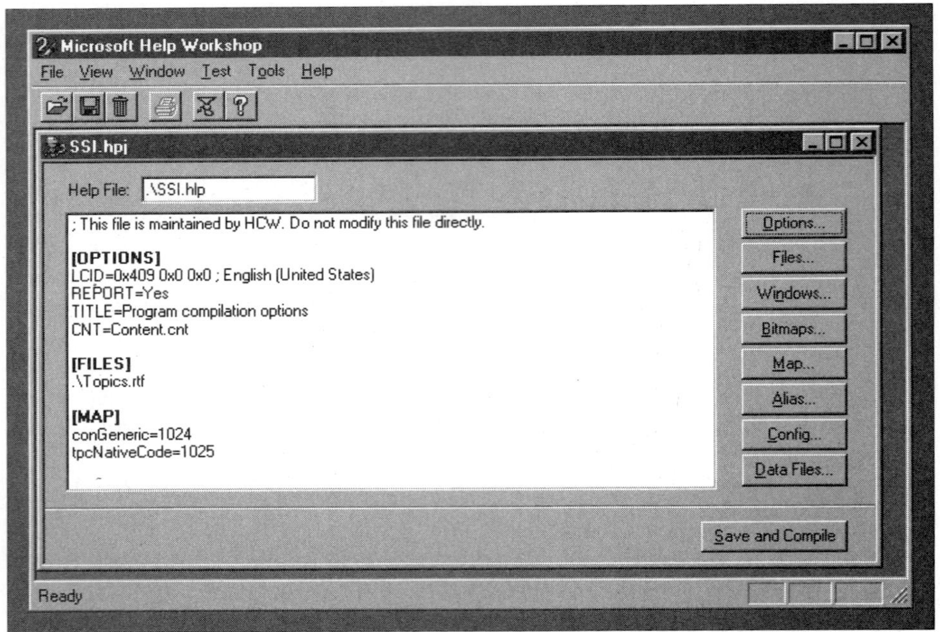

Figure 15-13: Microsoft Help Workshop – Project window

As shown in Figure 15-13, the Project window contains a multiline list box that describes the elements of the Help system. It also contains buttons to manipulate those elements. In this chapter, you will look at the existing elements of a Help system that already has been created. You do not edit the contents of the list box directly. Rather, you select an item in the list box, and use the buttons on the right-hand side of the Project window to add new elements to the list box or make changes to existing elements. The Help project file shown in this chapter already has been created. The hands-on steps in this section illustrate how to view different parts of the project file.

To open a Help project file:

1. Start **Help Workshop.** Help Workshop is an MDI application with options to open project files and compile those source files into an .hlp file. Remember, you may need to install this application from the Visual Basic CD-ROM.
2. Click **File** then **Open**. Click the project file named **Chapter.15\Help\SSI.hpj.** Depending on the version of Help Workshop you are running, you may see a dialog indicating that the version is not compatible with the DOS-based version or some similar dialog. Click OK. These version differences should not be a problem.

A project file is made up of sections. The project file shown in Figure 15-13 is made up of three sections named Options, Files, and Map. Note that section names are enclosed in brackets. If you are familiar with the syntax of .ini files, you will find the syntax of a Help Workshop project file very familiar; each has sections. Within each section, there are statements to configure a particular Help directive. These statements resemble assignment statements.

- The Options section contains configuration information used to specify how the Help file is compiled.
- The Files section specifies the different RTF files that are compiled in the Help file.
- The Map section associates a numeric ID with an existing topicID.

These are but 3 sections of the 14 sections that are supported by a Help project file. Refer to the "Sections in Project Files" Help topic for a complete list of the different sections supported. Within each section are statements. Each statement consists of a directive followed by an equal sign (=) followed by a value. Again, there are many other statements than the ones shown in this example.

In this example, the Options section contains two significant directives. The TITLE directive specifies the title that will appear on the title bar of the Help Topics dialog. The CNT directive identifies the name of another type of file called a contents file. Contents files will be discussed in a moment.

The FILES section contains the name of the RTF file(s) used to create the Help file. In this example, all the Help topics are stored in one RTF file so only one file is listed. Additional files would be listed in this section on separate lines.

The MAP section contains directives to associate a numeric ID with an existing topicID. The purpose of a MAP is to open a specific Help page from another program like Visual Basic. Again, the use of the MAP will become apparent later in the chapter.

Adding or changing the contents of each section is accomplished by selecting a section and clicking one of the buttons on the right-hand side of the Project window. Many of the settings are defined using the Options button, which activates the Options dialog shown in Figure 15-14.

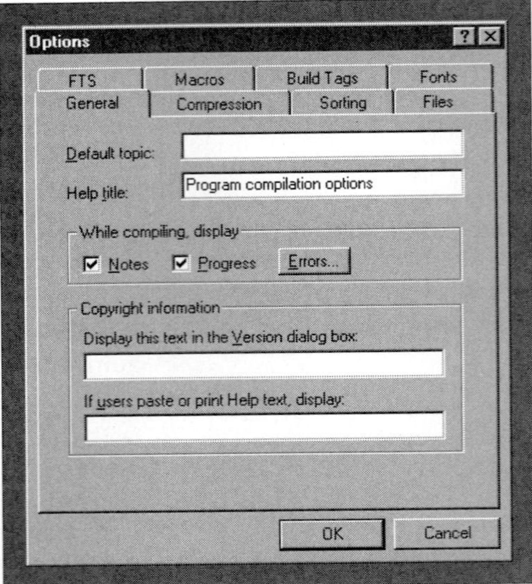

Figure 15-14: Options dialog – General tab

As shown in Figure 15-14, the Options dialog looks like any other dialog. It contains tabs to group related settings together. Of particular importance in this chapter is the General and Files tabs. The General tab is shown in Figure 15-14. It contains the Help title text box that is used to set the caption that is displayed in the Help window. The other tab used in this program is the Files tab, which is shown in Figure 15-15.

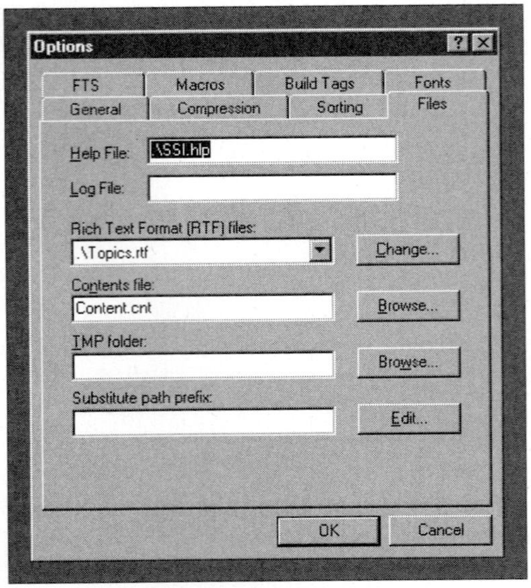

Figure 15-15: Options dialog – Files tab

As shown in Figure 15-15, the Files tab is used to manipulate the RTF files used to create the compiled Help file and the contents file used.

Understanding the Contents File

Tightly coupled with the project file is the contents file. This file contains the necessary information so a Help system can display a table of contents. This information is stored in a contents file with the extension of .cnt. The contents file contains three types of information.

- **Headings** appear as open or closed books. Headings can be nested. That is, a book can contain another book and so on.
- Inside headings a list of **topics** is displayed. A question mark icon is displayed to the left of a textual description.
- The contents file also can contain commands. Commands are used to execute Help macros and are not discussed in this chapter.

To view the contents file associated with a project:

1 Click **Open** on the **File** menu. Click the file named **Chapter.15\Help\Content.cnt** in the Open dialog. The contents file is shown in Figure 15-16.

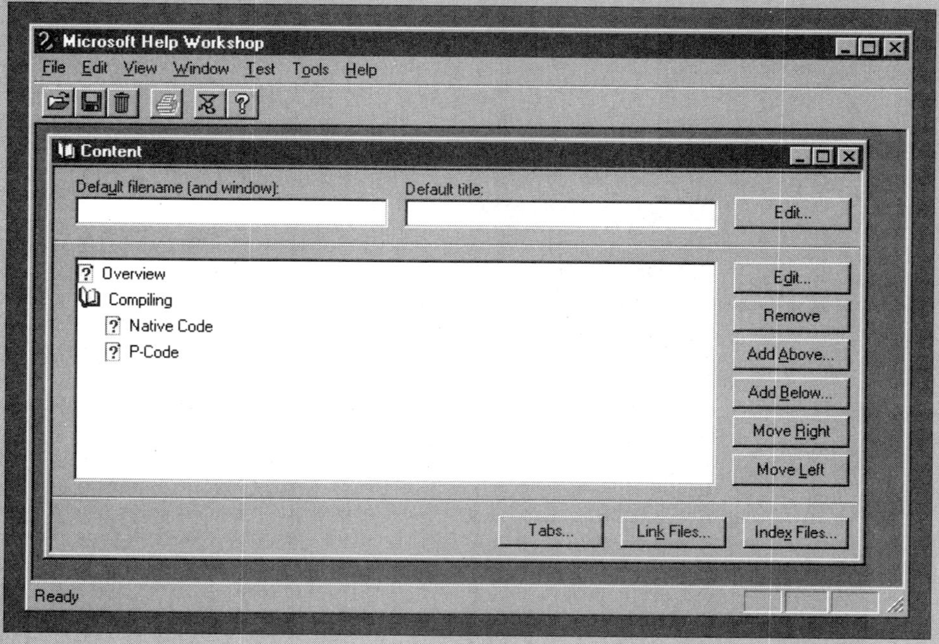

Figure 15-16: Content window

As shown in Figure 15-16, the Contents window contains a list box that displays a graphical representation of the table of contents as it will appear to the user. The only difference is that all the books appear open. Thus, the table of contents always appears fully expanded in the Contents window. The contents shown in Figure 15-16 have topics named "Overview," "Native Code," and "P-Code." There is one heading (book) named Compiling. Note the indenting of the items in Figure 15-16. The indenting of items in the Contents window has a similar effect as the indenting in the Menu Editor. Indenting a particular item causes that item to appear as a child in the table of contents. The command buttons on the right-hand side of the list box are used to add new items, change existing ones, and delete items. They also are used to change the indenting of an item hence the level the item appears in the contents hierarchy.

- The Edit button changes the attributes of the currently selected item.
- The Remove button deletes the currently selected item.
- The Add Above and Add Below buttons insert a new item above or below the currently selected item.
- The Move Right button increases the indent level of the currently selected item.
- The Move Left button decreases the indent level of the currently selected item.

The difficult part of using the Contents window is adding and editing new entries. When a new entry is added or an existing entry changed, the Edit Contents Tab Entry dialog appears, which is shown in Figure 15-17.

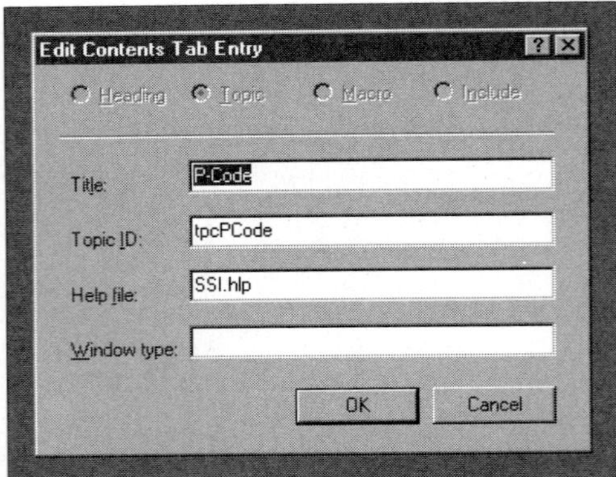

Figure 15-17: Edit Contents Tab Entry dialog

As shown in Figure 15-17, the dialog has several parts that correspond to the topics you created in the Word document. If the Heading option button is selected, only the Title text box is enabled. This is because there is not a topic associated with a title. Titles only are used as a means to group topics together. If the Topic option button is selected, all the text boxes are enabled. The following list describes the purpose of these text boxes:

- The Title text box contains the textual description that is displayed in the table of contents.

- The Topic ID text box contains the topicID of the desired topic. This name is the same as the topicID you specified in the footnote pertaining to a specific document when you edited the RTF file in Word.
- The Help file text box defines the name of the Help file, after it is compiled, where the topic can be located.
- The Window type text box is not used in this simple example.

To see how this process works, you now will examine a topic in the Content window.

To edit a line in the table of contents:

1. Make sure the **Content** window is active in Help Workshop.
2. Click the Item named **Native Code** then click the second **Edit** button. The Edit dialog will appear.
3. Click **Cancel** to close the dialog.

At this point, you have seen all the elements needed to create a Help system. The final step in the process is to compile each of these source files into the .hlp file that can be used by WinHelp.exe. This file is not an executable file in the true sense of the word. Rather, a data file is processed by WinHelp to display Help information.

To compile a Help project file:

1. Make sure the project file is opened inside Help Workshop.
2. Click **Compile** on the **File** menu on the Help Workshop menu bar. The Compile a Help File dialog will appear as shown in Figure 15-18.

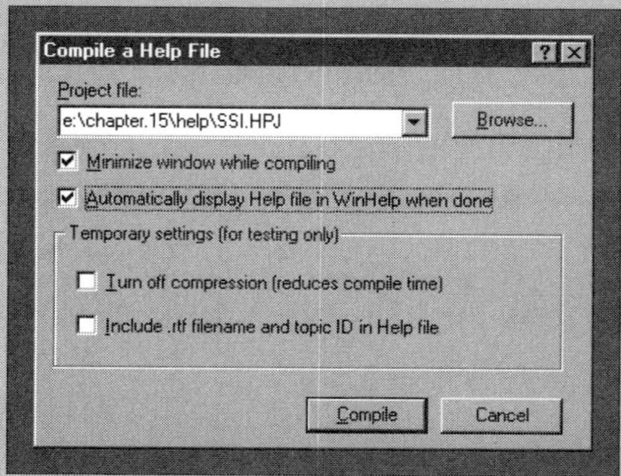

Figure 15-18: Compile a Help File dialog

3 Complete the information shown in Figure 15-18. Make sure to replace the drive designator as needed. Click **Compile**. After the file is compiled, WinHelp is started and displays the Help file so you can test it.

4 Exit Help Workshop.

At this point, you would run WinHelp.exe and load the Help file named SSI.hlp to display the help for the program. You also could double-click the file itself using Windows Explorer. You need to be able to display the Help system from a Visual Basic program, however.

Displaying Context-Sensitive Help

Most well-designed and implemented programs support what is known as context-sensitive help. Conceptually, context-sensitive help is very easy to understand. When the user presses the F1 key, a Help topic should be displayed that pertains to the current control or form that has focus. Implementing context-sensitive help requires cooperation between Visual Basic and Help Workshop. The key to the process is specifying an Integer number in Help Workshop that uniquely identifies a particular Help topic. Then, in Visual Basic you set the HelpContextID property for a particular control or form.

The example in this chapter that demonstrates context-sensitive help is both very generic and simple. It does illustrate the process of displaying a context-sensitive Help topic for a particular dialog, however. This concept can be extended easily to work with any other form or active control on a form.

First, lets look at the process of specifying an Integer number for a particular Help topic. This is accomplished using the Project window in Help Workshop. Remember, the project for this Help system contains a section called MAP. This section is edited by clicking the Map button on the form, which causes the Map dialog to be displayed. The Map dialog is shown in Figure 15-19.

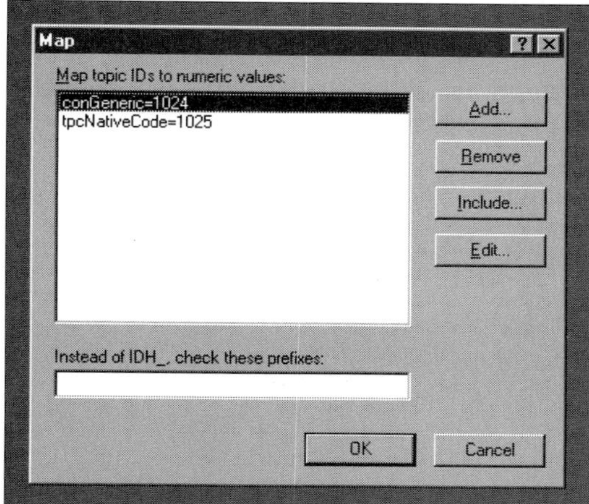

Figure 15-19: Map dialog

As shown in Figure 15-19, there are buttons to add, edit and delete Maps. The key to the process is the Add Map Entry and Edit Map Entry dialogs. These dialogs have the same fields. The Edit Map Entry dialog is shown in Figure 15-20.

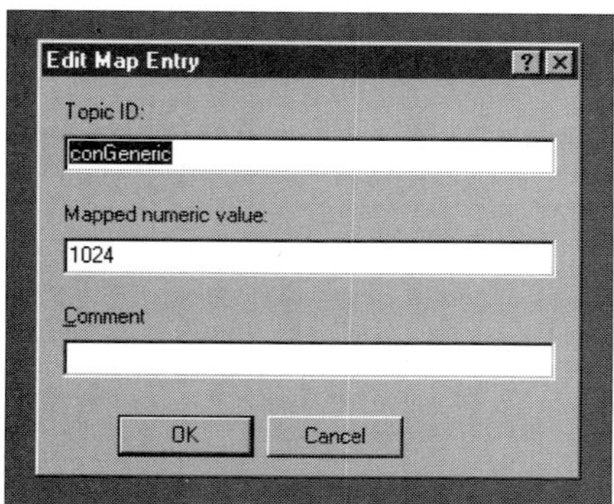

Figure 15-20: Edit Map Entry dialog

As shown in Figure 15-20, there are three text boxes used to edit a Map.

- The Topic ID text box contains the name of a topic to be mapped. The topicID should correspond to the name of a topic specified in the footnote of the Word document.
- The Mapped numeric value text box is an Integer number that defines the mapped value.
- The Comment text box is used to define a comment for the specific Map.

Displaying the Help File from Visual Basic

The other responsibility of the developer is to display specific Help information for the user. Most users are accustomed to getting help from a Help menu on the menu bar, by pressing the F1 key, or by clicking a command button with a caption of Help. There are several techniques you can use to display Help information from a Visual Basic program.

- The Show method of the CommonDialog control can be used to display a Help topic.
- You can set the HelpContextID property of a Visual Basic control or form to display context-sensitive help when the user presses the F1 key.
- You can display Help information by calling Windows DLLs.

Displaying Context-Sensitive Help from Visual Basic

As mentioned, the key to displaying context-sensitive help is specifying the integer contextID of the Help topic. All you need to do to implement context-sensitive help for a dialog or other form is to set the HelpContextID property of the form or dialog to the Integer value you used for the Help topic in Help Workshop. In this case, the value is 1024. A generic dialog already has been created so you can see how this process works. The dialog does nothing. Its purpose is to display a particular Help topic when the user presses the F1 key.

To display context-sensitive help:

1. Start **Visual Basic** then load the project named **Chapter.15\Startup\SSI.vbp.**
2. Activate the Code window for the form named **frmSSI,** then enter the following statements in the Form_Load event procedure. Make sure to replace the path name of the Help file as necessary depending on the drive you are using.

```
App.HelpFile = "A:\Chapter.15\Help\SSI.hlp"
frmSSI.HelpContextID = 1024
txtMin.HelpContextID = 1024
txtMax.HelpContextID = 1024
```

3. Activate the Form window for the form named **frmDlg,** then open the **Properties** window.
4. Set the HelpContextID property for the form to **1024.**
5. Test the program. Click **Dialog** on the **Window** menu to activate the dialog. Press **F1**. The Help page pertaining to the generic dialog should be displayed.

Suppose that your program had several dialogs that needed context-sensitive help. In this situation, you could set the contextID of each form to a different value and map those IDs to separate topics.

Displaying Help Using the CommonDialog Control

In many of the chapters in this book, you have seen how to use the CommonDialog control to perform common tasks like opening and saving files. The CommonDialog control supports another common task—displaying Help files. The technique you use to display Help files using the common dialog is the same as you used to perform other tasks using the control—you set the properties pertaining to the control, including the Flags property, to control the behavior of the dialog. Then you call a method actually to perform the task. To display a Help page, you again set specific properties and call the ShowHelp method pertaining to the common dialog.

- The HelpCommand property determines the type of online help that is displayed. It can be set to one of several constant values described later in this chapter.
- The HelpContextID property is used to display context-sensitive help for the current control or form.
- The HelpFile property contains the name of the Help file for your application. If the user can change the installation location of the Help file for your application, then the current file location should be set and retrieved using the Windows Registry.
- The HelpKey property is used with the HelpCommand property to specify a specific help topic to be displayed.

Before delving into all different possibilities for displaying Help files, you will first see how to use the CommonDialog control to display the Help system you created in the previous section of this chapter.

To display a Help system using the CommonDialog control:

1. Create an instance of the CommonDialog control on the form **frmSSI**, then set the Name property to **cdl1.**
2. Enter the following statements in the **mnuHelpOnClick_Click** event procedure:

```
cdl1.HelpCommand = cdlHelpHelpOnHelp
cdl1.ShowHelp
```

3. Test the program. Click **Help On Help** on the **Help** menu. The Windows Help dialog telling the user how to use the Help system is displayed.

The above code set the Help command for the cdlHelpHelpOnHelp. This causes the Help system to display the Windows system Help file telling the user how to use the Help system itself. Then the ShowHelp method is called to display the Help topic. Help On Help is but one of many commands that you as the developer can use to display Help files. The following list describes some of the other Help command constants that are useful:

- cdlHelpCommand executes a Help macro.
- cdlHelpContents displays the Help contents for the particular Help file.
- cdlHelpHelpIndex displays the index for the Help file.

In the previous example, you displayed a standard Windows Help file. In the steps that follow, you will see how to display any Help file—specifically, the one you created in the previous section. To display the contents of a particular Help file, you set the HelpFile property. Generally, you should consider installing the Help file(s) pertaining to your application to the Windows directory containing Help files. This directory usually is Windows\Help. In addition to defining a specific file, you also need to tell the CommonDialog control what to display pertaining to that Help file. In this example, you will see how to display a specific Help topic.

To display a Help topic using the CommonDialog control:

1 Enter the following statements in the **cmdHelp_Click** event procedure on the main form:

```
cdl1.HelpFile = "A:\Chapter.15\Help\SSI.hlp"
cdl1.HelpCommand = cdlHelpContents
cdl1.HelpKey = "tpcOverview"
cdl1.ShowHelp
```

2 Test the program. Click the **Help** button on the main form to display the Overview page.

Displaying Help by Calling DLLs

Displaying Help using the common dialog has limitations. To better control how Help is displayed, there is a DLL function named WinHelpA to accomplish the task. The following code segment shows the Declare statement for this function:

```
Declare Function WinHelp Lib "user32" _
    Alias "WinHelpA" _
    (ByVal hWnd As Long, _
    ByVal lpHelpFile As String, _
    ByVal wCommand As Long, _
    ByVal dwData As Long) As Long
```

As shown in the previous code segment, the function takes four arguments. The first is the window handle of the parent window, and the second is the name of the Help file that will be loaded. The use of the wCommand and dwData arguments is more interesting. wCommand can contain one of the following constant values:

```
Public Const HELP_COMMAND = &H102&
Public Const HELP_CONTENTS = &H3&
```

```
Public Const HELP_CONTEXT = &H1
Public Const HELP_CONTEXTPOPUP = &H8&
Public Const HELP_FORCEFILE = &H9&
Public Const HELP_HELPONHELP = &H4
Public Const HELP_INDEX = &H3
Public Const HELP_KEY = &H101
Public Const HELP_MULTIKEY = &H201&
Public Const HELP_PARTIALKEY = &H105&
Public Const HELP_QUIT = &H2
Public Const HELP_SETCONTENTS = &H5&
Public Const HELP_SETINDEX = &H5
Public Const HELP_SETWINPOS = &H203&
```

These are the different commands that are supported by WinHelp. Depending on which command is used, you supply a different value to the dwData argument. In this example, you will see how to display a particular Help topic by using the HELP_CONTEXT command. The data for this command is a Long Integer data type containing the Map entry for a particular topic. In the existing Help contents file for the program, two Map entries have been defined having the values 1024 and 1025.

To display Help using a DLL:

1. Enter the following statements in the **cmdHelpDll_Click** event procedure. Note that the constants used for the command, and the Declare statement for the DLL, already have been written and exist in the form's file.

```
Dim pstrHelpFile As String
Dim plngTopic As Long
Dim plngReturn As Long
pstrHelpFile = "A:\Chapter.15\Help\SSI.hlp"
plngTopic = 1025
plngReturn = WinHelp(Me.hWnd, pstrHelpFile, _
    HELP_CONTEXT, plngTopic)
```

2. Make sure to save the project as any DLL error may cause Visual Basic to crash.
3. Test the program. Click the **Help Dll** command button. The Help page for the topic appears in the Help window.

Again, the goal of this chapter is not to demonstrate how to exploit every feature of the Help system. Rather, it is intended to illustrate the basic fundamental topics related to creating and calling a Help file. As such, use of the other commands pertaining to the DLL is left as an exercise for the reader.

SUMMARY

This chapter has presented three separate topics related to creating a program distribution and creating a robust program as seen by the end user. These topics included program compilation, program distribution, and creating Help files.

- How a program is compiled can have a material effect on the performance of a program. Visual Basic can create two types of executable files. P-code, also known as pseudocode, is intermediate interpreted code that is read by the Visual Basic run-time library before it is executed. Another type of code is native code. This type of executable file does not require the same capabilities of the Visual Basic run-time library. Because native code is not interpreted, it generally runs faster than comparable p-code.
- When a program is compiled into native code, there are several optimization options that can be applied to the executable file to improve performance. First, programs can be optimized for speed or space. There also is an option to improve program performance when the program is run on a Pentium Pro processor. Advanced options can improve program performance further. These options should be used with great care, however, as Visual Basic will not check for common error conditions like numeric overflow and underflow.
- Like many other languages, Visual Basic supports conditional compilation. This allows you to include or exclude statements conditionally from an executable file. Conditional compilation is useful when building software that must be customized for specific users or to include debugging code while the program is being developed and exclude that code when the program is distributed.
- Creating a distributable program requires that you use another application called the Visual Basic Setup Wizard. The Setup Wizard takes care of compiling the application, if necessary, and identifying any dependent files needed for the program to run. For example, a program may require specific .ocx files for an ActiveX control to work. All the files needed to run a program are compressed and copied to a distribution area on the disk. This distribution area can be a single directory, which commonly is used for a CD-ROM distribution, or multiple directories. Multiple directories typically are used when software will be distributed on floppy disks.

The final section of this chapter described the fundamental topics related to creating a Help system for a Visual Basic program. The process of creating a Help system can be divided into two parts. The Help topic pages themselves are created using an editor that operates on RTF files. In this chapter, Word was used. The other part of the process consists of using Help Workshop to define the general characteristics of the Help system, and compile the project and Help topic files into a single Help file with the extension .hlp.

QUESTIONS

1. Which of the following statements are true?
   a. Visual Basic can compile files to p-code.
   b. Visual Basic can compile files to native code.
   c. Optimization may be performed on native code.
   d. All of the above.
   e. None of the above.

2. In general, _______________.
   a. native code runs faster than p-code
   b. native code runs slower than p-code
   c. the performance of native code is about the same as p-code
   d. both a and c
   e. all of the above

3. Which of the following statements are true about the Setup Wizard?
   a. It creates an executable file named Setup.exe that is run by the user.
   b. It must be run from inside Visual Basic.
   c. It collects all the dependent files necessary for the program to run.
   d. Both a and c.
   e. All of the above.

4. Which of the following files are used by the Setup Wizard?
   a. Setup.lst.
   b. Vb5Dep.ini.
   c. Setup.ini.
   d. Both a and b.
   e. All of the above.

5. Which of the following statements are true about the DLL base address?
   a. The DLL always is loaded at the base address.
   b. The DLL may be loaded at the base address if the address is not in use.
   c. The DLL base address cannot be changed.
   d. Changing the DLL base address will never impact the performance of the DLL.
   e. None of the above.
6. What are the two ways to create a software distribution?
   a. Run the Setup Wizard.
   b. Use the Setup Toolkit.
   c. Use the RegEdit program.
   d. Both a and b.
   e. All of the above.
7. The Distribution Method dialog in the Setup Wizard will allow you to ____________.
   a. create the program distribution on floppy disks
   b. create the program distribution in a single directory
   c. create the program distribution in multiple directories
   d. both b and c
   e. all of the above
8. A ________________ file is required for a program to run on a remote computer.
   a. Composite
   b. Required
   c. Dependency
   d. None of the above
   e. All of the above
9. Which of the following are configuration files used by the Setup Wizard to configure itself?
   a. VB.exe.
   b. Setup.lst.
   c. vb5Dep.ini.
   d. Both b and c.
   e. All of the above.
10. Which of the following statements are true regarding the DLL base address?
    a. It is the address where Windows attempts to load a particular DLL.
    b. It must be the same for all DLLs.
    c. It should be different for all the DLLs you create.
    d. Both a and b.
    e. Both a and c.

11. List two software tools used to create Help files.
   a. Word.
   b. Help Developer.
   c. Help Workshop.
   d. Both a and b.
   e. Both a and c.

12. What is another name for a Help page?
   a. Document.
   b. Topic.
   c. Window.
   d. Metafile.
   e. None of the above.

13. What is the term used to refer to a Help topic that causes a different Help page to be activated when the user clicks a specific string of characters?
   a. Hyperlink.
   b. Popup.
   c. Link.
   d. Jump.
   e. None of the above.

14. What is the term used to display ToolTip-like text when the user clicks a specific string of characters?
   a. Hyperlink.
   b. Popup.
   c. Link.
   d. Jump.
   e. None of the above.

15. Which of the following statements are true about Help topic files?
   a. They are RTF files.
   b. Each topic is separated by a page break.
   c. A topic is identified by a footnote.
   d. Both a and b.
   e. All of the above.

16. What are the two types of windows supported by Help Workshop?
   a. Project files.
   b. Contents files.
   c. Form files.
   d. Both a and b.
   e. Both b and c.

17. Which of the following are valid sections in a project file?
  a. Options.
  b. Files.
  c. Map.
  d. Both a and b.
  e. All of the above.

18. Which types of information are stored in a contents file?
  a. Headings.
  b. Topics.
  c. Items.
  d. Both a and b.
  e. Both b and c.

19. To display context-sensitive help you must ________________.
  a. use the Content window to map a topic to an Integer topicID
  b. define the topicID in Word
  c. use the Project window
  d. all of the above
  e. none of the above

20. To display the Help system from Visual Basic, you can ________________.
  a. use the CommonDialog control
  b. set the HelpFile property of the App object
  c. set the HelpContextID for a form or control
  d. all of the above
  e. none of the above

EXERCISES

1. In this exercise you will create a program with a long run time and compare the performance of several different compiler options.
   a. Create a new project and set the Name property of the form to **frmExercise1**. Save the form using the name **Chapter.15\Exercise\frmExercise1.frm** and the project using the name **Chapter.15\Exercise\Exercise1.vbp.**
   b. Create two arrays of 100,000 elements of type Long. In the first array, initialize all the values so the contents of the array element are the same as its subscript. Initialize the second array so the contents of the element are the contents of the corresponding element in the first array multiplied by two (2). Note that depending on the speed of your computer, you may need to increase or decrease the size of the array.
   c. Compile the program to both p-code and native code and run the program. Record the time it takes to execute the program.
   d. Compile the program to native code again but this time select each of the different optimization options and record the execution time for each different option.
   e. Using the Advanced Optimizations dialog, remove each of the error checks and compile the program again. Test the executable file to see the effect on performance, if any.
2. In this exercise you will create a distributable program.
   a. Create a new project and set the Name property of the form to **frmExercise2**. Save the form using the name **Chapter.15\Exercise\frmExercise2.frm** and the project using the name **Chapter.15\Exercise\Exercise2.vbp.**
   b. Add a rich text box and CommonDialog control to the form. Write the necessary code using the CommonDialog control to open a file and display it in the rich text box. The purpose of this is to create dependencies rather than to create a robust program that uses these two controls.
   c. Save the project then exit Visual Basic.
   d. Start the Visual Basic Setup Wizard. Complete the necessary dialogs so the following will occur: the executable file should be rebuilt, the distribution should be saved to multiple directories on the hard disk, and a dependency file should be created.
   e. After you have created all the dialogs, execute the **Setup.exe** file to test the installation.

3. In this exercise you will create a simple Help system and a program to test it. The program will have two command buttons named Calculate and Reset. Assume that Calculate will calculate the payment of a loan. Each of these should have a Help topic.

a. In Microsoft Word, create a Help topic file.

b. Create a topic named **tpcCalculate**. As this topic will be used to calculate the payment on a loan, the Help page should describe three input parameters including the loan amount, the term, and the interest rate.

c. For each of these three parameters, create a popup that will display a valid range of input values. That is, when the user clicks the words loan amount, term, or interest rate, a popup should appear. For the loan amount assume a range of $1,000 to 250,000. For the term, assume a period of between 1 and 30 years. For the interest rate, assume a range of between 6 and 12 percent.

d. Create a second topic named **tpcClear**. This topic should contain a description that simply says all the input values will be cleared.

e. Create a jump between these two Help pages.

f. Make sure to save the document in RTF format. Save the document using the name **Chapter.15\Exercise\Exercise3.rtf**.

g. Using Help Workshop, create Help project and contents files as needed. Edit the files so the topics file you just created will be loaded. Also create a table of contents for the Help file. The table of contents should contain a book named **Exercise3** and two topics. These should be the same as the two topics you just created.

h. Compile the program as **Chapter15\Exercise\Exercise3.hlp**.

i. Create a new project and set the Name property of the form to **frmExercise3**. Save the form using the name **Chapter.15\Exercise\frmExercise3.frm** and the project using the name **Chapter.15\Exercise\Exercise3.vbp**.

j. Create three command buttons with the captions **Calculate**, **Clear**, and **Help**.

k. When the Help button is clicked, the Help system should be activated. Create an instance of, and use, the CommonDialog control to accomplish this.

l. Using the App object and the HelpContextID property of the two other command buttons, display context-sensitive help so pressing F1 while the Calculate button has focus causes the tpcCalculate Help topic to be displayed. Display the other Help topic when F1 is pressed while the Clear command button has focus.

m. Test the program and Help system to verify that the Help topics are being displayed properly, and that the jumps and popups are working.

CHAPTER

16

Crystal Reports

Reporting Database Data

case ▶ American Distributors is a wholesale distributor of food products to national grocery stores. Like any organization, they need to print different reports including inventory reports, sales reports, and many others. They would like these reports to have the same elements as other reports found in business today; that is, the reports should support different fonts and have graphical elements like lines, boxes, and pictures. In this chapter, you will create an inventory report based on data stored in a database file that supports these different elements.

SECTION A

objectives

In this section you will:

- Create a simple report using Crystal Reports
- Use the different types of fields supported by Crystal Reports
- Print report subtotals and totals
- Use formulas
- Test a report

Creating a First Report

Previewing the Completed Application

The completed application for this chapter has very little to do with Visual Basic. Rather, the application is used to print reports using the Crystal Reports program. Crystal Reports is not expressly part of Visual Basic. Rather, it is a stand-alone program used to create, modify, and test reports. While Crystal Reports is distributed with the Professional and Enterprise editions of Visual Basic, it also can be used by itself to create reports. Crystal Reports consists of two separate software components.

- The Crystal Reports program is a stand-alone software package used to create, edit, and test reports.
- The Crystal control is an ActiveX control that allows Visual Basic to print reports created by the Crystal Reports program.

Any programming language that supports ActiveX technology can use reports created with Crystal Reports. Once a report has been created with Crystal Reports, a Visual Basic program (or other programs) can print the report using an ActiveX control called the **Crystal** control. This control can be added to a project just like any other ActiveX control.

This chapter does not attempt to discuss every feature of Crystal Reports. Crystal Reports is a very powerful program that could not possibly be fully discussed in a single chapter. Rather, the purpose of this chapter is to present the basic techniques you use to create a Crystal Report, and how to print a report from a Visual Basic program. You should be able to apply the concepts and techniques presented in this chapter as a stepping stone to more complex reports.

The completed program in this chapter is very simple. It contains a menu that allows you to print reports and a list box that allows you to select the data to be printed.

To preview the completed application:

1 Start **Visual Basic** then load the project named **Chapter.16\Complete\AD_C.vbp.** The completed form for the program is shown in Figure 16-1.

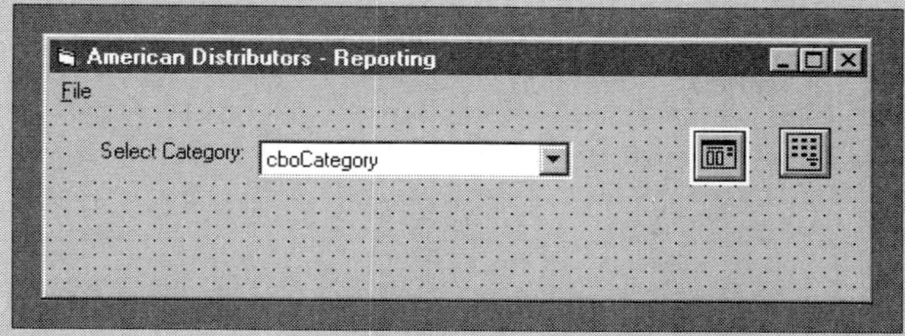

Figure 16-1: Completed form

2 Run the program.
3 Click **Open** on the **File** menu, then open the file named **Chapter.16\Complete\AD.mdb**. Set the drive designator as necessary. The purpose of the code in this event procedure is to associate a database file with the Crystal control.
4 Click **Print** on the **File** menu, then **Inventory** on the **Print** submenu. This causes the Crystal Reports run-time window to be activated and the inventory report to be printed on the screen, as shown in Figure 16-2. Note that if you are using a drive other than the floppy drive, you will need to modify the code in this procedure to specify the path name of the file named Simple.rpt.

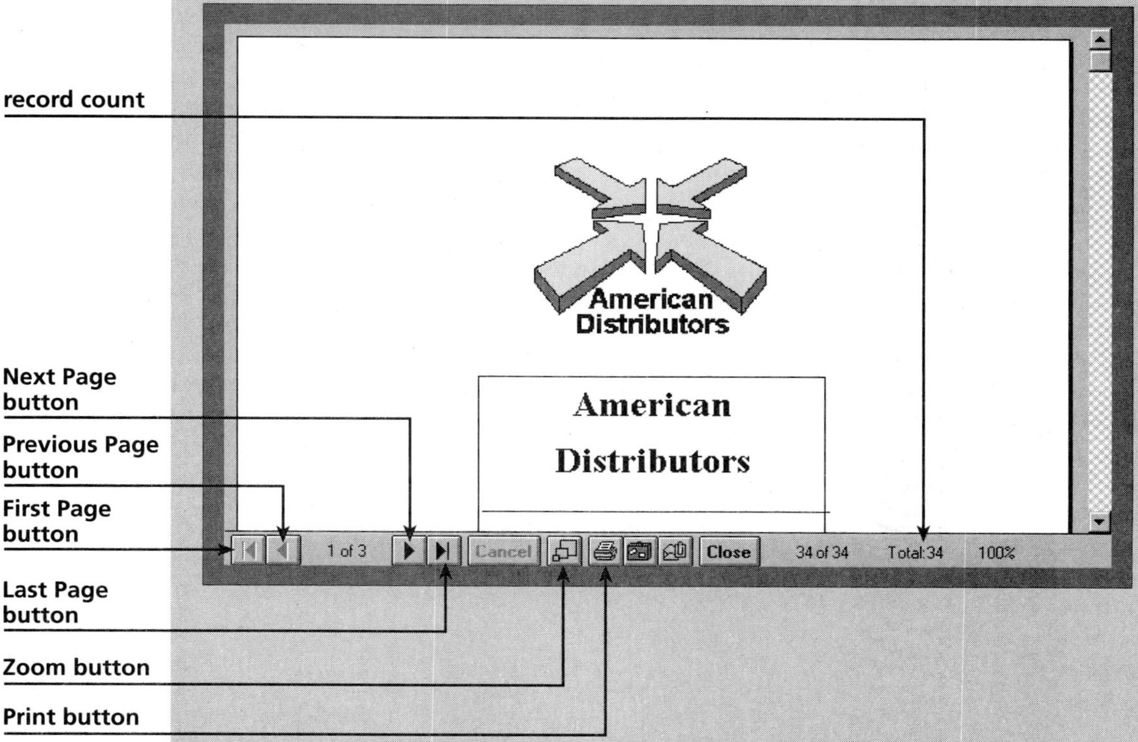

record count

Next Page button

Previous Page button

First Page button

Last Page button

Zoom button

Print button

Figure 16-2: Crystal Reports run-time window

As shown in Figure 16-2, the run-time window displays the first page of the selected report. It also contains buttons to locate different pages, zoom, and print the report to the printer. It also displays the number of detail records read.

5 Click the **Next Page** and **Previous Page** buttons to scroll through the report.

6 Click the **Zoom** button to change the magnification level. There are three different levels of magnification. Close the report viewer.

7 Select one of the categories from the combo box, then print the report again. Note that only the items from the selected category are printed.

8 Click the **Print** button to print the report to the printer. The report you will create in the following steps is the same report as the one shown in Figure 16-2. Having the printed report at your side will be helpful as you complete the steps in the chapter.

The report shown in Figure 16-2 was not created in Visual Basic. Rather, the report was designed and tested using Crystal Reports. The code in the program uses the Crystal control to establish a connection with Crystal Reports and print the report.

9 Exit Visual Basic.

The report consists of many parts called **sections**. These sections are common to nearly every report you create. For example, there are Title, Page header, and Page footer sections. The Page header and Page footer sections contain information that is printed at the top and bottom of every report page except the report Title. There also are sections called **groups**. A group section is used to print a subtotal in the report. In this example, there are subtotals printed whenever the inventory category or subcategory changes. There also is a Details section where the database records are printed. For each database record, there is one line printed in the report.

Other report elements include common items like a page number and current date. Also, there are graphical elements like lines and boxes to improve the visual appearance of the report. Finally, the report contains a picture—the logo for American Distributors.

Introducing Crystal Reports

Tools for creating reports have evolved considerably, just like most other software. In the past, when you created a report, you needed to write the code to control all the logic and formatting for the report. For example, consider a common type of report like a control break report. A **control break report** is a type of report that formats and prints subtotals for groups of records. For example, consider the inventory report for this chapter. The report could be printed such that each product in inventory is printed on a single line and a total of all items printed at the end of the report. The report likely would be very hard to read if there were more than a few different items, however. To make the report easier to read, it would be reasonable to break the inventory report down into groups of items. For example, assume that each inventory item for American Distributors belonged to a certain category and that each category was broken down into subcategories. In a situation like this, you could sort the report by category and further sort each category by subcategory. Each time the subcategory changes, a control break occurs and you could print the summary information pertaining to the current subcategory. When the category changes, summary information would be printed for all the different subcategories within a category.

Without Crystal Reports, you would need to create a Visual Basic program that would open a recordset. The code then would need to examine each record in the recordset. For each record, the code would need to test whether or not a control break occurred (a change in the category or subcategory). If there was a control break, then subtotals would need to be printed. For each detail record, you would need to print a detail line. Additionally, your code would need to keep track of page numbers, and whether a line will fit on a page or a new page would need to be printed.

This code is time consuming and tedious to create. When creating a report with Crystal Reports, as the report developer you do not actually write any code to control the logic of the report. In other words, you do not create a Do loop to examine all the records in a table and print a line in the report for each record. Crystal Reports does that for you. Furthermore, you do not write any code to print subtotals or totals in the report. Again, Crystal Reports also does that for you. Consequently, you will find the process of report creation more a matter of creating fields in the report and completing a set of dialogs than writing a program.

A word about Crystal Reports terminology is in order. Crystal Reports does not use the same object-oriented terminology as Visual Basic. Crystal Reports refers to visible objects in the report as fields rather than control instances. Furthermore, the attributes of a field are not expressly called properties. You can think of a field as a control that has properties. You set the properties of a field using menu commands, however, instead of by using the Properties window. In this chapter, the term field, instead of control, will be used to maintain consistency with the Crystal Reports Help pages.

Like most other quality applications, Crystal Reports supports an extensive Help system. You need to be aware that the Help pages are accessed from Crystal Reports rather than from Visual Basic. This also is true for the Crystal control. If you want to access the Help pages for the Crystal control, use the Crystal Reports Help pages. The information is not contained in the Visual Basic Help pages.

The Crystal Reports User Interface

As mentioned, Crystal Reports is not part of Visual Basic. Rather, a stand-alone program is used to design and print reports based on some data source. These data sources can include text files, Jet Engine databases, and other types of databases.

There are two ways to create a report using Crystal Reports. The easiest way is to use an Expert. An Expert is much like a Wizard. As the report developer, you interact with an Expert by completing the fields in various dialogs. Reports also can be created manually by drawing fields in the report. The process is much like one used to create control instances on a form. Crystal Reports is started from the Start menu, rather than from Visual Basic, as Crystal Reports is not actually part of Visual Basic. The program typically is found on the same menu as Visual Basic.

To start Crystal Reports and identify its components:

1. Click **Start, Programs, Microsoft Visual Basic 5.0, Crystal Reports** to start Crystal Reports and maximize the window. The Crystal Reports window will appear as shown in Figure 16-3.

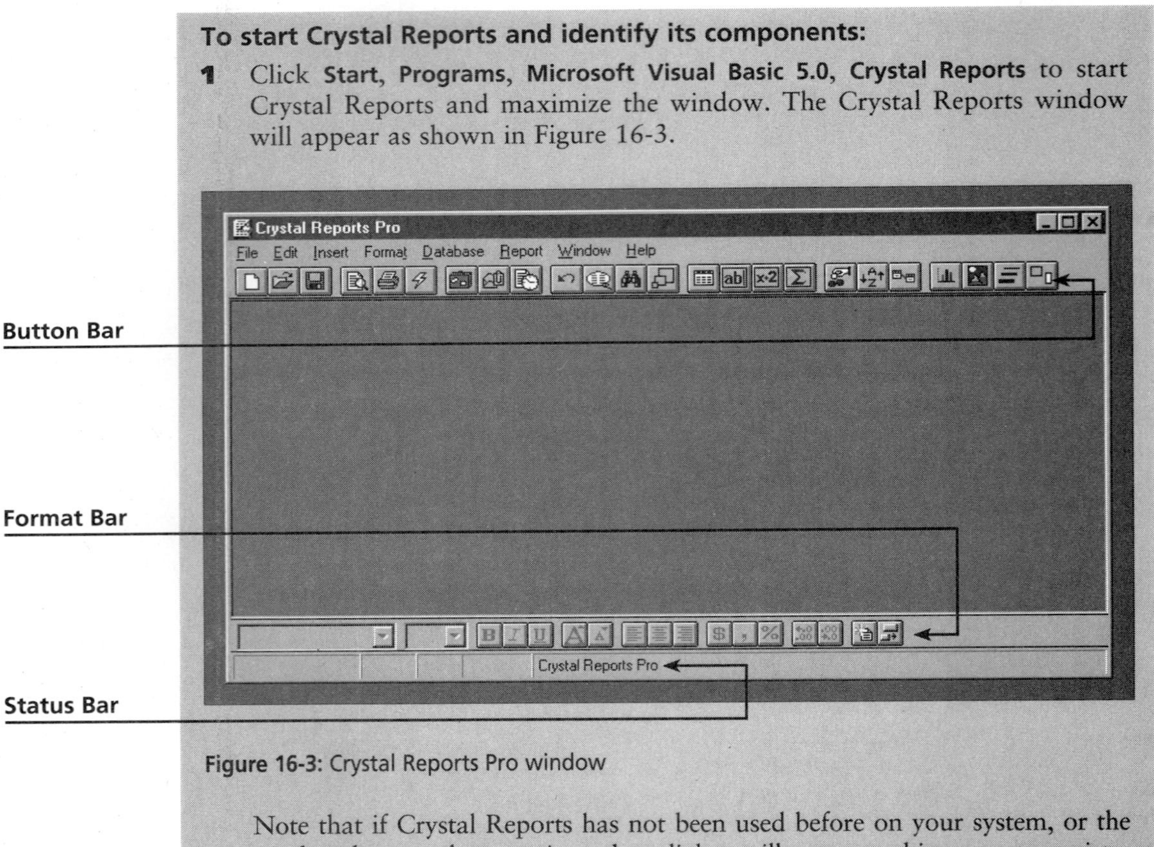

Figure 16-3: Crystal Reports Pro window

Note that if Crystal Reports has not been used before on your system, or the product has not been registered, a dialog will appear asking you to register Crystal Reports. You either can register Crystal Reports now or just click the **Close** button [X] in this dialog to continue without registering Crystal Reports.

As shown in Figure 16-3, Crystal Reports is an MDI application. The MDI parent window works as the container for the reports you create. Each open report appears as a separate MDI child window. As such, you can develop multiple reports concurrently in the same instance of Crystal Reports. Each report you create is saved on the disk as a file with the extension ".rpt". These files are not ASCII files. As such, only Crystal Reports can understand them.

Like most applications, there is a Menu Bar and a Button Bar at the top of the form. The commands on the menu bar are used to create new reports and edit existing ones. At the bottom of the MDI parent window is the Format Bar. This toolbar is used to set the formatting attributes of the objects drawn in the report. There also is a Status Bar on the bottom of the MDI parent window. By default, when the program first is started, there is no open report. Creating a new report is accomplished using the New command on the File menu. Editing existing reports is accomplished using the Open command on the File menu.

The Crystal Reports interface is a visual interface. That is, when you create fields on a report you see a visual representation of how the page will look when it is printed.

As stated earlier, the easiest way to create a new report is to use an Expert. Figure 16-4 shows the buttons to start the different Experts supported by Crystal Reports.

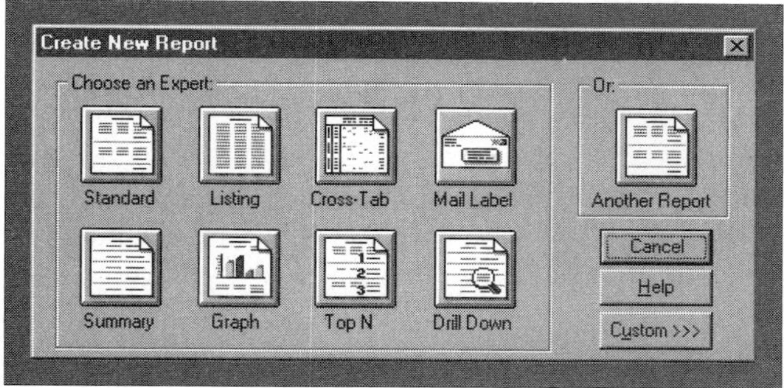

Figure 16-4: Create New Report dialog

- A **Standard** report usually contains a report title and page title. For each detail record found in the data file, one or more lines are printed. It also is possible to print subtotals and totals. The report you will create for American Distributors is similar to a Standard report.
- A **Listing** report typically contains a list of data in two or more columns. This type of report would be useful to print a list of names or addresses.
- A **Cross-Tab** report is used to cross-tabulate data. In essence, the rows in the data appear as columns in the report and the columns in the data appear as the rows.
- A **Mail Label** report is used to print mailing labels.
- A **Summary** report displays information summarized from the underlying data. It is much like a Standard report with no detail lines.
- A **Graph** report will summarize the data from an underlying file and print a graph.
- A **Top N** report is used to print the most significant records. For example, a Top N report could be used to print the top 10 selling inventory items.

- Conceptually, a **Drill Down** report is akin to a drill down interface like you have seen with Windows Explorer or when you created programs using the TreeView control. It is used to present the data in a hierarchical manner.

No matter which type of Expert you use, a tabbed dialog appears similar to the one shown in Figure 16-5.

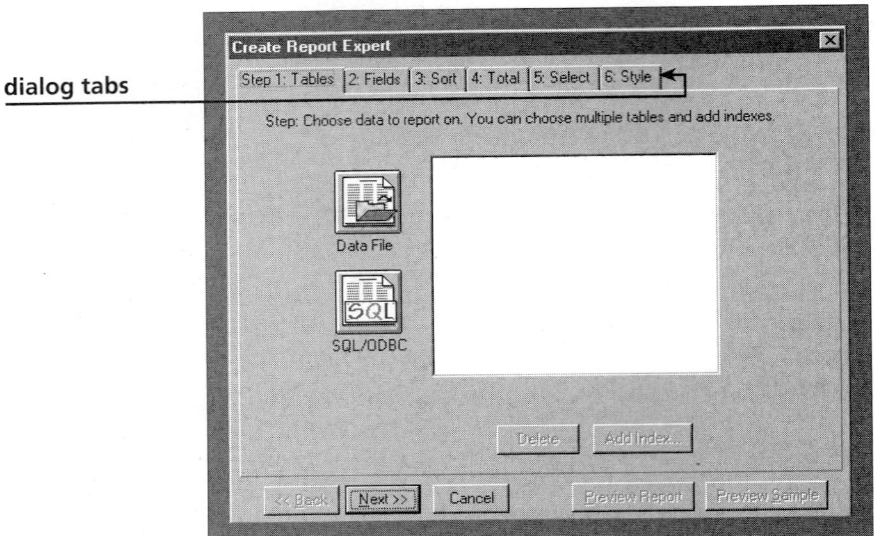

Figure 16-5: Create Report Expert

Each Expert contains its own series of tabs. As the developer, you generally complete the information on each tab working from left to right. Once you have specified all the information about the report, you click the Preview Report or Preview Sample buttons to generate the report. There are two important points to make about the Experts. First, once you preview the report, you cannot use the Expert to modify it. As such, you should be careful to define all the information about the report before previewing it. Second, you manually can modify reports created by an Expert. As such, you may find it helpful to use an Expert to define the general characteristics of the report. Then, you can modify the report created by the Expert and customize it for your particular needs. The steps in this chapter will not include creating a report using an Expert; that process is straightforward.

The second way to create a report is to create a custom report manually. When you create a report manually, you must create explicitly each of the fields that make up the report. You create custom reports and reports with an Expert by selecting options on the Create New Report menu as shown in Figure 16-6.

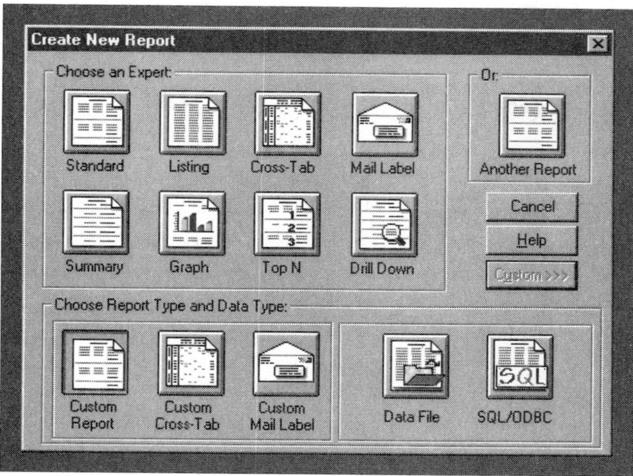

Figure 16-6: Create New Report dialog

As shown in Figure 16-6 the Create New Report dialog contains buttons to create different types of Standard reports using an Expert, or to create a custom report. Additionally, there are buttons to select the data file to be used with the report. A report always is based on some kind of data file. In this chapter, you will create reports based on the data contained in a Jet database. You can just as easily create reports that are based on data in other databases or ASCII files.

To create a new report:

1. Click **New** on the **File** menu to activate the Create New Report dialog.
2. On the Create New Report dialog, click the **Custom** button. This will expand the dialog so it displays the options necessary to create a custom report.
3. Click the **Data File** button to associate the report with a database file. A dialog will appear allowing you to select a file. Click the file named **Chapter.16\Startup\AD.mdb.** Set the drive designator as necessary. The report is created and shown in Figure 16-7.

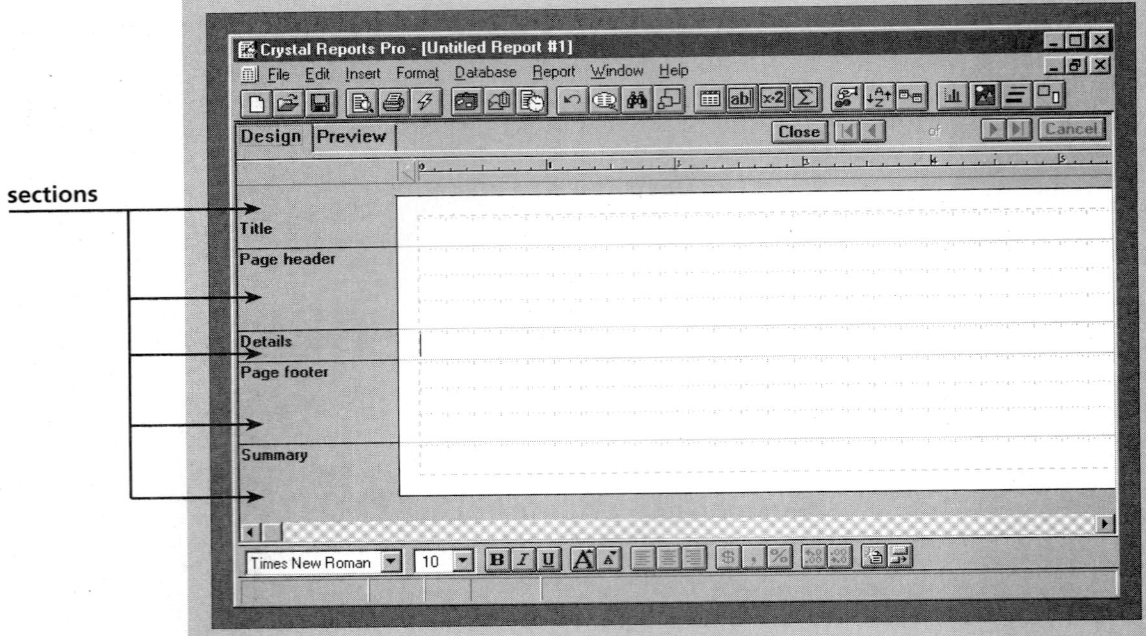

Figure 16-7: New report

Note that when the report is created, the Insert Database Field dialog appears (this dialog is not shown in Figure 16-7). Crystal Reports assumes that one of the first activities you will perform is to add the database fields you want to use to the report. This dialog is not modal so you can interact with other Crystal Reports windows while the dialog is open.

4 Click **Save As** on the **File** menu to save the report. Save the report using the name **Chapter.16\Startup\Simple.rpt**.

As shown in Figure 16-7, the new report consists of five sections.

- The **Title** section contains the report title. This title is printed only on the first page of the report.
- The **Page header** section contains the information that is displayed at the top of every page.
- The **Details** section contains the actual report data. Typically, one line is printed for each record in the report. It is analogous to printing the current record in the Details section for each record in a recordset.
- The **Page footer** section contains the information that is displayed at the bottom of every page.
- The **Summary** section is displayed at the end of the report.

GUI Design ▶ tip

Generally, either the Page header or Page footer section contains the page number, the date the report was printed, and the report name. If you are creating several reports for an organization, consider adopting consistent standards for the placement of this information on all the reports you create. This way, the user will be able to quickly identify the report, and the information that is common to all reports.

Depending on the current configuration of Crystal Reports, some of the toolbars may or may not be visible and other options may vary slightly. Clicking Options on the File menu will activate the File Options dialog. The following list highlights some of the configurable options you can set from this tabbed dialog:

- The **Layout** tab controls the visual appearance of the report and the toolbars that are displayed.
- The **New Report** tab contains options that define the default data source for a report. There are options, by default, to create reports from Jet database files (.mdb), and to create reports that execute SQL statements to connect to other types of data sources. Any database that supports a standard called Open Database Connectivity (ODBC) can be used with Crystal Reports.
- The **Database** tab contains options to define the default folder for database files and various optimization options for processing database files.
- The **SQL** tab contains options that are used when using an SQL server, likely running on a remote computer. You use this tab to specify the server name and any login/password information needed to gain access to the specified server.
- The Reporting tab contains options to control whether data is saved with the report and when data is read from the underlying data file.
- The **Fields** tab is used to set default formatting attributes for the different types of fields you create on a report. Note that Crystal Reports converts all data into one of five data types: String, Number, Currency, Date, and Boolean.
- The **Fonts** tab sets the default fonts used for different sections in the report.

Page Margins

Like any other program that works with a printed page, Crystal Reports allows you to define page margins. While Crystal Reports sets a default page margin for you, the margins can be changed to suit the particular needs of your report. This is accomplished by clicking Page Margins on the File menu, which activates the Page Margins dialog. It is possible to assign different values for the top, bottom, left, and right page margins.

To change the page margins:

1. Click **Page Margins** on the **File** menu.
2. Set each of the page margins to **1"**.
3. Click **OK** to apply the changes.

Programming tip

There are different techniques you can use to align the fields visually on a page. For example, you can set the page margins to zero (0) and align all the fields to the physical page or you can set the page margins and align the field to the edge of the page margins. Which technique to use is a matter of personal preference. As you work with Crystal Reports, you will find that there are many ways to accomplish the same task.

Creating Report Fields

The next step in creating a report is to create fields (objects) on it. The process of creating fields on a report is similar to drawing control instances on a form. Instead of creating control instances using the Toolbox, however, you insert fields using the commands on the Insert menu. The order in which you create the fields in the report is immaterial. You may decide to work visually from the top of the report to the bottom. You also may decide to get the data fields and formulas working, then work on the prompts and visual alignment. Crystal Reports is flexible enough that you can create the fields in the report, and set the general report characteristics in any order you choose.

All the visual elements on a report are considered fields. You do not create a program as such in Crystal Reports. Rather, you create a report by creating fields of different types in the various sections of the report. Crystal Reports supports four kinds of fields as shown in the following list:

- A **database** field represents a field in the selected database file. The selected database file is the file that you associated with the report when the report first was created. A database field is similar to a bound text box.
- A **text** field contains literal text. Text fields commonly are used to describe the contents of a database field much like a label is used to describe the contents of a Visual Basic text box.
- A **formula** field is used to perform computations on data. This data can be information from a database field or information from the database itself. Formula fields also can be used to call intrinsic functions supported by Crystal Reports.
- A **special** field is used to display data that pertains to nearly every report. This includes data like a page number or the current date.

While they are not expressly referred to as fields, you also can add lines, boxes, and pictures to enhance the report's appearance visually.

In the remainder of this section, you need to learn how to create, and when to use, each type of field and how to format each field. In this section, you will create the simplest type of field first and then see the different techniques you can use to format it. The techniques related to formatting a field pertain to all types of fields, not just a text field. Once you learn how to format a text field, you can apply the same techniques to all other field types.

Text Fields

A text field is analogous to a Visual Basic label. A text field displays literal text to describe a database field or to define report and page titles. Inserting a text field is very simple. You click Text Field on the Insert menu to activate the Edit Text Field dialog as shown in Figure 16-8.

Figure 16-8: Edit Text Field dialog

As shown in Figure 16-8, there is a text box in which you specify the text that will appear in the field. Clicking the Accept button causes the text field to be created and closes the dialog. Clicking the Cancel button closes the dialog without creating the field. If the Accept button is clicked, an outline of the field appears in the report. Unlike Visual Basic, Crystal Reports defines a default size for the field based on its contents. You move the insertion point to the desired section, position it in the report designer, and then click the left mouse button to anchor the field to the report. To see how text fields are created, you will define the report title.

To create text fields:

1. Click **Text Field** on the **Insert** menu to activate the Edit Text Field dialog.
2. Enter the text **Inventory Report** in the dialog, then click the **Accept** button. The dialog closes and a rectangular box is displayed in the report.
3. Note that as you move the mouse, the field is moved from section to section. It is important that you always insert fields in the correct section. Click the mouse while it is positioned in the **Title** section to position the text field in the report. The text "Inventory Report" will appear in the text field after it is placed in the report.

Note that both the horizontal and vertical size of the text field was determined automatically by Crystal Reports. In Crystal Reports, you do not set explicitly the height of a line. The line height is determined by the height of the text that will be displayed on the line.

Conceptually, Crystal Reports has design and run modes much like Visual Basic. In design mode, you draw fields in the report and format those fields. Run, or preview, mode is used to test the report you created. You can toggle back and forth between these two modes by clicking the Design and Preview tabs.

To preview a report:

1. Click the **Preview** tab. Crystal Reports will load the data from the database and display the report. By default, the report is displayed in page view. You can zoom in on the report by clicking Zoom on the Report menu. The only information displayed in the report is the one text field you just created. You have not yet created the fields to display data from the database file.
2. Click **Zoom** on the **Report** menu to zoom in on the data in the report.
3. Click the **Design** tab to return to design mode.

At this point the report is very simple. It merely displays a text field using the standard formatting that was applied to the text field when it was created. You now will see how to move existing fields and format those fields to improve the appearance of the report.

Formatting Text and Manipulating Fields

You will often find yourself moving and resizing the fields created on a report. The techniques to do this are very similar to the techniques you use in Visual Basic.

- To reposition a field, click the field to activate it and drag the field to its new location in the report.
- To resize a field, click the field to activate it and use the sizing handles to change the size of the field. Note that the vertical height of a field is determined by the height of the text stored in the field and cannot be changed explicitly.
- To delete a field, click the field and press the Delete key.
- You can select multiple fields by holding down the Shift key, then clicking the mouse on specific fields.

If you have become accustomed to using the copy and paste capabilities of Visual Basic to create multiple control instances, you will find Crystal Reports rather limiting. Crystal Reports will not let you select a text field, copy that field to the Clipboard, and paste the copy back on the form. Rather, you must use the Insert menu to add each field.

In addition to repositioning a field, it often is desirable to change the formatting attributes of a field. The easiest way to format a field is to select the field(s), then use the Format Bar at the bottom of the Crystal Reports window to change the formatting attributes. The buttons on the Format Bar are straightforward. The following list describes its general capabilities:

- There are two drop-down combo boxes to select the font and font size of the selected field(s).
- The first button group will apply or remove boldface, italic, and underline attributes.
- The next button group will increase or decrease the font size by one (1) point.
- The next button group will left justify, right justify, or center the text in the selected field. Note that the justification is relative to the field not the margins in the report.
- The next two button groups only apply to fields that contain numeric data. The first group adds formatting symbols to the field, and the second changes the number of decimal places that are displayed in the numeric field.
- The last button group applies styles and provides an auto arrange capability.

You now can use these formatting tools to improve the appearance of the text field you just created. Generally, report titles should have a larger font and often are centered on the page.

To format a field:

1. Make sure the text field you just created is selected. Note that because the field is not numeric, the buttons pertaining to numeric fields are disabled.
2. On the Format Bar at the bottom of the window, set the font size to **28** point, then set the font to **bold**.
3. **Underline** the text. You will align the text on the page in a moment.

Another way to format a field is to use the Format dialog corresponding to the underlying data type of the field. Crystal Reports supports the following formatting dialogs: Format String, Format Number, or Format Date. Selecting the field, then clicking Field on the Format menu activates one of the Format dialogs. Another way to activate a Format dialog is to right-click a field, then click Change Format. The appropriate Format dialog will be selected based on the underlying data type of the field.

Which dialog appears depends on the data type of the field. Text fields are equivalent to the Visual Basic String data type. A field is considered a numeric field when the data in the field is bound to a numeric database field. Numeric fields also are used to display page numbers, and the result of numeric formulas. Date fields are used when the underlying data type is Date. If the field is bound to a Date database field, then the field also is considered a date field. Also, there are special fields to display the current date, which also are considered date fields. The important concept to remember is that Crystal Reports defines the data type for you. You do not declare explicitly a field as having a specific data type.

The Format String dialog has options that differ from the options on the Format Bar. Also, options are the same as those found on the Format Bar. In most complex software packages, there are multiple ways to achieve the same task, and Crystal Reports is no different. The Format String dialog supports options to prevent a particular field from being printed in the report, and change the alignment of the field. Also, you can check the Print on multiple lines check box to allow the text to span a single line. If this box is checked, you also should set the maximum number of lines.

The Format Number dialog has many more options than the Format String dialog and is shown in Figure 16-9. This dialog is used for numeric fields.

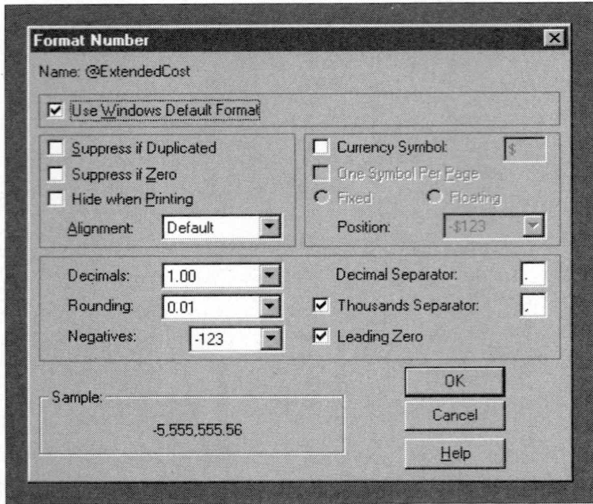

Figure 16-9: Format Number dialog

As shown in Figure 16-9, the dialog contains many options to customize the appearance of numeric data. The following list highlights the purpose of the different objects in the dialog:

- Like text fields, there is a frame that has options to control whether or not the selected field is printed in the report. There is an additional option to control whether the field is printed if the current value is zero (0).
- The objects in the next frame control whether a currency symbol appears, and the placement and appearance of that symbol.
- The next section controls how the number itself appears in the report. You can change the decimal separator and thousands separator. The other boxes control how many digits appear to the right of the decimal place, and whether the number is rounded.

When the underlying data type is Date, the Format Date dialog is used to format the fields. This dialog is shown in Figure 16-10.

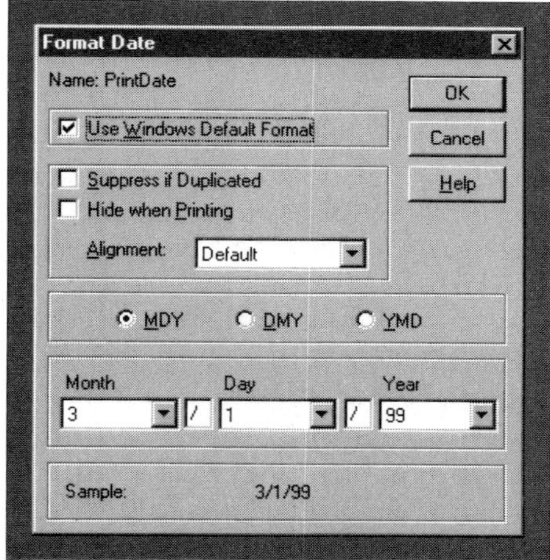

Figure 16-10: Format Date dialog

As shown in Figure 16-10, you have considerable flexibility in formatting dates. You can use the same options used in the other dialogs to suppress printing of the field. In addition, several options are unique to date values.

- You can change the order of the different date parts. That is, the date can be printed in month/day/year order, day/month/year order, or year/month/day order.
- The list boxes allow you to control the formatting of each date part.
- There also are text boxes allowing you to change the character that separates the different date components. By default, this character is a forward slash.

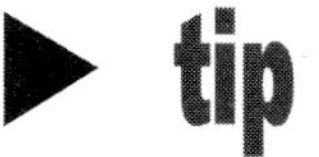

In addition to selecting these dialogs on the menu bar, Crystal Reports supports context-sensitive popup menus. You can select a field or group of fields and right-click the mouse button to activate the context-sensitive popup menu. This often is the quickest way to activate the desired dialog.

Formatting Borders and Colors

It also is possible to create different types of borders around a field and change the color of a field. This is accomplished by selecting a field and clicking Borders and Colors on the Format menu to activate the dialog. The Format Border and Colors dialog is shown in Figure 16-11.

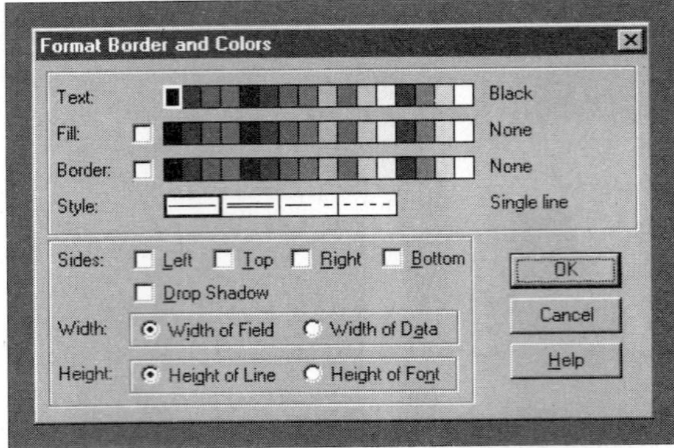

Figure 16-11: Format Border and Colors dialog

As shown in Figure 16-11, you can check the Fill and Border check boxes to define a fill color and border color for the field. The Sides section is a bit more interesting. The Left, Top, Right, and Bottom check boxes are used to draw a line (the type of line is based on the current style), along the four different sides of a field. Thus, if you wanted to draw a box around the field, you could check all four sides.

At this point, your report has very little data in it, so performing a hands-on exercise for each of the formatting tasks would be difficult. Instead, as you create the remaining report elements, you will format those elements.

A simple design strategy is used in this report that is common to many different reports. Formatting attributes are applied to fields based on the level of summarization. That is, detail information appears in a normal typeface. Subtotals and totals are bolded so they stand out. Furthermore, a single line is drawn for subtotals and a double line is drawn under the grand total. Again, this is to make the grand total stand out and visually indicate the end of the report. In general, the more important the data, the more it should stand out.

Section Formatting

In addition to formatting a particular object, there also are formats that you can apply to a particular section. You may have noticed that the size of a section changes automatically depending on the size of its contents. That is, if you increase the font size of the data in a particular section, the size of the section will increase accordingly. Furthermore, the size of a section corresponds to the visual size when the report is run. Sometimes, the initial or suggested size of a section is not the size you want. By default, Crystal Reports sizes a section based on the height of the fields drawn in it. By increasing the size of a section beyond the vertical space needed to display the fields, you create vertical white space in the section. For example, you may want more or less space between the detail lines in the report to improve readability. In this case, you can decrease or increase the size of the Details section accordingly. To change the size of a section, you move the mouse pointer over the horizontal line that divides the section. The mouse pointer changes to a vertical double-headed arrow. You can drag the mouse up or down to change the size of the section accordingly.

There also are formatting attributes you can apply to a particular section. This is accomplished using the Format Section dialog. You can activate this dialog by right-clicking the mouse button in the gray region of the section that contains the section name. For example, to format the Title section, you would right-click the mouse button in the gray area on the left-hand side of the report window that contained the text "Title". The Format Section dialog is shown in Figure 16-12.

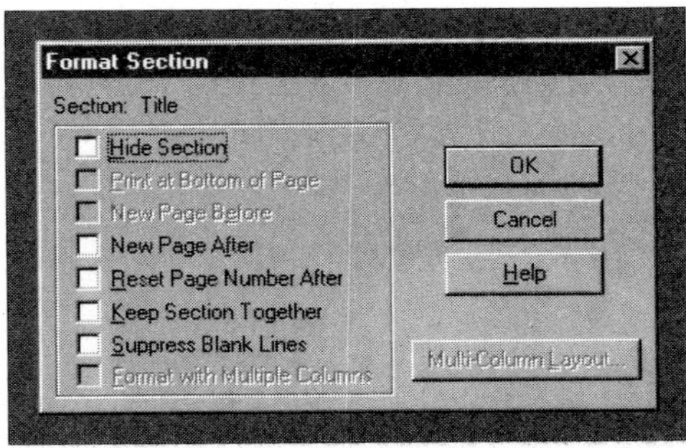

Figure 16-12: Format Section dialog

As shown in Figure 16-12, some of the options in the Format Section dialog are disabled. Which options are enabled and disabled depends on the type of section currently selected. This is because some options have no meaning for certain types of sections. The following list identifies the purpose of the different check boxes:

- **Hide Section** will cause the section not to be printed. For example, if you were printing a summary report and did not want to print the detail lines, you can check this option.
- **Print at Bottom of Page** will cause subtotals to be printed only at the bottom of the page. This may cause the bottom margin of some pages to increase.
- **New Page Before** will cause a new page to be started before printing the section.
- **New Page After** will cause a new page to be started after printing the section.
- **Reset Page Number After** will cause the page number to be reset after the page is printed. If you were printing a large report that contained information organized by different offices, it may be useful to reset the page number for each office. That way, each office could receive page one of the report.
- **Keep Section Together** will cause the section to be printed on the same page, if possible. Of course, a section may span multiple pages.
- **Suppress Blank Lines** will prevent a blank line from printing.
- The remaining options only are used when a multicolumn report is used. Multicolumn reports are not described in this chapter.

In this example, you will modify the Title section so the report title will appear on its own page and center the text that appears in the report title. The purpose of this task is to illustrate some of the difficulties with the Crystal Reports formatting capabilities. While Crystal Reports displays a horizontal ruler, it does not display a vertical ruler so you can see the height of a section or the exact vertical placement of a field relative to a section. In this example, you want to display a report title centered on a physical page. Thus, the text fields need to be in the Title section centered on a page. To accomplish this, you need to increase the size of the section and move the text field down so the text does not appear at the top of the page. Achieving the desired formatting requires a bit of trial and error because it is not possible to determine precisely the exact vertical placement of the fields on a section.

The only solution to the problem is to make a best guess about the vertical position of a field, then toggle to preview mode to see the result. You most likely will have to repeat this process to get the formatting correct.

To format a section:

1. Right-click the **Title section**, then click **Format Section** on the popup menu.
2. In the Format Section dialog, check the **New Page After** check box, then click **OK** to close the dialog.
3. Increase the size of the Title section to about the size of the report window.
4. Move the text field containing the caption **Inventory Report** in the Title section to the bottom of the screen.
5. Add two more text fields having a caption of **American** and **Distributors**. Set the font size to **24** point and the font attribute to **bold**. Refer to the report you printed at the beginning of the chapter for the exact placement of the text.
6. Toggle to **preview** mode then look at the full-page view to see the placement of the text box in the section. Toggle back and forth between the **preview** and **design** modes adjusting both the size of the section and the placement of the text box until the caption is centered both horizontally and vertically on the page.

Graphical Fields

You can insert graphical objects to improve significantly the appearance of a report to the end user. These include lines, boxes, and pictures. Lines and boxes are similar functionally to the Visual Basic Line and Shape controls. The process of creating lines and boxes in a report is nearly identical to the process you use in Visual Basic. A picture is something akin to a PictureBox control. It is used to display a graphical image in a report.

The process of creating a line is very simple. You click Line on the Insert menu. The mouse pointer changes to a pencil icon. You drag the mouse pointer to specify the start and end points of the line. Lines drawn in Crystal Reports have limitations. They always are horizontal or vertical lines. You cannot create a diagonal line. Also, you cannot change a vertical line into a horizontal line or a horizontal line into a vertical line. To do this, the line must be deleted and recreated.

The process to create a box is the same as the process to create a line. You click Box on the Insert menu. Again, the mouse pointer changes to a pencil icon. You drag the mouse pointer to specify the region of the box. You can edit the formatting characteristics of the box by clicking the box, right-clicking the mouse button, and then clicking Change Format on the popup menu. This causes the Box Format dialog to be displayed. A box supports the following customizable formatting elements:

- You can change both the border color and fill color of the box.
- The width of the border is customizable.
- The border can have a solid line or different forms of a dashed line.

In this example, you will create both a line and box on the Title page. The box will surround the text fields and the line will divide the text "American Distributors" from the text "Inventory Report".

To create a box and line on the Title page:

1. Scroll so the **Title** section is visible.
2. Click **Box** on the **Insert** menu. The mouse pointer will change to a pencil icon.
3. Create a box surrounding the page title text. Note that you also may need to increase the size of the section. Again, refer to the printed report for the exact placement.
4. Click **Line** on the **Insert** menu. The mouse pointer will change to a pencil icon.
5. Draw a line between the text **American Distributors** and the text **Inventory Report.**
6. Toggle to preview mode to see the box and lines in the report.

Graphical elements can dramatically improve the appearance of a report. Too many graphical elements in a report, however, can make it look cluttered. Thus, when and where to create graphical elements is somewhat subjective. In general, use graphical elements to divide sections or logical elements.

In addition to adding lines and boxes to a report, you also can insert graphical images in a report.

Adding Pictures in a Report

Inserting a picture in a report also is quite simple. Crystal Reports supports the following types of graphical files: bitmap files (.bmp), graphical interchange files (.gif), PC Paintbrush files (.pcx), TARGA files (.tga), and TIF files (.tif).

In this example, you will insert the company logo in the report. This logo is in .tif format and should appear in the Page header section of the report.

To insert a graphical image in a report:

1. Make sure the **Title** section is visible.
2. Click **Picture** on the **Insert** menu.
3. The Choose Picture File dialog will appear. Click the picture file named **Chapter.16\Startup\Logo.tif.** Make sure to specify the disk drive designator as necessary.
4. The image will appear in the report with the sizing handles activated. Move the image to the Title section in the report, then center it above the box you just created.

The initial size of the image in the report is the same as the actual size of the image. While the sizing handles can be used to resize the image, you should use care not to change significantly the relative dimensions of an image. If you do, the image will be stretched to fill the new region, and will appear distorted. Also, an image cannot span from one report section to another.

If you create a large image that needs to be displayed on every page of a long report, the image is regenerated for each page of the report. As such, if you print the report to a file, the file will be quite large. Also, if you have a slow printer, the report will be very time consuming to print.

Special Fields

Special fields are used to simplify common tasks. They are used for tasks like printing a page number on each page, or printing the current date in the report. The following list summarizes the different special fields supported by Crystal Reports:

- A **page number** field is used to display the current page number in the report. As such, it usually appears in the report's Page header or Page footer section.
- A **record number** field is used to print a counter associated with each detail record. As such, this type of field usually appears in the Details section of the report.

- A **group number** field is used for control break reports. This allows you to display a number associated with a control break. Control break reports are discussed later in the chapter.
- A **print date** field is used to display the current date in the report. The Page header or Page footer sections are suitable to display date fields.

Almost all the reports you create should contain both a date and a page number. One exception to this rule is printing mailing labels. Also, consider a situation when printing invoices and you are assured that an invoice always will fit on a single page. In this situation, page numbers are not necessary.

To create special fields:

1 Click **Special Field** on the **Insert** menu, then click **Print Date Field** on the **Special Field** submenu.

2 Position the date field in the Page header section in the report. Use the copy of the report you already printed to determine the position of the various fields.

3 Click **Special Field** on the **Insert** menu, then **Page Number Field** on the **Special Field** submenu.

4 Position the page number field in the Page footer section in the report.

5 Create two text fields to describe the special fields you just created with a caption of **Page:** and **Date:**.

6 Create a text field with the caption **Inventory Report** in the Page header section. Use a **14** point, **bold, underlined** font.

7 Draw a line across the top of the Page footer section.

8 Test the report.

At this point your report does not print any data. To print data from a Jet database or other data source, you use database fields.

Database Fields

Before inserting a database field, a word is in order about how Crystal Reports saves the data associated with a report. As you test a report, you frequently will toggle between the design and preview modes. If you make changes to the database data using Visual Basic or Access, the changed report data may not be read back into Crystal Reports. In the Crystal Reports development environment, Crystal Reports will, by default, read the database data the first time that preview mode is activated. As you toggle back and forth between the design and preview modes, however, Crystal Reports will use data that is cached in memory rather than rereading the database file when possible. To force Crystal Reports to reread a database file you click Refresh Report Data on the Report menu.

It also is possible to save data in the report. In this case, the data is read from the database file and stored in the report file itself. This is accomplished by clicking

Save Data with Report on the File menu. You can force Crystal Reports to read the database file again by clicking Refresh Report Data on the Report menu.

Inserting a database field is accomplished by activating the Insert Database Field dialog, which is shown in Figure 16-13.

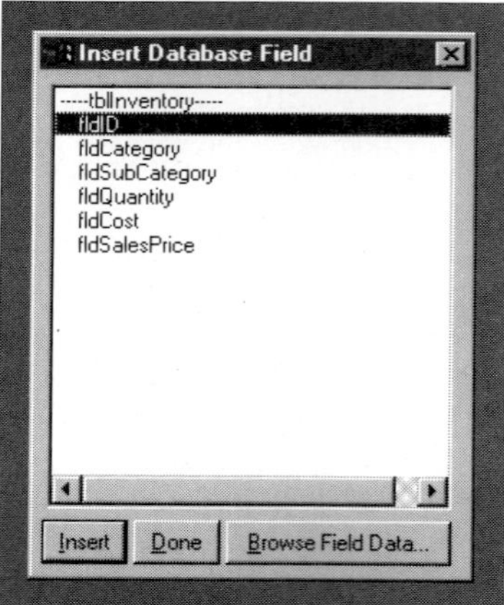

Figure 16-13: Insert Database Field dialog

As shown in Figure 16-13, the database table and fields in the table are listed in the dialog. In Figure 16-13, there is one table named tblInventory. The fields pertaining to each table appear under the table name and are indented. The Insert button is used to add the database field to the report. The Done button closes the dialog. The Browse Field Data button will display the actual data for a few records corresponding to the selected field.

To create the database field in the report, you select the desired field and click the Insert button. After clicking the Insert button, move the insertion point to the desired section in the report and click the mouse button. This causes the field to be inserted in the report. If the field is inserted into the Details section of the report, a corresponding text field is created automatically with a caption that is the same as the field's name just above the field in the Page header section. Note that this dialog is not modal.

To create a database field in the report:

1. Click **Database Field** on the **Insert** menu to activate the dialog, if necessary.
2. Double-click the field named **fldID**, then position the field on the Details section in the report.
3. Repeat Step 2 for the fields named **fldQuantity** and **fldCost**.
4. To create a more professional-looking report, you should change the caption of these fields and format them as necessary. Change the captions for the three text fields that were created automatically to **ID Number**, **Quantity**, and **Cost**. Set font to **Bold**, **Underline**, and **12 point**.

5 Test the report. The detail records should appear on one line. There should be 34 detail records printed.

You have seen how to display both text and database fields on a report. It often is necessary to perform computations based on data that is stored in a database table. This is accomplished using formula fields.

Formula Fields

Creating a formula field is a little more difficult than creating a text or database field. Conceptually, creating a formula field is like writing a string or arithmetic expression in Visual Basic. You can use literal values, like constant numbers, and arithmetic operators, like (+, -, *, /). The variables you use in a formula field work a bit differently than the variables used in a Visual Basic expression. Typically, the variables used in a formula field consist of fields from the database or database fields you already have defined. Finally, Crystal Reports supports a rich set of intrinsic functions that you can use to create a formula field.

Syntactically, a formula field looks much different than the syntax you are accustomed to in Visual Basic. Every formula has a name that begins with an @ sign. You click Insert Formula Field to activate a dialog allowing you to specify a name for the formula field. After you have assigned a name to a formula field, the Edit Formula dialog appears as shown in Figure 16-14.

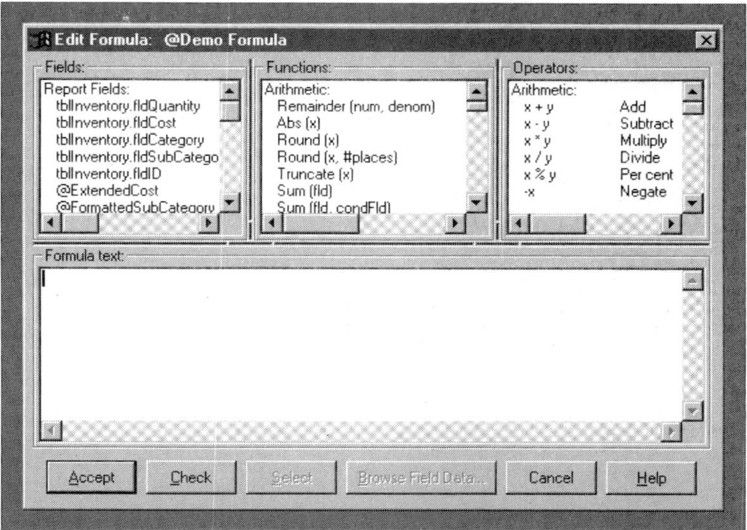

Figure 16-14: Edit Formula dialog

As shown in Figure 16-14 the dialog consists of the following four sections:

- The **Fields** section is used to select the database fields to be used in a formula.
- The **Functions** section is used to call mathematical and string manipulation functions. These functions typically are applied to database fields.
- The **Operators** section is used to perform arithmetic operations on database fields.
- As fields, functions, and operators are selected, the formula is displayed in the **Formula text** section.

The Fields, Functions, and Operators sections are just a convenience for the developer, as you could just type the formula in the Formula text text box. To use the Fields, Functions, and Operators sections, you click the insertion point in the Formula text text box, then click the desired field, function, or operator. If you make a mistake, you can select part of the formula and delete it. The Formula text text box really is nothing more than a simple Text Editor.

The buttons at the bottom of the dialog also are significant.

- When you click the **Accept** button, Crystal Reports verifies that the formula's syntax is correct. If it is, then the formula is added and you then can position it on the report. If the formula is not correct, a message box will be displayed and the Edit Formula dialog will not close. You either can correct the syntax or cancel the formula. Crystal Reports will not allow you to add a formula unless the syntax is correct.
- The **Check** button allows you to check the formula as you are creating or editing it. If the syntax is correct, a message box with the caption No Errors Found will appear. Otherwise, a message will be displayed that indicates the source of the error.
- The **Select** button is enabled only when a field, function, or operator is selected. Highlighting one of those items and clicking the Select button will add the item to the Formula text text box at the location of the insertion point.
- The **Browse Field Data** button only is enabled when a field in the Fields section is selected. Clicking this button will cause Crystal Reports to establish a connection with the database, and display a few records from the selected field.
- The **Cancel** button cancels the new formula or cancels editing of an existing formula.

Before creating a formula, consider the following valid formula:

```
{tblInventory.fldQuantity} * {tblInventory.fldCost}
```

The above formula is made up of two database fields that are multiplied together. First, note that each field is enclosed in braces {}. The field consists of both the database table name and the field name. Also note that the formula is like the right-hand side of an arithmetic expression. The left-hand side of the expression does not exist, however.

In this example, you will create a simple formula to compute the extended cost of an inventory item. The extended cost is computed by multiplying the quantity database field by the cost field.

To create a formula field:

1. Click **Formula Field** on the **Insert** menu.
2. In the Insert Formula dialog, enter the name **ExtendedCost** as the name of the new formula, then click the **OK** button. Note that you do not enter explicitly the @ character into the formula name. The Formula Editor automatically does this.
3. In the Fields section, click the field named **tblInventory.fldQuantity**, then click the **Select** button at the bottom of the dialog.
4. In the Operators section, click the **multiplication** operator (*), then click the **Select** button. Note that you also can just type the character in the Formula text text box.
5. In the Fields section, click the field named **tblInventory.fldCost**, then click the **Select** button. At this point the formula should look like the one shown in Figure 16-15.

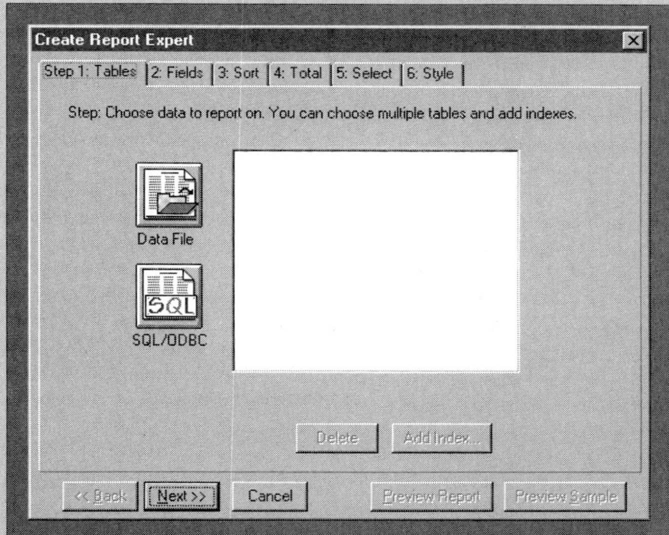

Figure 16-15: Edit Formula dialog

6. Click the **Check** button to validate the syntax of the formula. If the formula is correct, a dialog will appear telling you that no errors were found.
7. Click the **Accept** button to create the formula. Once the dialog is closed, a rectangular box appears in the report window.
8. Move the box to the **Details** section, then position the formula field to the right of the cost field.

9 A text field was automatically created when you created the formula field in the previous steps. Modify the caption of the text field to **Extended Cost.** Set the formatting attributes so they are the same as the other column headings.

10 Test the report. Make sure the extended cost is being computed correctly.

Before proceeding, consider what happens when Crystal Reports is evaluating the formula you just wrote. Each time a detail record is read from the database, Crystal Reports evaluates all the formulas in the Details section. It does this for each detail record. Again, Crystal Reports is doing this automatically and transparently.

In addition to printing detail information, most reports also summarize information in some way. You frequently need to print subtotals and totals in a report.

Printing Totals

In addition to printing detail lines, it often is necessary to summarize a column of numbers. For example, in the inventory report, it would be useful to print a grand total of the values in the @ExtendedCost formula field. Like the other tasks you have performed, you do not need to write any code to compute the grand total. The steps involved to create a total are similar regardless of whether you are creating a grand total or just a subtotal.

1. Select the field you want to summarize. This typically is a numeric field in the Details section. As you will see later in the chapter, there also are sections to display subtotals. You cannot compute a subtotal or total based on another subtotal.
2. On the Insert menu, there are two options. The Grand Total option allows you to insert a grand total for a detail field. The Subtotal option will summarize the specific records rather than all the records. Subtotals will be explained in a moment.
3. The final step is to determine the operation you want to perform on the selected field in the Details section. A Sum operation will add all the values together. There are other functions to compute the Average, Maximum, Minimum, Count, Variance, and Standard Deviation of the values.

Computing a grand total for a field is accomplished with the Insert Grand Total dialog, which is shown in Figure 16-16.

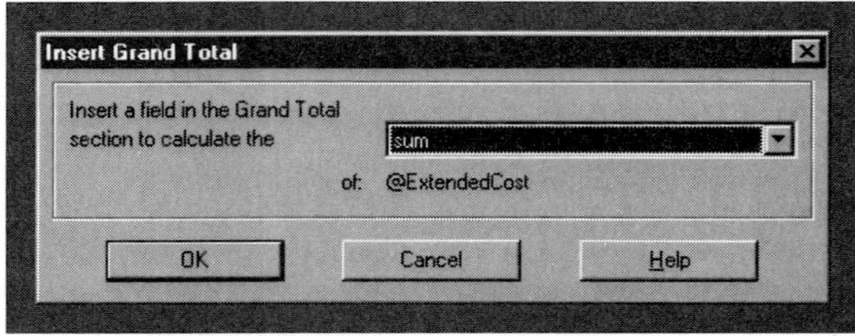

Figure 16-16: Insert Grand Total dialog

As shown in Figure 16-16, there is a list box with the value "sum", which will add the values of a field. To perform other operations, you select a different function in the list box. In this example, you will compute the grand total for all the extended cost values, and then format the grand total to improve the readability of the report.

To summarize the values for a column:

1. Click the **@ExtendedCost** field you already created in the Details section.
2. Click **Grand Total** on the **Insert** menu. Note that if you do not select a field, the command will be disabled.
3. Click **OK** to add the grand total. Note that a new section is added to the report named **Grand Total**, then the new field is added to the report.
4. Format the field. Select a **10** point **bold** font.
5. In this example, the grand total will appear with a double underline. Click **Border and Colors** on the **Format** menu. In the dialog, check the **Border** box, then select a **Black** border. Select the **double line** Line style. Check only the **Bottom** side check box. If all the boxes are checked, the border will appear as a box around the field.
6. Test the report. All the extended cost values are added together to create the grand total, which appears in the Grand Total section of the report.

In this example, you have a single formula field for each record. Again, this chapter is intended as an introduction to Crystal Reports. In many cases, you will have several computations for a single detail record. Furthermore, you may have one formula field that uses the result of another formula field. Crystal Reports supports both of these capabilities.

Control Break Reports

The report you have created so far is very simple. It contains the most basic elements of a report. Most reports are rarely this simple, however. Most reports require subtotals to be printed when the value of a specific field changes. For example, you may want to print a sales report with sales totals for each salesperson. This type of report commonly is referred to as a **control break report.** To create a control break in a report, you insert another type of section called a group section, and complete the information in the Group Section dialog, which is shown in Figure 16-17.

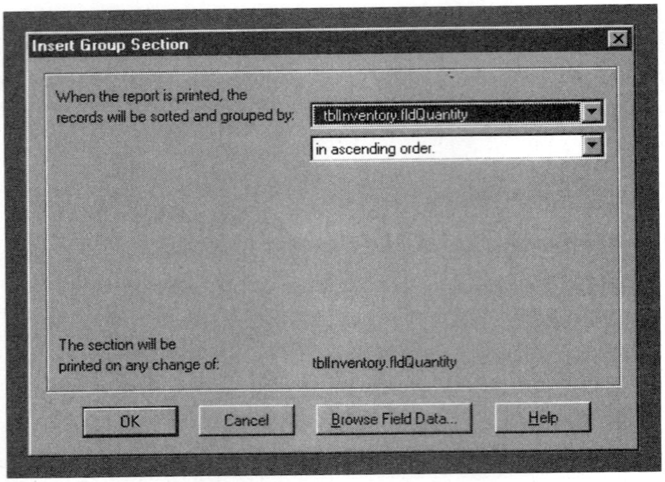

Figure 16-17: Insert Group Section dialog

As shown in Figure 16-17, the Insert Group Section dialog contains a list box to select a field. The field name you select is the field to be summarized. If you click the OK button, the new section will appear in the report.

In this example, you will create two group sections—one for the category and the other for the subcategory. In each of these sections, you will print the subtotal for the extended cost values. When you create multiple group sections, the order in which you create the group sections is important. In this example, the data should be summarized by category. For all the items having the same category, the items further are sorted by subcategory. Thus, a category can be thought of as the primary group section, and the subcategory can be thought of as the secondary section. In Crystal Reports, you should create the primary group section first, the secondary group section next, and so on.

To create a group section:

1. Click **Group Section** on the **Insert** menu to activate the Insert Group Section dialog.
2. In the list box at the top of the dialog, select the field named **tblInventory.fldCategory**. Click **OK** to add the section.
3. Click **Group Section** on the **Insert** menu again to insert another group section.
4. In the list box at the top of the dialog, select the field named **tblInventory.fldSubCategory**. Click **OK** to add the section.

Generally, the purpose of creating group sections is to print subtotals. In this example, you will print a subtotal that sums the values in the extended cost column for a particular subcategory when the value for the subcategory changes.

When the value of the category changes, you also will print a subtotal for all the records in that category. The subtotal includes all the subcategories within the same category. These values will be printed in the appropriate section. There are two ways to create these subtotals. You can create a formula field and use the Sum function. There also is a quick way to print a subtotal in a group section for a particular field. Using this technique, printing a subtotal is a three-step process (assuming that you already have created the necessary group sections).

1. Select the field in the Details section for which you want to create a subtotal.
2. Click Insert Subtotal to activate the Insert Subtotal dialog.
3. Select the group section you want to subtotal. The subtotal field is added to the footer for the selected group section and positioned below the value that exists in the Details section.

To print subtotals:

1. Activate the detail formula field named **@ExtendedCost** in the Details section.
2. Click **Subtotal** on the **Insert** menu.
3. In the Insert Subtotal dialog box, click the group section named **Group #2 tblInventory.fldSubCategory**, then click **OK** to add the new field. Note that the new field appears in the fldSubCategory group.
4. Activate the formula field in the Details section named **@ExtendedCost.**
5. Click **Subtotal** on the **Insert** menu.
6. In the Insert Subtotal dialog, select the group section named **Group #1 tblInventory.fldCategory**, then click **OK** to add the new field. Note that the field appears in the fldCategory group.
7. These fields also should be formatted so they stand out in the report. For the subcategory, set the font to **bold**. Set the border so a **black** border appears on the top of the field. For the category, set the font to **bold**. Set the border so a **black** border appears on the bottom of the field.
8. Test the report. Subtotals for both the category and subcategory should be printed.

String Formulas

Like Visual Basic, you can create formulas that operate on strings and use conversion functions that convert numeric values to strings. It is possible to concatenate strings and call various intrinsic functions on strings. String concatenation in Crystal Reports works like string concatenation in Visual Basic except that the concatenation operator is the plus character (+), instead of the ampersand character (&). The functions to convert numeric values to strings and manipulate strings are considerably different than those found in Visual Basic.

In this example, you will use string concatenation to build a string to appear in both the category and subcategory group footers. One part of the string will be the literal value "Category" or "Subcategory." The other part will be the actual name of the category or subcategory. The technique used in this example is to create a formula field that concatenates the literal string "Category" to the database field fldCategory.

To create a string formula:

1. Insert a formula field named **FormattedSubCategory** with the following contents:

   ```
   "Sub Category: " + {tblInventory.fldSubCategory}
   ```

2. Add the formula field to the **Subcategory** group footer.
3. Insert a formula field named **FormattedCategory** with the following contents:

   ```
   "Category: " + {tblInventory.fldCategory}
   ```

4. Add the formula field to the **Category** group footer.
5. For both of the formula fields, set the font to **bold**.
6. Test the report. The text strings should appear next to both the category and subcategory subtotals.

These two formulas are simple. A literal string is concatenated to a String field in the database. Because both arguments have the same type, no string conversion needs to be performed. A word is in order about what Crystal Reports is doing behind the scenes to display the category or subcategory for the correct record. When a control break occurs, the fields in the corresponding Group footer section are displayed. When this happens, you must consider the state of the current record. Consider the situation when a control break is happening for a subcategory. Assume the previous subcategory was Beets and the new subcategory is Corn. In the Group footer section, the value of the field is the old value Beets, rather than the new value Corn. After the Group footer section for Beets is displayed, the contents of the Group header section for Corn would be displayed, At this point, the current record is the first Corn record. Crystal Reports controls all this program logic for you.

Intrinsic Functions

Special fields, text fields, and database fields cannot be used to call any intrinsic functions. Only formula fields can. You have seen how to perform basic operations with formula fields by multiplying numbers and concatenating strings. You also can call intrinsic functions to perform type conversions and compute statistics, and many more. All the intrinsic functions supported by Crystal Reports appear in the Functions list box in the Edit Formula dialog.

If you examine the functions supported by Crystal Reports, you will see that many functions have the same name and syntax as comparable Visual Basic functions. You also will find there are several functions unique to Crystal Reports. Intrinsic functions are like those in Visual Basic in that they take arguments. These arguments can be other fields and literal values.

One of the features that would be useful in this report is a count of the number of different inventory items there are in a particular category or subcategory. To determine the number of items, you again create a formula field using the Count function.

Syntax

Count(*field***)**
Count(*field*, *condField***)**

Dissection

- The **Count** function finds the number of detail records for a group or grand total.
- *Field* identifies the database field or other formula field to be examined.
- The optional *condField*, if used, is the name of the character, number, or dollar value field that triggers *field* to print whenever its value changes. This option is typically used in a control break report.

Code Example

```
Count({tblInventory.fldID})
Count({tblInventory.fldID},
    {tblInventory.fldCategory})
```

Code Dissection

The first of the two functions determines the number of detail records in the report. The second form of the function likely would be used in a control break report. In this example, the count of records is printed whenever the value of the field fldCategory changes.

Note that the syntax of the Count function appears on two lines without any kind of continuation character. The Formula text text box ignores carriage returns in a formula. The carriage return appears in the above formula because the line is too long to appear on one line in this book.

You could create a formula field and add this function to it. This would display the count of records. A prompt also should be displayed to identify the purpose of the value to the reader of the report. While you could create a text field adjacent to the formula field, you can create one formula field to display a prompt followed by the number of records in one field. This requires that you perform three tasks. The first is to determine the count of records. The second is to convert that number to a string. Finally, you can concatenate the literal prompt to that string containing the number of records. You already have seen how to use the Count function and do string concatenation. You have not seen the function to convert a number to a string, however. This is accomplished using the ToText intrinsic function.

Syntax	**ToText**(*x*, #places)
Dissection	■ The **ToText** function converts a number to text. If the #places argument is used, the text is rounded. ■ The *x* argument contains a numeric field that is converted to text. ■ The #places argument contains an Integer number specifying the number of decimal points to appear in the text. Note that the value is rounded not truncated.
Code Example	`ToText({tblInventory.fldCost},2)`
Code Dissection	Assuming that fldCost is a number, this function rounds the number to two decimal places and converts the number to a string.

One of the complexities of using formulas in Crystal Reports is that a complex formula cannot be broken down into multiple statements as is possible in Visual Basic. Consider the following formula to compute the count of records for a category, convert the value to a string, and concatenate a text literal to the string:

```
ToText(Count ({tblInventory.fldID},
    {tblInventory.fldCategory} ),0) + " Records"
```

First, note that the following statement exists as one continuous line in the Formula Editor. As you can see, the syntactical difficulty arises because all the intrinsic procedure calls and operators are encapsulated into a single formula. The following steps occur as the formula is evaluated:

1. The count of records in fldCategory is determined (Count is evaluated).
2. The count is converted to a text value (ToText is evaluated).
3. The two strings are concatenated (+ is evaluated).

In this example, you will compute the record count for both the category and subcategory Group footer sections:

To use intrinsic functions:

1 Using the Formula Editor, create the following formula named **CountCategory**: Note that the formula should be entered on one line even though it appears on multiple lines in this book.

```
ToText(Count({tblInventory.fldID},{tblInventory.
fldCategory} ),0) + " Records"
```

2 Add the formula to the footer for the Category group.

3 Using the Formula Editor, create the following formula named **CountSubcategory** to the SubCategory group:

```
ToText(Count({tblInventory.fldID},{tblInventory.
fldCategory} ),0) + " Records"
```

4 Make sure both fields appear along the left margin and both are formatted with a **bold** font to remain consistent with the other information displayed in the group section.

5 Test the report.

These are but a few of the formulas supported by Crystal Reports. For example, many other functions are particular to creating reports based on a particular range of dates.

Selecting Specific Records

By default, Crystal Reports will print all the records in a table or query. This is not always the desired action, however. There may be times when you want to print records that satisfy specific criteria. For example, you may want to print records having a specific range of dates, or any other criteria. Conceptually, this is analogous to a WHERE clause. In fact, the syntax is similar to a WHERE clause without the word WHERE.

In Crystal Reports, you select specific records from a database table by creating a selection formula. The same Edit Formula dialog is used to create a selection formula as the dialog used to create a formula field. Like the condition list in a WHERE clause, however, the result must be a Boolean value. Consider the following Selection formula:

```
{tblInventory.fldCategory} = "Frozen Vegetables"
```

This selection formula causes only those records to be selected where the value of the field fldCategory is "Frozen Vegetables".

To create a selection formula:

1 Click **Edit Selection Formula** on the **Report** menu, then click **Record** on the **Edit Selection Formula** submenu. Enter the following formula in the Formula Editor:

```
{tblInventory.fldCategory} = "Frozen Vegetables"
```

2 Click **Accept** and test the report. Crystal Reports will display a dialog asking you whether you want to use saved data or refresh data. Click **Refresh Data.** The report preview should contain only those records for the category **Frozen Vegetables.**

3 Exit Crystal Reports. The remainder of the chapter shows how to execute the report just created from Visual Basic.

More complex selection formulas can be created. Selection formulas can contain other logical operators. You also can use relational operators like And, Or, and Not.

Sorting

When printing control break reports, how the records are sorted is an important consideration. If the records are not sorted so they correspond to the control breaks, the breaks will not occur as you would expect, and the report will be incorrect. Crystal Reports is intelligent about sorting control break reports. As you add group sections to a report, Crystal Reports modifies the sort criteria so the data will be sorted correctly. You can modify the sorting characteristics that Crystal Reports uses with the Record Sort Order dialog, which is shown in Figure 16-18.

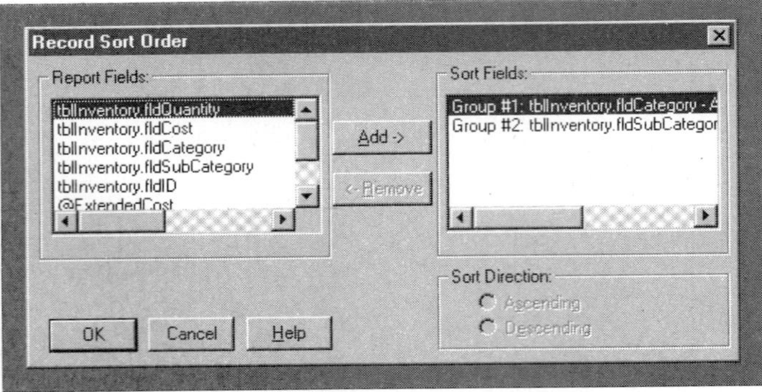

Figure 16-18: Record Sort Order dialog

As shown in Figure 16-18, the two group sections you created are listed in the Sort Fields list box. Again, Crystal Reports does this automatically. You can add additional sort fields by selecting a field in the Report Fields list box, and clicking the Add button.

SECTION B

objectives

In this section you will:

- Connect a Visual Basic program to Crystal Reports using the Crystal control
- Set the properties of the Crystal control to change report characteristics and report data

Using the Crystal Control

Using the Crystal Control

In the previous section, you saw how to use the Crystal Reports program to create, edit, debug, and test a report. In this section, you will see how to use the Crystal control to display a report from a Visual Basic program. The Crystal control is an ActiveX control, so it must be added on the Toolbox before a Visual Basic program can use it. Like the CommonDialog control, the Crystal control is invisible at run time.

Syntax	Crystal control
Properties	■ The **Action** property is used to print a report. The report is printed when the Action property is set to one (1). The reason for the Action property is historical. Early versions of controls, like the Crystal control, did not support methods. Rather, setting a property to a specific value simulated the effect of calling a method. This property typically was named Action. ■ The **ReportFileName** property is a string that identifies the path and file name of the report to be printed. ■ The **SelectionFormula** property changes the records that are selected and appear in the report. ■ The **WindowTitle** property is a string. The WindowTitle appears on the title bar of the Crystal Reports run-time window.

Like you have done many times before, you will begin by creating a simple example, then expand on that example. In the simplest possible case, you only need to create an instance of the Crystal control on the form, set the ReportFileName property to specify the report you want to print, then set the Action property to one (1) to print the report.

To print a report using the Crystal control:

1. Start **Visual Basic** then open the project named **Chapter.16\Startup\AD_S.vbp**.
2. Click **Components** on the **Project** menu, then locate the entry **Crystal Reports Control 4.6**. Add a reference to the control in the project.
3. Create an instance of the control on the form, then set the Name property to **cry1**.
4. Activate the **Property Pages** dialog for the control as shown in Figure 16-19.

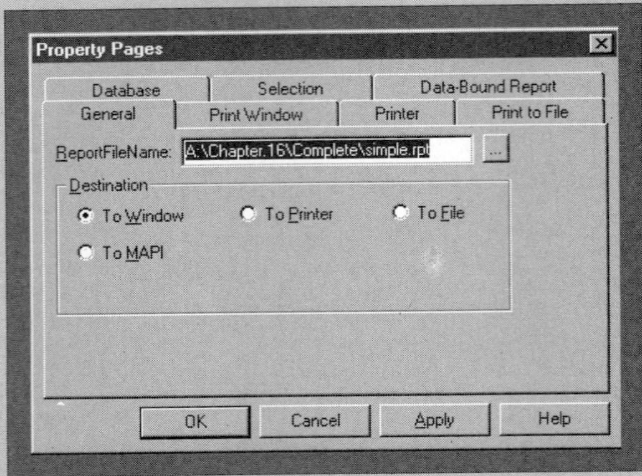

Figure 16-19: Property Pages dialog

5. Set the properties as shown in Figure 16-19. Click **OK**.
6. Enter the following statement in the **mnuFilePrintInventory_Click** event procedure:

```
cry1.Action = 1
```

7. Test the program. Click **Print** on the **File** menu, then click **Inventory** on the **Print** submenu to print the inventory report to the string. Note that the selection filter still applies to the selected records.

While using the Property Pages dialog to print the report will work, this technique has several limitations. First, if you wanted to print multiple reports from the same program, you would have to create one instance of the Crystal control for each report you wanted to print. As you know from your experience with the CommonDialog control, it is more efficient to minimize the number of control instances and use the same instance for many tasks. This same technique can be used with the Crystal control. Additionally, you can set properties dynamically at run time to change the report destination and other characteristics. In this example, suppose you wanted the user to be able to print two different reports. Also, assume that you wanted to allow the user to print the report to the printer or screen and allow the user to change the number of copies of the report that are printed.

The most logical way to accomplish this is to set the ReportFileName property dynamically at run time so the same instance of the Crystal control can be used for multiple reports. To specify the report destination and number of copies, you can use the CommonDialog control allowing the user to select the report destination and number of copies. After the user selects this information, the appropriate properties of the Crystal control can be set.

Another useful feature would be to allow the user to select different report data dynamically at run time. For example, suppose you wanted the user to be able to select a specific category or all categories. Remember, in the previous section you created a selection formula. You also can define a selection formula at run time for a report by setting the SelectionFormula property. The process to define a selection formula is much like the process you used to create an SQL WHERE clause. That is, you create a string variable that makes up the WHERE clause. This is accomplished through string concatenation. To illustrate how to set the selection formula, consider the following statement. This statement assumes that cry1 represents an instance of the Crystal control and that cboCategory is a combo box that has been loaded with the valid categories of the different inventory items.

```
cry1.SelectionFormula = "{tblInventory.fldCategory}" & _
    " = " & " '" & cboCategory & "' "
```

Note the following about the preceding statement and remember the syntax of a WHERE clause and the process you went through to define the string argument for that clause. In this situation, you are creating a selection formula like the one you created in Crystal Reports in the previous section. Note that the syntax to reference a field in a table is the same. The table name is followed by the field name and the two are separated by a period. Also note that the name is enclosed in brackets just like it was when you created the formula in the Formula Editor.

The formula will be used to select different categories, or all categories if there is not a specific category selected. When you entered a category in the Crystal Reports Formula Editor, the category, because it was a string, was surrounded by double quotes. In Visual Basic, the same string must be surrounded by single quotation marks.

To select and print reports dynamically at run time:

1 Enter the following statements in the **mnuFilePrintInventory_Click** event procedure:

```
On Error GoTo CancelError
    cry1.ReportFileName = _
        "A:\Chapter.16\Complete\Simple.rpt"
```

```
        cry1.WindowTitle = _
            "American Distributors - Inventory Report"
        If cboCategory.ListIndex = -1 Then
            cry1.SelectionFormula = ""
        Else
            cry1.SelectionFormula = _
                "{tblInventory.fldCategory}" & _
                " = " & " '" & cboCategory & "' "
        End If
        cry1.Destination = crptToWindow
        cry1.Action = 1
    CancelError:
```

2 Test the program. Click **Open** on the **File** menu. Click the **Chapter.16\Startup\AD.mdb** database file from the common dialog. Select the drive designator as necessary. This causes the database to be opened and the distinct categories to be read in the combo box.

3 Click one of the categories from the combo box. Click **Print** on the **File** menu, then **Inventory** on the **Print** submenu to print the same inventory report but select only the categories that you selected.

The code to use the CommonDialog control to open a file should be familiar along with the use of the error handler. The use of the Crystal control is new so the syntax requires further explanation.

```
If cboCategory.ListIndex = -1 Then
    cry1.SelectionFormula = ""
Else
    cry1.SelectionFormula = _
        "{tblInventory.fldCategory}" & _
        " = " & " '" & cboCategory & "' "
End If
```

The If statement first determines whether a particular category has been selected. If not, the SelectionFormula property is set to an empty string causing all the records to be selected. If a category is selected in the ComboBox control, then the SelectionFormula is built based on the currently selected item. Remember, the text of the currently selected item in a combo box is stored in the default property.

```
cry1.Destination = crptToWindow
cry1.Action = 1
```

The final statements cause the report to be printed on the screen.

While there are many other properties related to the Crystal control, the use of the previous properties should provide a foundation for the remaining properties supported. As you work with additional Crystal control properties, remember you are setting properties for particular report components just as you did when you were using Crystal Reports. The only difference is that you are setting those same properties from Visual Basic.

SUMMARY

This chapter has presented the fundamental concepts of report creation with Crystal Reports and how to print reports and dynamically change the properties at run time. Although you can create more complex reports than the ones presented here, the techniques are the same. You create a report made up of sections. The simplest report contains five sections. If you want to add control breaks to a report, you can add additional sections for each control break. The process of creating a report can be divided roughly into the following well-defined set of tasks:

- All reports are divided into sections. The different sections in a report control the information that is printed when a report title is printed, when a page break occurs, when a detail line is printed, or when a control break occurs.
- Data is printed in a section because a field was created in a particular section. Four types of fields can be used including database fields, text fields, formula fields, and special fields.
- Only formula fields can evaluate expressions and call intrinsic functions.
- There is a variation of a formula field called a selection formula that is used to determine which records are printed in a report. Conceptually, the purpose of a selection formula is the same as an SQL WHERE clause.

Getting Visual Basic to print a report is accomplished with the Crystal control. You create an instance of the Crystal control on a form, and set its properties to define the name of the report you want to print, whether to print the report on the screen or to the printer, and other characteristics pertaining to the report.

QUESTIONS

1. Which of the following statements are true pertaining to Crystal Reports?
   a. Crystal Reports is a stand-alone program and not part of Visual Basic.
   b. Visual Basic programs can access Crystal Reports using the Crystal control.
   c. You execute Crystal Reports from Visual Basic.
   d. Both a and b.
   e. Both b and c.
2. What are the default sections created on a new report?
   a. Page title, Page header, Details, Page footer, Page summary.
   b. Page title, Page header, Details, Page footer, Summary.
   c. Title, Page header, Details, Page footer, Summary.
   d. Title, Header, Details, Footer, Summary.
   e. None of the above.
3. Which of the following are valid types of fields in Crystal Reports?
   a. Text, formula, data, special.
   b. TextBox, label, formula, DatabaseType.
   c. Text, formula, label, database, special.
   d. Text, formula, database, special.
   e. Label, formula, database, special.
4. Which of the following graphical elements are supported by Crystal Reports?
   a. Line, Shape, PictureBox.
   b. Line, Box, Picture.
   c. Line, Rectangle, PictureBox.
   d. Arrow, Box, Picture.
   e. None of the above.
5. To increase the height of a detail line you ____________.
   a. set the Distance property
   b. explicitly change the height of a field
   c. set the Height property
   d. change the size of the Details section
   e. look at the vertical ruler
6. Which of the following are valid special fields?
   a. Page, current record, date.
   b. Page, record number, current date.
   c. Current page, record number, date.
   d. Page, record, date.
   e. Page number, record number, print date.

7. To create a field that will display data from a database, you create a __________ field.
   a. Database
   b. Formula
   c. Text
   d. Special
   e. None of the above.
8. To create a field that will display a prompt you create a ___________ field.
   a. prompt
   b. text
   c. label
   d. formula
   e. database
9. Which of the following statements are true about formulas?
   a. A formula begins with an & character.
   b. A formula has a name.
   c. Database fields are enclosed in square brackets ([ ]).
   d. None of the above.
   e. All of the above.
10. Which of the statements are true about a grand total?
    a. It appears in the Grand Total section.
    b. There can be multiple Grand Total sections.
    c. A grand total field is based on a detail field.
    d. Both a and c.
    e. All of the above.
11. Which of the following functions are supported by a total?
    a. Sum.
    b. Average.
    c. Maximum.
    d. Standard Deviation.
    e. All of the above.
12. ___________ fields can use intrinsic functions.
    a. formula
    b. database
    c. text
    d. special
    e. All of the above.

13. Which of the following statements are true related to the Crystal control?
    a. It is an intrinsic control.
    b. It allows you to create reports directly from Visual Basic.
    c. The ShowPrinter method is used to print a report.
    d. All of the above.
    e. None of the above.

For Questions 14 through 20 assume the following: there is a table named tblSales having numeric fields named fldQuantity and fldPrice. Each record has a unique ID specified by the fldID field that is a text string.

14. Create the code for a formula field that will multiply the field named **fldQuantity** by the field named **fldPrice**.
15. Create the code for a formula field that will multiply the field named **fldQuantity** by the field named **fldPrice** and reduce that amount by 10% (a 10 percent discount).
16. Create the code for a formula field that will multiply the fields **fldQuantity** by **fldPrice,** round the number to 0 decimal places and convert the number to a string.
17. Create the code for a formula field that will count the number of records printed.
18. Create the code for a formula field that will count the number of records printed and concatenate that value to the string literal Records Printed.
19. Write the necessary code to set the SelectionFormula property such that the only record selected will be where the value of **fldPrice** is greater than $100.00.
20. Write the necessary statement to print the report identified by the Crystal control named **cryReport**.

EXERCISES

In each of the following exercises, you will use the database named **Sample.mdb**, which has the following structure:

tblSample
- fldSampleID
- fldSampleLocation
- fldSampleDate
- fldElement
- fldAmount

The information contains chemical samples for different locations. fldSampleID is a unique key that identifies the record. fldSampleLocation is an integer. This value represents a physical location where a chemical sample was taken. The remaining fields contain the date of the sample, a chemical being sampled, and the amount of the specific chemical found in the sample.

1. In this exercise, you will create a control break report consisting of a Page header, a Page footer, and a Details section. The records should be sorted by sample location. For records having the same sample location, sort the record by the element (chemical name). Finally, order those records by date. This report should have a primary control break for the location, and a secondary control break for the element.

a. Start **Crystal reports** and create a report named **Chapter.16\Exercise\Exercise1.rpt.**
b. Create a page heading for the report to print the page number.
c. Draw a line between the Page heading and the Details sections.
d. In the Details section, print each of the five fields. Create a column header for each column.
e. Create a page footer that contains a line and the current date, and a text field to identify the report. The text field should have the caption **Basic Sample Report.**
f. Add a control break to the report such that each time the sample location changes, the number of records is printed for the location.
g. Add a second control break that will print the average of a specific element when the element name changes for a particular location.
h. Create a report title with a box. In the report title, display the text **Exercise 1 Sample Report.**
i. Save and test the report.

2. In this exercise, you will print a summary that will list the average amount of all chemicals (elements) for all locations. That is, you should sort the records by element name. For each element, print the element name and the average amount in that element.

a. Start **Crystal Reports** and create a report named **Chapter.16\Exercise\Exercise2.rpt.**
b. Add a report name of **Element Summary Report** to the page header.
c. Add the page number and date printed to the page footer.
d. Sort the report by the field named **fldElement.**
e. Add the fields named **fldElement** and **fldAmount** to the Details section.
f. Create a control break on the field named **fldElement.**
g. Create the necessary formula field to print the average of all the samples for the current element. The formula field should be in the footer for the control break.

h. Hide the Details section.
i. Save and test the report.

3. In this exercise, you will use the Crystal control.
   a. Create a new project and set the Name property of the form to **frmExercise3**. Save the form using the name **Chapter.16\Exercise\frmExercise3.frm** and the project using the name **Chapter.16\Exercise\Exercise3.vbp.**
   b. Add the Crystal control and the CommonDialog control to the project.
   c. Create a File menu with an Open submenu that will use the common dialog to get the report name of a file. Using the techniques presented in the chapter, print the selected report to the screen.
   d. Save and test the project.

objectives

In this appendix you will:

- Prepare a Visual Basic program for debugging
- Identify the cause of, and diagnosis for, errors in a program
- Trace the execution of a program
- Set breakpoints and watch expressions

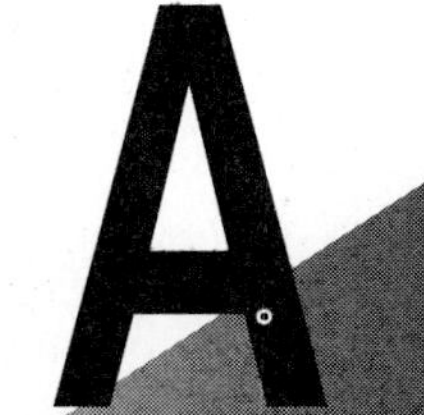

APPENDIX A

Debugging

Techniques for Resolving Errors in a Visual Basic Program

The demonstration program in this appendix is made up of a Standard EXE project and an ActiveX DLL project combined into a project group. The program is designed to illustrate different debugging and error handling techniques to help you identify specific programming problems, and diagnose them using different types of projects.

Identifying Programming Errors

As you have no doubt discovered, you seldom will write a program that works perfectly the first time. You also likely have discovered that locating and correcting programming errors can be a time consuming and tedious process. Programming errors can be categorized into three different types: syntax, run-time, and logic.

- A **syntax error** occurs when you write a statement that Visual Basic cannot understand; that is, a statement that violates the rules of the Visual Basic language. For example, you may misspell a keyword or try to reference a property that is not supported by a particular object.
- A **run-time error** occurs when a program is executing. Run-time errors occur for many reasons. For example, an expression may be evaluated that causes numeric overflow or underflow to occur (attempting to store too large or small a number in a variable of a specific data type). Nearly all run-time errors can be trapped using an error handler.
- A **logic error** occurs when the program does not perform as intended and produces incorrect results. Logic errors may or may not result in run-time errors.

The distinction between logic and run-time errors is not always clear. A logic error would occur if you intended to add two numbers together but wrote statements to multiply them instead. When the program is run, the multiplication could generate an overflow run-time error. In this example, the logic error in turn causes a run-time error. Or you may write a statement that stores a value in an incorrect text box. In this situation, your program likely will produce incorrect results but not generate a run-time error.

Detecting and correcting run-time and logic errors is made much simpler because of the tools provided by the Visual Basic IDE. Using these tools to identify programming errors collectively is referred to as **debugging**.

Preparing a Program for Debugging

Visual Basic checks for syntax errors when a program is compiled. How a program is compiled, and how errors are handled, depend on settings in the Options dialog. The Options dialog can be activated from the Tools menu. These settings are saved to the Visual Basic environment, so you should verify that they are correct for the project you are trying to debug. Figure A-1 shows the Error Trapping and Compile options that pertain to debugging.

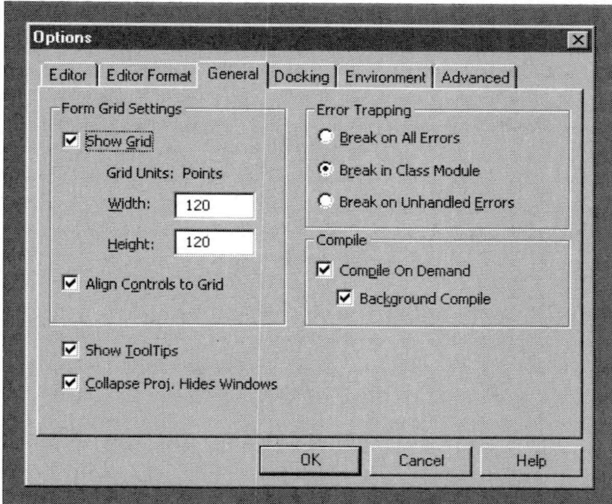

Figure A-1: Options dialog

As shown in Figure A-1, the Compile section contains two check boxes.

- If the **Compile On Demand** check box is checked, Visual Basic will compile the current procedure and analyze it for syntax errors just before the procedure is run. Note that the entire procedure is examined rather than each line one at a time. In this situation, a procedure only will be compiled when it is called for the first time; that is, Visual Basic will not find all the syntax errors in a project until you execute all the procedures in the project. While you are writing and testing programs, checking this box will cause your programs to start much faster because the entire project does not need to be compiled prior to executing. If the Compile On Demand check box is not checked, the syntax of an entire program is checked before the program begins executing.
- If the **Background Compile** check box is checked, a program will be compiled while the computer is idle during run time. The Background Compile check box option can improve run-time execution speed the first time procedures are executed. This option is available only when Compile On Demand is checked.

How Visual Basic handles run-time errors depends on settings in the Error Trapping section in the Options dialog. These options become important when you are debugging class modules, error handlers, and project groups. The three options in this section control the behavior of Visual Basic when a run-time error occurs:

- When **Break on All Errors** is selected, any run-time error will cause Visual Basic to enter break mode and highlight the offending statement in the module where the error occurred regardless of the type of module.
- When **Break in Class Module** is selected, errors in class modules that are not handled by an On Error statement cause Visual Basic to enter break mode and highlight the offending statement in the Code window.

- When **Break on Unhandled Errors** is selected, Visual Basic enters break mode when a run-time error occurs that is not handled by an On Error statement.

To illustrate the effect of these different options, the debugging program contains a class module and three command buttons. When and where an error occurs depend on the settings of these options. The following code already has been created in the Mult method of the class module named clsDebug. The function is nonsensical. It multiplies two numbers together. The purpose of the example is to illustrate the different ways Visual Basic will treat a run-time error. As such, all the procedures in this appendix are very simple so the errors are obvious. Using each different error-trapping option, you will generate run-time errors in both a form and class module. The run-time error that occurs is the same in each circumstance. It is an overflow error generated because an attempt is made to multiply two integer numbers together that produce a result that is greater than 32767:

```
Public Function Mult(pintArg1 As Integer, _
    pintArg2 As Integer) As Integer
    Mult = pintArg1 * pintArg2
End Function
```

The Break Mode command button on the form contains code to create an instance of the class and call the Mult function with arguments that will generate a run-time error. It also contains code to perform the same multiplication operation in the Click event procedure for the button itself.

```
Private Sub cmdBreakMode_Click( )
On Error Resume Next
    Dim pintResult As Integer
    Dim d As New clsDebug
    pintResult = 32000 * 32000
    pintResult = d.Mult(32000, 32000)
    Exit Sub
cmdError:
    Debug.Print Err.Number
    Debug.Print Err.Description
End Sub
```

This code performs the same multiplication operation both in the command button's Click event procedure and in the class module. One statement will cause a run-time error in the command button's Click event procedure. The other will cause a run-time error in the class module.

To examine the error trapping options:

1. Open the project group **Appendix.A\Complete\Debug.vbg.** On the General tab in the Options dialog click the **Break on All Errors** option button in the Error Trapping section. Test the program. Click the **Break Mode** command button. The error dialog appears as shown in Figure A-2.

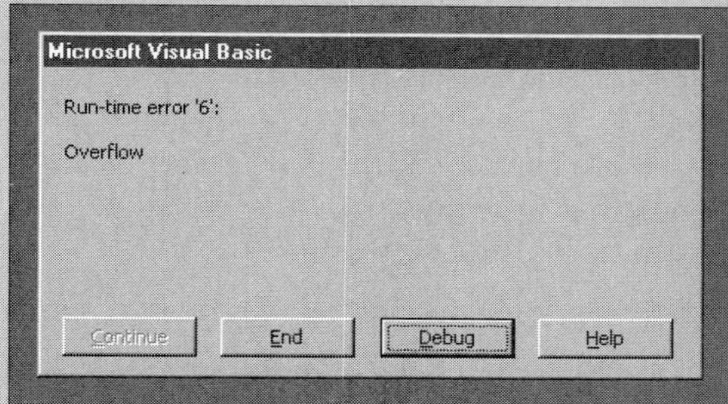

Figure A-2: Overflow error message

2. Click **Debug** to highlight the offending statement:

```
pintResult = 32000 * 32000
```

This error occurred in the command button's Click event procedure even though it contained an error handler. Had one of the other option buttons in the Error Trapping section been clicked, the run-time error would have been trapped by the error handler, and execution would have continued. End the program.

3. Click **Break in Class Module** in the Options dialog, then test the program again. This time, the statement that caused the error is in the class module.

```
Mult = pintArg1 * pintArg2
```

From the organization of the code in the Click event procedure, the call to the Mult method in the class module appears after the attempt to multiply the same numbers in the event procedure. Thus, the error handler trapped the error that occurred in the previous set of steps, but because you clicked Break in Class Module, the unhandled error in the class module is raised. End the program.

4. Click **Break on Unhandled Errors** in the Options dialog, then test the program again. This time, no run-time error occurs. In this situation, an error is raised in the class module. Visual Basic returns the error code to the calling procedure, which in this case is the Click event procedure. The code in the event procedure then handles the error in the class module.

Which error trapping mode to use depends on the code that you are debugging. For example, if you are working with a class module that you believe to be working correctly, you generally do not want to trap the errors in that module. Rather, you want the class module to return any errors to the client using the class.

There also may be times when you want to test your error handlers to see if they are working as you expect. That is, you want to be able to see all the run-time errors that are occurring, whether or not there is an active error handler. In this situation, the Break on All Errors option button is useful. Remember, these debugging tools are just that—tools. You undoubtedly will find your own way to use these tools and when.

Visual Basic Debugging Tools

In the previous example, you saw the different types of modules that will generate a run-time error depending on the error trapping settings. This is fine when an error in your code actually generates a run-time error. There are other types of errors that can occur, which do not actually cause a run-time error, however. In these cases, there is no error to be trapped. In these situations, you need to learn how to control, in more detail, the execution of a program.

The Visual Basic debugging tools consist of commands that allow you to suspend temporarily the execution of your program by entering break mode, and then follow the execution of statements and procedures. You can execute each statement in the program line by line and have your program stop executing when a specific statement is reached or when the value of a variable or object changes.

Whenever you suspend the execution of your program, you do so to try to identify a particular problem. This involves looking at the values of the variables and object properties in your program to see if they contain correct data. You can look at the contents of variables and objects using the Immediate, Watch, and Local windows. You use the debugging commands in conjunction with these windows as tools to help you locate and fix run-time and logic errors in your program.

Tracing Program Execution

Often a program contains logic errors; that is, it produces incorrect results, but does not necessarily generate a run-time error or the actual cause of a run-time error is not apparent. This is when the debugging tools are most useful. When a program is producing incorrect results, but you are not sure why, it often is helpful to step through the statements in a program. There are several commands that allow you to follow the execution of your program.

- The **Step Into** button allows you to execute one statement at a time and then Visual Basic enters break mode. If the statement is a procedure call, the procedure declaration for the procedure that will be executed next is highlighted in the Code window.

- The **Step Over** button works like the Step Into button. If the statement is a procedure call, however, then all the statements in the procedure are executed, and Visual Basic will enter break mode just before executing the statement following the procedure call.
- The **Step Out** button is similar to the Step Over button. When clicked, the Step Out button will execute all the remaining statements in the current procedure.
- You can alter the flow of execution during break mode by clicking a statement in the Code window, clicking Debug, and then clicking Set Next Statement.

In addition to stepping through every statement in every procedure in a program, you can step through parts of a program or pause the program and continue executing statements one at a time. When you are debugging a procedure that calls other procedures, you do not have to trace through the statements in a procedure when you know it works correctly. You can use the Step Over button to execute all the statements in a procedure and suspend execution from the statement following that procedure. Furthermore, you can suspend execution at any time by clicking the Break button at run time.

Again, how you use these tools depends on the problem you are trying to fix, and where you suspect the problem is occurring. To illustrate the different ways that you can step through a program, a simple example is again in order. It is intended to illustrate how to locate a specific module that contains an error and how to locate the code that is causing the error. In this example, there only are three procedures in question. In a large program, however, it is likely that you may need to examine many more procedures to locate the cause of an error.

Programming tip

As you debug programs, you may find it useful to display the Debug toolbar. Clicking Debug, then Toolbars on the View menu can accomplish this.

In this example, you will examine the code to compute the area of a rectangle (length * width), and the volume of a three-dimensional rectangle (length * width * height). This example again is very simple, and the procedures are subdivided more than those you usually would write in practice. Again, the focus of the example is to trace the execution of various procedures. As such, the procedures are kept very simple. Consider the following code in the form module:

```
Private Sub cmdTrace_Click( )
    Dim pintArea As Integer
    Dim pintVolume As Long
    pintArea = Area(txtLength, txtWidth)
    pintVolume = Volume(pintArea, txtHeight)
    txtVolume = pintVolume
End Sub
Private Function Area(l As Integer, w As Integer)
    Area = l * w
End Function
```

```
' The following statement contains the logic error.
Private Function Volume(a As Integer, h As Integer)
    Volume = a / h
End Function
```

In the above code, the area of a rectangle is computed by multiplying the length by the width. The result then is used as an argument in the call to the Volume function. This function has an error. Instead of multiplying the area by the height, the area is divided by the height. You now can use the various execution tracing techniques to examine the flow of execution in a program.

To trace a program's execution flow:

1. Press the **F8** key to start the program. As before, enter the values **1**, **2** and **3** in the text boxes and click **Trace**. At this point, the program is running but no statement is executing. The program is waiting for an event to occur.
2. Enter the values **1**, **2**, and **3**, as the length, width, and height, then click the **Trace** command button.
3. The event procedure named **cmdTrace_Click** is highlighted in the Code window indicating that the procedure is about to be executed.
4. Press the **F8** key again. The following statement is highlighted and is the next statement to be executed:

   ```
   pintArea = Area(txtLength, txtWidth)
   ```

5. Move the insertion point over the arguments named txtLength and txtWidth. Note that a ToolTip appears containing the current value of these two arguments. This is a quick way to determine the current value of a property or variable.
6. Press the **F8** key again to execute the statement. In this case, the function is called and the Function procedure named **Area** is highlighted indicating that this procedure is about to be executed.
7. Continue to press the **F8** key. You will see the Area function execute and return, then the Volume function called. Eventually, you will see no statement highlighted in the Code window. At this point, there is no statement executing and Visual Basic again is waiting for an event to occur. End the program.

You also can step over a function procedure when it is working correctly.

To step over a Function or Sub procedure:

1. Start the program by pressing the **F8** key. When the following statement is highlighted, press **Shift+F8** to step over the Area function call:

   ```
   pintArea = Area(txtLength, txtWidth)
   ```

2 The function executes. The next statement that will be executed is the call to the Volume function. End the program.

Stepping through the statements that are executing, examining which statements are executing, and then looking at the values of variables and properties as they are manipulated are all important parts of the debugging process. While stepping through all the statements in a program is useful, it has serious limitations. Imagine that you had to execute 10,000 statements to reach the point where you suspected the problem in a program was occurring. In this situation, you can tell Visual Basic to suspend execution when a particular statement is reached, then from that point, examine the statements that are executing one at a time.

Setting Breakpoints

When you suspect a problem is occurring in a particular procedure or that a particular statement is not correct, you can suspend execution of a program at any executable statement by setting a breakpoint. A **breakpoint** is a program line you specify where the program will stop execution and enter break mode. As such, you only can set breakpoints on statements containing executable code. That is, you cannot set a breakpoint on a line containing a variable declaration. Setting a breakpoint can be accomplished by locating a statement in the Code window and clicking the Toggle Breakpoint button or pressing the F9 key. The Toggle Breakpoint button is available only when the Code window is active. Note that breakpoints are not persistent between invocations of Visual Basic. Thus, if you have several breakpoints set for a particular debugging session, they will disappear the next time you start Visual Basic.

It also is possible to set a breakpoint by clicking the mouse in the left margin of the Code window containing an executable statement. This causes the line to be highlighted and a breakpoint set. Clicking the line again will remove the breakpoint.

When a breakpoint is set on a line, the line will appear in a highlighted color. To clear a breakpoint, click the line in the program where a breakpoint is set and click the Toggle Breakpoint button. When you run the program and the statement containing the breakpoint is reached, Visual Basic will suspend execution of the program and enter break mode just before executing the statement containing the breakpoint. The line will appear highlighted. Once in break mode, you can use the Immediate window and the Step Into or Step Over buttons to find problems in the code. For example, if you have determined that a function such as Pmt is producing incorrect results, you might want to set a breakpoint just before the function is called, and then look at the values of the arguments to determine which one is not correct.

To set a breakpoint:

1. Activate the Code window for the form module.
2. Set a breakpoint on the following line:

   ```
   pintArea = Area(txtLength, txtWidth)
   ```

3. Test the program. Enter values for the length, width, and height, then click the **Trace** command button. The program will enter break mode just before executing the statement. End the program.

The process to create and destroy breakpoints is the same for all breakpoints. You can create as many or as few breakpoints as you need. Again, where to set a breakpoint and how many breakpoints to set is up to you and the debugging task at hand.

Using the Immediate Window

Another debugging tool is the Immediate window. You use the **Immediate** window to look at the values of variables and object properties and to change those values. There are two ways to use the Immediate window:

- You can use the **Debug.Print** method in a program. When this method is called, the values of its arguments are printed in the Immediate window.
- You also can type Print statements directly in the Immediate window to look at values of both variables and object properties in the program. You can type statements in the Immediate window only while a program is in break mode or design mode. Most statements are valid only in break mode.
- You also can execute a procedure simply by typing its name and arguments in the Immediate window.

In the following example, you will use the Immediate window to examine the value of variables and call a function explicitly.

To display values in the Immediate window:

1. Start the program. Enter values for the length, width, and height. Then click the **Trace** command button. The breakpoint you set in the previous steps should be highlighted.
2. Click **Immediate** on the **View** menu to open the Immediate window and enter the following statement:

   ```
   Print txtLength
   ```

   The value you entered for the length will appear in the Immediate window.

3 Enter the following assignment statement in the Immediate window:

```
txtArea = Area(10,10)
```

This causes the Area function to be called and the result stored in the text box named txtArea. As you can see, you can execute assignment statements in the Immediate window, just as the statement has been entered in your code. This can help you to test whether or not a particular function is running correctly.

Again, when to use the Immediate window to display the value of variables and properties is a matter of personal choice.

Adding Watch Expressions

Watch expressions are similar to breakpoints, but **watch expressions** allow you to suspend execution when a condition is True or when the value of an object or variable changes. Like breakpoints, watch expressions can be created, changed, or deleted while a program is in design mode or break mode. Like breakpoints, watch expressions are not preserved after you close a project or exit Visual Basic. The more watch expressions you define, the longer it will take your program to execute, because Visual Basic must check each watch expression for every statement that is executed. When you debug a program, use watch expressions sparingly.

Visual Basic uses the Add Watch dialog to add a watch expression to the project. Figure A-3 shows the Add Watch dialog.

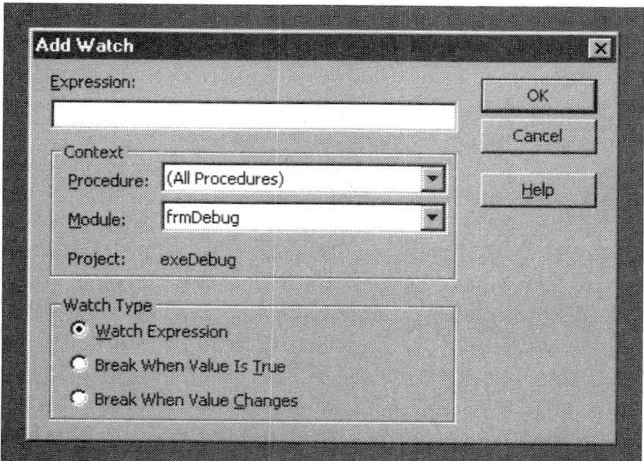

Figure A-3: Add Watch dialog

The Add Watch dialog contains three sections:

- The **Expression** text box is where you enter the expression you want Visual Basic to evaluate. If you want to watch the value of a variable, enter the variable name. You can copy the expression or variable from the Code window to the Add Watch dialog using the Copy and Paste commands to avoid typographical errors. The watch expression can be a variable, a property, or procedure call.

- The **Context** section sets the scope of the expression to watch. This is useful if you have variables of the same name in different procedures. **Module** refers to the form or other module in your project that should be watched.
- The **Watch Type** section tells Visual Basic how to respond to the watch expression. If the **Watch Expression** option button is selected, Visual Basic will display the value of the expression in the Watch window but the program will not enter break mode when the expression becomes True or changes. You should consider selecting the Watch Expression option button if you print the value of a variable frequently when you reach a breakpoint. This option also is useful for tracing the value of a variable when you are using the Step Into button to watch the contents of a variable in detail. If the **Break When Value Is True** option button is selected, Visual Basic will enter break mode whenever the expression is True. If the **Break When Value Changes** option button is selected, Visual Basic will enter break mode whenever a statement changes the value of the watch expression.

Consider setting a breakpoint in a loop that has many iterations. For example, you may have a Do loop that iterates hundreds or thousands of times. In this situation, setting a breakpoint in a loop may not be effective for debugging because you would need to resume execution each time through the loop. In these situations, a watch expression may be useful.

The command button with the caption Watch contains the following code in its Click event procedure. This code consists of nested For loops to initialize a 100-by-100 two-dimensional array.

```
Private Sub cmdWatch_Click( )
    Dim pintArray(100, 100)
    Dim pintX As Integer
    Dim pintY As Integer
    For pintX = 0 To 99
        For pintY = 0 To 99
            pintArray(pintX, pintY) = 10
        Next
    Next
End Sub
```

In this example, you will set different watch expressions to trace the execution of the event procedure.

To set and use watch expressions:

1. Click **Add Watch** on the **Debug** menu to activate the Add Watch dialog.
2. For each watch expression, set the module to **frmDebug**, then the procedure to **cmdWatch_Click**.
3. Enter the expression **pintX = 84** in the Expression text box, then click the **Break When Value Is True** option button in the **Watch Type** section. Click **OK** to add the watch expression.
4. Open the Add Watch dialog again. Enter the expression **pintY** in the Expression text box, then click the **Watch Expression** option button in the **Watch Type** section. Click **OK**.
5. Click **Watch Window** on the **View** menu to activate the Watches window as shown in Figure A-4. Note that Figure A-4 shows the Watches window while the program is running.

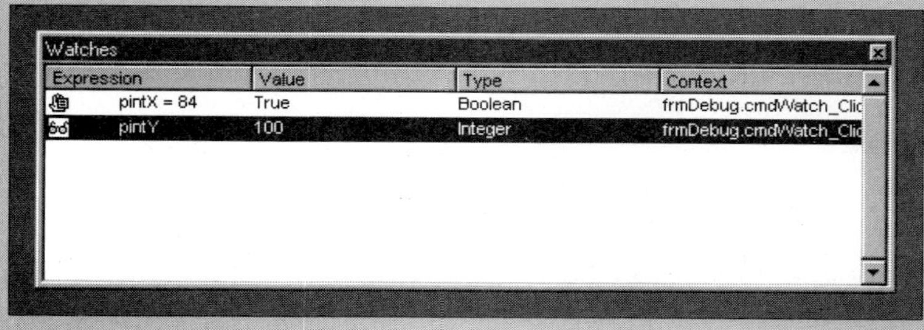

Figure A-4: Watches window

6. Test the program. Click the **Watch** command button.

Setting watch expressions is particularly useful when you know that a particular variable contains an incorrect value. In this situation, set a watch expression that will occur when the value of a particular variable changes.

The Locals Window

Another useful window is the Locals window. The Locals window displays the local variables pertaining to the currently executing procedure. As the current procedure changes from one procedure to another, the Locals window is updated to display the local variables pertaining to the new procedure. Figure A-5 shows the Locals window.

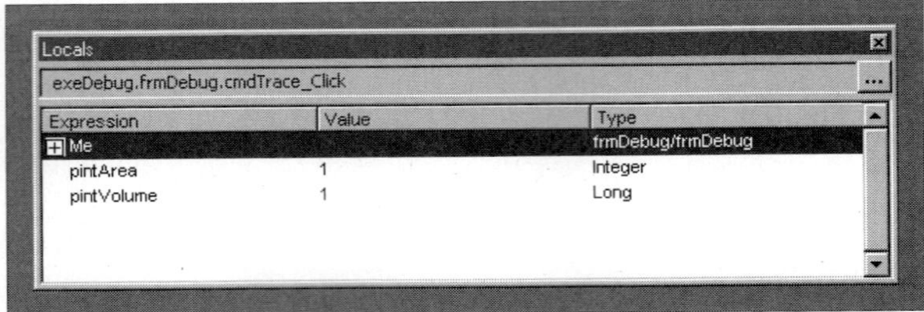

Figure A-5: Locals window

As shown in Figure A-5, the currently executing procedure is named cmdTrace_Click. It contains two local variables named pintArea and pintVolume. Note that you can change the values of these variables by clicking the Value column and changing a variable's values.

Error Handling Techniques

Closely related to the topic of debugging is the topic of error handling. Throughout this book, you have created error handlers to trap all types of run-time errors. You have created error handlers to trap numeric overflow and underflow conditions. You also have created error handlers to trap file and database errors. With a bit of design and foresight, you can improve the error handling capabilities of a program significantly while reducing the code you need to write for those error handlers.

For example, consider a program that manipulates DAO objects, or a program that performs input and output operations on files. In large programs, you may have several procedures that perform these operations, and each procedure has its own error handler. In situations like this, the error handling code in each procedure may be the same, or almost the same, as the error handlers in other procedures. In situations like this, you can reduce the code you need to write significantly by creating a Function procedure to process a category or group of errors. When a run-time error occurs in a procedure, the error handler for that procedure will be invoked. That error handler should in turn call the Function procedure to process the error. This is known as a **centralized error handler.**

SUMMARY

This appendix has presented a brief overview of the tools that can be used to debug programs. These tools include tracing the execution of a program, setting breakpoints and watch expressions, and using the Immediate window. These tools typically are not used independently of each other. Rather they commonly are used in conjunction with each other to detect and correct errors. As you become more familiar with these tools, you likely will develop your own techniques to debug programs.

o b j e c t i v e s

In this appendix you will:

- Drag and drop objects between programs

APPENDIX B

Understanding OLE Drag and Drop Operations

Communicating Data Between Programs

Programs and their data can also communicate with each other using what is known as OLE drag and drop. The capabilities of OLE drag and drop allow you to copy and paste data between programs and perform operations on that data.

Introducing OLE Drag and Drop

When you use **OLE drag and drop** you are essentially copying the data from one application into another application. There are many situations where OLE drag and drop can have a positive impact on a program's user interface. For example, you can drag an RTF or text file from the Windows Explorer into a rich text box. The rich text box can then be directed to open the dragged file. You can also perform complex drag and drop operations by dragging a range of cells from an Excel spreadsheet and dropping them into the DBGrid control. You can also drag pictures and other objects.

The easiest way to perform an OLE drag and drop operation is to use a control that supports automatic OLE dragging and dropping. The Image, PictureBox, TextBox, RichTextBox, MaskedEditBox, and DBGrid controls all support automatic OLE drag and drop operations. The best way to illustrate how an automatic OLE drag and drop operation works is by means of an example.

To perform an OLE drag and drop operation:

1. Start Visual Basic and open the project file **Appendix.B\AppB.vbp**. The form contains two instances of the RichTextBox control which support automatic and manual OLE drag and drop operations. The RichTextBox control supports OLE objects in addition to text.
2. Test the program. Activate **Windows Explorer** and locate the file **Appendix.B\Demo.txt**; click and hold down the mouse button (drag). Move the pointer to the top rich text box on the form and release the mouse button (drop). An icon appears in the Rich text box having the caption Demo.txt.
3. Double-click the file in the rich text box. Windows will start an instance of Notepad and display the file. Close Notepad.
4. Drag the same file to the second rich text box. This rich text box is set to manual OLE drop mode. The code in its event procedures opens the text file.
5. Drag a list of files from Windows Explorer to the list box on the form. Using manual OLE drag and drop, the file names are added to the list box.

Automatic and manual OLE drag and drop capabilities are made possible by the OLEDragMode and OLEDropMode properties. In the previous examples, the list box and second rich text box are using manual OLEDropMode. The first rich text box is automatic.

Whenever, an OLE drag and drop operation is performed, there are two control instances and frequently two programs involved in the operation. These are referred to as the source and the target. The **source** contains the data that is being dragged. In the previous example, Windows Explorer is the source. The **target** (rich text box or list box) is where the data is dropped. Because the rich text box supports automatic dragging and dropping, it is not necessary to write any code to complete the operation. Some controls, however, are more limited in that drag and drop operations must be performed manually. That is, you must write code to complete an OLE drag and drop operation. You may also want to write your own code to determine the behavior of a specific OLE drag and drop operation.

Manual OLE Drag and Drop Operations

When automatic drop mode is used with the rich text box, an object reference is stored in the rich text box. However, suppose you wanted to change the default behavior so that dragging a text or RTF file into the rich text box would cause the file to be opened. To accomplish this, you must understand the OLE events pertaining to dragging and dropping, how to respond to those events, and the OLE objects used in the process. When using manual OLE dropping, the OLEDropMode property of the target object should be set to Manual. When an object is then dropped on the target, the OLEDragDrop event occurs.

Syntax	**Private Sub** *target*_**OLEDragDrop(***data* **As DataObject**, *effect* **As Long**, *button* **As Integer**, *shift* **As Integer**, *x* **As Single**, *y* **As Single**)
Definition	The OLEDragDrop event occurs when manual OLE dropping is enabled and an object is dropped on the target.
Dissection	■ The *target* can be any object that supports manual OLE dropping. ■ The *data* contains a reference to a DataObject object, which contains the actual data that is being dropped. ■ The *effect* is a long integer that is set by the target. Setting this value allows the source to take appropriate action. For example, data may be copied or moved. ■ The *button* is a bit field defining the state of the mouse button when it was depressed. ■ The *shift* argument is a bit field that indicates the state of the Shift, Ctrl, and Alt keys. ■ The *x* and *y* arguments identify the current position of the mouse pointer.

When OLE data is dragged and dropped, information about the object is stored in yet another object called the **DataObject** object. Different types of data can be stored in the DataObject. For example, you can store bitmaps, rtf files, text files and many others.

Object	DataObject
Definition	The **DataObject** object is a container for the data being transferred between the OLE source and target controls.

Properties	The **Files** property contains a list of file names. It is used when the data type stored in the DataObject is of type vbCFFiles. This data type is used when the OLE source is a program such as Windows Explorer.
Methods	The **Clear** method is valid only for the OLE source. It removes the data associated with the DataObject object. The **GetFormat** method gets the type of data stored in the DataObject object. Data types include bitmaps, text, etc. The **GetData** method returns the data stored in the DataObject object. It is used by the OLE target. The data can be one of several types as identified by the GetFormat method. The **SetData** method is used by the OLE source to store data in the DataObject object.

Suppose you wanted the user to be able to drag a list of file names into a list box from the Windows Explorer. Each file dragged should appear in the list box. As you know, you can select multiple files in the Windows Explorer and drag those files to other programs. When a file is dragged from the Windows Explorer, the data type (returned by the DataObject's GetFormat method) is vbCFFiles. Other programs may set the data type to another constant like vbCFText to indicate a file is a text file. Refer to the GetFormat method pertaining to the DataObject using the Help system for a complete list of the constants.

When Windows Explorer is used as an OLE data source, the type of data associated with the source is vbCFFiles. Before dropping information on a target, the target must determine the type of object being dropped and how to process the file. Consider the following For loop.

```
Private Sub lstDrop_OLEDragDrop(Data As DataObject, _
    Effect As Long, Button As Integer, _
    Shift As Integer, X As Single, Y As Single)
    Dim pintCurrent As Integer
    If Data.GetFormat(vbCFFiles) Then
        For pintCurrent = 1 To Data.Files.Count
            lstDrop.AddItem (Data.Files(pintCurrent))
        Next
    End If
End Sub
```

The lstDrop_OLEDragDrop event procedure occurs when an OLE object is dropped on the target. In this case, the list box named lstDrop. Note that the OLE drop mode has been set to manual. The above loop first calls the GetFormat method pertaining to the Data object (a reference to the DataObject object). If the data is of type vbCFFiles, then the For loop is executed. Otherwise it is not. It is logical to make this test as it does not make sense to load anything but a list of files in the list box.

Carefully consider the syntax of the For loop. When the type of data stored in the DataObject is vbCFFiles, then the Files property contains a collection of strings. Each of these strings represents a file. The Files collection is a bit peculiar. It does not support the For Each loop nor does it support a string key. Thus, the above For loop must be used to examine the files in the collection. For each file selected, the filename is then added to the list box named lstDrop.

As an extension of the previous concept, you can also use the Files collection and the format of the DataObject to open files when dropped onto a control. In this example, you will again use the rich text box. The following code however, will check that the selected file is of the proper type by checking the file's extension then opening that file in the RichTextBox control.

```
Dim pstrFile As String
Dim pintFile As Integer
If Data.Files.Count = 1 Then
    If InStr(1, Data.Files(1), ".txt") Or _
        InStr(1, Data.Files(1), ".rtf") Then
        rtfFile.LoadFile Data.Files(1)
    End If
End If
```

This code is very similar to the code for the list box. The first If statement checks that only one file is selected. If this is the case, then the file is checked to make sure that it has a suffix of .txt or .rtf. If it does, then the LoadFile method is called on the rich text box.

Much more complex operations can be performed using OLE drag and drop than those presented in this brief appendix. This appendix is only intended to provide you with an idea of how OLE drag and drop works.

Index

B

D

E

G

J

K

N

S

T

U

V

W

MICROSOFT INTERNET EXPLORER, VERSION 4.0, AND SOFTWARE RELATED COMPONENTS. END-USER LICENSE AGREEMENT FOR MICROSOFT SOFTWARE

IMPORTANT. READ CAREFULLY: This Microsoft End-User License Agreement ("EULA") is a legal agreement between you (either a individual or a single entity) and Microsoft Corporation for the Microsoft software product(s) identified above which may include associated software components, media, printed materials, and "online" or electronic documentation ("SOFTWARE PRODUCT"). By installing, copying, or otherwise using the SOFTWARE PRODUCT, you agree to be bound by the terms of this EULA. If you do not agree to the terms of this EULA, do not install or use the SOFTWARE PRODUCT. If the SOFTWARE PRODUCT was purchased by you, you may return it to your place of purchase for a full refund. The SOFTWARE PRODUCT is protected by copyright laws and international copyright treaties, as well as other intellectual property laws and treaties. The SOFTWARE PRODUCT is licensed, not sold.

1. Grant of License. The SOFTWARE PRODUCT is licensed as follows: Installation and Use: Microsoft grants you the right to install and use copies of the SOFTWARE PRODUCT on your computers running validly licensed copies of the operating system for which the SOFTWARE PRODUCT was designed [e.g., Windows® 95; Windows NT®, Windows 3.x, Macintosh, etc.]. Backup Copies: You may also make copies of the SOFTWARE PRODUCT as may be necessary for backup and archival purposes. Components: Certain software components of the SOFTWARE PRODUCT are subject to the following additional provisions: DCOM95. You may only use copies of the DCOM95 component on computer(s) for which you have licensed Microsoft Windows operating system platforms. NetMeeting: NetMeeting contains technology that enables applications to be shared between two or more computers, even if an application is installed on only one of the computers. You may use this technology with all Microsoft application products for multi-party conferences. For non-Microsoft applications, you should consult the accompanying license agreement or contact the licensor to determine whether application sharing is permitted by the licensor. Internet Assistants and Internet Viewers: You may reproduce and distribute an unlimited number of copies of these components of the SOFTWARE PRODUCT; provided each copy shall be a true and complete copy, including all copyright and trademark notices, and shall be accompanied by a copy of this EULA. Copies of these components may be distributed as a standalone product or included with your own product. Microsoft Agent: You may distribute Microsoft Agent and its associated characters and speech engines in accordance with terms of a separate end user license agreement. See the "EULA.htm" file located at http://www.microsoft.com/workshop/prog/agent/ for further details.

2. Description of Other Rights and Limitations. Maintenance of Copyright Notices: You must not remove or alter any copyright notices on all copies of the SOFTWARE PRODUCT. Distribution: You may not distribute copies of the SOFTWARE PRODUCT to third parties. Prohibition on Reverse Engineering, Decompilation, and Disassembly: You may not reverse engineer, decompile, or disassemble the SOFTWARE PRODUCT, except and only to the extent that such activity is expressly permitted by applicable law notwithstanding this limitation. Rental: You may not rent, lease, or lend the SOFTWARE PRODUCT. Transfer: You may permanently transfer all of your rights under this EULA, provided the recipient agrees to the terms of this EULA. Support Services: Microsoft may provide you with support services related to the SOFTWARE PRODUCT ("Support Services"). Use of Support Services is governed by the Microsoft polices and programs described in the user manual, in "on line" documentation and/or other Microsoft-provided materials. Any supplemental software code provided to you as part of the Support Services shall be considered part of the SOFTWARE PRODUCT and subject to the terms and conditions of this EULA. With respect to technical information you provide to Microsoft as part of the Support Services, Microsoft may use such information for its business purposes, including for product support and development. Microsoft will not utilize such technical information in a form that personally identifies you. Compliance with Applicable Laws: You must comply with all applicable laws regarding use of the SOFTWARE PRODUCT.

3. Termination. Without prejudice to any other rights, Microsoft may terminate this EULA if you fail to comply with the terms and conditions of this EULA. In such event, you must destroy all copies of the SOFTWARE PRODUCT.

4. Copyright. All title, including but not limited to copyrights, in and to the SOFTWARE PRODUCT and any copies thereof are owned by Microsoft or its suppliers. All title and intellectual property rights in and to the content which may be accessed through use of the SOFTWARE PRODUCT is the property of the respective content owner and may be protected by applicable copyright or other intellectual property laws and treaties. This EULA grants you no rights to use such content. All rights not expressly granted are reserved by Microsoft.

5. U.S. Government Restricted Rights. The SOFTWARE PRODUCT is provided with RESTRICTED RIGHTS. Use, duplication, or disclosure by the Government is subject to restrictions as set forth in subparagraph (c)(1)(ii) of the Rights in Technical Data and Computer Software clause at DFARS 252.227-7013 or subparagraphs (c)(1) and (2) of the Commercial Computer Software Restricted Rights at 48 CFR 52.227-19, as applicable. Manufacturer is Microsoft Corporation/One Microsoft Way/Redmond, WA 98052-6399.

6. Export Restrictions. You agree that you will not export or re-export the SOFTWARE PRODUCT to any country, person, entity or end user subject to U.S.A. export restrictions. Restricted countries currently include, but are not necessarily limited to Cuba, Iran, Iraq, Libya, North Korea, Sudan, and Syria. You warrant and represent that neither the U.S.A. Bureau of Export Administration nor any other federal agency has suspended, revoked or denied your export privileges.

7. Note on Java Support. The SOFTWARE PRODUCT may contain support for programs written in Java. Java technology is not fault tolerant and is not designed, manufactured, or intended for use or resale as on-line control equipment in hazardous environments requiring fail-safe performance, such as in the operation of nuclear facilities, aircraft navigation or communication systems, air traffic control, direct life support machines, or weapons systems, in which the failure of Java technology could lead directly to death, personal injury, or severe physical or environmental damage.

8. No Warranties. Microsoft expressly disclaims any warranty for the SOFTWARE PRODUCT. THE SOFTWARE PRODUCT AND ANY RELATED DOCUMENTATION IS PROVIDED "AS IS" WITHOUT WARRANTY OF ANY KIND, EITHER EXPRESS OR IMPLIED, INCLUDING, WITHOUT LIMITATION, THE IMPLIED WARRANTIES OR MERCHANTABILITY, FITNESS FOR A PARTICULAR PURPOSE, OR NONINFRINGEMENT. THE ENTIRE RISK ARISING OUT OF USE OR PERFORMANCE OF THE SOFTWARE PRODUCT REMAINS WITH YOU.

9. Limitation of Liability. To the maximum extent permitted by applicable law, in no event shall Microsoft or its suppliers be liable for any special, incidental, indirect, or consequential damages whatsoever (including, without limitation, damages for loss of business profits, business interruption, loss of business information, or any other pecuniary loss) arising out of the use of or inability to use the SOFTWARE PRODUCT or the provision of or failure to provide Support Services, even if Microsoft has been advised of the possibility of such damages. In any case, Microsoft's entire liability under any provision of this EULA shall be limited to the greater of the amount actually paid by you for the SOFTWARE PRODUCT or US$5.00; provided however, if you have entered into a Microsoft Support Services Agreement, Microsoft's entire liability regarding Support Services shall be governed by the terms of that agreement. Because some states and jurisdictions do not allow the exclusion or limitation of liability, the above limitation may not apply to you.

10. Miscellaneous. This EULA is governed by the laws of the State of Washington, U.S.A. If you acquired this product in Canada, this EULA is governed by the laws of the Province of Ontario, Canada. Each of the parties hereto irrevocably attorns to the jurisdiction of the courts of the Province of Ontario and further agrees to commence any litigation which may arise hereunder in the courts located in the Judicial District of York, Province of Ontario. If this product was acquired outside the United States, then local law may apply.

Should you have any questions concerning this EULA, or if you desire to contact Microsoft for any reason, please contact the Microsoft subsidiary serving your country, or write: Microsoft Sales Information Center/One Microsoft Way/Redmond, WA 98052-6399.